A User's Guide to Data Protection

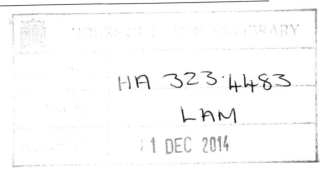

A User's Guide to Data Protection

Paul Lambert BA, LLB, LLM, CTMA

Lecturer, Solicitor

Bloomsbury Professional

Bloomsbury Professional Ltd, Maxwelton House, 41–43 Boltro Road, Haywards Heath, West Sussex, RH16 1BJ

© Bloomsbury Professional Ltd 2013

Bloomsbury Professional is an imprint of Bloomsbury Publishing plc

A CIP Catalogue record for this book is available from the British Library.

ISBN 978 1 84766 980 3

Typeset by Columns Design XML Ltd, Reading
Printed and bound in Great Britain by CPI Group (UK) Ltd, Croydon, CR0 4YY

Contents

Part 1: How to Comply with the Data Protection Regime

Contents

Contents

Contents

Contents

Part 3: Outward-Facing Organisational DP Obligations

Contents

Contents

Contents

Contents

Contents

'Technology has … altered the way we work. It is no longer really necessary to go into "an office" to make viable contribution to an organisation. We can work at home, in coffee bars, in airports, on trains using wifi and 3G telephone services utilising an increasingly diverse range of devices from laptops to tablet computers to smart phones in order to access emails and "attend" online meetings.'[1]

'[P]ersonal data … are more and more processed and archived.'[1]

The importance of consent[2] cannot be overestimated.

'There is an inherent security issue with many of these online exchanges which if often overlooked. Emails are not particularly secure.'[3]

'A blog [or social networking post] is a bit like a tattoo: a good idea at the time but you might live to regret it.'[4]

1 Davies, C, Editorial, *Communications Law*, (2012)(17), pp 38–39.
2 Costa, L., and Poullet, Y, 'Privacy and the Regulation of 2012,' *Computer Law & Security Review*, (2012)(28), pp. 254–262, at 256.
3 Ferretti, F, 'A European Perspective on Data Processing Consent Through the Re-Conceptualiation of European Data Protection's Looking Glass After the Lisbon Treaty: Taking Rights seriously,' *European Review of Private Law*, (2012)(20), pp. 473–506.
4 Davies, C, Editorial, *Communications Law*, (2012)(17), pp. 38–39.

Abbreviations

These abbreviations shall be used throughout.

DPA: UK Data Protection Act 1998;

DPD95: EU Data Protection Directive 1995 (Directive 95/46/EC of the European Parliament and of the Council of 24 October 1995 on the protection of individuals with regard to the processing of personal data and on the free movement of such data);

DPR: EU draft Proposed Data Protection Regulation (Proposal for a Regulation of the European Parliament and of the Council on the protection of individuals with regard to the processing of personal data and on the free movement of such data (General Data Protection Regulation) COM(2012) 11 final).

(This DPR would replace the DPD95 and be directly effective throughout the EU without the need for separate sets of national implementing legislation);

ePD: Directive 2002/58/EC of the European Parliament and of the Council of 12 July 2002 concerning the processing of personal data and the protection of privacy in the electronic communications sector (Directive on privacy and electronic communications). This is also known as the ePrivacy Directive (ePD);

WP29 EU Article 29 Working Party on Data Protection;

Personal data: Any data or information identifying or relating to the individual data subject (see DPD detailed definition below);

Abbreviations

Data subject: The individual who the personal data relates to (see DPD95 detailed definition below);

Data controller: The organisation collecting, processing and holding the personal data (see DPD95 detailed definition below);

Data processor: An outsourced third party organisation or related entity carrying out certain defined outsourced activities for and on behalf of the main data controller with the personal data eg outsourced payroll, outsourced direct marketing, etc (see DPD95 detailed definition below);

ICO Information Commissioner's Office ie the main UK data protection regulator;

Member State: means a member State of the European Union (EU);

PECR: Privacy and Electronic Communications (EC Directive) Regulations 2003;

PECR Amendment Regulations: Privacy and Electronic Communications (EC Directive) (Amendment) Regulations 2011;

Commission: means the EU Commission;

EEA: means the European Economic Area, comprising the EU plus Iceland, Liechtenstein and Norway. (Note, Switzerland has a similar type arrangement with the EU.)

List of Statutes

A more detailed Table of Statutes, with references to the text, can be found at p. xlv

Access to Health Records Act 1990
Access to Justice Act 1999
Access to Medical Reports Act 1988
Access to Personal Files Act 1987
Adoption Act 1976
Anti-terrorism, Crime and Security Act 2001
Banking and Financial Dealings Act 1971
Broadcasting Act 1990
Broadcasting Act 1996
Business Names Act 1985
Charities Act 1993, 2006
Charities Act (Northern Ireland) 2008
Children Act 1989
Communications Act 2003
Companies Act 1985
Computer Misuse Act 1990
Communications Act 2003
Constitutional Reform Act 2005
Consumer Credit Act 1974
Copyright, Designs and Patents Act 1988
Coroners and Justice Act 2009
Courts and Legal Services Act 1990
Crime and Disorder Act 1998
Crime (International Co-operation) Act 2003
Crime and Security Act 2010
Criminal Damage Act 1971
Criminal Justice Act 1988, 2003
Criminal Justice and Courts Services Act 2000
Criminal Justice and Immigration Act 2008
Criminal Justice and Police Act 2001
Criminal Justice and Public Order Act 1994
Data Protection Act 1984

List of Statutes

Data Protection Act 1998
Defamation Act 1996
Digital Economy Act 2010
Disability Discrimination Act 1995
Education Act 1996
Education Reform Act 1988
Employers Liability (Compulsory Insurance) Act 1969
Employment Act 2002
Employment Rights Act 1996
Enterprise Act 2002
Equality Act 2010
Finance Act 1998
Financial Services Act 1986
Financial Services and Markets Act 2000
Football Spectators Act 1989
Fraud Act 2006
Freedom of Information Act 2000
Freedom of Information (Scotland) Act 2002
Further and Higher Education Act 1992
Gas Act 1986
Health and Safety at Work Act 1974
Health and Social Care Act 2001, 2008
Health and Social Care (Community Health and Standards) Act 2003
Health and Social Services and Social Security Adjudications Act 1983
Housing Act 1985
Housing Act 1988
Human Fertilisation and Embryology Act 1990
Human Rights Act 1998
Human Tissue Act 2004
Immigration, Asylum and Nationality Act 2006
Information Acts
Interception of Communications Act 1985
Interpretation Act 1978, 1889
Insurance Companies Act 1982
Interception of Communications Act 1985
Interpretation Act 1978
Jobseekers Act 1995
Local Authority Social Services Act 1970
Local Government Act 1972
Local Government Act 2000
Malicious Communications Act 1988
Medical Act 1983
Mental Capacity Act 2005
National Health Service Act 1977

National Health Services Act 2006
National Health Service and Community Care Act 1990
Office of Communications Act 2002
Official Secrets Act 1989
Opticians Act 1989
Osteopaths Act 1993
Pension Schemes Act 1993
Personal Files Act 1987
Pharmacy Act 1954
Police Act 1996, 1997
Police and Criminal Evidence Act 1984 (PACE)
Police and Justice Act 2006
Powers of Criminal Courts (Sentencing) Act 2000
Prison Act 1952
Probation Service Act 1993
Proceeds of Crime Act 2002
Professions Supplementary to Medicine Act 1960
Protection from Harassment Act 1997
Protection of Children Act 1978
Protection of Freedoms Act 2012
Protection of Vulnerable Groups (Scotland) Act 2007
Public Records Act 1958
Race Relations Act 1976
Race Relations (Amendment) Act 2000
Regulation of Investigatory Power Act 2000
Regulation of Investigatory Power (Scotland) Act 2000
Rehabilitation of Offenders Act 1974
Representation of the People Act 1983
Representation of the People Act 2000
Safeguarding Vulnerable Groups Act 2006
School Standards and Framework Act 1998
Serious Crime Act 2007
Serious Organised Crime and Police Act 2005
Sex Discrimination Act 1975
Social Security Act 1989
Social Security Administration Act 1992
Social Security Contributions and Benefits Act 1992
Statistics and Registration Act 2007
Superannuation Act 1972
Taxes Management Act 1970
Terrorism Act 2000
Theft Act 1968
Trade Union and Labour Relations (Consolidation) Act 1992
Transfer of Undertakings (Protection of Employment)

List of Statutes

List of Statutory Instruments

A more detailed Table of Statutory Instruments, with references to the text, can be found at p. xlix

Adoption Agency Regulations 1983
Adoption Rules 1984
Banking Coordination (Second Council Directive) Regulations 1992
Civil Procedure Rules 1998
Consumer Credit (Credit Reference Agency) Regulations 1977
Consumer Credit (Credit Reference Agency) Regulations 2000
Consumer Protection (Contracts Concluded by Means of Distance Communications) Regulations 2000
Data Protection Act 1998 (Commencement) Order 2000
Data Protection Act 1998 (Commencement No 2) Order 2000
Data Protection Act 1998 (Commencement No 2) Order 2008
Data Protection Act 1998 (Commencement No 3) Order 2008
Data Protection (Conditions under paragraph 3 of Part II of Schedule 1) Order 2000
Data Protection (Corporate Finance Exemption) Order 2000
Data Protection (Crown Appointments) Order 2000
Data Protection (Designated Codes of Practice) Order 2000
Data Protection (Designated Codes of Practice)(No 2) Order 2000
Data Protection (Fees under section 19(7)) Regulations 2000
Data Protection (Functions of Designated Authorities) Order 2000
Data Protection (International Cooperation) Order 2000
Data Protection (Miscellaneous Subject Access Exemptions) Order 2000
Data Protection (Miscellaneous Subject Access Exemptions) (Amendment) Order 2000
Data Protection (Monetary Penalties) Order 2010
Data Protection (Monetary Penalties) (Maximum Penalty and Notices) Regulations 2010
Data Protection (National Security Appeals) Regulations 2000
Data Protection (Notification and Notification Fees) Regulations 2000
Data Protection (Notification and Notification Fees) (Amendment) Regulations 2001

List of Statutory Instruments

Data Protection (Notification and Notification Fees) (Amendment) Regulations 2009

Data Protection (Processing of Sensitive Personal Data) Order 2000, 2006, 2009, 2012

Data Protection (Processing of Sensitive Personal Data) (Elected Representatives) Order 2002

Data Protection (Processing of Sensitive Personal Data) (Elected Representatives) (Amendment) Order 2002, 2010

Data Protection Registration Fee Order 1991

Data Protection (Subject Access Modification) (Education) Order 2000

Data Protection (Subject Access Modification) (Health) Order 2000

Data Protection (Subject Access Modification) (Social Work) Order 2000

Data Protection (Subject Access Modification) (Social Work) Amendment Order 2011

Data Protection Registration Fee Order 1991

Data Protection (Subject Access) (Fees and Miscellaneous Provisions) Regulations 2000

Data Protection (Subject Access) (Fees and Miscellaneous Provisions)(Amendment) Regulations 2001

Data Protection (Subject Access Modification)(Social Work)(Amendment) Order 2005

Data Protection Tribunal (Enforcement Appeals) Rules 2000

Data Protection Tribunal (National Security Appeals) Rules 2000

Data Protection Tribunal (National Security Appeals) (Telecommunications) Rules 2000

Data Retention (EC Directive) Regulations 2007, 2009

Education (School Records) Regulations 1989

Education (Special Educational Needs) Regulations 1994

Electronic Commerce (EC Directive) Regulations 2002

Electronic Communications (Universal Service) Order 2003

Environmental Information (Fees and Appropriate Limits) Regulations 2004

Environmental Information Regulations 2004

Family Proceedings Courts (Children Act 1989) Rules 1991

Family Proceedings Rules 1991

Freedom of Information and Data Protection (Appropriate Limit and Fees) Regulations 2004

Health Professions Order 2001

Health Service (Control of Patient Information) Regulations 2002

Information Tribunal (Enforcement Appeals) Rules 2005

Information Tribunal (Enforcement Appeals)(Amendment) Rules 2002

Information Tribunal (Enforcement Appeals)(Amendment) Rules 2005

Information Tribunal (National Security Appeals) Rules 2005

INSPIRE Regulations

Insurance Companies (Third Insurance Directives) Regulations 1994

List of European/International Legislation

More detailed Tables of EU, EC and International Material can be found at p. liii

Aarhus Convention on Access to Information, Public Participation in Decision making and Access to Justice in Environmental Matters 1998

Charter of Fundamental Rights of the European Union 2009

CIS Convention on the Use of Information technology for Customs Purposes 1995

Commission Decision 2004/91 of December 7, 2004 amending Decision 2001/497 as Regards the Introduction of an Alternative Set of Standard Clauses for Transfer of Personal Data to Third Counties

Commission decision 2004/535 on the Adequate Protection of Personal Data Contained in Passenger Name Record of Air Passengers Transferred to the United States Bureau of Customs and Border Protection

Convention for the Processing of Individuals with Regard to the Automatic Processing of Personal Data 1981

Convention on Mutual Assistance between Customs Administrations 1967

Convention on Mutual Assistance in Criminal Matters 2000

Council of Europe Convention 1981

Council of Europe Convention for the Protection of Individuals with Regard to the Automatic Processing of Personal Data (Treaty 108) 1981

Council Decision 2004/496 on the Agreement Between the European Community and the United States of America on the Processing and Transfer of PNR Data by Air carriers to the United States of America on the Transfer and processing of PNR data by Carriers to the United States Department of Homeland Security, Bureau of Customs and Border Protection

Council Directive 73/148 (Council Directive 73/148/EEC of 21 May 1973 on the abolition of restrictions on movement and residence within the Community for nationals of Member States with regard to establishment and the provision of services)

Council Directive 89/552 ()Council Directive 89/552/EEC of 3 October 1989 on the coordination of certain provisions laid down by Law, Regulation or Administrative Action in Member States concerning the pursuit of television broadcasting activities

List of European/International Legislation

Council Directive 95/46 (Directive 95/46/EC of the European Parliament and of the Council of 24 October 1995 on the protection of individuals with regard to the processing of personal data and on the free movement of such data) (DPD95)

Council Directive 1997/7/EC (Directive 97/7/EC of the European Parliament and of the Council of 20 May 1997 on the protection of consumers in respect of distance contracts – Statement by the Council and the Parliament re Article 6 (1) – Statement by the Commission re Article 3 (1), first indent-)(Distance Selling Directive)

Council Directive 97/66 (Directive 97/66/EC of the European Parliament and of the Council of 15 December 1997 concerning the processing of personal data and the protection of privacy in the telecommunications sector)(Telecoms Data Protection Directive)

Council Directive 98/34 (Directive 98/34/EC of the European Parliament and of the Council of 22 June 1998 laying down a procedure for the provision of information in the field of technical standards and regulations and of rules on Information Society services)

Council Directive 98/48 (Directive 98/48/EC of the European Parliament and of the Council of 20 July 1998 amending Directive 98/34/EC laying down a procedure for the provision of information in the field of technical standards and regulations)

Council Directive 99/5 (Directive 1999/5/EC of the European Parliament and of the Council of 9 March 1999 on radio equipment and telecommunications terminal equipment and the mutual recognition of their conformity)

Council Directive 2000/31(Directive 2000/31/EC of the European Parliament and of the Council of 8 June 2000 on certain legal aspects of information society services, in particular electronic commerce, in the Internal Market ('Directive on electronic commerce') (eCommerce Directive)

Council Directive 2002/21 Directive 2002/21/EC of the European Parliament and of the Council of 7 March 2002 on a common regulatory framework for electronic communications networks and services (Framework Directive)

Council Directive 2002/22 (Directive 2002/22/EC of the European Parliament and of the Council of 7 March 2002 on universal service and users' rights relating to electronic communications networks and services (Universal Service Directive)

Council Directive 2002/58 (Directive 2002/58/EC of the European Parliament and of the Council of 12 July 2002 concerning the processing of personal data and the protection of privacy in the electronic communications sector (Directive on privacy and electronic communications))(ePD or ePrivacy Data Protection Directive)

Council Directive 2003/98 (Directive 2003/98/EC of the European Parliament and of the Council of 17 November 2003 on the re-use of public sector information)

Council Directive 2009/136/EC (Directive 2009/136/EC of the European Parliament and of the Council of 25 November 2009 amending Directive 2002/22/EC on universal service and users' rights relating to electronic communications networks and services, Directive 2002/58/EC concerning the processing of personal data and the protection of privacy in the electronic communications sector and Regulation (EC) No 2006/2004 on cooperation between national authorities responsible for the enforcement of consumer protection laws)

Council Regulation (EC) 2299/89 (Council Regulation (EEC) No 2299/89 of 24 July 1989 on a code of conduct for computerized reservation systems)

Council Regulation 1035/97 (Council Regulation (EC) No 1035/97 of 2 June 1997 establishing a European Monitoring Centre on Racism and Xenophobia)

Council Regulation 2725/2000 (Council Regulation (EC) No 2725/2000 of 11 December 2000 concerning the establishment of 'Eurodac' for the comparison of fingerprints for the effective application of the Dublin Convention)

Council Regulation 2424/2001 (Council Regulation (EC) No 2424/2001 of 6 December 2001 on the development of the second generation Schengen Information System (SIS II))

Council Regulation 2580/2001 (Council Regulation (EC) No 2580/2001 of 27 December 2001 on specific restrictive measures directed against certain persons and entities with a view to combating terrorism)

Council Regulation 45/2001 (Regulation (EC) 45/2001 of the European Parliament and of the Council of 18 December 2000 on the Protection of Individuals with Regard to the processing of personal data by the Community Institutions and Bodies and on the Free Movement of Such Data)

Council Regulation 2252/2004 (Council Regulation (EC) No 2252/2004 of 13 December 2004 on standards for security features and biometrics in passports and travel documents issued by Member States)

Council Regulation 871/2004 (Council Regulation (EC) No 871/2004 of 29 April 2004 concerning the introduction of some new functions for the Schengen Information System, including in the fight against terrorism)

Cybercrime Convention

Decision 2001/497 of June 15, 2001 on Standard Contractual Clauses for the Transfer of Personal Data to Third Countries under Directive 95/46

Directive 95/46 on the Protection of Individuals with Regard to the Processing of Personal Data and on the Free Movement of the Data (Directive on Data Protection)(DPD95)

Directive on the Protection of Individuals with Regard to the Processing of Personal Data [2013], draft

Directive 97/7 on the Protection of Consumers in Respect of Distance Contracts

Directive 97/66 Concerning the Processing of Personal Data and the Protection of Privacy in the Telecommunications Sector (Telecommunications Directive)

Directive 98/48 amending Directive 98/34 (Directive 98/48/EC of the European Parliament and of the Council of 20 July 1998 amending Directive 98/34/EC laying down a procedure for the provision of information in the field of technical standards and regulations)

Directive 99/67 amending Directive 93/49 (Commission Directive 1999/67/EC of 28 June 1999 amending Directive 93/49/EEC setting out the schedule indicating the conditions to be met by ornamental plant propagating material and ornamental plants pursuant to Council Directive 91/682/EEC)

Directive 2002/59/EC Establishing a Community Vessel Traffic Monitoring and Information System

Directive 2002/19 on Access to and Interconnection of Electronic Communications Networks and Associated Facilities

Directive 2002/21 on a Common Regulatory Framework for Electronic Communications Networks and Services

Directive 2002/22 on Universal Service and Users' Rights Relating to Electronic Communications Networks and Services

Directive 2002/58 Concerning the Processing of Personal Data and the protection of Privacy in the Electronic Communications Sector Privacy and Electronic Communications Directive

Directive 2002/96 on Waste Electrical and Electronic Equipment (WEEE)

Directive 2003/4 Public Access to Environmental Information

Directive 2005/18 on the Retention of Data Generated or processing in Connection with the Provision or Publicly Available Electronic Communications Services or of Public Communications Networks

Directive 2006/24 on the Retention of Data Generated or Processed in Connection with the Provision of Publicly Available Electronic Communications Services or of Public Communications Networks and Amended Directive 2002/58

Directive 2009/136/EC Relating to Electronic Communications Networks and Services

Draft Regulation on the Protection of Individuals with Regard to the Data Protection [2013]

Draft Directive on the Protection of Individuals with Regard to the Processing of Personal Data [2013]

Dublin Convention 1990 (Convention determining the State responsible for examining applications for asylum lodged in one of the Member States of the European Communities – Dublin Convention)

EC Treaty

Eurodac Convention 1996

Europol Convention on the Establishment of a European Police Force

European Convention for the Protection of Human Rights and Fundamental Freedoms 1950 (European Convention on Human Rights)

Europol Convention

Lisbon Treaty 2009

Mutual Assistance Convention

Nice Charter of Fundamental Rights 2000

Organisation for Economic Co-operation and Development (OECD) Guidelines Concerning the Protection of Privacy and Trans-border Flows of Personal Data

Proposed Regulation on the Protection of Individuals with Regard to the Data Protection [2013], draft

Proposed Directive on the Protection of Individuals with Regard to the Processing of Personal Data [2013], draft

Regulation 515/97 on Mutual Assistance Between Administrative Authorities of the Member States

Regulation 45/2001 on the Protection of Individuals with Regard to the Processing of Personal Data by the Community Institutions and Bodies and on the Free Movement of Such Data

Regulation on the Protection of Individuals with Regard to the Data Protection [2013], draft

Regulation 343/2003 (Dublin II Regulation)

Regulation 1987/2006 (Schengen II/SIS II)

Rome EC Treaty 1957

Single European Act 1987

Strasbourg Convention

Treaty 108 of the Council of Europe Convention for the Protection of Individuals with Regard to Automatic Processing of Personal Data 1981

Treaty of Amsterdam

Treaty on European Union

Treaty on European Union consolidated

UNCITRAL Model Law on Electronic Commerce

Universal Declaration of Human Rights 1948

WP29

Opinion 8/2001 (Opinion 8/2001 on the processing of personal data in the employment context)

Opinion 7/2003 (Opinion 7/2003 on the re-use of public sector information and the protection of personal data)

Opinion 4/2007 (Opinion 4/2007 on the concept of personal data)

Opinion 1/2010 (Opinion 1/2010 on the concepts of 'controller' and 'processor')

Opinion 2/2010 (Opinion 2/2010 on online behavioural advertising)

Article 29 working party opinion on the processing of personal data in the employment context 8/2001

Opinion 3/2009 on the Draft Commission Decision on standard contractual clauses for the transfer of personal data to processors established in third countries, under Directive 95/46/EC (data controller to data processor)

FAQs in order to address some issues raised by the entry into force of the EU Commission Decision 2010/87/EU of 5 February 2010 on standard contractual clauses for the transfer of personal data to processors established in third countries under Directive 95/46/EC 2010

Opinion 3/2002on the data protection provisions of a Commission proposal for a Directive on the harmonisation of the laws, regulations and administrative provisions of the Member States concerning credit for consumers

Working document on the surveillance of electronic communications in the workplace 2002

Recommendation 1/2001 on Employee Evaluation Data 2001

Recommendation 1/2007 on the Standard Application for Approval of Binding Corporate Rules for the Transfer of Personal Data

The Future of Privacy Joint contribution to the Consultation of the European Commission on the legal framework for the fundamental right to protection of personal data 2009

Table of Cases

Table of Cases

Table of Statutes

Table of Statutes

Table of Statutory Instruments

Table of Statutory Instruments

Table of Statutory Instruments

Table of European Regulations

Table of European Regulations

Table of European Directives

Table of European Directives

Table of Treaties and Conventions

Part I
Data Protection

How to Comply with the Data Protection Regime

Chapter 1

Data Protection

What is Data Protection?

1.01 Data protection aims to protect the privacy and personal information of individuals. It provides a regulatory protection regime around personal informational privacy, or personal data. Personal data is data or information which relates to or identifies, directly or indirectly, an individual.

The data protection legal regime governs when and how organisations may collect and process personal data.

This applied to all sorts of personal information, from general to highly confidential and sensitive. Examples of the later include sensitive health data and details of criminal convictions.

The data protection regime is twofold in the sense of: (a) providing obligations (which are inward-facing and outward-facing, see below) which organisations must comply with; and (b) providing individuals or data subjects as they are known, with various data protection rights which they or the Information Commissioner's Office (ICO) can invoke or enforce as appropriate. Significantly, there are proposals to expand the ability to invoke the data protection rights to privacy groups and collective non governmental type organisations (see proposed EU Data Protection Regulation (DPR), replacing the DPD95). The DPR will bring 'comprehensive reform'[1] to the EU and UK data protection regime.

Organisations, as part of their compliance obligations, must register or notify the ICO in relation to their data processing activities.

Certain specific sections of industry and certain specific activities (eg data transfers abroad, direct marketing, cookies), also have additional data protection compliance rules.

---

1   In Brief, *Communications Law* (2012) (17), p. 3.

In terms of individuals, they can invoke their rights directly with organisations, with the ICO and also via the courts in legal proceedings. Compensation can also be awarded. In addition, criminal offences can be prosecuted. Data protection compliance is therefore very important.

As regards implementing compliance frameworks, an organisation must have defined structures, policies and teams in place to ensure that it knows what personal data it has, for what purposes, ensure that it is held fairly, lawfully and in compliance with the data protection regime, and that it is safely secured against damage and loss. The cost of loss, and of security breach, can be significant both financially and publicly. Breaches which are criminal offences can be prosecuted. In addition, personal liability can attach to organisational personnel separate and in addition to the organisation itself.

The Importance of Data Protection

1.02 A recent Editorial in the *Computer Law & Security Review* notes that '[p]rivacy and data protection issues are never far from the horizon at the moment. There are waves of discussion in this area ... and currently that wave is riding high.'[2] The increasing 'centralisation of information through the computerisation of various records has made the right of privacy a fundamental concern.'[3] Data protection is important, increasingly topical and an issue of legally required compliance for all organisations. More importantly it is part of management and organisational best practice. Individuals, employees and customers expect that their personal data will be respected by organisations. They are increasingly aware of their rights, and increasingly they enforce said rights.

1.03 The coverage of data protection has also increased in the mainstream media. This is due in part to a large number of recent data loss and data breach incidents. These have involved the personal data of millions of individuals being lost by commercial organisations, but also trusted government entities.

Even more recently the issue of online abuse, which involves amongst other things privacy and data protection, has also been hitting

---

2   Editorial, Saxby, S., *Computer Law & Security Review* (2012) (28), 251–253, at 251.

3   'Personal Data Protection and Privacy,' Counsel of Europe, available at http://hub. coe.int/web/coe-portal/what-we-do/rule-of-law/personal-data?dynLink=true&layout Id=35&dlgroupId=10226&fromArticleId=, accessed on 18 January 2013.

the headlines. Tragically, such online abuse can, and does, result in and contribute to actual suicide. This is a particular concern in relation to children and teenagers.

1.04 All organisations collect and process personal data. Whether they are big or new start-ups, they need to comply with the data protection regime. Many issues enhance the importance of getting organisational data protection understanding and compliance right from day one. These include investigations, fines, prosecutions, being ordered to *delete* databases and adverse publicity.

1.05 In addition, organisations often fail to realise that data protection compliance is frequently an issue of dual compliance. They need to be looking both *inward* and *outward*. Internally, they have to be data protection compliant in relation to all of their employees' (and contractors') personal data, which traditionally may have related to HR files and employee contracts, but now includes issues of electronic communications, social networking, internet usage, filtering, monitoring abuse, on-site activity, off-site activity, etc.

1.06 Separately, organisations have to be concerned about other sets of personal data, such as those relating to persons outside of the organisation, eg customers, prospects, etc. Comprehensive data protection compliance is also required here. The consequences are significant for non compliance.

1.07 Substantial fines have been imposed in a number of recent cases. In some instances also, organisations have been ordered to delete their databases. In a new technology start-up situation, this can be the company's most valuable asset. Even in an established organisation, it can be a valuable asset.

1.08 Up until recently the issue of data loss was a small story. More recently, however, the loss of personal data files of millions of individuals in the UK – and from official governmental sources – makes UK data loss a front page issue. There is increased scrutiny from the ICO, and others, and new regulation is forthcoming. Organisations must look at security issues with increasing rigour.

1.09 In the UK and elsewhere there are enhanced obligations to report all data losses; as well as discussion to have enhanced financial penalties, and in some instances personal director responsibility for data loss. The need for compliance is now a boardroom issue and an important issue of corporate compliance. Proactive and complete data protection compliance is also a matter of good corporate governance, brand loyalty and a means to ensuring user and customer goodwill.

1.10 The frequency and scale of recent breaches of security eg Sony's Playstation Network (70 million individuals' personal data[4] in one instance, and 25 million in another[5]) make the topicality and importance of data security compliance for personal data ever more important. The largest UK data loss appears to be Revenue and Customs loss of discs with the names, dates of birth, bank and address details for 25 million UK individuals.[6]

1.11 There are many new UK cases involving substantial fines for data protection breaches. The Brighton and Sussex University Hospitals NHS Trust had a fine of £325,000 imposed by the ICO in relation to a data loss incident.[7] Zurich Insurance was fined £2.3m for losing data in relation to 46,000 individual customers.[8] Sony was fined £250,000.

Apart from data loss incidents, two Spam texters were fined a total of £440,000 in respect of text Spam their marketing company had sent (*ICO v Christopher Niebel and Gary McNeish*, 2012).[9] The size of the penalty is significant. However, possibly more significant is that it involves director liability. In a further significant development, the ICO has also recently issued a substantial fine in relation to breach of the data protection regime by way of incorrect storage and processing when the financial data and files of individual customers were mixed up.

---

4   See, for example, Martin, G., 'Sony Data Loss Biggest Ever,' *Boston Herald*, 27 April, 2011, available at http://bostonherald.com/business/technology/general/view/2011_0427sony_data_loss_biggest_ever, accessed on 18 January 2013.

5   See, for example, Arthur, C., 'Sony Suffers Second Data Breach With Theft of 25m More User Details,' *Guardian*, 3 May, 2011, available at http://www.guardian.co.uk/technology/blog/2011/may/03/sony-data-breach-online-entertainment, accessed on 18 January 2013.

6   See, for example, 'Brown Apologises for Record Loss, Prime Minister Gordon Brown has said he "Profoundly Regrets" the Loss of 25 Million Child Benefit Records,' *BBC*, 21 November, 2007, available at http://news.bbc.co.uk/2/hi/7104945.stm, accessed on 22 August, 2011.

7   See, for example, 'Largest Ever Fine for Data Loss Highlights Need for Audited Data Wiping,' *ReturnOnIt*, available at http://www.returnonit.co.uk/largest-ever-fine-for-data-loss-highlights-need-for-audited-data-wiping.php, accessed on 22 August, 2012.

8   See, for example, Oates, J., 'UK Insurer Hit With Biggest Ever Data Loss Fine,' *The Register*, 24 August, 2010, available at http://www.theregister.co.uk/2010/08/24/data_loss_fine/, accessed on 22 August, 2012. This was imposed by the Financial Services Authority (FSA).

9   Available at http://www.ico.gov.uk/news/latest_news/2012/spam-texters-fined-nearly-half-a-million-pounds-28112012.aspx, accessed 22 January 2013.

Potentially, a customer could have suffered financial loss and adverse consequences. This was the ICO case of Prudential. Prudential was fined £50,000.

In another case, a health trust was fined £225,000 in relation to third party unauthorised access to files held at a disused building.[10] A Barclays bank employee was fined in a court prosecution for unauthorised access to bank records for personal reasons under s 55 of the DPA. She was fined at Derby Crown Court.[11]

1.12 National data protection authorities are increasingly pro-active and undertake audits of data protection compliance frameworks, as well as incidents of breaches. Facebook internationally has been audited by one of the EU data protection authorities.[12] The ICO is also involved in dealing with personal data issues relating to the recent phone hacking scandal which parallels the Leveson Inquiry.[13] This ICO investigation is called Operation Motorman.[14]

The Data Protection Regime

1.13 Personal data protection is enshrined in the EU DPD95 and the DPA in the UK. The DPA implements the DPD95 in the UK, as does respective national legislation in the other EU Member States.

Outward-Facing Data Protection Compliance

1.14 The data protection regime as implemented in the DPA creates legal obligations which organisations must comply with when collecting and processing the personal data of individuals. '[I]f someone can

10 Belfast Health and Social Care (BHSC) Trust, available at http://www.ico.gov.uk/news/latest_news/2012/belfast-trust-fined-225000-after-leaving-thousands-of-patient-records-in-disused-hospital-19062012.aspx, accessed 22 January 2013.
11 Available at http://www.ico.gov.uk/news/latest_news/2012/bank-employee-fined-for-reading-partners-ex-wifes-statements-06122012.aspx, accessed 22 January 2013.
12 The audit relates to Facebook internationally, outside of the US and Canada. See first stage of the audit report, of 21 December 2011 at http://dataprotection.ie/view doc.asp?m=&fn=/documents/Facebook%20Report/final%20report/report.pdf, accessed on 18 January 2013. It is entitled *Facebook Ireland Limited, Report of Audit*, and was conducted by the Irish Data Protection Commissioner's Office. Note also complaints and access requests referred to at Europe Against Facebook, available at http://europe-v-facebook.org/EN/en.html, accessed on 18 January 2013.
13 Available at http://www.levesoninquiry.org.uk/.
14 For more details see 'Operation Motorman – Steve Whittamore Notebooks,' ICO website, available at http://www.ico.gov.uk/for_the_public/topic_specific_guides/operation_motorman.aspx, accessed on 18 January 2013.

be distinguished from other people, data protection legislation is applicable.'[15] This applies to customers and prospective customers, hence there are outward-facing obligations. It can also apply to non-customers who may be using a particular website but are not a registered customer, if their personal data is being collected.

Inward-Facing Data Protection Compliance

1.15 The data protection regime also applies to the organisation in its dealings regarding the personal data of its employees. Equally, where the organisation is engaging third party independent contractors but is collecting, processing and using their personal data, the data protection regime will also apply. Hence, the data protection regime in relation to organisations is inward-facing.

1.16 As well as creating legal compliance obligations for organisations, the data protection regime enshrines certain rights or data protection rights for individuals in terms of ensuring their ability to know what personal data is being collected, to consent – or not consent – to the collection of their personal data, and to control the uses to which their personal data may be put. There is also a mechanism through which individuals can complain to data controllers holding their personal data, the ICO and also via the courts directly.

Information Commissioner

1.17 In order to ensure that the duties are complied with, and the rights of individuals vindicated, there is an official authority established in each Member State to monitor and act as appropriate in relation to the efficient operation of the data protection regime. This role is fulfilled in the UK by the ICO.

Why Data Protection?

1.18 Why have a data protection regime? We have a data protection regime because of the legal and political recognition that society respects the personal privacy and informational privacy of individuals. In the context of data protection, that means respect for, control of, and security in relation to informational personal data. The DPA protects

---

15 Costa, L, and Poullet, Y, 'Privacy and the Regulation of 2012,' *Computer Law & Security Review* (2012) (28), pp. 254–262, at 256.

personal data relating to individuals, which includes employees, contractors, customers and users.

Data protection exists in order to ensure:

- Privacy in relation to personal information;
- The consent of individuals is obtained to collect and process personal data;
- Security in respect for the right to privacy and personal information;
- Protection against privacy and informational privacy abuse;
- Protection against privacy theft and identity theft;
- Protection against unsolicited direct marketing (DM);
- Remedies are available to individual data subjects.

The threats to personal data and informational privacy have increased as the ease with which personal data can be collected and transferred electronically. This has increased further with digital technology, computer processing power and the rise of Internet 2.0 and social networking.[16]

Summary Data Protection Rules

1.19 Data controllers must comply with a number of data protection issues, perhaps the foremost of which relate to:

- Fairness;
- Transparency;
- Consent;
- Accuracy;
- Security;
- Proper procedures for processing.

The collecting, use and onward transfer of personal data must be fair, legitimate and transparent.

Transparency (and access to one's personal data) is increasingly being emphasised in importance in relation to the internet and social networking sphere. While this is beginning to be examined and there have been improvements with some websites, there is still a long way to go. Some have more improvements to make, even including the

---

16 Note generally, comments of the ICO in relation to Privacy by Design (PbD), and the report *Privacy by Design* (2008), available at http://www.ico.gov.uk/for_organisations/data_protection/topic_guides/privacy_by_design.aspx, accessed on 18 January 2013.

implementation of privacy policies and statements, reporting mechanisms and procedures. These also need to be assessed at the front and back end. In the recent Prudential case where a fine of £50,000 was issued, there was potential financial loss to the data subject.

The personal data must be correct and accurate. The reason is that damage or harm to the individual data subject can be a consequence of inaccurately held personal data. For example, a credit rating could be adversely affected through incorrect or wrong personal data records regarding personal payment histories.

There is a general obligation in terms of safeguarding personal data. Organisations must assess and implement security measures to protect personal data. Increasingly, this is also being considered in relation to the developing cloud environment and the increasing use of data processors and third parties.[17]

There is also an obligation on data controllers to register or notify the ICO as regards their data processing activities.

If personal data is permitted to be transferred to third countries, it must qualify under a specific exemption, as well as the general security conditions.

Data controllers can have a duty of care to individuals as regards their personal data being processed by the organisation, particularly if loss or damage arises.

Data controllers and data processors have obligations in certain circumstances to have legal contracts in place between them. Data processors process and deal with personal data for, and on behalf of, a data controller in relation to specific defined tasks, eg activities such as outsourced payroll, HR, marketing, market research, customer satisfaction surveys, etc.

General Criteria for Data Processing

1.20 Generally, in order to lawfully collect and process personal data, a data controller should be aware that:

- The individual data subject must consent to the collection and processing of their personal data;
- The data subject may say that they object to processing or continued processing;

---

17 In relation to cloud generally, one recent article is *W Kuan Hon and Christopher Millard*, 'Data Export Cloud Computing – How Can Personal Data be Transferred Outside the EEA? The Cloud of Unknowing,' SCRIPTed, (2012) (9:1), available at http://script-ed.org/?page_id=302, accessed 22 January 2012.

- Legal data protection requirements are complied with;
- The prior information requirements, Data Protection Principles, Legitimate Processing Conditions, Sensitive Personal Data Legitimate Processing Conditions (in the case of sensitive personal data), and security obligations are required to be complied with;
- The rights and interests of the individual data subject must be respected and complied with.

The interests of the data controller can sometimes be relevant in particular instances in deciding what data processing is necessary and permitted.

Data Protection Overview

1.21 The DPA, implementing the DPD95, sets out a number of structures, obligations, rights and implementing criteria which are together the basis of the legal data protection regime in the UK.

The main criteria and obligations to be respected and complied with in order to be able to legally collect and process personal data include,

- The definitions of personal data and the data protection regime;
- The Data Protection Principles, also known as the 'data quality principles';
- The Legitimate Processing Conditions;
- The requirement that processing of personal data be 'legitimate' under at least one of the Legitimate Processing Conditions;
- Recognising the two categories of personal data covered by the data protection regime, namely, *sensitive* personal data and *non-sensitive* general personal data;
- In the case of sensitive personal data, complying with the additional Sensitive Personal Data Legitimate Processing Conditions;
- Ensuring the fair obtaining of all personal data collected and processed;
- Taking and ensuring appropriate security measures in relation to all processing activities;
- Implementing formal legal contracts when engaging or dealing with third party data processors (eg outsourcing data processing tasks or activities);
- Complying with the separate criteria in relation to *automated decision making processes* or *automated decisions*;
- Complying with the legal criteria for direct marketing (DM);
- A duty of care can exist in relation to the individual data subjects whose personal data the organisation is collecting and processing;

- The transfer of personal data outside of the EEA is strictly controlled. Personal data may not be transferred outside of the EEA unless specifically permitted under the data protection regime;
- Access requests, or requests by individuals for copies of their personal data held by the organisation, must be complied with (with limited exceptions);
- Registration obligations by organisations must be complied with;
- Implementing internal privacy policies and terms;
- Implementing outward facing privacy policies for customers, etc;
- Implementing outward facing website privacy statements (generally a data protection policy covers organisation-wide activities, whereas a website privacy statement governs only the online collection and processing of personal data);
- Implementing mobile, computer and internet usage policies;
- Implementing data loss, data breach, incident handling and incident reporting policies and associated reaction plans;[18]
- Keeping abreast of the increasing trend towards sector/issue specific rules eg Spam; direct marketing (DM); industry codes of conduct[19] in relation to personal data, etc;
- Complying with new legal developments.

The EEA is wider that the EU Member States and includes Iceland, Liechtenstein and Norway. Switzerland has a similar type arrangement with the EU. EU data protection law frequently refers to the EEA generally meaning the EU Member States plus the EEA countries.

Legitimate Processing

1.22 There is a prohibition on the collection and processing of personal data and sensitive personal data unless:

- The processing complies with the Data Protection Principles; and;
- The processing comes within one of a limited number of specified conditions (the Legitimate Processing Conditions);
- The processing must also comply with the security requirements.

---

18 Note, for example, the ICO PECR security breach notifications – guidance for service providers, available at http://www.ico.gov.uk/for_organisations/guidance_index/data_protection_and_privacy_and_electronic_communications.aspx#privacy, accessed on 22 August, 2012.
19 The DPA and the EU data protection regime provide for codes of conduct being agreed with national data protection authorities such as the ICO in relation to specific industry sectors.

Definitions

1.23 The DPA contains a number of key definitions. These are central to understanding the data protection regime, and ultimately complying with it. These are essentially the building blocks of the data protection regime. While these can be 'complex concepts,'[20] organisations need to fully understand them. Some examples of the matters defined include:

- Data subject;
- Data controller;
- Data processor;
- Personal data;
- Processing;
- Relevant filing system;
- Sensitive personal data.

The definitions are found in greater detail in Chapter 3.

---

20 Hallinan, D., Friedewald, M., and McCarthy, P., 'Citizens' Perceptions of Data Protection and Privacy in Europe' *Computer Law & Security Review* (2012) (28), pp. 263–272, at 263.

Chapter 2

Sources of Data Protection Law

Introduction

2.01 Organisations and individuals need to consider a number of sources of the law and policy underpinning the data protection regime. In addition, there are a growing number of sources of interpretation and understanding of data protection law. Reliance on the DPA alone can, therefore, be insufficient. Data protection is therefore arguably quite different from many other areas of legal practice. In order to fully understand the data protection regime, one has to look beyond the text, or first principles, of the DPA.

What are the sources of data protection law and policy?

UK DPA

2.02 Primarily, the data protection regime in the UK is governed by the DPA. In addition, it is also necessary to have regard to a number of other sources of law, policy and the interpretation of the data protection regime. It is also necessary to look out for any amendments to same.

UK Secondary Legislation

2.03 In addition to the DPA, various statutory instruments need to be considered, which include:

- Adoption Agency Regulations 1983;
- Adoption Rules 1984;
- Banking Coordination (Second Council Directive) Regulations 1992;
- Civil Procedure Rules 1998;

- Consumer Credit (Credit Reference Agency) Regulations 1977;
- Consumer Credit (Credit Reference Agency) Regulations 2000;
- Consumer Protection (Contracts Concluded by Means of Distance Communications) Regulations 2000;
- Data Protection Act 1998 (Commencement) Order 2000;
- Data Protection Act 1998 (Commencement No 2) Order 2000;
- Data Protection Act 1998 (Commencement No 2) Order 2008;
- Data Protection (Corporate Finance Exemption) Order 2000;
- Data Protection (Conditions under paragraph 3 of Part II of Schedule 1) Order 2000;
- Data Protection (Crown Appointments) Order 2000;
- Data Protection (Designated Codes of Practice) Order 2000;
- Data Protection (Designated Codes of Practice) (No 2) Order 2000;
- Data Protection (Fees under section 19(7)) Regulations 2000;
- Data Protection (Functions of Designated Authorities) Order 2000;
- Data Protection (International Cooperation) Order 2000;
- Data Protection (Miscellaneous Subject Access Exemptions) Order 2000;
- Data Protection (Miscellaneous Subject Access Exemptions) (Amendment) Order 2000;
- Data Protection (Monetary Penalties) (Maximum Penalty and Notices) Regulations 2010;
- Data Protection (National Security Appeals) Regulations 2000;
- Data Protection (Notification and Notification Fees) Regulations 2000;
- Data Protection (Notification and Notification Fees) (Amendment) Regulations 2001;
- Data Protection (Notification and Notification Fees) (Amendment) Regulations 2009;
- Data Protection (Processing of Sensitive Personal Data) Order 2000;
- Data Protection (Processing of Sensitive Personal Data) Order 2006;
- Data Protection (Processing of Sensitive Personal Data) Order 2009;
- Data Protection (Processing of Sensitive Personal Data) (Elected Representatives) Order 2002;
- Data Protection (Processing of Sensitive Personal Data) (Elected Representatives) (Amendment) Order 2002;
- Data Protection Registration Fee Order 1991;
- Data Protection (Subject Access Modification) (Health) Order 2000;

- Data Protection (Subject Access Modification) (Education) Order 2000;
- Data Protection (Subject Access Modification) (Social Work) Order 2000;
- Data Protection (Processing of Sensitive Personal Data) Order 2000;
- Data Protection Registration Fee Order 1991;
- Data Protection (Subject Access) (Fees and Miscellaneous Provisions) Regulations 2000;
- Data Protection (Subject Access) (Fees and Miscellaneous Provisions) (Amendment) Regulations 2001;
- Data Protection (Subject Access Modification) (Social Work) (Amendment) Order 2005;
- Data Protection Tribunal (Enforcement Appeals) Rules 2000;
- Data Protection Tribunal (National Security Appeals) Rules 2000;
- Data Protection Tribunal (National Security Appeals) (Telecommunications) Rules 2000;
- Data Retention (EC Directive) Regulations 2007;
- Education (School Records) Regulations 1989;
- Education (Special Educational Needs) Regulations 1994;
- Electronic Commerce (EC Directive) Regulations 2002;
- Electronic Communications (Universal Service) Order 2003;
- Environmental Information (Fees and Appropriate Limits) Regulations 2004;
- Environmental Information Regulations 2004;
- Family Proceedings Courts (Children Act 1989) Rules 1991;
- Family Proceedings Rules 1991;
- Freedom of Information and Data Protection (Appropriate Limit and Fees) Regulations 2004;[1]
- Health Professions Order 2001;
- Health Service (Control of Patient Information) Regulations 2002;
- Information Tribunal (Enforcement Appeals) Rules 2005;
- Information Tribunal (Enforcement Appeals) (Amendment) Rules 2002;
- Information Tribunal (Enforcement Appeals) (Amendment) Rules 2005;
- Information Tribunal (National Security Appeals) Rules 2005;

---

1   The Freedom of Information and Data Protection (Appropriate Limit and Fees) Regulations 2004, available at http://www.legislation.gov.uk/uksi/2004/3244/contents/made, accessed on 18 January 2013.

- INSPIRE Regulations;[2]
- Insurance Companies (Third Insurance Directives) Regulations 1994;
- Investment Services Regulations 1995;
- Magistrates Courts (Adoption) Rules 1984;
- Magistrates Courts (Children and Young Persons) Rules 1992;
- Magistrates Courts (Criminal Justice (Children)) Rules 1992;
- Open Ended Investment Companies (Investment Companies with variable Capital) Regulations 1996;
- Parental Orders (Human Fertilisation and Embryology) Regulations 1994;
- Pharmacists and Pharmacy Technicians Order 2007;
- Police Act 1997 (Criminal Records) Regulations 2002;
- Police Act 1997 (Criminal Records) (Amendment) Regulations 2007;
- Privacy and Electronic Communications (EC Directive) Regulations 2003 (PECR);[3]
- Privacy and Electronic Communications (EC Directive) (Amendment) Regulations 2004;
- Privacy and Electronic Communications (EC Directive) (Amendment) Regulations 2011 (PECR Amendment Regulations);
- Privacy and Electronic Communications (EC Directive) Regulations 2003;
- Regulations of Investigatory Powers (Interception of Communications: Code of Practice) Order 2002;
- Regulation of Investigatory Powers (Communications Data) Order 2003;
- Regulation of Investigatory Powers (Communications Data) (Additional Functions and Amendment) Order 2006;
- Rehabilitation of Offenders (Exceptions) (Amendment) Order 2001;
- Rehabilitation of Offenders (Exceptions) (Amendment) (No 2) Order 2001;
- Representation of People (England and Wales) Regulations 2001;
- Representation of People (England and Wales) (Amendment) Regulations 2001;
- Representation of People Regulations 1986;

---

2   The INSPIRE Regulations, 2009, available at http://www.legislation.gov.uk/uksi/2009/3157/contents/made, accessed on 18 January 2013.
3   The Privacy and Electronic Communications (EC Directive) Regulations, 2003, available at http://www.legislation.gov.uk/uksi/2003/2426/contents/made, accessed on 18 January 2013.

- Telecommunications (Data Protection and Privacy) (Direct Marketing) Regulations 1998;
- Telecommunications (Data Protection and Privacy) Regulations 1999;
- Telecommunications (Data Protection and Privacy) Regulations 2000;
- Telecommunications (Data Protection and Privacy) (Amendment) Regulations 2000;
- Telecommunications (Lawful Business Practice) (Interception of Communications) Regulations 2000;
- Transfer of Undertakings (Protection of Employment) Regulations 2006;
- Unfair Terms in Consumer Contracts Regulations 1999;
- Waste Electrical and Electronic Equipment Regulations 2006;
- Directive 2002/58 on Privacy and Electronic Communications (ePrivacy Directive) amended by Directive 2009/136 (Cookie Regulation Directive).

It is also necessary to look out for any amendments to same.

EU Data Protection Law

2.04 The main sources of EU data protection law include:

- DPD95;
- EPD;
- DPR (and the new Directive (once enacted);
- Regulation (EC) No 45/2001 of the European Parliament and of the Council of 18 December 2000 on the protection of individuals with regard to the processing of personal data by the EU institutions and bodies and on the free movement of such data.[4]

It is also necessary to constantly keep abreast of all amendments to same.

The EU review of the DPD95 and the proposed update of the DPD95 via the draft DPR (and associated Directive) are arguably the most important developments in EU and UK data protection since 1995 (see

---

4   Regulation (EC) No 45/2001 of the European Parliament and of the Council of 18 December 2000 on the protection of individuals with regard to the processing of personal data by the EU institutions and bodies and on the free movement of such data, Regulation (EC) No 45/2001, OJ L 8, 12.1.2001, available at http://eur-lex.europa.eu/LexUriServ/LexUriServ.do?uri=OJ:L:2001:008:0001:0022:en:PDF, accessed on 18 January 2013.

Part 4). There will be significant implications for organisations and data protection practice.

Case law

2.05 Increasingly data protection cases (and cases which involve direct or indirect reference to personal data and information impacting the data protection regime) are coming to be litigated and determined before the courts.

One of the reasons is that individuals are increasingly aware of their rights under the data protection regime. A further reason is technological developments have enhanced the potential abuse of personal data, from Spam, unsolicited direct marketing (DM), hacking and data loss, phishing, email and internet scams, and litigation related access to personal data.

The case law which is relevant, whether influential or binding, to applying and interpreting the UK data protection regime include:

- Case studies and documentation from the ICO;
- Case complaints adjudicated by the ICO and or Tribunal;
- Cases in England and Wales;
- Cases in Scotland;
- European Court of Justice (ECJ) cases;
- European Court of Human Rights (ECHR) cases;
- Relevant cases in other EU Member States and or Common Law jurisdictions.

Some of the relevant cases are summarised at the end of the book.

ICO Guides

2.06 The ICO provides a number of guides and interpretations in relation to specific data protection issues and industry sectors. There are currently guides for:

- Audits;
- CCTV;
- Credit and finance;
- Crime mapping;
- Data processing;
- Data sharing;
- Data protection - general;
- Deletion;

- Education;
- Employment;
- Identity scanning;
- International transfer;
- Marketing;
- Monetary penalties;
- MPs and elected officials;
- Notification;
- Online;
- Personal data;
- Privacy and electronic communications - general;
- Privacy by design;
- Privacy notice;
- Relevant filing system;
- RFID tags;
- Security;
- Data subject access;
- Telecommunications.[5]

ICO Determinations

2.07　In addition, there is a body of decided decisions in relation to complaints filed by individuals with the ICO on various issues. These include the ICO's Office in England and Wales[6] and the ICO's Office in Scotland.[7] They can assist in considering identical and similar situations regarding issues of data protection compliance.[8]

Legal Textbooks

2.08　There are an increasing number of data protection legal textbooks and guides. Frequently also, IT legal textbooks will have chapters or sections dedicated to data protection. Some examples of the former include:

5　See, for example, ICO at http://www.ico.gov.uk/for_organisations/guidance_index/data_protection_and_privacy_and_electronic_communications.aspx#crime, accessed on 18 January 2013.

6　Available at http://www.ico.gov.uk/.

7　Available at http://www.ico.gov.uk/about_us/our_organisation/scotland.aspx.

8　In relation to the ICO and National Authorities generally regarding data protection not DPD95; and also Greenleaf, G., 'Independence of Data Privacy Authorities (Part 1): International Standards,' *Computer Law & Security Review* (2012) (28), pp. 3–13.

- Data Protection Law and Practice, Rosemary Jay (2012);
- Data Protection Strategy, Richard Morgan and Ruth Boardman (2012);
- Data Protection Compliance in the UK: A Pocket Guide, Rosemary Jay and Jenna Clarke (2008);
- Data Protection: Law and Practice, Rosemary Jay and Angus Hamilton (2007);
- Data Protection Law, David Bainbridge (2005);
- Data Protection: A Practical Guide to UK and EU Law, Peter Carey (2008);
- Property Rights in Personal Data, A European Perspective, Nadezhda Purtova (2012);
- Data Protection: Legal Compliance and Good Practice for Employers, Lynda A.C. Macdonald (2008);
- Data Protection in the Financial Services Industry, Mandy Webster (2006);
- Data Protection and Compliance in Context, Stewart Room (2007);
- European Data Protection Law: Corporate Compliance and Regulation, Christopher Kuner (2007);
- Data Protection for Financial Firms: A Practical Guide to Managing Privacy and Information Risk, Tim Gough, ed. (2009);
- Data Protection for Voluntary Organisations, Paul Ticher (2009);
- Data Protection for Virtual Data Centers, Jason Buffington (2010);
- Effective Data Protection: Managing Information in an Era of Change, Mandy Webster (2011);
- Data Protection & Privacy: Jurisdictional Comparisons, general editor: Monika Kuschewsky (2012);
- Implementation of the Data Protection Directive in Relation to Medical Research in Europe, D. Beyleveld *et al* (2005);
- Research Ethics Committees, Data Protection and Medical Research in European Countries, D. Beyleveld, D. Townend and J. Wright (2005);
- Data Protection and Employment Practices, Susan Singleton (2005);
- Data Protection: A Practical for Employers, Engineering Employers' Federation (2005);
- The New Data Protection Liabilities & Risks for Direct Marketers: Handbook, Rosemary Smith, and Jenny Moseley (2005);
- Data Protection in the NHS, Murray Earle (2003);
- Data Protection Strategy, Implementing Data Protection Compliance, Richard Morgan and Ruth Boardman (2012);

- Data Protection & the Pensions Industry: Implications of the Data Protection Act, Clare Fawke & Louise Townsend (2002);
- Data Protection Law: Approaching its Rationale, Logic and Limits, Lee A. Bygrave (2002);
- Regulating Spam: A European Perspective After the Adoption of the E-Privacy Directive, L. Asscher, and S.A. Hoogcarspel (2006);
- Information and Decisional Privacy, Madeleine Schachter (2003);
- Privacy on the Line, The Politics of Wiretapping and Encryption, Whitfield Diffie and Susan Landau (1998);
- European Data Protection Law: Corporate Regulation and Compliance, Christopher Kuner (2007).
- First Report on the Implementation of the Data Protection Directive (95/46/EC) (ie DPD95);
- Encyclopedia of Data Protection.

Some examples of the latter include:

- E-Commerce and Convergence: A Guide to the Law of Digital Media, Mike Butler, ed. (2012);
- Information Technology Law, Ian J. Lloyd (2011);
- Information Technology Law: The Law and Society, Andrew Murray (2010) (chapters 18 and 19);
- Concise European IT Law, Alfred Büllesbach *et al* (2010);
- Information Technology Law: The Law and Society, Andrew Murray (2010);
- The EU Regulatory Framework for Electronic Communications Handbook, Michael Ryan (2010));
- Law and the Internet, Lilian Edwards and Charlotte Waelde, eds. (2009) (chapters 14–21);
- Introduction to Information Technology Law, David Bainbridge (2008);
- Internet Law and Regulation, Graham J.H. Smith (2007) (chapter 7);
- Information Technology Law, Diane Rowland, Elizabeth Macdonald (2005);
- Computer Law: The Law and Regulation of Information Technology, Chris Reed and John Angel, eds. (2007) (chapters 10 and 11);
- Outsourcing – The Legal Contract, Rachel Burnett (2005);
- Outsourcing IT: The Legal Aspects: Planning, Contracting, Managing and the Law, Rachel Burnett (2009);
- A Business Guide to Information Security: How to Protect Your Company's IT Assets, Reduce Risks and Understand the Law, Alan Calder (2005);

- The New Legal Framework for E-Commerce in Europe, L. Edwards, ed. (2005);
- Communications Law Handbook, Mike Conradi, ed. (2009);
- Government and Information: The Law Relating to Access, Disclosure and their Regulation, Birkinshaw and Varney (2012).

Legal Journals

2.09 There are also relevant learned journals and articles published in relation to data protection compliance and developing data protection issues. Some examples include:

- *Data Protection Law and Practice*;
- *Communications Law*;
- *Journal of Information Law and Technology* (JILT), available at http://elj:warick.ac.uk;
- *Computers and Law* from the Society of Computers and Law, available at www.scl.org;
- *SCRIPTed*;
- *Computer Law and Security Review*.

WP29

2.10 In terms of the interpretation and understanding of the data protection regime in the UK, the Article 29 Working Party of the EU (WP29), established under Article 29 of the DPD95 is also required to be consulted. This is an influential body in relation to addressing and interpreting the data protection regime as well as problem areas in data protection practice. It is also influential as it is comprised of members from the respective data protection authorities in the EU, including the ICO.

WP29 issues working papers, opinions and related documentation. It is available at:

- http://ec.europa.eu/justice/policies/privacy/workinggroup/index_en.htm.

European Data Protection Supervisor

2.11 The European Data Protection Supervisor is also worth consulting and is arguably increasing in prominence and importance. Details are available at:

* http://www.edps.europa.eu/EDPSWEB/edps/EDPS).

Council of Europe

2.12 There are various important reference materials in relation to data protection and privacy emanating from the Council of Europe, such as:

* Council of Europe Convention on data protection, No 108 of 1981;
* Recommendation R(85) 20 on Direct Marketing;
* Recommendation R(86) 1 on Social Security;
* Recommendation R(97) 1 on the Media;
* Recommendation R(97) 5 on Health Data;
* Etc.

These and other documents are available at, http://www.coe.int/t/dghl/standardsetting/dataprotection/Documents_TPD_en.asp.

The Council of Europe Convention on data protection[9] of 1981 predates the DPD95 and is incorporated into the national law of many EU and other states (40 plus) prior to the DPD95. The Council of Europe is also reviewing and updating the Convention.[10]

Other Data Protection Authorities

2.13 Issues which may not yet be decided or formally reported on in the UK can sometimes have been considered elsewhere. It can therefore be useful to consider the decisions and logic behind decisions, reports and opinions of:

---

9   Convention for the Protection of Individuals with regard to Automatic Processing of Personal Data, Council of Europe (1982), available at http://conventions.coe.int/Treaty/en/Treaties/Html/108.htm, accessed on 18 January 2013. 'Draft Convention for the Protection of Individuals with Regards to Automatic Processing of Personal Data,' *International Legal Materials* (1980) (19), pp. 284–298.

10 See Kierkegaard, S., et al, '30 Years On – The Review of the Council of Europe Data Protection Convention 108,' *Computer Law & Security Review*, (2011) (27), pp. 223–231.

- Data Protection Authorities of other EU Member States and EEA Member States;
- Data Protection Authorities of other states, eg Canada.

The European Data Protection Supervisor provides links to the data protection authorities in the EU at:

- http://ec.europa.eu/justice/policies/privacy/nationalcomm/index_ en.htm.

Other Official Sources

2.14 Related issues can sometimes arise under freedom of information legislation.

Tribunals can also be relevant, none more so than the current Leveson Inquiry, particularly in terms of protection for personal data, security, deliberate breaches, hacking, etc, and the ICO and Operation Motorman. The report and ultimate recommendations of the Leveson Inquiry are also of interest from a data protection perspective (see below, Part 4).

Key/Topical Issues

2.15 Some of the key developments and issues which also influence the data protection regime and how it is interpreted include:

- Security requirements for business;
- Employee monitoring and consent;
- Spam and direct marketing;
- The relationship between the data controller and the data processor, and which relationship needs to be formalised in contract pursuant to the DPA;
- Disposal of computer hardware. Particular care is needed when considering the disposal of IT hardware, equipment and software. They may still contain personal data files. This can continue to be the case even when it appears that files have been wiped or deleted. There are many examples accessible personal data still being available even after it is believed to have been deleted and the device handed over to a third part, or worse sold on. The new recipient could be able to access the original personal data and records. This could quite easily be a breach of a number of principles in the data protection regime. It is always advised to take professional legal, IT and or forensic advice when considering disposing of computer devices;

- Websites and social networking compliance with the data protection regime;
- Online abuse.

Data Protection Websites and Blogs

2.16 There are number of privacy and data protection websites and blogs, such as Datonomy, available at http://www.datonomy.eu/, the Data Protection Forum at www.dpforum.org.uk and the Society of Computers and Law at www.scl.org.

Other Laws

2.17 Other laws can also be relevant in considering personal data and privacy.[11] Examples include:

- IT law;
- Contract law;
- Consumer law;
- eCommerce law;
- Financial services law;
- Health law;
- Computer crime and theft laws;
- Abuse and harassment laws.

Conferences

2.18 There are a variety of conferences, annual events and training organisations related to data protection. Some will be organised by professional conference firms while others are non-profit technology, legal or related organisations.

Reference

2.19 Useful reference material is available as set out below.

The DPA is at: http://www.legislation.gov.uk/ukpga/1998/29/section/2

---

11 See review of particular laws in Delfino, R., 'European Union Legislation and Actions,' *European Review of Contract Law* (2011) (7), pp. 547–551, which includes reference to data protection law.

The ICO is at: http://www.ico.gov.uk/

The EU Commission is at: http://ec.europa.eu/justice/data-protection/index_en.htm

The WP29 is at: http://ec.europa.eu/justice/policies/privacy/working group/index_en.htm

The ECJ website is at: http://europa.eu/about-eu/institutions-bodies/court-justice/index_en.htm

ECJ cases[12] are at: http://curia.europa.eu/juris/recherche.jsf?language=en

The ECHR website is at: http://www.echr.coe.int/ECHR/Home page_En/

---

12 Tzanou, M., 'Balancing Fundamental Rights, United in Diversity? Some Reflections on the Recent Case Law of the European Court of Justice on Data Protection,' *CYELP* (2010) (6), pp. 53–74.

Chapter 3

Definitions

Introduction

3.01 It is critical to understanding the data protection regime to know and appreciate the definitions of key terms which underpin the legal measures implementing the data protection regime. The definitions are the building blocks for the data protection regime. They are contained in the DPA and DPD95. There are also definitions in the new proposed DPR (Regulation) which should also be considered as these will update the EU data protection legal regime. It will also become the main EU data protection legal measure for many years to come.

The various definitions are referred to below.

DPA Definitions

3.02 Section 1 of the DPA sets out the following definitions,

'data'   means information which,

    (a)   is being processed by means of equipment operating automatically in response to instructions given for that purpose,

    (b)   is recorded with the intention that it should be processed by means of such equipment,

    (c)   is recorded as part of a relevant filing system or with the intention that it should form part of a relevant filing system,

    (d)   does not fall within paragraph (a), (b) or (c) but forms part of an accessible record as defined by s 68; or

(e) is recorded information held by a public authority and does not fall within any of the above;

'data controller' means, subject to sub-s (4), a person who (either alone or jointly or in common with other persons) determines the purposes for which and the manner in which any personal data are, or are to be, processed;

'data processor' in relation to personal data, means any person (other than an employee of the data controller) who processes the data on behalf of the data controller;

'data subject' means an individual who is the subject of personal data;

'personal data' means data which relate to a living individual who can be identified,

- from those data, or

- from those data and other information which is in the possession of, or is likely to come into the possession of, the data controller,

and includes any expression of opinion about the individual and any indication of the intentions of the data controller or any other person in respect of the individual;

'processing' in relation to information or data, means obtaining, recording or holding the information or data or carrying out any operation or set of operations on the information or data, including,

- organisation, adaptation or alteration of the information or data,

- retrieval, consultation or use of the information or data,

- disclosure of the information or data by transmission, dissemination or otherwise making available, or

- alignment, combination, blocking, erasure or destruction of the information or data;

'public authority' means a public authority as defined by the Freedom of Information Act 2000 or a Scottish public authority as defined by the Freedom of Information (Scotland) Act 2002;

'relevant filing system'	means any set of information relating to individuals to the extent that, although the information is not processed by means of equipment operating automatically in response to instructions given for that purpose, the set is structured, either by reference to individuals or by reference to criteria relating to individuals, in such a way that specific information relating to a particular individual is readily accessible;
'obtaining' or 'recording'	in relation to personal data, includes obtaining or recording the information to be contained in the data;
'using' or 'disclosing'	in relation to personal data, includes using or disclosing the information contained in the data.

In determining for the purposes of the DPA whether any information is recorded with the intention:

- that it should be processed by means of equipment operating automatically in response to instructions given for that purpose; or
- that it should form part of a relevant filing system,

it is immaterial that it is intended to be so processed or to form part of such a system only after being transferred to a country or territory outside the EEA.

Where personal data are processed only for purposes for which they are required by or under any enactment to be processed, the person on whom the obligation to process the data is imposed by or under that enactment is for the purposes of the DPA the data controller.

In paragraph (e) of the definition of 'data' in sub-s (1), the reference to information 'held' by a public authority shall be construed in accordance with s 3(2) of the Freedom of Information Act 2000 or s 3(2), (4) and (5) of the Freedom of Information (Scotland) Act 2002. Where:

- s 7 of the Freedom of Information Act 2000 prevents Parts I to V of that Act; or
- s 7(1) of the Freedom of Information (Scotland) Act 2002 prevents that Act from applying to certain information held by a public authority, that information is not to be treated for the purposes of paragraph (e) of the definition of 'data' in sub-s (1) as held by a public authority.

Section 2 of the DPA also sets out the following definition of sensitive personal data. It is personal data consisting of information as to:

- the racial or ethnic origin of the data subject;
- their political opinions;
- their religious beliefs or other beliefs of a similar nature;
- whether they are a member of a trade union (within the meaning of the Trade Union and Labour Relations (Consolidation) Act 1992);
- their physical or mental health or condition;
- their sexual life;
- the commission or alleged commission of any offence; or
- any proceedings for any offence committed or alleged to have been committed, the disposal of such proceedings or the sentence of any court in such proceedings.

Sensitive personal data contains higher compliance obligations and conditions.

DPD95 Definitions

3.03 Article 2 of the DPD sets out the following definitions,

'personal data'	shall mean any information relating to an identified or identifiable natural person ('data subject'); an identifiable person is one who can be identified, directly or indirectly, in particular by reference to an identification number or to one or more factors specific to his physical, physiological, mental, economic, cultural or social identity;
'processing of personal Data' ('processing')	shall mean any operation or set of operations which is performed upon personal data, whether or not by automatic means, such as collection, recording, organisation, storage, adaptation or alteration, retrieval, consultation, use, disclosure by transmission, dissemination or otherwise making available, alignment or combination, blocking, erasure or destruction;
'personal data filing system' ('filing system')	shall mean any structured set of personal data which are accessible according to specific criteria, whether centralised, decentralised or dispersed on a functional or geographical basis;

'controller' [as in data controller]	shall mean the natural or legal person, public authority, agency or any other body which alone or jointly with others determines the purposes and means of the processing of personal data; where the purposes and means of processing are determined by national or EU laws or regulations, the controller or the specific criteria for his nomination may be designated by national or EU law;
'processor' [as in data processor]	shall mean a natural or legal person, public authority, agency or any other body which processes personal data on behalf of the data controller;
'third party'	shall mean any natural or legal person, public authority, agency or any other body other than the data subject, the data controller, the data processor and the persons who, under the direct authority of the data controller or the data processor, are authorised to process the data;
'recipient'	shall mean a natural or legal person, public authority, agency or any other body to whom data are disclosed, whether a third party or not; however, authorities which may receive data in the framework of a particular inquiry shall not be regarded as recipients;
'the data subject's consent'	shall mean any freely given specific and informed indication of their wishes by which the data subject signifies their agreement to personal data relating to them being processed.

DPR Definitions

3.04   Article 4 of the new draft DPR sets out the following definitions,

'data subject'	means an identified natural person or a natural person who can be identified, directly or indirectly, by means reasonably likely to be used by the data controller or by any other natural or legal person, in particular by reference to an identification number, location data, online identifier or to one or more factors specific to the physical, physiological, genetic, mental, economic, cultural or social identity of that person;

'personal data'	means any information relating to a data subject;
'processing'	means any operation or set of operations which is performed upon personal data or sets of personal data, whether or not by automated means, such as collection, recording, organisation, structuring, storage, adaptation or alteration, retrieval, consultation, use, disclosure by transmission, dissemination or otherwise making available, alignment or combination, erasure or destruction;
'filing system'	means any structured set of personal data which are accessible according to specific criteria, whether centralised, decentralised or dispersed on a functional or geographical basis;
'controller'	means the natural or legal person, public authority, agency or any other body which alone or jointly with others determines the purposes, conditions and means of the processing of personal data; where the purposes, conditions and means of processing are determined by EU law or Member State law, the data controller or the specific criteria for his nomination may be designated by EU law or by Member State law;
'processor'	means a natural or legal person, public authority, agency or any other body which processes personal data on behalf of the data controller;
'recipient'	means a natural or legal person, public authority, agency or any other body to which the personal data are disclosed;
'the data subject's consent'	means any freely given specific, informed and explicit indication of his or her wishes by which the data subject, either by a statement or by a clear affirmative action, signifies agreement to personal data relating to them being processed;
'personal data breach'	means a breach of security leading to the accidental or unlawful destruction, loss, alteration, unauthorised disclosure of, or access to, personal data transmitted, stored or otherwise processed;
'genetic data'	means all data, of whatever type, concerning the characteristics of an individual which are inherited or acquired during early prenatal development;

'biometric data'	means any data relating to the physical, physiological or behavioural characteristics of an individual which allow their unique identification, such as facial images, or dactyloscopic data;
'data concerning health'	means any information which relates to the physical or mental health of an individual, or to the provision of health services to the individual;
'main establishment'	means as regards the data controller, the place of its establishment in the EU where the main decisions as to the purposes, conditions and means of the processing of personal data are taken; if no decisions as to the purposes, conditions and means of the processing of personal data are taken in the EU, the main establishment is the place where the main processing activities in the context of the activities of an establishment of a data controller in the EU take place. As regards the data processor, 'main establishment' means the place of its central administration in the EU;
'representative'	means any natural or legal person established in the EU who, explicitly designated by the data controller, acts and may be addressed by any Supervisory Authority and other bodies in the EU instead of the data controller, with regard to the obligations of the data controller under the Regulation;
'enterprise'	means any entity engaged in an economic activity, irrespective of its legal form, thus including, in particular, natural and legal persons, partnerships or associations regularly engaged in an economic activity;
'group of undertakings'	means a controlling undertaking and its controlled undertakings;
'binding corporate rules'	means personal data protection policies which are adhered to by a data controller or data processor established on the territory of a Member State of the EU for transfers or a set of transfers of personal data to a data controller or data processor in one or more third countries within a group of undertakings;
'child'	means any person below the age of 18 years;
'Supervisory Authority'	means a public authority which is established by a Member State in accordance with Article 46.

Two Categories of Personal Data

3.05 Organisations need to be familiar with two separate categories of personal data in relation to their data protection actions and compliance obligations. It also affects what personal data they may collect in the first instance.

The first is general personal data. Unless specified otherwise, all personal data falls into this category. The second category is sensitive personal data. The importance of sensitive personal data is that it triggers additional and more onerous obligations of compliance and initial collection conditions.

Why is there a distinction? Certain categories of personal data are more important, personal and sensitive to individuals over other categories of personal data. This is recognised in the data protection regime. Additional rules are put in place. Firstly, sensitive personal data is defined differently. Secondly, in order to collect and process sensitive personal data, an organisation must satisfy additional processing conditions, in addition to the Data Protection Principles and the general Legitimate Processing Conditions, namely complying with the Sensitive Personal Data Legitimate Processing Conditions.

DPA: Sensitive Personal Data

3.06 Section 2 of the DPA defines Sensitive Personal Data as consisting of information as to:

- the racial or ethnic origin of the data subject;
- political opinions;
- religious beliefs or other beliefs of a similar nature;
- whether a member of a trade union (within the meaning of the Trade Union and Labour Relations (Consolidation) Act 1992);
- physical or mental health or condition;
- sexual life;
- the commission or alleged commission of any offence; or
- any proceedings for any offence committed or alleged to have been committed, the disposal of such proceedings or the sentence of any court in such proceedings.

DPD95: Sensitive Personal Data

3.07 Article 8 of the DPD95 refers to the processing of special categories of data. It states:

- Member States shall prohibit the processing of personal data revealing racial or ethnic origin, political opinions, religious or philosophical beliefs, trade-union membership, and the processing of data concerning health or sex life;
- the above paragraph 1 shall not apply where:
  - the data subject has given their explicit consent to the processing of those data, except where the laws of the Member State provide that the prohibition referred to in paragraph 1 may not be lifted by the data subject's giving his consent; or
  - processing is necessary for the purposes of carrying out the obligations and specific rights of the data controller in the field of employment law in so far as it is authorised by national law providing for adequate safeguards; or
  - processing is necessary to protect the vital interests of the data subject or of another person where the data subject is physically or legally incapable of giving their consent; or
  - processing is carried out in the course of its legitimate activities with appropriate guarantees by a foundation, association or any other non-profit-seeking body with a political, philosophical, religious or trade-union aim and on condition that the processing relates solely to the members of the body or to persons who have regular contact with it in connection with its purposes and that the data are not disclosed to a third party without the consent of the data subjects; or
  - the processing relates to data which are manifestly made public by the data subject or is necessary for the establishment, exercise or defence of legal claims;
- Paragraph 1 above shall not apply where processing of the data is required for the purposes of preventive medicine, medical diagnosis, the provision of care or treatment or the management of health-care services, and where those data are processed by a health professional subject under national law or rules established by national competent bodies to the obligation of professional secrecy or by another person also subject to an equivalent obligation of secrecy;
- Subject to the provision of suitable safeguards, Member States may, for reasons of substantial public interest, lay down exemptions in addition to those laid down in paragraph 2 (bullet 2) either by national law or by decision of the Supervisory Authority;
- Processing of data relating to offences, criminal convictions or security measures may be carried out only under the control of official authority, or if suitable specific safeguards are provided under national law, subject to derogations which may be granted by

the Member State under national provisions providing suitable specific safeguards. However, a complete register of criminal convictions may be kept only under the control of official authority. Member States may provide that data relating to administrative sanctions or judgements in civil cases shall also be processed under the control of official authority.

Member States shall determine the conditions under which a national identification number or any other identifier of general application may be processed.

DPR: Sensitive Personal Data

3.08   Article 9 of the DPR relates to the processing of special categories of personal data. Article 9(1) states that the processing of personal data, revealing race or ethnic origin, political opinions, religion or beliefs, trade-union membership, and the processing of genetic data or data concerning health or sex life or criminal convictions or related security measures shall be prohibited.

Article 9(2) provides that paragraph 1 (above) shall not apply where:

- the data subject has given consent to the processing of those personal data, subject to the conditions laid down in Articles 7 and 8, except where EU law or Member State law provide that the prohibition referred to in paragraph 1 may not be lifted by the data subject; or
- processing is necessary for the purposes of carrying out the obligations and exercising specific rights of the data controller in the field of employment law in so far as it is authorised by EU law or Member State law providing for adequate safeguards; or
- processing is necessary to protect the vital interests of the data subject or of another person where the data subject is physically or legally incapable of giving consent; or
- processing is carried out in the course of its legitimate activities with appropriate safeguards by a foundation, association or any other non-profit seeking body with a political, philosophical, religious or trade-union aim and on condition that the processing relates solely to the members or to former members of the body or to persons who have regular contact with it in connection with its purposes and that the data are not disclosed outside that body without the consent of the data subjects; or
- the processing relates to personal data which are manifestly made public by the data subject; or

- processing is necessary for the establishment, exercise or defence of legal claims; or
- processing is necessary for the performance of a task carried out in the public interest, on the basis of EU law, or Member State law which shall provide for suitable measures to safeguard the data subject's legitimate interests; or
- processing of data concerning health is necessary for health purposes and subject to the conditions and safeguards referred to in Article 81; or
- processing is necessary for historical, statistical or scientific research purposes subject to the conditions and safeguards referred to in Article 83; or
- processing of data relating to criminal convictions or related security measures is carried out either under the control of official authority or when the processing is necessary for compliance with a legal or regulatory obligation to which a data controller is subject, or for the performance of a task carried out for important public interest reasons, and in so far as authorised by EU law or Member State law providing for adequate safeguards. A complete register of criminal convictions shall be kept only under the control of official authority.

Article 9(3) empowers the Commission to adopt delegated acts for the purpose of further specifying the criteria, conditions and appropriate safeguards for the processing of the special categories of personal data referred to in paragraph 1 and the exemptions laid down in paragraph 2.

Conclusion

3.09 It is important for organisations to distinguish, in advance of collecting personal data, whether the proposed data collection relates to general personal data or sensitive personal data. They also need to be able to confirm compliance procedures in advance of collecting and maintaining personal data and particularly sensitive personal data. The organisation could be asked to demonstrate at a future date that it obtained consent, and general compliance. If it cannot, it may have to delete the data, have committed breaches and offences, and potentially face fines and or being sued by the data subject. Depending on the circumstances, personal liability can also arise.

Chapter 4

History and EU Data Protection

Introduction

4.01 The legal discussion in relation to privacy is frequently linked to the Warren and Brandeis's legal article in 1890 entitled 'The Right to Privacy' published in the Harvard Law Review.[1] Arguably, data protection is the modern coalface of the debate in relation to privacy and privacy protection.[2] The EU data protection regime can be considered as setting standards in certain areas of informational privacy protection – which have come to be followed in other jurisdictions internationally beyond the EU.[3] There have also been calls for international level data protection rules. Certainly, if this was to come to pass, it could add greater certainty for both organisations, the industry and individual data subjects.

History of Data Protection

4.02 The growth of the processing of information relating to individuals in electronic computer data format from the 1970s onwards, led to ever increasing concerns regarding such processing. Existing laws

---

1   Warren, S., and Brandeis, L., 'The Right to Privacy," *Harvard Law Review* (1890) (IV), p. 193.
2   See JB Rule, J.B., and G Greenleaf, G., eds, *Global Privacy Protection – The First Generation* (Cheltenham: Elgar, 2008).
3   See Birnhack, M., 'The EU Data Protection Directive: An Engine of a Global Regime,' *Computer Law & Security Report* (2008) (2), p. 508, at 512.

were 'insufficient to deal with concerns about the amount of information relating to individuals that was held by organisations in electronic form.'[4] The purpose behind the DPA was largely to promote openness and transparency of information held about individuals in filing systems, whether manual or computerised, and to protect the privacy and data protection interests and rights of such individuals.[5]

The main EU data protection instrument is the DPD95.[6] This is implemented in the UK by the DPA.

However, even prior to the Directive in 1995 concern for informational privacy in the computer environment was recognised in an early data protection regime. The Council of Europe proposed and enacted the Convention for the Protection of Individuals with Regard to Automatic Processing of Personal Data Done at Strasbourg on the 28 January, 1981.[7] The UK implemented the DPA 1984. Ultimately this was replaced with the DPA in 1998 to implement the DPD95. It is also implemented in secondary legislation relating to data protection.[8]

There were also a number of official investigations and proposed bills regarding privacy and data protection. The Younger Committee on Privacy[9] proposed ten recommendations and principles regarding personal data. It proposed the following principles:

- Information should be regarded as held for a specific purpose and should not be used, without appropriate authorisation, for other purposes;
- Access to information should be confined to those authorised to have it for the purpose for which it was supplied;
- The amount of information collected and held should be the minimum necessary for the achievement of a specified purpose;

4   Carey, P., *Data Protection, A Practical Guide to UK and EU Law* (Oxford: OUP, 2009), p. 1. Also, Bainbridge, D., *Data Protection* (CLT, 2000), p. 2.
5   MacDonald, Lynda, A.C., *Data Protection: Legal Compliance and Good Practice for Employers* (London: Tottel, 2008), p. 33.
6   D'Afflitto, R.I., 'European Union Directive on Personal Privacy Rights and Computerised Information,' *Villanova Law Review* (1996) (41), pp. 305–324.
7   Council of Europe Convention for the Protection of Individuals with Regard to Automatic Processing of Personal Data Done at Strasbourg on the 28 January, 1981, available at http://conventions.coe.int/Treaty/en/Treaties/Html/108.htm, accessed on 18 January 2013. Also, Convention for the Protection of Individuals with Regard to Automatic Processing of Personal Data,' *International Legal Materials* (1981) (20), pp. 317–325.
8   See generally Carey, P., *Data Protection, A Practical Guide to UK and EU Law* (Oxford, OUP, 2009), chapter 1.
9   Younger Committee on Privacy, Cmnd 5012 (1972).

- In computerised systems handling information for statistical purposes, adequate provision should be made in their design and programs for separating identities from the rest of the data;
- There should be arrangements whereby a subject can be told about the information held concerning them;
- The level of security to be achieved by a system should be specified in advance by the user and should include precautions against the deliberate abuse or misuse of information;
- A monitoring system should be provided to facilitate the detection of any violation of the security system;
- In the design of information systems, periods should be specified beyond which the information should not be retained;
- Data held should be accurate. There should be machinery for the correction of inaccuracy and updating of information;
- Care should be taken in coding value judgements.

This was followed by the Lindrop Committee[10] on how best to proceed to protect privacy and personal data. The Committee uses the term 'data privacy' to mean the individual data subject's right to control the circulation of data about them.[11] While specific recommendations were made, these were not enacted. Ultimately, the DPA 1984 was enacted following on from the Council of Europe Convention 1981 relating to data processing. It is entitled 'Convention for the Protection of Individuals with regard to the Automatic Processing of Personal Data.' The Convention sets out the following principles and requirements, namely, the personal data must be:

- obtained and processed fairly and lawfully;
- stored for specified and legitimate purposes and not used in a way incompatible with those purposes;
- adequate, relevant and not excessive in relation to the purposes for which they are stored;
- accurate and, where necessary, kept up to date;
- preserved in a form which permits identification of the data subjects for no longer than is required for the purpose for which those data are stored.

In addition, the Convention provides that:

- Personal data revealing racial origin, political opinions or religious or other beliefs, as well as personal data concerning health or

---

10   Lindrop Committee, Cmnd 7341 (1978).
11   Referred to in Carey, P., above, p. 3.

sexual life, may not be processed automatically unless domestic law provides appropriate safeguards. The same shall apply to personal data relating to criminal convictions;

- Appropriate security measures shall be taken for the protection of personal data stored in automated data files against accidental or unauthorised destruction or accidental loss as well as against unauthorised access, alteration or dissemination;
- Any person shall be enabled:
  - to establish the existence of an automated personal data file, its main purposes, as well as the identity and habitual residence or principal place of business of the controller of the file;
  - to obtain at reasonable intervals and without excessive delay or expense confirmation of whether personal data relating to them are stored in the automated data file as well as communication to them of such data in an intelligible form;
  - to obtain, as the case may be, rectification or erasure of such data if these have been processed contrary to the provisions of domestic law giving effect to the basic principles set out in Articles 5 and 6 of the convention;
  - to have a remedy if a request for confirmation or, as the case may be, communication, rectification or erasure are not complied with.[12]

Data Protection Act

4.03 The DPA implements the provisions of the EU DPA95 on the protection of individuals with regard to the processing of personal data and on the free movement of such data. The DPA95 ensures data protection and a common data protection regime across Member States in the EU. It is also extended to EEA Member States.

The DPA of 1998 was commenced on 1 March 2000 in the UK.[13]

The DPA has important implications for business and organisations which collect, process and deal in information relating to living individuals, and in particular customers and employees. It contains stringent data protection measures to safeguard personal informational

---

12 Convention Articles 5–8.
13 There was also a previous Data Protection Act in the UK, namely, the Data Protection Act 1984. The DPA of 1998 repealed the DPA of 1984. The DPA was passed into law on 1 March 2000 pursuant to the Data Protection Act (Commencement) Order 2000 (SI 2000/183).

privacy and to ensure that personal data is not misused or used for purposes that are incompatible with data protection legislation.

Legal Instruments

4.04   The introduction or Recitals to the European legal instruments, while not legally binding like the main text of the provisions, are still influential in terms of interpreting the data protection regime, and also highlight some of the history, philosophy and policy behind particular data protections laws and provisions.

DPD95 Recitals

4.05   The DPD95 provides the overarching framework for data protection in the EU and EEA.[14] The Directive provides the Data Protection Principles, Legitimate Processing Conditions, security requirements, individual data subject rights, fair collection and processing rules, restriction of trans-border data flows or transfers of personal data and sensitive personal data rules. The DPD95 at a headline level also provides for:

● Privacy and data protection;
● Harmonisation of such measures throughout the EU.

Some of the pertinent Recitals to the DPD include the following themes which are also illustrative of the aims, and intentions and implementation of the DPD95.

Harmonisation

Recital 1 of DPD95 states that the objectives of the EU include creating an ever closer union among the peoples of Europe, fostering closer relations between the States belonging to the EU, ensuring economic and social progress by common action to eliminate the barriers which divide Europe, encouraging the constant improvement of the living conditions of its peoples, preserving and strengthening peace and liberty and promoting democracy on the basis of the fundamental rights recognised in the constitution and laws of the Member States and in the European Convention for the Protection of Human Rights and Fundamental Freedoms.

---

14   EU Member States plus Iceland, Liechtenstein and Norway.

Privacy/Data Protection/Fundamental Rights/Sectors

Recital 2 states that whereas data-processing systems are designed to serve, they must, whatever the nationality or residence of natural persons, respect their fundamental rights and freedoms, notably the right to privacy, and contribute to economic and social progress, trade expansion and the well-being of individuals.

Recital 3 states that personal data should be able to flow freely from one Member State to another, but also that the fundamental rights of individuals should be safeguarded.

Recital 22 states that Member States shall more precisely define in the laws they enact or when bringing into force the measures taken under the Directive the general circumstances in which processing is lawful. In particular Article 5, in conjunction with Articles 7 and 8, allows Member States, independently of general rules, to provide for special processing conditions for specific sectors and for the various categories of data covered by Article 8.

Recital 23 states that Member States are empowered to ensure the implementation of the protection of individuals both by means of a general law on the protection of individuals as regards the processing of personal data and by sectorial laws such as those relating, for example, to statistical institutes.

Recital 26 states that the principles of protection must apply to any information concerning an identified *or identifiable* person. To determine whether a person is identifiable, account should be taken of *all* the *means likely* reasonably to be used either by the data controller or by any other person *to identify the said person*. The principles of protection shall not apply to data rendered anonymous in such a way that the data subject is no longer identifiable. Codes of conduct within the meaning of Article 27 may be a useful instrument for providing guidance as to the ways in which data may be rendered anonymous and retained in a form in which identification of the data subject is no longer possible.

Recital 27 states that the protection of individuals must apply as much to automatic processing of data as to manual processing. The scope of this protection must not in effect depend on the techniques used. Otherwise this would create a serious risk of circumvention. As regards manual processing, the Directive covers only filing systems, not unstructured files. In particular, the content of a filing system must be structured according to specific criteria relating to individuals allowing easy access to the personal data. The different criteria for determining the constituents of a structured set of personal data, and the different criteria governing access to such a set, may be laid down by each

Member State. Files or sets of files as well as their cover pages, which are not structured according to specific criteria, shall under no circumstances fall within the scope of the Directive.

Recital 28 states that any processing of personal data must be lawful and fair to the individuals concerned. In particular, the data must be adequate, relevant and not excessive in relation to the purposes for which they are processed. Such purposes must be explicit and legitimate and must be determined at the time of collection of the data. Whereas the purposes of processing further to collection shall not be incompatible with the purposes as they were originally specified.

Recital 30 states that in order to be lawful, the processing of personal data must in addition be carried out with the *consent* of the data subject or be necessary for the conclusion or performance of a contract binding on the data subject, or as a legal requirement, or for the performance of a task carried out in the public interest or in the exercise of official authority, or in the legitimate interests of a natural or legal person, provided that the interests or the rights and freedoms of the data subject are not overriding. In order to maintain a balance between the interests involved while guaranteeing effective competition, Member States may determine the circumstances in which personal data may be used or disclosed to a third party in the context of the legitimate ordinary business activities of companies and other bodies. Member States may similarly specify the conditions under which personal data may be disclosed to a third party for the purposes of marketing whether carried out commercially or by a charitable organisation or by any other association or foundation, of a political nature for example, subject to the provisions allowing a data subject to object to the processing of data regarding them, at no cost and without having to state his reasons.

Recital 31 states that the processing of personal data must equally be regarded as lawful where it is carried out in order to protect an interest which is essential for the data subject's life.

Recital 33 states that data which are capable by their nature of infringing fundamental freedoms or privacy should not be processed unless the data subject gives his *explicit* consent. However, derogations from this prohibition must be explicitly provided for in respect of specific needs, in particular where the processing of these data is carried out for certain health-related purposes by persons subject to a legal obligation of professional secrecy or in the course of legitimate activities by certain associations or foundations the purpose of which is to permit the exercise of fundamental freedoms.

Recital 38 states that if the processing of data is to be fair, the data subject must be in a position to learn of the existence of a processing operation and, where data are collected from them, must be given accurate and full information, bearing in mind the circumstances of the collection.

Recital 39 states that certain processing operations involve data which the controller has not collected directly from the data subject; whereas, furthermore, data can be legitimately disclosed to a third party, even if the disclosure was not anticipated at the time the data were collected from the data subject; whereas, in all these cases, the data subject should be informed when the data are recorded or at the latest when the data are first disclosed to a third party.

Recital 68 states that the principles set out in the Directive regarding the protection of the rights and freedoms of individuals, notably their right to privacy, with regard to the processing of personal data may be supplemented or clarified, in particular as far as certain sectors are concerned, by specific rules based on those principles.

Technology/Increased Processing

Recital 4 states that increasingly frequent recourse is being had in the EU to the processing of personal data in the various spheres of economic and social activity. The progress made in information technology is making the processing and exchange of such data considerably easier.

Recital 5 states that the economic and social integration resulting from the establishment and functioning of the internal market will necessarily lead to a substantial increase in cross-border flows of personal data between all those involved in a private or public capacity in economic and social activity in the Member States. The exchange of personal data between undertakings in different Member States is set to increase. The national authorities in the various Member States are being called upon by virtue of EU law to collaborate and exchange personal data so as to be able to perform their duties or carry out tasks on behalf of an authority in another Member State within the context of the area without internal frontiers as constituted by the internal market.

Recital 6 states that the increase in scientific and technical cooperation and the coordinated introduction of new telecommunications networks in the EU necessitate and facilitate cross-border flows of personal data.

Recital 10 states that the object of the national laws on the processing of personal data is to protect fundamental rights and freedoms, notably the right to privacy, which is recognised both in Article 8 of the European Convention for the Protection of Human Rights and Fundamental Freedoms and in the general principles of EU law. The approximation of those laws must not result in any lessening of the protection they afford but must, on the contrary, seek to ensure a high level of protection in the EU.

Barriers

Recital 7 states that the difference in levels of protection of the rights and freedoms of individuals, notably the right to privacy, with regard to the processing of personal data afforded in the Member States may prevent the transmission of such data from the territory of one Member State to that of another Member State. This difference may therefore constitute an obstacle to the pursuit of a number of economic activities at EU level, distort competition and impede authorities in the discharge of their responsibilities under EU law. This difference in levels of protection is due to the existence of a wide variety of national laws, regulations and administrative provisions.

Recital 8 states that in order to remove the obstacles to flows of personal data, the level of protection of the rights and freedoms of individuals with regard to the processing of such data must be equivalent in all Member States. This objective is vital to the internal market but cannot be achieved by the Member States alone, especially in view of the scale of the divergences which currently exist between the relevant laws in the Member States and the need to coordinate the laws of the Member States so as to ensure that the cross-border flow of personal data is regulated in a consistent manner that is in keeping with the objective of the internal market as provided for in Article 7a of the Treaty. EU action to approximate those laws is therefore needed.

Recital 9 states that given the equivalent protection resulting from the approximation of national laws, the Member States will no longer be able to inhibit the free movement between them of personal data on grounds relating to protection of the rights and freedoms of individuals, and in particular the right to privacy. Member States will be left a margin for manoeuvre, which may, in the context of implementation of the Directive, also be exercised by the business and social partners. Member States will therefore be able to specify in their national law the general conditions governing the lawfulness of data processing. In doing so the Member States shall strive to improve the protection currently provided by their legislation. Within the limits of this margin for manoeuvre and in accordance with EU law, disparities could arise in the implementation of the Directive, and this could have an effect on the movement of data within a Member State as well as within the EU.

Convention

Recital 11 states that the principles of the protection of the rights and freedoms of individuals, notably the right to privacy, which are contained in the Directive, give substance to and amplify those contained in the Council of Europe Convention of 28 January 1981 for the Protection of Individuals with regard to Automatic Processing of Personal Data.

Domestic Exemption

Recital 12 states that the protection principles must apply to all processing of personal data by any person whose activities are governed by EU law. There should be excluded the processing of data carried out by a natural person in the exercise of activities which are exclusively personal or domestic, such as correspondence and the holding of records of addresses.

Political/Economic Policy

Recital 13 states that the activities regarding public safety, defence, State security or the activities of the State in the area of criminal laws fall outside the scope of EU law, without prejudice to the obligations incumbent upon Member States under the Treaty establishing the European Community. The processing of personal data that is necessary to safeguard the economic well-being of the State does not fall within the scope of the Directive where such processing relates to State security matters.

Recital 71 states that the Directive does not stand in the way of a Member State's regulating marketing activities aimed at consumers residing in territory in so far as such regulation does not concern the protection of individuals with regard to the processing of personal data.

Recital 72 states that the Directive allows the principle of public access to official documents to be taken into account when implementing the principles set out in the Directive.

Future Proof

Recital 14 states that given the importance of the developments under way, in the framework of the information society, of the techniques used to capture, transmit, manipulate, record, store or communicate sound and image data relating to natural persons, the Directive should be applicable to processing involving such data.

Definitions/Structured Data/Automated

Recital 15 states that the processing of such data is covered by the Directive only if it is automated or if the data processed are contained or are intended to be contained in a filing system structured according to specific criteria relating to individuals, so as to permit easy access to the personal data in question.

Security/Defence/Criminal Law

Recital 16 states that the processing of sound and image data, such as in cases of video surveillance, does not come within the scope of the Directive if it is carried out for the purposes of public security, defence, national security or in the course of State activities relating to the area of criminal law or of other activities which do not come within the scope of EU law.

Journalism

Recital 17 states that as far as the processing of sound and image data carried out for purposes of journalism or the purposes of literary or artistic expression is concerned, in particular in the audiovisual field, the principles of the Directive are to apply in a restricted manner according to the provisions laid down in Article 9.

Member States/Jurisdiction

Recital 18 states that in order to ensure that individuals are not deprived of the protection to which they are entitled under the Directive, any processing of personal data in the EU must be carried out in accordance with the law of one of the Member States. Processing carried out under the responsibility of a data controller who is established in a Member State should be governed by the law of that State.

Recital 19 states that establishment on the territory of a Member State implies the effective and real exercise of activity through stable arrangements. The legal form of such an establishment, whether simply branch or a subsidiary with a legal personality, is not the determining factor in this respect. When a single data controller is established on the territory of several Member States, particularly by means of subsidiaries, he must ensure, in order to avoid any circumvention of national rules, that each of the establishments fulfils the obligations imposed by the national law applicable to its activities.

Third Party Controllers and EU Data Subjects

Recital 20 states that the fact that the processing of data is carried out by a person established in a third country must not stand in the way of the protection of individuals provided for in the Directive. The processing should be governed by the law of the Member State in which the means used are located, and there should be guarantees to ensure that the rights and obligations provided for in the Directive are respected in practice.

Criminal Exclusion

Recital 21 states that the Directive is without prejudice to the rules of territoriality applicable in criminal matters.

Balance

Recital 25 states that the principles of protection must be reflected, on the one hand, in the obligations imposed on persons, public authorities, enterprises, agencies or other bodies responsible for processing, in particular regarding data quality, technical security, notification to the Supervisory Authority, and the circumstances under which processing can be carried out, and, on the other hand, in the right conferred on individuals, the data on whom are the subject of processing, to be informed that processing is taking place, to consult the data, to request corrections and even to object to processing in certain circumstances.

Security and Technical Security

Recital 25 also refers to security and states that whereas the principles of protection must be reflected, on the one hand, in the obligations imposed on persons, public authorities, enterprises, agencies or other bodies responsible for processing, in particular regarding data quality, technical security, notification to the Supervisory Authority, and the circumstances under which processing can be carried out, and, on the other hand, in the right conferred on individuals, the data on whom are the subject of processing, to be informed that processing is taking place, to consult the data, to request corrections and even to object to processing in certain circumstances.

Historical, Statistical or Scientific Purposes

Recital 29 states that the further processing of personal data for historical, statistical or scientific purposes is not generally to be considered incompatible with the purposes for which the data have previously been collected provided that Member States furnish suitable safeguards; whereas these safeguards must in particular rule out the use of the data in support of measures or decisions regarding any particular individual.

Official Authority

Recital 32 states that it is for national legislation to determine whether the data controller performing a task carried out in the public interest or in the exercise of official authority should be a public administration or another natural or legal person governed by public law, or by private law such as a professional association.

Public Health and Social Protection

Recital 34 states that Member States must also be authorised, when justified by grounds of important public interest, to derogate from the prohibition on processing sensitive categories of data where important reasons of public interest so justify in areas such as public health and social protection – especially in order to ensure the quality and cost-effectiveness of the procedures used for settling claims for benefits and services in the health insurance system – scientific research and government statistics. It is incumbent on them, however, to provide specific and suitable safeguards so as to protect the fundamental rights and the privacy of individuals.

Legal Policy/Religion

Recital 35 states that the processing of personal data by official authorities for achieving aims, laid down in constitutional law or international public law, of officially recognised religious associations is carried out on important grounds of public interest.

Elections

Recital 36 states that where, in the course of electoral activities, the operation of the democratic system requires that, in certain Member States, political parties compile data on people's political opinion and that the processing of such data may be permitted for reasons of important public interest, provided that appropriate safeguards are established.

Journalism, Art, Etc

Recital 37 states that the processing of personal data for purposes of journalism or for purposes of literary of artistic expression, in particular

in the audiovisual field, should qualify for exemption from the requirements of certain provisions of the Directive in so far as necessary to
reconcile the fundamental rights of individuals with freedom of information and notably the right to receive and impart information, as
guaranteed in particular in Article 10 of the European Convention for
the Protection of Human Rights and Fundamental Freedoms. Member
States should therefore lay down exemptions and derogations necessary
for the purpose of balance between fundamental rights as regards
general measures on the legitimacy of data processing, measures on the
transfer of data to third countries and the power of the Supervisory
Authority. This should not, however, lead Member States to lay down
exemptions from the measures to ensure security of processing;
whereas at least the Supervisory Authority responsible for this sector
should also be provided with certain ex-post powers, eg to publish a
regular report or to refer matters to the judicial authorities.

Exemptions

Recital 40 states that it is not necessary to impose this obligation if the
data subject already has the information; whereas, moreover, there will
be no such obligation if the recording or disclosure are expressly
provided for by law or if the provision of information to the data
subject proves impossible or would involve disproportionate efforts,
which could be the case where processing is for historical, statistical or
scientific purposes; whereas, in this regard, the number of data subjects,
the age of the data, and any compensatory measures adopted may be
taken into consideration.

Access Right to Personal Data

Recital 41 states that any person must be able to exercise the right of
access to data relating to them which are being processed, in order to
verify in particular the accuracy of the data and the lawfulness of the
processing. Every data subject must also have the right to know the
logic involved in the automatic processing of data concerning them, at
least in the case of the automated decisions referred to in Article 15(1);
whereas this right must not adversely affect trade secrets or intellectual
property and in particular the copyright protecting the software. These
considerations must not, however, result in the data subject being
refused all information.

Health Data Access

Recital 42 states that Member States may, in the interest of the data
subject or so as to protect the rights and freedoms of others, restrict

rights of access and information. They may, for example, specify that access to medical data may be obtained only through a health professional.

State Interests, Security, Defence, Safety, Economy, Criminal Law

Recital 43 states that restrictions on the rights of access and information and on certain obligations of the data controller may similarly be imposed by Member States in so far as they are necessary to safeguard, for example, national security, defence, public safety, or important economic or financial interests of a Member State or the EU, as well as criminal investigations and prosecutions and action in respect of breaches of ethics in the regulated professions. The list of exceptions and limitations should include the tasks of monitoring, inspection or regulation necessary in the three last-mentioned areas concerning public security, economic or financial interests and crime prevention. The listing of tasks in these three areas does not affect the legitimacy of exceptions or restrictions for reasons of State security or defence.

Member State Derogations

Recital 44 states that Member States may also be led, by virtue of the provisions of EU law, to derogate from the provisions of the Directive concerning the right of access, the obligation to inform individuals, and the quality of data, in order to secure certain of the purposes referred to above.

Right to Object to Processing

Recital 45 states that in cases where data might lawfully be processed on grounds of public interest, official authority or the legitimate interests of a natural or legal person, any data subject should nevertheless be entitled, on legitimate and compelling grounds relating to his particular situation, to object to the processing of any data relating to them; whereas Member States may nevertheless lay down national provisions to the contrary.

Security

Recital 46 states that the protection of the rights and freedoms of data subjects with regard to the processing of personal data requires that appropriate technical and organisational measures be taken, both *at the time of the design* of the processing system *and at the time of the processing* itself, particularly in order to maintain security and thereby to prevent any unauthorised processing; whereas it is incumbent on the

Member States to ensure that data controllers comply with these measures; whereas these measures must ensure an *appropriate level of security*, taking into account the *state of the art* and the *costs* of their implementation in relation to the *risks* inherent in the processing and the *nature of the data* to be protected.

Transmission

Recital 47 states that where a message containing personal data is transmitted by means of a telecommunications or electronic mail service, the sole purpose of which is the transmission of such messages, the data controller in respect of the personal data contained in the message will normally be considered to be the person from whom the message originates, rather than the person offering the transmission services; whereas, nevertheless, those offering such services will normally be considered data controllers in respect of the processing of the additional personal data necessary for the operation of the service.

Registration and Processing Purpose(s)

Recital 48 states that the procedures for notifying the Supervisory Authority are designed to ensure disclosure of the purposes and main features of any processing operation for the purpose of verification that the operation is in accordance with the national measures taken under the Directive.

Recital 49 states that in order to avoid unsuitable administrative formalities, exemptions from the obligation to notify and simplification of the notification required may be provided for by Member States in cases where processing is unlikely adversely to affect the rights and freedoms of data subjects, provided that it is in accordance with a measure taken by a Member State specifying its limits. Whereas exemption or simplification may similarly be provided for by Member States where a person appointed by the data controller ensures that the processing carried out is not likely adversely to affect the rights and freedoms of data subjects. Such a data protection official, whether or not an employee of the data controller, must be in a position to exercise his functions in complete independence.

Recital 50 states that exemption or simplification could be provided for in cases of processing operations whose sole purpose is the keeping of a register intended, according to national law, to provide information to the public and open to consultation by the public or by any person demonstrating a legitimate interest.

Recital 51 states that nevertheless, simplification or exemption from the obligation to notify shall not release the data controller from any of the other obligations resulting from the Directive.

Specific Processing Risks

Recital 53 states that certain processing operation are likely to pose specific risks to the rights and freedoms of data subjects by virtue of their nature, their scope or their purposes, such as that of excluding individuals from a right, benefit or a contract, or by virtue of the *specific use of new technologies*. It is for Member States, if they so wish, to specify such risks in their legislation.

Recital 54 states that with regard to all the processing undertaken in society, the amount posing such specific risks should be very limited; whereas Member States must provide that the Supervisory Authority, or the data protection official in cooperation with the authority, can check such processing prior to it being carried out. Following this prior check, the Supervisory Authority may, according to its national law, give an opinion or an authorisation regarding the processing; whereas such checking may equally take place in the course of the preparation either of a measure of the national parliament or of a measure based on such a legislative measure, which defines the nature of the processing and lays down appropriate safeguards.

Court and Judicial Remedy

Recital 55 states that if the data controller fails to respect the rights of data subjects, national legislation must provide for a judicial remedy; whereas any damage which a person may suffer as a result of unlawful processing must be compensated for by the data controller, who may be exempted from liability if they prove that they are not responsible for the damage, in particular cases where fault is established on the part of the data subject or in case of force majeure. Sanctions must be imposed on any person, whether governed by private of public law, who fails to comply with the national measures taken under the Directive.

TBDFs

Recital 56 states that cross-border flows of personal data are necessary to the expansion of international trade. The protection of individuals guaranteed in the EU by the Directive does not stand in the way of transfers of personal data to third countries which ensure an adequate level of protection. The adequacy of the level of protection afforded by a third country must be assessed in the light of all the circumstances surrounding the transfer operation or set of transfer operations.

Recital 57 states that, on the other hand, the transfer of personal data to a third country which does not ensure an adequate level of protection must be prohibited.

Recital 59 states that particular measures may be taken to compensate for the lack of protection in a third country in cases where the data controller offers appropriate safeguards. Provision must be made for procedures for negotiations between the EU and such third countries.

Recital 60 states that transfers to third countries may be effected only in full compliance with the provisions adopted by the Member States pursuant to the Directive, and in particular Article 8.

Recital 66 states that where, with regard to the transfer of data to third countries, the application of the Directive calls for the conferment of powers of implementation on the Commission and the establishment of a procedure as laid down in Council Decision 87/373/EEC (1).

Consent

Recital 58 states that where provisions should be made for exemptions from this prohibition in certain circumstances where the data subject has given their consent, where the transfer is necessary in relation to a contract or a legal claim, and where protection of an important public interest so requires (for example in cases of international transfers of data between tax or customs administrations, between services competent for social security matters, or where the transfer is made from a register established by law and intended for consultation by the public or persons having a legitimate interest) where in this case such a transfer should not involve the entirety of the data or entire categories of the data contained in the register and, when the register is intended for consultation by persons having a legitimate interest, the transfer should be made only at the request of those persons or if they are to be the recipients.

Information Commissioner/National Authorities

Recital 62 states that the establishment in Member States of Supervisory Authorities, exercising their functions with complete independence, is an essential component of the protection of individuals with regard to the processing of personal data.

Recital 63 states that such authorities must have the necessary means to perform their duties, including powers of investigation and intervention, particularly in cases of complaints from individuals, and powers to engage in legal proceedings. Such authorities must help to ensure transparency of processing in the Member States within whose jurisdiction they fall.

Recital 64 states that the authorities in the different Member States will need to assist one another in performing their duties so as to ensure that the rules of protection are properly respected throughout the EU.

WP29

Recital 65 states that at EU level, a Working Party on the Protection of Individuals with regard to the Processing of Personal Data (ie WP29) must be set up and be completely independent in the performance of its functions. It must advise the Commission and, in particular, contribute to the uniform application of the national rules adopted pursuant to the Directive.

DPR Recitals

4.06 The Recitals to the proposed DPR are also instructive. They include,

Data Protection/Fundamental Right

Recital 1 states that the protection of natural persons in relation to the processing of personal data is a fundamental right. Article 8(1) of the Charter of Fundamental Rights of the European Union and Article 16(1) of the Treaty lay down that everyone has the right to the protection of personal data concerning them.

Recital 2 states that the processing of personal data is designed to serve, the principles and rules on the protection of individuals with regard to the processing of their personal data should, whatever the nationality or residence of natural persons, respect their fundamental rights and freedoms, notably the right to the protection of personal data. It should contribute to the accomplishment of an area of freedom, security and justice and of an economic union, to economic and social progress, the strengthening and the convergence of the economies within the internal market, and the well-being of individuals.

DPD

Recital 3 states that the DPD95 seeks to harmonise the protection of fundamental rights and freedoms of natural persons in respect of processing activities and to guarantee the free flow of personal data between Member States.

Processing Increase/Technology/Co-operation

Recital 4 states that the economic and social integration resulting from the functioning of the internal market has led to a substantial increase in cross-border flows. The exchange of data between economic and social, public and private actors across the EU increased. National authorities in the Member States are being called upon by EU law to cooperate and exchange personal data so as to be able to perform their duties or carry out tasks on behalf of an authority in another Member State.

Recital 5 states that the rapid technological developments and globalisation have brought new challenges for the protection of personal data. The scale of data sharing and collecting has increased spectacularly. Technology allows both private companies and public authorities to make use of personal data on an unprecedented scale in order to pursue their activities.

Individuals increasingly make personal information available publicly and globally.

Technology has transformed both the economy and social life, and is required to further facilitate the free flow of data within the EU and the transfer to third countries and international organisations, while ensuring a high level of the protection of personal data.

Need for Stronger Data Protection Regime Framework

Recital 6 states that the these developments require building a strong and more coherent data protection framework in the EU, backed by strong enforcement, given the importance to create the trust that will allow the digital economy to develop across the internal market. Individuals should have control of their own personal data and legal and practical certainty for individuals, economic operators and public authorities should be reinforced.

Recital 7 states that the objectives and principles of DPD95 remain sound, but it has not prevented fragmentation in the way data protection is implemented across the EU, legal uncertainty and a widespread public perception that there are significant risks for the protection of individuals associated notably with online activity. Differences in the level of protection of the rights and freedoms of individuals, notably to the right to the protection of personal data, with regard to the processing of personal data afforded in the Member States may prevent the free flow of personal data throughout the EU.

These differences may therefore constitute an obstacle to the pursuit of economic activities at the level of the EU, distort competition and impede authorities in the discharge of their responsibilities under EU law. This difference in levels of protection is due to the existence of differences in the implementation and application of DPD95.

Recital 8 states that in order to ensure consistent and high level of protection of individuals and to remove the obstacles to flows of personal data, the level of protection of the rights and freedoms of individuals with regard to the processing of such data should be equivalent in all Member States. Consistent and homogenous application of the rules for the protection of the fundamental rights and freedoms of natural persons with regard to the processing of personal data should be ensured throughout the EU.

Recital 9 states that the effective protection of personal data throughout the EU requires strengthening and detailing the rights of data subjects and the obligations of those who process and determine the processing of personal data, but also equivalent powers for monitoring and ensuring compliance with the rules for the protection of personal data and equivalent sanctions for offenders in the Member States.

Recital 10 states that Article 16(2) of the Treaty mandates the European Parliament and the Council to lay down the rules relating to the protection of individuals with regard to the processing of personal data and the rules relating to the free movement of personal data.

Recital 11 states that in order to ensure a consistent level of protection for individuals throughout the EU and to prevent divergences hampering the free movement of data within the internal market, a regulation is necessary to provide legal certainty and transparency for economic operators, including micro, small and medium-sized enterprises, and to provide individuals in all Member States with the same level of legally enforceable rights and obligations and responsibilities for data controllers and data processors, to ensure consistent monitoring of the processing of personal data, and equivalent sanctions in all Member States as well as effective co-operation by the supervisory authorities of different Member States. To take account of the specific situation of micro, small and medium-sized enterprises, the Regulation includes a number of derogations. In addition, the EU institutions and bodies, Member States and their supervisory authorities are encouraged to take account of the specific needs of micro, small and medium-sized enterprises (SMEs) in the application of the Regulation.

Recital 12 states that the protection afforded by the Regulation concerns natural persons, whatever their nationality or place of residence, in relation to the processing of personal data. With regard to the processing of data which concern legal persons and in particular undertakings established as legal persons, including the name and the form of the legal person and the contact details of the legal person, the protection of the Regulation should not be claimed by any person. This should also apply where the name of the legal person contains the names of one or more natural persons.

Technologically Neutral Protection

Recital 13 states that the protection of individuals should be technologically neutral and not depend on the techniques used. Otherwise this would create a serious risk of circumvention. The protection of individuals should apply to processing of personal data by automated means, as well as to manual processing, if the data are contained or are intended to be contained in a filing system. Files or sets of files as well as their cover pages, which are not structured according to specific criteria, should not fall within the scope of the Regulation.

Exclusion

Recital 14 states that the Regulation does not address issues of protection of fundamental rights and freedoms or the free flow of data related to activities which fall outside the scope of EU law, nor does it cover the processing of personal data by the EU institutions, bodies, offices and agencies, which are subject to Regulation (EC) No 45/200144, or the processing of personal data by the Member States when carrying out activities in relation to the common foreign and security policy of the EU.

Domestic

Recital 15 states that the Regulation should not apply to processing of personal data by a natural person, which are exclusively personal or domestic, such as correspondence and the holding of addresses, and without any gainful interest and thus without any connection with a professional or commercial activity. The exemption should also not apply to data controllers or data processors which provide the means for processing personal data for such personal or domestic activities.

Criminal Exemption

Recital 16 states that the protection of individuals with regard to the processing of personal data by competent authorities for the purposes of prevention, investigation, detection or prosecution of criminal offences or the execution of criminal penalties, and the free movement of such data, is subject of a specific legal instrument at EU level.

Therefore, the Regulation should not apply to the processing activities for those purposes. However, data processed by public authorities under the Regulation when used for the purposes of prevention, investigation, detection or prosecution of criminal offences or the execution of criminal penalties should be governed by the more specific legal instrument at EU level.

ISPs

Recital 17 states that the Regulation should be without prejudice to the application of Directive 2000/31/EC, in particular of the liability rules of intermediary service providers in Articles 12 to 15 of that Directive.

Official Documents

Recital 18 states that the Regulation allows the principle of public access to official documents to be taken into account when applying the provisions set out in the Regulation.

Location/Jurisdiction/Processing

Recital 19 states that any processing of personal data in the context of the activities of an establishment of a data controller or a data processor in the EU should be carried out in accordance with the Regulation, regardless of whether the processing itself takes place within the EU or not. Establishment implies the effective and real exercise of activity through stable arrangements. The legal form of such arrangements, whether through a branch or a subsidiary with a legal personality, is not the determining factor in this respect.

Recital 20 states that in order to ensure that individuals are not deprived of the protection to which they are entitled under the Regulation, the processing of personal data of data subjects residing in the EU by a data controller not established in the EU should be subject to the Regulation where the processing activities are related to the offering of goods or services to such data subjects, or to the monitoring of the behaviour of such data subjects.

Monitoring

Recital 21 states that in order to determine whether a processing activity can be considered to 'monitor the behaviour' of data subjects, it should be ascertained whether individuals are tracked on the internet with data processing techniques which consist of applying a 'profile' to an individual, particularly in order to take decisions concerning them or for analysing or predicting her or his personal preferences, behaviours and attitudes. Recital 22 states that where the national law of a Member State applies by virtue of public international law, the Regulation should also apply to a data controller not established in the EU, such as in a Member State's diplomatic mission or consular post.

Any Information

Recital 23 states that the principles of protection should apply to any information concerning an identified or identifiable person. To determine whether a person is identifiable, account should be taken of all the means likely reasonably to be used either by the data controller or by any other person to identify the individual. The principles of data protection should not apply to data rendered anonymous in such a way that the data subject is no longer identifiable.

Internet

Recital 24 states that when using online services, individuals may be associated with online identifiers provided by their devices, applications, tools and protocols, such as Internet Protocol addresses or cookie identifiers. This may leave traces which, combined with unique identifiers and other information received by the servers, may be used to create profiles of the individuals and identify them. It follows that identification numbers, location data, online identifiers or other specific factors as such need not necessarily be considered as personal data in all circumstances.

Consent

Recital 25 states that the consent should be given explicitly by any appropriate method enabling a freely given specific and informed indication of the data subject's wishes, either by a statement or by a clear affirmative action by the data subject, ensuring that individuals are aware that they give their consent to the processing of personal data, including by ticking a box when visiting an Internet website or by any other statement or conduct which clearly indicates in this context the data subject's acceptance of the proposed processing of their personal data. Silence or inactivity should therefore not constitute consent. Consent should cover all processing activities carried out for the same purpose or purposes. If the data subject's consent is to be given following an electronic request, the request must be clear, concise and not unnecessarily disruptive to the use of the service for which it is provided.

Health

Recital 26 states that the personal data relating to health should include in particular all data pertaining to the health status of a data subject; information about the registration of the individual for the provision of health services; information about payments or eligibility for healthcare with respect to the individual; a number, symbol or particular assigned to an individual to uniquely identify the individual for health purposes; any information about the individual collected in the course of the provision of health services to the individual; information derived from the testing or examination of a body part or bodily substance, including biological samples; identification of a person as provider of healthcare to the individual; or any information on eg a disease, disability, disease risk, medical history, clinical treatment, or the actual physiological or biomedical state of the data subject independent of its source, such as eg from a physician or other health professional, a hospital, a medical device, or an in vitro diagnostic test.

Establishment

Recital 27 states that the main establishment of a data controller in the EU should be determined according to objective criteria and should imply the effective and real exercise of management activities determining the main decisions as to the purposes, conditions and means of processing through stable arrangements. This criterion should not depend whether the processing of personal data is actually carried out at that location; the presence and use of technical means and technologies for processing personal data or processing activities do not, in themselves, constitute such main establishment and are therefore not determining criteria for a main establishment. The main establishment of the data processor should be the place of its central administration in the EU.

Group Companies

Recital 28 states that a group of undertakings should cover a controlling undertaking and its controlled undertakings, whereby the controlling undertaking should be the undertaking which can exercise a dominant influence over the other undertakings by virtue, for example, of ownership, financial participation or the rules which govern it or the power to have personal data protection rules implemented.

Children

Recital 29 states that the children deserve specific protection of their personal data, as they may be less aware of risks, consequences, safeguards and their rights in relation to the processing of personal data. To determine when an individual is a child, the Regulation should take over the definition laid down by the UN Convention on the Rights of the Child.

Lawful Processing

Recital 30 states that any processing of personal data should be lawful, fair and transparent in relation to the individuals concerned. In particular, the specific purposes for which the data are processed should be explicit and legitimate and determined at the time of the collection of the data. The data should be adequate, relevant and limited to the minimum necessary for the purposes for which the data is processed; this requires in particular ensuring that the data collected are not excessive and that the period for which the data are stored is limited to a strict minimum. Personal data should only be processed if the purpose of the processing could not be fulfilled by other means. Every reasonable step should be taken to ensure that instances of personal data which are inaccurate are rectified or deleted. In order to ensure that the data are not kept longer than necessary, time limits should be established by the controller for erasure or for a periodic review.

Recital 31 states that in order for processing to be lawful, personal data should be processed on the basis of the consent of the person concerned or some other legitimate basis, laid down by law, either in the Regulation or in other EU or Member State law as referred to in the Regulation.

Recital 35 states that the processing should be lawful where it is necessary in the context of a contract or the intended entering into a contract.

Recital 36 states that where processing is carried out in compliance with a legal obligation to which the data controller is subject or where processing is necessary for the performance of a task carried out in the public interest or in the exercise of an official authority, the processing should have a legal basis in EU law, or in a Member State law which meets the requirements of the Charter of Fundamental Rights of the European Union for any limitation of the rights and freedoms. It is also for EU or national law to determine whether the data controller performing a task carried out in the public interest or in the exercise of official authority should be a public administration or another natural or legal person governed by public law, or by private law such as a professional association.

Recital 37 states that the processing of personal data should equally be regarded as lawful where it is necessary to protect an interest which is essential for the data subject's life.

Recital 38 states that the legitimate interests of a data controller may provide a legal basis for processing, provided that the interests or the fundamental rights and freedoms of the data subject are not overriding. This would need careful assessment in particular where the data subject is a child, given that children deserve specific protection. The data subject should have the right to object the processing, on grounds relating to their particular situation and free of charge. To ensure transparency, the data controller should be obliged to explicitly inform the data subject on the legitimate interests pursued and on the right to object, and also be obliged to document these legitimate interests. Given that it is for the legislator to provide by law the legal basis for public authorities to process data, this legal ground should not apply for the processing by public authorities in the performance of their tasks.

Recital 39 states that the processing of data to the extent strictly necessary for the purposes of ensuring network and information security, ie the ability of a network or an information system to resist, at a given level of confidence, accidental events or unlawful or malicious actions that compromise the availability, authenticity, integrity and confidentiality of stored or transmitted data, and the security of the related services offered by, or accessible via, these networks and systems, by public authorities, Computer Emergency Response Teams (CERTs), Computer Security Incident Response Teams (CSIRTs), providers of electronic communications networks and services and by providers of security technologies and services, all constitute a legitimate interest of the concerned data controller. This could, for example, include preventing unauthorised access to electronic communications networks and malicious code distribution and stopping 'denial of service' attacks and damage to computer and electronic communication systems.

Recital 40 states that the processing of personal data for other purposes should be only allowed where the processing is compatible with those purposes for which the data have been initially collected, in particular where the processing is necessary for historical, statistical or scientific research purposes. Where the other purpose is not compatible with the initial one for which the data are collected, the data controller should obtain the consent of the data subject for this other purpose or should base the processing on another legitimate ground for lawful processing, in particular where provided by EU law or the law of the

Member State to which the data controller is subject. In any case, the application of the principles set out by the Regulation and in particular the information of the data subject on those other purposes should be ensured.

Consent

Recital 32 states that where processing is based on the data subject's consent, the data controller should have the burden of proving that the data subject has given the consent to the processing operation. In particular in the context of a written declaration on another matter, safeguards should ensure that the data subject is aware that and to what extent consent is given.

Recital 33 states that in order to ensure free consent, it should be clarified that consent does not provide a valid legal ground where the individual has no genuine and free choice and is subsequently not able to refuse or withdraw consent without detriment.

Recital 34 states that the consent should not provide a valid legal ground for the processing of personal data, where there is a clear imbalance between the data subject and the data controller. This is especially the case where the data subject is in a situation of dependence from the data controller, among others, where personal data are processed by the employer of employees' personal data in the employment context. Where the data controller is a public authority, there would be an imbalance only in the specific data processing operations where the public authority can impose an obligation by virtue of its relevant public powers and the consent cannot be deemed as freely given, taking into account the interest of the data subject.

Sensitive Personal Data

Recital 41 states that the personal data which is, by its nature, particularly sensitive and vulnerable in relation to fundamental rights or privacy, deserve specific protection. Such data should not be processed, unless the data subject gives his explicit consent. However, derogations from this prohibition should be explicitly provided for in respect of specific needs, in particular where the processing is carried out in the course of legitimate activities by certain associations or foundations the purpose of which is to permit the exercise of fundamental freedoms.

Recital 42 states that the derogating from the prohibition on processing sensitive categories of data should also be allowed if done by a law, and subject to suitable safeguards, so as to protect personal data and other fundamental rights, where grounds of public interest so justify and in particular for health purposes, including public health and social protection and the management of health-care services, especially in order to ensure the quality and cost-effectiveness of the procedures used for settling claims for benefits and services in the health insurance system, or for historical, statistical and scientific research purposes.

Official Processing/Religion

Recital 43 states that the processing of personal data by official authorities for achieving aims, laid down in constitutional law or international public law, of officially recognised religious associations is carried out on grounds of public interest.

Elections

Recital 44 states that where in the course of electoral activities, the operation of the democratic system requires in a Member State that political parties compile data on people's political opinions, the processing of such data may be permitted for reasons of public interest, provided that appropriate safeguards are established.

Access

Recital 45 states that if the data processed by a data controller do not permit the controller to identify a natural person, the data controller should not be obliged to acquire additional information in order to identify the data subject for the sole purpose of complying with any provision of the Regulation. In case of a request for access, the controller should be entitled to ask the data subject for further information to enable the data controller to locate the personal data which that person seeks.

Transparency/Children

Recital 46 states that the principle of transparency requires that any information addressed to the public or to the data subject should be easily accessible and easy to understand, and that clear and plain language is used. This is in particular relevant where in situations, such as online advertising, the proliferation of actors and the technological complexity of practice makes it difficult for the data subject to know and understand if personal data relating to them are being collected, by whom and for what purpose. Given that children deserve specific protection, any information and communication, where processing is addressed specifically to a child, should be in such a clear and plain language that the child can easily understand.

Exercising Rights

Recital 47 states that the modalities should be provided for facilitating the data subject's exercise of their rights provided by the Regulation, including mechanisms to request, free of charge, in particular access to data, rectification, erasure and to exercise the right to object. The data controller should be obliged to respond to requests of the data subject within a fixed deadline and give reasons, in case they do not comply with the data subject's request. Recital 48 States that the principles of fair and transparent processing require that the data subject should be informed in particular of the existence of the processing operation and its purposes, how long the data will be stored, on the existence of the right of access, rectification or erasure and on the right to lodge a complaint. Where the data are collected from the data subject, the data subject should also be informed whether they are obliged to provide the data and of the consequences, in cases they do not provide such data.

Recital 51 states that any person should have the right of access to data which has been collected concerning them, and to exercise this right easily, in order to be aware and verify the lawfulness of the processing. Every data subject should therefore have the right to know and obtain communication in particular for what purposes the data are processed, for what period, which recipients receive the data, what is the logic of the data that are undergoing the processing and what might be, at least when based on profiling, the consequences of such processing. This right should not adversely affect the rights and freedoms of others, including trade secrets or intellectual property and in particular the copyright protecting software. However, the result of these considerations should not be that all information is refused to the data subject.

Recital 52 states that the data controller should use all reasonable measures to verify the identity of a data subject that requests access, in particular in the context of online services and online identifiers. A data controller should not retain personal data for the unique purpose of being able to react to potential requests.

Prior Information

Recital 49 states that the information in relation to the processing of personal data relating to the data subject should be given to them at the time of collection, or, where the data are not collected from the data subject, within a reasonable period, depending on the circumstances of the case. Where data can be legitimately disclosed to another recipient, the data subject should be informed when the data are first disclosed to the recipient.

Recital 50 states, however, that it is not necessary to impose this obligation where the data subject already disposes of this information, or where the recording or disclosure of the data is expressly laid down by law, or where the provision of information to the data subject proves impossible or would involve disproportionate efforts. The latter could be particularly the case where processing is for historical, statistical or scientific research purposes; in this regard, the number of data subjects, the age of the data, and any compensatory measures adopted may be taken into consideration.

Rectification

Recital 53 states that any person should have the right to have personal data concerning them rectified and a 'right to be forgotten' where the retention of such data is not in compliance with the Regulation. In particular, data subjects should have the right that their personal data are erased and no longer processed, where the data are no longer necessary in relation to the purposes for which the data are collected or otherwise processed, where data subjects have withdrawn their consent for processing or where they object to the processing of personal data concerning them or where the processing of their personal data otherwise does not comply with the Regulation. This right is particularly relevant, when the data subject has given their consent as a child, when not being fully aware of the risks involved by the processing, and later wants to remove such personal data especially on the Internet. However, the further retention of the data should be allowed where it is necessary for historical, statistical and scientific research purposes, for reasons of public interest in the area of public health, for exercising the right of freedom of expression, when required by law or where there is a reason to restrict the processing of the data instead of erasing them.

Enhancing Right to Be Forgotten

Recital 54 states that to strengthen the 'right to be forgotten' in the online environment, the right to erasure should also be extended in such a way that a controller who has made the personal data public should be obliged to inform third parties which are processing such data that a data subject requests them to erase any links to, or copies or replications of that personal data. To ensure this information, the data controller should take all reasonable steps, including technical measures, in relation to data for the publication of which the data controller is responsible. In relation to a third party publication of personal data, the data controller should be considered responsible for the publication, where the data controller has authorised the publication by the third party.

Electronic Access

Recital 55 states that to further strengthen the control over their own data and their right of access, data subjects should have the right, where personal data are processed by electronic means and in a structured and commonly used format, to obtain a copy of the data concerning them also in commonly used electronic format. The data subject should also be allowed to transmit those data, which they have provided, from one automated application, such as a social network, into another one. This should apply where the data subject provided the data to the automated processing system, based on their consent or in the performance of a contract.

Right to Object

Recital 56 states that in cases where personal data might lawfully be processed to protect the vital interests of the data subject, or on grounds of public interest, official authority or the legitimate interests of a data controller, any data subject should nevertheless be entitled to object to the processing of any data relating to them. The burden of proof should be on the data controller to demonstrate that their legitimate interests may override the interests or the fundamental rights and freedoms of the data subject.

Direct Marketing

Recital 57 states that where personal data are processed for the purposes of direct marketing, the data subject should have the right to object to such processing free of charge and in a manner that can be easily and effectively invoked.

Automated Processing

Recital 58 states that every natural person should have the right not to be subject to a measure which is based on profiling by means of automated processing. However, such measure should be allowed when expressly authorised by law, carried out in the course of entering or performance of a contract, or when the data subject has given his consent. In any case, such processing should be subject to suitable safeguards, including specific information of the data subject and the right to obtain human intervention and that such measure should not concern a child.

Recital 59 states that the restrictions on specific principles and on the rights of information, access, rectification and erasure or on the right to data portability, the right to object, measures based on profiling, as well as on the communication of a personal data breach to a data subject and on certain related obligations of the data controllers may be imposed by EU or Member State law, as far as necessary and proportionate in a democratic society to safeguard public security, including the protection of human life especially in response to natural or man made disasters, the prevention, investigation and prosecution of criminal offences or of breaches of ethics for regulated professions, other public interests of the Union or of a Member State, in particular an important economic or financial interest of the Union or of a Member State, or the protection of the data subject or the rights and freedoms of others. Those restrictions should be in compliance with requirements set out by the Charter of Fundamental Rights of the European Union and by the European Convention for the Protection of Human Rights and Fundamental Freedoms.

Liability

Recital 60 states that the comprehensive responsibility and liability of the data controller for any processing of personal data carried out by the data controller or on the data controller's behalf should be established. In particular, the data controller should ensure and be obliged to demonstrate the compliance of each processing operation with the Regulation.

Policies and Measures

Recital 61 states that the protection of the rights and freedoms of data subjects with regard to the processing of personal data require that appropriate technical and organisational measures are taken, both at the time of the design of the processing and at the time of the processing itself, to ensure that the requirements of the Regulation are met. In order to ensure and demonstrate compliance with the Regulation, the data controller should adopt internal policies and implement appropriate measures, which meet in particular the principles of data protection by design and data protection by default.

Recital 62 states that the protection of the rights and freedoms of data subjects as well as the responsibility and liability of data controllers and data processor, also in relation to the monitoring by and measures of supervisory authorities, requires a clear attribution of the responsibilities under the Regulation, including where a data controller determines the purposes, conditions and means of the processing jointly with other data controllers or where a processing operation is carried out on behalf of a data controller.

Recital 65 states that in order to demonstrate compliance with the Regulation, the data controller or data processor should document each processing operation. Each data controller and data processor should be obliged to co-operate with the Supervisory Authority and make this documentation, on request, available to it, so that it might serve for monitoring those processing operations.

Third Counties

Recital 63 states that where a data controller not established in the EU is processing personal data of data subjects residing in the EU whose processing activities are related to the offering of goods or services to such data subjects, or to the monitoring their behaviour, the data controller should designate a representative, unless the data controller is established in a third country ensuring an adequate level of protection, or the data controller is a small or medium sized enterprise (SME) or a public authority or body or where the data controller is only occasionally offering goods or services to such data subjects. The representative should act on behalf of the data controller and may be addressed by any Supervisory Authority.

Recital 64 states that in order to determine whether a data controller is only occasionally offering goods and services to data subjects residing in the EU, it should be ascertained whether it is apparent from the data controller's overall activities that the offering of goods and services to such data subjects is ancillary to those main activities.

Security

Recital 66 states that in order to maintain security and to prevent processing in breach of the Regulation, the data controller or data processor should evaluate the risks inherent to the processing and implement measures to mitigate those risks. These measures should ensure an appropriate level of security, taking into account the state of the art and the costs of their implementation in relation to the risks and the nature of the personal data to be protected. When establishing technical standards and organisational measures to ensure security of processing, the Commission should promote technological neutrality, interoperability and innovation, and, where appropriate, cooperate with third countries.

Data Breach

Recital 67 states that a personal data breach may, if not addressed in an adequate and timely manner, result in substantial economic loss and social harm, including identity fraud, to the individual concerned. Therefore, as soon as the data controller becomes aware that such a breach has occurred, the data controller should notify the breach to the Supervisory Authority without undue delay and, where feasible, within 24 hours. Where this cannot be achieved within 24 hours, an explanation of the reasons for the delay should accompany the notification. The individuals whose personal data could be adversely affected by the breach should be notified without undue delay in order to allow them to take the necessary precautions. A breach should be considered as adversely affecting the personal data or privacy of a data subject where it could result in, for example, identity theft or fraud, physical harm, significant humiliation or damage to reputation. The notification should describe the nature of the personal data breach as well as recommendations as well as recommendations for the individual concerned to mitigate potential adverse effects. Notifications to data subjects should be made as soon as reasonably feasible, and in close cooperation with the Supervisory Authority and respecting guidance provided by it or other relevant authorities (eg law enforcement authorities). For example, the chance for data subjects to mitigate an immediate risk of harm would call for a prompt notification of data subjects whereas the need to implement appropriate measures against continuing or similar data breaches may justify a longer delay.

The Editorial of the *Computer Law & Security Review* recently notes that new data breach reporting laws are arising 'in response to a growth in unauthorised disclosures of personal information by public and private sector organisations.'[15]

Recital 68 states that in order to determine whether a personal data breach is notified to the Supervisory Authority and to the data subject without undue delay, it should be ascertained whether the data controller has implemented and applied appropriate technological protection and organisational measures to establish immediately whether a personal data breach has taken place and to inform promptly the Supervisory Authority and the data subject, before a damage to personal and economic interests occurs, taking into account in particular the nature and gravity of the personal data breach and its consequences and adverse effects for the data subject.

---

15   Editorial, Saxby, S., *Computer Law & Security Review* (2012) (28), 251–253, at 252.

Recital 69 states that in setting detailed rules concerning the format and procedures applicable to the notification of personal data breaches, due consideration should be given to the circumstances of the breach, including whether or not personal data had been protected by appropriate technical protection measures, effectively limiting the likelihood of identity fraud or other forms of misuse. Moreover, such rules and procedures should take into account the legitimate interests of law enforcement authorities in cases where early disclosure could unnecessarily hamper the investigation of the circumstances of a breach.

Registration/Notification

Recital 70 states that DPD95 provided for a general obligation to notify processing of personal data to the supervisory authorities. While this obligation produces administrative and financial burdens, it did not in all cases contribute to improving the protection of personal data. Therefore, such an indiscriminate general notification obligation should be abolished, and replaced by effective procedures and mechanism which focus instead on those processing operations which are likely to present specific risks to the rights and freedoms of data subjects by virtue of their nature, their scope or their purposes. In such cases, a data protection impact assessment should be carried out by the data controller or data processor prior to the processing, which should include in particular the envisaged measures, safeguards and mechanisms for ensuring the protection of personal data and for demonstrating the compliance with the Regulation.

Recital 71 states that this should in particular apply to newly established large scale filing systems, which aim at processing a considerable amount of personal data at regional, national or supranational level and which could affect a large number of data subjects.

Impact Assessments

Recital 72 states that there are circumstances under which it may be sensible and economic that the subject of a data protection impact assessment should be broader than a single project, for example where public authorities or bodies intend to establish a common application or processing platform or where several data controllers plan to introduce a common application or processing environment across an industry sector or segment or for a widely used horizontal activity.

Recital 73 states that the data protection impact assessments should be carried out by a public authority or public body if such an assessment has not already been made in the context of the adoption of the national law on which the performance of the tasks of the public authority or public body is based and which regulates the specific processing operation or set of operations in question.

Recital 74 states that where a data protection impact assessment indicates that processing operations involve a high degree of specific risks to the rights and freedoms of data subjects, such as excluding individuals from their right, or by the use of specific new technologies, the Supervisory Authority should be consulted, prior to the start of operations, on a risky processing which might not be in compliance with the Regulation, and to make proposals to remedy such situation. Such consultation should equally take place in the course of the preparation either of a measure by the national parliament or of a measure based on such legislative measure which defines the nature of the processing and lays down appropriate safeguards.

Public Sector

Recital 75 states that where the processing is carried out in the public sector or where, in the private sector, processing is carried out by a large enterprise, or where its core activities, regardless of the size of the enterprise, involve processing operations which require regular and systematic monitoring, a person should assist the data controller or data processor to monitor internal compliance with the Regulation. Such data protection officers, whether or not an employee of the data controller, should be in a position to perform their duties and tasks independently.

Industry Codes

Recital 76 states that the associations or other bodies representing categories of controllers should be encouraged to draw up codes of conduct, within the limits of the Regulation, so as to facilitate the effective application of the Regulation, taking account of the specific characteristics of the processing carried out in certain sectors.

Certification

Recital 77 states that in order to enhance transparency and compliance with the Regulation, the establishment of certification mechanisms, data protection seals and marks should be encouraged, allowing data subjects to quickly assess the level of data protection of relevant products and services. Recital (78) sates that cross-border flows of personal data are necessary for the expansion of international trade and international co-operation. The increase in these flows has raised new challenges and concerns with respect to the protection of personal data. However, when personal data are transferred from the EU to third countries or to international organisations, the level of protection of individuals guaranteed in the EU by the Regulation should not be undermined. In any event, transfers to third countries may only be carried out in full compliance with the Regulation.

Global Data Protection/TBDFs

Recital 79 states that the Regulation is without prejudice to international agreements concluded between the EU and third countries regulating the transfer of personal data including appropriate safeguards for the data subjects.

Recital 80 states that the Commission may decide with effect for the entire EU that certain third countries, or a territory or a processing sector within a third country, or an international organisation, offer an adequate level of data protection, thus providing legal certainty and uniformity throughout the EU as regards the third countries or international organisations which are considered to provide such level of protection. In these cases, transfers of personal data to these countries may take place without needing to obtain any further authorisation.

Recital 81 states that in line with the fundamental values on which the EU is founded, in particular the protection of human rights, the Commission should, in its assessment of the third country, take into account how a given third country respects the rule of law, access to justice as well as international human rights norms and standards.

TBDFs, White List, Etc

Recital 82 states that the Commission may equally recognise that a third country, or a territory or a processing sector within a third country, or an international organisation offers no adequate level of data protection. Consequently the transfer of personal data to that third country should be prohibited. In that case, provision should be made for consultations between the Commission and such third countries or international organisations.

Recital 83 states that in the absence of an adequacy decision, the data controller or data processor should take measures to compensate for the lack of data protection in a third country by way of appropriate safeguards for the data subject. Such appropriate safeguards may consist of making use of binding corporate rules, standard data protection clauses adopted by the Commission, standard data protection clauses adopted by a Supervisory Authority or contractual clauses authorised by a Supervisory Authority, or other suitable and proportionate measures justified in the light of all the circumstances surrounding a data transfer operation or set of data transfer operations and where authorised by a Supervisory Authority.

Recital 84 states that the possibility for the data controller or data processor to use standard data protection clauses adopted by the Commission or by a Supervisory Authority should neither prevent the possibility for data controllers or data processors to include the standard data protection clauses in a wider contract nor to add other clauses as long as they do not contradict, directly or indirectly, the standard contractual clauses adopted by the Commission or by a Supervisory Authority or prejudice the fundamental rights or freedoms of the data subjects.

Recital 85 states that a corporate group should be able to make use of approved binding corporate rules for its international transfers from the EU to organisations within the same corporate group of undertakings, as long as such corporate rules include essential principles and enforceable rights to ensure appropriate safeguards for transfers or categories of transfers of personal data.

Recital 86 states that provisions should be made for the possibility for transfers in certain circumstances where the data subject has given his consent, where the transfer is necessary in relation to a contract or a legal claim, where important grounds of public interest laid down by EU or Member State law so require or where the transfer is made from a register established by law and intended for consultation by the public or persons having a legitimate interest. In this latter case such a transfer should not involve the entirety of the data or entire categories of the data contained in the register and, when the register is intended for consultation by persons having a legitimate interest, the transfer should be made only at the request of those persons or if they are to be the recipients.

Recital 87 states that these derogations should in particular apply to data transfers required and necessary for the protection of important grounds of public interest, for example in cases of international data transfers between competition authorities, tax or customs administrations, financial supervisory authorities, between services competent for social security matters, or to competent authorities for the prevention, investigation, detection and prosecution of criminal offences.

Recital 88 states that the transfers which cannot be qualified as frequent or massive, could also be possible for the purposes of the legitimate interests pursued by the data controller or the data processor, when they have assessed all the circumstances surrounding the data transfer. For the purposes of processing for historical, statistical and scientific research purposes, the legitimate expectations of society for an increase of knowledge should be taken into consideration.

Recital 89 states that in any case, where the Commission has taken no decision on the adequate level of data protection in a third country, the data controller or data processor should make use of solutions that provide data subjects with a guarantee that they will continue to benefit from the fundamental rights and safeguards as regards processing of their data in the EU once this data has been transferred.

Recital 90 states that the some third countries enact laws, regulations and other legislative instruments which purport to directly regulate data processing activities of natural and legal persons under the jurisdiction of the Member States. The extraterritorial application of these laws, regulations and other legislative instruments may be in breach of international law and may impede the attainment of the protection of individuals guaranteed in the EU by the Regulation. Transfers should only be allowed where the conditions of the Regulation for a transfer to third countries are met. This may *inter alia* be the case where the disclosure is necessary for an important ground of public interest recognised in EU law or in a Member State law to which the data controller is subject. The conditions under which an important ground of public interest exists should be further specified by the Commission in a delegated act.

Recital 91 states that when personal data moves across borders it may put at increased risk the ability of individuals to exercise data protection rights in particular to protect themselves from the unlawful use or disclosure of that information. At the same time, Supervisory Authorities may find that they are unable to pursue complaints or conduct investigations relating to the activities outside their borders. Their efforts to work together in the cross-border context may also be hampered by insufficient preventative or remedial powers, inconsistent legal regimes, and practical obstacles like resource constraints. Therefore, there is a need to promote closer co-operation among data protection supervisory authorities to help them exchange information and carry out investigations with their international counterparts.

ICO/Supervisory Authorities

Recital 92 states that the establishment of Supervisory Authorities in Member States, exercising their functions with complete independence, is an essential component of the protection of individuals with regard to the processing of their personal data. Member States may establish more than one Supervisory Authority, to reflect their constitutional, organisational and administrative structure.

Recital 93 states that where a Member State establishes several supervisory authorities, it should establish by law mechanisms for ensuring the effective participation of those Supervisory Authorities in the consistency mechanism. That Member State should in particular designate the Supervisory Authority which functions as a single contact point for the effective participation of those authorities in the mechanism, to ensure swift and smooth co-operation with other supervisory authorities, the European Data Protection Board and the Commission.

Recital 94 states that each Supervisory Authority should be provided with the adequate financial and human resources, premises and infrastructure, which is necessary for the effective performance of their tasks, including for the tasks related to mutual assistance and cooperation with other Supervisory Authorities throughout the EU.

Recital 95 states that the general conditions for the members of the Supervisory Authority should be laid down by law in each Member State and should in particular provide that those members should be either appointed by the parliament or the government of the Member State, and include rules on the personal qualification of the members and the position of those members.

Recital 96 states that the Supervisory Authorities should monitor the application of the provisions pursuant to the Regulation and contribute to its consistent application throughout the EU, in order to protect natural persons in relation to the processing of their personal data and to facilitate the free flow of personal data within the internal market. For that purpose, the Supervisory Authorities should co-operate with each other and the Commission.

Processing in More than One Member State

Recital 97 states that where the processing of personal data in the context of the activities of an establishment of a data controller or a data processor in the EU takes place in more than one Member State, one single Supervisory Authority should be competent for monitoring the activities of the data controller or data processor throughout the EU and taking the related decisions, in order to increase the consistent application, provide legal certainty and reduce administrative burden for such data controllers and data processors.

One Stop Shop

Recital 98 states that the competent authority, providing such 'one-stop shop', should be the Supervisory Authority of the Member State in which the data controller or data processor has its main establishment.

Recital 99 states that the while the Regulation applies also to the activities of national courts, the competence of the Supervisory Authorities should not cover the processing of personal data when courts are acting in their judicial capacity, in order to safeguard the independence of judges in the performance of their judicial tasks. However, this exemption should be strictly limited to genuine judicial activities in court cases and not apply to other activities where judges might be involved in, in accordance with national law.

Recital 100 states that in order to ensure consistent monitoring and enforcement of the Regulation throughout the EU, the Supervisory Authorities should have in each Member State the same duties and effective powers, including powers of investigation, legally binding intervention, decisions and sanctions, particularly in cases of complaints from individuals, and to engage in legal proceedings. Investigative powers of Supervisory Authorities as regards access to premises should be exercised in conformity with EU law and national law. This concerns in particular the requirement to obtain a prior judicial authorisation.

Recital 101 states that each Supervisory Authority should hear complaints lodged by any data subject and should investigate the matter. The investigation following a complaint should be carried out, subject to judicial review, to the extent that is appropriate in the specific case. The Supervisory Authority should inform the data subject of the progress and the outcome of the complaint within a reasonable period. If the case requires further investigation or coordination with another Supervisory Authority, intermediate information should be given to the data subject.

DP Awareness

Recital 102 states that the awareness raising activities by Supervisory Authorities addressed to the public should include specific measures directed at data controllers and data processors, including micro, small and medium-sized enterprises (SMEs), as well as data subjects.

Recital 103 states that the Supervisory Authorities should assist each other in performing their duties and provide mutual assistance, so as to ensure the consistent application and enforcement of the Regulation in the internal market.

Recital 104 states that each Supervisory Authority should have the right to participate in joint operations between Supervisory Authorities. The requested Supervisory Authority should be obliged to respond to the request in a defined time period.

Recital 105 states that in order to ensure the consistent application of the Regulation throughout the EU, a consistency mechanism for co-operation between the Supervisory Authorities themselves and the Commission should be established. This mechanism should in particular apply where a Supervisory Authority intends to take a measure as regards processing operations that are related to the offering of goods or services to data subjects in several Member States, or to the monitoring such data subjects, or that might substantially affect the free flow of personal data. It should also apply where any Supervisory Authority or the Commission requests that the matter should be dealt with in the consistency mechanism. This mechanism should be without prejudice to any measures that the Commission may take in the exercise of its powers under the Treaties.

Recital 106 states that in application of the consistency mechanism, the European Data Protection Board should, within a determined period of time, issue an opinion, if a simple majority of its members so decides or if so requested by any Supervisory Authority or the Commission.

Recital 107 states that in order to ensure compliance with the Regulation, the Commission may adopt an opinion on this matter, or a decision, requiring the Supervisory Authority to suspend its draft measure.

Enforcement

Recital 108 states that there may be an urgent need to act in order to protect the interests of data subjects, in particular when the danger exists that the enforcement of a right of a data subject could be considerably impeded. Therefore, a Supervisory Authority should be able to adopt provisional measures with a specified period of validity when applying the consistency mechanism.

Recital 109 states that the application of this mechanism should be a condition for the legal validity and enforcement of the respective decision by a Supervisory Authority. In other cases of cross-border relevance, mutual assistance and joint investigations might be carried out between the concerned Supervisory Authorities on a bilateral or multilateral basis without triggering the consistency mechanism.

Recital 110 states that at EU level, a European Data Protection Board should be set up. It should replace the Working Party on the Protection of Individuals with Regard to the Processing of Personal Data established by DPD95. It should consist of a head of a Supervisory Authority of each Member State and of the European Data Protection Supervisor. The Commission should participate in its activities. The European Data Protection Board should contribute to the consistent application of the

Regulation throughout the EU, including by advising the Commission and promoting cooperation of the Supervisory Authorities throughout the EU. The European Data Protection Board should act independently when exercising its tasks.

Complaints to ICO

Recital 111 states that every data subject should have the right to lodge a complaint with a Supervisory Authority in any Member State and have the right to a judicial remedy if they consider that their rights under the Regulation are infringed or where the Supervisory Authority does not react on a complaint or does not act where such action is necessary to protect the rights of the data subject.

Recital 112 states that any body, organisation or association which aims to protects the rights and interests of data subjects in relation to the protection of their data and is constituted according to the law of a Member State should have the right to lodge a complaint with a Supervisory Authority or exercise the right to a judicial remedy on behalf of data subjects, or to lodge, independently of a data subject's complaint, an own complaint where it considers that a personal data breach has occurred.

Court Remedies

Recital 113 states that each natural or legal person should have the right to a judicial remedy against decisions of a Supervisory Authority concerning them. Proceedings against a Supervisory Authority should be brought before the courts of the Member State, where the Supervisory Authority is established.

Recital 114 states that the in order to strengthen the judicial protection of the data subject in situations where the competent Supervisory Authority is established in another Member State than the one where the data subject is residing, the data subject may request any body, organisation or association aiming to protect the rights and interests of data subjects in relation to the protection of their data to bring on the data subject's behalf proceedings against that Supervisory Authority to the competent court in the other Member State.

Recital 115 states that in situations where the competent Supervisory Authority established in another Member State does not act or has taken insufficient measures in relation to a complaint, the data subject may request the Supervisory Authority in the Member State of his or her habitual residence to bring proceedings against that Supervisory Authority to the competent court in the other Member State. The requested Supervisory Authority may decide, subject to judicial review, whether it is appropriate to follow the request or not.

Recital 116 states that for proceedings against a data controller or data processor, the plaintiff should have the choice to bring the action before the courts of the Member States where the data controller or data processor has an establishment or where the data subject resides, unless the data controller is a public authority acting in the exercise of its public powers.

Recital 117 states that where there are indications that parallel proceedings are pending before the courts in different Member States, the courts should be obliged to contact each other. The courts should have the possibility to suspend a case where a parallel case is pending in another Member State. Member States should ensure that court actions, in order to be effective, should allow the rapid adoption of measures to remedy or prevent an infringement of the Regulation.

Compensation

Recital 118 states that any damage which a person may suffer as a result of unlawful processing should be compensated by the data controller or data processor, who may be exempted from liability if they prove that they are not responsible for the damage, in particular where he establishes fault on the part of the data subject or in case of force majeure.

Penalties

Recital 119 states that penalties should be imposed to any person, whether governed by private or public law, who fails to comply with the Regulation. Member States should ensure that the penalties should be effective, proportionate and dissuasive and should take all measures to implement the penalties.

Sanctions

Recital 120 states that the in order to strengthen and harmonise administrative sanctions against infringements of the Regulation, each Supervisory Authority should have the power to sanction administrative offences. The Regulation should indicate these offences and the upper limit for the related administrative fines, which should be fixed in each individual case proportionate to the specific situation, with due regard in particular to the nature, gravity and duration of the breach. The consistency mechanism may also be used to cover divergences in the application of administrative sanctions.

Journalism

Recital 121 states that the processing of personal data solely for journalistic purposes, or for the purposes of artistic or literary expression should qualify for exemption from the requirements of certain provisions of the Regulation in order to reconcile the right to the protection of personal data with the right to freedom of expression, and notably the right to receive and impart information, as guaranteed in particular by Article 11 of the Charter of Fundamental Rights of the European Union. This should apply in particular to processing of personal data in the audiovisual field and in news archives and press libraries. Therefore, Member States should adopt legislative measures, which should lay down exemptions and derogations which are necessary for the purpose of balancing these fundamental rights. Such exemptions and derogations should be adopted by the Member States on general principles, on the rights of the data subject, on data controller and data processor, on the transfer of data to third countries or international organisations, on the independent Supervisory Authorities and on co-operation and consistency. This should not, however, lead Member States to lay down exemptions from the other provisions of the Regulation. In order to take account of the importance of the right to freedom of expression in every democratic society, it is necessary to interpret notions relating to that freedom, such as journalism, broadly.

Therefore, Member States should classify activities as 'journalistic' for the purpose of the exemptions and derogations to be laid down under the Regulation if the object of these activities is the disclosure to the public of information, opinions or ideas, irrespective of the medium which is used to transmit them. They should not be limited to media undertakings and may be undertaken for profit-making or for non-profit making purposes.

Health

Recital 122 states that the processing of personal data concerning health, as a special category of data which deserves higher protection, may often be justified by a number of legitimate reasons for the benefit of individuals and society as a whole, in particular in the context of ensuring continuity of cross-border healthcare. Therefore, the Regulation should provide for harmonised conditions for the processing of personal data concerning health, subject to specific and suitable safeguards so as to protect the fundamental rights and the personal data of individuals. This includes the right for individuals to have access to their personal data concerning their health, for example the data in their medical records containing such information as diagnosis, examination results, assessments by treating physicians and any treatment or interventions provided.

Recital 123 states that processing of personal data concerning health may be necessary for reasons of public interest in the areas of public health, without consent of the data subject. In that context, 'public health' should be interpreted as defined in Regulation (EC) No 1338/2008 of the European Parliament and of the Council of 16 December 2008 on EU statistics on public health and health and safety at work, meaning all elements related to health, namely, health status, including morbidity and disability, the determinants having an effect on that health status, health care needs, resources allocated to health care, the provision of, and universal access to, health care as well as health care expenditure and financing, and the causes of mortality. Such processing of personal data concerning health for reasons of public interest should not result in personal data being processed for other purposes by third parties, such as employers, insurance and banking companies.

Employment

Recital 124 states that the general principles on the protection of individuals with regard to the processing of personal data should also be applicable to the employment context. Therefore, in order to regulate the processing of employees' personal data in the employment context, Member States should be able, within the limits of the Regulation, to adopt by law specific rules for the processing of personal data in the employment sector.

Research

Recital 125 states that the processing of personal data for the purposes of historical, statistical or scientific research should, in order to be lawful, also respect other relevant legislation such as on clinical trials.

Recital 126 states that the scientific research for the purposes of the Regulation should include fundamental research, applied research, and privately funded research and in addition should take into account the EU's objective under Article 179(1) of the Treaty on the Functioning of the European Union of achieving a European Research Area.

Recital 127 states that, as regards the powers of the supervisory authorities to obtain from the data controller or data processor access personal data and access to its premises, Member States may adopt by law, within the limits of the Regulation, specific rules in order to safeguard the professional or other equivalent secrecy obligations, in so far as necessary to reconcile the right to the protection of personal data with an obligation of professional secrecy.

Religious Not Effected

Recital 128 states that the Regulation respects and does not prejudice the status under national law of churches and religious associations or communities in the Member States, as recognised in Article 17 of the Treaty on the Functioning of the European Union. As a consequence, where a church in a Member State applies, at the time of entry into force of the Regulation, comprehensive rules relating to the protection of individuals with regard to the processing of personal data, these existing rules should continue to apply if they are brought in line with the Regulation. Such churches and religious associations should be required to provide for the establishment of a completely independent Supervisory Authority.

Data Protection Rights and Laws

Recital 129 states that in order to fulfil the objectives of the Regulation, namely to protect the fundamental rights and freedoms of natural persons and in particular their right to the protection of personal data and to ensure the free movement of personal data within the EU, the power to adopt acts in accordance with Article 290 of the Treaty on the Functioning of the European Union should be delegated to the Commission. In particular, delegated acts should be adopted in respect of lawfulness of processing; specifying the criteria and conditions in relation to the consent of a child; processing of special categories of data; specifying the criteria and conditions for manifestly excessive requests and fees for exercising the rights of the data subject; criteria and requirements for the information to the data subject and in relation to the right of access; the right to be forgotten and to erasure; measures based on profiling; criteria and requirements in relation to the responsibility of the data controller and to data protection by design and by default; a data processor; criteria and requirements for the documentation and the security of processing; criteria and requirements for establishing a personal data breach and for its notification to the Supervisory Authority, and on the circumstances where a personal data breach is likely to adversely affect the data subject; the criteria and conditions for processing operations requiring a data protection impact assessment; the criteria and requirements for determining a high degree of specific risks which require prior consultation; designation and tasks of the data protection officer; codes of conduct; criteria and requirements for certification mechanisms; criteria and requirements for transfers by way of binding corporate rules; transfer derogations; administrative sanctions; processing for health purposes; processing in the employment context and processing for historical, statistical and scientific research purposes. It is of particular importance that the Commission carry out appropriate consultations during its preparatory work, including at an expert level. The Commission, when preparing and drawing-up delegated acts, should ensure a simultaneous, timely and appropriate transmission of relevant documents to the European Parliament and Council.

Recital 130 states that in order to ensure uniform conditions for the implementation of the Regulation, implementing powers should be conferred on the Commission for: specifying standard forms in relation to the processing of personal data of a child; standard procedures and forms for exercising the rights of data subjects; standard forms for the information to the data subject; standard forms and procedures in relation to the right of access; the right to data portability; standard forms in relation to the responsibility of the data controller to data protection by design and by default and to the documentation; specific requirements for the security of processing; the standard format and the procedures for the notification of a personal data breach to the Supervisory Authority and the communication of a personal data breach to the data subject; standards and procedures for a data protection impact assessment; forms and procedures for prior authorisation and prior consultation; technical standards and mechanisms for certification; the adequate level of protection afforded by a third country or a territory or a processing sector within that third country or an international organisation; disclosures not authorised by EU law; mutual assistance; joint operations; decisions under the consistency mechanism. Those powers should be exercised in accordance with Regulation (EU) No 182/2011 of the European Parliament and of the Council of 16 February 2011 laying down the rules and general principles concerning mechanisms for control by the Member States of the Commission's exercise of implementing powers.

These issues are becoming increasingly topical and important, both in terms of complying with the data protection regime, fines and penalties in the event of breach as well as civil remedies available to data subjects. Indeed, civil remedies already exist for data subjects under the DPD95 and DPA.

Standards/Forms

Recital 131 states that the examination procedure should be used for the adoption of specifying standard forms in relation to the consent of a child; standard procedures and forms for exercising the rights of data subjects; standard forms for the information to the data subject; standard forms and procedures in relation to the right of access; the right to data portability; standard forms in relation to the responsibility of the controller to data protection by design and by default and to the documentation; specific requirements for the security of processing; the standard format and the procedures for the notification of a personal data breach to the Supervisory Authority and the communication of a personal data breach to the data subject; standards and procedures for a data protection impact assessment; forms and procedures for prior authorisation and prior consultation; technical standards and mechanisms for certification; the adequate level of protection afforded by a third country or a territory or a processing sector within that third country or an international organisation; disclosures not authorised by EU law; mutual assistance; joint operations; decisions under the consistency mechanism, given that those acts are of general scope.

Third Countries

Recital 132 states that the Commission should adopt immediately applicable implementing acts where, in duly justified cases relating to a third country or territory or a processing sector within that third country or an international organisation which does not ensure an adequate level of protection, and relating to matters communicated by Supervisory Authorities under the consistency mechanism, imperative grounds of urgency so require.

Recital 133 states that since the objectives of the Regulation, namely to ensure an equivalent level of protection of individuals and the free flow of data throughout the EU, cannot be sufficiently achieved by the Member States and can, therefore, by reason of the scale or effects of the action, be better achieved at EU level, the EU may adopt measures, in accordance with the principle of subsidiarity as set out in Article 5 of the Treaty on European Union. In accordance with the principle of proportionality as set out in that Article, the Regulation does not go beyond what is necessary in order to achieve that objective.

DPD Repeal

Recital 134 states that DPD95 should be repealed by the Regulation. However, Commission decisions adopted and authorisations by Supervisory Authorities based on DPD95 should remain in force.

ePD Amended

Recital 135 states that the Regulation should apply to all matters concerning the protection of fundamental rights and freedom vis-à-vis the processing of personal data, which are not subject to specific obligations with the same objective set out in ePD, including the obligations on the data controller and the rights of individuals. In order to clarify the relationship between the Regulation and ePD, the latter Directive should be amended accordingly.

Schengen

Recital 136 states that as regards Iceland and Norway, the Regulation constitutes a development of provisions of the Schengen acquis to the extent that it applies to the processing of personal data by authorities involved in the implementation of that acquis, as provided for by the Agreement concluded by the Council of the European Union and the Republic of Iceland and the Kingdom of Norway concerning the association of those two States with the implementation, application and development of the Schengen acquis.

Recital 137 states that as regards Switzerland, the Regulation constitutes a development of provisions of the Schengen acquis to the extent that it applies to the processing of personal data by authorities involved in the implementation of that acquis, as provided for by the Agreement between the European Union, the European Community and the Swiss Confederation concerning the association of the Swiss Confederation with the implementation, application and development of the Schengen acquis.

Recital 138 states that, as regards Liechtenstein, the Regulation constitutes a development of provisions of the Schengen acquis to the extent that it applies to the processing of personal data by authorities involved in the implementation of that acquis, as provided for by the Protocol between the European Union, the European Community, the Swiss Confederation and the Principality of Liechtenstein on the accession of the Principality of Liechtenstein to the Agreement between the European Union, the European Community and the Swiss Confederation on the Swiss Confederation's association with the implementation, application and development of the Schengen acquis.

Proportionality

Recital 139 states that in view of the fact that, as underlined by the Court of Justice of the European Union, the right to the protection of personal data is not an absolute right, but must be considered in relation to its function in society and be balanced with other fundamental rights, in accordance with the principle of proportionality, the Regulation respects all fundamental rights and observes the principles recognised in the Charter of Fundamental Rights of the European Union as enshrined in the Treaties, notably the right to respect for private and family life, home and communications, the right to the protection of personal data, the freedom of thought, conscience and religion, the freedom of expression and information, the freedom to conduct a business, the right to an effective remedy and to a fair trial as well as cultural, religious and linguistic diversity.

DPD95: General Provisions

4.07 Chapter I of DPD95 contains the general provisions of the Directive. Article 1 refers to the object of the Directive. In particular Article 1(1) states that in accordance with the Directive, Member States shall protect the fundamental rights and freedoms of natural persons, and in particular their right to privacy with respect to the processing of personal data. Article 1(2) provides that Member States shall neither restrict nor prohibit the free flow of personal data between Member States for reasons connected with the protection afforded under Article 1(1).

DPR: General Provisions

4.08 Chapter I of the DPR contains the general provisions. Article 1 of Chapter 1 refers to the subject matter and objectives. Particularly, Article 1(1) states that the DPR lays down rules relating to the protection of individuals with regard to the processing of personal data and rules relating to the free movement of personal data.

Article 2(2) states that the DPR protects the fundamental rights and freedoms of natural persons, and in particular their right to the protection of personal data. Article 3(3) provides that the free movement of personal data within the EU shall neither be restricted nor prohibited for reasons connected with the protection of individuals with regard to the processing of personal data.

Article 2 relates to material scope. Article 2(1) provides that the DPR applies to the processing of personal data wholly or partly by automated means, and to the processing other than by automated means of personal data which form part of a filing system or are intended to form part of a filing system.

However, Article 2(2) makes clear that the DPR does not apply to the processing of personal data:

- in the course of an activity which falls outside the scope of EU law, in particular concerning national security;
- by the EU institutions, bodies, offices and agencies;
- by the Member States when carrying out activities which fall within the scope of Chapter 2 of the Treaty on European Union;
- by a natural person without any gainful interest in the course of its own exclusively personal or household activity;
- by competent authorities for the purposes of prevention, investigation, detection or prosecution of criminal offences or the execution of criminal penalties.

In addition, Article 3(3) states that the DPR shall be without prejudice to the application of Directive 2000/31/EC, ie the eCommerce Directive,[16] in particular of the liability rules of intermediary service providers in Articles 12 to 15 of that Directive.[17] That refers to the three specific and limited ISP defences.[18]

Article 3 relates to territorial scope. Article 3(1) states that the DPR applies to the processing of personal data in the context of the activities of an establishment of a data controller or a data processor in the EU. Further, Article 2(2) states that the DPR applies to the processing of personal data of data subjects residing in the EU by a data controller not established in the EU, where the processing activities are related to: (a) the offering of goods or services to such data subjects in the EU; or (b) the monitoring of their behaviour.

---

16 Directive 2000/31/EC of the European Parliament and of the Council of 8 June 2000 on certain legal aspects of information society services, in particular electronic commerce, in the Internal Market (Directive on eCommerce). Note also UNCITRAL Model Law on Electronic Commerce; 'UNCITRAL Model Law on Electronic Commerce,' *Tulane Journal of International and Comparative Law* (1999) (7), pp. 237–250.

17 Article 12 relates to mere conduit; Article 13 relates to caching; and Article 14 relates to hosting, ie the three separate and limited ecommerce defences.

18 Note that there are only three such defences, not four, five, etc.

Article 3(3) states that the DPR applies to the processing of personal data by a data controller not established in the EU, but in a place where the national law of a Member State applies by virtue of public international law.

DPD95: Scope

4.09 Article 3 relates to scope. Article 3(1) states that the DPD shall apply to the processing of personal data wholly or partly by automatic means, and to the processing otherwise than by automatic means of personal data which form part of a filing system or are intended to form part of a filing system.

It does not apply, however, according to Article 3(2), to the processing of personal data:

● in the course of an activity which falls outside the scope of EU law, such as those provided for by Titles V and VI of the Treaty on European Union and in any case to processing operations concerning public security, defence, State security (including the economic well-being of the State when the processing operation relates to State security matters) and the activities of the State in areas of criminal law;

● by a natural person in the course of a purely personal or household activity.

DPD95: National Laws

4.10 Article 4 relates to the national law applicable. Under Article 4(1) each Member State shall apply the national provisions it adopts pursuant to the Directive to the processing of personal data where:

● the processing is carried out in the context of the activities of an establishment of the data controller on the territory of the Member State; when the same data controller is established on the territory of several Member States, he must take the necessary measures to ensure that each of these establishments complies with the obligations laid down by the national law applicable;

● the data controller is not established on the Member State's territory, but in a place where its national law applies by virtue of international public law;

● the data controller is not established on EU territory and, for purposes of processing personal data makes use of equipment, automated or otherwise, situated on the territory of the said Member State, unless such equipment is used only for purposes of transit through the territory of the EU.

Under Article 4(2) it is provided that in the circumstances referred to in paragraph 1 third bullet, the data controller must designate a representative established in the territory of that Member State, without prejudice to legal actions which could be initiated against the data controller itself.

DPD95: Data Protection Principles (Data Quality Principles)

4.11 The Data Protection Principles are also known as the data quality principles, as referred to in the DPD95. Section I relates to principles relating to data quality. Article 6(1) provides that Member States shall provide that personal data must be:

(a) processed fairly and lawfully;

(b) collected for specified, explicit and legitimate purposes and not further processed in a way incompatible with those purposes. Further processing of data for historical, statistical or scientific purposes shall not be considered as incompatible provided that Member States provide appropriate safeguards;

(c) adequate, relevant and not excessive in relation to the purposes for which they are collected and/or further processed;

(d) accurate and, where necessary, kept up to date; every reasonable step must be taken to ensure that data which are inaccurate or incomplete, having regard to the purposes for which they were collected or for which they are further processed, are erased or rectified;

(e) kept in a form which permits identification of data subjects for no longer than is necessary for the purposes for which the data were collected or for which they are further processed. Member States shall lay down appropriate safeguards for personal data stored for longer periods for historical, statistical or scientific use.

Article 6(2) provides that it shall be for the data controller to ensure that Article 6(1) is complied with.

DPD95: Legitimate Data Processing Conditions

4.12 Section II refers to the criteria for making data processing legitimate.

Article 7 provides that Member States shall provide that personal data may be processed only if:

(a) the data subject has unambiguously given his consent; or
(b) processing is necessary for the performance of a contract to which the data subject is party or in order to take steps at the request of the data subject prior to entering into a contract; or
(c) processing is necessary for compliance with a legal obligation to which the data controller is subject; or
(d) processing is necessary in order to protect the vital interests of the data subject; or
(e) processing is necessary for the performance of a task carried out in the public interest or in the exercise of official authority vested in the data controller or in a third party to whom the data are disclosed; or
(f) processing is necessary for the purposes of the legitimate interests pursued by the data controller or by the third party or parties to whom the data are disclosed, except where such interests are overridden by the interests for fundamental rights and freedoms of the data subject which require protection under Article 1(1).

DPR: Data Processing Principles

4.13 Chapter II refers to the Data Protection Principles. Article 5 relates to principles relating to personal data processing.

Personal data must be:

(a) processed lawfully, fairly and in a transparent manner in relation to the data subject;
(b) collected for specified, explicit and legitimate purposes and not further processed in a way incompatible with those purposes;
(c) adequate, relevant, and limited to the minimum necessary in relation to the purposes for which they are processed; they shall only be processed if, and as long as, the purposes could not be fulfilled by processing information that does not involve personal data;
(d) accurate and kept up to date; every reasonable step must be taken to ensure that personal data that are inaccurate, having regard to the purposes for which they are processed, are erased or rectified without delay;
(e) kept in a form which permits identification of data subjects for no longer than is necessary for the purposes for which the personal data are processed; personal data may be stored for longer periods

insofar as the data will be processed solely for historical, statistical or scientific research purposes in accordance with the rules and conditions of Article 83 and if a periodic review is carried out to assess the necessity to continue the storage;

(f) processed under the responsibility and liability of the data controller, who shall ensure and demonstrate for each processing operation the compliance with the provisions of the Regulation.

DPR: Legitimate Processing Conditions

4.14   Article 6 of the DPR refers to the lawfulness of processing. Article 6(1) provides that processing of personal data shall be lawful only if and to the extent that at least one of the following applies:

(a) the data subject has given consent to the processing of their personal data for one or more specific purposes;

(b) processing is necessary for the performance of a contract to which the data subject is party or in order to take steps at the request of the data subject prior to entering into a contract;

(c) processing is necessary for compliance with a legal obligation to which the data controller is subject;

(d) processing is necessary in order to protect the vital interests of the data subject;

(e) processing is necessary for the performance of a task carried out in the public interest or in the exercise of official authority vested in the data controller;

(f) processing is necessary for the purposes of the legitimate interests pursued by a controller, except where such interests are overridden by the interests or fundamental rights and freedoms of the data subject which require protection of personal data, in particular where the data subject is a child. This shall not apply to processing carried out by public authorities in the performance of their tasks.

Under Article 6(2) processing of personal data which is necessary for the purposes of historical, statistical or scientific research shall be lawful subject to the conditions and safeguards referred to in Article 83.

Article 6(3) states that the basis of the processing referred to in points (c) and (e) of Article 6(1) must be provided for in:

● EU law; or
● the law of the Member State to which the data controller is subject.

The law of the Member State must meet an objective of public interest or must be necessary to protect the rights and freedoms of others, respect the essence of the right to the protection of personal data and be proportionate to the legitimate aim pursued (Article 6(3)).

According to Article 6(4), where the purpose of further processing is not compatible with the one for which the personal data have been collected, the processing must have a legal basis at least in one of the grounds referred to in points (a) to (e) of Article 6(1). This shall in particular apply to any change of terms and general conditions of a contract (Article 6(4)).

Article 6(5) provides that the Commission shall be empowered to adopt delegated acts in accordance with Article 86 for the purpose of further specifying the conditions referred to in point (f) of Article 6(1) for various sectors and data processing situations, including as regards the processing of personal data related to a child.

DPR: Consent Conditions

4.15 Article 7 relates to the conditions for consent. In particular Article 7(1) provides that the data controller shall bear the burden of proof for the data subject's consent to the processing of their personal data for specified purposes.

Under Article 7(2), if the data subject's consent is to be given in the context of a written declaration which also concerns another matter, the requirement to give consent must be presented distinguishable in its appearance from this other matter.

The data subject shall have the right to withdraw his or her consent at any time under Article 7(3). The withdrawal of consent shall not affect the lawfulness of processing based on consent before its withdrawal.

Consent shall not provide a legal basis for the processing, where there is a significant imbalance between the position of the data subject and the data controller, per Article 7(4).

Conclusion

4.16 Privacy and data protection are evolving in terms of how technology is changing how personal data are collected, used and processed. The current data protection legal regime is perceived as requiring updating. The DPD95 was enacted in 1995, prior to social networking, cloud computing, mass data storage, data mining, electronic profiling, Web 2.0 and the threats to the data security surrounding personal data. This was even before the spotlight centred on abuse issues. Data protection needs to evolve to deal with, or at least more explicitly deal with, these issues. This is partly the reason for the proposed EU DPR.

This is important for the issues it addresses as well as the current legal provisions it enhances. As a Regulation as opposed to a Directive, it means that it is directly applicable in the UK without the need for a Directive or national implementing legislation such as the DPA. The law and practice of the UK will be changed as will many of the obligations of organisations. This will also differ more for organisations in particular sectors.

There must be better awareness and more hands on board management responsibility, planning and data protection assessment in advance of product or service launch via the Privacy by Design (PbD/DPbD) concept (see Part 4). There is explicit recognition of children under the data protection regime for the first time. Data protection compliance is now required to be much more considered and planned.

Chapter 5

Data Protection Principles

Introduction

5.01 All organisations which collect and process personal data must comply with the obligations of the UK data protection regime. It is, therefore, very important to be familiar with the data protection regime. This is set out in the DPA of 1998, which commenced on 1 March 2000.

When Data Protection Provisions Apply

5.02 The circumstances in which UK data protection provisions are important. The data protection regime applies:

- to the collection and processing of personal data where the data controller is established in the UK (and the data are processed in the context of the establishment);
- to data controllers not established in UK or the EEA, or who make use of equipment situated in UK to process personal data (otherwise than for the purpose of transit to UK).

Fair Processing Requirements

5.03 The DPA provides details as to what constitutes fair processing and identifies the information that must be given to data subjects not only where the personal data is obtained directly from the data subjects but also when it is obtained indirectly. It also refers to the times at which this information needs to be given.

Organisations cannot collect and process personal data unless they:

- Comply with the registration requirements;

- Comply with the Data Protection Principles (also known as the data quality principles);
- Ensure the processing is carried out in accordance with the Legitimate Processing Conditions (and the Sensitive Personal Data Legitimate Processing Conditions in the case of sensitive personal data);
- Provide specific information to data subjects in advance of the collection and processing of personal data, known as the Prior Information Requirements;
- Security requirements.

These all serve as pre-conditions to lawful data processing of personal data.

Data Protection Principles (also known as Data Quality Principles)

5.04 Schedule 1 Part 1 of the DPA sets out the Data Protection Principles. Personal data shall be processed fairly and lawfully and, in particular, shall not be processed unless at least one of the conditions in Schedule 2 is met, and in the case of sensitive personal data, at least one of the conditions in Schedule 3 is also met.

Schedule 2 contains the general personal data Legitimate Processing Conditions.

Schedule 3 contains the personal data Sensitive Personal Data Legitimate Processing Conditions.

These Data Protection Principles state that:

- Personal data shall be obtained only for one or more specified and lawful purposes, and shall not be further processed in any manner incompatible with that purpose or those purposes;
- Personal data shall be adequate, relevant and not excessive in relation to the purpose or purposes for which they are processed;
- Personal data shall be accurate and, where necessary, kept up to date;
- Personal data processed for any purpose or purposes shall not be kept for longer than is necessary for that purpose or those purposes;
- Personal data shall be processed in accordance with the rights of data subjects under the DPA;
- Appropriate technical and organisational measures shall be taken against unauthorised or unlawful processing of personal data and

against accidental loss or destruction of, or damage to, personal data (ie the security conditions);

- Personal data shall not be transferred to a country or territory outside the EEA unless that country or territory ensures an adequate level of protection for the rights and freedoms of data subjects in relation to the processing of personal data.

There are thus eight Data Protection Principles to be complied with by all data controllers. It can, therefore, be summarised that all personal data must be:

(1) fairly and lawfully processed;
(2) processed for limited purposes;
(3) adequate, relevant and not excessive;
(4) accurate and up to date;
(5) not kept for longer than is necessary;
(6) processed in line with data subject rights;
(7) secure; and
(8) not transferred to other countries without adequate protection.

Section 4(4) of the DPA states that 'it shall be the duty of a data controller to comply with the Data Protection Principles in relation to all personal data with respect to which [it] is the data controller.'

Interpreting the Data Protection Principles

5.05 The DPA also contains certain guidance which assists in interpreting the Data Protection Principles. These are contained in Schedule 1, Part I.

First Data Protection Principle

5.06 The first Data Protection Principle states that personal data must be:

- fairly and lawfully processed.

The collection and processing must be fair and transparent. It must, therefore, be in a manner which is not covert or deceptive. The requirement incorporates an obligation that information must be provided to the individual data subject in relation to the data controller and the details of the collection and processing. The prior information requirement and conditions must be satisfied.

In relation to the first Data Protection Principle, Schedule 1 states, *inter alia*, that, in determining for the purposes of the first principle whether personal data are processed fairly, regard is to be had to the method by which they are obtained, including in particular whether any person from whom they are obtained is deceived or misled as to the purpose or purposes for which they are to be processed (Schedule 1, Part 1, s 1(1)).

Under Schedule 1, Part II, s 1(2) it is provided that subject to paragraph 2, for the purposes of the first principle, data are to be treated as obtained fairly if they consist of information obtained from a person who:

● is authorised by or under any enactment to supply it, or
● is required to supply it by or under any enactment or by any convention or other instrument imposing an international obligation on the UK.

Under Schedule 1, Part II, s 2(1) it is provided that subject to paragraph 3, for the purposes of the first principle, personal data are not to be treated as processed fairly unless:

● in the case of data obtained from the data subject, the data controller ensures so far as practicable that the data subject has, is provided with, or has made readily available to them, the information specified in sub-paragraph (3); and
● in any other case, the data controller ensures so far as practicable that, before the relevant time or as soon as practicable after that time, the data subject has, is provided with, or has made readily available to them, the information specified in sub-paragraph (3).
  Under Schedule 1, Part II, s 2(2) it is provided that the 'the relevant time' (in sub-paragraph 1(b) above) means
  (a) the time when the data controller first processes the data; or
  (b) in a case where at that time disclosure to a third party within a reasonable period is envisaged,
● if the data are in fact disclosed to such a person within that period, the time when the data are first disclosed;
● if within that period the data controller becomes, or ought to become, aware that the data are unlikely to be disclosed to such a person within that period, the time when the data controller does become, or ought to become, so aware; or
● in any other case, the end of that period.

In addition, it states that the information referred to in sub-paragraph (1) is as follows, namely;

(a) the identity of the data controller;
(b) if he has nominated a representative for the purposes of the DPA, the identity of that representative;
(c) the purpose or purposes for which the data are intended to be processed; and
(d) any further information which is necessary, having regard to the specific circumstances in which the data are or are to be processed, to enable processing in respect of the data subject to be fair.

Under Schedule 1, Part II, s 3(1) it provides that paragraph 2(1)(b) does not apply where either of the primary conditions in sub-paragraph (2), together with such further conditions as may be prescribed by the Secretary of State by order, are met.

Under Schedule 1, Part II, s 3(2) it provides that the primary conditions referred to in sub-paragraph (1) are:

(a) that the provision of that information would involve a disproportionate effort; or
(b) that the recording of the information to be contained in the data by, or the disclosure of the data by, the data controller is necessary for compliance with any legal obligation to which the data controller is subject, other than an obligation imposed by contract.

The second to fifth Data Protection Principles relate to data quality.

Second Data Protection Principle

5.07 The second Data Protection Principle states that personal data must be:

• processed for limited purposes.

Therefore, the intended purposes must be enumerated and set out, both by the organisation, in the registration notification, and provided to the individual data subject in a transparent manner.

Third Data Protection Principle

5.08 The third Data Protection Principle states that personal data must be:

• adequate, relevant and not excessive.

This indicates that the processing must be adequate for the fair and lawful purpose; it must be relevant to that specific purpose; and must not be disproportionate or excessive in relation to that purpose.

Fourth Data Protection Principle

5.09 The fourth Data Protection Principle states that personal data must be:

- accurate and up to date.

The personal data must be correct and accurate. Given that personal data can become out of date, and consequently increase the risk of adverse consequences for the individual data subject, there is an obligation to ensure that the personal data is kept up to data. This means continually assessing the data and updating, correcting or deleting it as appropriate. It also implies a finite end to processing activities.

Fifth Data Protection Principle

5.10 The fifth Data Protection Principle states that personal data must be:

- not kept for longer than is necessary.

Once the purpose is accomplished, the need is over and there does not continue to be a current purpose continuing for to keep and process the personal data. It must be kept no longer than necessary in relation to the original collection and processing purpose. This is partly why it is important for the original purpose to be properly set out. Again, it implies a finite end to processing activities.

Sixth Data Protection Principle

5.11 The sixth Data Protection Principle states that personal data must be:

- processed in line with the data subject's rights.

The rights of data subjects can be summarised as including:

- Right of access (s 7 DPA);
- Right to establish if personal data exists (s 7(1)(a) DPA);
- Right to be informed of the logic in automatic decision taking (s 7(1)(d);

- Right to prevent processing likely to cause damage or distress (s 18 DPA);
- Right to prevent processing for direct marketing (s 11 DPA);
- Right to prevent automated decision taking (s 12 DPA);
- Right in relation to exempt manual data (s 12A DPA);
- Right to compensation (s 13 DPA);
- Right to rectify inaccurate data (s 14 DPA);
- Right to rectification, blocking, erasure and destruction (s 14 DPA);
- Right to complain to ICO (see s 42 DPA);
- Right to go to court (see s 15 DPA).

There are exemptions in relation to the access right, such as in relation to repeat requests, confidentiality of references, sensitive business forecasting, negotiations, professional legal privilege, crime and taxation.

Exemptions also arise as regards the rights in relation to processing causing damage or distress, such as third party information interests, or serious harm arsing in the event of disclosure.

Seventh Data Protection Principle

5.12 The seventh Data Protection Principle states that personal data must be;

- secure.

This is critically important, and is increasingly emphasised with the significant number of official and commercial data breach and data loss incidents. In addition, there is an increasing emphasis that organisations should not only inform the ICO but also individual data subjects in the event of data breach. The latter can be justified if it would be necessary for individuals to change passwords, etc in order to minimise damage, loss or distress from the misuse of the personal data the subject of the breach.

Organisations should also consider that it may be more difficult to explain a data breach incident if the security is lapse, nor to defend a claim for compensation if there was less than optimum security proportionate to the cost, organisation, types of data, and risks involved.

Security considerations also arise as regards outsourcing to data processors; transfers abroad; the new world of cloud computing; internet and website usage; online abuse; and social networking websites. Sony was fined £250,000 for data breach.

Eighth Data Protection Principle

5.13 The eighth Data Protection Principle states that personal data must be:

● not transferred to other countries without adequate protection.

Personal data, as a default position may, not be transferred outside of the EEA. In order to do so, there must be a situation of determined adequate protection arising as envisaged and provided under the data protection regime. This includes examples such as safe harbour, binding corporate rules, specific contract clauses, passenger records to US, etc.

There are exemptions to the default ban, however. Schedule 4 to the DPA sets out cases where the eighth Data Protection Principle does not apply. It states:

● The data subject has given his consent to the transfer;
● The transfer is necessary:
   ● for the performance of a contract between the data subject and the data controller; or
   ● for the taking of steps at the request of the data subject with a view to his entering into a contract with the data controller;
● The transfer is necessary:
   ● for the conclusion of a contract between the data controller and a person other than the data subject which,
      (i) is entered into at the request of the data subject; or
      (ii) is in the interests of the data subject; or
   ● for the performance of such a contract;
● The transfer is necessary for reasons of substantial public interest;
● The Secretary of State may by order specify:
   ● circumstances in which a transfer is to be taken for the purposes of sub-paragraph (1) to be necessary for reasons of substantial public interest; and
   ● circumstances in which a transfer which is not required by or under an enactment is not to be taken for the purpose of sub-paragraph (1) to be necessary for reasons of substantial public interest;
● The transfer:
   ● is necessary for the purpose of, or in connection with, any legal proceedings (including prospective legal proceedings);
   ● is necessary for the purpose of obtaining legal advice; or
   ● is otherwise necessary for the purposes of establishing, exercising or defending legal rights;

- The transfer is necessary in order to protect the vital interests of the data subject;
- The transfer is part of the personal data on a public register and any conditions subject to which the register is open to inspection are complied with by any person to whom the data are or may be disclosed after the transfer;
- The transfer is made on terms which are of a kind approved by the Commissioner as ensuring adequate safeguards for the rights and freedoms of data subjects;
- The transfer has been authorised by the Commissioner as being made in such a manner as to ensure adequate safeguards for the rights and freedoms of data subjects.

Chapter 6

Ordinary Personal Data Legitimate Processing Conditions

Introduction

6.01 Organisations when obtaining and processing personal data must not mislead and must also provide a number of prior information requirements to the individual data subjects.

Without these it would be deemed that there is unfair obtaining and processing. In addition, organisations must satisfy and meet one of the Legitimate Processing Conditions.

General Legitimate Processing Conditions

6.02 The Legitimate Processing Conditions are required to be complied with, in addition to the Data Protection Principles. Schedule 2 to the DPA contains the general Legitimate Processing Conditions. In order to collect and process personal data, in addition to complying with the above Data Protection Principles, organisations must comply or fall within one of the following general personal data Legitimate Processing Conditions.

Schedule 2 to the DPA contains conditions relevant for the purposes of the first Data Protection Principle, in particular the processing of personal data. It states:

1   The data subject has given his consent to the processing;
2   The processing is necessary:
    (a)   for the performance of a contract to which the data subject is a party; or
    (b)   for the taking of steps at the request of the data subject with a view to entering into a contract;

3   The processing is necessary for compliance with any legal obliga-
    tion to which the data controller is subject, other than an obligation
    imposed by contract;
4   The processing is necessary in order to protect the vital interests of
    the data subject;
5   The processing is necessary:
    (a)   for the administration of justice;
        (aa) for the exercise of any functions of either House of
            Parliament;
    (b)   for the exercise of any functions conferred on any person by
        or under any enactment;
    (c)   for the exercise of any functions of the Crown, a Minister of
        the Crown or a government department; or
    (d)   for the exercise of any other functions of a public nature
        exercised in the public interest by any personal;
6   (1)   The processing is necessary for the purposes of legitimate
        interests pursued by the data controller or by the third party or
        parties to whom the data are disclosed, except where the
        processing is unwarranted in any particular case by reason of
        prejudice to the rights and freedoms or legitimate interests of
        the data subject;

The Secretary of State may by order specify particular circumstances in
which this condition is, or is not, to be taken to be satisfied. There are,
therefore, six general Legitimate Processing Conditions. Frequently, an
organisation would seek to fall within the legitimate interests condition
above.

    These conditions might be summarised as follows:

●   The data subject has given consent;
●   The processing is necessary for performance of contract to which
    data subject is a party;
●   The processing is necessary to take steps at request of the data
    subject prior to entering into contract;
●   The processing is necessary for compliance with a legal obligation
    (other than contractually imposed obligation);
●   It is necessary to protect the vital interests of the data subject;
●   It is necessary for the administration of justice, performance of
    statutory function or function of public nature;
●   The processing is necessary for legitimate interests pursued by data
    controller except where unwarranted.

Sensitive personal data legitimate processing conditions

6.03   In the case of sensitive personal data, an organisation must, in addition to complying with the Data Protection Principles, be able to comply or fall within one of the Sensitive Personal Data Legitimate Processing Conditions.

Schedule 3 to the DPA sets out the conditions relevant for the purposes of the first Data Protection Principle in particular in relation to the processing of sensitive personal data. It sets out the following provisions:

1   The data subject has given his explicit consent to the processing of the personal data;

2   (1)   The processing is necessary for the purposes of exercising or performing any right or obligation which is conferred or imposed by law on the data controller in connection with employment;

   (2)   The Secretary of State may by order,
      (a)   exclude the application of sub-paragraph (1) in such cases as may be specified; or
      (b)   provide that, in such cases as may be specified, the condition in sub-paragraph (1) is not to be regarded as satisfied unless such further conditions as may be specified in the order are also satisfied;

3   The processing is necessary:
   (a)   in order to protect the vital interests of the data subject or another person, in a case where;
      (i) consent cannot be given by or on behalf of the data subject; or
      (ii) the data controller cannot reasonably be expected to obtain the consent of the data subject; or
   (b)   in order to protect the vital interests of another person, in a case where consent by or on behalf of the data subject has been unreasonably withheld;

4   The processing:
   (a)   is carried out in the course of its legitimate activities by any body or association which;
      (i) is not established or conducted for profit; and
      (ii) exists for political, philosophical, religious or trade-union purposes;
   (b)   is carried out with appropriate safeguards for the rights and freedoms of data subjects;
   (c)   relates only to individuals who either are members of the

body or association or have regular contact with it in connection with its purposes; and

(d)   does not involve disclosure of the personal data to a third party without the consent of the data subject;

5   The information contained in the personal data has been made public as a result of steps deliberately taken by the data subject;

6   The processing:

(a)   is necessary for the purpose of, or in connection with, any legal proceedings (including prospective legal proceedings);

(b)   is necessary for the purpose of obtaining legal advice; or

(c)   is otherwise necessary for the purposes of establishing, exercising or defending legal rights.

7   (1)   The processing is necessary,

(a)   for the administration of justice;

(aa)   for the exercise of any functions of either House of Parliament;

(b)   for the exercise of any functions conferred on any person by or under an enactment; or

(c)   for the exercise of any functions of the Crown, a Minister of the Crown or a government department;

(2)   The Secretary of State may by order,

(a)   exclude the application of sub-paragraph (1) in such cases as may be specified; or

(b)   provide that, in such cases as may be specified, the condition in sub-paragraph (1) is not to be regarded as satisfied unless such further conditions as may be specified in the order are also satisfied.

7A   (1)   The processing,

(a)   is either,

(i)   the disclosure of sensitive personal data by a person as a member of an anti-fraud organisation or otherwise in accordance with any arrangements made by such an organisation; or

(ii)   any other processing by that person or another person of sensitive personal data so disclosed; and

(b)   is necessary for the purposes of preventing fraud or a particular kind of fraud;

(2)   In this paragraph 'an anti-fraud organisation' means any unincorporated association, body corporate or other person which enables or facilitates any sharing of information to prevent fraud or a particular kind of fraud or which has any of these functions as its purpose or one of its purposes;

8 (1) The processing is necessary for medical purposes and is undertaken by,
  (a) a health professional; or
  (b) a person who in the circumstances owes a duty of confidentiality which is equivalent to that which would arise if that person were a health professional;

  (2) In this paragraph 'medical purposes' includes the purposes of preventative medicine, medical diagnosis, medical research, the provision of care and treatment and the management of healthcare services;

9 (1) The processing,
  (a) is of sensitive personal data consisting of information as to racial or ethnic origin;
  (b) is necessary for the purpose of identifying or keeping under review the existence or absence of equality of opportunity or treatment between persons of different racial or ethnic origins, with a view to enabling such equality to be promoted or maintained; and
  (c) is carried out with appropriate safeguards for the rights and freedoms of data subjects;

  (2) The Secretary of State may by order specify circumstances in which processing falling within sub-paragraph (1)(a) and (b) is, or is not, to be taken for the purposes of sub-paragraph (1)(c) to be carried out with appropriate safeguards for the rights and freedoms of data subjects.

These sensitive personal data legitimate processing conditions may be summarised as follows:

● The individual who the sensitive personal data is about has given explicit consent to the processing;
● The processing is necessary to comply with employment law;
● The processing is necessary to protect the vital interests of,
  – the individual (in a case where the individual's consent cannot be given or reasonably obtained); or
  – another person (in a case where the individual's consent has been unreasonably withheld).
● The processing is carried out by a not-for-profit organisation and does not involve disclosing personal data to a third party, unless the individual consents. Extra limitations apply to this condition;
● The individual has deliberately made the information public;
● The processing is necessary in relation to legal proceedings; for obtaining legal advice; or otherwise for establishing, exercising or defending legal rights;

- The processing is necessary for administering justice, or for exercising statutory or governmental functions;
- The processing is necessary in relation to preventing fraud;
- The processing is necessary for medical purposes, and is undertaken by a health professional or by someone who is subject to an equivalent duty of confidentiality;
- The processing is necessary for monitoring equality of opportunity, and is carried out with appropriate safeguards for the rights of individuals.

Furthermore, regulations enacted also set out further obligations in relation to the processing of sensitive personal data.

Chapter 7

Processing Pre-Conditions: DPA Prior Information Requirements

Introduction

7.01 Organisations even prior to obtaining and processing are generally obliged to provide certain information to individual data subjects. This is in order that data subjects can be properly be informed, and can decide whether to consent or not, to the proposed data collection and data processing.

DPA

7.02 The DPA in Sch 1, Part II provides as follows:

1 (1) In determining for the purposes of the first principle whether personal data are processed fairly, regard is to be had to the method by which they are obtained, including in particular whether any person from whom they are obtained is deceived or misled as to the purpose or purposes for which they are to be processed;

   (2) Subject to paragraph 2, for the purposes of the first principle data are to be treated as obtained fairly if they consist of information obtained from a person who,

     (a) is authorised by or under any enactment to supply it; or

     (b) is required to supply it by or under any enactment or by any convention or other instrument imposing an international obligation on the United Kingdom;

2 (1) Subject to paragraph 3, for the purposes of the first principle personal data are not to be treated as processed fairly unless,

     (a) in the case of data obtained from the data subject, the data controller ensures so far as practicable that the data subject has, is provided with, or has made readily available to them, the information specified in sub-paragraph (3); and

    (b) in any other case, the data controller ensures so far as practicable that, before the relevant time or as soon as practicable after that time, the data subject has, is provided with, or has made readily available to them, the information specified in sub-paragraph (3);

(2) In sub-paragraph (1)(b) 'the relevant time' means,

    (a) the time when the data controller first processes the data; or

    (b) in a case where at that time disclosure to a third party within a reasonable period is envisaged,

       (i) if the data are in fact disclosed to such a person within that period, the time when the data are first disclosed;

      (ii) if within that period the data controller becomes, or ought to become, aware that the data are unlikely to be disclosed to such a person within that period, the time when the data controller does become, or ought to become, so aware; or

     (iii) in any other case, the end of that period;

(3) The information referred to in sub-paragraph (1) is as follows, namely,

    (a) the identity of the data controller;

    (b) if he has nominated a representative for the purposes of the DPA, the identity of that representative;

    (c) the purpose or purposes for which the data are intended to be processed; and

    (d) any further information which is necessary, having regard to the specific circumstances in which the data are or are to be processed, to enable processing in respect of the data subject to be fair.

DPD95: Prior Information Requirements – Directly Obtained Data

7.03 Article 10 of the DPD95 provides for information in cases of collection of personal data from the individual data subject. It states that Member States shall provide that the data controller or its representative must provide a data subject from which data relating to them is collected with at least the following information, except where they already have it, namely:

- the identity of the data controller and of his representative, if any;
- the purposes of the processing for which the data are intended;
- any further information such as:
  - the recipients or categories of recipients of the data;
  - whether replies to the questions are obligatory or voluntary, as well as the possible consequences of failure to reply;
  - the existence of the right of access to and the right to rectify the data concerning them,

in so far as such further information is necessary, having regard to the specific circumstances in which the data are collected, to guarantee fair processing in respect of the data subject.

DPD95: Prior Information Requirements – Indirectly Obtained Data

7.04   Article 11 of the DPD95 provides and distinguishes information where the data have not been obtained from the individual data subject. In this case, where the data have not been obtained from the data subject, Member States shall provide that the data controller or his representative must at the time of undertaking the recording of personal data or if a disclosure to a third party is envisaged, no later than the time when the data are first disclosed provide the data subject with at least the following information, except where he already has it:

- the identity of the data controller and of his representative, if any;
- the purposes of the processing;
- any further information such as:
  - the categories of data concerned;
  - the recipients or categories of recipients;
  - the existence of the right of access to and the right to rectify the data concerning them,

in so far as such further information is necessary, having regard to the specific circumstances in which the data are processed, to guarantee fair processing in respect of the data subject (Article 11(1)).

Article 11(2) of DPD95 provides that Article 11(1) shall not apply where, in particular for processing for statistical purposes or for the purposes of historical or scientific research, the provision of such information proves impossible or would involve a disproportionate effort or if recording or disclosure is expressly laid down by law. In these cases Member States shall provide appropriate safeguards.

DPR: Prior Information Requirements

7.05 Article 14(1) of the DPR provides in relation to information to the data subject that, where personal data relating to a data subject are collected, the data controller shall provide the data subject with at least the following information:

- the identity and the contact details of the data controller and, if any, of the data controller's representative and of the data protection officer;
- the purposes of the processing for which the personal data are intended, including the contract terms and general conditions where the processing is based on Article 6(1)(b) and the legitimate interests pursued by the data controller where the processing is based on Article 6(1)(f);
- the period for which the personal data will be stored;
- the existence of the right to request from the data controller access to and rectification or erasure of the personal data concerning the data subject or to object to the processing of such personal data;
- the right to lodge a complaint to the Supervisory Authority and the contact details of the Supervisory Authority;
- the recipients or categories of recipients of the personal data;
- where applicable, that the data controller intends to transfer to a third country or international organisation and on the level of protection afforded by that third country or international organisation by reference to an adequacy decision by the Commission;
- any further information necessary to guarantee fair processing in respect of the data subject, having regard to the specific circumstances in which the personal data are collected.

Article 14(2) provides that where the personal data are collected from the data subject, the data controller shall inform the data subject, in addition to the information referred to in Article 11(1), whether the provision of personal data is obligatory or voluntary, as well as the possible consequences of failure to provide such data.

Article 14(3) provides that where the personal data are not collected from the data subject, the data controller shall inform the data subject, in addition to the information referred to in Article 11(1), from which source the personal data originate.

Article 14(4) provides that the data controller shall provide the information referred to in Article 11(1), (2) and (3):

- at the time when the personal data are obtained from the data subject; or
- where the personal data are not collected from the data subject, at the time of the recording or within a reasonable period after the collection, having regard to the specific circumstances in which the data are collected or otherwise processed, or, if a disclosure to another recipient is envisaged, and at the latest when the data are first disclosed.

Article 14(5) provides that paragraphs 1 to 4 shall not apply, where:

- the data subject has already the information referred to in Article 11(1), (2) and (3); or
- the data are not collected from the data subject and the provision of such information proves impossible or would involve a disproportionate effort; or
- the data are not collected from the data subject and recording or disclosure is expressly laid down by law; or
- the data are not collected from the data subject and the provision of such information will impair the rights and freedoms of others, as defined in EU law or Member State law in accordance with Article 21.

Article 14(6) provides that in the case referred to in point (b) of paragraph 5, the controller shall provide appropriate measures to protect the data subject's legitimate interests.

Article 14(7) provides that the Commission shall be empowered to adopt delegated acts in accordance with Article 86 for the purpose of further specifying the criteria for categories of recipients referred to in Article 14(1)(f), the requirements for the notice of potential access referred to in Article 14(1)(g), the criteria for the further information necessary referred to in Article 14(1)(h) for specific sectors and situations, and the conditions and appropriate safeguards for the exceptions laid down in Article 14(5)(b). In doing so, the Commission shall take the appropriate measures for micro, small and medium-sized-enterprises (SMEs).

Article 14(8) further provides that the Commission may lay down standard forms for providing the information referred to in Article 14(1) to (3), taking into account the specific characteristics and needs of various sectors and data processing situations where necessary. Those implementing acts shall be adopted in accordance with the examination procedure referred to in Article 87(2).

Chapter 8

Exemptions

Introduction

8.01 In considering compliance obligations it is also important to consider the exemptions that may apply. In the context of the DPA, these include exemptions applying in particular to the following:

- National security;
- Crime and taxation;
- Health;
- Education;
- Social work;
- Regulatory activity;
- Journalism, literature and art;
- Research, history and statistics;
- Public authority personnel records;
- Public disclosure;
- Corporate finance;
- Examination marks;
- Examination scripts;
- Legal professional privilege;
- Self incrimination;
- Disclosures required by law;
- Legal proceedings and advice;
- Domestic purposes;
- Confidential references;
- Armed forces;
- Judicial appointments, honours and dignities;
- Crown employment or Ministerial appointments;
- Management forecasts;
- Negotiations;

- Human fertilisation and embryology;
- Adoption records and reports;
- Special educational needs;
- Parental records and reports;
- Parliamentary privilege.

Part IV of the DPA refers to exemptions. Section 27(1) provides that references in any of the Data Protection Principles or any provision of Parts II and III to personal data or to the processing of personal data do not include references to data or processing which by virtue of this Part are exempt from that principle or other provision.

Section 27(2) states that in this Part 'the subject information provisions' means:

- the first Data Protection Principle to the extent to which it requires compliance with paragraph 2 of Part II of Sch 1; and
- s 7.

Section 27(3) states that in this Part 'the non-disclosure provisions' means the provisions specified in sub-s (4) to the extent to which they are inconsistent with the disclosure in question.

Further, s 27(4) states that the provisions referred to in sub-s (3) are:

- the first data protection principle, except to the extent to which it requires compliance with the conditions in Schs 2 and 3;
- the second, third, fourth and fifth Data Protection Principles; and
- ss 10 and 14(1) to (3).

Section 27(5) states that except as provided by this Part of the DPA, the subject information provisions shall have effect notwithstanding any enactment or rule of law prohibiting or restricting the disclosure, or authorising the withholding, of information.

There is a caveat, however, similar to the three specific e-commerce activity defences, in that just because a particular exemption exists does not always mean that it applies generally, universally and regardless of the factual situation. There can, on occasion be criteria and conditions applicable to meet, and to maintain, a particular exemption. When considering whether a particular exemption applies, the full text of the exemption needs to be considered.

Separately, it can also be noted that recently the Leveson Report in considering the journalism 'exemption' has suggested that it may have been too widely drafted, and also considered the history of the particular section. The Report has suggested that the DPA be amended to ensure a more balanced journalism exemption provision. At the time of writing, it appears that both government parties, as well as the main opposition party, are in favour of the suggested amendment and restriction.

DPA: National Security Exception

8.02   Section 28 of the DPA refers to national security. Section 28(2) provides that personal data are exempt from any of the provisions of:

- the Data Protection Principles;
- Parts II, III and V; and
- Sections 54A and 55,

if the exemption from that provision is required for the purpose of safeguarding national security.

Section 28(2) states that subject to sub-s (4), a certificate signed by a Minister of the Crown certifying that exemption from all or any of the provisions mentioned in sub-s (1) is or at any time was required for the purpose there mentioned in respect of any personal data shall be conclusive evidence of that fact.

Section 28(3)A states that certificate under sub-s (2) may identify the personal data to which it applies by means of a general description and may be expressed to have prospective effect.

Section 28(4) provides that any person directly affected by the issuing of a certificate under sub-s (2) may appeal to the Tribunal against the certificate.

Section 28(5) provides that if on an appeal under sub-s (4), the Tribunal finds that, applying the principles applied by the court on an application for judicial review, the Minister did not have reasonable grounds for issuing the certificate, the Tribunal may allow the appeal and quash the certificate.

Section 28(6) provides that where in any proceedings under or by virtue of the DPA it is claimed by a data controller that a certificate under sub-s (2) which identifies the personal data to which it applies by means of a general description applies to any personal data, any other party to the proceedings may appeal to the Tribunal on the ground that the certificate does not apply to the personal data in question and, subject to any determination under sub-s (7), the certificate shall be conclusively presumed so to apply.

Section 28(7) provides that on any appeal under sub-s (6), the Tribunal may determine that the certificate does not so apply.

Section 28(8)A provides that document purporting to be a certificate under sub-s (2) shall be received in evidence and deemed to be such a certificate unless the contrary is proved.

Section 28(9)A provides that document which purports to be certified by or on behalf of a Minister of the Crown as a true copy of a certificate issued by that Minister under sub-s (2) shall in any legal proceedings be evidence (or, in Scotland, sufficient evidence) of that certificate.

Section 28(10) provides that the power conferred by sub-s (2) on a Minister of the Crown shall not be exercisable except by a Minister who is a member of the Cabinet or by the Attorney General or the Lord Advocate.

Section 28(11) provides that no power conferred by any provision of Part V may be exercised in relation to personal data which by virtue of this section are exempt from that provision.

Section 28(12) provides that sch 6 shall have effect in relation to appeals under sub-s (4) or sub-s(6) and the proceedings of the Tribunal in respect of any such appeal.

DPA: Crime and Taxation Exceptions

8.03 Section 29 of the DPA relates to crime and taxation. Section 29(1) provides that personal data processed for any of the following purposes:

- the prevention or detection of crime;
- the apprehension or prosecution of offenders; or
- the assessment or collection of any tax or duty or of any imposition of a similar nature,

are exempt from the first data protection principle (except to the extent to which it requires compliance with the conditions in sch 2 and 3) and s 7 in any case to the extent to which the application of those provisions to the data would be likely to prejudice any of the matters mentioned in this sub-section.

Section 29(2) provides that personal data which:

- are processed for the purpose of discharging statutory functions; and
- consist of information obtained for such a purpose from a person who had it in his possession for any of the purposes mentioned in sub-s (1),

are exempt from the subject information provisions to the same extent as personal data processed for any of the purposes mentioned in that sub-section.

However, under s 29(3) it is provided that personal data are exempt from the non-disclosure provisions in any case in which:

- the disclosure is for any of the purposes mentioned in sub-s (1); and,
- the application of those provisions in relation to the disclosure would be likely to prejudice any of the matters mentioned in that sub-section.

Section 29(4) provides that personal data in respect of which the data controller is a relevant authority and which:

- consist of a classification applied to the data subject as part of a system of risk assessment which is operated by that authority for either of the following purposes:
    - the assessment or collection of any tax or duty or any imposition of a similar nature; or
    - the prevention or detection of crime, or apprehension or prosecution of offenders, where the offence concerned involves any unlawful claim for any payment out of, or any unlawful application of, public funds; and
- are processed for either of those purposes,

are exempt from s 7 to the extent to which the exemption is required in the interests of the operation of the system.

Section 29(5) provides that in sub-s (4) – 'public funds' includes funds provided by any EU institution; "relevant authority" means: (a) a government department, (b) a local authority, or (c) any other authority administering housing benefit or council tax benefit.

DPA: Health, Education and Social Work Exception

8.04 Section 30 of the DPA relates to health, education and social work. Section 30(1) provides that the Secretary of State may by order exempt from the subject information provisions, or modify those provisions in relation to, personal data consisting of information as to the physical or mental health or condition of the data subject.

Section 30(2) provides that the Secretary of State may by order exempt from the subject information provisions, or modify those provisions in relation to:

- personal data in respect of which the data controller is the proprietor of, or a teacher at, a school, and which consist of information relating to persons who are or have been pupils at the school; or
- personal data in respect of which the data controller is an education authority in Scotland, and which consist of information relating to persons who are receiving, or have received, further education provided by the authority.

Section 30(3) provides that the Secretary of State may by order exempt from the subject information provisions, or modify those provisions in relation to, personal data of such other descriptions as may be specified in the order, being information:

- processed by government departments or local authorities or by voluntary organisations or other bodies designated by or under the order; and
- appearing to them to be processed in the course of, or for the purposes of, carrying out social work in relation to the data subject or other individuals,

but the Secretary of State shall not under this sub-section confer any exemption or make any modification except so far as he considers that the application to the data of those provisions (or of those provisions without modification) would be likely to prejudice the carrying out of social work.

Section 30(4) provides that an order under this section may make different provision in relation to data consisting of information of different descriptions.

Section 30(5) provides that in this section 'education authority' and 'further education' have the same meaning as in the Education (Scotland) Act 1980 ("the 1980 Act"), and 'proprietor':

- in relation to a school in England or Wales, has the same meaning as in the Education Act 1996;
- in relation to a school in Scotland, means:
  - in the case of a self-governing school, the board of management within the meaning of the Self-Governing Schools etc (Scotland) Act 1989;
  - in the case of an independent school, the proprietor within the meaning of the 1980 Act;
  - in the case of a grant-aided school, the managers within the meaning of the 1980 Act; and
  - in the case of a public school, the education authority within the meaning of the 1980 Act; and

in relation to a school in Northern Ireland, has the same meaning as in the Education and Libraries (Northern Ireland) Order 1986 and includes, in the case of a controlled school, the Board of Governors of the school.

DPA: Regulatory Activity Exception

8.05 Section 31 of the DPA relates to regulatory activity. Section 31(1) provides that personal data processed for the purposes of discharging functions to which this sub-section applies are exempt from the subject information provisions in any case to the extent to which the application of those provisions to the data would be likely to prejudice the proper discharge of those functions.

Section 31(2) provides that sub-s (1) applies to any relevant function which is designed:

- for protecting members of the public against:
  - financial loss due to dishonesty, malpractice or other seriously improper conduct by, or the unfitness or incompetence of, persons concerned in the provision of banking, insurance, investment or other financial services or in the management of bodies corporate;
  - financial loss due to the conduct of discharged or undischarged bankrupts; or
  - dishonesty, malpractice or other seriously improper conduct by, or the unfitness or incompetence of, persons authorised to carry on any profession or other activity;
- for protecting charities or community interest companies against misconduct or mismanagement (whether by trustees, directors or other persons) in their administration;
- for protecting the property of charities or community interest companies from loss or misapplication;
- for the recovery of the property of charities or community interest companies;
- for securing the health, safety and welfare of persons at work; or
- for protecting persons other than persons at work against risk to health or safety arising out of or in connection with the actions of persons at work.

Section 31(3) provides that in sub-s (2) 'relevant function' means: (a) any function conferred on any person by or under any enactment, (b) any function of the Crown, a Minister of the Crown or a government department, or (c) any other function which is of a public nature and is exercised in the public interest.

Section 31(4) provides that personal data processed for the purpose of discharging any function which:

- is conferred by or under any enactment on;
  - the Parliamentary Commissioner for Administration;
  - the Commission for Local Administration in England or, the Commission for Local Administration in Wales;
  - the Health Service Commissioner for England or, the Health Service Commissioner for Wales;
  - the Public Services Ombudsman for Wales;
  - the Assembly Ombudsman for Northern Ireland;
  - the Northern Ireland Commissioner for Complaints; or
  - the Scottish Public Services Ombudsman; and
- is designed for protecting members of the public against;
  - maladministration by public bodies;
  - failures in services provided by public bodies; or
  - a failure of a public body to provide a service which it was a function of the body to provide,

are exempt from the subject information provisions in any case to the extent to which the application of those provisions to the data would be likely to prejudice the proper discharge of that function.

Section 31(4A) provides that personal data processed for the purpose of discharging any function which is conferred by or under Part XVI of the Financial Services and Markets Act 2000 on the body established by the Financial Services Authority for the purposes of that Part are exempt from the subject information provisions in any case to the extent to which the application of those provisions to the data would be likely to prejudice the proper discharge of the function.

Section 31(4B) provides that personal data processed for the purposes of discharging any function of the Legal Services Board are exempt from the subject information provisions in any case to the extent to which the application of those provisions to the data would be likely to prejudice the proper discharge of the function.

Section 31(4C) provides that personal data processed for the purposes of the function of considering a complaint under the scheme established under Part 6 of the Legal Services Act 2007 (legal complaints) are exempt from the subject information provisions in any case to the extent to which the application of those provisions to the data would be likely to prejudice the proper discharge of the function.

Section 31(5) provides that personal data processed for the purpose of discharging any function which:

- is conferred by or under any enactment on the the Office of Fair Trading; and
- is designed:
  - for protecting members of the public against conduct which may adversely affect their interests by persons carrying on a business;
  - for regulating agreements or conduct which have as their object or effect the prevention, restriction or distortion of competition in connection with any commercial activity; or
  - for regulating conduct on the part of one or more undertakings which amounts to the abuse of a dominant position in a market,

are exempt from the subject information provisions in any case to the extent to which the application of those provisions to the data would be likely to prejudice the proper discharge of that function.

Section 31(5A) provides that personal data processed by a CPC enforcer for the purpose of discharging any function conferred on such a body by or under the CPC Regulation are exempt from the subject information provisions in any case to the extent to which the application of those provisions to the data would be likely to prejudice the proper discharge of that function.

Section 31(5B) provides that in sub-s (5A):

- 'CPC enforcer' has the meaning in s 213(5A) of the Enterprise Act 2002 but does not include the Office of Fair Trading;
- 'CPC Regulation' has the meaning in s 235A of that Act.

Section 31(6) provides that personal data processed for the purpose of the function of considering a complaint under s 113(1) or (2) or 114(1) or (3) of the Health and Social Care (Community Health and Standards) Act 2003, or s 24D, 26 or 26ZB of the Children Act 1989, are exempt from the subject information provisions in any case to the extent to which the application of those provisions to the data would be likely to prejudice the proper discharge of that function.

Section 31(7) provides that personal data processed for the purpose of discharging any function which is conferred by or under Part 3 of the Local Government Act 2000 on:

- the monitoring officer of a relevant authority;
- an ethical standards officer; or
- the Public Services Ombudsman for Wales,

are exempt from the subject information provisions in any case to the extent to which the application of those provisions to the data would be likely to prejudice the proper discharge of that function.

Section 31(8) provides that in sub-s (7), (a) 'relevant authority' has the meaning given by s 49(6) of the Local Government Act 2000, and (b) any reference to the monitoring officer of a relevant authority, or to an ethical standards officer, has the same meaning as in Part 3 of that Act.

DPA: Journalism, Literature and Art Exception

8.06 Section 32 of the DPA relates to journalism, literature and art. Section 32(1) provides that personal data which are processed only for the special purposes are exempt from any provision to which this sub-section relates if:

- the processing is undertaken with a view to the publication by any person of any journalistic, literary or artistic material;
- the data controller reasonably believes that, having regard in particular to the special importance of the public interest in freedom of expression, publication would be in the public interest; and
- the data controller reasonably believes that, in all the circumstances, compliance with that provision is incompatible with the special purposes.

Section 32(2) provides that sub-s (1) relates to the provisions of:

- the data protection principles except the seventh Data Protection Principle;
- s 7;
- s 10;
- s 12; and
- s 14(1) to (3).

Section 32(3) provides that in considering for the purposes of sub-s (1)(b) whether the belief of a data controller that publication would be in the public interest was or is a reasonable one, regard may be had to its compliance with any code of practice which:

- is relevant to the publication in question; and
- is designated by the Secretary of State by order for the purposes of this subsection.

Section 32(4) provides that where at any time ('the relevant time') in any proceedings against a data controller under ss 7(9), 10(4), 12(8) or 14 or by virtue of s 13 the data controller claims, or it appears to the court, that any personal data to which the proceedings relate are being processed:

- only for the special purposes; and
- with a view to the publication by any person of any journalistic, literary or artistic material which, at the time twenty-four hours immediately before the relevant time, had not previously been published by the data controller,

the court shall stay the proceedings until either of the conditions in sub-s (5) is met.

Section 32(5) that those conditions are (a) that a determination of the ICO under s 45 with respect to the data in question takes effect, or (b) in a case where the proceedings were stayed on the making of a claim, that the claim is withdrawn.

Section 32(6) states that for the purposes of the DPA 'publish,' in relation to journalistic, literary or artistic material, means make available to the public or any section of the public.

DPA: Research, History and Statistics Exceptions

8.07 Section 33 refers to research, history and statistics. Section 33(1) provides that in this section 'research purposes' includes statistical or historical purposes; 'the relevant conditions,' in relation to any processing of personal data, means the conditions:

- that the data are not processed to support measures or decisions with respect to particular individuals; and
- that the data are not processed in such a way that substantial damage or substantial distress is, or is likely to be, caused to any data subject.

For the purposes of the second Data Protection Principle, the further processing of personal data only for research purposes in compliance with the relevant conditions is not to be regarded as incompatible with the purposes for which they were obtained (s 33(2)).

Personal data which are processed only for research purposes in compliance with the relevant conditions may, notwithstanding the fifth Data Protection Principle, be kept indefinitely (s 33(3)).

Section 33(4) provides that personal data which are processed only for research purposes are exempt from s 7 if (a) they are processed in compliance with the relevant conditions, and (b) the results of the research or any resulting statistics are not made available in a form which identifies data subjects or any of them.

Section 33(5) provides that for the purposes of sub-s (2) to (4) personal data are not to be treated as processed otherwise than for research purposes merely because the data are disclosed (a) to any person, for research purposes only, (b) to the data subject or a person acting on his behalf, (c) at the request, or with the consent, of the data subject or a person acting on his behalf, or (d) in circumstances in which the person making the disclosure has reasonable grounds for believing that the disclosure falls within paragraph (a), (b) or (c).

DPA: Manual Data Held by Public Authorities Exception

8.08 Section 33A refers to manual data held by public authorities. Section 33A(1) provides that personal data falling within paragraph (e) of the definition of 'data' in s 1(1) are exempt from:

- the first, second, third, fifth, seventh and eighth Data Protection Principles;
- the sixth Data Protection Principle except so far as it relates to the rights conferred on data subjects by ss 7 and 14;
- ss 10 to 12;
- s 13, except so far as it relates to damage caused by a contravention of s 7 or of the fourth Data Protection Principle and to any distress which is also suffered by reason of that contravention;
- Part III; and
- s 55.

Section 33A(2) provides that personal data which fall within paragraph (e) of the definition of 'data' in s 1(1) and relate to appointments or removals, pay, discipline, superannuation or other personnel matters, in relation to:

- service in any of the armed forces of the Crown;
- service in any office or employment under the Crown or under any public authority; or
- service in any office or employment, or under any contract for services, in respect of which power to take action, or to determine or approve the action taken, in such matters is vested in Her Majesty, any Minister of the Crown, the National Assembly for Wales, any Northern Ireland Minister (within the meaning of the Freedom of Information Act 2000) or any public authority,

are also exempt from the remaining Data Protection Principles and the remaining provisions of Part II.

DPA: Information Available to the Public by or Under Enactment Exception

8.09 Section 34 refers to information available to the public by or under enactment. Personal data are exempt from:

- the subject information provisions;
- the fourth Data Protection Principle and s 14(1) to (3); and
- the non-disclosure provisions,

if the data consist of information which the data controller is obliged by or under any enactment other than an enactment contained in the Freedom of Information Act 2000 to make available to the public, whether by publishing it, by making it available for inspection, or otherwise and whether gratuitously or on payment of a fee.

DPA: Disclosures Required by Law or Made in Connection with Legal Proceedings etc Exceptions

8.10 Section 35 refers to disclosures required by law or made in connection with legal proceedings etc. Section 35(1) provides that personal data are exempt from the non-disclosure provisions where the disclosure is required by or under any enactment, by any rule of law or by the order of a court.

Section 35(2) provides that personal data are exempt from the non-disclosure provisions where the disclosure is necessary:

- for the purpose of, or in connection with, any legal proceedings (including prospective legal proceedings); or
- for the purpose of obtaining legal advice,

or is otherwise necessary for the purposes of establishing, exercising or defending legal rights.

DPA: Parliamentary Privilege Exception

8.11 Section 35A refers to Parliamentary privilege. Personal data are exempt from:

- the first Data Protection Principle, except to the extent to which it requires compliance with the conditions in Schedules 2 and 3;

- the second, third, fourth and fifth Data Protection Principles;
- s 7; and
- ss 10 and 14(1) to (3);

if the exemption is required for the purpose of avoiding an infringement of the privileges of either House of Parliament.

DPA: Domestic Purposes Exception

8.12 Section 36 refers to domestic purposes. Personal data processed by an individual only for the purposes of that individual's personal, family or household affairs (including recreational purposes) are exempt from the data protection principles and the provisions of Parts II and III.

DPA: Miscellaneous Exemptions

8.13 Section 37 refers to certain miscellaneous exemptions. Schedule 7 (which confers further miscellaneous exemptions) has effect.

DPA: Powers to Make Further Exemptions by Order

8.14 Section 38 provides that powers to make further exemptions by order. Section 38(1) provides that the Secretary of State may by order exempt from the subject information provisions personal data consisting of information the disclosure of which is prohibited or restricted by or under any enactment if and to the extent that he considers it necessary for the safeguarding of the interests of the data subject or the rights and freedoms of any other individual that the prohibition or restriction ought to prevail over those provisions.

Section 38(2) provides that the Secretary of State may by order exempt from the non-disclosure provisions any disclosures of personal data made in circumstances specified in the order, if he considers the exemption is necessary for the safeguarding of the interests of the data subject or the rights and freedoms of any other individual.

DPD95: Exemptions

8.15 Section VI of the DPD95 refers to the exemptions and restrictions. Article 13(1) provides that Member States may adopt legislative measures to restrict the scope of the obligations and rights provided for in Articles 6(1), 10, 11(1), 12 and 21 when such a restriction constitutes a necessary measures to safeguard:

● national security;
● defence;
● public security;
● the prevention, investigation, detection and prosecution of criminal offences, or of breaches of ethics for regulated professions;
● an important economic or financial interest of a Member State or of the European EU, including monetary, budgetary and taxation matters;
● a monitoring, inspection or regulatory function connected, even occasionally, with the exercise of official authority in cases referred to in (c), (d) and (e);
● the protection of the data subject or of the rights and freedoms of others.

Article 13(2) provides that subject to adequate legal safeguards, in particular that the data are not used for taking measures or decisions regarding any particular individual, Member States may, where there is clearly no risk of breaching the privacy of the data subject, restrict by a legislative measure the rights provided for in Article 12 when data are processed solely for purposes of scientific research or are kept in personal form for a period which does not exceed the period necessary for the sole purpose of creating statistics.

Conclusion

8.16 The exemptions are important when and where applicable. They will often be more relevant to particular sectors. Generally, the exemptions appear to be less litigated than other areas of data protection.

Chapter 9

Individual Data Subject Rights

Introduction

9.01   The data protection regime provides, or enshrines, a number of rights to individuals in relation to their informational data and informational privacy. Transparency and consent are very important aspects of respecting and enabling such right to be vindicated, utilised and enforced by data subjects. Individual data subjects have a right of access to personal data. Certain fees may be charged. There are also time limits to be complied with by data controller in relation to replying to a data subject access request.

Individuals also have a right to prevent data processing for direct marketing (DM) purposes.

The individual data subject has a right to prevent processing likely to cause damage or distress.

A further right relates to automated decision taking, which relates to automated decisions being taken without human oversight or intervention. The traditional example often used is adverse credit decisions being taken automatically. However, it can equally encompass such adverse decisions and activities as so called neutral algorithmic processing and arranging of information and result outputs. Examples could include search rankings and priorities; search suggestions; search prompts; autosuggest; autocomplete; etc. Other examples could arise in relation to profiling and advertising related activities.

Importantly, individual data subjects have specific rights in relation to rectification, blocking, erasure and destruction.

Individual data subject are also entitled to compensation, as well as being entitled to complain to the ICO and to the courts to obtain judicial remedies.

Recital 10 of the DPD95 also refers to rights and states that whereas the object of the national laws on the processing of personal data is to protect fundamental rights and freedoms, notably the right to privacy, which is recognised both in Article 8 of the European Convention for the Protection of Human Rights and Fundamental Freedoms and in the general principles of EU law. For that reason, the approximation of those laws must not result in any lessening of the protection they afford but must, on the contrary, seek to ensure a high level of protection in the EU.

Data Protection Principles

9.02 The eight Data Drotection Principles require that personal data are;

(1) fairly and lawfully processed;
(2) processed for limited purposes;
(3) adequate, relevant and not excessive;
(4) accurate and up to date;
(5) not kept for longer than is necessary;
(6) processed in line with your rights;
(7) secure; and
(8) not transferred to other countries without adequate protection.

Rights for Individual Data Subjects

9.03 The DPA contains a number of important rights for individuals in respect of their personal data, such as;

- the prior information that has to be given to them by data controllers;
- access to personal data;
- the right to object into processing;
- not being forced to make an access request as a condition of recruitment, employment or provision of a service;
- not being subjected to 'automated decision making processes.'

The rights are expanding and are becoming more explicit. It is import-ant that organisations keep abreast of the expanding rights and obliga-tions. The data protection rights enshrined in the data protection regime for individuals are set out in the Data Protection Principles and, in particular, in ss 7–15 of the DPA. They include the following;

- Individuals have a right to be informed by organisation as to their identity when they are collecting and processing the individual's personal data.

- The organisation must disclose to the individual the purpose for which it is collecting and processing the individual's personal data.
- If the organisation is forwarding on the personal data to third party recipients, it must disclose this to the individual as well as identify the third party recipients. If it is permitted to transfer the personal data outside of the county, the organisation must then also identify which third party country will be receiving the personal data.
- Organisations must answer and comply with requests from the individual in relation to their data protection rights.

This includes requests for access to a copy of the personal data held in relation to the individual. This is known as a personal data access request.

The rights of data subjects can be summarised as including:

- Right of access (s 7 DPA);
- Right to establish if personal data exists (s 7(1)(a) DPA);
- Right to be informed of the logic in automatic decision taking (s 7(1)(d));
- Right to prevent processing likely to cause damage or distress (s 18 DPA);
- Right to prevent processing for direct marketing (s 11 DPA);
- Right to prevent automated decision taking (s 12 DPA);
- Right in relation to exempt manual data (s 12A DPA);
- Right to compensation (s 13 DPA);
- Right to rectify inaccurate data (s 14 DPA);
- Right to rectification, blocking, erasure and destruction (s 14 DPA);
- Right to complain to ICO (see s 42 DPA);
- Right to go to court (see s 15 DPA).

Recipients of Right

9.04 The data protection rights apply generally in relation any individuals whose personal data are being collected and processed. Specifically, it can include:

- Employees;
- Other workers such as contractors, temps, casual staff;
- Agency staff;
- Ex-employees and retired employees;
- Spouses and family members;
- Job applicants, including unsuccessful applicants;
- Volunteers;

- Apprentices and trainees;
- Customers and clients;
- Prospective customer and clients;
- Suppliers;[1]
- Members;
- Users.

DPA: Access Right

9.05 Part II of the DPA refers to the rights of data subjects and others. In particular, s 7 refers to the right of access to personal data. This applies to data subjects. It is a data subject right. Section 7(1) provides that subject to the following provisions of this section and to s 8, 9 and 9A, an individual is entitled:

- to be informed by any data controller whether personal data of which that individual is the data subject are being processed by or on behalf of that data controller;
- if that is the case, to be given by the data controller a description of:
    - the personal data of which that individual is the data subject;
    - the purposes for which they are being or are to be processed; and
    - the recipients or classes of recipients to whom they are or may be disclosed;
- to have communicated to them in an intelligible form:
    - the information constituting any personal data of which that individual is the data subject; and
    - any information available to the data controller as to the source of those data; and
- where the processing by automatic means of personal data of which that individual is the data subject for the purpose of evaluating matters relating to them such as, for example, his performance at work, his credit worthiness, his reliability or his conduct, has constituted or is likely to constitute the sole basis for any decision significantly affecting them, to be informed by the data controller of the logic involved in that decision-taking.

Section 7(2)A provides that a data controller is not obliged to supply any information under sub-s (1) unless he has received:

---

1   MacDonald, Lynday A.C., *Data Protection: Legal Compliance and Good Practice for Employers* (London: Tottel, 2008), p. 41.

- a request in writing; and
- except in prescribed cases, such fee (not exceeding the prescribed maximum) as he may require.

Section 7(3) provides that where a data controller:

- reasonably requires further information in order to satisfy them as to the identity of the person making a request under this section and to locate the information which that person seeks; and
- has informed them of that requirement,

the data controller is not obliged to comply with the request unless he is supplied with that further information.

Section 7(4) provides that where a data controller cannot comply with the request without disclosing information relating to another individual who can be identified from that information, he is not obliged to comply with the request unless:

- the other individual has consented to the disclosure of the information to the person making the request; or
- it is reasonable in all the circumstances to comply with the request without the consent of the other individual.

Section 7(5) provides that in sub-s (4) the reference to information relating to another individual includes a reference to information identifying that individual as the source of the information sought by the request; and that sub-section is not to be construed as excusing a data controller from communicating so much of the information sought by the request as can be communicated without disclosing the identity of the other individual concerned, whether by the omission of names or other identifying particulars or otherwise.

Section 7(6) provides that in determining for the purposes of sub-s (4)(b) whether it is reasonable in all the circumstances to comply with the request without the consent of the other individual concerned, regard shall be had, in particular, to:

- any duty of confidentiality owed to the other individual;
- any steps taken by the data controller with a view to seeking the consent of the other individual;
- whether the other individual is capable of giving consent; and
- any express refusal of consent by the other individual.

Section 7(7) provides that an individual making a request under this section may, in such cases as may be prescribed, specify that his request is limited to personal data of any prescribed description.

Section 7(8) provides that subject to sub-s (4), a data controller shall comply with a request under this section promptly and in any event before the end of the prescribed period beginning with the relevant day.

Section 7(9) provides that if a court is satisfied on the application of any person who has made a request under the foregoing provisions of this section that the data controller in question has failed to comply with the request in contravention of those provisions, the court may order them to comply with the request.

Section 7(10) also provides that in this section:

- 'prescribed' means prescribed by the Secretary of State by regulations;
- 'the prescribed maximum' means such amount as may be prescribed;
- 'the prescribed period' means forty days or such other period as may be prescribed;
- 'the relevant day,' in relation to a request under this section, means the day on which the data controller receives the request or, if later, the first day on which the data controller has both the required fee and the information referred to in sub-s (3).

Section 7(11) provides that different amounts or periods may be prescribed under this section in relation to different cases.

Section 7(12) provides that a person is a relevant person for the purposes of sub-s (4)(c) if he:

- is a person referred to in paragraph 4(a) or (b) or paragraph 8(a) or (b) of Sch 11;
- is employed by an education authority (within the meaning of paragraph 6 of Schedule 11) in pursuance of its functions relating to education and the information relates to them, or he supplied the information in his capacity as such an employee; or
- is the person making the request.

Section 7(12) provides that a person is a relevant person for the purposes of sub-s (4)(c) if he:

- is a person referred to in paragraph 1(p) or (q) of the Schedule to the Data Protection (Subject Access Modification)(Social Work) Order 2000; or
- is or has been employed by any person or body referred to in paragraph 1 of that Schedule in connection with functions which are or have been exercised in relation to the data consisting of the information; or
- has provided for reward a service similar to a service provided in

the exercise of any functions specified in paragraph 1(a)(i), (b), (c) or (d) of that Schedule,

and the information relates to them or he supplied the information in his official capacity or, as the case may be, in connection with the provision of that service.

Section 8 refers to provisions supplementary to s 7. Section 8(1) provides that the Secretary of State may by regulations provide that, in such cases as may be prescribed, a request for information under any provision of sub-s (1) of s 7 is to be treated as extending also to information under other provisions of that sub-section.

Section 8(2) provides that the obligation imposed by s 7(1)(c)(i) must be complied with by supplying the data subject with a copy of the information in permanent form unless:

- the supply of such a copy is not possible or would involve disproportionate effort; or
- the data subject agrees otherwise;

and where any of the information referred to in s 7(1)(c)(i) is expressed in terms which are not intelligible without explanation the copy must be accompanied by an explanation of those terms.

Section 8(3) provides that where a data controller has previously complied with a request made under s 7 by an individual, the data controller is not obliged to comply with a subsequent identical or similar request under that section by that individual unless a reasonable interval has elapsed between compliance with the previous request and the making of the current request.

Section 8(4) provides that in determining for the purposes of sub-s (3) whether requests under s 7 are made at reasonable intervals, regard shall be had to the nature of the data, the purpose for which the data are processed and the frequency with which the data are altered.

Section 8(5) provides that s 7(1)(d) is not to be regarded as requiring the provision of information as to the logic involved in any decision-taking if, and to the extent that, the information constitutes a trade secret.

Section 8(6) provides that the information to be supplied pursuant to a request under s 7 must be supplied by reference to the data in question at the time when the request is received, except that it may take account of any amendment or deletion made between that time and the time when the information is supplied, being an amendment or deletion that would have been made regardless of the receipt of the request.

Section 8(7) provides that for the purposes of s 7(4) and (5) another individual can be identified from the information being disclosed if he can be identified from that information, or from that and any other information which, in the reasonable belief of the data controller, is likely to be in, or to come into, the possession of the data subject making the request.

It is important to consider that being informed only verbally may not always, or at all, be a proper vindication of the data subjects' access right. This is particularly so where large sets of personal data, or complex details involving personal data, are involved. Generally, personal data is provided in hardcopy. However, in particular circumstances, certain data controllers prefer to furnish personal data in electronic format where large volumes of materials are involved. If a data controller was to refuse to furnish the personal data required, on the basis that it had verbally communicated same, this would jar with the accepted understanding of the data access right. It could also be argued that the data controller was not allowing access to the personal data to be effectively and properly accessed. Note, however, the recent case of *Durham County Council v Dunn* [2012] EWCA Civ 1654, which while acknowledging the legitimacy of copies of documents, appears to suggest that other avenues also arise. An organisation should be cautious in embarking in data access disclosures other than in a documented and written manner. Some would also query whether interpreting the data access right as some sort of a *data communicated right* as appears to be suggested in part of *Durham* as compatible with the DPA and DPD95.

Credit Reference Agencies

9.06 Section 9 refers to the application of s 7 where the data controller is a credit reference agency.

Section 9(1) provides that where the data controller is a credit reference agency, s 7 has effect subject to the provisions of this section.

Section 9(2) provides that an individual making a request under s 7 may limit his request to personal data, relevant to his financial standing, and shall be taken to have so limited his request unless the request shows a contrary intention.

Section 9(3) provides that where the data controller receives a request under s 7 in a case where personal data, of which the individual making the request is the data subject, are being processed by or on behalf of the data controller, the obligation to supply information under that section includes an obligation to give the individual making the request a statement, in such form as may be prescribed by the Secretary of State by regulations, of the individual's rights:

- under s 159 of the Consumer Credit Act 1974; and
- to the extent required by the prescribed form, under the Act.

Public Authorities

9.07 Section 9A relates to unstructured personal data held by public authorities. Section 9A(1) provides that in this section 'unstructured personal data' means any personal data falling within paragraph (e) of the definition of 'data' in s 1(1), other than information which is recorded as part of, or with the intention that it should form part of, any set of information relating to individuals to the extent that the set is structured by reference to individuals or by reference to criteria relating to individuals.

Section 9A(2) provides that a public authority is not obliged to comply with sub-s (1) of s 7 in relation to any unstructured personal data unless the request under that section contains a description of the data.

Section 9A(3) provides that even if the data are described by the data subject in his request, a public authority is not obliged to comply with subsection (1) of s 7 in relation to unstructured personal data if the authority estimates that the cost of complying with the request so far as relating to those data would exceed the appropriate limit.

Section 9A(4) provides that sub-s (3) does not exempt the public authority from its obligation to comply with paragraph (a) of s 7(1) in relation to the unstructured personal data unless the estimated cost of complying with that paragraph alone in relation to those data would exceed the appropriate limit.

Section 9A(5) provides that in sub-s (3) and (4) 'the appropriate limit' means such amount as may be prescribed by the Secretary of State by regulations, and different amounts may be prescribed in relation to different cases.

Section 9A(6) provides that any estimate for the purposes of the section must be made in accordance with regulations under s 12(5) of the Freedom of Information Act 2000.

DPD95: Access Right

9.08 Article 12 of the DPD95 provides for the right of access, and states, Member States shall guarantee every data subject the right to obtain from the data controller:

- without constraint at reasonable intervals and without excessive delay or expense

: • confirmation as to whether or not data relating to them are being processed and information at least as to the purposes of the processing, the categories of data concerned, and the recipients or categories of recipients to whom the data are disclosed;

- communication to them in an intelligible form of the data undergoing processing and of any available information as to their source;

- knowledge of the logic involved in any automatic processing of data concerning them at least in the case of the automated decisions referred to in Article 15(1);

- as appropriate the rectification, erasure or blocking of data the processing of which does not comply with the provisions of DPD95, in particular because of the incomplete or inaccurate nature of the data (12(b));

- notification to third parties to whom the data have been disclosed of any rectification, erasure or blocking carried out in compliance with (b), unless this proves impossible or involves a disproportionate effort.

Intelligible form is generally meant and understood as including copies of the relevant personal data or document containing it. It could be often ineffective and difficult for an individual merely to receive verbal communications, particularly where large sets of personal data are involved. Less scrupulous data controllers could also seek to circumvent the spirit and letter of the data protection regime if actual copies were not required. In any event, the data protection regime provides that certain charges can be applied in relation to copies being provided to data subjects in compliance with their access rights.

In practice, certain websites are also developing tools in order to provide access to certain sets of personal data electronically as opposed to furnishing in hard copy format.

DPR: Access Right

9.09 Article 15 of the DPR relates to the right of access for the data subject and provides:

- The data subject shall have the right to obtain from the controller at any time, on request, confirmation as to whether or not personal data relating to the data subject are being processed. Where such personal data are being processed, the data controller shall provide the following information:

- the purposes of the processing;
- the categories of personal data concerned;
- the recipients or categories of recipients to whom the personal data are to be or have been disclosed, in particular to recipients in third countries;
- the period for which the personal data will be stored;
- the existence of the right to request from the data controller rectification or erasure of personal data concerning the data subject or to object to the processing of such personal data;
- the right to lodge a complaint to the Supervisory Authority and the contact details of the Supervisory Authority;
- communication of the personal data undergoing processing and of any available information as to their source (15(1)(g));
- the significance and envisaged consequences of such processing, at least in the case of measures referred to in Article 20;

- The data subject shall have the right to obtain from the data controller communication of the personal data undergoing processing. Where the data subject makes the request in electronic form, the information shall be provided in electronic form, unless otherwise requested by the data subject;
- The Commission shall be empowered to adopt delegated acts in accordance with Article 86 for the purpose of further specifying the criteria and requirements for the communication to the data subject of the content of the personal data referred to in point (g) of paragraph 1;
- The Commission may specify standard forms and procedures for requesting and granting access to the information referred to in paragraph 1, including for verification of the identity of the data subject and communicating the personal data to the data subject, taking into account the specific features and necessities of various sectors and data processing situations. Those implementing acts shall be adopted in accordance with the examination procedure referred to in Article 87(2).

Dealing with Access Requests

9.10 One commentary[2] refers to the advisability of having a process flow chart in place. The main components referred to include:

- Data subject calls or asks for personal data;

---

2   Morgan, R., and Boardman, R., *Data Protection Strategy* (London: Sweet & Maxwell, 2003), p. 252.

- Data subject access request form issued;
- Data subject access request form returned plus appropriate fee if requested);
- Personal data located, whether by legal department, data protection personnel, etc;
- Examining same in relation to whether any third party information; health data; exempt data;
- Data reviewed by legal department;
- Personal data copy issues to data subject.

The ICO provides the following guidance or checklist,[3]

1. Is this a subject access request?
   No – Handle the query as part of the normal course of business.
   Yes – Go to 2.

2. Is there enough information to be sure of the requester's identity?
   No – If the requester's identity is unclear, ask them to provide evidence to confirm it. For example, one may ask for a piece of information held in your records that the person would be expected to know, such as membership details, or a witnessed copy of their signature. Once satisfied, go to 3.
   Yes – Go to 3.

3. Is any other information required to find the records they want?
   No – Go to 4.
   Yes – One will need to ask the individual promptly for any other information reasonably needed to find the records they want. One might want to ask them to narrow down their request. For example, if keeping all customers' information on one computer system and suppliers' information on another, one could ask what relationship they had with the organisation. Or, one could ask when they had dealings with the organisation. However, they do have the right to ask for everything held about them and this could mean a very wide search. The organisation has 40 calendar days to respond to a subject access request after receiving any further information one needs and any fee charged. Go to 4.

4. Are you going to charge a fee?
   No – Go to 5.

---

3. *Data Protection Good Practice Note, Checklist for Handling Requests for Personal Information* (subject access requests), ICO, available at http://www.ico.gov. uk/for_organisations/data_protection/subject_access_requests.aspx, accessed on 18 January 2013.

Yes – If there is a fee one must ask the individual promptly for one. The maximum that can be charged is £10 unless medical or education records are involved (see guidance on our website). The 40 calendar days in which one must respond starts when one receives the fee and all necessary information to help one find the records. Go to 5.

5   Does the organisation hold any information about the person?
     No – If one holds no personal information at all about the individual one must tell them this.
     Yes – Go to 6.

6   Will the information be changed between receiving the request and sending the response?
     No – Go to 7.
     Yes – One can still make routine amendments and deletions to personal information after receiving a request. However, one must not make any changes to the records as a result of receiving the request, even if one finds inaccurate or embarrassing information on the record. Go to 7.

7   Does it include any information about other people?
     No – Go to 8.
     Yes – One will not have to supply the information unless the other people mentioned have given their consent, or it is reasonable to supply the information without their consent. Even when the other person's information should not be disclosed, one should still supply as much as possible by editing the references to other people. Go to 8.

8   Is the organisation obliged to supply the information?
     No – If all the information held about the requester is exempt, then one can reply stating that one does not hold any of their personal information required to be revealed.
     Yes – Go to 9.

9   Does it include any complex terms or codes?
     No – Go to 10.
     Yes One must make sure that these are explained so the information can be understood. Go to 10.

10   Prepare the response.[4]

4   *Data Protection Good Practice Note, Checklist for Handling Requests for Personal Information* (subject access requests), ICO, available at http://www.ico.gov.uk/for_organisations/data_protection/subject_access_requests.aspx, accessed on 18 January 2013.

DPA: Right to Prevent Data Processing Likely to Cause Damage or Distress

9.11 Section 10 of the DPA refers to the right to prevent processing likely to cause damage or distress.

Section 10(1) provides that subject to sub-s (2), an individual is entitled at any time by notice in writing to a data controller to require the data controller at the end of such period as is reasonable in the circumstances to cease, or not to begin, processing, or processing for a specified purpose or in a specified manner, any personal data in respect of which he is the data subject, on the ground that, for specified reasons:

- the processing of those data or their processing for that purpose or in that manner is causing or is likely to cause substantial damage or substantial distress to them or to another; and
- that damage or distress is or would be unwarranted.

Section 10(2) provides that sub-s (1) does not apply:

- in a case where any of the conditions in paragraphs 1 to 4 of Sch 2 is met; or
- in such other cases as may be prescribed by the Secretary of State by order.

Section 10(3) provides that the data controller must within twenty-one days of receiving a notice under sub-s (1) ('the data subject notice') give the individual who gave it a written notice:

- stating that he has complied or intends to comply with the data subject notice; or
- stating his reasons for regarding the data subject notice as to any extent unjustified and the extent (if any) to which he has complied or intends to comply with it.

Section 10(4) provides that if a court is satisfied, on the application of any person who has given a notice under sub-s (1) which appears to the court to be justified (or to be justified to any extent), that the data controller in question has failed to comply with the notice, the court may order them to take such steps for complying with the notice (or for complying with it to that extent) as the court thinks fit.

Section 10(5) provides that the failure by a data subject to exercise the right conferred by sub-s (1) or s 11(1) does not affect any other right conferred on them by this Part.

This may well have renewed importance and application application in relation to online abuse and social networking abuse.

DPA: Right to Prevent Data Processing for Direct Marketing (DM)

9.12 Section 11 of the DPA relates to the right to prevent processing for purposes of direct marketing (DM).

Section 11(1) provides that an individual is entitled at any time by notice in writing to a data controller to require the data controller at the end of such period as is reasonable in the circumstances to cease, or not to begin, processing for the purposes of direct marketing personal data in respect of which he is the data subject.

Section 11(2) provides that if the court is satisfied, on the application of any person who has given a notice under sub-s (1), that the data controller has failed to comply with the notice, the court may order them to take such steps for complying with the notice as the court thinks fit.

Section 11(2A) provides that this section shall not apply in relation to the processing of such data as are mentioned in paragraph (1) of regulation 8 of the Telecommunications (Data Protection and Privacy) Regulations 1999 (processing of telecommunications billing data for certain marketing purposes) for the purposes mentioned in paragraph (2) of that regulation.

Section 11(3) provides that in this section, 'direct marketing' means the communication (by whatever means) of any advertising or marketing material which is directed to particular individuals.

DPA: Automated Decision Taking/Making Processes

9.13 Data controllers may not take decisions which produce legal effects concerning a data subject or which otherwise significantly affect a data subject and which are based solely on processing by automatic means of personal data and which are intended to evaluate certain personal matters relating to the data subject such as, performance at work, credit worthiness, reliability of conduct.

Section 12 provides for the rights in relation to automated decision-taking. Section 12(1) provides that an individual is entitled at any time, by notice in writing to any data controller, to require the data controller to ensure that no decision taken by or on behalf of the data controller which significantly affects that individual is based solely on the processing by automatic means of personal data in respect of which that individual is the data subject for the purpose of evaluating matters relating to them such as, for example, his performance at work, his creditworthiness, his reliability or his conduct.

Section 12(2) provides that where, in a case where no notice under sub-s (1) has effect, a decision which significantly affects an individual is based solely on such processing as is mentioned in sub-s (1):

- the data controller must as soon as reasonably practicable notify the individual that the decision was taken on that basis; and
- the individual is entitled, within twenty-one days of receiving that notification from the data controller, by notice in writing to require the data controller to reconsider the decision or to take a new decision otherwise than on that basis (12(2)(b)).

Section 12(3) provides that the data controller must, within twenty-one days of receiving a notice under sub-s (2)(b) ('the data subject notice') give the individual a written notice specifying the steps that he intends to take to comply with the data subject notice.

Section 12(4) provides that a notice under sub-s (1) does not have effect in relation to an exempt decision; and nothing in sub-s (2) applies to an exempt decision.

Section 12(5) provides that in sub-s (4) 'exempt decision' means any decision:

- in respect of which the condition in sub-s (6) and the condition in sub-s (7) are met; or
- which is made in such other circumstances as may be prescribed by the Secretary of State by order.

Section 12(6) provides that the condition in this sub-s is that the decision:

- is taken in the course of steps taken;
    - for the purpose of considering whether to enter into a contract with the data subject;
    - with a view to entering into such a contract; or
    - in the course of performing such a contract; or
- is authorised or required by or under any enactment.

Section 12(7) provides that the condition in this sub-s is that either:

- the effect of the decision is to grant a request of the data subject; or
- steps have been taken to safeguard the legitimate interests of the data subject (for example, by allowing them to make representations).

Section 12(8) provides that if a court is satisfied on the application of a data subject that a person taking a decision in respect of them (the 'responsible person') has failed to comply with sub-s (1) or (2)(b), the court may order the responsible person to reconsider the decision, or to take a new decision which is not based solely on such processing as is mentioned in sub-s (1).

Section 12(9) provides that an order under sub-s (8) shall not affect the rights of any person other than the data subject and the responsible person.

Section 12 of the DPA provides rights in relation to automated decision-taking. It states:

(1) An individual is entitled at any time, by notice in writing to any data controller, to require the data controller to ensure that no decision taken by or on behalf of the data controller which significantly affects that individual is based solely on the processing by automatic means of personal data in respect of which that individual is the data subject for the purpose of evaluating matters relating to them such as, for example, his performance at work, his creditworthiness, his reliability or his conduct;

(2) Where, in a case where no notice under sub-s (1) has effect, a decision which significantly affects an individual is based solely on such processing as is mentioned in sub-s (1);

    (a) the data controller must as soon as reasonably practicable notify the individual that the decision was taken on that basis; and

    (b) the individual is entitled, within twenty-one days of receiving that notification from the data controller, by notice in writing to require the data controller to reconsider the decision or to take a new decision otherwise than on that basis;

(3) The data controller must, within twenty-one days of receiving a notice under sub-s (2)(b) ('the data subject notice') give the individual a written notice specifying the steps that he intends to take to comply with the data subject notice;

(4) A notice under sub-s (1) does not have effect in relation to an exempt decision; and nothing in sub-s (2) applies to an exempt decision;

(5) In subsection (4) 'exempt decision' means any decision:

    (a) in respect of which the condition in sub-s (6) and the condition in sub-s (7) are met; or

    (b) which is made in such other circumstances as may be prescribed by the Secretary of State by order;

(6) The condition in this sub–s is that the decision:

    (a) is taken in the course of steps taken;

(i) for the purpose of considering whether to enter into a contract with the data subject;

(ii) with a view to entering into such a contract; or

(iii) in the course of performing such a contract; or

(b) is authorised or required by or under any enactment;

(7) The condition in this sub-s is that either:

(a) the effect of the decision is to grant a request of the data subject; or

(b) steps have been taken to safeguard the legitimate interests of the data subject (for example, by allowing them to make representations);

(8) If a court is satisfied on the application of a data subject that a person taking a decision in respect of them ('the responsible person') has failed to comply with sub-s (1) or (2)(b), the court may order the responsible person to reconsider the decision, or to take a new decision which is not based solely on such processing as is mentioned in sub-s (1);

(9) An order under sub-s (8) shall not affect the rights of any person other than the data subject and the responsible person.

DPD95: Right Against Automated Individual Decisions

9.14 Article 15 of the DPD95 provides for the right against automated individual decisions. Section 15(1) states that Member States shall grant the right to every person not to be subject to a decision which produces legal effects concerning them or significantly affects them and which is based solely on automated processing of data intended to evaluate certain personal aspects relating to them, such as his performance at work, creditworthiness, reliability, conduct, etc.

Section 15(2) states that subject to the other Articles of this Directive, Member States shall provide that a person may be subjected to a decision of the kind referred to in Article 15(1) if that decision:

- is taken in the course of the entering into or performance of a contract, provided the request for the entering into or the performance of the contract, lodged by the data subject, has been satisfied or that there are suitable measures to safeguard his legitimate interests, such as arrangements allowing them to put his point of view; or

- is authorised by a law which also lays down measures to safeguard the data subject's legitimate interests.

DPD95: Right to Object

9.15 Section VII of the DPD95 refers to the data subject's right to object. Article 14 refers to the data subject's right to object. It provides that Member States shall grant the data subject the right:

- at least in the cases referred to in Article 7 (e) and (f), to object at any time on compelling legitimate grounds relating to his particular situation to the processing of data relating to them, save where otherwise provided by national legislation. Where there is a justified objection, the processing instigated by the data controller may no longer involve those data;
- to object, on request and free of charge, to the processing of personal data relating to them which the data controller anticipates being processed for the purposes of direct marketing, or to be informed before personal data are disclosed for the first time to third parties or used on their behalf for the purposes of direct marketing, and to be expressly offered the right to object free of charge to such disclosures or uses.

It also provides that Member States shall take the necessary measures to ensure that data subjects are aware of the existence of the right.

DPD95: Right Against Automated Individual Decisions

9.16 Article 15 of DPD95 refers to automated individual decisions. Article 15(1) provides that Member States shall grant the right to every person not to be subject to a decision which produces legal effects concerning them or significantly affects them and which is based solely on automated processing of data intended to evaluate certain personal aspects relating to them, such as his performance at work, creditworthiness, reliability, conduct, etc.

Article 15(2) provides that subject to the other Articles of the Directive, Member States shall provide that a person may be subjected to a decision of the kind referred to in paragraph 1 if that decision:

- is taken in the course of the entering into or performance of a contract, provided the request for the entering into or the performance of the contract, lodged by the data subject, has been satisfied or that there are suitable measures to safeguard his legitimate interests, such as arrangements allowing them to put his point of view; or
- is authorised by a law which also lays down measures to safeguard the data subject's legitimate interests.

DPA: Rectification, Blocking, Erasure and Destruction Rights

9.17 Section 14 of the DPA provides user rights in relation to rectification, blocking, erasure and destruction.

Section 14(1) provides that if a court is satisfied on the application of a data subject that personal data of which the applicant is the subject are inaccurate, the court may order the data controller to rectify, block, erase or destroy those data and any other personal data in respect of which he is the data controller and which contain an expression of opinion which appears to the court to be based on the inaccurate data.

Section 14(2) provides that sub-s (1) applies whether or not the data accurately record information received or obtained by the data controller from the data subject or a third party but where the data accurately record such information, then:

- if the requirements mentioned in paragraph 7 of Part II of Schedule 1 have been complied with, the court may, instead of making an order under sub-s (1), make an order requiring the data to be supplemented by such statement of the true facts relating to the matters dealt with by the data as the court may approve (14(2)(a)); and
- if all or any of those requirements have not been complied with, the court may, instead of making an order under that sub-section, make such order as it thinks fit for securing compliance with those requirements with or without a further order requiring the data to be supplemented by such a statement as is mentioned in the above paragraph (a).

Section 14(3) provides that where the court:

- makes an order under sub-s (1); or
- is satisfied on the application of a data subject that personal data of which he was the data subject and which have been rectified, blocked, erased or destroyed were inaccurate,

it may, where it considers it reasonably practicable, order the data controller to notify third parties to whom the data have been disclosed of the rectification, blocking, erasure or destruction.

Section 14(4) provides that if a court is satisfied on the application of a data subject:

- that he has suffered damage by reason of any contravention by a data controller of any of the requirements of the DPA in respect of any personal data, in circumstances entitling them to compensation under s 13; and

• that there is a substantial risk of further contravention in respect of those data in such circumstances,

the court may order the rectification, blocking, erasure or destruction of any of those data.

Section 14(5) provides that where the court makes an order under sub-s (4) it may, where it considers it reasonably practicable, order the data controller to notify third parties to whom the data have been disclosed of the rectification, blocking, erasure or destruction.

Section 14(6) provides that in determining whether it is reasonably practicable to require such notification as is mentioned in sub-s (3) or (5) the court shall have regard, in particular, to the number of persons who would have to be notified.

Again, this can apply in relation to various forms of online and social networking abuse.

DPD: Rectification, Erasure or Blocking

9.18 Article 12 of the DPD95 provides for the right of access, and states, Member States shall guarantee every data subject the right to obtain from the data controller:

(a) ...
(b) as appropriate the rectification, erasure or blocking of data the processing of which does not comply with the provisions of the DPD95, in particular because of the incomplete or inaccurate nature of the data;
(c) notification to third parties to whom the data have been disclosed of any rectification, erasure or blocking carried out in compliance with (b), unless this proves impossible or involves a disproportionate effort.

DPR: Rectification Right

9.19 Section 3 of the DPR refers to rectification and erasure. Article 16 relates to the right to rectification. It provides that the data subject shall have the right to obtain from the data controller the rectification of personal data relating to them which are inaccurate. The data subject shall have the right to obtain completion of incomplete personal data, including by way of supplementing a corrective statement.

DPR: Erasure Right/Right to be Forgotten

9.20 Article 17 of the DPR provides for the enhanced right to be forgotten and to erasure.

Article 17(1) provides that the data subject shall have the right to obtain from the controller the erasure of personal data relating to them and the abstention from further dissemination of such data, especially in relation to personal data which are made available by the data subject while he or she was a child, where one of the following grounds applies:

- the data are no longer necessary in relation to the purposes for which they were collected or otherwise processed;
- the data subject withdraws consent on which the processing is based according to point (a) of Article 6(1), or when the storage period consented to has expired, and where there is no other legal ground for the processing of the data;
- the data subject objects to the processing of personal data pursuant to Article 19;
- the processing of the data does not comply with the Regulation for other reasons.

Article 17(2) provides that where the data controller referred to in paragraph 1 has made the personal data public, it shall take all reasonable steps, including technical measures, in relation to data for the publication of which the data controller is responsible, to inform third parties which are processing such data, that a data subject requests them to erase any links to, or copy or replication of that personal data. Where the data controller has authorised a third party publication of personal data, the data controller shall be considered responsible for that publication.

Article 17(3) provides that the data controller shall carry out the erasure without delay, except to the extent that the retention of the personal data is necessary:

- for exercising the right of freedom of expression in accordance with Article 80;
- for reasons of public interest in the area of public health in accordance with Article 81;
- for historical, statistical and scientific research purposes in accordance with Article 83;
- for compliance with a legal obligation to retain the personal data by EU or Member State law to which the data controller is subject; Member State laws shall meet an objective of public interest,

respect the essence of the right to the protection of personal data and be proportionate to the legitimate aim pursued;

- in the cases referred to in paragraph 4.

Article 17(4) provides that instead of erasure, the data controller shall restrict processing of personal data where:

- their accuracy is contested by the data subject, for a period enabling the controller to verify the accuracy of the data;
- the data controller no longer needs the personal data for the accomplishment of its task but they have to be maintained for purposes of proof;
- the processing is unlawful and the data subject opposes their erasure and requests the restriction of their use instead;
- the data subject requests to transmit the personal data into another automated processing system in accordance with Article 18(2).

Article 17(5) provides that personal data referred to in paragraph 4 may, with the exception of storage, only be processed for purposes of proof, or with the data subject's consent, or for the protection of the rights of another natural or legal person or for an objective of public interest.

Article 17(6) provides that where processing of personal data is restricted pursuant to paragraph 4, the data controller shall inform the data subject before lifting the restriction on processing.

Article 17(7) provides that the data controller shall implement mechanisms to ensure that the time limits established for the erasure of personal data and/or for a periodic review of the need for the storage of the data are observed.

Article 17(8) provides that where the erasure is carried out, the data controller shall not otherwise process such personal data.

Article 17(9) provides that the Commission shall be empowered to adopt delegated acts in accordance with Article 86 for the purpose of further specifying:

- the criteria and requirements for the application of Article 17(1) for specific sectors and in specific data processing situations;
- the conditions for deleting links, copies or replications of personal data from publicly available communication services as referred to in Article 17(2);
- the criteria and conditions for restricting the processing of personal data referred to in Article 17(4).

Synodinou[5] refers to the "right to oblivion" and notes in relation to her research that media rights are not immune to the right to be forgotten. Examples are given where cases have been successful in preventing particular media stories dragging up past events long after they had occurred, including court cases.[6] Indeed, many countries already obscure party names from decisions and judgments so as to render them anonymous, such as in Germany, Austria, Greece, Finland, Belgium, Hungary, the Netherlands, Poland and Portugal.[7] The right to be forgotten has also been recognised in France and Belgium.[8] A recent UK case also granted anonymity to the Plaintiff,[9] as did the Canadian Supreme Court in an online abuse case.[10] To be successful, however, it can be important to change party initials. For example, while the parties and director defendants in a Berlin Facebook data protection case were reduced initials, reducing one party's name to 'M.Z.' may not have been fully effective.[11]

DPA: Compensation for Data Subjects

9.21–9.23 Section 13 of the DPA refers to compensation for failure to comply with certain requirements.

Section 13(1) provides that an individual who suffers damage by reason of any contravention by a data controller of any of the requirements of the DPA is entitled to compensation from the data controller for that damage.

---

5   Synodinou, Tatiana-Eleni, 'The Media Coverage of Court Proceedings in Europe: Striking a Balance Between Freedom of Expression and Fair Process,' *Computer Law & Security Review* (2012)(28), pp. 208–219, at 217.
6   *Ibid*, p. 218.
7   *Ibid*, p. 218 and fn 106, p. 218.
8   Synodinou, Tatiana-Eleni, 'The Media Coverage of Court Proceedings in Europe: Striking a Balance Between Freedom of Expression and Fair Process,' *Computer Law & Security Review* (2012)(28), pp. 208–219, at 217.
9   See *XY v Facebook*, which also said that the website was a publisher. *XY v Facebook*, McCloskey J, [2012] NIQB 96, 30 November 2012.
10   AB v Bragg Communications, 27 September 2012 Available at http://www.scc-csc.gc.ca/case-dossier/cms-sgd/sum-som-eng.aspx?cas=34240, accessed 22 January 2013.
11   See *The Federal Association of Consumer Organisations and Consumer Groups, Federal Consumer Association, GB v Facebook Ireland Limited, MA, JB, DG, PT and the Chairman MZ*, [names redacted], [redacted] Reach, [redacted] Quay, Dublin, Ireland.

Article 13(2) provides that an individual who suffers distress by reason of any contravention by a data controller of any of the requirements of the Act is entitled to compensation from the data controller for that distress if:

- the individual also suffers damage by reason of the contravention; or
- the contravention relates to the processing of personal data for the special purposes.

Section 13(3) provides that in proceedings brought against a person by virtue of this section it is a defence to prove that he had taken such care as in all the circumstances was reasonably required to comply with the requirement concerned.

This is an area which will continue to grow in importance. The facts upon which the *Prudential* case could well have potentially resulted in actual financial loss and damage to a data subject. While the ICO implemented a fine of £50,000, the possibility of civil compensation would also have been a potential possibility.

In another case, a businessman successfully sued a company for Spamming them.[12] Another victim of Spam also sued and received £750 for a single Spam message received.[13]

In the US there have been cases by service providers, in addition to individual recipients of Spam. In 2006 Microsoft is also understood to have successfully sued in the UK for £45,000 in relation to a Spam company.[14]

The trend in Spam laws appears to be to permitting recipients, service providers and a regulator to be able to sue Spammers. Indeed, Regulation 30(1) PECR Amendment provides that 'A person who suffers damage by reason of any contravention … by any other person shall be entitled to bring proceedings for compensation from that person for that damage.'

Injunctions can be possible for Spam, as well as other areas involving data protection rights.

More recently the ICO has fined the promoters behind a Spam company a total of £440,000 (ICO v Niebel, McNeish and Tetrus Telecoms, 2012).

The area of compensation and civil litigation in vindication of data protection rights will continue to develop. While the scale of monetary claims, and awards, can differ as between the US and the UK, it is

---

12   Hart, H., "Cutting Down on Spam," *Solicitors Journal*, 10 March, 2005, 290.
13   Young, T., "Courts Put Price on Unsolicited Email," *Computing*, 15 March, 2007, 14
14   *Microsoft v Paul Martin McDonald* [2006] EWHC 3410 (Ch).

noted that Facebook has been willing to settle social networking privacy and advertising litigation for approx. $20 million. This related to the unlawful use of personal data in relation to the Beacon project. Indeed, it appears that this figure could have risen significantly.

It is certainly possible that data subjects, and indeed data subjects who have not suffered financial loss, can still suffer damage.

DPA: Requiring Data Disclosure

9.24 Appendix 2 s 57 refers to avoidance of certain contractual terms relating to organisation access to health records.

Appendix 2 s 57(1) provides that any term or condition of a contract is void in so far as it purports to require an individual:

- to supply any other person with a record to which this section applies, or with a copy of such a record or a part of such a record; or
- to produce to any other person such a record, copy or part.

Appendix 2 s 57(2) provides that this section applies to any record which:

- has been or is to be obtained by a data subject in the exercise of the right conferred by section 7; and
- consists of the information contained in any health record as defined by s 68(2).

Jurisdiction

9.25 DPR Recital 19 states that any processing of personal data in the context of the activities of an establishment of a data controller or a data processor in the EU should be carried out in accordance with the Regulation, regardless of whether the processing itself takes place within the EU or not. Establishment implies the effective and real exercise of activity through stable arrangements. The legal form of such arrangements, whether through a branch or a subsidiary with a legal personality, is not the determining factor in this respect.

Recital 20 of the DPR states that in order to ensure that individuals are not deprived of the protection to which they are entitled under the Regulation, the processing of personal data of data subjects residing in the EU by a data controller not established in the EU should be subject to the Regulation where the processing activities are related to the offering of goods or services to such data subjects, or to the monitoring of the behaviour of such data subjects.

Section 15 of the DPA refers to jurisdiction and procedure. Section 15(1) provides that the jurisdiction conferred by ss 7 to 14 is exercisable by the High Court or a county court or, in Scotland, by the Court of Session or the sheriff.

Section 15(2) of the DPA provides that for the purpose of determining any question whether an applicant under sub-s (9) of s 7 is entitled to the information which he seeks (including any question whether any relevant data are exempt from that section by virtue of Part IV) a court may require the information constituting any data processed by or on behalf of the data controller and any information as to the logic involved in any decision-taking as mentioned in s 7(1)(d) to be made available for its own inspection but shall not, pending the determination of that question in the applicant's favour, require the information sought by the applicant to be disclosed to them or his representatives whether by discovery (or, in Scotland, recovery) or otherwise.

Complaints to ICO

9.26 Recital 111 of the DPR states that every data subject should have the right to lodge a complaint with a Supervisory Authority in any Member State and have the right to a judicial remedy if they consider that their rights under the Regulation are infringed or where the Supervisory Authority does not react on a complaint or does not act where such action is necessary to protect the rights of the data subject.

Organisational Privacy Groups

9.27 Recital 112 of the DPR states that any body, organisation or association which aims to protects the rights and interests of data subjects in relation to the protection of their data and is constituted according to the law of a Member State should have the right to lodge a complaint with a Supervisory Authority or exercise the right to a judicial remedy on behalf of data subjects, or to lodge, independently of a data subject's complaint, an own complaint where it considers that a personal data breach has occurred.

While the DPR provides for privacy groups and entities litigating (and advocating), there appears to be noting explicitly preventing this occurring under the data protection regime as it presently stands.

Court Remedies

9.28   Recital 113 of the DPR states that each natural or legal person should have the right to a judicial remedy against decisions of a Supervisory Authority concerning them. Proceedings against a Supervisory Authority should be brought before the courts of the Member State, where the Supervisory Authority is established.

Different Supervisory Authorities

9.29   Recital 114 of the DPR states that the in order to strengthen the judicial protection of the data subject in situations where the competent Supervisory Authority is established in another Member State than the one where the data subject is residing, the data subject may request any body, organisation or association aiming to protect the rights and interests of data subjects in relation to the protection of their data to bring on the data subject's behalf proceedings against that Supervisory Authority to the competent court in the other Member State.

Recital 115 states that in situations where the competent Supervisory Authority established in another Member State does not act or has taken insufficient measures in relation to a complaint, the data subject may request the Supervisory Authority in the Member State of his or her habitual residence to bring proceedings against that Supervisory Authority to the competent court in the other Member State. The requested Supervisory Authority may decide, subject to judicial review, whether it is appropriate to follow the request or not.

Plaintiff Choice of Jurisdictions and Courts

9.30   Recital 116 of the DPR states that for proceedings against a data controller or data processor, the plaintiff should have the choice to bring the action before the courts of the Member States where the data controller or data processor has an establishment or where the data subject resides, unless the data controller is a public authority acting in the exercise of its public powers.

Recital 117 states that where there are indications that parallel proceedings are pending before the courts in different Member States, the courts should be obliged to contact each other. The courts should have the possibility to suspend a case where a parallel case is pending in another Member State. Member States should ensure that court actions, in order to be effective, should allow the rapid adoption of measures to remedy or prevent an infringement of the Regulation.

Compensation

9.31 Recital 118 of the DPR states that any damage which a person may suffer as a result of unlawful processing should be compensated by the data controller or data processor, who may be exempted from liability if they prove that they are not responsible for the damage, in particular where he establishes fault on the part of the data subject or in case of force majeure.

Penalties

9.32 Recital 119 of the DPR states that penalties should be imposed to any person, whether governed by private or public law, who fails to comply with the Regulation. Member States should ensure that the penalties should be effective, proportionate and dissuasive and should take all measures to implement the penalties.

Sanctions

9.33 Recital 120 of the DPR states that the in order to strengthen and harmonise administrative sanctions against infringements of the Regulation, each Supervisory Authority should have the power to sanction administrative offences. The Regulation should indicate these offences and the upper limit for the related administrative fines, which should be fixed in each individual case proportionate to the specific situation, with due regard in particular to the nature, gravity and duration of the breach. The consistency mechanism may also be used to cover divergences in the application of administrative sanctions.

DPR: Right to Proportionality

9.34 Article 18 of the DPR refers to the right to data portability. Article 18(1) provides that the data subject shall have the right, where personal data are processed by electronic means and in a structured and commonly used format, to obtain from the controller a copy of data undergoing processing in an electronic and structured format which is commonly used and allows for further use by the data subject.

Article 18(2) provides that where the data subject has provided the personal data and the processing is based on consent or on a contract, the data subject shall have the right to transmit those personal data and any other information provided by the data subject and retained by an automated processing system, into another one, in an electronic format which is commonly used, without hindrance from the data controller from whom the personal data are withdrawn.

Article 18(3) provides that the Commission may specify the electronic format referred to in paragraph 1 and the technical standards, modalities and procedures for the transmission of personal data pursuant to paragraph 2. Those implementing acts shall be adopted in accordance with the examination procedure referred to in Article 87(2).

DPR: Right to Object and Profiling

9.35 Section 4 of the DPR refers to the right to object to processing and to profiling.

Article 19 of the DPR refers to the right to object. Article 19(1) provides that the data subject shall have the right to object, on grounds relating to their particular situation, at any time to the processing of personal data which is based on points (d), (e) and (f) of Article 6(1), unless the data controller demonstrates compelling legitimate grounds for the processing which override the interests or fundamental rights and freedoms of the data subject.

Article 19(2) provides that where personal data are processed for direct marketing purposes, the data subject shall have the right to object free of charge to the processing of their personal data for such marketing. This right shall be explicitly offered to the data subject in an intelligible manner and shall be clearly distinguishable from other information.

Article 19(3) provides that where an objection is upheld pursuant to Article 19(1) and (2), the data controller shall no longer use or otherwise process the personal data concerned.

DPR: Right Regarding Profiling

9.36 Article 20 of the DPR refers to measures based on profiling. Article 20(1) provides that every natural person shall have the right not to be subject to a measure which produces legal effects concerning this natural person or significantly affects this natural person, and which is based solely on automated processing intended to evaluate certain personal aspects relating to this natural person or to analyse or predict in particular the natural person's performance at work, economic situation, location, health, personal preferences, reliability or behaviour.

Article 20(2) provides that subject to the other provisions of the Regulation, a person may be subjected to a measure of the kind referred to in Article 20(1) only if the processing:

- is carried out in the course of the entering into, or performance of, a contract, where the request for the entering into or the performance of the contract, lodged by the data subject, has been satisfied or where suitable measures to safeguard the data subject's legitimate interests have been adduced, such as the right to obtain human intervention; or
- is expressly authorised by a EU or Member State law which also lays down suitable measures to safeguard the data subject's legitimate interests; or
- is based on the data subject's consent, subject to the conditions laid down in Article 7 and to suitable safeguards.

Article 20(3) provides that automated processing of personal data intended to evaluate certain personal aspects relating to a natural person shall not be based solely on the special categories of personal data referred to in Article 9.

Article 20(4) provides that in the cases referred to in Article 20(2), the information to be provided by the data controller under Article 14 shall include information as to the existence of processing for a measure of the kind referred to in Article 20(1) and the envisaged effects of such processing on the data subject.

Article 20(5) refers to the Commission shall be empowered to adopt delegated acts in accordance with Article 86 for the purpose of further specifying the criteria and conditions for suitable measures to safeguard the data subject's legitimate interests referred to in Article 20(2).

Conclusion

9.37 The rights are very important for organisations to recognise and protect. These need to be incorporated from day one, as it may not be possible to retrospectively become a complaint if the initial collection and processing was illegitimate. This is increasingly significant as data protection authorities become more proactive and as the levels of fines and penalties increase.

Cases to Consider

ICO complaints, cases and case studies which may be useful for organisations to consider

- *Prudential*;
- *Microsoft v Paul Martin McDonald*;
- *McCall v Facebook*;
- *ICO v Niebel, ICO v McNeish*;

- *Rugby Football Union v Viagogo Limited*;
- *Durham County Council v Dunn*;
- *British Gas*;
- *Brian Reed Beetson Robertson*;
- *Campbell v MGM*;
- *CCN Systems v Data Protection Registrar*;
- *Lindqvist v Kammaraklagaren*;
- *Commission v Bavarian Lager*;
- *Common Services Agency v Scottish Information Commissioner*;
- *Douglas v Hello!*;
- *Halford v UK*;
- *Von Hannover*;
- *Mosley*;
- *Motion Picture Association v BT*;
- *WP29 and Data Protection Authorities/Google* (re Google policy change and breaches);
- *Barclays/Lara Davies* prosecution;
- *Sony*.

Chapter 10

Notification and Registration

Introduction

10.01 Organisations are prohibited from carrying on data collection and processing without notification and registration. There are certain details and categories of information required to be registered. There are, however, certain exemptions available. The ICO maintain the register. If the organisation makes any changes to the registered details, these must then be updated in the register. Registrations also need to be reviewed and renewed.

Organisation Registration

10.02 Organisations are obliged to register with the ICO. Section 17 of the DPA prohibits data processing without registration. It provides that:

(1) Subject to the following provisions of this section, personal data must not be processed unless an entry in respect of the data controller is included in the register maintained by the ICO under s 19 (or is treated by notification regulations made by virtue of s 19(3) as being so included);

(2) Except where the processing is assessable processing for the purposes of s 22, sub-s (1) above does not apply in relation to personal data consisting of information which falls neither within paragraph (a) of the definition of 'data' in s 1(1) of the DPA nor within paragraph (b) of that definition;

(3) If it appears to the Secretary of State that processing of a particular description is unlikely to prejudice the rights and freedoms of data subjects, notification regulations may provide that, in such cases as

may be prescribed, sub-s (1) is not to apply in relation to processing of that description;

(4) Sub-section (1) does not apply in relation to any processing whose sole purpose is the maintenance of a public register.

Section 16 of the DPA also refers to registration and contains details of the 'registrable particulars' required in relation to a data controller when registering. The details which must be registered are:

- organisation name and address;
- if the organisation has nominated a representative for the purposes of the Act, the name and address of the representative, etc;
- a description of the personal data being or to be processed by or on behalf of the data controller and of the category or categories of data subject to which they relate;
- a description of the purpose or purposes for which the data are being or are to be processed;
- a description of any recipient or recipients to whom the data controller intends or may wish to disclose the data;
- the names, or a description of, any countries or territories outside the EEA to which the data controller directly or indirectly transfers, or intends or may wish directly or indirectly to transfer, the data;
- where the data controller is a public authority, a statement of that fact;
- in any case where:
  - personal data are being, or are intended to be, processed in circumstances in which the prohibition in sub-s (1) of s 17 is excluded by sub-s (2) or (3) of that section; and
  - the notification does not extend to those data, a statement of that fact, and
- such information about the data controller as may be prescribed under s 18(5A) (s 16(1)).

Section 16(2) refers to further definition in this Part of the DPA, namely:

'fees regulations'	means regulations made by theSecretary of Stateunder s 18(5) or 19(4) or (7);
'notification regulations'	means regulations made by the Secretary of Stateunder the other provisions of this Part;
'prescribed'	except where used in relation to fees regulations, means prescribed by notification regulations.

Section 16(3) DPA states that for the purposes of this Part of the Act, so far as it relates to the addresses of data controllers:

- the address of a registered company is that of its registered office; and
- the address of a person (other than a registered company) carrying on a business is that of its principal place of business in the UK.

Section 18 refers to notification by data controllers. Any data controller who wishes to be included in the register maintained under s 19 shall give a notification to the Commissioner under this section. A notification under this section must specify in accordance with notification regulations:

- the registrable particulars; and
- a general description of measures to be taken for the purpose of complying with the seventh Data Protection Principle (ie the required security measures).

Section 18(3) provides that notification regulations made by virtue of sub-s (2) may provide for the determination by the ICO, in accordance with any requirements of the regulations, of the form in which the registrable particulars and the description mentioned in sub-s (2)(b) are to be specified, including in particular the detail required for the purposes of s 16(1)(c), (d), (e) and (f) and sub-s (2)(b).

Under s 18(4) notification regulations may make provision as to the giving of notification:

- by partnerships; or
- in other cases where two or more persons are the data controllers in respect of any personal data.

Section 18(5) provides that the notification must be accompanied by such fee as may be prescribed by fees regulations. Section 26 of the DPA provides that the Secretary of State may make various fee regulations. Section 18(5A) provides that notification regulations may prescribe the information about the data controller which is required for the purpose of verifying the fee payable under sub-s (5). Section 18(6) provides that notification regulations may provide for any fee paid under sub-s (5) or s 19(4) to be refunded in prescribed circumstances.

Register of Notifications

10.03 The ICO is obliged, under s 19(1), to:

- maintain a register of persons who have given notification under s 18; and
- make an entry in the register in pursuance of each notification received by them under that section from a person in respect of whom no entry as data controller was for the time being included in the register.

Each entry in the register shall, under s 19(2), consist of:

- the registrable particulars notified under s 18 or, as the case requires, those particulars as amended in pursuance of s 20(4); and
- such other information as the ICO may be authorised or required by notification regulations to include in the register.

Section 19(3) provides that notification regulations may make provision as to the time as from which any entry in respect of a data controller is to be treated for the purposes of s 17 as having been made in the register.

Section 19(4) provides that no entry shall be retained in the register for more than the relevant time except on payment of such fee as may be prescribed by fees regulations.

Section 19(5) provides that in sub-s (4) 'the relevant time' means twelve months or such other period as may be prescribed by notification regulations; and different periods may be prescribed in relation to different cases.

Under s 19(6), the ICO:

- shall provide facilities for making the information contained in the entries in the register available for inspection (in visible and legible form) by members of the public at all reasonable hours and free of charge; and
- may provide such other facilities for making the information contained in those entries available to the public free of charge as he considers appropriate.

The ICO shall, in accordance with s 19(7), on payment of such fee, if any, as may be prescribed by fees regulations, supply any member of the public with a duly certified copy in writing of the particulars contained in any entry made in the register. Nothing in sub-s (6) or (7) applies to information which is included in an entry in the register only by reason of it falling within s 16(1)(h)(s 19(8)).

Duty to Notify Changes

10.04 There is also an obligation on data controllers to notify changes. Section 20 of the DPA provides for the duty to notify changes. Section 20(1) provides that for the purpose specified in sub-s (2), notification regulations shall include provision imposing on every person in respect of whom an entry as a data controller is for the time being included in the register maintained under s 19 a duty to notify to the ICO, in such circumstances and at such time or times and in such form as may be prescribed, such matters relating to the registrable particulars and measures taken as mentioned in s 18(2)(b) as may be prescribed.

There is an obligation to notify of any changes. Section 20(1) provides that for the purpose specified in sub-s (2), notification regulations shall include provision imposing on every person in respect of whom an entry as a data controller is for the time being included in the register maintained under s 19 a duty to notify to the ICO, in such circumstances and at such time or times and in such form as may be prescribed, such matters relating to the registrable particulars and measures taken as mentioned in s 18(2)(b) as may be prescribed.

Section 20(2) indicates that the purpose referred to in sub-s (1) is that of ensuring, so far as practicable, that at any time:

- the entries in the register maintained under s 19 contain current names and addresses and describe the current practice or intentions of the data controller with respect to the processing of personal data; and
- the ICO is provided with a general description of measures currently being taken as mentioned in s 18(2)(b).

Section 20(3) provides that sub-s (3) of section 18 has effect in relation to notification regulations made by virtue of sub-s (1) as it has effect in relation to notification regulations made by virtue of sub-s (2) of that section. Section 20(4) provides that on receiving any notification under notification regulations made by virtue of subsection (1), the ICO shall make such amendments of the relevant entry in the register maintained under s 19 as are necessary to take account of the change notification.

How Does an Organisation Register?

10.05 Where the organisation is required to register and notify, it must notify the ICO with details of:

- The name and identity of whom is the data controller;

- The purpose or purposes for which the personal data are being processed;
- To whom the personal data may be disclosed;
- Where the organisation is engaged with TBDFs or transfers of personal data abroad, it must set out the details in the registration;
- The organisational security measures used.

More specifically, the notification and registration process requires even more specific detailed information on certain specific criteria. One example is the description of the individual data subjects to whom the personal data relates and whose personal data is be used by the organisation. The ICO *Notification Handbook*[1] refers, for example to sections for:

- the name and address of the data controller;
- the company registration number (optional);
- contact details;
- general description of the processing of personal information being carried out by the data controller, including,
- the *purposes* for which personal information is being or is to be processed, eg debt collection or research;
- a description of the *data subjects* about whom data is or is to be held, eg employees or patients;
- a description of the *data classes*, eg employment details and financial details;
- a list of the *recipients* of data, eg Central Government and Financial Organisations; and
- information about whether data is transferred outside the EEA;
- security statement;
- trading names;
- statement of exempt processing;
- voluntary notification;
- representative name and address;
- fees; and
- the declaration.[2]

It provides that in relation to the general description of the processing of personal information, each notification must include a general description of the processing of personal information being carried

---

1   *ICO Notification Handbook*, ICO, available at http://www.ico.gov.uk/upload/documents/notifications_handbook_html/index.html, accessed on 18 January 2013.
2   *Ibid.*

out.[3] On the register this description is structured by reference to the purposes for which data is being processed.[4]

The ICO provides the following 'purpose' example registration details,

Provision of Financial Services and Advice

Data subjects are:	• customers and clients; • complainants, correspondents and enquirers; and • advisers, consultants and other professional experts.
Data classes are:	• personal details; • family, lifestyle and social circumstances; • employment details; • financial details; and • goods or services provided.
Recipients are:	• data subjects themselves; • relatives, guardians or other persons associated with the data subject; • business associates and other professional advisers; • financial organisations and advisers; and • ombudsmen and regulatory authorities.
Transfers:	• none outside the EEA.

It also refers to example 'business' purposes, such as,

Staff administration

Appointments or removals, pay, discipline, superannuation, work management or other personnel matters in relation to the staff of the data controller.

Advertising, marketing and public relations

Advertising or marketing the data controller's own business, activity, goods or services, and promoting public relations in connection with that business or activity, or those goods or services.

---

3   *ICO Notification Handbook*, ICO, available at http://www.ico.gov.uk/upload/documents/notifications_handbook_html/index.html, accessed on 18 January 2013, section 3.1.5.

4   *Ibid.*

Accounts and records

Keeping accounts relating to any business or other activity carried out by the data controller or deciding whether to accept any person as a customer or supplier or keeping records of purchases, sales or other transactions for the purpose of ensuring that the requisite payments and deliveries are made or services provided by them or to them in respect of those transactions, or for the purpose of making financial or management forecasts to assist them in the conduct of any such business or activity.[5]

It also refers to examples of other purposes,

Accounting and auditing

The provision of accounting and related services; the provision of an audit where such an audit is required by statute.

Administration of justice

Internal administration and management of courts of law or tribunals and discharge of court business.

Administration of membership records

The administration of membership records.

Advertising, marketing and public relations for others

Public relations work, advertising and marketing, including host mailings for other organisations and list broking.

Assessment and collection of taxes and other revenue

Assessment and collection of taxes, duties, levies and other revenue. You will be asked to indicate the type of tax or other revenue concerned.

Benefits, grants and loans administration

The administration of welfare and other benefits. You will be asked to indicate the type(s) of benefit you are administering.

Canvassing political support amongst the electorate

The seeking and maintenance of support amongst the electorate by the data controller.

Constituency casework

The carrying out of casework on behalf of individual constituents by elected representatives.

Consultancy and advisory services

---

5   *ICO Notification Handbook*, ICO, available at http://www.ico.gov.uk/upload/ documents/notifications_handbook_html/index.html, accessed on 18 January 2013.

Giving advice or rendering professional services. The provision of services of an advisory, consultancy or intermediary nature. You will be asked to indicate the nature of the services which you provide.

Credit referencing

The provision of information relating to the financial status of individuals or organisations on behalf of other organisations. This purpose is for use by credit reference agencies, not for organisations who merely contact or use credit reference agencies.

Crime prevention and prosecution of offenders

Crime prevention and detection and the apprehension and prosecution of offenders. This includes the use of most CCTV systems which are used for this purpose.

Debt administration and factoring

The tracing of consumer and commercial debtors and the collection on behalf of creditors. The purchasing of consumer or trade debts, including rentals and instalment credit payments, from business.

Education

The provision of education or training as a primary function or as a business activity.

Fundraising

Fundraising in support of the objectives of the data controller.

Health administration and services

The provision and administration of patient care.

Information and databank administration

Maintenance of information or databanks as a reference tool or general resource. This includes catalogues, lists, directories and bibliographic databases.

Insurance administration

The administration of life, health, pensions, property, motor and other insurance business. This applies only to insurance companies doing risk assessments, payment of claims and underwriting. Insurance consultants and intermediaries should use the provision of financial services and advice purpose.

Journalism and media

Processing by the data controller of any journalistic, literary or artistic material made or intended to be made available to the public or any section of the public.

Legal services

The provision of legal services, including advising and acting on behalf of clients.

Licensing and registration

The administration of licensing or maintenance of official registers.

Pastoral care

The administration of pastoral care by a vicar or other minister of religion.

Pensions administration

The administration of funded pensions or superannuation schemes. Data controllers using this purpose will usually be the trustees of pension funds.

Policing

The prevention and detection of crime; apprehension and prosecution of offenders; protection of life and property; maintenance of law and order; also rendering assistance to the public in accordance with force policies and procedures.

Private investigation

The provision on a commercial basis of investigatory services according to instruction given by clients.

Processing for not-for-profit organisations

Establishing or maintaining membership of or support for a body or association which is not established or conducted for profit, or providing or administering activities for individuals who are either members of the body or association or have regular contact with it.

An organisation that is a body or association not established or conducted for profit may be exempt from notification provided that the processing meets specific criteria. If you are a not-for-profit organisation, please call the notification helpline for guidance on whether the exemptions cover your organisation's processing.

Property management

The management and administration of land, property and residential property and the estate management of other organisations.

Provision of financial services and advice

The provision of services as an intermediary in respect of any financial transactions including mortgage and insurance broking.

Realising the objectives of a charitable organisation or voluntary body

The provision of goods and services in order to realise the objectives of the charity or voluntary body.

Research

Research in any field, including market, health, lifestyle, scientific or technical research. You will be asked to indicate the nature of the research undertaken.

Trading/sharing in personal information

The sale, hire, exchange or disclosure of personal information to third parties in return for goods/services/benefit.[6]

Examples of the general types or classes of personal data, and which must be designated in processes, are also provided, as follows,

C200: Personal details

Included in this category is any information that identifies the data subject and their personal characteristics. Examples are name, address, contact details, age, sex, date of birth, physical description, and any identifier issued by a public body, eg National Insurance number.

C201: Family, lifestyle and social circumstances

Included in this category is any information relating to the family of the data subject and the data subject's lifestyle and social circumstances. Examples are details about current marriage and partnerships and marital history, details of family and other household members, habits, housing, travel details, leisure activities and membership of charitable or voluntary organisations.

C202: Education and training details

Included in this category is any information which relates to the education and any professional training of the data subject. Examples are academic records, qualifications, skills, training records, professional expertise, and student and pupil records.

C203: Employment details

Included in this category is any information relating to the employment of the data subject. Examples are employment and career history, recruitment and termination details, attendance records, health and safety records, performance appraisals, training records and security records.

6   *ICO Notification Handbook*, ICO, available at http://www.ico.gov.uk/upload/documents/notifications_handbook_html/index.html, accessed on 18 January 2013, section 3.1.8.

C204: Financial details

Included in this category is any information relating to the financial affairs of the data subject. Examples are income, salary, assets and investments, payments, creditworthiness, loans, benefits, grants, insurance details and pension information.

C205: Goods or services provided

Included in this category is any information relating to goods and services that have been provided. Examples are details of the goods or services supplied, licences issued, agreements and contracts.[7]

Sensitive personal data classes are also referenced, as follows,

C206: Racial or ethnic origin;

C207: Political opinions;

C208: Religious or other beliefs of a similar nature;

C209: Trade union membership;

C210: Physical or mental health or condition;

C211: Sexual life;

C212: Offences (including alleged offences);

C213: Criminal proceedings, outcomes and sentences.[8]

The recipient details must also be included, where the personal data is furnished to third parties. This is particularly so where it is proposed to make transfers outside the EEA.

The details and types of individual security measures must be described.

First Notification Regulations

10.06 Section 25 refers to the functions of ICO in relation to making of notification regulations.

Section 25(1) provides that as soon as practicable after the passing of the DPA, the ICO shall submit to the Secretary of State proposals as to the provisions to be included in the first notification regulations.

---

7 *ICO Notification Handbook*, ICO, available at http://www.ico.gov.uk/upload/documents/notifications_handbook_html/index.html, accessed on 18 January 2013.
8 *Ibid.*

Section 25(2) provides that the ICO shall keep under review the working of notification regulations and may from time to time submit to the Secretary of State proposals as to amendments to be made to the regulations.

Section 25(3) provides that the Secretary of State may from time to time require the ICO to consider any matter relating to notification regulations and to submit to them proposals as to amendments to be made to the regulations in connection with that matter.

Section 25(4) provides that before making any notification regulations, the Secretary of State shall: (a) consider any proposals made to them by the ICO under sub-s (2) or (3), and (b) consult the Commissioner.

Conclusion

10.07   The important things for organisations are to be aware of what classes of personal data are being collected, for what purposes and to notify these as part of the registration process. Any time that changes occur, including adding data collections or anticipating additional new purposed, updated registration details must be furnished (and new consents if required).

Chapter 11

Time Limits for Compliance

Introduction

11.01 There are various time limits referred to in the data protection regime for the accomplishment of particular tasks. Depending on the task at hand, non-compliance with a time limit could amount to a breach and or offence.

Time Limits

11.02 The DPA time limits include the following:

- An access request must be complied with within 40 calendar days;
- The data controller must reply within 21 days of receiving it to explain whether it is going to comply with the s 10 notice;
- Under s 11 DPA an individual can request the data controller to cease using personal information for direct marketing, including junk mail, sales calls, or email and text messages. The ICO states that in normal circumstances electronic communications should stop within 28 days of receiving the notice, and postal communications should stop within two months.
- Credit files should be supplied in seven calendar days.

Official Information (FOI and Environmental Information Regulations)

11.03 Organisations must reply to a request for official information within 20 working days.

Conclusion

When an organisation fails to comply within the required timeframe, this in itself is another breach. It may be taken into consideration by the ICO and or a court.

Chapter 12

Enforcement & Penalties for Non-Compliance

Introduction

12.01 There are a series of offences set out in the DPA. These are designed to ensure compliance with the data protection regime, from registration to fair use of personal data. Organisations must fully comply with their obligations. In addition to questions arising in relation to their continued use of personal data if it has not been collected fairly, investigations, prosecutions and financial penalties can also arise.

Organisations can now be fined up to £500,000 by the ICO for unwanted marketing phone calls and emails in accordance with the updated and amended PECR.

Offences by organisation can include:

- Failure of a data controller to notify (s 1(1));
- Failure to notify of changes to the notified entry details (s 21(2));
- Processing before the expiration of assessable processing time limits or receipt of assessable processing notice within such time (s 22(6)).

Breaches, Offences and Penalties

12.02 The DPA and the data protection regime set out the rules with which data controllers must obey. Breaches of these rules sometimes involve offences which are punishable by fines. The offences set out in the data protection regime include the following:

- Offences by data controllers who are required to register (s 17 and 21(1));
- Offences by any person who fails to comply with the duty imposed by notification regulations (s 21(2));

- Offences by any data controllers (not just those who are required to register);
- Offences by employees or agents of data controllers;
- Offences by data processors who are required to register;
- Offences by any data processors (not just those who are required to register);
- Offences by directors etc of organisations (s 61);
- Penalties for offences under the DPA;
- Offences by direct marketers;
- Penalties for offences under PECR and PECR Amendments;
- Offences for breach of assessment/assessment procedure (s 22(6));
- Offences for not making information available (s 24(4));
- Offences in relation to unlawfully obtaining, disclosing or procuring the disclosure or procuring the disclosure to another person of personal data (s 55);
- Offences of selling personal data if unlawfully obtained, disclosed or procured the disclosure or procured the disclosure to another person of personal data (s 55(4) and (5)).

See ICO penalties, fines and prosecutions details below.

Criminal Offences

12.03 The organisation can commit criminal offences in relation to its data processing activities, namely:

- Unlawful obtaining or disclosure of personal data;
- Selling and offering to sell personal data;
- Enforcing individual data subject access;
- Disclosure of information;
- Obstructing or failing to assist in the execution of a warrant;
- Processing without a register entry;
- Failing to notify changes regarding registration;
- Carrying on assessable processing;
- Failing to make certain particulars available;
- Failing to comply with a notice;
- Making a false statement in response to a notice.

Other Consequences of Breach

12.04 Some of the other consequences of a breach of the data protection regime include:

- Offences can be committed by the organisation and its officers;

- Processing focused offences;
- Access related offences;
- Offences for non-compliance with ICO and ICO related powers (eg enforcement notices; assessments; information notices; entry and inspection);
- Being sued by individual data subjects;
- Potentially being sued by rights based organisations and or class action type cases (eg Google re Apple);
- Publicity of an unwanted nature.

DPA: Prohibition on Processing Without Registration

12.05   Section 17 refers to the prohibition on processing without registration. Section 17(1) states that subject to the following provisions of this section, personal data must not be processed unless an entry in respect of the data controller is included in the register maintained by the Commissioner under s 19 (or is treated by notification regulations made by virtue of s 19(3) as being so included). Section 17(2) states that except where the processing is assessable processing for the purposes of s 22, sub-s (1) does not apply in relation to personal data consisting of information which falls neither within paragraph (a) of the definition of 'data' in s 1(1) nor within paragraph (b) of that definition. Section 17(3) states that if it appears to the Secretary of State that processing of a particular description is unlikely to prejudice the rights and freedoms of data subjects, notification regulations may provide that, in such cases as may be prescribed, sub-s (1) is not to apply in relation to processing of that description. Section 17(4) states that sub-s (1) does not apply in relation to any processing whose sole purpose is the maintenance of a public register.

DPA: Section 21 Offence of Prohibition on Processing Without Registration

12.06   Section 21 of the DPA refers to offences.

Section 21(1) provides that if s 17(1) (prohibition on processing without registration) is contravened, the data controller is guilty of an offence.

Section 21(2) provides that any person who fails to comply with the duty imposed by notification regulations made by virtue of s 20(1) is guilty of an offence.

Section 21(3) provides that it shall be a defence for a person charged with an offence under sub-s (2) to show that he exercised all due diligence to comply with the duty.

Accordingly, data controllers who keep personal data, without meeting their requirement to register are liable to be prosecuted.

However, it should be noted that section does not say 'all reasonable due diligence.' Therefore, it is arguable that the obligation on organisations is much higher. The legislators decided not to incorporate a reasonableness standard.

DPA: Offences for Breach of Assessment/Assessment Procedure

12.07   Section 22 refers to preliminary assessment by the Commissioner. Section 22(1) provides that in this section 'assessable processing' means processing which is of a description specified in an order made by the Secretary of State as appearing to them to be particularly likely:

- to cause substantial damage or substantial distress to data subjects, or
- otherwise significantly to prejudice the rights and freedoms of data subjects.

The ICO will give a notice to the data controller stating the extent to which the ICO is of the opinion that the processing is likely or unlikely to comply with the provisions of the Act.

Section 22(5) provides that no assessable processing in respect of which a notification has been given to the Commissioner shall be carried on unless either:

- the period of 28 days beginning with the day on which the notification is received by the Commissioner (or, in a case falling within sub-s (4), that period as extended under that sub-section) has elapsed, or
- before the end of that period (or that period as so extended) the data controller has received a notice from the Commissioner under sub-s (3) in respect of the processing.

Section 22(6) provides that where sub-s (5) is contravened, the data controller is guilty of an offence.

DPA: Offences Regarding Not Making Information Available

12.08   Section 23 refers to a power to make provision for appointment of data protection supervisors.

Section 24 refers to a duty of certain data controllers to make certain information available. Section 24(1) provides that subject to sub-s (3), where personal data are processed in a case where:

- by virtue of subsection (2) or (3) of s 17, sub-s (1) of that section does not apply to the processing, and
- the data controller has not notified the relevant particulars in respect of that processing under s 18,

the data controller must, within twenty-one days of receiving a written request from any person, make the relevant particulars available to that person in writing free of charge. Section 24(4) provides that any data controller who fails to comply with the duty imposed by sub-s (1) is guilty of an offence.

DPA: Failure to Comply With Notices

12.09   Section 40 of the DPA indicated that the ICO can issue enforcement notices to organisations when it feels the organisation is contravening the Data Protection Principles, specifying and requiring compliance. The ICO can also issue information notices to organisations requesting information or compliance under s 43. Section 44 also refers to special information notices.

Section 47(1) provides that there are offences for failure to comply with enforcement notices, information notices, and or special information notices.

DPA: Knowingly or Recklessly Making a False Statement

12.10   Section 47(2) refers to an offence of knowingly or recklessly making a false statement in relation to an information notice or special information notice.

DPA: Obstruction

12.11   Schedule 9 refers to powers of entry and inspection and warrants. There are offences of intentional obstruction of, or failure to give reasonable assistance in the execution of a warrant (Sch 9, s 12).

DPA: Offence Regarding Unlawful Obtaining or Procuring Personal Data

12.11A Section 55 provides that it is an offence for a person, knowingly or recklessly, without the consent of the data controller, to:

- Obtain or disclose personal data or the information contained in personal data;
- Procure the disclosure to another person of the information contained in personal data.

This refers to 'a person' and therefore includes directors, employees, agents and any other person.

There was a recent case resulting in successful convictions regarding blagging and unlawful access to the personal data relating to tenants. The case involved Philip Campbell Smith, Adam Spears, Graham Freeman and Daniel Summers. Amongst other things, the ICO again called for custodial sentences for breach of the data protection regime. This was also a theme in the Leveson recommendations.

The ICO states,

'The Department for Work and Pensions hold important information about each and every one of us. We are very pleased that a DWP staff member was alert to this attempt to blag information and that the call was halted before it was too late. The motive behind Mr Braun's action was financial. He knew that such an underhand method of obtaining the tenant's personal information was illegal but carried on regardless. This case shows that unscrupulous individuals will continue to try and blag peoples' details until a more appropriate range of deterrent punishments is available to the courts. There must be no further delay in introducing tougher powers to enforce the Data Protection Act beyond the current "fine only" regime.'[1]

The ICO also said,

'The scourge of data theft continues to threaten the privacy rights of the UK population. Whilst we welcome today's sentencing of the private investigator, Graham Freeman, and his three accomplices, the outcome of the case underlines the need for a comprehensive approach to deterring information theft. If SOCA had been restricted to pursuing this case solely using their powers under the Data Protection Act then these individuals would have been faced with a small fine and would have been able to continue their

---

1   'Private Detectives Jailed for Blaggig: ICO Statement,' ICO, 27 February, 2012, available at http://www.ico.gov.uk/news/latest_news/2012/statement-private-detectives-jailed-for-blagging-27022012.aspx, accessed on 18 January 2013.

activities the very next day. This is not good enough. Unscrupulous individuals will continue to try and obtain peoples' information through deception until there are strong punishments to fit the crime. We must not delay in getting a custodial sentence in place for section 55 offences under the Data Protection Act.'[2]

DPA: Record Offences

12.12   Section 56 provides that it is an offence for a person to require another person or a third party to:

- Supply them or her with a relevant record; or
- Produce a relevant record to them,

in connection with:

- The recruitment of that other person as an employee;
- The continued employment of that other person;
- Any contract for the provision of services to them by that other person; or
- Where a person is concerned with providing (for payment or not) goods, facilities or services to the public or a sector of the public, as a condition of providing or offering to provide any goods, facilities or services to that other person.

Again, this refers to any person.

There are exceptions to liability, such that:

- The imposition of the requirement was required or authorised by the law; or
- In particular circumstances the imposition of the requirements was justified as being in the public interest.

DPA: Offences by Direct Marketers under PECR/PECR Amendments

12.13   Offences arise in relation to activities referred to under PECR. These include:

- sending unsolicited marketing messages to individuals by fax, SMS, email or automated dialing machine;

---

2   'Private Detectives Jailed for Blaggig: ICO Statement,' ICO, 27 February, 2012, available at http://www.ico.gov.uk/news/latest_news/2012/statement-private-detectives-jailed-for-blagging-27022012.aspx, accessed on 18 January 2013.

- sending unsolicited marketing by fax, SMS, email or automated dialing machine to a business if it has objected to the receipt of such messages;
- marketing by telephone where the subscriber has objected to the receipt of such calls;
- failing to identify the caller or sender or failing to provide a physical address or a return e-mail address;
- failing to give customers the possibility of objecting to future email and SMS marketing messages with each message sent;
- concealing the identity of the sender on whose behalf the marketing communication was made.

Fines can be significant. Organisations can be fined up to £500,000 by the ICO for unwanted marketing phone calls and emails in accordance with the updated amended PECR. It is also envisaged that fines will increase significantly in potential under the proposed DPR.

Recently the ICO imposed combined fines of £440,000 in relation to the two promoters and directors of a company engaged in Spamming (*ICO v Niebel* and *ICO v McNeish*, 2012).

ICO Monetary Penalties

12.14 The ICO is also empowered under the Criminal Justice and Immigration Act 2008 to impose penalties of a monetary variety. Section 77 of the CJIA 2008 provides power to alter penalties for unlawfully obtaining etc personal data, as follows:

(1) The Secretary of State may by order provide for a person who is guilty of an offence under s 55 of the DPA (unlawful obtaining etc of personal data) to be liable:

    (a) on summary conviction, to imprisonment for a term not exceeding the specified period or to a fine not exceeding the statutory maximum or to both;

    (b) on conviction on indictment, to imprisonment for a term not exceeding the specified period or to a fine or to both;

(2) In sub-s (1)(a) and (b) 'specified period' means a period provided for by the order but the period must not exceed:

    (a) in the case of summary conviction, 12 months (or, in Northern Ireland, 6 months); and

    (b) in the case of conviction on indictment, two years;

(3) The Secretary of State must ensure that any specified period for England and Wales which, in the case of summary conviction, exceeds 6 months is to be read as a reference to 6 months so far as

it relates to an offence committed before the commencement of s 282(1) of the Criminal Justice Act 2003 (c. 44) (increase in sentencing powers of magistrates' courts from 6 to 12 months for certain offences triable either way);

(4) Before making an order under this section, the Secretary of State must consult:

    (a)   the Information Commissioner;

    (b)   such media organisations as the Secretary of State considers appropriate; and

    (c)   such other persons as the Secretary of State considers appropriate;

(5) An order under this section may, in particular, amend the DPA.

See examples of some of the recent ICO fines and monetary penalties referred to below.

Civil Sanctions under the DPA

12.15   This is an area which will continue to expand in future. Individual data subjects can also sue for compensation under the DPA. Where a person suffers damage as a result of a failure by a data controller or data processor to meet their data protection obligations, then the data controller or data processor may be subject to civil sanctions by the person affected. Damage suffered by a data subject will include damage to reputation, financial loss and mental distress.

   Section 13 of the DPA provides as follows:

- An individual who suffers damage by reason of any contravention by a data controller of any of the requirements of the DPA is entitled to compensation from the data controller for that damage;

- An individual who suffers distress by reason of any contravention by a data controller of any of the requirements of the DPA is entitled to compensation from the data controller for that distress if:

    - the individual also suffers damage by reason of the contravention; or

    - the contravention relates to the processing of personal data for the special purposes.

- In proceedings brought against a person by virtue of this section it is a defence to prove that one had taken such care as in all the circumstances was reasonably required to comply with the requirement concerned.

While there are certain conditions, the primary clause refers to 'any contravention' by the organisation. In terms of the defence, in order to be able to avail of it, an organisation will have to establish that it has 'taken such care as in all the circumstances was reasonably required.' This will vary from organisation to organisation, sector to sector, the type of personal data involved, the risks of damage, loss, etc, the nature of the security risks, the security measures and procedures adopted, the history of risk, loss and damage in the organisation and sector.

Certain types of data will convey inherent additional risks over others, such as loss of financial personal data. This can be argued to require higher obligations for the organisation.

One interesting area to consider going forward is online damage, such as viral publication, defamation, bulletin boards, discussion forums and websites (or sections of websites), and social networking websites. Where damage occurs as a result of misuse or loss of personal data or results in defamation, abuse and threats, liability could arise for the individual tortfeasors as well as the website.

While there are three eCommerce defences in the eCommerce Directive, one should recall that the data protection regime (and its civil rights, sanctions, duty of care and liability provisions) are separate and stand alone from the eCommerce Directive legal regime. Indeed, even in terms of the eCommerce defences one should also recall that (a) an organisation must first fall within an eCommerce defence, and not lose that defence, in order to avail of it; and (b) there is no automatic entitlement to an internet service provider (ISP) or website to a global eCommerce defence, as in fact there in not one eCommerce defence but three specific defences relating to specific and technical activities. Not all or every ISP activity will fall into one of these defences. Neither will one activity fall into all three defences.

It is also possible to conceive of a website which has no take down procedures, inadequate take down defences, or non-expeditious take down procedures or remedies, and which will face potential liability under privacy and data protection as well as eCommerce liability. For example, an imposter social networking profile which contains personal data and defamatory material could attract liability for the website operator under data protection, and under normal liability if none of the eCommerce defences were unavailable or were lost. The later could occur if, for example, the false impersonating profile was notified to the website (or it was otherwise aware) but it did not do anything.[3]

---

3   This is a complex and developing area of law, common law, civil law, Directive, forthcoming Regulation (DPR) and case law, both in the UK and internationally. A full detailed analysis is beyond this current work.

As indicated above, the issue of civil liability and litigation by data subjects to enforce their rights will continue. This will in part be fuelled by increased awareness but also by the increasingly publicised instances of data loss, data breach, damage and instances of abuse which involve personal data. The Facebook Beacon settlement, while in the US, for approx. $20 million emphasises the import of individuals seeking to vindicate their privacy and personal data rights. In the UK, while Prudential was fined £50,000, it is not inconceivable that loss, damage and financial loss may have ensued. Consider, further that this example appears to have related to a small number of individuals. However, what if thousands of customer suffered financial loss, damage, stress, delay, missed payments, lost flights, lost contracts, etc as a result of mixing up files, not completing files and transactions. These are all things which can occur, whether through process errors or software glitches. This is not at all farfetched, as customers of RBS bank will confirm. Google may also be sued re Apple breach.

While we are well aware of the press phone hacking scandal, the Leveson Inquiry and the ensuing litigation from many victims, as well as there being admissions, interception offences, etc, there are also personal data breach and data protection civil liability issues arising.

DPA: Director Liability and Offences

12.16 The potential for personal liability (s 61 DPA) is also a significant issue for an organisation and those within positions of authority where the organisation is involved in offences.

Employees can also be liable for offences if they obtain, disclose or procure the personal data in the organisation for their own purposes.

Section 61 of the DPA refers to liability of directors etc. Section 61(1) provides that where an offence under this Act has been committed by a body corporate and is proved to have been committed with the consent or connivance of or to be attributable to any neglect on the part of any director, manager, secretary or similar officer of the body corporate or any person who was purporting to act in any such capacity, he as well as the body corporate shall be guilty of that offence and be liable to be proceeded against and punished accordingly.

Section 61(2) provides that where the affairs of a body corporate are managed by its members sub-s (1) shall apply in relation to the acts and defaults of a member in connection with his functions of management as if he were a director of the body corporate.

Section 61(3) provides that where an offence under the DPA has been committed by a Scottish partnership and the contravention in question is proved to have occurred with the consent or connivance of, or to be attributable to any neglect on the part of, a partner, he as well as the partnership shall be guilty of that offence and shall be liable to be proceeded against and punished accordingly.

One interesting case involves Facebook. In a data protection related case in Berlin, not only was the company sued but the directors were also personally named and included in the case. One of the reasons specified was to ensure that the directors made sure that the Board of the company made the appropriate amendments to ensure the breaches were rectified and would not re-occur. A further interesting aspect of the case is that while the directors were included personally, their names were redacted to initials. One such set of initials was 'M.Z.'[4]

DPA: Offences by Data Processors

12.17 Data processors can also commit offences. These include:

- failure of a data processor to register;
- failure to notify the ICO of changes and change of address;
- provision of false or misleading information when applying for registration;
- failure to comply with notices;
- disclosure of personal data without authorisation of data controller.

DPD95: Courts

12.18 Chapter III of the DPD refers to judicial remedies, liability and sanctions. Article 22 refers to remedies. It provides that without prejudice to any administrative remedy for which provision may be made, inter alia before the Supervisory Authority referred to in Article 28, prior to referral to the judicial authority, Member States shall provide for the right of every person to a judicial remedy for any breach of the rights guaranteed them by the national law applicable to the processing in question.

---

4   See *The Federal Association of Consumer Organisations and Consumer Groups, Federal Consumer Association, GB v Facebook Ireland Limited, MA, JB, DG, PT and the Chairman MZ*, [names redacted], [redacted] Reach, [redacted] Quay, Dublin, Ireland.

DPD95: Damages and Compensation

12.19 Article 23 of DPD95 refers to liability. Article 23(1) provides that Member States shall provide that any person who has suffered damage as a result of an unlawful processing operation or of any act incompatible with the national provisions adopted pursuant to the Directive is entitled to receive compensation from the data controller for the damage suffered. Article 23(2) provides that the data controller may be exempted from this liability, in whole or in part, if he proves that he is not responsible for the event giving rise to the damage.

The increase in profiling, advertising and marketing, as well as the separate issue of online abuse, will continue to increase the potential instances where damages and compensation will arise.

DPD95: Sanctions

12.20 Article 24 of DPD95 refers to sanctions. It provides that the Member States shall adopt suitable measures to ensure the full implementation of the provisions of the Directive and shall in particular lay down the sanctions to be imposed in case of infringement of the provisions adopted pursuant to the Directive.

DPR: Remedies

12.21 Chapter VIII of the DPR refers to remedies, liability and sanctions. Article 73 refers to right to lodge a complaint with a Supervisory Authority. Article 73(1) provides that without prejudice to any other administrative or judicial remedy, every data subject shall have the right to lodge a complaint with a Supervisory Authority in any Member State if they consider that the processing of personal data relating to them does not comply with the Regulation.

Article 73(2) provides that any body, organisation or association which aims to protect data subjects' rights and interests concerning the protection of their personal data and has been properly constituted according to the law of a Member State shall have the right to lodge a complaint with a Supervisory Authority in any Member State on behalf of one or more data subjects if it considers that a data subject's rights under the Regulation have been infringed as a result of the processing of personal data.

Article 73(3) provides that independently of a data subject's complaint, any body, organisation or association referred to in paragraph 2 shall have the right to lodge a complaint with a Supervisory Authority in any Member State, if it considers that a personal data breach has occurred.

Article 74 refers to the right to a judicial remedy against a Supervisory Authority.

Article 74(1) refers to and provides that each natural or legal person shall have the right to a judicial remedy against decisions of a Supervisory Authority concerning them.

Article 74(2) provides that each data subject shall have the right to a judicial remedy obliging the Supervisory Authority to act on a complaint in the absence of a decision necessary to protect their rights, or where the Supervisory Authority does not inform the data subject within three months on the progress or outcome of the complaint pursuant to point (b) of Article 52(1).

Article 74(3) provides that proceedings against a Supervisory Authority shall be brought before the courts of the Member State where the Supervisory Authority is established.

Article 74(4) provides that a data subject which is concerned by a decision of a Supervisory Authority in another Member State than where the data subject has its habitual residence, may request the Supervisory Authority of the Member State where it has its habitual residence to bring proceedings on its behalf against the competent Supervisory Authority in the other Member State.

Article 74(5) provides that the Member States shall enforce final decisions by the courts referred to in the Article.

Article 75 refers to the right to a judicial remedy against a data controller or data processor. Article 75(1) provides that without prejudice to any available administrative remedy, including the right to lodge a complaint with a Supervisory Authority as referred to in Article 73, every natural person shall have the right to a judicial remedy if they consider that their rights under the Regulation have been infringed as a result of the processing of their personal data in non-compliance with the Regulation.

Article 75(2) provides that proceedings against a data controller or a data processor shall be brought before the courts of the Member State where the data controller or data processor has an establishment.

Alternatively, such proceedings may be brought before the courts of the Member State where the data subject has its habitual residence, unless the data controller is a public authority acting in the exercise of its public powers.

Article 75(3) provides that where proceedings are pending in the consistency mechanism referred to in Article 58, which concern the same measure, decision or practice, a court may suspend the proceedings brought before it, except where the urgency of the matter for the protection of the data subject's rights does not allow to wait for the outcome of the procedure in the consistency mechanism.

Article 75(4) provides that the Member States shall enforce final decisions by the courts referred to in this.

Article 76 refers to common rules for court proceedings. Under Article 76(1) any body, organisation or association referred to in Article 73(2) shall have the right to exercise the rights referred to in Articles 74 and 75 on behalf of one or more data subjects. Article 7(2) provides that each Supervisory Authority shall have the right to engage in legal proceedings and bring an action to court, in order to enforce the provisions of the Regulation or to ensure consistency of the protection of personal data within the EU.

Article 76(3) provides that where a competent court of a Member State has reasonable grounds to believe that parallel proceedings are being conducted in another Member State, it shall contact the competent court in the other Member State to confirm the existence of such parallel proceedings.

Article 76(4) provides that if such parallel proceedings in another Member State concern the same measure, decision or practice, the court may suspend the proceedings.

Article 76(5) provides that Member States shall ensure that court actions available under national law allow for the rapid adoption of measures including interim measures, designed to terminate any alleged infringement and to prevent any further impairment of the interests involved.

Article 77 refers to the right to compensation and liability. Under Article 77(1) any person who has suffered damage as a result of an unlawful processing operation or of an action incompatible with the Regulation shall have the right to receive compensation from the data controller or the data processor for the damage suffered.

Article 77(2) provides that where more than one data controller or processor is involved in the processing, each data controller or data processor shall be jointly and severally liable for the entire amount of the damage.

Article 77(3) the data controller or the data processor may be exempted from this liability, in whole or in part, if the data controller or the data processor proves that they are not responsible for the event giving rise to the damage.

Article 78 refers to penalties. Article 78(1) provides that Member States shall lay down the rules on penalties, applicable to infringements of the provisions of the Regulation and shall take all measures necessary to ensure that they are implemented, including where the data controller did not comply with the obligation to designate a representative. The penalties provided for must be effective, proportionate and dissuasive.

Article 78(2) where the data controller has established a representative, any penalties shall be applied to the representative, without prejudice to any penalties which could be initiated against the data controller.

Article 78(3) provides that each Member State shall notify to the Commission those provisions of its law which it adopts pursuant to paragraph 1, by the date specified in Article 91(2) at the latest and, without delay, any subsequent amendment affecting them

Article 79 relates to administrative sanctions. Article 79(1) provides that each Supervisory Authority shall be empowered to impose administrative sanctions in accordance with this Article.

Article 79(2) provides that the administrative sanction shall be in each individual case effective, proportionate and dissuasive. The amount of the administrative fine shall be fixed with due regard to the nature, gravity and duration of the breach, the intentional or negligent character of the infringement, the degree of responsibility of the natural or legal person and of previous breaches by this person, the technical and organisational measures and procedures implemented pursuant to Article 23 and the degree of cooperation with the Supervisory Authority in order to remedy the breach.

Article 79(3) provides that in case of a first and unintentional non-compliance with the Regulation, a warning in writing may be given and no sanction imposed, where:

- a natural person is processing personal data without a commercial interest; or
- an enterprise or an organisation employing fewer than 250 persons is processing personal data only as an activity ancillary to its main activities.

Article 79(4) provides that the Supervisory Authority shall impose a fine up to €250,000, or in case of an enterprise up to 0.5 percent of its annual worldwide turnover, to anyone who, intentionally or negligently:

- does not provide the mechanisms for requests by data subjects or does not respond promptly or not in the required format to data subjects pursuant to Articles 12(1) and (2);
- charges a fee for the information or for responses to the requests of data subjects in violation of Article 12(4).

Article 79(1) provides that the Supervisory Authority shall impose a fine up to €500,000, or in case of an enterprise up to 1% of its annual worldwide turnover, to anyone who, intentionally or negligently:

- does not provide the information, or does provide incomplete information, or does not provide the information in a sufficiently transparent manner, to the data subject pursuant to Article 11, Article 12(3) and Article 14;
- does not provide access for the data subject or does not rectify personal data pursuant to Articles 15 and 16 or does not communicate the relevant information to a recipient pursuant to Article 13;
- does not comply with the right to be forgotten or to erasure, or fails to put mechanisms in place to ensure that the time limits are observed or does not take all necessary steps to inform third parties that a data subjects requests to erase any links to, or copy or replication of the personal data pursuant Article 17;
- does not provide a copy of the personal data in electronic format or hinders the data subject to transmit the personal data to another application in violation of Article 18;
- does not or not sufficiently determine the respective responsibilities with data controllers pursuant to Article 24;
- does not or not sufficiently maintain the documentation pursuant to Article 28, Article 31(4), and Article 44(3);
- does not comply, in cases where special categories of data are not involved, pursuant to Articles 80, 82 and 83 with rules in relation to freedom of expression or with rules on the processing in the employment context or with the conditions for processing for historical, statistical and scientific research purposes.

Article 79(16) provides that the Supervisory Authority shall impose a fine up to €1,000,000 or, in case of an enterprise up to 2 percent of its annual worldwide turnover, to anyone who, intentionally or negligently:

- processes personal data without any or sufficient legal basis for the processing or does not comply with the conditions for consent pursuant to Articles 6, 7 and 8;
- processes special categories of data in violation of Articles 9 and 81;
- does not comply with an objection or the requirement pursuant to Article 19;
- does not comply with the conditions in relation to measures based on profiling pursuant to Article 20;
- does not adopt internal policies or does not implement appropriate

measures for ensuring and demonstrating compliance pursuant to Articles 22, 23 and 30;

- does not designate a representative pursuant to Article 25;
- processes or instructs the processing of personal data in violation of the obligations in relation to processing on behalf of a data controller pursuant to Articles 26 and 27;
- does not alert on or notify a personal data breach or does not timely or completely notify the data breach to the Supervisory Authority or to the data subject pursuant to Articles 31 and 32;
- does not carry out a data protection impact assessment pursuant or processes personal data without prior authorisation or prior consultation of the Supervisory Authority pursuant to Articles 33 and 34;
- does not designate a data protection officer or does not ensure the conditions for fulfilling the tasks pursuant to Articles 35, 36 and 37;
- misuses a data protection seal or mark in the meaning of Article 39;
- carries out or instructs a data transfer to a third country or an international organisation that is not allowed by an adequacy decision or by appropriate safeguards or by a derogation pursuant to Articles 40 to 44;
- does not comply with an order or a temporary or definite ban on processing or the suspension of data flows by the Supervisory Authority pursuant to Article 53(1);
- does not comply with the obligations to assist or respond or provide relevant information to, or access to premises by, the Supervisory Authority pursuant to Article 28(3), Article 29, Article 34(6) and Article 53(2);
- does not comply with the rules for safeguarding professional secrecy pursuant to Article 84.

Article 79(1) provides that the Commission shall be empowered to adopt delegated acts in accordance with Article 86 for the purpose of updating the amounts of the administrative fines referred to in Article 79(4), (5) and (6), taking into account the criteria referred to in Article 79(2).

Powers and Functions of the ICO

12.22   The ICO has a number of registration, promotion, investigation and enforcement powers and functions under the DPA. These include:

- the obligation to check each application for registration;
- to assess whether especially risky or dangerous types of processing are involved;
- to prepare and publish codes of practice for guidance in applying data protection law in particular areas;
- cases;
- investigations;
- complaints;
- audits;
- fines.

ICO: Preliminary Assessment

12.23 Section 22 refers to preliminary assessment by the ICO. Section 22(1) provides that in the section 'assessable processing' means processing which is of a description specified in an order made by the Secretary of State as appearing to them to be particularly likely:

- to cause substantial damage or substantial distress to data subjects; or
- otherwise significantly to prejudice the rights and freedoms of data subjects.

Section 22(2) provides that on receiving notification from any data controller under s 18 or under notification regulations made by virtue of s 20 the ICO shall consider:

- whether any of the processing to which the notification relates is assessable processing, and
- if so, whether the assessable processing is likely to comply with the provisions of the Act.

Section 22(3) provides that subject to sub-s (4), the ICO shall, within the period of twenty-eight days beginning with the day on which he receives a notification which relates to assessable processing, give a notice to the data controller stating the extent to which the ICO is of the opinion that the processing is likely or unlikely to comply with the provisions of the DPA.

Section 22(4) provides that before the end of the period referred to in sub-s (3) the ICO may, by reason of special circumstances, extend that period on one occasion only by notice to the data controller by such further period not exceeding fourteen days as the ICO may specify in the notice.

Section 22(5) provides that no assessable processing in respect of which a notification has been given to the ICO as mentioned in sub-s (2) shall be carried on unless either:

- the period of twenty-eight days beginning with the day on which the notification is received by the ICO (or, in a case falling within sub-s (4), that period as extended under that sub-section) has elapsed, or
- before the end of that period (or that period as so extended) the data controller has received a notice from the ICO under sub-s (3) in respect of the processing.

Section 22(6) provides that where sub-s (5) is contravened, the data controller is guilty of an offence.

Section 22(7) provides that the Secretary of State may by order amend sub-s (3), (4) and (5) by substituting for the number of days for the time being specified there a different number specified in the order.

ICO: Financial Penalties

12.24 The ICO can issue monetary penalty notices or fines.[5] This is where serious breaches occur which are deliberate and with knowledge or where there ought to be knowledge of the breach and of the likely damage. This is in accordance with the ICO's powers as per the Criminal Justice and Immigration Act of 2008. Organisations can be fined up to £500,000 by the ICO for unwanted marketing phone calls and emails in accordance with the updated amended PECR.

ICO: Inspections

12.25 The ICO may also undertake inspections of organisations. This is where the ICO suspects that there may be a breach of the DPA and it obtains a warrant to search the organisational premises. In such an instance the ICO may enter, search, inspect, examine, test equipment, inspect and seize documents, materials, etc. Obstructing such an inspection will be a criminal offence. Legal advices should be immediately sought in relation to such incidents.

---

5   In accordance with the powers of the ICO under the Criminal Justice and Immigration Act 2008.

DPA: Data Protection Supervisors

12.26   Section 23 refers to a power to make provision for appointment of data protection supervisors.

Section 23(1) provides that the Secretary of State may by order:

- make provision under which a data controller may appoint a person to act as a data protection supervisor responsible in particular for monitoring in an independent manner the data controller's compliance with the provisions of the DPA; and
- provide that, in relation to any data controller who has appointed a data protection supervisor in accordance with the provisions of the order and who complies with such conditions as may be specified in the order, the provisions of this Part are to have effect subject to such exemptions or other modifications as may be specified in the order.

Section 23(2) provides that an order under the section may:

- impose duties on data protection supervisors in relation to the ICO; and
- confer functions on the ICO in relation to data protection supervisors.

Section 24 refers to a duty of certain data controllers to make certain information available.

Section 24(1) provides that subject to sub-s (3), where personal data are processed in a case where:

(a) by virtue of subs-s (2) or (3) of s 17, sub-s (1) of that section does not apply to the processing; and

(b) the data controller has not notified the relevant particulars in respect of that processing under s 18,

the data controller must, within twenty-one days of receiving a written request from any person, make the relevant particulars available to that person in writing free of charge.

Section 24(2) provides that in the section 'the relevant particulars' means the particulars referred to in paragraphs (a) to (f) of s 16(1).

Section 24(3) provides that the section has effect subject to any exemption conferred for the purposes of the section by notification regulations.

Section 24(4) provides that any data controller who fails to comply with the duty imposed by sub-s (1) is guilty of an offence.

Section 24(5) provides that it shall be a defence for a person charged with an offence under sub-s (4) to show that he exercised all due diligence to comply with the duty.

Recent ICO Data Loss/Data Breaches, Fines and Convictions

12.27

Issue	Date	Party	Breach	Penalty
Data breach	2 January 2013	Sony	Hack breach	£250,000
Unlawful access Customer financial data Bank employee	6 November 2012	Lara Davies	Bank employee obtained unlawfully access to bank statements of her partner's ex-wife. Court prosecution. Pleaded guilty to 11 DPA offences.	Court conviction. Fined. Lost job.
Spam	28 November 2012	Christopher Niebel and Gary McNeish, joint owners ofTetrus Telecoms.	An ICO monetary penalty was issued. The company had sent millions of unlawful spam texts to the public over the past three years.	£300,000 £140,000
Data Loss/Data Breach Unlawful disclosure Sensitive data	22 November 2012	Plymouth City Council	An ICO monetary penalty issued for a serious breach of the seventh data protection principle. A social worker sent part of a report relating to family A, to family B due to printing issues. The photocopied report contained confidential and highly sensitive personal data relating to the two parents and their four children, including of allegations of child neglect in on-going care proceedings.	£60,000

Issue	Date	Party	Breach	Penalty
Incorrect storage and processing Potential loss and damage Financial institution	6 November 2012	Prudential	An ICO monetary penalty issued after a mix-up over the administration of two customers' accounts led to tens of thousands of pounds, meant for an individual's retirement fund, ending up in the wrong account.	£50,000
Data Loss/Data Breach Unlawful disclosure Sensitive data	25 October 2012	Stoke-on-Trent City Council	An ICO monetary penalty issued following a serious breach of the Data Protection Act that led to sensitive information about a child protection legal case being emailed to the wrong person.	£120,000
Data Loss/Data Breach Police	16 October 2012	Greater Manchester Police	An ICO monetary penalty issued after the theft of a memory stick containing sensitive personal data from an officer's home. The device, which had no password protection, contained details of more than a thousand people with links to serious crime investigations.	£150,000
Data Loss/Data Breach Charity	10 October 2012	Norwood Ravenswood Ltd	An ICO monetary penalty issued after highly sensitive information about the care of four young children was lost after being left outside a London home. This was a charity which was fined.	£70,000

Issue	Date	Party	Breach	Penalty
Data Loss/Data Breach	11 September 2012	Scottish Borders Council	An ICO monetary penalty issued after former employees' pension records were found in an over-filled paper recycle bank in a supermarket car park.	£250,000
Unlawful disclosure Sensitive data	6 August 2012	Torbay Care Trust	An ICO monetary penalty issued after sensitive personal information relating to 1,373 employees was published on the Trust's website.	£175,000
Unlawful disclosure Sensitive data	12 July 2012	St George's Healthcare NHS Trust	An ICO monetary penalty issued after a vulnerable individual's sensitive medical details were sent to the wrong address.	£60,000
Data Loss/Data Breach	5 July 2012	Welcome Financial Services Limited	An ICO monetary penalty issued following a serious breach of the Data Protection Act. The breach led to the personal data of more than half a million customers being lost.	£150,000
Data Loss/Data Breach Sensitive data	19 June 2012	Belfast Health and Social Care Trust	An ICO monetary penalty issued following a serious breach of the Data Protection Act. The breach led to the sensitive personal data of thousands of patients and staff being compromised. The Trust also failed to report the incident to the ICO.	£225,000

Issue	Date	Party	Breach	Penalty
Unlawful disclosure Sensitive data	6 June 2012	Telford & Wrekin Council	An ICO monetary penalty issued for two serious breaches of the seventh data protection principle. A Social Worker sent a core assessment report to the child's sibling instead of the mother. The assessment contained confidential and highly sensitive personal data. Whilst investigating the first incident, a second incident was reported to the ICO involving the inappropriate disclosure of foster carer names and addresses to the children's mother. Both children had to be re-homed.	£90,000
Unlawful disclosure Sensitive data Security	1 June 2012	Brighton and Sussex University Hospitals NHS Trust	An ICO monetary penalty issued following the discovery of highly sensitive personal data belonging to tens of thousands of patients and staff – including some relating to HIV and Genito Urinary Medicine patients – on hard drives sold on an Internet auction site in October and November 2010.	£325,000

Issue	Date	Party	Breach	Penalty
Unlawful disclosure Sensitive data	21 May 2012	Central London Community Healthcare NHS Trust	An ICO monetary penalty issued for a serious contravention of the DPA, which occurred when sensitive personal data was faxed to an incorrect and unidentified number. The contravention was repeated on 45 occasions over a number of weeks and compromised 59 data subjects' personal data.	£90,000
Data Loss/Data Breach Sensitive data	15 May 2012	London Borough of Barnet	An ICO monetary penalty issued following the loss of sensitive information relating to 15 vulnerable children or young people, during a burglary at an employee's home.	£70,000
Unlawful disclosure Sensitive data	30 April 2012	Aneurin Bevan Health Board	An ICO monetary penalty issued following an incident where a sensitive report – containing explicit details relating to a patient's health – was sent to the wrong person.	£70,000
Unlawful disclosure Sensitive data	14 March 2012	Lancashire Constabulary	An ICO monetary penalty issued following the discovery of a missing person's report containing sensitive personal information about a missing 15 year old girl.	£70,000

Issue	Date	Party	Breach	Penalty
Unlawful disclosure Sensitive data	15 February 2012	Cheshire East Council	An ICO monetary penalty issued after an email containing sensitive personal information about an individual of concern to the police was distributed to 180 unintended recipients.	£80,000
Data Loss/Data Breach Sensitive data	13 February 2012	Croydon Council	An ICO monetary penalty issued after a bag containing papers relating to the care of a child sex abuse victim was stolen from a London pub.	£100,000
Unlawful disclosure Sensitive data	13 February 2012	Norfolk County Council	An ICO monetary penalty issued for disclosing information about allegations against a parent and the welfare of their child to the wrong recipient.	£80,000
Unlawful disclosure Sensitive data	30 January 2012	Midlothian Council	An ICO monetary penalty issued for disclosing sensitive personal data relating to children and their carers to the wrong recipients on five separate occasions. The penalty is the first that the ICO has served against an organisation in Scotland.	£140,000
Unlawful disclosure Sensitive data	6 December 2011	Powys County Council	An ICO monetary penalty issued for a serious breach of the Data Protection Act after the details of a child protection case were sent to the wrong recipient.	£130,000

Issue	Date	Party	Breach	Penalty
Unlawful disclosure Sensitive data	28 November 2011	North Somerset Council	An ICO monetary penalty issued for a serious breach of the Data Protection Act where a council employee sent five emails, two of which contained highly sensitive and confidential information about a child's serious case review, to the wrong NHS employee.	£60,000
Unlawful disclosure Sensitive data	28 November 2011	Worcestershire County Council	An ICO monetary penalty issued for an incident where a member of staff emailed highly sensitive personal information about a large number of vulnerable people to 23 unintended recipients.	£80,000
Unlawful disclosure Sensitive data	9 June 2011	Surrey County Council	An ICO monetary penalty issued for a serious breach of the Data Protection Act after sensitive personal information was emailed to the wrong recipients on three separate occasions.	£120,000
Unlawful disclosure Sensitive data Security	10 May 2011	Andrew Jonathan Crossley, formerly trading as solicitors firmACS Law	An ICO monetary penalty issued for failing to keep sensitive personal information relating to around 6,000 people secure.	£1,000

Issue	Date	Party	Breach	Penalty
Data Loss/Data Breach Laptop Encryption	8 February 2011	Ealing Council	An ICO monetary penalty issued following the loss of an unencrypted laptop which contained personal information. Ealing Council breached the Data Protection Act by issuing an unencrypted laptop to a member of staff in breach of its own policies.	£80,000
Data Loss/Data Breach Laptop Encryption	8 February 2011	Hounslow Council	An ICO monetary penalty issued following the loss of an unencrypted laptop which contained personal information. Hounslow Council breached the Act by failing to have a written contract in place with Ealing Council. Hounslow Council also did not monitor Ealing Council's procedures for operating the service securely.	£70,000

Conclusion

12.28   If a request for information or other notice is received from the ICO it may be appropriate to seek immediate legal advice. The ICO can also issue enforcement notices. In addition, the ICO may also issue monetary penalty notices or fines.[6] Organisations should ensure proper policies; awareness and ongoing training are in operation across all personnel whom have an impact and responsibility regarding data protection operations. It appears that fines, prosecutions and data subject damage and access litigation will increase.

---

6   In accordance with the powers of the ICO under the Criminal Justice and Immigration Act 2008.

Chapter 13

Security of Personal Data

Introduction

13.01 'Personally identifiable information (PII) data has become the prime target of hackers and cyber-criminals. It can be exploited in many ways, from identity theft, spamming and phishing right through to cyber-espionage.'[1] The data protection regime sets information and data security obligations on all data controllers, as well as data processors. These IT and personal data security requirements must be complied with. While security risks have increased with the internet,[2] security issues are not just limited to the organisation's internet.

The increasing instances of data security breach, including through inadequate security, as well as internet usage and social networking, cloud computing and online abuse will all increase the attention on security and data protection. Sony was recently fined £250,000.

Appropriate Security Measures

13.02 There are specific requirements with regard to the security measures that need to be implemented under the DPA.

Organisations and data controller must take appropriate security measures against unauthorised access to, or unauthorised alteration, disclosure or destruction of, the data, in particular where the processing involves the transmission of data over a network, and against all other

---

1 Rozenberg, Y., 'Challenges in PII Data Protection,' *Computer Fraud & Security* (2012), pp, 5–9, at 5.
2 'Security of the Internet and the Known Unknowns,' *Communications of the ACM* (2012)(55), pp. 35–37.

unlawful forms of processing. As these risks grow,[3] so too must the effort of the organisation. It cannot be a case that one solution, on one occasion, will be sufficient.

The requirements regarding security of processing are contained in the seventh Data Protection Principle (DPA Sch 1 s 7). The data controller must take appropriate technical and organisational measures against unauthorised or unlawful processing of personal data and against accidental loss or destruction of, or damage to personal data.

The data controller must ensure the following,

'*Appropriate technical* and *organisational* measures shall be taken against *unauthorised* or *unlawful* processing of personal data and against accidental *loss* or *destruction* of, or *damage* to personal data.'

Ensuring Appropriate Security Measures

13.03 What are security and 'appropriate technical and organisational measures'? What must the organisation do? In determining appropriate technical and organisational measures, a data controller may have regard to:

- the state of technological development and the cost of implementing any measures;
- the harm that might result from such unauthorised or unlawful processing or accidental loss, destruction or damage; and
- the nature of the data to be protected.

The seventh Data Protection Principle contained in Sch 1 to the DPA refers to security.

DPA Sch 1 s 9 provides that having regard to the state of technological development and the cost of implementing any measures, the measures must ensure a level of security appropriate to:

- the harm that might result from such unauthorised or unlawful processing or accidental loss, destruction or damage as are mentioned in the seventh principle; and
- the nature of the data to be protected.

---

3   See, for example, 'The Cybersecurity Risk,' *Communications of the ACM* (2012)(55), pp. 29–32.

DPA: Security Level

13.04   The eighth Data Protection Principle interpretative guidance contained in Sch 1 to the DPA refers to security.

DPA Sch 1, s 13 provides that an adequate level of protection is one which is adequate in all the circumstances of the case, having regard in particular to:

- the nature of the personal data;
- the country or territory of origin of the information contained in the data;
- the country or territory of final destination of that information;
- the purposes for which and period during which the data are intended to be processed;
- the law in force in the country or territory in question;
- the international obligations of that country or territory;
- any relevant codes of conduct or other rules which are enforceable in that country or territory (whether generally or by arrangement in particular cases); and
- any security measures taken in respect of the data in that country or territory.

DPA Sch 1, s 14 provides that the eighth Data Protection Principle does not apply to a transfer falling within any paragraph of Sch 4, except in such circumstances and to such extent as the Secretary of State may by order provide.

DPA Sch 1, s 15(1) provides that where:

- in any proceedings under the DPA any question arises as to whether the requirement of the eighth Data Protection Principle as to an adequate level of protection is met in relation to the transfer of any personal data to a country or territory outside the EEA; and
- an EU Community finding has been made in relation to transfers of the kind in question,

that question is to be determined in accordance with that finding.

DPA Sch 1, s 15(2) provides that in sub-paragraph (1) 'Community finding' means a finding of the European Commission, under the procedure provided for in Article 31(2) of the DPD95, that a country or territory outside the EEA does, or does not, ensure an adequate level of protection within the meaning of Article 25(2) of DPD95.

DPA: Employees and Security

13.05   DPA Sch 1, s 10 provides that the data controller must take reasonable steps to ensure the reliability of any employees of the organisation who have access to the personal data.

Organisations should be aware that they could be held liable, whether with the ICO or in a civil court, in relation to data breaches and data security breaches occasioned by their employees. Organisations may also begin to face claims in relation to online abuse caused, initiated or participated in by their employees while using the organisation's network and devices. Indeed, this applies in relation to their other servants and agents also.

DPA: Engaging Data Processors

13.06   Data processors[4] also have obligations in relation to processing personal data and security.

DPA Sch 1 s 11 provides that where processing of personal data is carried out by a data processor on behalf of a data controller, the data controller must in order to comply with the seventh principle:

- choose a data processor providing sufficient guarantees in respect of the technical and organisational security measures governing the processing to be carried out; and
- take reasonable steps to ensure compliance with those measures.

Where processing of personal data is carried out by a data processor on behalf of a data controller, then the data controller must have a contract in writing with the data processor, containing certain clauses and obligations.

DPA Schedule 1 s 12 provides that where processing of personal data is carried out by a data processor on behalf of a data controller, the data controller is not to be regarded as complying with the seventh principle unless:

- the processing is carried out under a contract:
    - which is made or evidenced in writing; and
    - under which the data processor is to act only on instructions from the data controller, and

---

4   Note generally, for example, Morgan, R., 'Data Controllers, Data Processors and Data Sharers,' SCL *Computers and Law*, 04 March, 2011.

- the contract requires the data processor to comply with obligations equivalent to those imposed on a data controller by the seventh principle.

The contracts with data processors must address the following:

- Processing must be carried out in pursuance of a contract in writing;
- Contract must provide that the data processor carries out the processing only on and subject to the instructions of the data controller;
- Data processor must comply with the above *security* requirements.

There are also certain other requirements. The data controller:

- Must ensure data processors provide sufficient guarantees in respect of the technical security measures and organisational measures governing the processing;
- Must take reasonable steps to ensure compliance with these measures.

There are specific requirements were data processors are engaged and relied upon. Where data controllers engage data processors then the data controller must:

- have a contract in writing or other equivalent form which provides that the data processor will act only on instructions of the data controller and that is will comply with the data security measures to which the data controller is subject;
- ensure that the data processor provide sufficient guarantees in respect of the technical security measures and organisational measures it implements;
- takes reasonable steps to ensure compliance with such matters.

What actions should an organisation take if third parties process their organisation's data? Organisations should consider:

- Ideally, that an organisation should have advance procedures and policies in place to cater for such an eventuality, for example ensuring that an appropriate senior manager/board member has an assigned role and takes responsibility for date protection compliance, including dealing with breaches, and also having a documented IT security incident handling procedure policy in place. Needless to say, it must be properly policed, implemented, reviewed and updated appropriately;

- Once a breach does occur, a proper procedure can assist in containing the breach and recovering from same; assessing the ongoing risk; notify the breach as appropriate; evaluating and reacting to the breach and the risk;
- All of the appropriate personnel within the organisation should be aware of the procedures and consulted as appropriate, including for example managing director, legal, IT, media/press officer;
- A part of the procedure will have a designated list of external contact points, some or all of whom may need to be notified and contacted, as appropriate;
- Obviously the nature of organisations, and of breaches themselves, differ and the IT security incident handling procedure policy will need to be tailored. After all, the cause of a data security breach can be any of a number of potential reasons;
- Also, such a policy while covering breaches of data protection and privacy, may well encompass wider issues, such as outsourcing, backups, disaster recovery, business continuity, etc;
- If you do business in other jurisdictions you may need to take additional measures. For example, if you own or have access to personal information of Californian residents then you may have a legal duty to notify those individuals if that information (such as names and credit card details) has been accessed illegally.

WP29: Security

13.07　The influential EU Article 29 Working Party has published a document relating to personal data and information security. This was published on 29 May 2002. It refers to the surveillance of employee's electronic communications. In terms of compliance it raises a number of policy concerns for organisations to consider when dealing with their policies and activities regarding such personal data. It suggests that organisations asking if the proposed processing of the employee's personal data is:

- Transparent?
- Necessary?
- Fair?
- Proportionate?
- For what purpose?

It also suggests that organisations should consider if each proposed processing activity can be achieved through some other less obtrusive means.

It also refers to informing those outside of the organisation as appropriate in relation to the proposed processing.

It also refers to issues of proportionality in suggesting that an organisation in processing personal data should adopt the minimum processing necessary, and pursuing a strategy of prevention versus detection. Detection leans more towards blanket monitoring of employees, whereas prevention is viewed as more appropriate and employee privacy friendly. Of course, where some issue comes to the organisation's attention, they could then investigate that issue, as opposed to actively monitoring all employees 24/7. An example would be using IT filtering systems, which alert the IT manager that there may be an issue to look at further, rather than the IT manager actively looking at and monitoring all employee communications.

DPD95: Confidentiality

13.08 Section VIII of the DPD refers to confidentiality and security of processing. Article 16 refers to the confidentiality of processing. It provides that any person acting under the authority of the data controller or of the data processor, including the data processor, who has access to personal data must not process them except on instructions from the data controller, unless required to do so by law.

DPD95: Security

13.09 Article 17 of the DPD refers to security of processing.

Article 17(1) provides that Member States shall provide that the data controller must implement appropriate technical and organisational measures to protect personal data against accidental or unlawful destruction or accidental loss, alteration, unauthorised disclosure or access, in particular where the processing involves the transmission of data over a network, and against all other unlawful forms of processing. It also provides that having regard to the state of the art and the cost of their implementation, such measures shall ensure a level of security appropriate to the risks represented by the processing and the nature of the data to be protected.

Article 17(2) provides that Member States shall provide that the data controller must, where processing is carried out on his behalf, choose a data processor providing sufficient guarantees in respect of the technical security measures and organisational measures governing the processing to be carried out, and must ensure compliance with those measures.

Article 17(3) provides that the carrying out of processing by way of a data processor must be governed by a contract or legal act binding the data processor to the data controller and stipulating in particular that:

- the data processor shall act only on instructions from the data controller;
- the obligations set out in Article 17(1), as defined by the law of the Member State in,

which the data processor is established, shall also be incumbent on the data processor.

Article 17(4) provides that for the purposes of keeping proof, the parts of the contract or the legal act relating to data protection and the requirements relating to the measures referred to in Article 17(1) shall be in writing or in another equivalent form.

DPR: Security

13.10   Section 2 of the DPR relates to data security. Article 30 specifically refers to security of processing.

Section 2(1) provides that the data controller and the data processor shall implement appropriate technical and organisational measures to ensure a level of security appropriate to the risks represented by the processing and the nature of the personal data to be protected, having regard to the state of the art and the costs of their implementation.

Section 2(2) provides that the data controller and the data processor shall, following an evaluation of the risks, take the measures referred to in paragraph 1 to protect personal data against accidental or unlawful destruction or accidental loss and to prevent any unlawful forms of processing, in particular any unauthorised disclosure, dissemination or access, or alteration of personal data.

Section 2(3) provides that the Commission shall be empowered to adopt delegated acts in accordance with Article 86 for the purpose of further specifying the criteria and conditions for the technical and organisational measures referred to in Article 30(1) and (2), including the determinations of what constitutes the state of the art, for specific sectors and in specific data processing situations, in particular taking account of developments in technology and solutions for privacy by design and data protection by default, unless Article 30(4) applies.

Section 2(4) provides that the Commission may adopt, where necessary, implementing acts for specifying the requirements laid down in Article 30(1) and (2) to various situations, in particular to,

- prevent any unauthorised access to personal data;
- prevent any unauthorised disclosure, reading, copying, modification, erasure or removal of personal data;
- ensure the verification of the lawfulness of processing operations.

In addition, those implementing acts shall be adopted in accordance with the examination procedure referred to in Article 87(2).

If the Commission begins to issue particular security requirements, processes, etc, as appears to be envisaged in the DPR, this will mean yet another area for organisations to keep abreast of. Of course, there are many advantages for such a consolidated and timely method of enhancing security.

DPR: Notification of Security Breaches

13.11   Article 31 of the DPR refers to notification of a personal data breach[5] to the Supervisory Authority.

Article 31(1) provides that in the case of a personal data breach, the data controller shall without undue delay and, where feasible, not later than 24 hours after having become aware of it, notify the personal data breach to the Supervisory Authority. The notification to the Supervisory Authority shall be accompanied by a reasoned justification in cases where it is not made within 24 hours.

Article 31(2) provides that pursuant to point (f) of Article 26(2), the data processor shall alert and inform the data controller immediately after the establishment of a personal data breach.

Article 31(3) provides that the notification referred to in Article 31(1) must at least:

- describe the nature of the personal data breach including the categories and number of data subjects concerned and the categories and number of data records concerned;
- communicate the identity and contact details of the data protection officer or other contact point where more information can be obtained;
- recommend measures to mitigate the possible adverse effects of the personal data breach;
- describe the consequences of the personal data breach;

5   Note, for example, Wainman, P., 'Data Protection Breaches: Today and Tomorrow,' SCL *Computers and Law*, 30 June 2012. Also see Dekker, M., Dr., Christoffer Karsberg, C. and Daskala, B., *Cyber Incident Reporting in the EU* (2012).

- describe the measures proposed or taken by the data controller to address the personal data breach.

Article 31(4) provides that data controller shall document any personal data breaches, comprising the facts surrounding the breach, its effects and the remedial action taken. This documentation must enable the Supervisory Authority to verify compliance with this Article. The documentation shall only include the information necessary for that purpose.

Article 31(5) provides that the Commission shall be empowered to adopt delegated acts in accordance with Article 86 for the purpose of further specifying the criteria and requirements for establishing the data breach referred to in Article 31(1) and (2) and for the particular circumstances in which a data controller and a data processor is required to notify the personal data breach.

Article 31(6) provides that the Commission may lay down the standard format of such notification to the Supervisory Authority, the procedures applicable to the notification requirement and the form and the modalities for the documentation referred to in paragraph 4, including the time limits for erasure of the information contained therein. Those implementing acts shall be adopted in accordance with the examination procedure referred to in Article 87(2).

DPR: Notification of Personal Data Breach to Data Subject

13.12 Article 32 of the DPR refers to communication of a personal data breach[6] to the data subject.

Article 32(1) provides that when the personal data breach is likely to adversely affect the protection of the personal data or privacy of the data subject, the data controller shall, after the notification referred to in Article 31; communicate the personal data breach to the data subject without undue delay.

Article 32(2) provides that the communication to the data subject referred to in paragraph 1 shall describe the nature of the personal data breach and contain at least the information and the recommendations provided for in points (b) and (c) (bullets 2 and 3 of Article 31(3).

Article 32(3) provides that the communication of a personal data breach to the data subject shall not be required if the data controller demonstrates to the satisfaction of the Supervisory Authority that it has

---

6   Note, for example, Wainman, P., 'Data Protection Breaches: Today and Tomorrow,' SCL *Computers and Law*, 30 June 2012. Also see Dekker, M., Dr., Christoffer Karsberg, C. andDaskala, B., *Cyber Incident Reporting in the EU* (2012).

implemented appropriate technological protection measures, and that those measures were applied to the data concerned by the personal data breach. Such technological protection measures shall render the data unintelligible to any person who is not authorised to access it.

Article 32(4) provides that without prejudice to the data controller's obligation to communicate the personal data breach to the data subject, if the data controller has not already communicated the personal data breach to the data subject of the personal data breach, the Supervisory Authority, having considered the likely adverse effects of the breach, may require it to do so.

Article 32(5) provides that the Commission shall be empowered to adopt delegated acts in accordance with Article 86 for the purpose of further specifying the criteria and requirements as to the circumstances in which a personal data breach is likely to adversely affect the personal data referred to in paragraph 1.

Article 32(6) provides that the Commission may lay down the format of the communication to the data subject referred to in paragraph 1 and the procedures applicable to that communication.

Those implementing acts shall be adopted in accordance with the examination procedure referred to in Article 87(2).

Organisational Security Awareness

13.13 There is an issue of ensuring security awareness within the organisation. Data controllers and data processors must take all reasonable steps to ensure that persons employed by them and other persons at the place of work, are aware of and comply with the relevant security measures (note DPA Schedule 1, s 10).

Identifying and Controlling Organisational IT Security

13.14 Who needs to be in charge of IT and data security in an organisation? What organisational security measures should be in place?

The DPA does not require that a named individual be appointed with responsibility for security compliance. However, there are specific organisational responsibilities, regarding security, which are set out in the DPA and these include a specific requirement that all staff are aware of and comply with the security standards set out in the data protection regime.

These security requirements apply where an organisation collects and processes any personal data. Typically personal data would include information which identifies living individuals such as employees or customers. Accordingly, for most organisations, data protection compliance is likely to be an issue that crosses various aspects of the business such as human resources, IT and customer support. It is not necessarily just an IT function. An organisational decision as to who should be responsible for IT and data security should be made with this in mind.

The security standards set out in the Data Protection Act can be summarised as obliging the organisation to take 'appropriate' security measures to guard against unauthorised access, alteration, disclosure or destruction of any personal data.

In determining what is 'appropriate,' the organisation can have regard to the state of technological development and the cost of implementing the security measures. However, the organisation is obliged to ensure that the measures it decides to adopt provide a level of security appropriate to the harm that might result from a security compromise given the nature of the data concerned. For example, a hospital processing sensitive health data would be expected to adopt a particularly high security standard while a corner shop processing personal data for a paper round might be subject to a less onerous standard.

In light of some high profile cases of data theft or loss, readers should note also that the ICO's office has taken the view that an appropriate level of security for laptop computers used in the financial services and health industries requires the use of encryption in respect of the data stored on the hard drive (over and above the use of user name and password log-in requirements).

In adopting security measures within an organisation, they should note that the legal standard governing personal data is over and above any other legal obligations of confidentiality which could be owed to third parties at common law or under a contract which contains confidentiality provisions.

Appraising Employees

13.15 What guidance should be given to an organisation's employees regarding IT and data security? An organisation might consider these issues.

The overriding principle here is that, for it to be effective, an employee must have clear notice of all aspects of your IT and data security policy. The following might be included.

General Policy: You should reserve the right to monitor use of the computer and telephone system, including email. Disclosure of sensitive or confidential information about the company or personal data about any individual without authorisation should be forbidden.

Email: Employees should be made aware that email is an essential business tool but not without its risks. Business communications should be suitable and not too chatty or contain inappropriate material. Personal use of email must be reasonable.

Internet Access: Downloading of any software without approval should be forbidden. No improper or illegal activities (hacking, etc) should be tolerated. Access to certain types of websites (abuse, adult, criminal, hate, violent, etc) should be expressly restricted. Origination or dissemination of inappropriate material should be forbidden.

Mobile Telephones and Devices: Downloading of any software without approval should be forbidden. No improper or illegal activities (hacking, etc) should be tolerated. Access to certain types of websites (adult, criminal, hate, violent, etc) should be expressly restricted. Origination or dissemination of inappropriate material should be forbidden.

Vehicles: Increasingly tracking and other data from vehicles can be related to identified employees. It is important for organisations to consider these personal data issues.

Internet Social Networking: Downloading of any software without approval should be forbidden. No improper or illegal activities (hacking, etc) should be tolerated. Access to certain types of websites (adult, criminal, hate, violent, etc) should be expressly restricted. Origination or dissemination of inappropriate material should be forbidden, eg abuse.

Software Installation & Management: Purchase and/or installation of software not approved by you should be forbidden. All software must be required to be tested before installation on the system to ensure that it is free from viruses, malware, etc.

Password Security: Clear guidelines as to the use of passwords should be given including the strength of password required, the importance of keeping one's password confidential, the changing of passwords at regular intervals and (in the light of recent events) the application of password security to laptops, mobile phones and PDAs. At least, in some businesses, stronger encryption may be appropriate and employees should be required to comply with procedures in this regard. Carrying company data on vulnerable media such as memory sticks should be discouraged.

Connecting Hardware: Employees should be required not to connect any hardware (memory sticks, hard drives, etc) without following specified procedures and obtaining appropriate authorisation.

Remote Access: For many businesses, remote access, including web-based remote access, is a vital tool. However, policies should deal with such matter as accessing remotely from insecure locations as internet cafes, etc and emphasise the importance of logging off effectively.

Organisational Security Measures

13.16 What measures should an organisation take? Some suggestions may include:

- Ensure you have the appropriate security equipment and software to protect your systems if you grant third party access. If providing access to a third party involves your business opening its systems up to a public network such as the Internet it is essential that suitable security measures are taken;
- Obtain a complete listing of the IT provider personnel who have access to your systems and detail their level, status (full time/ contractor) and ensure that their employment contracts incorporate terms similar to above;

Third parties should be granted access to your systems only when the

- relevant individuals in your organisation (eg a business manager, in conjunction with IT staff) have agreed that there is a business need for such access to be granted. Access should only be for a temporary period and renewed at regular intervals;
- Third party computer accounts should be monitored (subject to legal agreements between the organisation and the third party and in accordance with legal requirements) and disabled as soon as access is no longer required;
- Ensure that sensitive files segregated in secure areas/computer systems and available only to qualified persons;
- Ensure that you have inventoried the various types of data being stored and classified it according to how important it is and how costly it would be your company if it were lost or stolen;
- Scan computers (especially servers) for unauthorised programs that transmit information to third parties such as hackers;
- Programs that have a hidden purpose are known as Trojans. Individuals may have inadvertently or deliberately downloaded free programs from the Internet that send back information such as passwords to hackers or Internet usage information to marketers to build up trends of people's tastes;

- Ensure that third parties only have access to information and computer settings on a 'need-to-know' basis;
- The System Administrator for your computer systems should set up computer accounts for third parties so that these third parties do not have access to all information on your systems or have the permission to install non standard software and change computer settings;
- When engaging an external business to destroy records or electronic media, ensure references are checked. Draft a contract setting out the terms of the relationship. Ensure that destruction is done on-site and require that a certificate of destruction be issued upon completion.

Breach Laws to Consider

13.17   What laws might affect an organisation if an organisation has an IT or data security breach? Suggested legal issues and laws to consider include:

- DPD;
- DPD95;
- ePD;
- Electronic Commerce (EC) Regulations 2002;
- Criminal Damage Act 1971;
- Evidence;
- Fraud Act 2006;
- Theft Act 1968;
- Civil liability law;
- Protection of Children Act 1978;
- Criminal Justice and Public Order Act 1994;
- European Convention on Human Rights;
- PECR/PECR Amendment.

Other issues to consider include:

- Official guidance and current stated positions of regulators and guidance bodies;
- International standards organisations eg technical security standards, etc.

Third Party Security Providers

13.18 What actions should an organisation take if a third party is responsible for IT security or has access to its IT system? Some issues to consider include:

- This is becoming increasingly popular in practice through outsourcing arrangements and vendor agreements;
- It is prudent to understand the security framework and document stakeholder exposure throughout it;
- Measures to take with the organisation's IT provider;
- Ensure that one engages lawyers to draft appropriate contracts that secure what your IT provider is securing;
- Ensure that confidentiality clauses are included to protect all of your intellectual property assets;
- Have the IT provider supply a complete security document outlining the hardware, topology, software and methodologies deployed;
- Ensure that the IT provider has staff participate in regular training programs to keep abreast of technical and legal issues?;
- Ensure that the IT provider develops a security breach response plan in the event that your company experiences a data breach; also develop security guidelines for laptops and other portable computing devices when transported off-site;
- Have the IT provider ensure that all employees follow strict password and virus protection procedures and develop a mechanism where employees are required to change passwords often, using foolproof methods especially for terminating employees;
- Ensure that the IT provider has a records retention/disposal schedule for personally identifiable information, whether stored in paper, micrographic or magnetic/electronic (computer) media.

Council Resolution 2002/C43/02: Raising Awareness

13.19 EU Council Resolution 2002/C43/02 of 28 January, 2002 indicates the recognition and official concern in relation to the loss of personal data, and the fact that technology has changed significantly since the DPD in 1995.

It refers to the dangers of information loss, attacks on organisations, and issues of network and information security for organisations and individuals.

It indicated that EU Member States should engage in information campaigns addressing the issues of security and personal data.

It recognises the need to promote best practice, such as the internationally recognised standards for IT and security set by international and standards setting organisation eg ISO 15408.

It also recognises the increase in eGovernment and the need to promote secure eGovernment.

It also notes that in the increase of attacks on the security of personal data though technology, some of the solutions may also come from new technologies. Some of these are referred to as privacy enhancing technologies, or PETs.[7] (See P6D and DP6D, Part 4.)

In addition it also refers to the increase of mobile and wireless communications technologies and the need for introducing and enhancing wireless security.

Keeping on top of the increasing threats to information security is an ongoing task. The threats are ever changing, and so equally should be the effort to prevent breaches, and to deal with them if and when they occur. Some of the most current information security threats are highlighted annually by various IT security vendors as well as police and investigative officials. Many security risk reports are published annually.

ICO Guidance

13.20 The ICO has also issued a guide entitled *A Practical Guide to IT Security, Ideal for Small Businesses*[8] which is useful. The ICO has also commented in relation to encryption issues.[9]

The ICO also provides the following tips and suggestions[10] for maintaining and implementing IT security for personal data, namely,

For computer security

- Install a firewall and virus-checking on the computers;
- Make sure that the operating system is set up to receive automatic updates;
- Protect the computer by downloading the latest patches or security updates, which should cover vulnerabilities;

---

7   See, for example, Beric, B, Carlisle, G. 'Investigating the Legal Protection of Data, Information and Knowledge Under the EU Data Protection Regime,' *International Review of Law*, Computers & Technology (2009)(23), pp. 189–201.
8   Available at http://www.ico.gov.uk/, accessed on 18 January 2013.
9   Available at http://www.ico.gov.uk/news/current_topics/Our_approach_to_encryption.aspx, accessed on 18 January 2013.
10 Available at http://www.ico.gov.uk/for_organisations/data_protection/security_measures.aspx, accessed on 18 January 2013.

- Only allow staff access to the information they need to do their job and do not let them share passwords;
- Encrypt any personal information held electronically that would cause damage or distress if it were lost or stolen;
- Take regular back-ups of the information on your computer system and keep them in a separate place so that if one loses computers, one does not lose the information;
- Securely remove all personal information before disposing of old computers (by using technology or destroying the hard disk);
- Consider installing an anti-spyware tool. Spyware can secretly monitor ones computer activities etc. Spyware can be unwittingly installed within other file and program downloads, and their use is often malicious. They can capture passwords, banking credentials and credit card details, and then relay them back to fraudsters. Anti-spyware helps to monitor and protect the computer from spyware threats, and it is often free to use and update.

For Using Emails Securely

- Consider whether the content of the email should be encrypted or password protected. The IT or security team should be able to assist with encryption;
- When starting to type in the name of the recipient, some email software will suggest similar addresses one has used before. If one has previously emailed several people whose name or address starts the same way – eg 'Dave' – the auto-complete function may bring up several 'Dave's.' Make sure to choose the right address before clicking send;
- If one wants to send an email to a recipient without revealing their address to other recipients, make sure to use blind carbon copy (bcc), not carbon copy (cc). When one uses cc every recipient of the message will be able to see the address it was sent to;
- Be careful when using a group email address. Check who is in the group and make sure you really want to send your message to everyone;
- If sending a sensitive email from a secure server to an insecure recipient, security will be threatened. One may need to check that the recipient's arrangements are secure enough before sending the message.

For Using Faxes Securely

- Consider whether sending the information by a means other than fax is more appropriate, such as using a courier service or secure email. Make sure to only send the information that is required;
- Make sure to double check the fax number you are using. It is best to dial from a directory of previously verified numbers;
- Check that you are sending a fax to a recipient with adequate security measures in place. For example, the fax should not be left uncollected in an open plan office;
- If the fax is sensitive, ask the recipient to confirm that they are at the fax machine, they are ready to receive the document, and there is sufficient paper in the machine;
- Ring up or email to make sure the whole document has been received safely;
- Use a cover sheet. This will let anyone know who the information is for and whether it is confidential or sensitive, without them having to look at the contents.

For Other Security

- Shred all your confidential paper waste;
- Check the physical security of your premises;
- Train the staff:
  - so they know what is expected of them;
  - to be wary of people who may try to trick them into giving out personal details;
  - so that they can be prosecuted if they deliberately give out personal details without permission;
  - to use a strong password – these are long (at least seven characters) and have a combination of upper and lower case letters, numbers and the special keyboard characters like the asterisk or currency symbols;
  - not to send offensive emails about other people, their private lives or anything else that could bring your organisation into disrepute;
  - not to believe emails that appear to come from your bank that ask for your account, credit card details or your password (a bank would never ask for this information in this way);
  - not to open Spam – not even to unsubscribe or ask for no more mailings. Tell them to delete the email and either get

Spam filters on your computers or use an email provider that offers this service.[11]

ICO: Security Breaches

13.21 The ICO advises that under the revised Regulations (PECR), public electronic communications service providers are required to notify the ICO if a personal data breach occurs.

A personal data breach id defined to mean:

'a breach of security leading the accidental or unlawful destruction, loss, alteration, unauthorised disclosure of, or access to, personal data transmitted, stored or otherwise processed in connection with the provisions of a public electronic communications service.'

The ICO advises[12] that the following must be complied with,

Keep a log of personal data breaches

You must keep a record of all personal data breaches in an inventory or log. It must contain:

- the facts surrounding the breach;
- the effects of that breach; and
- remedial action taken.

We have produced a template log to help you record the information you need.

Notify breaches to the ICO

You must notify the ICO of any personal data breaches. This notification must include at least a description of:

- the nature of the breach;
- the consequences of the breach; and
- the measures taken or proposed to be taken by the provider to address the breach.

To make this process easier, we suggest that you send your log to us on a monthly basis. This means one will not have to record the information twice and will meet the organisation's requirement to notify any security breaches without unnecessary delay.

---

11 Available at http://www.ico.gov.uk/for_organisations/data_protection/security_measures.aspx, accessed on 18 January 2013.
12 Available at http://www.ico.gov.uk/for_organisations/privacy_and_electronic_communications/the_guide/security_breaches.aspx, accessed on 18 January 2013.

However, if the breach is of a particularly serious nature you need to notify us about the breach as soon as possible, by filling in the security breach notification form (PECR).

When thinking about whether a breach is of a serious nature, we recommend that one considers:

- the type and sensitivity of the data involved;
- the impact it could have on the individual, such as distress or embarrassment; and
- the potential harm, such as financial loss, fraud, theft of identity.

Please email all security breach notifications to us at datasecurity breach@ico.gsi.gov.uk.

Failure to comply with the requirement to submit breach notifications can incur a £1,000 fine.

For more practical information on how to notify us about PECR security breaches please see our guidance for service providers.

Notify breaches to your subscribers

You may also need to tell your subscribers. If the breach is likely to adversely affect their personal data or privacy you need to, without unnecessary delay, notify them of the breach. You need to tell them:

- the nature of the breach;
- contact details for your organisation where they can get more information; and
- how they can mitigate any possible adverse impact of the breach.

You do not need to tell your subscribers about a breach if you can demonstrate that you have measures in place which would render the data unintelligible and that those measures were applied to the data concerned in the breach.

If you don't tell subscribers, the ICO can require you do so, if it considers the breach is likely to have an adverse effect on them.[13]

Disposal of Computer Hardware

13.22   Particular care is needed when considering the disposal of IT hardware, equipment and software. They may still contain personal data files. It may also include commercial or other confidential information relating to the organisation. This can continue to be the case even when

---

13   Available   at   http://www.ico.gov.uk/for_organisations/data_protection/security_ measures.aspx, accessed on 18 January 2013.

it appears that files have been wiped or deleted. It is always advised to take professional legal, IT and or forensic advice.

Disposal can occur from the organisation. However, organisations need to be aware that there can be a security breach as well a breach of the data protection regime if devices and hardware are donated to charity or otherwise given away but there remains corporate and personal data on the devices. Even when it appears data may be deleted, it can sometimes be recovered with the right skills. There have also been instances where equipment is meant to be decommissioned and disposed of but employees or contractors do not fulfil the job, and the devices get into third party hands with data still on them.

This can raise other issues. If an employee leaves, they will be leaving their company laptop, etc behind. This can be reassigned to another employee. However, is the new employee appropriately designated to access to the level and importance of the data on the laptop? Hierarchies of access control need to be considered.

Particular sensitivity also arises if it is intended to recycle or give to charity particular devices. Real consideration should be given to the personal data (and other data) thereon in deciding if and how to so dispose of such devices.

Conclusion

13.23 Security is a legal data protection compliance requirement, as well as best business practice. This is one of the more prominent areas of compliance where time never stands still. The security risks and needs must constantly be appraised and updated. It is also essential to ensure that outsourced data processing activities are also undertaken in an appropriately secure manner. Increasingly the area of appraisals and procedures surrounding security breaches and data loss instances is regulated. If such an event arises, the ICO as well as individual data subjects may have to be informed. Liability issues should also be a constant concern for organisations as regards security and risk.

Chapter 14

Outsourcing and Data Processors

Introduction

14.01 While many organisations may feel they do not engage third parties to deal with their personal data and databases, closer inspection often indicates that this is not correct. Many organisations, and across all sectors of activity, engage third parties or outsource certain of their internal processing activities.[1]

One example is where an organisation may find it more convenient to outsource its payroll functions to an organisation specialising in such activities. It is necessary, therefore, that the employee personal data, or certain of it, is transferred to the third party organisation for processing. This third party is a data processor acting for the organisation. A contract must be in place and appropriate security standards implemented.

Sometime organisations outsource other activities, such as marketing, recruitment, employment of consultants or agents or part time employees. Organisations increasingly outsource market research and customer satisfaction surveys to third parties. These are all data controllers where personal data is involved.

If an organisation must transfer or export personal data outside of the EEA and lawfully permit transfers outside of the ban restriction, it must satisfy, as appropriate:

- An export to one of the safe permitted countries; or
- An export to the US under the Safe harbour program; or

---

1   See generally Alsenoy, V. Van, 'Allocating Responsibility Among Controllers, Processors, and 'Everything In Between': The Definition of Actors and Roles in Directive 95/46/EC,' *Computer Law & Security Review* (2012)(28), pp. 25–43; Morgan, R., 'Data Controllers, Data Processors and Data Sharers,' SCL *Computers and Law*, 04 March, 2011.

- An export pursuant to the accepted standard contractual clauses; or
- An export pursuant to the accepted binding corporate rules.

Data Processors and Security

14.02 Data processors also have obligations in relation to processing personal data and security.

Where processing of personal data is carried out by a data processor on behalf of a data controller, then the data controller must have a contract in writing in place with the data processor, containing certain clauses and obligations.

The contracts with data processors must address the following:

- Processing must be carried out in pursuance of a contract in writing or another equivalent form;
- Contract must provide that the data processor carries out the processing only on and subject to the instructions of the data controller;
- Data processor must comply with the 'security' requirements (see above).

There are also certain other requirements. The data controller:

- Must ensure data processor provides sufficient guarantees in respect of the technical security measures and organisational measures governing the processing;
- Must take reasonable steps to ensure compliance with these measures.

Cloud and data security issues also arise to be considered.

DPA: Engaging Data Processors

14.03 DPA Sch 1, s 11 provides that where processing of personal data is carried out by a data processor on behalf of a data controller, the data controller in order to comply with the seventh principle must:

- choose a data processor providing sufficient guarantees in respect of the technical and organisational security measures governing the processing to be carried out; and
- take reasonable steps to ensure compliance with those measures.

DPA Sch 1 s 12 provides that where processing of personal data is carried out by a data processor on behalf of a data controller, the data controller is not to be regarded as complying with the seventh principle unless:

- the processing is carried out under a contract:
  - which is made or evidenced in writing; and
  - under which the data processor is to act only on instructions from the data controller, and
- the contract requires the data processor to comply with obligations equivalent to those imposed on a data controller by the seventh principle.

Relying on Third Party Data Processors

14.04 There are specific requirements where data processors are engaged. Where data controllers engage data processors then the data controller must:

- have a contract in writing or other equipment form which provides that the data processor will act only on instructions of the data controller and that is will comply with the data security measures to which the data controller is subject;
- ensure the data processor provide sufficient guarantees in respect of the technical security measures and organisational measures it implements;
- takes reasonable steps to ensure compliance with such matters.

What actions should an organisation take if third parties process their organisation's data? Organisations should consider:

- Advance procedures and policies in place to ensure and cater for such an eventuality
- Ensuring that an appropriate senior manager/board member has an assigned role and takes responsibility for date protection compliance, including dealing with breaches, and also having a documented IT security incident handling procedure policy in place. Needless to say, it must be properly policed, implemented, reviewed and updated appropriately;
- Once a breach does occur, a proper procedure can assist in containing the breach and recovering from same; assessing the ongoing risk; notify the breach as appropriate; evaluating and reacting to the breach and the risk;
- All of the appropriate personnel within the organisation should be

aware of the procedures and consulted as appropriate, including for example managing director, legal, IT, media/press officer;

- A part of the procedure will have a designated list of external contact points, some or all of whom may need to be notified and contacted, as appropriate;

- Obviously the nature of organisations, and of the breaches themselves, differ and the IT security incident handling procedure policy will need to be tailored. After all, the cause of a data security breach can be any of a number of potential reasons;

- Also, such a policy while covering breaches of data protection and privacy, may well encompass wider issues, such as outsourcing, backups, disaster recovery, business continuity, etc;

- If doing business in other jurisdictions one may need to take additional measures. For example, if owning or having access to personal information of Californian residents then one may have a legal duty to notify those individuals if that information (such as names and credit card details) has been accessed illegally.

Conclusion

14.05 It is also important that the organisation undertake ongoing assessments and checks regarding the operation of the data processing undertaken by the data processor. This should also include the security and compliance measures. Issues of risk, security breach and data protection compliance must be assessed on an ongoing basis.

Chapter 15

Other Data Protection Issues

Introduction

15.01 Data protection covers many separate but important topics. Many of these are directly relevant to many organisations. Unfortunately, all of these cannot be adequately covered in a book such as this. However, it may assist to briefly refer to some of these.

Medical and Health Data

15.02 Medical and health data comprise one of the categories of sensitive personal data. Hence, there are greater conditions and compliance obligations. There is also a greater need for higher security measures. The concerns in relation to medical and health data increase once such data is held in electronic form and electronic databases. There is a need for enhanced practical and security procedures.[1]

There are various and increasing forms of recording personal health and related data regarding individuals, held in databases or biobanks.[2] One of the concerns is also the increasing possibility for profiling

---

1 Sandea, I., 'Analysis of the Legal Aspects Concerning Data Protection in Electronic Medical Registry," *Applied Medical Informatics*,' (2009)(25), pp. 16–20.
2 Bygrave, Lee A., 'The Body as Data? Biobank Regulation via the "Back door" of Data Protection Law,' *Law, Innovation & Technology* (2010)(2), pp. 1–25.

individuals from bioinformatic and genetic data.[3] The issue of consent in relation to bio data and biobanks is an issue of increasing concern.[4]

Genome Data

15.03 A related and growing area is genomic,[5] genome research and the implications for individuals' privacy and personal data. Individual may be concerned with what happens with their own DNA gene sequence, information regarding predispositions to diseases, how this may affect them, and how doctors, employers, insurers, and government may access and use such personal data. One recent text relating to this area is *The Governance of Genetic Information, Who Decides?* by Widdows and Mulle.[6]

Body Scanners

15.04 The introduction of body scanning technology in airports has been controversial.[7] While the prime argument in favour relates to airline security and terrorism, not everyone is convinced, and those challenged to produce evidence of successful attacks prevented, have been less forthcoming.

The main controversy centres on the ability of the body scanners to provide a complete, graphic, internal and intrusive image of a person's naked body once they walk through the scanner. There are of course different types and different settings. However, the introduction of body scanners is a perfect example of the introduction of a new technology without considering the privacy and data protection implications in advance. Later versions of body scanners have been developed which produce a line image drawing, not a biological naked image. They are equally capable of highlighting contraband material. Privacy designed body scanners can be equally effective.

---

3   Azmi, I.M., 'Bioinformatics and Genetic Privacy: The Impact of the Personal Data Protection Act 2010,' *Computer Law & Security Review* (2011)(27), pp. 394–401.
4   See, for example, Taupitz, J., and Weigel, J., 'The Necessity of Broad Consent and Complementary Regulations for the Protection of Personal Data in Biobanks: What Can We Learn from the German Case?' *Public Health Genomics* (2012)(15), pp. 263–271.
5   Curren, L., et al, 'Identifiability, Genomics, and UK Data Protection Law,' *European Journal of Health Law* (2010)(17), pp. 329–344.
6   Widdows, H., and Mullen, C., eds, 'Frontmatter, The Governance of Genetic Information, Who Decides?' *Cambridge Law, Medicine and Ethics* (2009).
7   See, for example, Mironenko, O., 'Body Scanners Versus Privacy and Data Protection,' *Computer Law & Security Review* (2011)(27), pp. 232–244.

Investigation, Discovery and Evidence

15.05 The issue of electronic evidence is important and critical, whether for the organisation or the data subject wishing to use such evidence. It is recommended that organisations consider these issues proactively in advance rather than hoping to be able to deal with them adequately in a reactive manner.

Cloud

15.06 The popularity of cloud computing and virtualisation services with users, enterprise and increasingly official organisations is ever increasing. However, there are real concerns in relation to privacy, data protection, data security,[8] continuity, discovery, liability, record keeping, etc.[9] One commentator refers to cloud computing as 'the privacy storm on the horizon.'[10] Any organisation considering cloud services needs to carefully consider the advantages, disadvantages, assessments and contract assurances that will be required. Such organisations, as well as the service operators, also need to assure themselves as to how they ensure data protection compliance.

New Hardware Devices

15.07 The arrival of new devices, from smartphones, combined devices and even communications devices on devices (such as RFID tags), emphasise that organisations need to be much more aware and considered in their policies and risk assessments under the data protection regime.

---

8   See for example, Soghoian, C., 'Caught in the Cloud: Privacy, Encryption, and Government Back Doors in the Web 2.0 Era,' *Journal of Telecommunications & High Technology Law* (2010)(8), pp. 359–424.

9   ICO, *Guidance on the Use of Cloud Computing*, available at http://www.ico.gov. uk/for_organisations/data_protection/topic_guides/online/cloud_computing.aspx, accessed on 14 October, 2012; Article 29 Working Party, *Opinion 05/2012 on Cloud Computing*, WP 196, 1 July 2012; Lanois, P., 'Caught in the Clouds: The Web 2.0, Cloud Computing, and Privacy?,' *Northwestern Journal of Technology and Intellectual Property* (2010)(9), pp. 29–49; Pinguelo, F.M., and Muller, B.W., 'Avoid the Rainy Day: Survey of US Cloud Computing Caselaw,' *Boston College Intellectual Property & Technology Forum* (2011), 1–7; Kattan, I.R., 'Cloudy Privacy Protections: Why the Stored Communications Act Fails to Protect the Privacy of Communications Stored in the Cloud,' *Vandenburg Journal of Entertainment and Technology Law* (2010–2011)(13), pp. 617–656.

10 DeVere, A.C., 'Cloud Computing: Privacy Storm on the Horizon?' *Albany Law Journal* (2010)(20), pp. 365–373.

On-Site/Off-Site

15.08 Organisations have to tackle the issues presented by employees not just working on-site, but also travelling and working at home or other locations off-site. This can impact, for example, the security and security risks regarding the personal data collected and processed by the organisation. It also means that devices may be taken off-site and or that third party devices may exist and which are utilised to access the organisation's systems remotely.

Online Abuse

15.09 The increasingly evident problem of online abuse such as cyberbullying, trolling, defamation copying and utilising personal data to abuse and blackmail children, teenagers, etc, are issues which need to be considered by all organisations, as well as policy makers.

What is New?

15.10 The proposed Data Protection Regulation (DPR) will overhaul and modernise the data protection regime throughout the EU (and elsewhere). UK organisations will be affected and will have to prepare for the upcoming regime. What will the new data protection regime under the forthcoming EU DPR do? Some of the specific changes and updates for organisations are highlighted in Part 4 of the book.

The whole area of transfers of personal data outside of the EEA (TBDFs) is regularly changing, for example, as new countries are added to a white list of permitted export countries after having been examined on behalf of the EU Commission. There are also other changes such as contractual clauses and binding corporate rules (BCR). If an organisation needs to consider the possibility of data transfer exports to non-EEA countries, the current most up to data transfer rules should be assessed, as well as appropriate professional advices. It may be necessary to have specific legal contracts in place. These rules may also be sector specific for certain industries eg airlines flying to US from Europe. WP29 is also an important resource for organisations.

Further topical issues are regularly being analysed by WP29. These issues may be consulted at, http://ec.europa.eu/justice/policies/privacy/workinggroup/index_en.htm.

Conclusion

15.11   Data protection compliance is never a one size fits all or a single one time policy document. The nature of what amounts to personal data and the activities to which such data can be processed for are ever changing. Those within an organisation, therefore, need to be constantly alert to compliance issues and changes. Organisations also need to be constantly alert to new issues and dangers.

Part 2
Inward-Facing Organisational DP Obligations

Chapter 16

Processing Employee Personal Data

Introduction

16.01 Organisations sometimes focus on their customer related data compliance issues. It is important for new and existing organisations to look inwards, as there are important inward facing data protection obligations. Personal data includes the personal data of employees also. The employees of the organisation also have data subject rights which must be respected.

The variety of inward-facing data protection issues which organisations need to deal with on a daily basis is ever increasing. Some of these include whether to allow employees to bring their own devices (BYOD) into the organisation and to permit them to place organisational data onto such devices. If so, a particular BYOD policy needs to be considered and implemented.

The ability for organisations to track their employees off-site is also a new consideration. This can include technologies on board vehicles as well as satellite and location technologies. It also includes the organisation's (and employee's BYOD) smart phone (and other) devices.

Clearly, there are many more means by which new and or expanded sets of personal data may be collected and used by an organisation. However, it is equally necessary to consider the data protection compliance issues at the earliest opportunity.

Inward-Facing Issues

16.02 Organisations must comply with the data protection regime as regards their inward facing personal data. This primarily relates to the employees of the organisation. This raises a number of issues both in terms of whom are the employees, what personal data is being collected and processed, for what purpose or purposes, where is it located, does anyone else obtain the data, etc, and how the organisation ensures that it is data protection compliant in relation to same.

In relation to employee personal data, organisations must ensure compliance with the:

- Data Protection Principles;
- The Legitimate Processing Conditions;
- The Sensitive Personal Data Legitimate Processing Conditions;
- The security requirements.

Who Is Covered?

16.03 Who is covered by the inward facing organisational data protection obligations? While full time employees are the most obvious example, they are not the only ones. Organisations must consider the inward facing personal data of:

- Full time employees;
- Part time employees;
- Other workers such as temps and casual staff;
- Agency staff;
- Contractors;
- Ex-employees;
- Retired employees;
- Spouses;
- Job applicants, including unsuccessful applicants;
- Volunteers;
- Apprentices and trainees;
- Work experience staff.

Where an organisation engages with any of the above, it will have to ensure that the data protection regime is complied with.

Compliance with the Data Protection Principles

16.04 In dealing with employee personal data, as well as potential employees and any of the categories outlined above, it is necessary for the organisation to comply with the Data Protection Principles.

The eight Data Protection Principles apply in the work environment as well as elsewhere. Employee personal data must be:

(1) fairly and lawfully processed;
(2) processed for limited purposes;

(3) adequate, relevant and not excessive;
(4) accurate and up to date;
(5) not kept for longer than is necessary;
(6) processed in line with employee data protection rights;
(7) secure; and
(8) not transferred to other countries without adequate protection.[1]

All eight of the principles must be complied with. Compliance with the Data Protection Principles applies to all employee and inward-facing personal data collected and or processed by an organisation. It also applies regardless of registration requirements.

Ordinary Personal Data Legitimate Processing Conditions

16.05 When dealing with the above inward-facing categories of employees, agents, contractors, etc, the Legitimate Processing Conditions are required to be complied with, *in addition* to the Data Protection Principles.

Schedule 2 of the DPA contains the general Legitimate Processing Conditions eg employee non sensitive personal data. In order to comply with the general personal data Legitimate Processing Conditions, the organisation must fall within *one* of the following conditions, namely:

- The individual whom the personal data is about has consented to the processing.
- The processing is necessary:
  - in relation to a contract which the individual has entered into; or
  - because the individual has asked for something to be done so they can enter into a contract.
- The processing is necessary because of a legal obligation that applies to the organisation (except an obligation imposed by a contract);
- The processing is necessary to protect the individual's 'vital interests.' This condition only applies in cases of life or death, such as where an employee's medical history is disclosed to a hospital's A&E department treating them after a serious road accident;
- The processing is necessary for administering justice, or for exercising statutory, governmental, or other public functions;

1   See Schedule 1, Part 1, section 1 to the DPA.

- The processing is in accordance with the 'legitimate interests' condition.

DPA Schedule 2C contains conditions relevant for the purposes of the first Data Protection Principle, in particular the processing of personal data. It states:

1 The data subject has given his consent to the processing;
2 The processing is necessary:
   (a) for the performance of a contract to which the data subject is a party; or
   (b) for the taking of steps at the request of the data subject with a view to entering into a contract;
3 The processing is necessary for compliance with any legal obligation to which the data controller is subject, other than an obligation imposed by contract;
4 The processing is necessary in order to protect the vital interests of the data subject;
5 The processing is necessary:
   (a) for the administration of justice;
       (aa) for the exercise of any functions of either House of Parliament;
   (b) for the exercise of any functions conferred on any person by or under any enactment;
   (c) for the exercise of any functions of the Crown, a Minister of the Crown or a government department; or
   (d) for the exercise of any other functions of a public nature exercised in the public interest by any person.
6 (1) The processing is necessary for the purposes of legitimate interests pursued by the data controller or by the third party or parties to whom the data are disclosed, except where the processing is unwarranted in any particular case by reason of prejudice to the rights and freedoms or legitimate interests of the data subject;
   (2) The Secretary of State may by order specify particular circumstances in which this condition is, or is not, to be taken to be satisfied.

There are, therefore, six general Legitimate Processing Conditions. Frequently, an organisation would seek to fall within the legitimate interests condition above. These might be summarised as follows:

- The employee has given explicit consent;
- Processing necessary for performance of *contract* to which the employee is a party;

- Processing is necessary to take steps at request of the employee prior to entering into contract;
- Processing is necessary for compliance with legal obligation (other than contractual obligation);
- Necessary to prevent injury or other damage to health of the employee or serious loss or damage to property of the employee or to protect vital interests;
- Necessary for the administration of justice, performance of statutory function or function of public nature performed in public interest;
- Processing necessary for *legitimate interests* pursued by data controller except where unwarranted.

Legitimate Processing and Organisation's Employees

16.06 Unlike certain other areas, the legitimate processing of employee personal data does not require employee consent. However, many organisations would have originally expected and proceeded on the basis that consent was so required. They would have incorporated (deemed) consent clauses into employment contracts, etc.

As indicated above, DPA Schedule 2 enables organisations to rely upon the legitimate processing condition that processing is necessary for the purposes of *legitimate interests* pursued by the data controller or by the third party or parties to whom the data are disclosed, except where the processing is unwarranted in any particular case by reason of prejudice to the rights and freedoms or legitimate interests of the data subject.

An alternative could be to say that the processing is necessary as part of a contract to which the employee is a party, in particular the employment contract.

Sensitive Personal Data Legitimate Processing Conditions

16.07 Organisations may also feel the need on occasion to store and use sensitive personal data in relation to employees, such as medical and health data. In the case of sensitive personal data, an organisation must in addition to satisfying all of the Data Protection Principles, be able to comply or fall within one of the Sensitive Personal Data Legitimate Processing Conditions.

Schedule 3 to the DPA sets out conditions relevant for the purposes of the first Data Protection Principle in particular in relation to the processing of Sensitive Personal Data. In the context of employees and inward-facing personal data, it provides:

1   The employee data subject has given his or her explicit consent to the processing of the personal data;

2   (1)   The processing is necessary for the purposes of exercising or performing any right or obligation which is conferred or imposed by law on the data controller in connection with employment;

        (2)   The Secretary of State may by order,

            (a)   exclude the application of sub-paragraph (1) in such cases as may be specified; or

            (b)   provide that, in such cases as may be specified, the condition in sub-paragraph (1) is not to be regarded as satisfied unless such further conditions as may be specified in the order are also satisfied;

3   The processing is necessary:

    (a)   in order to protect the vital interests of the employee data subject or another person, in a case where,

        (i)   consent cannot be given by or on behalf of the employee data subject; or

        (ii)   the data controller cannot reasonably be expected to obtain the consent of the employee data subject; or

    (b)   in order to protect the vital interests of another person, in a case where consent by or on behalf of the employee data subject has been unreasonably withheld;

4   The processing:

    (a)   is carried out in the course of its legitimate activities by any body or association which,

        (i)   is not established or conducted for profit; and

        (ii)   exists for political, philosophical, religious or trade-union purposes;

    (b)   is carried out with appropriate safeguards for the rights and freedoms of data subjects;

    (c)   relates only to individuals who either are members of the body or association or have regular contact with it in connection with its purposes; and

    (d)   does not involve disclosure of the employee personal data to a third party without the consent of the employee data subject;

5   The information contained in the personal data has been made public as a result of steps deliberately taken by the employee data subject;

6   The processing:

(a) is necessary for the purpose of, or in connection with, any legal proceedings (including prospective legal proceedings);

(b) is necessary for the purpose of obtaining legal advice; or

(c) is otherwise necessary for the purposes of establishing, exercising or defending legal rights;

7 (1) The processing is necessary:

for the administration of justice;

(aa) for the exercise of any functions of either House of Parliament;

(b) for the exercise of any functions conferred on any person by or under an enactment; or

(c) for the exercise of any functions of the Crown, a Minister of the Crown or a government department;

(2) The Secretary of State may by order:

(a) exclude the application of sub-paragraph (1) in such cases as may be specified; or

(b) provide that, in such cases as may be specified, the condition in sub-paragraph (1) is not to be regarded as satisfied unless such further conditions as may be specified in the order are also satisfied;

7A (1) The processing:

(a) is either,

(i) the disclosure of sensitive personal data by a person as a member of an anti-fraud organisation or otherwise in accordance with any arrangements made by such an organisation; or

(ii) any other processing by that person or another person of sensitive personal data so disclosed; and

(b) is necessary for the purposes of preventing fraud or a particular kind of fraud;

(2) In this paragraph 'an anti-fraud organisation' means any unincorporated association, body corporate or other person which enables or facilitates any sharing of information to prevent fraud or a particular kind of fraud or which has any of these functions as its purpose or one of its purposes;

8 (1) The processing is necessary for medical purposes and is undertaken by,

(a) a health professional; or

(b) a person who in the circumstances owes a duty of confidentiality which is equivalent to that which would arise if that person were a health professional;

(2) In this paragraph 'medical purposes' includes the purposes of preventative medicine, medical diagnosis, medical research,

the provision of care and treatment and the management of healthcare services;

9   (1)   The processing,

      (a)   is of sensitive personal data consisting of information as to racial or ethnic origin;

      (b)   is necessary for the purpose of identifying or keeping under review the existence or absence of equality of opportunity or treatment between persons of different racial or ethnic origins, with a view to enabling such equality to be promoted or maintained; and

      (c)   is carried out with appropriate safeguards for the rights and freedoms of employee data subjects;

    (2)   The Secretary of State may by order specify circumstances in which processing falling within sub-paragraph (1)(a) and (b) is, or is not, to be taken for the purposes of sub-paragraph (1)(c) to be carried out with appropriate safeguards for the rights and freedoms of data subjects.

These Sensitive Personal Data Legitimate Processing conditions may be summarised as follows:

- The employee whom the sensitive personal data is about has given explicit consent to the processing;
- The processing is necessary so that the organisation can comply with employment law;
- The processing is necessary to protect the vital interests of,
  - the employee (in a case where the employee's consent cannot be given or reasonably obtained); or
  - another person (in a case where the individual's consent has been unreasonably withheld);
- The processing is carried out by a not-for-profit organisation and does not involve disclosing personal data to a third party, unless the employee consents. Extra limitations apply to this condition;
- The employee has deliberately made the information public;
- The processing is necessary in relation to legal proceedings, for obtaining legal advice; or otherwise for establishing, exercising or defending legal rights;
- The processing is necessary for administering justice, or for exercising statutory or governmental functions;
- The processing is necessary for medical purposes, and is undertaken by a health professional or by someone who is subject to an equivalent duty of confidentiality;

- The processing is necessary for monitoring equality of opportunity, and is carried out with appropriate safeguards for the rights of individuals.

Furthermore, regulations also set out further obligations in relation to the processing of sensitive personal data.

Sensitive Data Legitimate Processing and Organisation's Employees

16.08 However, where sensitive personal data is involved, the organisation may have to obtain consent, unless otherwise specifically permitted in relation to one of the other particular purpose conditions set out above.

Consent

16.09 If it is the case that none of the condition criteria apply or permit a specific data processing use, then the organisation must obtain appropriate consent.

In considering the legitimising criteria the organisation should pay particular attention to the conditional word 'necessary.' If not strictly necessary, and demonstrably so, in the event that it is ever necessary to justify it when subsequently queried, it means that it may be necessary to fall back to the consent criteria.

Explicit consent, for example, with sensitive personal data usage, can mean having to obtain written consent. There is also a reference to freely given consent. Where employee consent is utilised or required, an issue can sometimes arise as to whether it is voluntarily and freely given. If the employee feels forced into giving consent they, or the DPC, might subsequently say that the consent is invalid, thus compromising the legitimacy of the processing.

Compliance and Policies

16.10 It is essential for all organisations to implement appropriate written policies. These will vary, as there are different types of policy. In addition, each policy will be specifically tailored to meet the needs and circumstances of the particular organisation.

Once finalised, the policy or policies should be properly and effectively communicated to all employees. It may also have to be made available to others who work in or for the organisation eg contractors.

Those in the organisation with responsibility for dealing with personal data also need to be particularly familiarised with the policies, security measures, data protection processes, as well as effectively trained in relation to all aspects of data protection compliance.

As with all legal, business and organisational policies relating to regulatory compliance, data protection policies need to be regularly monitored and updated as requirement dictates. This can be because of legal changes, ICO guideline changes, business and activity changes, changing security and risk requirements, changing technology, etc.

ICO Codes

16.11 It is recommended that the organisation consult the most relevant ICO guidance and codes in terms of implementing, or tailoring, IT data processing and data protection compliance practices.[2]

Responsible Person for Data Protection Compliance

16.12 Organisations will have to appoint a particular identified person in the organisation to deal with and be responsible for all data protection processes and related compliance issues. This includes ensuring that the organisation is data protection compliant in accordance with the DPA and the ICO Employment Practices Code.[3]

In addition to a data protection supervisor or officer it is also recommended that an individual at Board level be appointed to be responsible for overseeing and dealing with data protection compliance within the organisation. The contemporary importance and significance of data protection ensures that it is now clearly a boardroom issue.

Responsibilities include ongoing compliance, policies, strategies, processes, training, monitoring, reviewing and updating, coordinating, engaging appropriate expertise and advices, audits, PbD, education, courses, notification and registration, incident response, etc as regards data protection.

---

2   ICO Employment Practices Code, available at http://www.ico.gov.uk/upload/ documents/library/data_protection/detailed_specialist_guides/employment_practices _code.pdf, accessed on 18 January 2013.
3   *Ibid.*

HR and Contracts

16.13 The organisation's contracts of employment need to incorporate appropriate notifications, consent clauses (only if appropriate), and references to the organisational policies relevant to data protection, such as corporate communications usage policies, internet policies, devices, security, breaches, etc. There may also be reference to where these policies are located and where the latest and most up to date version will always be available. This might be a staff handbook, intranet, etc.

These documents will all be different depending on the organisation, the sector and the data protection practices ie the types of personal data, what it is used for and why. Issues such as compliance, security and confidentiality should be emphasised.

Training

16.14 Staff induction sessions as well as ongoing staff training should all incorporate guidance in relation to dealing with and handling personal data.

Employee Handbooks

16.15 Most organisations provide an employee handbook to their employees. These handbooks should contain guidance and polices of data protection, corporate communications, usage policies, etc.

Notices, Communications, Internet, Intranet

16.16 All of these provide an opportunity for the organisation to set out and reinforce the organisational requirements regarding the data protection regime. These can be user friendly and instantaneous, and hence provide an easy means of notifying new and urgent changes, notices, etc.

HR Department

16.17 While the HR department or HR Director will be required to be familiar with data protection, the role and responsibility of operating data protection compliance is not a HR role. It needs to be someone outside of the employment and HR function. However, the person responsible for data protection will need to liaise regularly with the HR department, including training and keeping HR personnel up to date in relation to new developments in data protection compliance.

DPA: Employees and Security

16.18 The security of employee personal data is an essential obligation under the data protection regime.

DPA Sch 1, s 10 provides that the data controller must take reasonable steps to ensure the reliability of any employees of the organisation who have access to the personal data.

Lynda McDonald[4] refers to security indicating that the following would be required to be checked, namely:

- Access to buildings, computer rooms and offices where personal data is held;
- Access to computer and other equipment where unauthorised access could have a detrimental effect on security;
- That manual records are put away at night in locked filing cabinets before the cleaners arrive;
- That passwords are not written down so that others can access them;
- That strict rules are in force within the business about what personal information can be accessed by which organisations, for example, the information that line managers can access about their staff may be different to (and less than) that which an HR manager can access;
- That there is an efficient and effective security system in place to prevent employees from seeing other employee data;
- That mechanisms are in place to detect any breach of security, and procedures in place to investigate such breaches;
- That all staff have undergone training on the organisation's data protection policy and how it works in practice, either as part of their induction or at specialist sessions which are appropriate to their job role, position and function.[5]

Even where an employee is working off site or at home, or indeed travelling, it is still the organisation's responsibility to ensure appropriate security measures and processes are in place.

---

4   MacDonald, Lynda A.C., *Data Protection: Legal Compliance and Good Practice for Employers* (London: Tottel, 2008), pp. 11–12.

5   MacDonald, Lynda A.C., *Data Protection: Legal Compliance and Good Practice for Employers* (London: Tottel, 2008), pp. 11–12.

These scenarios are increasingly prominent but the organisation should ensure that they occur on a planned and permission basis. Unregulated activities enhance the level of risk as well as increasing the level on unknown, uncontrollable activities.

Access Requests by Employees

16.19 Employees are individuals and are hence able to rely upon their data protection rights, such as requesting a copy of the personal data relating to them. In the instance of an employee access request being made, the organisation should assess the request to see if the appropriate fee has been paid (£10.00) and whether any exemptions apply which would prevent a disclosure being made. In addition, while the employee's personal data may have to be disclosed, certain third party personal data should be taken out or redacted. It may also be the case that clarification may have to be obtained to further clarify what particular personal data is being sought. It should not be a mere mechanism to avoid so complying.

The access request must be complied with within forty calendar days.

MacDonald[6] refers to some examples of the types of employee related personal data that may relate to access requests, such as:

- Performance reviews or appraisals;
- Sickness records;
- Warnings or minutes of disciplinary interviews;
- Training records;
- Statements about pay;
- Emails or electronic documents of which they are the subject;
- Expressions of opinion regarding eg prospects for promotion.

Information relating to automated individual decisions regarding employees are also relevant and may be requested.

Conclusion

16.20 Organisations need to actively have considered data protection compliance issues and the recording of compliance even before an employee is engaged. Data protection and personal data arises at recruitment, selection and interview stages. The organisation must also

---

6   MacDonald, Lynda A.C., *Data Protection: Legal Compliance and Good Practice for Employers* (London: Tottel, 2008), p. 51.

note relevant policies. Unless data protection issues and policy issues are properly incorporated into the employment relationship, the organisation may be non-compliant. In addition, it may not be able to enforce and rely upon particular contract terms, policies, employee obligations, disciplinary rules and such like.

Chapter 17

Employee Data Protection Rights

Introduction

17.01 Just as other parties whose personal data are being collected and processed have data protection rights, employees also have data subject rights.

The Data Protection Rights of Employees

17.02 The rights of employees can be summarised as including:

- Right of access (s 7 DPA);
- Right to establish if personal data exists (s 7(1)(a) DPA);
- Right to be informed of the logic in automatic decision taking (s 7(1)(d);
- Right to prevent processing likely to cause damage or distress (s 18 DPA);
- Right to prevent processing for direct marketing (s 11 DPA);
- Right to prevent automated decision taking (s 12 DPA);
- Right in relation to exempt manual data (s 12A DPA);
- Right to compensation (s 13 DPA);
- Right to rectify inaccurate data (s 14 DPA);
- Right to rectification, blocking, erasure and destruction (s 14 DPA);
- Right to complain to ICO (see s 42 DPA);
- Right to go to court (see s 15 DPA).

Employee Access Right

17.03 Part II of the DPA refers to the rights of data subjects and others. In particular, s 7 refers to the right of access to personal data. This applies to employee data subjects. It is a data subject right.

Section 7(1) provides that subject to the following provisions of this section and to sections 8, 9 and 9A, an employee is entitled:

- to be informed by any data controller whether personal data of which that individual is the employee data subject are being processed by or on behalf of that data controller,
- if that is the case, to be given by the data controller a description of:
    - the personal data of which that individual is the employee data subject;
    - the purposes for which they are being or are to be processed; and
    - the recipients or classes of recipients to whom they are or may be disclosed,
- to have communicated to them in an intelligible form:
    - the information constituting any personal data of which that individual is the data subject; and
    - any information available to the data controller as to the source of those data; and
- where the processing by automatic means of personal data of which that employee is the data subject for the purpose of evaluating matters relating to them such as, for example, his performance at work, his creditworthiness, his reliability or his conduct, has constituted or is likely to constitute the sole basis for any decision significantly affecting them, to be informed by the data controller of the logic involved in that decision-taking.

Therefore, and employee is entitled to the above.

Section 7(2)A provides that a data controller is not obliged to supply any information under subsection (1) unless he has received:

- a request in writing; and
- except in prescribed cases, such fee (not exceeding the prescribed maximum) as he may require.

Section 7(3) provides that where a data controller:

- reasonably requires further information in order to satisfy them as to the identity of the person making a request under this section and to locate the information which that person seeks; and

- has informed them of that requirement,

the data controller is not obliged to comply with the request unless he is supplied with that further information.

Section 7(4) provides that where a data controller cannot comply with the request without disclosing information relating to another individual who can be identified from that information, he is not obliged to comply with the request unless:

- the other individual has consented to the disclosure of the information to the person making the request; or
- it is reasonable in all the circumstances to comply with the request without the consent of the other individual.

Section 7(5) provides that in sub-s (4) the reference to information relating to another individual includes a reference to information identifying that individual as the source of the information sought by the request; and that subsection is not to be construed as excusing a data controller from communicating so much of the information sought by the request as can be communicated without disclosing the identity of the other individual concerned, whether by the omission of names or other identifying particulars or otherwise.

Section 7(6) provides that in determining for the purposes of subsection (4)(b) whether it is reasonable in all the circumstances to comply with the request without the consent of the other individual concerned, regard shall be had, in particular, to:

- any duty of confidentiality owed to the other individual;
- any steps taken by the data controller with a view to seeking the consent of the other individual;
- whether the other individual is capable of giving consent; and
- any express refusal of consent by the other individual.

Section 7(7) provides that an individual making a request under this section may, in such cases as may be prescribed, specify that his request is limited to personal data of any prescribed description.

Section 7(8) provides that subject to sub-s (4), a data controller shall comply with a request under this section promptly and in any event before the end of the prescribed period beginning with the relevant day.

Section 7(9) provides that if a court is satisfied on the application of any person who has made a request under the foregoing provisions of this section that the data controller in question has failed to comply with the request in contravention of those provisions, the court may order them to comply with the request.

Section 7(10) also provides that in this section:

- 'prescribed' means prescribed by the Secretary of State by regulations;
- 'the prescribed maximum' means such amount as may be prescribed;
- 'the prescribed period' means forty days or such other period as may be prescribed;
- 'the relevant day,' in relation to a request under this section, means the day on which the data controller receives the request or, if later, the first day on which the data controller has both the required fee and the information referred to in subsection (3).

Section 7(11) provides that different amounts or periods may be prescribed under this section in relation to different cases.

Section 7(12) provides that a person is a relevant person for the purposes of subsection (4)(c) if he:

- is a person referred to in para 4(a) or (b) or para 8(a) or (b) of Sch 11;
- is employed by an education authority (within the meaning of para 6 of Schedule 11) in pursuance of its functions relating to education and the information relates to them, or he supplied the information in his capacity as such an employee; or
- is the person making the request.

Section 7(12) provides that a person is a relevant person for the purposes of sub-s (4)(c) if he:

- is a person referred to in para 1(p) or (q) of the Schedule to the Data Protection (Subject Access Modification) (Social Work) Order 2000; or
- is or has been employed by any person or body referred to in para 1 of that Schedule in connection with functions which are or have been exercised in relation to the data consisting of the information; or
- has provided for reward a service similar to a service provided in the exercise of any functions specified in paragraph 1(a)(i), (b), (c) or (d) of that Schedule,

and the information relates to them or he supplied the information in his official capacity or, as the case may be, in connection with the provision of that service.

Section 8 refers to provisions supplementary to s 7.

Section 8(1) provides that the Secretary of State may by regulations provide that, in such cases as may be prescribed, a request for information under any provision of subsection (1) of section 7 is to be treated as extending also to information under other provisions of that subsection.

Section 8(2) provides that the obligation imposed by s 7(1)(c)(i) must be complied with by supplying the data subject with a copy of the information in permanent form unless:

- the supply of such a copy is not possible or would involve disproportionate effort; or
- the data subject agrees otherwise,

and where any of the information referred to in s 7(1)(c)(i) is expressed in terms which are not intelligible without explanation the copy must be accompanied by an explanation of those terms.

Section 8(3) provides that where a data controller has previously complied with a request made under s 7 by an individual, the data controller is not obliged to comply with a subsequent identical or similar request under that section by that individual unless a reasonable interval has elapsed between compliance with the previous request and the making of the current request.

Section 8(4) provides that in determining for the purposes of sub-s (3) whether requests under s 7 are made at reasonable intervals, regard shall be had to the nature of the data, the purpose for which the data are processed and the frequency with which the data are altered.

Section 8(5) provides that s 7(1)(d) is not to be regarded as requiring the provision of information as to the logic involved in any decision-taking if, and to the extent that, the information constitutes a trade secret.

Section 8(6) provides that the information to be supplied pursuant to a request under section 7 must be supplied by reference to the data in question at the time when the request is received, except that it may take account of any amendment or deletion made between that time and the time when the information is supplied, being an amendment or deletion that would have been made regardless of the receipt of the request.

Section 8(7) provides that for the purposes of s 7(4) and (5) another individual can be identified from the information being disclosed if he can be identified from that information, or from that and any other information which, in the reasonable belief of the data controller, is likely to be in, or to come into, the possession of the data subject making the request.

Section 9 refers to the application of s 7 where data controller is credit reference agency.

Section 9(1) provides that where the data controller is a credit reference agency, s 7 has effect subject to the provisions of this section.

Section 9(2) provides that an individual making a request under s 7 may limit his request to personal data relevant to his financial standing, and shall be taken to have so limited his request unless the request shows a contrary intention.

Section 9(3) provides that where the data controller receives a request under s 7 in a case where personal data of which the individual making the request is the data subject are being processed by or on behalf of the data controller, the obligation to supply information under that section includes an obligation to give the individual making the request a statement, in such form as may be prescribed by the Secretary of State by regulations, of the individual's rights:

- under s 159 of the Consumer Credit Act 1974; and
- to the extent required by the prescribed form, under this Act.

Section 9A relates to unstructured personal data held by public authorities.

Section 9A(1) provides that in this section 'unstructured personal data' means any personal data falling within paragraph (e) of the definition of 'data' in s 1(1), other than information which is recorded as part of, or with the intention that it should form part of, any set of information relating to individuals to the extent that the set is structured by reference to individuals or by reference to criteria relating to individuals.

Section 9A(2) provides that public authority is not obliged to comply with sub-s (1) of s 7 in relation to any unstructured personal data unless the request under that section contains a description of the data.

Section 9A(3) provides that even if the data are described by the data subject in his request, a public authority is not obliged to comply with sub-s (1) of s 7 in relation to unstructured personal data if the authority estimates that the cost of complying with the request so far as relating to those data would exceed the appropriate limit.

Section 9A(4) provides that sub-s (3) does not exempt the public authority from its obligation to comply with para (a) of s 7(1) in relation to the unstructured personal data unless the estimated cost of complying with that paragraph alone in relation to those data would exceed the appropriate limit.

Section 9A(5) provides that in sub-s (3) and sub-s (4) 'the appropriate limit' means such amount as may be prescribed by the Secretary of State by regulations, and different amounts may be prescribed in relation to different cases.

Section 9A(6) provides that any estimate for the purposes of this section must be made in accordance with regulations under s 12(5) of the Freedom of Information Act 2000.

DPD95: Access Right

17.04 Article 12 of the DPD provides for the right of access, and states, Member States shall guarantee every data subject the right to obtain from the controller:

(a) without constraint at reasonable intervals and without excessive delay or expense:
- confirmation as to whether or not data relating to them are being processed and information at least as to the purposes of the processing, the categories of data concerned, and the recipients or categories of recipients to whom the data are disclosed;
- communication to them in an intelligible form of the data undergoing processing and of any available information as to their source;
- knowledge of the logic involved in any automatic processing of data concerning them at least in the case of the automated decisions referred to in Article 15(1);

(b) as appropriate the rectification, erasure or blocking of data the processing of which does not comply with the provisions of this Directive, in particular because of the incomplete or inaccurate nature of the data;

(c) notification to third parties to whom the data have been disclosed of any rectification, erasure or blocking carried out in compliance with (b), unless this proves impossible or involves a disproportionate effort.

DPR: Access Right

17.05 Article 15 of the DPR relates to the right of access for the data subject and provides:

1. The data subject shall have the right to obtain from the data controller at any time, on request, confirmation as to whether or not personal data relating to the data subject are being processed. Where such personal data are being processed, the data controller shall provide the following information:
   (a) the purposes of the processing;

    (b)   the categories of personal data concerned;

    (c)   the recipients or categories of recipients to whom the personal data are to be or have been disclosed, in particular to recipients in third countries;

    (d)   the period for which the personal data will be stored;

    (e)   the existence of the right to request from the data controller rectification or erasure of personal data concerning the data subject or to object to the processing of such personal data;

    (f)   the right to lodge a complaint to the Supervisory Authority and the contact details of the Supervisory Authority;

    (g)   communication of the personal data undergoing processing and of any available information as to their source;

    (h)   the significance and envisaged consequences of such processing, at least in the case of measures referred to in Article 20;

2.   The data subject shall have the right to obtain from the data controller communication of the personal data undergoing processing. Where the data subject makes the request in electronic form, the information shall be provided in electronic form, unless otherwise requested by the data subject;

3.   The Commission shall be empowered to adopt delegated acts in accordance with Article 86 for the purpose of further specifying the criteria and requirements for the communication to the data subject of the content of the personal data referred to in point (g) of para 1;

4.   The Commission may specify standard forms and procedures for requesting and granting access to the information referred to in para 1, including for verification of the identity of the data subject and communicating the personal data to the data subject, taking into account the specific features and necessities of various sectors and data processing situations. Those implementing acts shall be adopted in accordance with the examination procedure referred to in Article 87(2).

DPA: Right to Prevent Data Processing Likely to Cause Damage or Distress

17.06 Section 10 of the DPA refers to the right to prevent processing likely to cause damage or distress.

Section 10(1) provides that subject to sub-s (2), an individual is entitled at any time by notice in writing to a data controller to require the data controller at the end of such period as is reasonable in the circumstances to cease, or not to begin, processing, or processing for a specified purpose or in a specified manner, any personal data in respect of which he is the data subject, on the ground that, for specified reasons:

- the processing of those data or their processing for that purpose or in that manner is causing or is likely to cause substantial damage or substantial distress to them or to another; and
- that damage or distress is or would be unwarranted.

Section 10(2) provides that sub-s (1) does not apply:

- in a case where any of the conditions in paras 1 to 4 of Schedule 2 is met; or
- in such other cases as may be prescribed by the Secretary of State by order.

Section 10(3) provides that the data controller must within twenty-one days of receiving a notice under sub-s (1) ('the data subject notice') give the individual who gave it a written notice:

- stating that he has complied or intends to comply with the data subject notice; or
- stating his reasons for regarding the data subject notice as to any extent unjustified and the extent (if any) to which he has complied or intends to comply with it.

Section 10(4) provides that if a court is satisfied, on the application of any person who has given a notice under sub-s (1) which appears to the court to be justified (or to be justified to any extent), that the data controller in question has failed to comply with the notice, the court may order them to take such steps for complying with the notice (or for complying with it to that extent) as the court thinks fit.

Section 10(5) provides that the failure by a data subject to exercise the right conferred by sub-s (1) or s 11(1) does not affect any other right conferred on them by this part.

DPA: Right to Prevent Data Processing for DM

17.07   Section 11 of the DPA relates to the right to prevent processing for purposes of direct marketing (DM).

Section 11(1) provides that an individual is entitled at any time by notice in writing to a data controller to require the data controller at the end of such period as is reasonable in the circumstances to cease, or not to begin, processing for the purposes of direct marketing personal data in respect of which he is the data subject.

Section 11(2) provides that if the court is satisfied, on the application of any person who has given a notice under sub-s (1), that the data controller has failed to comply with the notice, the court may order them to take such steps for complying with the notice as the court thinks fit.

Section 11(2A) provides that this section shall not apply in relation to the processing of such data as are mentioned in para (1) of regulation 8 of the Telecommunications (Data Protection and Privacy) Regulations 1999 (processing of telecommunications billing data for certain marketing purposes) for the purposes mentioned in para (2) of that regulation.

Section 11(3) provides that in this section 'direct marketing' means the communication (by whatever means) of any advertising or marketing material which is directed to particular individuals.

DPA: Automated Decision Taking/Making Processes

17.08　Data controllers may not take decisions which produce legal effects concerning a data subject or which otherwise significantly affect a data subject and which are based solely on processing by automatic means of personal data and which are intended to evaluate certain personal matters relating to the data subject such as, performance at work, credit worthiness, reliability of conduct.

Section 12 provides for the rights in relation to automated decision-taking.

Section 12(1) provides that an individual is entitled at any time, by notice in writing to any data controller, to require the data controller to ensure that no decision taken by or on behalf of the data controller which significantly affects that individual is based solely on the processing by automatic means of personal data in respect of which that individual is the data subject for the purpose of evaluating matters relating to them such as, for example, his performance at work, his creditworthiness, his reliability or his conduct.

Section 12(2) provides that where, in a case where no notice under sub-s (1) has effect, a decision which significantly affects an individual is based solely on such processing as is mentioned in sub-s (1):

- the data controller must as soon as reasonably practicable notify the individual that the decision was taken on that basis; and
- the individual is entitled, within twenty-one days of receiving that notification from the data controller, by notice in writing to require the data controller to reconsider the decision or to take a new decision otherwise than on that basis.

Section 12(3) provides that the data controller must, within twenty-one days of receiving a notice under sub-s (2)(b) ('the data subject notice') give the individual a written notice specifying the steps that he intends to take to comply with the data subject notice.

Section 12(4) provides that a notice under sub-s (1) does not have effect in relation to an exempt decision; and nothing in sub-s (2) applies to an exempt decision.

Section 12(5) provides that in subsection (4) 'exempt decision' means any decision:

- in respect of which the condition in sub-s (6) and the condition in sub-s (7) are met; or
- which is made in such other circumstances as may be prescribed by the Secretary of State by order.

Section 12(6) provides that the condition in this sub-section is that the decision:

(a) is taken in the course of steps taken:
    (i) for the purpose of considering whether to enter into a contract with the data subject;
    (ii) with a view to entering into such a contract; or
    (iii) in the course of performing such a contract, or
(b) is authorised or required by or under any enactment.

Section 12(7) provides that the condition in this sub-section is that either:

- the effect of the decision is to grant a request of the data subject; or
- steps have been taken to safeguard the legitimate interests of the data subject (for example, by allowing them to make representations).

Section 12(8) provides that if a court is satisfied on the application of a data subject that a person taking a decision in respect of them (the 'responsible person') has failed to comply with sub-s (1) or (2)(b), the court may order the responsible person to reconsider the decision, or to take a new decision which is not based solely on such processing as is mentioned in subsection (1).

Section 12(9) provides that an order under sub-s (8) shall not affect the rights of any person other than the data subject and the responsible person.

Section 12 of the DPA provides Rights in relation to automated decision-taking. It states:

(1) An individual is entitled at any time, by notice in writing to any data controller, to require the data controller to ensure that no decision taken by or on behalf of the data controller which significantly affects that individual is based solely on the processing by automatic means of personal data in respect of which that individual is the data subject for the purpose of evaluating matters relating to them such as, for example, his performance at work, his creditworthiness, his reliability or his conduct;

(2) Where, in a case where no notice under sub-s (1) has effect, a decision which significantly affects an individual is based solely on such processing as is mentioned in sub-s (1):

    (a) the data controller must as soon as reasonably practicable notify the individual that the decision was taken on that basis; and

    (b) the individual is entitled, within twenty-one days of receiving that notification from the data controller, by notice in writing to require the data controller to reconsider the decision or to take a new decision otherwise than on that basis.

(3) The data controller must, within twenty-one days of receiving a notice under sub-s (2)(b) ("the data subject notice") give the individual a written notice specifying the steps that he intends to take to comply with the data subject notice;

(4) A notice under sub-s (1) does not have effect in relation to an exempt decision; and nothing in sub-s (2) applies to an exempt decision;

(5) In sub-s (4) "exempt decision" means any decision:

    (a) in respect of which the condition in subsection (6) and the condition in sub-s (7) are met; or

    (b) which is made in such other circumstances as may be prescribed by the Secretary of State by order;

(6) The condition in this sub-section is that the decision:

    (a) is taken in the course of steps taken,

        (i) for the purpose of considering whether to enter into a contract with the data subject,

        (ii) with a view to entering into such a contract; or

        (iii) in the course of performing such a contract; or

    (b) is authorised or required by or under any enactment;

(7) The condition in this sub-section is that either:

    (a) the effect of the decision is to grant a request of the data subject; or

    (b) steps have been taken to safeguard the legitimate interests of the data subject (for example, by allowing them to make representations);

(8) If a court is satisfied on the application of a data subject that a person taking a decision in respect of them ('the responsible person') has failed to comply with sub-s (1) or (2)(b), the court may order the responsible person to reconsider the decision, or to take a new decision which is not based solely on such processing as is mentioned in sub-s (1);

(9) An order under sub-s (8) shall not affect the rights of any person other than the data subject and the responsible person.

DPD95: Right Against Automated Individual Decisions

17.09 Article 15 of the DPD95 provides for the right against automated individual decisions. Article 15(1) states that Member States shall grant the right to every person not to be subject to a decision which produces legal effects concerning them or significantly affects them and which is based solely on automated processing of data intended to evaluate certain personal aspects relating to them, such as his performance at work, creditworthiness, reliability, conduct, etc.

Article 15(2) states that subject to the other Articles of this Directive, Member States shall provide that a person may be subjected to a decision of the kind referred to in paragraph 1 if that decision:

● is taken in the course of the entering into or performance of a contract, provided the request for the entering into or the performance of the contract, lodged by the data subject, has been satisfied or that there are suitable measures to safeguard his legitimate interests, such as arrangements allowing them to put his point of view; or

● is authorised by a law which also lays down measures to safeguard the data subject's legitimate interests.

DPD95: Right to Object

17.10 Article 14 of the DPD95 provides for the data subject's right to object. It states that, Member States shall grant the data subject the right:

● at least in the cases referred to in Article 7(e) and (f), to object at any time on compelling legitimate grounds relating to his particular situation to the processing of data relating to them, save where otherwise provided by national legislation. Where there is a justified objection, the processing instigated by the data controller may no longer involve those data;

- to object, on request and free of charge, to the processing of personal data relating to them which the data controller anticipates being processed for the purposes of direct marketing, or to be informed before personal data are disclosed for the first time to third parties or used on their behalf for the purposes of direct marketing, and to be expressly offered the right to object free of charge to such disclosures or uses.

It also provides that Member States shall take the necessary measures to ensure that data subjects are aware of the existence of the right.

DPD95: Right to Object

17.11 Section VII of the DPD refers to the data subject's right to object. Article 14 refers to the data subject's right to object. It provides that Member States shall grant the data subject the right:

- at least in the cases referred to in Article 7 (e) and (f), to object at any time on compelling legitimate grounds relating to his particular situation to the processing of data relating to them, save where otherwise provided by national legislation. Where there is a justified objection, the processing instigated by the data controller may no longer involve those data;
- to object, on request and free of charge, to the processing of personal data relating to them which the data controller anticipates being processed for the purposes of direct marketing, or to be informed before personal data are disclosed for the first time to third parties or used on their behalf for the purposes of direct marketing, and to be expressly offered the right to object free of charge to such disclosures or uses.

Member States shall take the necessary measures to ensure that data subjects are aware of the existence of the right referred to in the first subparagraph of (b).

DPD95: Right Against Automated Individual Decisions

17.12 Article 15 refers to automated individual decisions. Article 15(1) provides that Member States shall grant the right to every person not to be subject to a decision which produces legal effects concerning them or significantly affects them and which is based solely on automated processing of data intended to evaluate certain personal aspects relating to them, such as his performance at work, creditworthiness, reliability, conduct, etc.

Article 15(2) provides that subject to the other Articles of this Directive, Member States shall provide that a person may be subjected to a decision of the kind referred to in paragraph 1 if that decision:

● is taken in the course of the entering into or performance of a contract, provided the request for the entering into or the performance of the contract, lodged by the data subject, has been satisfied or that there are suitable measures to safeguard his legitimate interests, such as arrangements allowing them to put his point of view; or

● is authorised by a law which also lays down measures to safeguard the data subject's legitimate interests.

DPR: Rectification Right

17.13 Section 3 of the DPR refers to rectification and erasure. Article 16 refers to the right to rectification. It provides that the data subject shall have the right to obtain from the data controller the rectification of personal data relating to them which are inaccurate. The data subject shall have the right to obtain completion of incomplete personal data, including by way of supplementing a corrective statement.

DPR: Erasure Right/Right to be Forgotten

17.14 Article 17 of the DPR refers to the expanded right to be forgotten and to erasure. Article 17(1) provides that the data subject shall have the right to obtain from the data controller the erasure of personal data relating to them and the abstention from further dissemination of such data, especially in relation to personal data which are made available by the data subject while he or she was a child, where one of the following grounds applies:

● the data are no longer necessary in relation to the purposes for which they were collected or otherwise processed;

● the data subject withdraws consent on which the processing is based according to point (a) of Article 6(1), or when the storage period consented to has expired, and where there is no other legal ground for the processing of the data;

● the data subject objects to the processing of personal data pursuant to Article 19;

● the processing of the data does not comply with the Regulation for other reasons.

Article 17(2) provides that where the data controller referred to in para 1 has made the personal data public, it shall take all reasonable steps, including technical measures, in relation to data for the publication of which the data controller is responsible, to inform third parties which are processing such data, that a data subject requests them to erase any links to, or copy or replication of that personal data. Where the data controller has authorised a third party publication of personal data, the data controller shall be considered responsible for that publication.

Article 17(3) provides that the data controller shall carry out the erasure without delay, except to the extent that the retention of the personal data is necessary:

- for exercising the right of freedom of expression in accordance with Article 80;
- for reasons of public interest in the area of public health in accordance with Article 81;
- for historical, statistical and scientific research purposes in accordance with Article 83;
- for compliance with a legal obligation to retain the personal data by EU or Member State law to which the data controller is subject; Member State laws shall meet an objective of public interest, respect the essence of the right to the protection of personal data and be proportionate to the legitimate aim pursued;
- in the cases referred to in paragraph 4.

Article 17(4) provides that instead of erasure, the data controller shall restrict processing of personal data where:

- their accuracy is contested by the data subject, for a period enabling the data controller to verify the accuracy of the data;
- the data controller no longer needs the personal data for the accomplishment of its task but they have to be maintained for purposes of proof;
- the processing is unlawful and the data subject opposes their erasure and requests the restriction of their use instead;
- the data subject requests to transmit the personal data into another automated processing system in accordance with Article 18(2).

Article 17(5) provides that personal data referred to in para 4 may, with the exception of storage, only be processed for purposes of proof, or with the data subject's consent, or for the protection of the rights of another natural or legal person or for an objective of public interest.

Article 17(6) provides that where processing of personal data is restricted pursuant to para 4, the data controller shall inform the data subject before lifting the restriction on processing.

Article 17(7) provides that the data controller shall implement mechanisms to ensure that the time limits established for the erasure of personal data and/or for a periodic review of the need for the storage of the data are observed.

Article 17(8) provides that where the erasure is carried out, the data controller shall not otherwise process such personal data.

Article 17(9) provides that the Commission shall be empowered to adopt delegated acts in accordance with Article 86 for the purpose of further specifying:

- the criteria and requirements for the application of paragraph 1 for specific sectors and in specific data processing situations;
- the conditions for deleting links, copies or replications of personal data from publicly available communication services as referred to in paragraph 2;
- the criteria and conditions for restricting the processing of personal data referred to in paragraph 4.

DPA: Rectification, Blocking, Erasure and Destruction Rights

17.15 Section 14 of the DPA provides user rights in relation to rectification, blocking, erasure and destruction.

Section 14(1) provides that if a court is satisfied on the application of a data subject that personal data of which the applicant is the subject are inaccurate, the court may order the data controller to rectify, block, erase or destroy those data and any other personal data in respect of which he is the data controller and which contain an expression of opinion which appears to the court to be based on the inaccurate data.

Section 14(2) provides that sub-s (1) applies whether or not the data accurately record information received or obtained by the data controller from the data subject or a third party but where the data accurately record such information, then:

- if the requirements mentioned in para 7 of Part II of sch 1 have been complied with, the court may, instead of making an order under sub-s (1), make an order requiring the data to be supplemented by such statement of the true facts relating to the matters dealt with by the data as the court may approve; and
- if all or any of those requirements have not been complied with, the court may, instead of making an order under that subsection, make

such order as it thinks fit for securing compliance with those requirements with or without a further order requiring the data to be supplemented by such a statement as is mentioned in paragraph (a).

Section 14(3) provides that where the court:

- makes an order under sub-s (1); or
- is satisfied on the application of a data subject that personal data of which he was the data subject and which have been rectified, blocked, erased or destroyed were inaccurate,

it may, where it considers it reasonably practicable, order the data controller to notify third parties to whom the data have been disclosed of the rectification, blocking, erasure or destruction.

Section 14(4) provides that if a court is satisfied on the application of a data subject:

- that he has suffered damage by reason of any contravention by a data controller of any of the requirements of the DPA in respect of any personal data, in circumstances entitling them to compensation under s 13; and
- that there is a substantial risk of further contravention in respect of those data in such circumstances,

the court may order the rectification, blocking, erasure or destruction of any of those data.

Section 14(5) provides that where the court makes an order under sub-s (4) it may, where it considers it reasonably practicable, order the data controller to notify third parties to whom the data have been disclosed of the rectification, blocking, erasure or destruction.

Section 14(6) provides that in determining whether it is reasonably practicable to require such notification as is mentioned in sub-s (3) or (5) the court shall have regard, in particular, to the number of persons who would have to be notified.

DPD95: Rectification, Erasure and Blocking

17.16 Article 12, which relates to the right of access, also provides for rectification, erasure and blocking. It states that Member States shall guarantee every data subject the right to obtain from the data controller,

'(b) as appropriate the rectification, erasure or blocking of data the processing of which does not comply with the provisions of this Directive, in particular because of the incomplete or inaccurate nature of the data;

(c) notification to third parties to whom the data have been disclosed of any rectification, erasure or blocking carried out in compliance with (b), unless this proves impossible or involves a disproportionate effort.'

DPR: Rectification Right

17.17   Section 3 of the DPR refers to rectification and erasure. Article 16 relates to the right to rectification. It provides that the data subject shall have the right to obtain from the data controller the rectification of personal data relating to them which are inaccurate. The data subject shall have the right to obtain completion of incomplete personal data, including by way of supplementing a corrective statement.

DPR: Erasure Right/Right to be Forgotten

17.18   Article 17 of the DPR provides for the right to be forgotten and to erasure.

Article 17(1) provides that the data subject shall have the right to obtain from the controller the erasure of personal data relating to them and the abstention from further dissemination of such data, especially in relation to personal data which are made available by the data subject while he or she was a child, where one of the following grounds applies:

- the data are no longer necessary in relation to the purposes for which they were collected or otherwise processed;
- the data subject withdraws consent on which the processing is based according to point (a) of Article 6(1), or when the storage period consented to has expired, and where there is no other legal ground for the processing of the data;
- the data subject objects to the processing of personal data pursuant to Article 19;
- the processing of the data does not comply with the Regulation for other reasons.

Article 17(2) provides that where the data controller referred to in para 1 has made the personal data public, it shall take all reasonable steps, including technical measures, in relation to data for the publication of which the data controller is responsible, to inform third parties which are processing such data, that a data subject requests them to erase any links to, or copy or replication of that personal data. Where the data controller has authorised a third party publication of personal data, the data controller shall be considered responsible for that publication.

Article 17(3) provides that the data controller shall carry out the erasure without delay, except to the extent that the retention of the personal data is necessary:

- for exercising the right of freedom of expression in accordance with Article 80;
- for reasons of public interest in the area of public health in accordance with Article 81;
- for historical, statistical and scientific research purposes in accordance with Article 83;
- for compliance with a legal obligation to retain the personal data by EU or Member State law to which the data controller is subject; Member State laws shall meet an objective of public interest, respect the essence of the right to the protection of personal data and be proportionate to the legitimate aim pursued;
- in the cases referred to in paragraph 4.

Article 17(4) provides that instead of erasure, the data controller shall restrict processing of personal data where:

- their accuracy is contested by the data subject, for a period enabling the data controller to verify the accuracy of the data;
- the data controller no longer needs the personal data for the accomplishment of its task but they have to be maintained for purposes of proof;
- the processing is unlawful and the data subject opposes their erasure and requests the restriction of their use instead;
- the data subject requests to transmit the personal data into another automated processing system in accordance with Article 18(2).

Article 17(5) provides that personal data referred to in para 4 may, with the exception of storage, only be processed for purposes of proof, or with the data subject's consent, or for the protection of the rights of another natural or legal person or for an objective of public interest.

Article 17(6) provides that where processing of personal data is restricted pursuant to para 4, the data controller shall inform the data subject before lifting the restriction on processing.

Article 17(7) provides that the data controller shall implement mechanisms to ensure that the time limits established for the erasure of personal data and/or for a periodic review of the need for the storage of the data are observed.

Article 17(8) provides that where the erasure is carried out, the data controller shall not otherwise process such personal data.

Article 17(9) provides that the Commission shall be empowered to adopt delegated acts in accordance with Article 86 for the purpose of further specifying:

- the criteria and requirements for the application of paragraph 1 for specific sectors and in specific data processing situations;
- the conditions for deleting links, copies or replications of personal data from publicly available communication services as referred to in paragraph 2;
- the criteria and conditions for restricting the processing of personal data referred to in paragraph 4.

DPR: Right to Proportionality

17.19 Article 18 refers to the right to data portability. Article 18(1) provides that the data subject shall have the right, where personal data are processed by electronic means and in a structured and commonly used format, to obtain from the data controller a copy of data undergoing processing in an electronic and structured format which is commonly used and allows for further use by the data subject.

Article 18(2) provides that where the data subject has provided the personal data and the processing is based on consent or on a contract, the data subject shall have the right to transmit those personal data and any other information provided by the data subject and retained by an automated processing system, into another one, in an electronic format which is commonly used, without hindrance from the data controller from whom the personal data are withdrawn.

Article 18(3) provides that the Commission may specify the electronic format referred to in para 1 and the technical standards, modalities and procedures for the transmission of personal data pursuant to para 2. Those implementing acts shall be adopted in accordance with the examination procedure referred to in Article 87(2).

DPR: Right to Object and Profiling

17.20 Section 4 of the DPR refers to the right to object and profiling.

Article 19 of the DPR refers to the right to object. Article 19(1) provides that the data subject shall have the right to object, on grounds relating to their particular situation, at any time to the processing of personal data which is based on points (d), (e) and (f) of Article 6(1), unless the data controller demonstrates compelling legitimate grounds for the processing which override the interests or fundamental rights and freedoms of the data subject.

Article 19(2) provides that where personal data are processed for direct marketing purposes, the data subject shall have the right to object free of charge to the processing of their personal data for such marketing. This right shall be explicitly offered to the data subject in an intelligible manner and shall be clearly distinguishable from other information.

Article 19(3) provides that where an objection is upheld pursuant to paras 1 and 2, the data controller shall no longer use or otherwise process the personal data concerned.

DPR: Right re Profiling

17.21   Article 20 of the DPR refers to measures based on profiling. Article 20(1) provides that every natural person shall have the right not to be subject to a measure which produces legal effects concerning this natural person or significantly affects this natural person, and which is based solely on automated processing intended to evaluate certain personal aspects relating to this natural person or to analyse or predict in particular the natural person's performance at work, economic situation, location, health, personal preferences, reliability or behaviour.

Article 20(2) provides that subject to the other provisions of the Regulation, a person may be subjected to a measure of the kind referred to in para 1 only if the processing:

- is carried out in the course of the entering into, or performance of, a contract, where the request for the entering into or the performance of the contract, lodged by the data subject, has been satisfied or where suitable measures to safeguard the data subject's legitimate interests have been adduced, such as the right to obtain human intervention; or
- is expressly authorised by a EU or Member State law which also lays down suitable measures to safeguard the data subject's legitimate interests; or
- is based on the data subject's consent, subject to the conditions laid down in Article 7 and to suitable safeguards.

Article 20(3) provides that automated processing of personal data intended to evaluate certain personal aspects relating to a natural person shall not be based solely on the special categories of personal data referred to in Article 9.

Article 20(4) provides that in the cases referred to in para 2, the information to be provided by the data controller under Article 14 shall include information as to the existence of processing for a measure of the kind referred to in para 1 and the envisaged effects of such processing on the data subject.

Article 20(5) refers to the Commission shall be empowered to adopt delegated acts in accordance with Article 86 for the purpose of further specifying the criteria and conditions for suitable measures to safeguard the data subject's legitimate interests referred to in para 2.

DPA: Requiring Data Disclosure

17.22 Section 57 of the DPA prohibits an organisation from forcing or requiring the production by data subjects of personal data records to them in relation to recruitment or employment. For example, organisations may be prohibited from forcing employees to disclose genetic data.

Compensation for Data Subjects

17.23 Section 13 of the DPA refers to compensation for failure to comply with certain requirements.

Section 13(1) provides that an individual who suffers damage by reason of any contravention by a data controller of any of the requirements of the DPAis entitled to compensation from the data controller for that damage.

Article 13(2) provides that an individual who suffers distress by reason of any contravention by a data controller of any of the requirements of the DPA is entitled to compensation from the data controller for that distress if:

- the individual also suffers damage by reason of the contravention; or
- the contravention relates to the processing of personal data for the special purposes.

Section 13(3) provides that in proceedings brought against a person by virtue of the section it is a defence to prove that he had taken such care as in all the circumstances was reasonably required to comply with the requirement concerned.

Jurisdiction

17.24 Section 15 of the DPA refers to jurisdiction and procedure.

Section 15(1) provides that the jurisdiction conferred by ss 7 to 14 is exercisable by the High Court or a county court or, in Scotland, by the Court of Session or the sheriff.

Section 15(2) provides that for the purpose of determining any question whether an applicant under sub-s (9) of s 7 is entitled to the information which he seeks (including any question whether any relevant data are exempt from that section by virtue of Part IV) a court may require the information constituting any data processed by or on behalf of the data controller and any information as to the logic involved in any decision-taking as mentioned in s 7(1)(d) to be made available for its own inspection but shall not, pending the determination of that question in the applicant's favour, require the information sought by the applicant to be disclosed to them or his representatives whether by discovery (or, in Scotland, recovery) or otherwise.

Conclusion

17.25 Organisations need to respect the data protection rights of their employees, and even potential employees. In addition, particular care and attention needs to be paid to access requests from employees. Compliance is an ongoing issue as, for example, new changes and business practices will always present new challenges internally.

Chapter 18

Employee Considerations

Introduction

18.01 A large number of issues arise in terms of dealing with employee personal data, both in terms of audits, access, planning and compliance.

Contract

18.02 The starting point for informing and appraising employees of the importance of data protection, confidentiality and security in the organisation, and in relation to the employee's personal data should be to begin with the employment contract. There should be clauses referring to data protection and also to security.

Policies

18.03 There should also be policies relating to data protection furnished to all actual (and prospective) employees. These need to be updated regularly as the issues covered change constantly.

These policies may be separate or may be incorporated into an employee handbook.

Organisations need to be aware that if there is an important change made, unless this is notified and recorded to employees, the organisation may not be able to rely upon the changed clause. For example, if there is a new activity banned or regulated in an updated policy but the new policy is not notified to employees, it may be impossible to use the new policy to disciple an errant employee. They and their lawyers will strongly argue that the new policy was not notified, is not part of the employment relationship, and would be unlawful to apply. There are many examples of this problem occurring in practice.

Data Protection Policy

18.04 In considering what policies to implement, the organisation will have to consider many issues and separate policies, with data protection being just one. Others include health and safety, environmental, etc. The data protection policy will perhaps be the most dynamic given the wide range of data, individuals, processes, activities and technologies involved, and which are ever changing. Someone within the organisation needs to be responsible for examining and implementing ongoing changes as the requirement arises.

Internet Usage Policy

18.05 In addition to a general data protection policy, further specific data protection related policies may be required. The foremost of these relates to the employees' use of the internet on the organisation's systems.

Mobile and Device Usage Policies

18.06 Increasingly, employees use not just desktop computers but also laptops, mobile phones, smart phones, handheld devices, Blackberrys, iPads, etc. Unless explicitly incorporated into one of the above policies, then additional, or extended, policies need to be implemented. One particular issue for an organisation to consider is the employees' own devices, employee devices the bills for which are paid by the organisation, and devices supplied and paid for by the organisation. Somewhat different considerations may need to be applied.

Vehicle Use Policy

18.07 Vehicles must also be considered by organisations in terms of policy and employee usage. Increasingly tracking and other data from vehicles can be related to identified employees. Sometimes this may be as a result of the organisation furnishing a vehicle to the employee for work related business. However, this need not be the case. Even where an employee is using their own vehicle, it is possible for the organisation to be collecting or accessing personal data. In addition, organisations must also be aware that vehicle technology, both in-built and added, can result in greater collections of data, including personal data, being potentially accessible. Tracking, incident and accident reports, etc are just some examples. It is important for organisations to consider these personal data issues.

Transfers of Undertaking

18.08 Transfers of undertakings or TUPE[1], as it is known, refers to organisations being transferred to a new owner, whether in whole or in part. Situations like this are an everyday part of the commercial business environment.

The Transfer of Undertakings (Protection of Employment) Regulations 2006 provides certain protections for employees where the business is being transferred to a new owner. While primarily directed at the protection of employees' employment related rights, it is also noteworthy in that employee personal data will also be transferred to the new employer or organisation. There are various types of personal data to consider. The same rights, interests, terms, contracts, etc as applied with the old employer are to apply with the new employer, which included data protection user rights, and possibly corporate communications usage, etc.

Evidence

18.09 Disputes naturally arise between employers and employees from time to time. In such disputes the organisation may need to rely upon documents, information and materials which will contain personal data. While this may fit under the legitimate interests and legal interest provisions, employers should be careful about using less obvious personal data. This might include private emails communications over which an employee may argue privacy and confidentiality. Particular concerns arise in cases where covert monitoring has been used. Before commencing covert activities of this type the organisation should seek advices. Otherwise, any evidence gathered may possibly be ruled inadmissible subsequently.

Organisations also need to be careful in that computer, electronic and mobile data can change, expire and or be amended quickly. It can be important to act quickly. Advance policies, procedures and protocols assist in this regard.

---

1   See generally, MacDonald, Lynda A.C., *Data Protection: Legal Compliance and Good Practice for Employers* (London: Tottel, 2008), pp. 44–48.

Enforceability

18.10   An important issue for all organisations to consider is that if they ever wish to be able to discipline an errant employee, including up to dismissal, consequent upon their activities regarding personal data, internet usage, security breach, etc, the organisation needs to be able to point to a breach of an explicit contract or policy clause. If the breach is not explicit, or there is not written into the policy and contract, the employee can argue that there is no breach, perhaps regardless of the seriousness of the instant issue arising.

While online abuse is an issue to be dealt with, organisations need to be conscious of reputational damage from such incidents. However, they also need to consider what would happen if any of their employees are involved, whether by way of participation or orchestration, in an incident of abuse. One would have to consider what the contracts and policies say, as well as develop reaction strategies.

Conclusion

18.11   These are all issues that need to be addressed well in advance of an incident arising. It may be too late to start implementing policies, etc, after the event.

Employee data protection compliance is a complicated and ongoing obligation for organisations. It also needs to involve the data protection officers, appropriate board member, human resources, IT personnel and legal. On occasion, others may also have to become involved also.

Chapter 19

Employee Monitoring Issues

Introduction

19.01   One of the more contentious areas of employee data protection practice relates to the issue of the monitoring of employee email, internet, etc usage.

One of the reasons is that employers may not be familiar enough with their obligations under the data protection regime. Employers are concerned at certain risks that can arise as result of the activities of employees in the workplace but sometimes proceed without considering data protection.

Sample Legal Issues Arising

19.02   Some examples of the legal issues and concerns that can arise for employers and organisations as a result of the actions of their employees include:

- Vicarious Liability;
- Defamation;
- Copyright infringement;
- Confidentiality breaches and leaks;
- Data protection;
- Contract;
- Inadvertent contract formation;
- Harassment;
- Abuse;
- Discrimination;
- Computer crime;
- Interception offences;
- Criminal damage;

- Data loss;
- Data damage;
- Computer crime;
- Criminal damage;
- eCommerce law;
- Arms and dual use good export restrictions;
- Non-fatal offences against the person;
- Child pornography;
- Policies;
- On-site/off-site
- Bring your own device (BYOD), etc;
- Online abuse;
- Etc.

These are examples of an expanding list of concerns for organisations. Obviously, some of these will be recalibrated in importance depending on the type of organisation, the business sector and what its activities are. Confidentiality, for example, may be critically important for certain organisations, but less important for other organisations.

Employee Misuse of the Email, Internet, Etc

19.03 Even before the recent increase in data breach and data loss examples, there is a significant number of examples where problems have arisen for organisations as a result of the activities of certain employees. Increasingly, organisations face the problem that the activity of an errant employee on the internet, television or social networks can go viral instantly on a global scale, with adverse reputational damage for the organisation.

There are many instances where organisations have felt the need to dismiss employees. Some examples include Norwich EU Healthcare; Lois Franxhi; Royal & Sun Alliance Liverpool (77); C&W Birmingham (6); Rolls Royce Bristol (5); Claire Swire/Bradley Chait; Ford; Weil Gotshal; Sellafield, etc. As these instances are ever expanding it would be impossible to provide a definitive list.

The frequency and scale of recent breaches of security eg Sony Playstation (70 million individual's personal data[1] and 25 million in

---

1   See, for example, Martin, G., "Sony Data Loss Biggest Ever," *Boston Herald*, 27 April, 2011, available at http://bostonherald.com/business/technology/general/view/2011_0427sony_data_loss_biggest_ever, accessed on 22 August, 2012.

another[2]) make the topicality and importance of data security compliance ever more important. The largest UK data loss appears to be from Revenue and Customs loss of discs with the names, dates of birth, bank and address details for 25 million individuals.[3] Marks and Spencer was also involved in a data breach.

There are many new UK cases involving substantial fines for data protection breaches. The Brighton and Sussex University Hospitals NHS Trust had a fine of £325,000 imposed by the ICO in relation to a data loss incident.[4] Zurich Insurance was fined £2.3m for losing data in relation to 46,000 individual customers.[5] Sony was fined £250,000.

HP suspended 150 employees in one instance, which is one of the potential actions available.

Prudential was also fined in relation to the mishandling of personal data, while a Barclays employee was fined in court for personal use and access to customer account personal data.

In a more creative solution Ford issued a deletion amnesty to 20,000 employees to delete objected to material before a new or amended policy would kick in.

We now look at some of the legal concerns referred to above in greater detail.

Contract

19.04 It is possible for employees to agree and enter into contract via electronic communications. This is increasingly a concern since the legal recognition of electronic contract in the eCommerce legislation.

This can include the inadvertent creation of legally binding contracts for the organsiation.

---

2 See, for example, Arthur, C., 'Sony Suffers Second Data Breach With Theft of 25m More User Details,' *Guardian*, 3 May, 2011, available at http://www.guardian.co.uk/technology/blog/2011/may/03/sony-data-breach-online-entertainment, accessed on 22 August, 2012.

3 See, for example, 'Brown Apologises for Record Loss, Prime Minister Gordon Brown has said he "Profoundly Regrets" the Loss of 25 Million Child Benefit Records,' *BBC*, 21 November, 2007, available at http://news.bbc.co.uk/2/hi/7104945.stm, accessed on 22 August, 2011.

4 See, for example, 'Largest Ever Fine for Data Loss Highlights Need for Audited Data Wiping,' *ReturnOnIt*, available at http://www.returnonit.co.uk/largest-ever-fine-for-data-loss-highlights-need-for-audited-data-wiping.php, accessed on 22 August, 2012.

5 See, for example, Oates, J., 'UK Insurer Hit With Biggest Ever Data Loss Fine,' *The Register*, 24 August, 2010, available at http://www.theregister.co.uk/2010/08/24/data_loss_fine/, accessed on 22 August, 2012. This was imposed by the Financial Services Authority (FSA).

In addition, it is possible that an employee may create or agree particular contract terms, delivery dates, etc, electronically which they would not otherwise do.

These can be contracts, or terms, which the organisation would not like to be bound by.

It is also possible that breach of contract issues could arise.

Employment Equality

19.05   It can be illegal to discriminate, or permit discrimination, on grounds of, for example:

- Gender;
- Race;
- Age;
- Sexual Orientation;
- Family Status;
- Religious Beliefs;
- Disability;
- Member of minority groups.

Instances of such discrimination can occur on the organisations computer systems. Even though the organisation may not be initially aware of the instance, it can still have legal consequences.

Harassment

19.06   Harassment via the organisation's computer systems is also something which could cause consequences for an organisation. Examples could include the circulation of written words, pictures or other material which a person may reasonably regard as offensive. The organisation could be held liable for employees' discriminatory actions unless it took reasonable steps to prevent them, or to deal with them appropriately once they arise. See Protection from Harassment Act 1997.

Online Abuse

19.07   This is a growing problem. However, it is also an issue for organisations when their employees are the victims of perpetrators of online abuse. It is only a matter of time before organisations are sued for the actions of their employees using the organisation's systems.

Organisations can also assist in tackling these issues, and some indeed have more of an ability to do so than others.

Child Pornography

19.08   There is a serious risk and concern for organisations where this could occur on the organisation's computer systems or devices. See, for example, the Protection of Children Act of 1978, Criminal Justice Act of 1988, and the Criminal Justice and Public Order Act of 1994.

Dealing with the Employee Risks

19.09   It is important for all organisations to engage in a process of risk assessment of exposures which can be created as a result of their employee's use of its computer systems and devices.

Organisations should:

- Identify the areas of risk;
- Assess and evaluate those risks;
- Engage in a process to eliminate/reduce the risks identifies as appropriate.
- Formalising an overall body of employee corporate communications usage policies;
- Implement appropriate and lawful technical solutions appropriate to dealing with the identified risks;
- Implement an ongoing strategy to schedule reviews of the new and emerging risks, and to update and or implement appropriate procedures and policies, including the existing employee corporate communications usage policies.

Employee Corporate Communications Usage Policies

19.10   Given the general risks, and the risks specific to an organisation identified in a review process, it is critical that the organisation implement appropriate policies in an overall body of employee corporate communications usage policies.

It is important to note that there is no one fixed solution, or one single policy on its own which is sufficient to deal with these issues. Equally, a single policy on its own would not be sufficient to give comfort to the organisation in terms of (a) dealing with the risks and issues, and (b) ensuring that the organisation has implemented suffi-cient policies that allows it to act appropriately to meet specific risks, including disposal, as they arise.

For example, if an organisation discovers a particular unauthorised activity on its computer systems undertaken by one of its employees, eg illegal file sharing an employee hosting an illegal gambling website on its servers, it may decide that it wishes to dismiss the errant employee. But can it legally dismiss the employee? In the first instance, the organisation should ideally be in the position of being able to point to a specific clause in the employees written contract of employment and a specific breach, or breaches, of one or more of the organisation's employee corporate communications usage policies.

If it can, then the likelihood is that the organisation's legal advisors would be comfortable recommending that the dismissal is warranted, justified and lawful. However, if the answer is no, in that there is no written clause which is clearly breached as a result of the specific activities, even though carried out during the hours of employment, at the organisation's office, on the organisations computer system and utilising the organisation's computer servers, the organisation would not have any legal comfort in dismissing the employee.

The organisation may not be able to obtain pro-dismissal legal advices. If the company decided to proceed with the dismissal in any event it could run the legal risk that the employee may decide to legally challenge the dismissal under employment law. The employee would be assisted in that there is no express written clause which is breached. Unfortunately, the organisation may have to defend such an action on the basis of common law or implied obligations and duties owed by the employee. There may be no guarantee of success.

Focus of Organisational Communications Usage Policies

19.11 Organisations have a need for a comprehensive suite of organi-sational communications usage policies. This includes use of the organisations devices, telephone, voicemail, email and Internet. The policies need to address:

- Telephone;
- Email;
- Internet;
- Mobile and portable devices;
- Home and off-site usage;
- Vehicle usage.

This will involve and ongoing task, not just a one off exercise. It also needs coordinated team responsibility.

Key Issues to Organisational Communications Usage Policies

19.12 The key aspects to consider in relation to the employee corporate communications usage policies, include:

- Ownership;
- Usage;
- Authorisation;
- Confidentiality;
- Authentication;
- Retention and Storage;
- Viruses;
- Disciplinary Matters;
- Security;
- Awareness;
- Transparency.

These will vary depending on each organisation.

From a data protection regime perspective, one of the key issues for an organisation is the ability to monitor employees when needed.

Data Protection and Employee Monitoring

19.13 Organisations may wish to monitor for various reasons. Some of these include:

- Continuity of operations during staff illness;
- Maintenance;
- Preventing/investigating allegations of misuse;
- Assessing/verifying compliance with software licensing obligations;
- Complying with legal and regulatory requests for information;
- Etc.

Organisations may also wish to monitor in order to prevent risks and to identify problems as they arise. When issues arise they will wish to deal appropriately with the employee.

Employers and agencies recruiting for them need to carefully consider the legality of internet and social networking monitoring of employees and applicants. It is a growing practice by all accounts, and appears more permissible in the US than the EU. However, organisations should not assume that they are permitted to monitor, records, keep files, and make decisions based upon personal information and personal data gathered online unknown to the individual employee or applicant.[6]

The issue of the right to privacy of the employee and the rights and interests of the organisation arise. The issue of the right to privacy is a complex subject beyond the scope of this discussion. However, it is an expanding area, particularly after the introduction of the Human Rights Act 1998.[7] Monitoring raises interlinking issues of privacy, human rights and data protection.

Human Right

19.14 The Human Rights Act 1998[8] means that the European Convention for the Protection of Human Rights and Fundamental Freedoms[9] is now incorporated into and applicable in the UK.

This means that Article 8 of European Convention for the Protection of Human Rights and Fundamental Freedoms is an important consideration. It provides that everyone has right to private and family life, and their home and correspondence. It states that:

(1) Everyone has the right to respect for his private and family life, his home and his correspondence;

(2) There shall be no interference by a public authority with the

---

6   See, for example, Brandenburg, C., 'The Newest Way to Screen Job Applicants: A Social Networker's Nightmare,' Federal Communications Law Journal (2007–2008)(60), p. 597; Gersen, D., Your Image, Employers Investigate Job Candidates Online More than Ever. What can You Do to Protect Yourself?' Student Law (2007–2008)(36), p. 24; Levinson, A.R., 'Industrial Justice: Privacy Protection for the Employed,' Cornell Journal of Law and Public Policy (2009)(18), pp. 609–688; Byrnside, I., 'Six Degrees of Separation: The Legal Ramifications of Employers Using Social Networking Sites to Research Applicants,' Vanderbilt Journal of Entertainment and Technology Law (2008)(2), pp. 445–477; and Maher, M., 'You've Got Messages, Modern Technology Recruiting Through text Messaging and the Intrusiveness of Facebook,' Texas Review of Entertainment and Sports Law (2007)(8), pp. 125–151.

7   Human Rights Act, 1998, available at http://www.legislation.gov.uk/ukpga/1998/42/contents, accessed on 18 January 2013.

8   Human Rights Act, 1998, available at http://www.legislation.gov.uk/ukpga/1998/42/contents, accessed on 18 January 2013.

9   Available at http://www.echr.coe.int/NR/rdonlyres/D5CC24A7-DC13–4318-B457–5C9014916D7A/0/CONVENTION_ENG_WEB.pdf, accessed on 18 August, 2012. See also Balla, R., 'Constitutionalism – Reform on Data Protection Law and Human Rights,' Cerentul Juridic (2011)(47), pp. 61–74.

exercise of this right except such as is in accordance with the law and is necessary in a democratic society in the interests of national security, public safety or the economic well-being of the country, for the prevention of disorder or crime, for the protection of health or morals, or for the protection of the rights and freedoms of others.[10]

The *Halford* case is an example of the interface of human rights and data protection. The Leveson inquiry press hacking is also relevant.

Application of Data Protection Regime

19.15 In terms of employee monitoring, employers are entitled to exercise reasonable control and supervision over their employees and their use of organisational resources.

Employers are also entitled to promulgate policies to protect their property and good name and to ensure that they do not become inadvertently liable for the mis-behaviour of employees.

Equally, however, employees do retain privacy rights and data protection rights that must be respected by the organisation.

Organisations must consider:

- The culture of organisation;
- Whether there is understanding and expectation that employees can use the organisation's computers for personal use;
- Whether the organisation accessing the employee's communications without permission would be unfair and unlawful obtaining.

Monitoring involves careful consideration of policy, practice as well as interrelated legal issues of Privacy/Human Rights/Data Protection.

Monitoring or accessing employee emails or tracking of employee web browsing without permission would likely be unfair obtaining. It is important, therefore, that organisations have appropriate mechanisms and policies to reduce the risks, and then also to deal with issues as they arise. Reactively responding and trying to set up policies once a problem has arisen should be avoided. As pointed out above, if it is not explicitly in place before the incident, then a bad policy cannot be relied upon in invoking particular terms against the employee.

---

10   Available at http://www.echr.coe.int/NR/rdonlyres/D5CC24A7-DC13–4318-B457–5C9014916D7A/0/CONVENTION_ENG_WEB.pdf, accessed on 18 January 2013.

ILO Code

19.16 Organisations should also consider the ILO code recommendations. The ILO Code of Practice on Protection of Workers Personal Data[11] recommends that:

- Employees must be informed in advance of reasons, time schedule, methods and techniques used and the personal data collected;
- The monitoring must minimise the intrusion on privacy of employees;
- Secret monitoring must be in conformity with legislation or on foot of suspicion of criminal activity or serious wrongdoing;
- Continuous monitoring should only occur if required for health and safety or protection of property.

WP29: Processing in the Employment Context

19.17 The WP29 has long been concerned about employee monitoring and surveillance issues in terms of privacy and personal data. It issued an Opinion in September 2001 entitled Opinion 8/2001 on the Processing of Personal Data in the Employment Context.[12] It states that 'no business interest may ever prevail on the principles of transparency, lawful processing, legitimisation, proportionality, necessity and others contained in data protection laws.'

WP29 states that when processing workers' personal data, employers should always bear in mind fundamental data protection principles such as the following:

- FINALITY: Data must be collected for a specified, explicit and legitimate purpose and not further processed in a way incompatible with those purposes;
- TRANSPARENCY: As a very minimum, workers need to know which data is the employer collecting about them (directly or from other sources), which are the purposes of processing operations envisaged or carried out with these data presently or in the future. Transparency is also assured by granting the data subject the right

---

11 Available at http://www.ilo.org/wcmsp5/groups/public/—ed_protect/—protrav/—safework/documents/normativeinstrument/wcms_107797.pdf, accessed on 18 January 2013.
12 Opinion 8/2001 on the processing of personal data in the employment context. Available at http://ec.europa.eu/justice/policies/privacy/workinggroup/wpdocs/2001_en.htm, accessed on 18 January 2013.

to access to his/her personal data and with the data controllers' obligation of notifying supervisory authorities as provided in national law;

- LEGITIMACY: The processing of workers' personal data must be legitimate. Article 7 of the Directive lists the criteria making the processing legitimate;
- PROPORTIONALITY: The personal data must be adequate, relevant and not excessive in relation to the purposes for which they are collected and/or further processed. Assuming that workers have been informed about the processing operation and assuming that such processing activity is legitimate and proportionate, such a processing still needs to be fair with the worker;
- ACCURACY AND RETENTION OF THE DATA: Employment records must be accurate and, where necessary, kept up to date. The employer must take every reasonable step to ensure that data inaccurate or incomplete, having regard to the purposes for which they were collected or further processed, are erased or rectified;
- SECURITY: The employer must implement appropriate technical and organisational measures at the workplace to guarantee that the personal data of his workers is kept secured. Particular protection should be granted as regards unauthorised disclosure or access;
- AWARENESS OF THE STAFF: Staff in charge or with responsibilities in the processing of personal data of other workers need to know about data protection and receive proper training. Without an adequate training of the staff handling personal data, there could never be appropriate respect for the privacy of workers in the workplace.[13]

In relation to consent the WP29 adds that it has taken the view that where as a necessary and unavoidable consequence of the employment relationship an employer has to process personal data it is misleading if it seeks to legitimise this processing through consent.[14] Reliance on consent should be confined to cases where the worker has a genuine free choice and is subsequently able to withdraw the consent without detriment.[15]

13 Available at http://ec.europa.eu/justice/policies/privacy/docs/wpdocs/2001/wp48en.pdf, accessed on 18 January 2013.
14 *Ibid.*
15 *Ibid.*

WP29: Electronic Communications

19.18   The WP29 also issued an opinion in 2008 on the review of the Directive 2002/58/EC on privacy and electronic communications (e-Privacy Directive).[16] It was entitled Opinion 2/2008 on the review of the Directive 2002/58/EC on privacy and electronic communications (ePrivacy Directive) and was adopted on 15 May, 2008.

Under the heading Privacy by Design (PbD) it states that it advocates the application of the principle of *data minimisation* and the deployment of Privacy Enhancing Technologies (PETs) by data controllers. It also calls upon European legislators to make provision for a re-enforcement of said principle, by reiterating Recitals 9 and 30 of the ePrivacy Directive in a new paragraph in Article 1 of this Directive.[17]

It also notes that Article 5(1) imposes an obligation to ensure confidentiality of communications irrespective of the nature of the network and whether the communication crosses borders to non-EU member states.[18]

Electronic communications were also considered in WP29 Opinion 8/2006 on the review of the regulatory Framework for Electronic Communications and Services, with focus on the ePrivacy Directive.[19]

The WP29 also issued a working document on the surveillance of electronic communications in the workplace on 29 May 2002.[20]

It also issued Opinion 4/2007 on the concept of personal data which is also relevant in considering the definition of personal data.[21]

In relation to employee health records it is worth examining Working Document on the processing of personal data relating to health in electronic health records (EHR).[22]

---

16   Opinion 2/2008 on the review of the Directive 2002/58/EC on privacy and electronic communications (ePrivacy Directive), available at http://ec.europa.eu/justice/policies/privacy/docs/wpdocs/2008/wp150_en.pdf, accessed on 18 January 2013.

17   *Ibid*, p. 6.

18   *Ibid*.

19   Available at http://ec.europa.eu/justice/policies/privacy/docs/wpdocs/2006/wp126_en.pdf, accessed on 18 January 2013.

20   Working document on the surveillance of electronic communications in the workplace, WP 55, adopted on 29 May, 2002, available at http://ec.europa.eu/justice/policies/privacy/docs/wpdocs/2002/wp55_en.pdf, accessed on 18 January 2013.

21   Available at http://ec.europa.eu/justice/policies/privacy/docs/wpdocs/2007/wp136_en.pdf, accessed 18 January 2013.

22   Available at http://ec.europa.eu/justice/policies/privacy/docs/wpdocs/2007/wp131_en.pdf, accessed on 18 January 2013.

When outsourcing and dealing with data processors it is worth considering Opinion 1/2010 on the concepts of data 'controller' and data 'processor.'[23]

In relation to video surveillance, the WP29 issued Opinion 4/2004 on the Processing of Personal Data by means of Video Surveillance.[24]

Employment Contracts, Terms, Policies

19.19   As indicated above, organisations need to consider:

- Whether the contract provision been properly incorporated?;
- Issues of limitation of liability;
- Issues of exclusion of warranties;
- Disclaimers;
- Graduated disclaimers;
- Ongoing risk assessment;
- Continual review and updating.

Registration Requirements

19.20   The data protection regime imposes registration requirements with the ICO.

The ICO sets out the following guidance questions in relation to assessing an organisation's registration requirements, namely:

- Is the organisation processing personal information?;
- Is the organisation processing on computer?;
- Is the organisation a data controller?;
- Is the organisation only processing personal information for personal, family or household affairs (including recreational purposes)?;
- Is the organisation processing personal information for any of the following purposes?;
- Is the organisation only processing personal information to maintain a public register?;
- Is the organisation a not-for-profit organisation?;

23 Available at http://ec.europa.eu/justice/policies/privacy/docs/wpdocs/2010/wp169_en.pdf, accessed on 18 January 2013.
24 Available at http://ec.europa.eu/justice/policies/privacy/docs/wpdocs/2004/wp89_en.pdf, accessed on 18 January 2013.

- As a not-for-profit organisation is all of the processing covered by the following descriptions?;
- The organisation may not have to notify if the only processing carried out is for one or more of these purposes:
  - Staff administration;
  - Advertising, marketing and public relations;
  - Accounts and records;
- The organisation does not have to notify if processing for the purpose of judicial functions.[25]

The ICO also asks these guidance questions:

- Does the organisation really need this information about an individual?;
- Does the organisation know what it is going to use it for?;
- Do the employees whose information the organisation has know that it has got it, and are they likely to understand what it will be used for?;
- If the organisation is asked to pass on personal information, would the people about whom the organisation hold information expect the organisation to do this?;
- Is the organisation satisfied that the information is being held securely, whether on paper or on computer?;
- Is the organisation website secure?;
- Does the organisation need to notify the ICO, and if so, is the notification up to date?[26]

The ICO has also issued a useful data protection notification handbook, *A Complete Guide to Notification*.[27] This is available online.

Registration Exemptions

19.21 The ICO advises that the following may have exemption from registration:

- Data controllers who only process personal information for:
  - staff administration (including payroll);

---

25 Available at http://ec.europa.eu/justice/policies/privacy/docs/wpdocs/2004/wp89_en.pdf, accessed on 18 January 2013, pp. 11–26.

26 Available at http://ec.europa.eu/justice/policies/privacy/docs/wpdocs/2004/wp89_en.pdf, accessed on 18 January 2013, pp. 29–30.

27 Available at http://www.ico.gov.uk/for_organisations/data_protection/notification/need_to_notify.aspx, accessed on 18 January 2013.

- advertising, marketing and public relations (in connection with their own business activity); and
- accounts and records;
- Some not-for-profit organisations;
- Processing personal information for personal, family or household affairs (including recreational purposes);
- Maintenance of a public register;
- Processing personal information for judicial functions;
- Processing personal information without an automated system such as a computer.[28]

However, even if exempt from registration, the other obligations and compliance rules set out in the data protection regime still apply once there is personal data being processed.

Registration Issues

19.22 Some of the registration, and registration planning, issues to consider are:

- The data controller;
- The legal entity of the data controller;
- The categories of general personal data collected and processed;
- The categories of sensitive personal data collected and processed;
- The purposes and uses for the collection and processing;
- Where there are two or more related purposes, separate registration details must be supplied;
- Where there are two or more unrelated purposes, separate registrations may be required;
- Whether there are any data processors involved;
- Location of personal data;
- Trans-border data flows with the personal data;
- Disclosures of personal data to third parties, if so occurring,
- Security requirements apply;
- Annual renewal;
- Update if there are significant changes.

---

28 A Brief Guide to Notification, ICO, p. 9, available at www.ico.gov.uk, accessed on 18 January 2013.

Processing Compliance Rules

19.23 If an organisation is collecting and processing personal data, it must comply with the DPA and data protection regime in respect of:

- Data Protection Principles;
- Non-sensitive personal data Legitimate Processing Conditions;
- Sensitive personal data Legitimate Processing Conditions;
- Direct marketing (DM) requirements;
- Security requirements;
- Registration requirements;
- Data processor contract requirements;
- Transfer requirements.

Suggested Guidelines

19.24 Some suggested guidelines to consider generally are set out below. However, it is always suggested that appropriate professional legal and technical advice be sought in particular circumstances:

- Comply with the processing compliance rules set out above;
- Ensure fair obtaining, collecting and processing of personal data;
- Compliance must be ensured at the time of data capture NOT subsequently;
- Get it right first time;
- The lessons of *British Gas* and other examples are that in a worst case you may have to delete the database and start again from the beginning, or re-do your collection and notification process;
- Consider and decide upon opt-in or op-out consent;
- Consider the purpose or purposes for the data collection and which must be specified;
- Provide information to the data subject when collecting;
- Consider whether the data subject is the source (direct) or whether a third-party is the source (indirect);
- Specifying in the registration may not be enough, it may have to be earlier;
- Specified and lawful;
- Use or purpose to which the data collected will be put must be clear and defined. Otherwise it could be deemed too vague and unfair and ultimately an unfair collection which would undermine the initial consent given;
- If disclosure occurs, it must be specified, clear and defined;
- Security measures must be assessed and implemented;
- Security includes physical security;

- Security also includes technical security;
- Measures must be put in place to prevent loss, alteration or destruction;
- Other legislation may also apply such as in relation to hacking, criminal damage, etc;
- The personal data must be kept accurate and kept up to date;
- Personal data must be kept for no longer than is necessary;
- Consider that there are many different types of personal data;
- The organisational or business need requirement must be identified;
- How personal data is collected is must be considered, planned and recorded;
- Check Data Protection Principles;
- Check Legitimate Processing Conditions;
- Explicit consent may be required for collecting and processing sensitive personal data;
- Identify and deal with new processes and procedures in advance to ensure data protection compliance. One cannot assume that the organisation can obtain a fair and lawful consent after a go-live;
- Identify new contacts, contracts, collections and consents in advance to ensure data protection compliance;
- Identify direct marketing (DM) changes and campaigns in advance to ensure data protection compliance.

The Rights of Employee Data Subjects

19.25 The rights of data subjects can be summarised as including:

- Right of access (s 7 DPA);
- Right to establish if personal data exists (s 7(1)(a) DPA);
- Right to be informed of the logic in automatic decision taking (s 7(1)(d);
- Right to prevent processing likely to cause damage or distress (s 18 DPA);
- Right to prevent processing for direct marketing (s 11 DPA);
- Right to prevent automated decision taking (s 12 DPA);
- Right in relation to exempt manual data (s 12A DPA);
- Right to compensation (s 13 DPA);
- Right to rectify inaccurate data (s 14 DPA);
- Right to rectification, blocking, erasure and destruction (s 14 DPA);
- Right to complain to ICO (see s 42 DPA);
- Right to go to court (see s 15 DPA).

Conclusion

19.26 Organisations at different times may feel a tension to engage in monitoring of employees. No matter how tempting, this needs to be checked in order to remain data protection compliant. While there are naturally risks and issues to deal with, the starting point will always be one of proportionate responses which ensure data protection compliance.

Part 3

Outward-Facing Organisational DP Obligations

Chapter 20

Outward Facing Issues

Introduction

20.01 Beyond the inward-facing employee related sphere, organisations also need to consider the outward-facing sphere. For many organisations the outward-facing data protection issues frequently dominate more. They can also be the most contentious. These issues raise significant data protection concerns and compliance issues to be dealt with.

Some of the queries that can arise include:

- What are the forms of outward facing personal data to consider?;
- How to comply with the data protection regime when dealing with existing customers?;
- How do organisations contact potential customers yet remain data protection compliant?;
- Can an organisation engage in direct marketing (DM)?;
- Do users who are not customers raise additional issues?;
- Do security considerations still arise?;
- Are there higher security obligations for customers and users?

The general increase in internet usage, profiling, advertising, marketing and social networking are also important issues to consider. Abuse whether online or via social networking or related websites is increasingly recognised as a problem to be dealt with. Civil sanctions and actions are likely to increase in the instances where it needs to be invoked.

Types of Outward Facing Personal Data: Customers, Prospects & Users

20.02 What forms of outward facing personal data must organisations be concerned with? The types of personal data which are considered related to:

- Current customers;
- Past customers;
- Prospective customers;
- Users whom may not be registered customers.

Organisations will be often concerned with collecting personal preferences, account details, etc from customers and leads. Direct marketing (DM) and additional avenues for commercialisation are also a frequent business imperative.

In addition, there may be individuals who access the organisations website but who are not actual customers. Indeed, they may never become customers. Yet certain personal data may still be collected by the organisation. In this instance, it is also necessary for the organisation to comply with the Data Protection Principles and related obligations.

How to be Outward Facing Compliant: Customers, Prospects and Users

20.03 How can an organisation focus on the elements that will ensure data protection compliance when dealing with the personal data of customers, prospects and/or users. In terms of personal data collected and processed relating to the above categories, the following must be complied with, namely, the

- Prior information requirements;
- Data Protection Principles;
- Legitimate Processing Conditions;
- Sensitive Personal Data Legitimate Processing Conditions;
- Security requirements;
- Notification requirements.

Particular considerations can also arise in relation to users whom may not be customers in the normal and contractual sense.

adopt this model should seek professional advice beforehand. It is quite easy for an organisation to feel that it is compliant, but then for additional activities, commercialisation and or direct marketing to occur which may not be transparent, fair or warranted.

In any event, the Data Protection Principles must be complied with regardless of the particular Legitimate Processing Condition.

Customers, Etc, Sensitive Personal Data Legitimate Processing Conditions

20.07 Organisations generally, or more frequently organisation involved in particular sectors, may wish to know certain information which falls within the sensitive personal data categories eg health data; sexual data. In the case of customers, etc, sensitive personal data, an organisation must, in addition to the Data Protection Principles, be able to comply or fall within one of the Sensitive Personal Data Legitimate Processing Conditions.

Schedule 3 of the DPA sets out conditions relevant for the purposes of the first Data Protection Principle in particular in relation to the Sensitive Personal Data Legitimate Processing Conditions. It states:

1　The customers have given explicit consent to the processing of the personal data;

2　(1)　The processing is necessary for the purposes of exercising or performing any right or obligation which is conferred or imposed by law on the data controller in connection with employment;

　　(2)　The Secretary of State may by order,

　　　　(a)　exclude the application of sub-para (1) in such cases as may be specified; or

　　　　(b)　provide that, in such cases as may be specified, the condition in sub-para (1) is not to be regarded as satisfied unless such further conditions as may be specified in the order are also satisfied;

3　The processing is necessary:

　　(a)　in order to protect the vital interests of the data subject or another person, in a case where,

　　　　(i) consent cannot be given by or on behalf of the data subject; or

　　　　(ii) the data controller cannot reasonably be expected to obtain the consent of the data subject; or

    (b)   in order to protect the vital interests of another person, in a case where consent by or on behalf of the data subject has been unreasonably withheld;

4   The processing:

    (a)   is carried out in the course of its legitimate activities by any body or association which;

       (i) is not established or conducted for profit; and

      (ii) exists for political, philosophical, religious or trade-union purposes;

    (b)   is carried out with appropriate safeguards for the rights and freedoms of data subjects;

    (c)   relates only to individuals who either are members of the body or association or have regular contact with it in connection with its purposes; and

    (d)   does not involve disclosure of the personal data to a third party without the consent of the data subject;

5   The information contained in the personal data has been made public as a result of steps deliberately taken by the data subject;

6   The processing:

    (a)   is necessary for the purpose of, or in connection with, any legal proceedings (including prospective legal proceedings);

    (b)   is necessary for the purpose of obtaining legal advice; or

    (c)   is otherwise necessary for the purposes of establishing, exercising or defending legal rights;

7   (1)   The processing is necessary, for the administration of justice;

      (aa) for the exercise of any functions of either House of Parliament;

    (b)   for the exercise of any functions conferred on any person by or under an enactment; or

    (c)   for the exercise of any functions of the Crown, a Minister of the Crown or a government department;

(2)   The Secretary of State may by order:

    (a)   exclude the application of sub-para (1) in such cases as may be specified; or,

    (b)   provide that, in such cases as may be specified, the condition in sub-paragraph (1) is not to be regarded as satisfied unless such further conditions as may be specified in the order are also satisfied;

7A (1)   The processing,

    (a)   is either;

(i) the disclosure of sensitive personal data by a person as a member of an anti-fraud organisation or otherwise in accordance with any arrangements made by such an organisation; or

(ii) any other processing by that person or another person of sensitive personal data so disclosed; and

(b) is necessary for the purposes of preventing fraud or a particular kind of fraud;

(2) In this paragraph "an anti-fraud organisation" means any unincorporated association, body corporate or other person which enables or facilitates any sharing of information to prevent fraud or a particular kind of fraud or which has any of these functions as its purpose or one of its purposes;

8 (1) The processing is necessary for medical purposes and is undertaken by,

(a) a health professional; or

(b) a person who in the circumstances owes a duty of confidentiality which is equivalent to that which would arise if that person were a health professional;

(2) In this paragraph "medical purposes" includes the purposes of preventative medicine, medical diagnosis, medical research, the provision of care and treatment and the management of healthcare services;

9 (1) The processing,

(a) is of sensitive personal data consisting of information as to racial or ethnic origin;

(b) is necessary for the purpose of identifying or keeping under review the existence or absence of equality of opportunity or treatment between persons of different racial or ethnic origins, with a view to enabling such equality to be promoted or maintained; and

(c) is carried out with appropriate safeguards for the rights and freedoms of data subjects;

(2) The Secretary of State may by order specify circumstances in which processing falling within sub-para (1)(a) and (b) is, or is not, to be taken for the purposes of sub-para (1)(c) to be carried out with appropriate safeguards for the rights and freedoms of data subjects.

These customers, etc, Sensitive Personal Data Legitimate Processing Conditions may be summarised as follows:

- The customers, etc, whom the sensitive personal data is about, has given explicit consent to the processing;

- The processing is necessary so that the organisation can comply with employment law;
- The processing is necessary to protect the vital interests of:
  - the customer, etc (in a case where the customers, etcs consent cannot be given or reasonably obtained); or
  - another person (in a case where the customers, etcs consent has been unreasonably withheld);
- The processing is carried out by a not-for-profit organisation and does not involve disclosing personal data to a third party, unless the customer, etc consents. Extra limitations apply to this condition;
- The customers, etc has deliberately made the information public;
- The processing is necessary in relation to legal proceedings; for obtaining legal advice; or otherwise for establishing, exercising or defending legal rights;
- The processing is necessary for administering justice, or for exercising statutory or governmental functions;
- The processing is necessary for medical purposes, and is undertaken by a health professional or by someone who is subject to an equivalent duty of confidentiality;
- The processing is necessary for monitoring equality of opportunity, and is carried out with appropriate safeguards for the rights of individuals.

Furthermore, regulations enacted also set out further obligations in relation to the processing of sensitive personal data.

It should be noted that the ability of an organisation to actually come within one of the Sensitive Personal Data Legitimate Processing Conditions is more restricted that the general personal data conditions. This is because the data protection regime considers that organisations have less legitimate interest in the processing of sensitive personal data. It also recognises the greater importance that legislators and individuals attach to the sensitive categories of personal data.

Customers, Etc, and Security Requirements

20.08 What security issues arise for customer, etc related personal data? Customers, etc, will be concerned to ensure that their personal data is not inadvertently disclosed or used in a manner which they have not consented to and are unaware of. This is a legal requirement under the data protection regime. Appropriate security measures must also be established.

In the case of outward facing personal data, such categories will generally present significant differences to employee related personal data. Generally there will be more customer, etc related personal data. It will also be more widely accessible within the organisation. Fewer people within an organisation need to have access to employee files and personal data. Customers, etc, personal data tends to be spread across more than one single location or database. Frequently, the personal data are obtained through a variety of sources, and which are more diverse than inward facing personal data. This all means that there are greater security issues and access issues to be considered by the organisation.

Increasingly, attacks and breaches that come to public attention tend to relate to outward facing personal data. This means that there is greater reason to maintain and or enhance these security measures to avoid the consequences of publicity, official enquiries, enforcement proceedings, or complaints and or proceedings from data subjects.

Security is also an issue to carefully consider in relation to the new and developing areas of cloud computing, outsourcing, and new models and categories of data processing.

Notification Requirements

20.09 Organisations collecting and processing customer, etc, personal data will also have to consider notification requirement issues. The notification registration details will have to specify the categories of customer, etc personal data being collected, for what purposes and activities, and also whether there are any third party recipients and transfers (TBDFs). The notification also needs to outline details of the security measures.

Direct Marketing (DM)

20.10 Most commercial organisations will wish to engage in direct marketing (DM). For some organisations this will be an important core activity. Section 11(3) of the DPA provides that 'direct marketing' means the communication (by whatever means) of any advertising or marketing material which is directed to particular individuals.

The DPA and data protection regime has extensive provisions dealing with direct marketing. There are requirements to inform the data subject that they may object by a written request and free of charge to their personal data being used for direct marketing (DM) purposes.

If the data controller anticipates that personal data kept by it will be processed for purposes of direct marketing it must inform the persons to whom the data relates that they may object by means of a request in writing to the data controller and free of charge.

However, s 11 of the DPA provides a right to prevent processing for purposes of direct marketing. A customer is entitled at any time by notice in writing to a data controller to require the data controller at the end of such period (as is reasonable in the circumstances) to cease, or not to begin, processing for the purposes of direct marketing (DM) personal data in respect of which he is the data subject (s 11(1)).

If a court is satisfied, on the application of any person who has given a notice under sub-s (1), that the data controller has failed to comply with the notice, the court may order them to take such steps for complying with the notice as the court thinks fit (s 11(2)).[1]

Two individuals were recently fined £440,000 by the ICO for sending unsolicited marketing Spam messages (*ICO v Niebel* and *ICO v McNeish*).

Consequences of Non-Compliance

20.11 If the organisation fails to assess and organise compliance procedures in advance of undertaking the collection and processing of personal data of customers, etc, it will inevitable be operating in breach of the data protection regime. Any personal data collected will be illicit.

Equally, if originally compliant but during operation one of the Data Protection Principles, Legitimate Processing Conditions, and/or security requirements are breached, the personal data processed will be questionable, particularly if new personal data is involved or has new activities and uses.

What are the consequences? The collection and/or processing are illegal. The organisation, as the data controller, can be the subject of complaints, investigations and enforcement proceedings from the ICO. Depending on the severity of the non-compliance, prosecutions can also involve the directors and employees of the organisation, in addition to the organisation itself.

If convicted, the organisation could face significant fines. These will be in addition to the bad publicity and media attention which a prosecution can bring.

---

1   Section 11 (2A) of the DPA provides that this section shall not apply in relation to the processing of such data as are mentioned in para (1) of regulation 8 of the Telecommunications (Data Protection and Privacy) Regulations 1999 (processing of telecommunications billing data for certain marketing purposes) for the purposes mentioned in para (2) of that regulation.

There can be other consequences too. If the organisation relies heavily on direct marketing (DM), or is a particular type of internet company, the customer database of personal data can be one of the most significant assets of the organisation. If the database is collected in breach of the data protection regime, the organisation will not be able to establish compliant data collections and consents. It could, therefore, be ordered to delete the database.

Alternatively, an organisation may wish to sell its business or to seek investors for the business. This is frequently the case in the technology sector. However, as part of a potential purchaser or investor assessing whether to proceed, it will undertake a due diligence examination of the processes, procedures and documentation of the organisation. It will request to see documented evidence of data protection compliance and that the valuable database, etc, are fully data protection compliant. If this cannot be established, serious question marks will arise and the transaction may not proceed.

Users Versus Customers

20.12 Do separate issues arise for users and their personal data? Where someone is a customer, there is more direct contact and therefore more direct means for the organisation to engage with the customer in a measured contract formation process. Consequently, it is possible to ensure compliance though a considered and documented data protection compliance process and to engage consent appropriately at an early stage from the individual customer or potential customer.

Users, however, may not be customers. Therefore, customer contact models which incorporate consent or other data protection legitimising procedures for customers may leave a gap where non customer users are not presented with the same documentation, notices and sign up document sets. Organisations therefore need to consider users as separate from normal customers. They must assess where the organisation interacts with such users, physically or online, and what personal data may be collected. Where personal data is collected from users, the organisation needs to ensure compliance. This may mean that the organisation needs to have a separate additional set of notices, policies and consent documentation in relation to users.

Conclusion

20.13 When organisations begin to look outwards, a separate range of data collection possibilities will arise. The avenues for data collection are more diverse. In addition, the intended uses which the organisation will put this type of personal data will be potentially greater. The Data Protection Principles and Legitimate Processing Conditions require particular consideration and configuration to the intended data processing activities of customer, etc personal data. Different security and enforcement risks can arise and need to be protected against. It cannot be assumed that everyone that the organisation may wish to collect personal data from will be an actual customer. Therefore, organisations need to consider how to ensure separate consent and notifications to this category of person. An example of this may be cookies which may obtain personal data (see later).

Chapter 21

Cookies and Electronic Communications

Introduction

21.01   Cookies are software files used to speed up interactions with websites. However, they can also be used to monitor individuals, create profiles and assist direct marketing (DM) to individuals.[1] There are, therefore, obvious concerns in relation to privacy and data protection.

The use of cookies is controversial. This is because cookies can be covert and non-transparent. Policy makers are therefore concerned that the use of cookies should be regulated by the data protection regime to protect internet users.

The ePD was amended by Directive 2009/136/EC, in particular Article 5(3), to ensure that the use of cookies would be predicated upon user consent and transparent.

Cookie Amendment

21.02   The concern in relation to cookies and data protection has led to Article 5.3 of ePD[2] being amended by Directive 2009/136/EC[3] in relation to how cookies can be used.

---

1   See, for example, Newson, A., Duffy, A., and Cheng, C., 'Cookies Compliance: The Practicalities,' SCL *Computers and Law*, 29 February, 2012.
2   Directive 2002/58/EC, the ePrivacy Directive.
3   Directive 2009/136/EC of the European Parliament and of the Council of 25 November 2009 amending Directive 2002/22/EC on universal service and users' rights relating to electronic communications networks and services, Directive 2002/58/EC concerning the processing of personal data and the protection of privacy in the electronic communications sector and Regulation (EC) No 2006/2004 on cooperation between national authorities responsible for the enforcement of consumer protection laws.

The amended Article 5.3 reads,

'Member States shall ensure that the storing of information, or the gaining of access to information already stored, in the terminal equipment of a subscriber or user is only allowed on condition that the subscriber or user concerned has given his or her consent, having been provided with clear and comprehensive information, in accordance with [DPD95], inter alia, about the purposes of the processing. This shall not prevent any technical storage or access for the sole purpose of carrying out the transmission of a communication over an electronic communications network, or as strictly necessary in order for the provider of an information society service explicitly requested by the subscriber or user to provide the service.'

The Privacy and Electronic Communications (EC Directive)(Amendment) Regulations 2011 (the PECR Amendment Regulations) introduce these changes in the UK.

New Cookie Rules

21.03   The ICO updated the guidance in relation to cookies in May 2012, entitled *Privacy and Electronic Communications Regulations, Guidance on the Rules on Use of Cookies and Similar Technologies*.[4]

It states, that the PECR[5] covers the use of cookies and similar technologies for storing information, and accessing information stored, on a user's equipment such as their computer or mobile device.

The PECR apply to cookies, and similar technologies, for storing information.[6] The PECR implements the ePD regarding the protection of privacy in the electronic communications sector. Users must be informed about cookies and given choices as regards cookie monitoring.[7] In 2009, the ePD was amended by Directive 2009/136/EC. This includes changes to Article 5(3) of the ePD requiring consent for the storage or access to information stored on a user's equipment. The UK amendments were introduced on 25 May 2011 through the Privacy and

---

4   *Privacy and Electronic Communications Regulations, Guidance on the Rules on Use of Cookies and Similar Technologies*, ICO, 2012. Available at http://www.ico.gov.uk/ for_organisations/privacy_and_electronic_communications/the_guide/cookies.aspx, accessed on 18 January 2013

5   Privacy and Electronic Communications (EC Directive) Regulations 2003.

6   *Privacy and Electronic Communications Regulations, Guidance on the Rules on Use of Cookies and Similar Technologies*, ICO, 2012. Available at http://www.ico.gov.uk/ for_organisations/privacy_and_electronic_communications/the_guide/cookies.aspx, accessed on 18 January 2013.

7   *Ibid.*

Electronic Communications (EC Directive)(Amendment) Regulations 2011 (the PECR Amendment Regulations).[8]

The new rules protect the privacy of internet users. The changes are prompted by concerns about online tracking of internet users eg online monitoring, tracking, accessing the devices of users, spyware, etc. The new rules prevent cookies being used without the knowledge, consent or agreement of users.[9] Organisations must now obtain consent to use cookies and similar technologies.[10]

ICO: Implementing the Rules

21.04 The ICO report also emphasises the importance of auditing cookies and websites using cookies, to ensure that users are provided with transparent information in advance relating to cookies and that organisations obtain user consent. New websites need to apply the new rules. Existing websites need to be reviewed and reconfigured to ensure user consent is obtained in order to use cookies.[11]

ICO: Definitions

21.05 The PECR Amendment Regulations apply not just to cookies but also to similar technologies used for collecting and storing user information, eg Local Shared Objects/'Flash Cookies,' web beacons or bugs.[12] There are also different types of cookies. For example, cookies can expire at the end of a browser session or can last for longer. The new PECR apply to both. Some of the PECR definitions are,

---

8   *Privacy and Electronic Communications Regulations, Guidance on the Rules on Use of Cookies and Similar Technologies*, ICO, 2012. Available at http://www.ico.gov.uk/ for_organisations/privacy_and_electronic_communications/the_guide/cookies.aspx, accessed on 18 January 2013.
9   *Ibid.*
10 *Ibid.*
11 *Ibid.*
12 *Ibid.*

Session cookies:	allow websites to link the actions of a user during a browser session. They may be used for a variety of purposes such as remembering what a user has put in their shopping basket as they browse around a site. They could also be used for security when a user is accessing internet banking or to facilitate use of webmail. These session cookies expire after a browser session so would not be stored long term. For this reason session cookies may sometimes be considered less privacy intrusive than persistent cookies;
Persistent cookies:	are stored on a users' device in between browser sessions which allows the preferences or actions of the user across a site (or in some cases across different websites) to be remembered. Persistent cookies may be used for a variety of purposes including remembering users' preferences and choices when using a site or to target advertising;
First and third party cookies:	Whether a cookie is 'first' or 'third' party refers to the website or domain placing the cookie. First party cookies in basic terms are cookies set by a website visited by the user – the website displayed in the URL window. Third party cookies are cookies that are set by a domain other than the one being visited by the user. If a user visits a website and a separate company sets a cookie through that website this would be a third party cookie;
Subscriber:	This means a person who is a party to a contract with a provider of public electronic communications services for the supply of such services. In this context the person who pays the bill for the internet connection (that is, the person legally responsible for the charges);
User:	This means any individual using a public electronic communications service. In this context a user would be the person sat at a computer or using a mobile device to browse the internet;
Terminal equipment:	The device a cookie is placed on, usually a computer or mobile device.[13]

---

13 *Privacy and Electronic Communications Regulations, Guidance on the Rules on Use of Cookies and Similar Technologies*, ICO, 2012. Available at http://www.ico.gov.uk/ for_organisations/privacy_and_electronic_communications/the_guide/cookies.aspx, accessed on 18 January 2013.

ICO: Consent

21.06   The new PECR Amendment Regulations require organisations to obtain user consent in order to use cookies. The DPD95 defines 'the data subject's consent' as,

'any freely given specific and informed indication of his wishes by which the data subject signifies his agreement to personal data relating to them being processed.'[14]

Consent must involve some form of communication where the individual knowingly indicates their acceptance. Hence, the prior information requirement. This may involve eg clicking an icon, sending an email or subscribing to a service. Users must be fully and transparently informed in advance, in order that they are able to fully understand the issues surrounding cookies and consent to cookies.[15]

ICO: 'Prior' Consent

21.07   The ICO indicated that 'prior' consent means that consent be obtained prior to the cookie being used.[16]

The use of cookies should be delayed until users have had the opportunity to understand cookies and decide. The prior information should be clear and comprehensive.[17]

If users make a one-off visit to a website, a persistent cookie should not be needed. Organisations should shorten the lifespan of cookies or even make them temporary session cookies.[18]

ICO: Implied Consent Basis For PECR Compliance

21.08   The ICO indicates that explicit consent provides the best certainty. Organisations collecting sensitive personal data, eg health data, always require explicit consent.[19]

Consent (implied or express) must be freely given, specific and informed. For implied consent, there has to be some action taken by the consenting individual from which their consent can be inferred. This might, for example, be visiting a website, moving from one page to another or clicking a particular button. In this instance, the individual

---

14 *Privacy and Electronic Communications Regulations, Guidance on the Rules on Use of Cookies and Similar Technologies*, ICO, 2012. Available at http://www.ico.gov.uk/ for_organisations/privacy_and_electronic_communications/the_guide/cookies.aspx, accessed on 18 January 2013.

15 *Ibid.*

16 *Ibid.*

17 *Ibid.*

18 *Ibid.*

19 *Ibid.*

has to have a reasonable understanding that by doing so they are agreeing to cookies.[20]

ICO: 'Specific and Informed'

21.09 However, merely visiting a website is not sufficient consent.[21] A user cannot 'give' consent if they are not aware that their actions are being interpreted as consent. If the user is not informed, there is no valid consent.[22]

If seeking to rely upon implied consent for cookies, it is important that the organisation seeking consent satisfy themselves that the user's actions are not only an explicit request for content or services but there is also an expression of the user's agreement that the organisation may use cookies.[23]

Clear and relevant information must be readily available to users, explaining what is likely to happen while the user is accessing the website and what choices the user has in terms of controlling what happens with cookies.[24] The ICO indicates that important factors may include the following.

The nature of the intended audience of the website:

Websites might be aimed at a tech savvy audience who understand what is going on. These websites would not necessarily need to provide very basic information about what cookies, are but may still need to give users detailed explanations of how the organisation uses cookies and similar technology.[25]

The way in which users expect to receive information from and on the website:

The more the information about cookies fits with the rest of the website, the more likely users are to read it. In turn, the more likely the website operator is able to assume that users understand and accept how the website works.[26]

The language used must be appropriate for the audience:

---

20 *Privacy and Electronic Communications Regulations, Guidance on the Rules on Use of Cookies and Similar Technologies*, ICO, 2012. Available at http://www.ico.gov.uk/ for_organisations/privacy_and_electronic_communications/the_guide/cookies.aspx, accessed on 18 January 2013.
21 *Ibid.*
22 *Ibid.*
23 *Ibid.*
24 *Ibid*
25 *Ibid.*
26 *Ibid.*

The ICI refers to the advice of the International Chambers of Commerce.[27]

ICO: 'Indication of Wishes'

21.10   Consent in the offline world can be given orally, in writing or it might be implied via a particular course of action.[28]

User actions can only give an indication if there is a shared understanding of what is happening. Without a clear notice, it is difficult to assume that the user was happy for cookies to be set. The ICO stresses the importance of providing more and better information to users about cookies.[29]

The ICO recognises that gaining explicit opt-in consent for analytics cookies is difficult. Implied consent might be the most practical and user-friendly option.[30] The key to valid implied consent in this context is increasing user knowledge.[31]

ICO: User or Subscriber Consent

21.11   The new PECR Amendment Regulations require that cookie consent should be obtained from the user or subscriber.[32]

The rules require the following,

'A person shall not store or gain access to information stored, in the terminal equipment of a subscriber or user unless the requirements of paragraph (2) are met.

(2)   The requirements are that the subscriber or user of that terminal equipment,
    (a)   is provided with clear and comprehensive information about the purposes of the storage of, or access to, that information; and
    (b)   has given his or her consent. (PECR Regulation 6).'[33]

---

27   *Privacy and Electronic Communications Regulations, Guidance on the Rules on Use of Cookies and Similar Technologies*, ICO, 2012. Available at http://www.ico.gov.uk/for_organisations/privacy_and_electronic_communications/the_guide/cookies.aspx, accessed on 18 January 2013.
28   *Ibid.*
29   *Ibid.*
30   *Ibid.*
31   *Ibid.*
32   *Ibid.*
33   *Ibid.*

Organisations (and website designers) must:

- inform users that the cookies are there;
- explain what the cookies are doing; and
- obtain user consent to store a cookie on the user's device.[34]

Since 2003, organisations using cookies are required to provide clear information to users. In May 2011 the existing rules were amended. The new revised PECR Amendment Regulations require clear prior information about the cookies and user consent to the cookie.[35]

ICO: Exception

21.12 There is an exception to the requirement to provide information about cookies and to obtain consent. This is where the use of the cookie is:

- for the sole purpose of carrying out the transmission of a communication over an electronic communications network; or
- where such storage or access is strictly necessary for the provision of an information society service requested by the subscriber or user.[36] [37]

'Strictly necessary' means that the storage or access must be essential, rather than reasonably necessary, for the exemption to apply. It must be essential to provide the service requested by the user, rather than merely essential for other uses the organisation may wish to make of that data. There may also be other legal requirements eg security required by the seventh Data Drotection Principle.[38]

Potential examples of the exception are cookies for the 'add to basket'/'proceed to checkout' button, so the website 'remembers' what the user chose on a previous page. This cookie is strictly necessary to

---

34 *Privacy and Electronic Communications Regulations, Guidance on the Rules on Use of Cookies and Similar Technologies*, ICO, 2012. Available at http://www.ico.gov.uk/ for_organisations/privacy_and_electronic_communications/the_guide/cookies.aspx, accessed on 18 January 2013.

35 *Ibid.*

36 *Ibid.* In defining an 'information society service' the Electronic Commerce (EC Directive) Regulations 2002 refer to 'any service normally provided for remuneration, at a distance, by means of electronic equipment for the processing (including digital compression) and storage of data, and at the individual request of a recipient of a service.'

37 *Ibid.*

38 *Ibid.*

provide the service the user requests (taking the purchase to the checkout). In this exception no consent is required.[39]

The ICO adds that the intention of the legislation is clearly that this exemption is viewed narrowly.[40]

ICO: Compliance Responsibility

21.13   The person setting the cookie is responsible for compliance. Where third party cookies are on a website, both parties will have a responsibility for ensuring users are clearly informed about the cookies and for obtaining user consent.[41]

Placing contractual obligations into agreements with web publishers may be advisable.[42]

Website designers must also consider the PECR Amendment Regulations. The development of new software, or upgrades, must be compliant with the new data protection requirements. Privacy by Design (PbD) can assist in compliance. This means that privacy and data protection compliance are designed into systems right from the start, not merely bolted on afterwards.[43] (See also Part 4).

UK organisations are subject to the new requirements even if the website is hosted abroad. The ICO adds that organisations outside of Europe, but whose websites target the European market or provide products or services to customers in Europe, should expect to comply.[44]

ICO: Browser Settings

21.14   The Directive and Regulations suggest browser settings may be one means of obtaining consent if they allow the subscriber to indicate their agreement to cookies.[45] However, relying solely on browser settings may not be sufficient.[46]

---

39   *Privacy and Electronic Communications Regulations, Guidance on the Rules on Use of Cookies and Similar Technologies*, ICO, 2012. Available at http://www.ico.gov.uk/ for_organisations/privacy_and_electronic_communications/the_guide/cookies.aspx, accessed on 18 January 2013.
40   *Ibid.*
41   *Ibid.*
42   *Ibid.*
43   *Ibid.*
44   *Ibid.*
45   *Ibid.*
46   *Ibid.*

ICO: Practical Advice

21.15 It is not enough simply to continue to comply with the old 2003 prior information requirements and allowing an opt out. The ICO states that the new law must be fully complied with.[47]

ICO: First Steps

21.16 Organisations should:

- Check what type of cookies (and similar technologies) they use and how they use them;
- Assess how intrusive the organisation cookies are;
- Where the organisation needs consent – decide what solution is best to obtain consent.[48]

ICO: Check Cookie Types and How Used

21.17 Organisations should audit their website[49] to analyse which cookies are strictly necessary, and also therefore which may not need consent.[50]

ICO: Assess Cookie Intrusiveness

21.18 The more intrusive the use of cookies, the more consideration is required.[51]

Some cookies create detailed user browsing profiles.[52] This can be very intrusive. The more privacy intrusive the cookie activity, the more important is the consent.[53] Privacy neutral cookies are at one end of the

---

47 *Privacy and Electronic Communications Regulations, Guidance on the Rules on Use of Cookies and Similar Technologies*, ICO, 2012. Available at http://www.ico.gov.uk/ for_organisations/privacy_and_electronic_communications/the_guide/cookies.aspx, accessed on 18 January 2013.
48 *Ibid.*
49 *Ibid.*
50 *Ibid.*
51 *Ibid.*
52 *Ibid.*
53 *Ibid.*

scale and more intrusive uses of the technology at the other. More information and detailed choices are required as the level of intrusiveness increases.[54]

ICO: Decide Consent Solution

21.19   Once the organisation knows what it does, how, and for what purpose, it needs to consider the best method for gaining consent. The more privacy intrusive the activity, the greater the need for meaningful consent.[55]

ICO: Conducting a Cookies Audit

21.20   An audit of cookies could involve the following:

- Identify which cookies are operating on the organisation's website;
- Confirm the purpose(s) of each cookies;
- Confirm whether the organisation links cookies to other information held about users – such as usernames;
- Identify what data each cookie holds;
- Confirm the type of cookie – session or persistent;
- If a persistent cookie, how long is the lifespan?;
- Is it a first or third party cookie?
- If it is a third party cookie, who is setting it?;
- Check that the privacy policy/statement provides accurate and clear information about each cookie.[56]

ICO: Providing Information About Cookies

21.21   The information should be sufficiently full and intelligible to allow users to clearly understand the potential consequences of allowing cookies. This compares with the transparency requirements of the first Data Protection Principle.[57]

---

54 *Privacy and Electronic Communications Regulations, Guidance on the Rules on Use of Cookies and Similar Technologies*, ICO, 2012. Available at http://www.ico.gov.uk/ for_organisations/privacy_and_electronic_communications/the_guide/cookies.aspx, accessed on 18 January 2013.
55 *Ibid.*
56 *Ibid.*
57 *Ibid.*

ICO: Getting Consent in Practice

21.22 Appropriate cookie consent depends on what the cookie is doing and the relationship with users.[58]

ICO: Pop Ups and Similar Techniques

21.23 Pop-ups, message bars and header bars may be an option for compliance if asking the user directly if they agree to the website putting something on their computer and if they click yes, this may be the consent.[59] The information must make the position absolutely clear to users.[60]

ICO: Terms and Conditions

21.24 Consent for the cookies may be gained online using the terms of use or terms and conditions to which the user agrees when they register or sign up.[61]

However, changing the terms of use alone, to include consent for cookies would not be sufficient. Consent has to be specific and informed. To satisfy the rules on cookies, organisations must make users aware of the changes and specifically that the changes refer to the use of cookies. Organisations need a positive indication that users understand and agree to the changes. This may include asking the user to tick a box to indicate that they consent to the new terms.[62]

Organisations must gain consent by giving the user specific information about what they are agreeing to and providing a way to show their acceptance. The ICO states that any attempt to gain consent that relies on users' ignorance about what they are agreeing to is unlikely to be compliant.[63]

---

58   *Privacy and Electronic Communications Regulations, Guidance on the Rules on Use of Cookies and Similar Technologies*, ICO, 2012. Available at http://www.ico.gov.uk/ for_organisations/privacy_and_electronic_communications/the_guide/cookies.aspx, accessed on 18 January 2013.
59   *Ibid.*
60   *Ibid.*
61   *Ibid.*
62   *Ibid.*
63   *Ibid.*

ICO: Settings-led Consent

21.25   Some cookies are deployed when a user makes a choice about how the website works or will be configured. Consent could be gained as part of the process by which the user confirms what they want to do or how they want the website to work for them.[64] Agreement for a language setting cookie could be integrated with the choice the user is already making if choosing a language.[65]

ICO: Feature-led Consent

21.26   Some objects are stored when a user chooses to use a particular feature of the website and or to personalise the content which the user is served by the website. If the user is clicking a button or agreeing to the functionality being 'switched on,' – one can also ask for their consent to set a cookie at this point. It must be clear to the user that by choosing to take a particular action, then certain things will happen, the organisation may interpret this as consent. The more complex or intrusive the activity, the more prior information, and clearer information, will have to be provided to the user.[66]

If a feature is provided by a third party, users must be made aware of this and given information on how the third party might use cookies (and similar technologies) so that the user is able to make an informed choice.[67] Apps, for example, are increasingly contentious.

ICO: Functional and Analytical Uses

21.27   Organisations may collect information about how people access and use the website, without the request of the user. Organisations must ensure that information provided is prominent. Users must make fully informed choices.[68]

Organisations should put in place a mechanism to obtain consent for analytical and functional cookies at the point the user logs in.[69]

---

64 *Privacy and Electronic Communications Regulations, Guidance on the Rules on Use of Cookies and Similar Technologies*, ICO, 2012. Available at http://www.ico.gov.uk/ for_organisations/privacy_and_electronic_communications/the_guide/cookies.aspx, accessed on 18 January 2013.
65 *Ibid.*
66 *Ibid.*
67 *Ibid.*
68 *Ibid.*
69 *Ibid.*

For users browsing and whom have no relationship with the organisation, websites should ensure the information provided to users about cookies is absolutely clear and is highlighted in a prominent place (not merely through a privacy policy/statement link). It must highlight the use of cookies and obtain agreement to set these cookies.[70]

If information about website use is passed to a third party, this must be absolutely clear to the user. Organisations should review what the third party does with the information about website visitors. Users must be able to alter their account settings to limit the sharing of visitor information. User options must be prominent, not hidden away.[71]

ICO: Third Party Cookies

21.28 Some websites allow third parties to use cookies. The process of consent for these cookies is more complex.[72]

ICO: Consent Mechanisms

21.29 The ICO[73] sets out possible mechanisms for gaining consent,

Relationship with the user or subscriber	Cookie type	Possible means of consent
Registered user of online banking	First party analytical cookies (session) and first party cookies used to tailor advertising on log in pages (persistent)	Highlighting the cookies and asking for consent from the user as they log into their account. Once this consent is obtained the option will not have to be provided on subsequent visits.

---

70 *Privacy and Electronic Communications Regulations, Guidance on the Rules on Use of Cookies and Similar Technologies*, ICO, 2012. Available at http://www.ico.gov.uk/for_organisations/privacy_and_electronic_communications/the_guide/cookies.aspx, accessed on 18 January 2013.

71 *Ibid.*

72 *Ibid.*

73 *Ibid.*

Occasional visitor to online magazine	Cookie to remember and tailor preferences for viewing and set up of the site (persistent)	The mechanism for the user to select or tailor their preferences 'Would you like us to remember your …' is amended to specifically flag that this process involves agreeing to a cookie. If the user selects the option to request that their preferences are remembered – having clearly had highlighted the role of the cookie in that process – the consent requirements would be satisfied.
User wishing to download game or App	First party cookie used to personalise the gaming experience (persistent)	In most cases the user will already be agreeing to terms and conditions to download the game or app. The way in which cookies are used is clearly and specifically highlighted in a prominent place in the process of agreement to these conditions (for example next to the 'I agree' box). Once this consent is obtained the option will not have to be provided each time the game is used.

Adapted from ICO *Privacy and Electronic Communications Regulations, Guidance on the rules on use of cookies and similar technologies.*

Sometimes a combination of solutions is required.[74]

---

74 *Privacy and Electronic Communications Regulations, Guidance on the Rules on Use of Cookies and Similar Technologies*, ICO, 2012. Available at http://www.ico.gov.uk/for_organisations/privacy_and_electronic_communications/the_guide/cookies.aspx, accessed on 18 January 2013.

ICO: Cookie Consent for More Than One Website

21.30 An organisation with several connected websites could obtain consent for cookies on each website in one place, eg when the user logged in on one website/the first website. It would have to be absolutely clear which websites the cookies relate to and what the cookies are used for and what the user is agreeing to.[75]

ICO: Changes to Cookie Use After Consent

21.31 If the purposes of the cookies change significantly after consent, organisations need to make users aware of the changes and allow them to make new choices. Users can provide consent to multiple cookies performing a set of functions.[76]

ICO: Withdrawing Cookie Consent

21.32 Users can choose to withdraw consent at any time. Organisations must provide information about how consent can be withdrawn. In this instance, cookies that have already been set must be removed. Organisations may explain the consequences of withdrawing consent, eg functionality impact.[77]

ICO: Alternatives to Cookies and Privacy

21.33 Sometimes functions performed by a cookie can be achieved through other means eg 'device fingerprinting'. Organisations must still inform users what is collected and how it is used.[78]

---

75 *Privacy and Electronic Communications Regulations, Guidance on the Rules on Use of Cookies and Similar Technologies*, ICO, 2012. Available at http://www.ico.gov.uk/ for_organisations/privacy_and_electronic_communications/the_guide/cookies.aspx, accessed on 18 January 2013.
76 *Ibid.*
77 *Ibid.*
78 *Ibid.*

ICO: Cookies and Personal Data

21.34   Organisations need to make sure they comply with the additional requirements of the DPA[79] in addition to cookie compliance.

ICO: Enforcement and Penalties

21.35   If organisations refuse or fail to comply, the ICO can take action.[80] These options[81] include,

Information notice: requiring organisations to provide the ICO with specified information within a certain time period;

Undertaking: fixing the organisation to a particular course of action to improve its compliance;

Enforcement notice: compelling the organisation to take specified action to bring ensure compliance with the Regulations. Failure to comply with an enforcement notice can be a criminal offence;

Monetary penalty notice: a monetary penalty notice requires an organisation to pay a monetary penalty as determined by the ICO, up to a maximum of £500,000. This power can be used in the most serious of cases and if specific criteria are met, if any person has seriously contravened the PECR and if the contravention was of a kind likely to cause substantial damage or substantial distress. The contravention must be deliberate or the person must have known or ought to have known that there was a risk that a contravention would occur and failed to take reasonable steps to prevent it.[82]

ICO: Enforcement of Cookie Rules

21.36   Enforcement will involve in most cases the ICO asking the organisation to respond to the complaint. It will explain what steps need to be taken to comply with the rules.[83]

---

79 *Privacy and Electronic Communications Regulations, Guidance on the Rules on Use of Cookies and Similar Technologies*, ICO, 2012. Available at http://www.ico.gov.uk/ for_organisations/privacy_and_electronic_communications/the_guide/cookies.aspx, accessed on 18 January 2013.
80 *Ibid.*
81 *Ibid.*
82 *Ibid.*
83 *Ibid.*

Formal action is considered if the organisation refuses. Further guidance is set out in the ICO Data Protection Regulatory Action Policy and Guidance on the issuing of monetary penalties.[84]

Organisations will need to be able to demonstrate they have taken sensible, measured action to move to compliance.[85]

Monetary penalties will be reserved for the most serious of breaches of the PECR rules.[86]

ICO: Do These Rules Apply to Intranets?

21.37   The ICO currently considers that the new rules do not apply in the same way to internal intranet systems.[87]

ICO: Can an Organisation Do Nothing?

21.38   No. It is the law. Compliance is required. The UK Regulations, and EU Directive of 2009, cannot be selectively ignored.[88]

ICO: Does the Same Apply for Mobile Devices?

21.39   Yes. The new requirements also apply to cookies set on mobile devices and other terminal equipment eg internet enabled televisions, games consoles, etc.[89]

ICO: Awareness

21.40   Organisations must educate consumers and users about cookies generally.[90]

---

84   *Privacy and Electronic Communications Regulations, Guidance on the Rules on Use of Cookies and Similar Technologies*, ICO, 2012. Available at http://www.ico.gov.uk/ for_organisations/privacy_and_electronic_communications/the_guide/cookies.aspx, accessed on 18 January 2013.

85   *Ibid.*
86   *Ibid.*
87   *Ibid.*
88   *Ibid.*
89   *Ibid.*
90   *Ibid.*

ICO: We only use analytical cookies – if nobody consents that will seriously restrict the amount of information we can get to improve and develop our website

21.41   The Regulations do not distinguish between analytical cookies and cookies used for other purposes. Analytical cookies do not fall within the 'strictly necessary' exception criteria. Organisations need to inform users about analytical cookies and obtain consent.[91]

However, the ICO appears less likely to take enforcement action in relation to purely analytical cookies.[92]

WP29: Online Behavioural Advertising Opinion

21.42   WP29 adopted an Opinion[93] on 22 June 2010 in relation to online behavioural advertising ('OBA'). OBA also entails tracking users internet activities and the building of profiles about them. These are later used to provide advertising matching their interests. These practices must not be carried out at the expense of individuals' rights to privacy and data protection, according to WP29.

The data protection regime safeguards must be respected. The Opinion refers to such safeguards.

Organisations are bound by Article 5(3) of ePD. Placing cookies or similar devices on users' terminal equipment or obtaining information through such devices is only allowed with the informed consent of the users. Organisations must create prior opt-in mechanisms requiring an affirmative action by users indicating their willingness to receive cookies and to the monitoring of their surfing behaviour for the purposes of serving tailored advertising. Organisations should: (i) limit in time the scope of the consent; (ii) offer the possibility to revoke it easily; and (iii), create visible tools to be displayed where the monitoring takes place.[94]

OBA enables the creation of very detailed user profiles which, in most cases, are deemed personal data. The DPD95 generally is also applicable, eg rights of access, rectification, erasure, retention, etc. Users must be provided with 'clear and comprehensive information.'[95]

---

91 *Privacy and Electronic Communications Regulations, Guidance on the Rules on Use of Cookies and Similar Technologies*, ICO, 2012. Available at http://www.ico.gov.uk/ for_organisations/privacy_and_electronic_communications/the_guide/cookies.aspx, accessed on 18 January 2013.
92 *Ibid.*
93 WP29, Opinion 2/2010 on Online Behavioural Advertising (WP 171).
94 *Ibid.*
95 *Ibid.*

The Opinion invites industry to undertake a dialogue with the WP29 with the view to put forward technical and other means to comply with the new rules.[96]

WP29 Opinion 2/2010: Issues

21.43 The Opinion states that online advertising and behavioural advertising raises important data protection and privacy concerns. User behaviour online is analysed in order to build extensive profiles about data subjects and their interests. Such profiles can be used to provide tailored advertising.

OBA is increasingly based on the use of tracking cookies (and similar devices). It is highly privacy intrusive.

The Opinion clarifies the legal framework applicable to behavioural advertising. It also invites industry to suggest technical and other solutions.

WP29 Opinion 2/2010: Online Behavioural Advertising

21.44 A broad range of methods are being used to create so called 'more relevant' advertisements to users. There are several methods, including contextual advertising, segmented advertising and behavioural advertising.

Behavioural advertising is advertising that is based on tracking user behaviour online. It tracks repeated site visits, interactions, keywords, online content production, order of visits and views, length of viewing, etc to develop a specific user profile and tailored adverts to match these inferred interests of the user.

Behavioural advertising involves: (a) advertising networks providers (also referred to as 'ad network providers'), who distribute behavioural advertising; (b) advertisers; and (c) publishers who are the website owners looking for revenues by selling space to display ads on their website(s).

WP29 Opinion 2/2010: Tracking Technologies

21.45 Most tracking for behavioural advertising uses information from the user's browser and computer terminal equipment. The main tracking technology used is cookies.

Tracking website visits and repeated visits enable the ad network provider to build a profile of the visitor to deliver personalised advertising. Cookies can have different life spans. 'Persistent cookies' either have a precise expiry date far in the future or until manually deleted.

---

96   WP29, Opinion 2/2010 on Online Behavioural Advertising (WP 171).

Most internet browsers offer the possibility to block third party cookies. Some browsers support 'private' browsing sessions that will automatically destroy (some) cookies on closing the browser.

Flash cookies, however, cannot be deleted through the traditional privacy settings of a web browser.

WP29 Opinion 2/2010: Building Profiles, Types of Identifiers

21.46   Predictive profiles are established by observing user behaviour over time, eg monitoring visited pages and ads viewed/clicked. Explicit profiles are created from personal data that data subjects themselves provide to a web service, eg by registering. Ad networks construct predictive profiles with a combination of tracking techniques, cookies and data mining software. Gender and age range can be deduced by analysing the pages the data subject visits and the ads viewed. Cookie data can be enriched with aggregated data derived from the behaviour of data subjects who exhibit similar behavioural patterns in other contexts. The location of the data subject is also a source of target profiling, obtained from eg user IP address.

WP29 Opinion 2/2010: Legal Framework Introduction

21.47   Article 5(1) of Directive 2002/58 protects the confidentiality of communications in general.

The protection of the confidentiality of communications in the case of cookies is provided in Article 5(3). Recital 66, adopted when the ePD was amended in 2009 and Recital 24 and 25 of the ePD are also relevant.

The Opinion also notes that DPD95 applies to matters not covered by the ePD whenever personal data are processed.

WP29 Opinion 2/2010: The Scope of Application of Article 5(3) and DPD95

21.48   Advertisers should consider Article 5(3) of the ePD and also DPD95.

WP29 Opinion 2/2010: Substantive Scope of Article 5(3)

21.49   Article 5(3) requires obtaining informed consent to lawfully store information or to gain access to information stored in the user's equipment. Tracking cookies are 'information' stored in the data subject's equipment. They are accessed by advertising network providers when data subjects visit a partner website. Article 5 (3) is therefore fully applicable. Hence, any storage of cookies or similar devices (irrespective of type) and any subsequent use of previously stored cookies to gain access to data subjects' information will have to comply with Article 5 (3).

Article 5 (3) applies to 'information.' It is not a prerequisite that this information is personal data within the meaning of DPD95. Recital 24 notes that 'terminal equipment of users ... and any information stored on such equipment are part of the private sphere of these users requiring protection under the European Convention.' The protection of the private sphere of the data subject triggers the obligations in Article 5 (3). WP29 Opinion 1/2008 confirms that Article 5 (3) is a general provision, applicable to electronic communication services but also any other services when these techniques are used. Article 5 (3) applies irrespectively of whether the entity placing the cookie is a data controller or a data processor.

WP29 Opinion 2/2010: Scope of DPD95

21.50 If the cookie information collected is personal data then, in addition to Article 5(3), DPD95 is also applicable.

Behavioural advertising often processes personal data (per Article 2 DPD95). For example, it normally collects user IP addresses which allows the tracking of users of a specific computer.

Users are 'singled out,' even if their names are not known. Furthermore, the information collected relates to, (ie is about) a person's characteristics or behaviour and is used to influence that particular person.

WP29 Opinion 2/2010: Interplay Between the Two Directives

21.51 Recital 10 of ePD states that DPD95 applies, 'to all matters concerning protection of fundamental rights and freedoms which are not specifically covered by the provisions of this Directive, including the obligations on the [data] controller and the rights of individuals.'

Article 5 (3) of the ePD and consent will be directly applicable. DPD95 will be fully applicable (except for provisions specifically addressed in the ePD, which mainly correspond to Article 7 of DPD95 on the legal grounds for data processing). The remaining provisions of DPD95 including the principles, data subject rights (such as access, erasure, right to object), confidentiality, security and international data transfers are fully applicable.

WP29 Opinion 2/2010: Territorial Scope of Article 5(3) and DPD95

21.52　The territorial scope of application of the above framework is determined by a combination of both Article 3 (1) of the ePD and Article 4.1 (a) and (c) of DPD95. Earlier WP29 Opinions give guidance on the concept of establishment and the use of equipment referred to in Article 4(1)(a) and (c) respectively as determinants for the applicability of DPD95. This also applies to advertising.

WP29 Opinion 2/2010: Roles and Responsibilities

21.53　Behavioural advertising involves ad network providers, publishers and advertisers. The role they play can establish their obligations.

WP29 Opinion 2/2010: Ad Network Providers

21.54　Article 5(3) applies regardless of whether the entity placing or reading the cookie is a data controller or a data processor. The obligation to obtain informed consent applies to ad network providers.

When personal data is involved, the ad network providers also act as data controller. Additional obligations arise from DPD95. The ad network providers control the purposes and means of processing.

The Opinion notes that they 'rent' space from publishers' web sites to place adverts; they set and/read cookie related information, collect IP addresses, use the information gathered on user surfing behaviour to build profiles and to select and deliver the ads to be displayed on the basis of this profile. They act as data controllers.

WP29 Opinion 2/2010: Publishers

21.55　Publishers rent out space on their websites for ad networks to place adverts.

The WP29 Opinion states that publishers have responsibility for the initial part of the data processing, namely the transfer of the IP address that takes place when individuals visit their websites. The publishers facilitate such transfer and co-determine the purposes for which it is carried out, ie to serve visitors with tailored advertising. Publishers will have some, but not all, responsibility as data controllers.

Publishers do not hold personal information; so it may not make sense to apply all DPD95 obligations, such as access right. However, the obligation to inform users of the data processing is applicable to publishers.

In addition, publishers are joint data controllers if they collect and transmit personal data regarding users, such as name, address, age, location, etc to the ad network provider. The publishers are therefore bound by the obligations of DPD95 regarding the part of the data processing under their control. In the ad network providers and publishers 'shall ensure that the complexity and the technicalities of the behavioural advertising system do not prevent them from finding appropriate ways to comply with data controllers' obligations and to ensure data subjects' rights.'

Service agreements between publishers and ad network providers should outline the roles and responsibilities of both parties.

WP29 Opinion 2/2010: Advertisers

21.56   When a user clicks an ad and visits the advertisers' website, the advertiser can track which campaign resulted in the click-through. If the advertiser captures the targeting information and combines it with the data subject's onsite surfing behaviour or registration data, then the advertiser is an independent data controller for this data processing.

WP29 Opinion 2/2010: Prior Informed Consent Obligation

21.57   The general rule contained in the first paragraph of Article 5 (3). The ePD was amended in 2009. The changes reinforce the need for users' informed prior consent.

WP29 Opinion 2/2010: Prior Consent to Engage in Behavioural Advertising

21.58   Pursuant to Article 5 (3), an ad network provider who wishes to store or gain access to information stored in a user's terminal equipment must: (i) provide the user with clear and comprehensive information in accordance with DPD95, inter alia, about the purposes of the processing; and (ii) it has obtained the user's consent to the storage of or access to information on their terminal equipment, after providing the information requested under (i).

Consent must be obtained before the cookie is placed and/or information stored in the user's terminal equipment is collected, referred to as prior consent. Informed consent can only be obtained if prior information about the sending and purposes of the cookie has been given to the user. For consent to be valid whatever the circumstances in which it is given, it must be freely given, specific and constitute an informed indication of the data subject's wishes. Consent must be obtained before the personal data are collected, as a necessary measure to ensure that data subjects can fully appreciate that they are consenting and what they are consenting to. Consent is also revocable.

WP29 Opinion 2/2010: Consent Via Browser Settings

21.59   Publishers and ad network providers often provide information in their general terms and conditions and/or privacy policies about third party cookies used for behavioural advertising. However, this does not meet the requirements of Article 5(3)amended, which places emphasis on providing prior information and obtaining prior consent (prior to the starting of the processing).

Recital 66 of the amended ePD indicates that the user consent may be expressed by using the appropriate settings of a browser or other application, 'where it is technically possible and effective, in accordance with the relevant provisions of [DPD95].' Consent can be given in different ways – where technically possible, effective and in accordance with the other relevant requirements for valid consent.

When may browser settings will meet the requirements of DPD95, and thus constitute a valid consent 'in accordance with [DPD95]?' WP29 considers that this will happen rarely.

The definition and requirements for valid consent per Article 2(h) of DPD95, means users cannot be deemed to have consented simply because they acquired/used a browser or other application which by default allows the collection and processing of their information. Average users are not aware of the tracking of their online behaviour, the purposes of the tracking, how to use browser settings to reject cookies, etc. User inaction cannot provide a clear and unambiguous indication of wishes.

WP29 Opinion 1/2008 states that 'The responsibility for [cookie] processing cannot be reduced to the responsibility of the user for taking or not taking certain precautions in his browser settings.' For browser settings to be able to deliver informed consent, it should not be possible to 'bypass' the choice made by the user in setting the browser (such as the 'respawned' practice).

Consent in bulk for any future processing without knowing the circumstances surrounding the processing cannot be valid consent.

Therefore, in order for browsers or any other application to be able to 'deliver' valid consent, they must deal with the following:

- Browsers which by default reject third party cookies and which require users to engage in an affirmative action to accept both the setting of and continued transmission of information contained in cookies by specific websites may be able to deliver valid and effective consent. (If the browser settings were predetermined to accept all cookies, such consent would not comply with Article 5 (3). Such consent cannot constitute a true indication of the data subject wishes. Such consent would not be specific nor prior (to the processing);

- Browsers should convey clear, comprehensive and fully visible information in order to ensure that consent is fully informed. To meet the requirements of DPD95 browsers should convey, on behalf of the ad network provider, the relevant information about the purposes of the cookies and the further processing. Generic warnings without explicit references to the ad network placing the cookie, are unsatisfactory.

The WP29 is of the view that unless the above requirements are met, providing information and facilitating user ability to reject cookies, cannot be informed consent per Article 5(3) of the ePD and in light of Article 2(h) of DPD95.

Browsers should require users to go through a privacy wizard when they first install or update the browser and provide for an easy way of exercising choice during use..

WP29 Opinion 2/2010: Consent and Opt-Out Options

21.60 Cookie opt-out mechanisms are welcomed by WP29 but it is noted that such opt-out mechanisms do not in principle deliver user consent. This mechanism is not an adequate mechanism to obtain average users informed consent. General users lack the basic understanding of the collection of any data, its uses, how the technology works and more importantly how and where to opt-out.

WP29 considers that cookie-based opt-out mechanisms do not provide average users with the effective means to consent to receive behavioural advertisement. They fail the requirements of Article 5 (3).

WP29 Opinion 2/2010: Prior Opt-In Consent Better For Informed Consent

21.61 WP29 prefers prior opt-in mechanisms, which require an affirmative user action to indicate consent before the cookie is sent to the data subject. Implicit consent does not always lead to unambiguous consent (as required by Article 7(a) of DPD95). In a previous Opinion, WP29 recommends the use of specific messages: 'In the case of cookies, the user should be informed when a cookie is intended to be received, stored or sent ... The message should specify, in generally understandable language, which information is intended to be stored in the cookie, for what purpose as well as the period of validity of the cookie.' After receiving such information, the user should be offered the possibility to indicate whether they want to be profiled for behavioural advertising. However, in accordance with Recital 25 of the ePD ('the right to refuse (cookies) may be offered once for the use of various devices to be installed on the user's terminal equipment ... during subsequent connections'), user acceptance of a cookie could be understood to be valid not only for the sending of the cookie but also for subsequent collection of data arising from such a cookie. This can mean, the consent obtained to place the cookie and use the information to send targeting advertising would cover subsequent 'readings' of the cookie that take place when the user visits a website partner of the ad network provider which placed the cookie.

However, taking into account that i) this practice would mean that individuals accept to be monitored 'once for ever,' and, ii) individuals might simply 'forget' that, for example, a year ago, they agreed to be monitored; WP29 considers that safeguards are needed.

First, organisations should limit the scope of the consent in terms of time. Consent to be monitored should not be 'for ever' but it should be valid for a limited period of time, for example, one year. After this period, ad network providers would need to obtain a new consent. Cookies can have a limited lifespan.

Second, risks should be further mitigated with additional information practices.

Third, consent can always be revoked. Data subjects should be offered the possibility to easily revoke their consent to monitoring for behavioural advertising. In this regard, the need to provide clear information about this possibility and how to exercise it is essential.

WP29 Opinion 2/2010: Informed Consent and Children

21.62   In Opinion 2/2009 the WP29 addresses the personal data of children. One problem relates to obtaining informed consent. In some cases, children's consent must be provided by parent or guardian. Ad network providers would need to provide notice to parents about the collection and the use of children's information and obtain their consent before collecting and further using their information for behavioural targeting of children.

In the light of the above and the vulnerability of children, WP29 feels that ad network providers should not offer interest categories intended to serve behavioural advertising or influence children.

WP29 Opinion 2/2010: Obligation to Provide Information for OBA

21.63   Transparency is a key condition for users to be able to consent to data collection and processing. Users may not know or understand the technology that supports behavioural advertising or that advertising is being targeted at them. Effective information must be provided to internet users. Only if users are adequately informed, will they be in a position to exercise their consent choices.

WP29 Opinion 2/2010: What Information Provided by Whom?

21.64   Article 5 (3) states that the user must be provided with information, 'in accordance with [DPD95], inter alia about the purposes of the processing.' Article 10 of DPD95 refers to the provision of this information.

With regard to behavioural advertising, data subjects should be informed about the identity of the advertising network provider and the purposes of the processing. The user should be clearly informed that cookies will allow the advertising provider to collect information about their visits to other websites, the advertisements they have been shown, which ones they have clicked on, timing, etc.

There should be a simple explanation on the uses of the cookie to create profiles to target advertising. Recital 25 of the ePD requires notices to be provided in a 'clear and comprehensive' manner. The Opinion notes that statements such as 'advertisers and other third parties may also use their own cookies or action tags' are clearly not sufficient.

Recital 25 requires the prior information to be 'as user friendly as possible.' The WP29 considers that providing a minimum of information directly on the screen, interactively, easily visible and understandable, would be the most effective way to comply. The information must be easily accessible and highly visible. It must not be hidden in general terms and conditions and/or privacy policies/statements.

Given the possibility for users to accept the monitoring once, to cover subsequent future readings of the cookie, it is essential for ad network providers to find ways to inform users periodically that monitoring is taking place. Unless users are given clear and unambiguous reminders, by easy means, of the monitoring, problems can arise. A monitoring symbol would be helpful to remind users of the monitoring but also to control whether they want to continue or even revoke their consent. Under Article 5 (3) of ePD, the obligation to provide the necessary prior (and post) information and obtain data subjects' consent ultimately lies with the entity that sends and reads the cookie. In most cases, this is the ad network provider. When publishers are joint-controllers, they are also bound by the obligation to provide information. Publishers have certain obligations from DPD95. They are bound by the obligation to provide information to users about the data processing that takes place as a result of the re-directing of their browser and also about the purposes for which the information will be used later on by ad network providers. The information should refer not only to the transfer of IP address for the purposes of displaying acts but also to further data processing carried out by the ad network providers, including setting up of cookies. Data Protection Authorities are to consider appropriate awareness raising measures.

WP29 Opinion 2/2010: Other Obligations from DPD95

21.65   In addition to Article 5(3), data controllers must ensure compliance with all the DPD95 obligations (which do not overlap with Article 5(3)).

WP29 Opinion 2/2010: Obligations and Special Categories of Data

21.66   Targeting users based on sensitive personal data opens the possibility of abuse. It can also lead to awkward situations which may arise if individuals receive advertising that reveals, for example, sexual preferences or political activity. Using interest categories that reveal sensitive data should be discouraged according to the WP29.

To use sensitive personal data, ad network providers must comply with Article 8 of DPD95. The only available legal ground that would legitimise such processing would be explicit, separate prior opt-in consent per Article 8(2)(a). An opt-out consent mechanism would not meet the requirement of the law. Such consent could not be obtained thorough browser settings. Explicit prior consent would be needed.

WP29 Opinion 2/2010: Compliance with Data Protection Principles

21.67 Article 6 of DPD95 must be respected by data controllers.

Behavioural advertising profiles could potentially be used for purposes other than advertising.

However, Article 6(1)(b) contains the purpose limitation principle. This prohibits processing which is not compatible with the purposes that legitimised the initial collection. Incompatible secondary uses contradict Art 6(b) of DPD95. Also, ad networks cannot enrich the information gathered for the purposes of behavioural advertisement with other information.

Secondary incompatible uses need additional legal grounds to do so per Article 7 of DP95. Hence, they will need to inform data subjects and, in most cases, obtain consent per Article 7(a).

Article 6(1)(e) requires data to be deleted when no longer necessary for the purpose for which the data were collected (retention principle). Compliance means limiting the storage of information. Organisations must specify and respect express time limits under which data will be retained.

Policies must ensure that information collected each time a cookie is read is immediately deleted or anonymised once the necessity for retaining it has expired. Each data controller needs to be able to justify the necessity for a given retention period.

When a user asks for a deletion of their profile or if they exercise their right to withdraw consent, this requires the ad network provider to erase or delete promptly the data subject's information.

WP29 Opinion 2/2010: Data Subjects Rights

21.68 Users and data subjects have rights of access, rectification, erasure and to object (Articles 12 and 14 of DPD95).

The WP29 refers to initiatives offering access to interest categories that data subjects have been labelled with based on the cookie ID number. These new tools may enable users not only to access the interest categories that related to them but also modify them and erase them.

These tools should be as visible as possible to users.

WP29 Opinion 2/2010: Other Obligations

21.69 Article 17 of the Directive imposes the obligation upon data controllers and data processors to apply technical and organisational measures to protect personal data against accidental or unlawful destruction loss, disclosure, and other forms of unlawful processing. Compliance with the security obligations require ad network providers to implement state of the art technical and organisational measures to ensure the security and confidentiality of the information.

Pursuant to Article 18 of DPD95, data controllers may have to notify the processing of personal data to data protection authorities, unless exempted.

If the data is transferred outside the EU, for example, to servers located in third countries, ad network providers must ensure compliance with the provisions on transfers of personal data to third countries (Articles 25 and 26 DPD95).

WP29 Opinion 2/2010: Recommendations

21.70 Individuals are often unaware that behavioural advertising and cookies enable advertisers to track them online, to build profiles and to serve tailored advertising. It is very doubtful whether users are aware of, much less that they consent to, being monitored for tailored advertising.

Notices in general terms and conditions and/or privacy policies, often in obscure language fall short of the requirements of data protection legislation. Organisations need to improve compliance efforts for the new rules.

The Opinion recommends as follows.

WP29 Opinion 2/2010: Applicable Laws

21.71 The EU legal framework for cookies is primarily Article 5(3) of the ePD.

Article 5(3) applies whenever 'information' such as a cookie is stored or retrieved from terminal equipment of an internet user. It is not a prerequisite that this information be personal data.

In addition, DPD95 applies to matters not specifically covered by the ePrivacy Directive whenever personal data are processed. Behavioural advertising is based on the use of identifiers that enable the creation of very detailed user profiles which, in most cases, are personal data.

Jurisdiction, Territorial Issues, Establishment

21.72 The DPD95 applies to the data processing that takes place when publishers and ad network providers engage in behavioural advertising, eg Article 4(1)(a) and (c) of DPD95 and eg Article 3 of the ePD.

There is other WP29 guidance also relevant.

WP29 Opinion 2/2010: Roles and Responsibilities

21.73 Ad network providers are bound by Article 5 (3) of the ePD as they place cookies and/or retrieve information from cookies already stored in users' terminal equipment. They are also data controllers as they determine the purposes and the essential means of the processing of data.

Publishers have certain data controller related responsibilities regarding processing in the first phase of the processing, ie, when they set up their websites to trigger the transfer of the IP address to ad network providers (which enables further processing). If publishers transfer directly identifiable personal data to ad network providers themselves, they will be deemed joint controllers.

WP29 Opinion 2/2010: Obligations and Rights Regarding Ad Network Providers

21.74 Article 5 (3) of the ePD requires prior informed consent by ad network providers.

Browser settings may only deliver consent in very limited circumstances. The browser must either alone or in combination with other means effectively convey clear, comprehensive and fully visible information about the processing.

Ad network providers should encourage and work with browser manufacturers/developers to implement privacy by design (PbD) in browsers.

Cookie-based opt out mechanisms in general do not constitute an adequate mechanism to obtain informed user consent. In most cases user consent is implied if they do not opt out. However, few people exercise the opt-out option, not because they have made an informed decision to accept behavioural advertising, but because they do not realise that the processing is taking place, nor how to exercise the opt out.

Ad network providers need to 'swiftly' move away from opt out mechanisms and create prior opt in mechanisms. Informed, valid consent requires an affirmative action by the data subject indicating their willingness to receive cookies and subsequent monitoring of their online surfing behaviour for the purposes of tailored advertising.

A users' acceptance to receive a cookie could also entail acceptance for the subsequent readings of the cookie, and hence for the monitoring of internet browsing (Recital 25 ePD). It would not be necessary to request consent for each reading of the cookie. However, to ensure that data subjects remain aware of the monitoring over time, ad network providers should:

i)   limit in time the scope of the consent;
ii) offer the possibility to easily revoke their consent to being monitored for behavioural advertising; and
iii) create a symbol or other tools which should be visible in all the websites where the monitoring takes place (the website partners of the ad network provider). This symbol would remind individuals of the monitoring but also help them to control whether they want to continue being monitored or wish to revoke their consent.

Network providers should ensure compliance with the obligations that arise from DPD95 which do not directly overlap with Article 5(3), namely, the purpose limitation principle, and security obligations.

Ad network providers should enable individuals to exercise their rights of access and rectification and erasure. The WP29 welcomes the practice of some ad network providers to offer data subjects the possibility to access and modify the interest categories in which they have been classified.

Ad network providers should implement retention policies which ensure that information collected each time that a cookie is read is automatically deleted after a set period of time (necessary for the purposes of the processing). This also applies for alternative tracking technologies eg JavaScript installed in the user's browser.

WP29 Opinion 2/2010: Ad Network Providers and Publishers

21.75 Providing highly visible information is a precondition for consent to be valid. Mentioning the practice of behavioural advertising in general terms and conditions and/or privacy policies can never suffice. Ad network providers/publishers must provide information to users in compliance with Article 10 of DPD95. They should ensure that individuals are told, at a minimum, who (ie which entity) is responsible for serving the cookie and collecting the related information. In addition, they should be informed in simple ways that (a) the cookie will be used to create profiles; (b) what type of information will be collected to build such profiles; (c) the fact that the profiles will be used to deliver targeted advertising and (d) that the cookie will enable the user identification across multiple websites.

Network providers and publishers should provide the information directly on the screen, interactively, if needed, through layered notices. It should be easily accessible and highly visible.

Icons placed on the publisher's website, around advertising, with links to additional information, can assist.

WP29: Opinion 16/2011 on OBA

21.76 WP29 Opinion 16/2011 on EASA/IAB Best Practice Recommendation on Online Behavioural Advertising (WP 188) was adopted on 08 December 2011.

Directive 2009/136/EC revised the ePD. One of the key changes concerns the mechanisms for implanting information in the user's terminal device eg cookies. The existing opt-out regime, where a user can object to the processing of information collected via terminal equipment (such as cookies) was rejected.

Instead, the standard became informed consent. These changes are important for the online behavioural advertising (OBA) industry relies heavily on cookies and similar technologies.

The consent rule reflects a growing concern amongst citizens, politicians, data protection authorities, consumer organisations and policy-makers that the technical possibilities to track individual internet behaviour over time, across different websites is increasing. Soon after the change, WP29 adopted Opinion 2/2010 on Online Behavioural Advertising (OBA). The opinion describes the roles and responsibilities of the different actors engaged in online behavioural advertising, and clarifies the applicable legal framework. The opinion focuses on the tracking of internet behaviour over time, across different websites as the source of the most important data protection concerns with regard to OBA.

In April 2011 the European Advertising Standards Alliance (EASA) and the Internet Advertising Bureau Europe (IAB), adopted a self-regulatory Best Practice Recommendation on online behavioural advertising ('EASA/IAB Code'). WP29 comments on this.

It states that the EASA/IAB Code per se is not adequate to ensure compliance with data protection regime.

WP29 Comment: EASA/IAB Notice (Principle I)

21.77   Under Article 5 (3) of the revised the ePD, consent must be informed. The user must have given their consent to store information or gain access to information stored in their terminal equipment after having been provided with clear and comprehensive information in accordance with DPD95, inter alia, about the purposes of the processing. In order to comply, the relevant information notice must be provided directly to the users in a clear and understandable form before the processing takes place. It is not enough for information to be 'available' somewhere in the website that the user visits.

Under the EASA/IAB Code, an icon will be used as an information notice for behavioural advertising. The icon links to an information website, www.youronlinechoices.eu. On this website, users can signal their willingness to opt out by selecting specific company names from a list of different advertising networks.

Given the current lack of user knowledge and awareness regarding behavioural advertising, this icon approach is not sufficient in itself to properly inform the users about the use of cookies per Article 5(3). This is due to the following reasons:

- Currently average users will not be able to recognise the icon's underlying meaning without any additional language;
- It is necessary to use clear language, allowing users to immediately understand that their activities are being tracked when they browse the web and that they may receive targeted ads;
- The mere use of the word 'advertising' alongside the icon is not enough to inform the user that the ad uses cookies for behavioural advertising. The wording as a minimum include 'personalised advertising';
- The icon can serve as additional information and as a reminder notice after the subscriber or user has provided consent for the

processing of his/her data for the purpose of behavioural advertising, not for the provision of prior information as required;

- The information should be correct and complete (Article 10 of DPD95). Opinion 2/2010 states that 'Ad network providers and publishers must provide information to users in compliance with Article 10 of [DPD95]. In practical terms, they should ensure that individuals are told, at a minimum, who (ie which entity) is responsible for serving the cookie and collecting the related information. In addition, they should be informed in simple ways that (a) the cookie will be used to create profiles; (b) what type of information will be collected to build such profiles; (c) the fact that the profiles will be used to deliver targeted advertising and (d) the fact that the cookie will enable the user's identification across multiple web sites. Network providers/publishers should provide the information directly on the screen, interactively, if needed, through layered notices. In any event it should be easily accessible and highly visible.'

The Code and the website do not meet the requirement set out at the revised ePD according to WP29.

WP29 Comment: EASA/IABUser Choice (Principle II)

21.78 In Opinion 2/2010, WP29 states that 'from the literal wording of Article 5 (3): i) consent must be obtained before the cookie is placed and/or information stored in the user's terminal equipment is collected, which is usually referred to as prior consent and ii) informed consent can only be obtained if prior information about the sending and purposes of the cookie has been given to the user. In this context, it is important to take into account that for consent to be valid whatever the circumstances in which it is given, it must be freely given, specific and constitute an informed indication of the data subject's wishes. Consent must be obtained before the personal data are collected, as a necessary measure to ensure that data subjects can fully appreciate that they are consenting and what they are consenting to. Furthermore, consent must be revocable.'

WP29 states that the EASA/IAB Code, instead of seeking consent, claims to provide for a way of exercising 'choice.' In fact it is a choice to opt out, as it offers the user the possibility to object to having his/her data collected and further processed for OBA. This 'choice' is not consistent with Article 5(3) of the revised ePD, as the data are in fact processed without user's consent and without providing the user with information before the processing takes place. Principle II does not meet the requirements of the revised ePD.

WP29 Comment: EASA/IAB User choice site www.youronlinechoices.eu

21.79   The "choice" approach could be modified to be compliant with the amended Article 5 (3) by creating an opt in cookie solution.

WP29 Comment: EASA/IAB Other Principles and Concerns

21.80   The OBA Best Practice Recommendation: A Sensitive segmentation (Principle IV). Special reference to children is commented upon by WP29.

The Code foresees a 12 year age threshold for the processing of children's data.

This should be 'subject to different mandatory requirements set forth in domestic law.'

The WP29 welcomes Part B of Principle IV, which dictates that a user's explicit consent is required prior to creating or targeting OBA segments which make use of sensitive personal data.

WP29 Comment: EASA/IAB Compliance and Enforcement (Principle VI)

21.81   The EASA/IAB Code includes measures for ensuring compliance of the signatory companies to its provisions, especially via the self-certification process which is subject to independent audit and complemented by a periodically renewable compliance 'seal.'

The WP29 recognises the need for internal industry compliance rules, but would like to stress the fact that the Code should in principle comply with the European legislative framework on data protection. In this context, it should be pointed out that it is the national regulators that are ultimately responsible for legal compliance and enforcement.

WP29 Comment: EASA/IAB Retention Period for Data Collected

21.82   Opinion 2/2010 notes 'Ad network providers should implement retention policies which ensure that information collected each time that a cookie is read is automatically deleted after a justified period of time (necessary for the purposes of the processing).' The collection and processing of data for behavioural advertising purposes must be kept to a minimum. The EASA/IAB Code does not contain any provisions on the amount of data collected and the retention period(s) for the specific purposes.

This information is absolutely necessary for a user to make a fully informed decision to consent to such profiling.

III. Some clarifications regarding cookies and consent

WP29 Comment: EASA/IAB OBA Recommendation

21.83 In some parts of the website www.youronlinechoices.eu it stated that '... in most cases the information used for providing you with these adverts is not personal, in that it does not identify you ...', and also that a cookie stores 'some basic, non-personal information on your PC to improve certain functionalities and customise the surfing experience.'

These arguments are used to conclude that the installation of cookies for the provision of behavioural advertising is not subject to the data protection legislation. The WP29 refers to its Opinion 2/2010 which outlines that behavioural advertising involves the processing of unique identifiers achieved through the use of cookies, or any kind of device fingerprinting. The use of unique identifiers allows for the tracking of users of a specific computer even when IP addresses are deleted or anonymised. Unique identifiers enable data subjects to be 'singled out' for the purpose of tracking user behaviour while browsing on different websites and thus qualify as personal data.

Article 5 (3) of the revised ePD is applicable independently of whether the information stored or accessed in the user's terminal equipment consists personal data or not.

WP29 Comment: EASA/IAB Consent Not Required for All Cookies

21.84 The EASA and IAB have also argued that the installation of each single cookie requires 'explicit' consent and thus will negatively impact on the surfing experience. The WP29 would like to clarify that consent is not required for every type of cookie, as there are different ways to use cookies with different purposes and requirements associated with them. According to Article 5(3) of the revised ePD, a cookie may be exempted from informed consent if it is 'necessary to carry out the transmission of an electronic communications network' or if 'it is strictly necessary in order to provide an information society service explicitly requested by the subscriber or user to provide that service.'

WP29 states that the following cookies would be exempted from informed consent:

- A secure login session cookie. This is a cookie designed to identify the user once logged-in and is necessary to recognise them, maintaining the consistency of the communication with the server over the communication network;
- A shopping basket cookie. It stores the reference of items the user has selected by clicking on a button (eg 'add to my shopping cart'). This cookie is thus necessary to provide an information society service explicitly requested by the user;
- Security cookies. Cookies which provide security that are essential to comply with the security requirements of the ePD or other legislation for an information society service explicitly requested by the user. For example, a cookie may be used to store a unique identifier to allow the information society service to provide additional assurance in the recognition of returning users. Attempted logins from previously unseen devices could prompt for additional security questions.

The WP29 further notes that although some cookies may be exempted from the informed consent required by Article 5 (3) of the ePD, DPD95 can also apply. Providers of information society services still have to comply with the obligation to inform users. There is sufficient opportunity to inform users about the usage of cookies prior to their being established.

WP29 Comment: EASA/IAB Pop Ups

21.85 Pop up screens are not the only way to obtain consent.
Other more user friendly ways to obtain consent include:

- A static information banner on top of a website requesting the user's consent to set cookies, with a link to a privacy statement with a more detailed explanation about the different data controllers and the purposes of the processing eg ICO website;
- A splash screen on entering the website explaining what cookies will be set, by what parties, if the user consents, eg breweries seeking to ensure their visitors are old enough to visit the website;
- A default setting prohibiting the transfer of data to external parties, requiring a user click to indicate consent for tracking purposes eg.German e-zine Heise with regard to cookies set and read by

Facebook with the help of its 'Like' button. By default, the button is light-grey. Only if the user clicks on the button, will it be highlighted and become able to set and receive user data;

- A default setting in browsers that would prevent the collection of behavioural data (Do not collect). Recital 66 of the amended DPD95 suggests browser settings as a way to obtain consent, provided that they are 'technically possible and effective, in accordance with the relevant provisions of [DPD95].' This is not an exception to Article 5 (3) but a reminder that consent can be given in different ways – where technically possible, effective and in accordance with the other relevant requirements for valid consent.

As a minimum, to meet the requirements of DPD95, users cannot be deemed to have consented simply because they acquired/used a browser or other application which by default enables the collection and processing of their information. To deliver valid and effective consent, they must require the user to engage in an affirmative action to accept both the setting of and continued transmission of information contained in cookies by specific websites.

Users should receive the relevant information on data processing as a preliminary step to installing the specific 'advertising' plug-in.

The WP29 welcomes recent initiatives by browser providers to develop privacy solutions such as Do Not Track, on the condition that such mechanisms truly enable users to express their consent on a case by case basis, without being tracked by default.

WP29 Comment: EASA/IAB Multiple Consent 'Pop Ups' Not Always Necessary

27.86 EASA and IAB assert users will have to click through consent requests continuously from one website to another. This does not take into account that once a user has expressed consent or refusal then there is no need to ask them again for consent for a cookie serving the same purpose and originating from the same provider. Hence, if a third party ad network on a website receives consent for an OBA cookie, this consent will not only be valid on other pages of the same website, but also for other websites that share the same OBA network. Consequently, for an average user, the number of consent requests will decrease as they navigate and expresses their choices.

Once the user has consented to receiving a specific cookie, the presence of the cookie can be used as a marker of such consent. As such, the current 'opt out' technology used by the advertising networks affiliated with the website www.youronlinechoices.eu could be re-engineered to provide an 'opt-in' approach. WP29 refers to an example:

- The first time a user comes in contact with an OBA provider (through a website visit), no cookie has been set, and thus no cookie will be sent to the ad network provider. The ad provider can display a message in an information area (including the area where the advertisement would appear) to propose a choice to the user:
  - Accept an 'opt-in' cookie for future behavioural advertising;
  - Refuse cookies for the purpose of behavioural advertising at the same time accepting a cookie containing the word 'REFUSE' so that this refusal can be recorded going forward;
  - Store no cookie at all. In that case, the user will be asked again about his choice during the next visit;
- When the user comes in contact with the same OBA provider again, the ad provider could adjust its behaviour according to three scenarios:
  - If there is an 'opt-in' cookie, the OBA provider can access and store cookies on the user's terminal and provide behavioural advertising;
  - If there is a 'REFUSE' cookie, the OBA provider will know that the user refuses future cookies (and thus behavioural advertising), and will stick to untargeted ads;
  - If there is no cookie at all, the OBA provider will consider that this is the user's first contact with them and will ask them about his choice.

WP29 recommends advertisers consider the above examples further.

The EASA and IAB www.youronlinechoice.eu website demonstrates clearly that choices related to OBA can be presented in a single page.

WP29: Opinion on ePD Cookie Amendment

21.87 The WP29 issued *Opinion 04/2012 on Cookie Consent Exemption* on 7 June, 2012.[97]

WP29 states that the new amendment has,

'reinforced the protection of users of electronic communication networks and services by requiring informed consent before information is stored or accessed

---

97 Opinion 04/2012 on Cookie Consent Exemption, Article 9 Working Party, 7 June, 2012, available at http://ec.europa.eu/justice/data-protection/article-29/documentation/opinion-recommendation/files/2012/wp194_en.pdf, accessed on 18 January 2013.

in the user's (or subscriber's) terminal device. The requirement applies to all types of information stored or accessed in the user's terminal device although the majority of discussion has centred on the usage of cookies.'[98]

Generally customer, etc, informed consent is required. However, now under Article 5(3), exemptions from requiring informed consent can apply to cookies if either:

- the cookie is used 'for the sole purpose of *carrying out the transmission* of a communication over an electronic communications network' (Condition A); *OR*
- the cookie is '*strictly necessary* in order for the provider of an information society service explicitly requested by the subscriber or user to *provide the service*' (Condition B).[99]

WP29: Condition A

21.88 The phrase 'sole purpose' in Condition A limits the types of processing using cookies. Simply using a cookie to assist, speed up or regulate the transmission over an electronic communications network is not sufficient. The transmission 'must *not be possible without* the use of the cookie.'[100]

Three issues arise, namely:

- The ability to route the information over the network, notably by identifying the communication endpoints;
- The ability to exchange data items in their intended order, notably by numbering data packets;
- The ability to detect transmission errors or data loss.[101]

Condition A 'encompasses cookies that fulfil at least one of the properties defined above for Internet communications.'[102]

---

98 Opinion 04/2012 on Cookie Consent Exemption, Article 9 Working Party, 7 June, 2012, available at http://ec.europa.eu/justice/data-protection/article-29/documentation/opinion-recommendation/files/2012/wp194_en.pdf, accessed on 18 January 2013. The Opinion explains how revised Article 5.3 impacts on the use of cookies but and potentially similar technologies.

99 *Ibid.*

100 *Ibid.*

101 *Ibid.*

102 *Ibid.*

WP29: Condition B

21.89 The Condition B exemption criteria are high.[103] A cookie matching CRITERION B has to pass two tests simultaneously, namely:

- The information society service is explicitly requested by the user: the user (or subscriber) by positive action requested a service with a clearly defined perimeter;
- The cookie is strictly needed to enable the information society service: if cookies are disabled, the service will not work.[104]

Recital 66 of Directive 2009/136/EC underlines that 'Exceptions to the obligation to provide information and offer the right to refuse should be limited to those situations where the technical storage or access is strictly necessary for the legitimate purpose of enabling the use of a specific service explicitly requested by the subscriber or user.' The Opinion states that there has to be a clear link between the strict necessity of a cookie and the delivery of the service explicitly requested by the user for the exemption to apply.

A cookie matching Condition B would need to pass the following tests:

- A cookie is necessary to provide a specific functionality to the user (or subscriber): if cookies are disabled, the functionality will not be available;
- This functionality has been explicitly requested by the user (or subscriber), as part of an information society service.[105]

WP29: Characteristics of a Cookie

21.90 Cookies are, according to the Opinion, often categorised according to whether they are 'session cookies' or 'persistent cookie';[106] or whether they are 'third party cookies' or not.[107]

---

103 Opinion 04/2012 on Cookie Consent Exemption, Article 9 Working Party, 7 June, 2012, available at http://ec.europa.eu/justice/data-protection/article-29/documentation/opinion-recommendation/files/2012/wp194_en.pdf, accessed on 18 January 2013. The Opinion explains how revised Article 5.3 impacts on the use of cookies but and potentially similar technologies.

104 *Ibid.*

105 *Ibid.*

106 A 'session cookie' is a cookie that is automatically deleted when the user closes his browser. A 'persistent cookie' is a cookie that remains stored in the user's terminal device until it reaches a defined expiration date (which can be minutes, days or several years in the future).

107 The Opinion uses the term 'third party cookie' to describe cookies that are set by data controllers that do not operate the website currently visited by the user.

A cookie exempted from consent should have a lifespan in direct relation to the original purpose used for, and must be set to expire once not needed, reflecting the reasonable expectations and consent of users.

'Third party' cookies are usually not 'strictly necessary' and relate to a service distinct from the service 'explicitly requested' by the user. Therefore, 'first party' session cookies are more likely exempted from consent than 'third party' persistent cookies. The Opinion states that ultimately, the purpose and the specific processing will determine whether or not a cookie can be exempted from consent according to Condition A or B. Permanently cookies on the user's computer are unlikely to be exempted.

WP29: Multipurpose Cookies

21.91 A cookie for several purposes may only be exempted from consent if all the distinct purposes for which the cookie is used are individually exempted from consent.

Tracking is unlikely to meet Condition A or B. A website would need to seek user consent for the tracking purpose.

If a website uses several, a single point of information and consent can be sufficient.

The Opinion gives examples of cookie use, such as:

- User-Input Cookies;
- Authentication Cookies;
- Field Code Changed;
- User Centric Security Cookies;
- Multimedia Player Session Cookies;
- Field Code Changed;
- UI Customisation Cookies;
- Social Plug-In Content Sharing Cookies.[108]

WP29: Non-Exempted Cookies

21.92 Some cookie uses do not fall into the Condition A or B exemptions. Examples include:

---

108 Opinion 04/2012 on Cookie Consent Exemption, Article 9 Working Party, 7 June, 2012, available at http://ec.europa.eu/justice/data-protection/article-29/ documentation/opinion-recommendation/files/2012/wp194_en.pdf, accessed on 18 January 2013. The Opinion explains how revised Article 5.3 impacts on the use of cookies but and potentially similar technologies.

- Social Plug-In Tracking Cookies;
- Third Party Advertising;
- First Party Analytics.

Social Plug-In Tracking Cookies can also be used to track individuals, both members and non-members, with third party cookies for additional purposes such as behavioural advertising, analytics, market research, etc. These cookies are not 'strictly necessary' to provide functionality explicitly requested by the user. Such tracking cookies cannot be exempt under Condition B. Without consent, there is unlikely a legal basis for social networking websites collecting data through social plug-ins about non-members of their network. By default, social plug-ins should thus not set a third party cookie in pages displayed to non-members.[109]

With regard to Third Party Advertising, the Opinion states that third party cookies used for behavioural advertising are not exempted from consent.[110] Consent is required for all related third party operational cookies.[111]

WP29: Opinion Summary and Guidelines

21.93 The Opinion provides the following guide of cookies which can be exempted from informed consent under certain conditions and if they are not used for additional purposes:

- User input cookies (session-id), for the duration of a session or persistent cookies limited to a few hours in some cases;
- Authentication cookies, used for authenticated services, for the duration of a session;
- User centric security cookies, used to detect authentication abuses, for a limited persistent duration;
- Multimedia content player session cookies, such as flash player cookies, for the duration of a session;
- Load balancing session cookies, for the duration of session;
- UI customisation persistent cookies, for the duration of a session (or slightly more);

---

109 Opinion 04/2012 on Cookie Consent Exemption, Article 9 Working Party, 7 June, 2012, available at http://ec.europa.eu/justice/data-protection/article-29/documentation/opinion-recommendation/files/2012/wp194_en.pdf, accessed on 18 January 2013. The Opinion explains how revised Article 5.3 impacts on the use of cookies but and potentially similar technologies.

110 This is already noted in Opinion 2/2010 and Opinion 16/2011.

111 *Ibid.*

- Third party social plug-in content sharing cookies, for logged in members of a social network.[112]

In relation to social networking websites, the WP29 notes that the use of third party social plug-in cookies for other purposes than to provide a functionality explicitly requested by their own members requires consent, notably if these purposes involve tracking users across websites.[113]

The WP29 notes[114] that third party advertising cookies cannot be exempted from consent, and further clarifies that consent would also be needed for operational purposes related to third party advertising such as frequency capping, financial logging, ad affiliation, click fraud detection, research and market analysis, product improvement and debugging.

While some operational purposes may distinguish one user from another, in principle these purposes do not justify the use of unique identifiers. There are discussions regarding the implementation of Do Not Track standard in Europe.[115]

Some primary guidelines offered by the Opinion include:

- When applying Condition B, it is important to examine what is strictly necessary from the point of view of the user, not the service provider;
- If a cookie is used for several purposes, it can only benefit from an exemption to informed consent, if each distinct purpose individually benefits from such an exemption;
- First party session cookies are far more likely to be exempted from consent than third party persistent cookies. However, the purpose of the cookie should always be the basis for evaluating if the exemption can be successfully applied, rather than a technical feature of the cookie.[116]

It is important to verify carefully if it fulfils one of the two exemption criteria in Article 5(3) as modified by Directive 2009/136/EC. If substantial doubts remain on whether or not an exemption criterion applies, websites should closely examine if there is an opportunity to gain consent from users in a simple clear way, thus avoiding legal uncertainty.[117]

---

112 This is already noted in Opinion 2/2010 and Opinion 16/2011.
113 *Ibid.*
114 *Ibid.*
115 *Ibid.*
116 *Ibid.*
117 *Ibid.*

ICO

21.94   In relation to cookies and the new PECR Amendment Regulations the ICO recommends that organisations:

- Check what type of cookies and similar technologies the organisation uses and how it uses them;
- Assess how intrusive the organisation cookies are;
- Where the organisation needs consent, decide what solution to obtain consent will be best in the circumstances.[118]

The ICO has issued guidance in terms of:

- The Guide to Privacy and Electronic Communications;[119]
- Privacy and Electronic Communications Regulations, Guidance on the Rules on Use of Cookies and Similar Technologies.[120]

In Opinion 2/2010, the WP29 notes that behavioural advertising must not be carried out at the expense of individuals' rights to privacy and data protection. The data protection regime sets forth specific safeguards which must be respected.

The advertising industry needs to comply with the precise requirements of the ePD.

Conclusion

21.95   While the technicalities of cookies can be a little complex, and it is sometimes easy for organisations to look straight at the potential data available via the use of cookies, it is critical for organisations to consider the new rules. Some cookie use may be permitted, but clearly some is not. Organisations and those responsible for web development need to reassess their current online practices to ensure full compliance.

---

118   *Privacy and Electronic Communications Regulations, Guidance on the Rules on Use of Cookies and Similar Technologies*, ICO (May, 2012), available at http://www.ico.gov.uk/for_organisations/privacy_and_electronic_communications/the_guide/cookies.aspx, accessed on 18 January 2013.

119   *The Guide to Privacy and Electronic Communications*, ICO (September, 2011), available at http://www.ico.gov.uk/for_organisations/privacy_and_electronic_communications/the_guide.aspx, accessed on 18 January 2013.

120   *Privacy and Electronic Communications Regulations, Guidance on the Rules on Use of Cookies and Similar Technologies*, ICO (May, 2012), available at http://www.ico.gov.uk/for_organisations/privacy_and_electronic_communications/the_guide/cookies.aspx, accessed on 18 January 2013.

It may mean a period of adjustment as organisations, and developers, come to grips with understanding what personal data is required and what may be gathered legitimately by permitted cookies.

Chapter 22

Enforcement Powers

Introduction

22.01 What happens if an organisation does not comply with the data protection regime when dealing with customers, etc, personal data?

When things go wrong, there can be legal and publicity consequences for the organisation. The impact of a data protection breach can mean an immediate cross team effort to deal with the data protection breach.

In dealing with an incident, and in planning for compliance with customer, etc personal data, organisations should be aware of the various ICO enforcement powers. These emphasise the importance of consequences for non-compliance. Enforcement proceedings can be issued by the ICO. Significant fines and penalties can result. Potentially also, individual customers may decide to sue for damage, loss and breach of their personal data rights.

Data protection compliance is also an important due diligence issue when organisations are reviewed at time of sale and purchase, and indeed at other times also. It can affect a sale or purchase as well as the value involved. In some instances where there is non compliance, a customer database, which in some instances is the most valuable asset of a commercial organisation, may have to be deleted. That is a real cost of non compliance and not getting things right from day one.

Enforcement Notices

22.02 In terms of the ICO, Part V of the DPA refers to enforcement actions. Section 40 provides that the ICO may issue enforcement notices to organisations. Under s 40(1), if the ICO is satisfied that a data controller has contravened or is contravening any of the Data

Protection Principles, in relation to the use of customer, etc personal data, the ICO may serve a notice (referred to as 'an enforcement notice'). The enforcement notice will require compliance by the organisation with the Data Protection Principles, or principle in question:

- to take within such time as may be specified in the notice, or to refrain from taking after such time as may be so specified, such steps as are so specified; and or
- to refrain from processing any personal data, or any personal data of a description specified in the notice, or to refrain from processing them for a purpose so specified or in a manner so specified, after such time as may be so specified.

The enforcement notice is, therefore, very wide in terms of what the ICO can require. It can encompass all types of non-compliance or breach in relation to customer, etc personal data. The ICO considers whether the contravention has caused or is likely to cause personal damage or distress, in deciding whether to serve an enforcement notice (s 40(2)). This would encompass non-compliance in terms of collecting and processing customer, etc personal data. However, the ICO may reserve such notices for more serious instances of non-compliance or breach. It may be argued that an actual data breach or data loss instance is naturally a serious incident and therefore may lean towards investigation and enforcement. This might be particularly the case if the breach has not been remedied by the time of notification of the breach to the ICO.

Section 40(3) provides an enforcement notice in respect of a contravention of the fourth Data Protection Principle (which requires the data controller to rectify, block, erase or destroy any inaccurate data) may also require the data controller to rectify, block, erase or destroy any other data held by it and containing an expression of opinion which appears to the ICO to be based on the inaccurate data.

Section 40(4) provides that an enforcement notice in respect of a contravention of the fourth Data Protection Principle, in the case of data which accurately record information received or obtained by the data controller from the data subject or a third party, may require the data controller either:

- to rectify, block, erase or destroy any inaccurate data and any other data held by it and containing an expression of opinion as mentioned in s 40(3); or
- to take such steps as are specified in the notice for securing compliance with the requirements specified in para 7 of Part II of Sch 1 and, if the ICO thinks fit, for supplementing the data with

such statement of the true facts relating to the matters dealt with by the data as the ICO may approve.

Section 40(5) provides that where:

- an enforcement notice requires the data controller to rectify, block, erase or destroy any personal data; or
- the ICO is satisfied that personal data which have been rectified, blocked, erased or destroyed had been processed in contravention of any of the data protection principles,

an enforcement notice may require the data controller to notify third parties to whom the data have been disclosed of the rectification, blocking, erasure or destruction.

Section 40(8) provides that if by reason of special circumstances the ICO considers that an enforcement notice should be complied with as a matter of urgency, it may include a statement to that effect; and in that event ss 40(7) shall not apply but the notice must not require the provisions of the notice to be complied with before the end of the period of seven days beginning with the day on which the notice is served.

Section 40(9) provides that notification regulations (as defined by s 16(2)) may make provision as to the effect of the service of an enforcement notice on any entry in the register maintained under s 19 which relates to the person on whom the notice is served. Section 40(10) provides that this section has effect subject to s 46(1).

Assessment Notices

22.03   Organisations also need to be aware of assessment notices that may be issued by the ICO. Section 41 relates to assessment notices. Section 40(1) provides that the ICO may serve a data controller within ss 41(2) with a notice (referred to as an 'assessment notice') for the purpose of enabling the ICO to determine whether the data controller has complied or is complying with the data protection principles.

Section 40(2) provides that a data controller comes within this subsection if a:

- government department;
- public authority designated for the purposes of this section by an order made by the Secretary of State; or
- person of a description designated for the purposes of this section by such an order.

Section 40(3) provides that an assessment notice is a notice which requires the data controller to do all, or any, of the following:

- permit the ICO to enter any specified premises;
- direct the ICO to any documents on the premises that are of a specified description;
- assist the ICO to view any information of a specified description that is capable of being viewed using equipment on the premises;
- comply with any request from the ICO for:
  - a copy of any of the documents to which the ICO is directed;
  - a copy (in such form as may be requested) of any of the information which the ICO is assisted to view;
- direct the ICO to any equipment or other material on the premises which is of a specified description;
- permit the ICO to inspect or examine any of the documents, information, equipment or material to which the ICO is directed or which the ICO is assisted to view;
- permit the ICO to observe the processing of any personal data that takes place on the premises;
- make available for interview by the ICO a specified number of persons of a specified description who process personal data on behalf of the data controller (or such number as are willing to be interviewed).

An assessment notice must, in relation to each requirement imposed by the notice, specify the time at which the requirement is to be complied with; or the period during which the requirement is to be complied with (s 40(5)). Section 40(6) provides that an assessment notice must also contain particulars of the rights of appeal conferred by s 48. Section 40(7) provides that the ICO may cancel an assessment notice. Section 40(8), (9), (10), (1) and (1) refer to the Secretary of State and provisions that may be made in relation to public authorities, which certain organisations may also have to consult.

Assessment Notices: Limitations

22.04 Section 41B refers to assessment notices and limitations. Section 41B(1) provides that a time specified in an assessment notice under s 41A(5) in relation to a requirement must not fall, and a period so specified must not begin, before the end of the period within which an appeal can be brought against the notice, and if such an appeal is brought the requirement need not be complied with pending the determination or withdrawal of the appeal.

Section 41B(2) provides that if by reason of special circumstances the ICO considers that it is necessary for the data controller to comply with a requirement in an assessment notice as a matter of urgency, the ICO may include in the notice a statement to that effect and a statement of the reasons for that conclusion; and in that event sub-s (1) applies in relation to the requirement as if for the words from 'within' to the end there were substituted of 7 days beginning with the day on which the notice is served.

Section 41B(3) provides that a requirement imposed by an assessment notice does not have effect in so far as compliance with it would result in the disclosure of:

● any communication between a professional legal adviser and the adviser's client in connection with the giving of legal advice with respect to the client's obligations, liabilities or rights under the DPA; or

● any communication between a professional legal adviser and the adviser's client, or between such an adviser or the adviser's client and any other person, made in connection with or in contemplation of proceedings under or arising out of DPA (including proceedings before the Tribunal) and for the purposes of such proceedings.

Section 41B(4) provides that in sub-s (3) references to the client of a professional legal adviser include references to any person representing such a client.

Section 41B(5) provides that nothing in s 41A authorises the ICO to serve an assessment notice on:

● a judge;
● a body specified in s 23(3) of the Freedom of Information Act 2000 (bodies dealing with security matters); or
● the Office for Standards in Education, Children's Services and Skills in so far as it is a data controller in respect of information processed for the purposes of functions exercisable by Her Majesty's Chief Inspector of Education, Children's Services and Skills by virtue of s 5(1)(a) of the Care Standards Act 2000.

Section 41B(6) provides that in this section 'judge' includes:

(a) a justice of the peace (or, in Northern Ireland, a lay magistrate);
(b) a member of a tribunal; and
(c) a clerk or other officer entitled to exercise the jurisdiction of a court or tribunal;

and in this subsection 'tribunal' means any tribunal in which legal proceedings may be brought.

Code of Practice About Assessment Notices

22.05 Section 41C refers to codes of practice about assessment notices. Section 41C(1) provides that the ICO must prepare and issue a code of practice as to the manner in which the ICO's functions under and in connection with s 41A are to be exercised.

Section 41C(2) provides that the code must in particular:

- specify factors to be considered in determining whether to serve an assessment notice on a data controller;
- specify descriptions of documents and information that:
  - are not to be examined or inspected in pursuance of an assessment notice; or
  - are to be so examined or inspected only by persons of a description specified in the code;
- deal with the nature of inspections and examinations carried out in pursuance of an assessment notice;
- deal with the nature of interviews carried out in pursuance of an assessment notice;
- deal with the preparation, issuing and publication by the Commissioner of assessment reports in respect of data controllers that have been served with assessment notices.

Section 41C(3) provides that the provisions of the code made by virtue of s 41C(2)(b) must, in particular, include provisions that relate to:

- documents and information concerning an individual's physical or mental health;
- documents and information concerning the provision of social care for an individual.

Section 41C(4) provides that an assessment report is a report which contains:

- a determination as to whether a data controller has complied or is complying with the data protection principles;
- recommendations as to any steps which the data controller ought to take, or refrain from taking, to ensure compliance with any of those principles; and
- such other matters as are specified in the code.

Section 41C(5) provides that the ICO may alter or replace the code.

Request for Assessment

22.06   Section 42 refers to a request for an assessment. Section 42(1) provides that a request may be made to the ICO by or on behalf of any person who is, or believes themselves to be, directly affected by any processing of personal data for an assessment as to whether it is likely or unlikely that the processing has been or is being carried out in compliance with the provisions of the DPA.

On receiving a request under this section, the ICO shall make an assessment in such manner as appears to it to be appropriate, unless it has not been supplied with such information as it may reasonably require in order to, satisfy it as to the identity of the person making the request, and enable it to identify the processing in question (s 42(2)).

Section 42(3) provides that the matters to which the ICO may have regard in determining in what manner it is appropriate to make an assessment include:

- the extent to which the request appears to it to raise a matter of substance;
- any undue delay in making the request; and
- whether or not the person making the request is entitled to make an application under s 7 in respect of the personal data in question.

Section 42(1) provides that where the ICO has received a request under this section it shall notify the person who made the request:

- whether it has made an assessment as a result of the request; and
- to the extent that it considers appropriate, having regard in particular to any exemption from s 7 applying in relation to the personal data concerned, of any view formed or action taken as a result of the request.

Information Notices

22.07   Section 43 refers to information notices. Section 43(1) provides that if the ICO:

- has received a request under s 42 in respect of any processing of personal data; or
- reasonably requires any information for the purpose of determining whether the data controller has complied or is complying with the Data Protection Principles,

it may serve the data controller with a notice ('an information notice') requiring the data controller, to furnish the ICO with specified information relating to the request or to compliance with the principles.

Section 43(1A) provides that in s 43(1) 'specified information' means information:

- specified, or described, in the information notice; or
- falling within a category which is specified, or described, in the information notice.

Section 43(1B) provides that the ICO may also specify in the information notice:

- the form in which the information must be furnished;
- the period within which, or the time and place at which, the information must be furnished.

Section 43(1A)(2) provides that an information notice must contain:

(a) in a case falling within sub-s (1)(a), a statement that the ICO has received a request under s 42 in relation to the specified processing; or

(b) in a case falling within sub-s (1)(b), a statement that the ICO regards the specified information as relevant for the purpose of determining whether the data controller has complied, or is complying, with the data protection principles and his reasons for regarding it as relevant for that purpose.

Section 43(1A)(3) provides that an information notice must also contain particulars of the rights of appeal conferred by s 48.

Section 43(1A)(4) provides that subject to sub-s (5), a period specified in an information notice under sub-s (1B)(b) must not end, and a time so specified must not fall, before the end of the period within which an appeal can be brought against the notice and, if such an appeal is brought, the information need not be furnished pending the determination or withdrawal of the appeal.

Section 43(1A)(5) provides that if by reason of special circumstances the ICO considers that the information is required as a matter of urgency, it may include in the notice a statement to that effect and a statement of its reasons for reaching that conclusion; and in that event sub-s (4) shall not apply, but the notice shall not require the information to be furnished before the end of the period of seven days beginning with the day on which the notice is served.

Section 43(1A)(6) provides that a person shall not be required by virtue of this section to furnish the ICO with any information in respect of:

(a) any communication between a professional legal adviser and his client in connection with the giving of legal advice to the client with respect to his obligations, liabilities or rights under the DPA; or

(b) any communication between a professional legal adviser and his client, or between such an adviser or his client and any other person, made in connection with or in contemplation of proceedings under or arising out of this Act (including proceedings before the Tribunal) and for the purposes of such proceedings.

Section 43(1A)(8) provides that a person shall not be required by virtue of this section to furnish the ICO with any information if the furnishing of that information would, by revealing evidence of the commission of any offence, other than an offence under the DPA or an offence within sub-s (8A), expose them to proceedings for that offence.

Section 43(8A) provides that the offences mentioned in sub-s (8) are:

- an offence under s 5 of the Perjury Act 1911 (false statements made otherwise than on oath);

- an offence under s 44(2) of the Criminal Law (Consolidation) (Scotland) Act 1995 (false statements made otherwise than on oath); or

- an offence under Article 10 of the Perjury (Northern Ireland) Order 1979 (false statutory declarations and other false unsworn statements).

Section 43(1A)(8B) provides that any relevant statement provided by a person in response to a requirement under this section may not be used in evidence against that person on a prosecution for any offence under the DPA (other than an offence under s 47) unless in the proceedings:

- in giving evidence the person provides information inconsistent with it; and

- evidence relating to it is adduced, or a question relating to it is asked, by that person or on that person's behalf.

Section 43(1A)(8C) provides that in sub-s (8B) 'relevant statement,' in relation to a requirement under this section, means an oral statement, or a written statement made for the purposes of the requirement.

Section 43(1A)(9) provides that the ICO may cancel an information notice.[1]

---

1 Section 43(1A)(10) provides that this section has effect subject to s 46(3).

Special Information Notices

22.08 Section 44 refers to special information notices. Section 44(1) provides that if the ICO:

(a) has received a request under s 42 in respect of any processing of personal data; or
(b) has reasonable grounds for suspecting that, in a case in which proceedings have been stayed under s 32, the personal data to which the proceedings relate:
    (i) are not being processed only for the special purposes; or
    (ii) are not being processed with a view to the publication by any person of any journalistic, literary or artistic material which has not previously been published by the data controller,

it may serve the data controller with a notice ('special information notice') requiring the data controller to furnish the ICO with specified information for the purpose specified in sub-s (2).

Section 44(1A) provides that in sub-s (1) 'specified information' means information:

- specified, or described, in the special information notice; or
- falling within a category which is specified, or described, in the special information notice.

Section 44(1B) provides that the ICO may also specify in the special information notice:

- the form in which the information must be furnished;
- the period within which, or the time and place at which, the information must be furnished.

Section 44(2) provides that purpose is the purpose of ascertaining:

- whether the personal data are being processed only for the special purposes; or
- whether they are being processed with a view to the publication by any person of any journalistic, literary or artistic material which has not previously been published by the data controller.

Section 44(3) provides that a special information notice must contain:

- in a case falling within paragraph (a) of sub-s (1), a statement that the ICO has received a request under s 42 in relation to the specified processing; or
- in a case falling within paragraph (b) of that sub-section, a

statement of the Commissioner's grounds for suspecting that the personal data are not being processed as mentioned in that paragraph.

Section 44(4) provides that a special information notice must also contain particulars of the rights of appeal conferred by s 48.

Section 44(5) provides that subject to sub-s (6), a period specified in a special information notice under sub-s (1B)(b) must not end, and a time so specified must not fall, before the end of the period within which an appeal can be brought against the notice and, if such an appeal is brought, the information need not be furnished pending the determination or withdrawal of the appeal.

Section 44(6) provides that if by reason of special circumstances the ICO considers that the information is required as a matter of urgency, he may include in the notice a statement to that effect and a statement of his reasons for reaching that conclusion; and in that event sub-s (5) shall not apply, but the notice shall not require the information to be furnished before the end of the period of seven days beginning with the day on which the notice is served.

Section 44(7) provides that a person shall not be required by virtue of this section to furnish the ICO with any information in respect of:

- any communication between a professional legal adviser and his client in connection with the giving of legal advice to the client with respect to his obligations, liabilities or rights under the DPA; or

- any communication between a professional legal adviser and his client, or between such an adviser or his client and any other person, made in connection with or in contemplation of proceedings under or arising out of the DPA (including proceedings before the Tribunal) and for the purposes of such proceedings.

Section 44(8) provides that in sub-s (7) references to the client of a professional legal adviser include references to any person representing such a client.

Section 44(9) provides that a person shall not be required by virtue of this section to furnish the ICO with any information if the furnishing of that information would, by revealing evidence of the commission of any offence, other than an offence under the DPA or an offence within sub-s (9A), expose them to proceedings for that offence.

Section 44(9A) provides that the offences mentioned in sub-s (9) are:

- an offence under s 5 of the Perjury Act 1911 (false statements made otherwise than on oath);

- an offence under s 44(2) of the Criminal Law (Consolidation) (Scotland) Act 1995 (false statements made otherwise than on oath); or
- an offence under Article 10 of the Perjury (Northern Ireland) Order 1979 (false statutory declarations and other false unsworn statements).

Section 44(9B) provides that any relevant statement provided by a person in response to a requirement under this section may not be used in evidence against that person on a prosecution for any offence under this Act (other than an offence under s 47) unless in the proceedings:

- in giving evidence the person provides information inconsistent with it; and
- evidence relating to it is adduced, or a question relating to it is asked, by that person or on that person's behalf.

Section 44(9C) provides that in sub-s (9B) 'relevant statement,' in relation to a requirement under this section, means an oral statement; or a written statement made for the purposes of the requirement.

Section 44(10) provides that the ICO may cancel a special information notice .

ICO Determination of Special Purposes

22.09 Section 45 refers to a determination by the ICO as to the special purposes. Section 45(1) provides that where at any time it appears to the ICO (whether as a result of the service of a special information notice or otherwise) that any personal data:

- are not being processed only for the special purposes; or
- are not being processed with a view to the publication by any person of any journalistic, literary or artistic material which has not previously been published by the data controller,

it may make a determination in writing to that effect.

Section 45(2) provides that notice of the determination shall be given to the data controller; and the notice must contain particulars of the right of appeal conferred by s 48.

Section 45(3) provides that a determination under s 45(1) shall not take effect until the end of the period within which an appeal can be brought and, where an appeal is brought, shall not take effect pending the determination or withdrawal of the appeal.

Restriction on Enforcement in Case of Processing for the Special Purposes

22.10 Section 46 refers to the restriction on enforcement in case of processing for the special purposes. Section 46(1) provides that the ICO may not at any time serve an enforcement notice on a data controller with respect to the processing of personal data for the special purposes unless:

- a determination under s 45(1) with respect to those data has taken effect; and
- the court has granted leave for the notice to be served.

Section 46(2) provides that the court shall not grant leave for the purposes of s 46(1)(b) unless it is satisfied:

- that the ICO has reason to suspect a contravention of the data protection principles which is of substantial public importance; and
- except where the case is one of urgency, that the data controller has been given notice, in accordance with rules of court, of the application for leave.

Section 46(3) provides that the ICO may not serve an information notice on a data controller with respect to the processing of personal data for the special purposes unless a determination under s 45(1) with respect to those data has taken effect.

Failure to Comply with Notice

22.11 Section 47 refers to the failure to comply with notice. Section 4(1) provides that a person who fails to comply with an enforcement notice, an information notice or a special information notice is guilty of an offence.

Section 4(2) provides that a person who, in purported compliance with an information notice or a special information notice:

- makes a statement which he knows to be false in a material respect; or
- recklessly makes a statement which is false in a material respect,

is guilty of an offence.

Section 4(3) provides that it is a defence for a person charged with an offence under s 47(1) to prove that he exercised all due diligence to comply with the notice in question.

Appeal

22.12 Section 48 refers to rights of appeal. Section 48(1) provides that a person on whom an enforcement notice, an assessment notice, an information notice or a special information notice has been served may appeal to the (Data Protection) Tribunal against the notice.

Section 48(2) provides that a person on whom an enforcement notice has been served may appeal to the Tribunal against the refusal of an application under s 41(2) for cancellation or variation of the notice.

Section 48(3) provides that where an enforcement notice, an assessment notice, an information notice or a special information notice contains a statement by the ICO in accordance with ss 40(8), 41B(2), 43(5) or 44(6) then, whether or not the person appeals against the notice, he may appeal against:

- the ICO's decision to include the statement in the notice; or
- the effect of the inclusion of the statement as respects any part of the notice.

Section 48(4) provides that a data controller in respect of whom a determination has been made under s 45 may appeal to the Tribunal against the determination.

Section 48(6) provides that sch 6 has effect in relation to appeals under this section and the proceedings of the Tribunal in respect of any such appeal.

Unlawful Obtaining Etc of Personal Data

22.13 Section 55 refers to unlawful obtaining etc, of personal data. Section 55(1) provides that a person must not knowingly or recklessly, without the consent of the data controller:

- obtain or disclose personal data or the information contained in personal data; or
- procure the disclosure to another person of the information contained in personal data.

Section 55(2) provides that s 55 (1) does not apply to a person who shows:

(a) that the obtaining, disclosing or procuring:
    (i) was necessary for the purpose of preventing or detecting crime; or
    (ii) was required or authorised by or under any enactment, by any rule of law or by the order of a court,

(b) that they acted in the reasonable belief that they had in law the right to obtain or disclose the data or information or, as the case may be, to procure the disclosure of the information to the other person;

(c) that they acted in the reasonable belief that they would have had the consent of the data controller if the data controller had known of the obtaining, disclosing or procuring and the circumstances of it; or

(d) that in the particular circumstances the obtaining, disclosing or procuring was justified as being in the public interest.

Section 55(3) provides that a person who contravenes s 55(1) is guilty of an offence.

Section 55(4) provides that a person who sells personal data is guilty of an offence if they had obtained the data in contravention of s 55(1).

Section 55(5) provides that a person who offers to sell personal data is guilty of an offence if:

- they had obtained the data in contravention of s 55(1); or
- they subsequently obtain the data in contravention of that subsection.

Section 55(6) provides that for the purposes of sub-s (5), an advertisement indicating that personal data are or may be for sale is an offer to sell the data.

Section 55(7) provides that s 1(2) does not apply for the purposes of this section; and for the purposes of ss 55(4) to (6), 'personal data' includes information extracted from personal data.

Section 55(8) provides that references in this section to personal data do not include references to personal data which by virtue of s 28 or 33A are exempt from this section.

Power of ICO to Impose Monetary Penalty

22.14 Section 55A refers to the power of the ICO to impose monetary penalty. Section 55A(1) provides that the ICO may serve a data controller with a monetary penalty notice if the ICO is satisfied that:

- there has been a serious contravention of s 4(4) by the data controller;
- the contravention was of a kind likely to cause substantial damage or substantial distress; and
- s 55A(2) or (3) applies.

Section 55A(2) provides that this subsection applies if the contravention was deliberate.

Section 55A(3) provides that this subsection applies if the data controller:

(a) knew or ought to have known:
    (i) that there was a risk that the contravention would occur; and
    (ii) that such a contravention would be of a kind likely to cause substantial damage or substantial distress, but
(b) failed to take reasonable steps to prevent the contravention.

Section 55A(3A) provides that the ICO may not be satisfied as mentioned in sub-s (1) by virtue of any matter which comes to the ICO's attention as a result of anything done in pursuance of:

● an assessment notice;
● an assessment under s 51(7).

Section 55A(4) provides that a monetary penalty notice is a notice requiring the data controller to pay to the ICO a monetary penalty of an amount determined by the ICO and specified in the notice.

Section 55A(5) provides that the amount determined by the ICO must not exceed the prescribed amount.

Section 55A(6) provides that the monetary penalty must be paid to the ICO within the period specified in the notice.

Section 55A(7) provides that the notice must contain such information as may be prescribed.

Section 55A(8) provides that any sum received by the ICO by virtue of this section must be paid into the Consolidated Fund.

Section 55A(9) provides that in this section:

● 'data controller' does not include the Crown Estate Commissioners or a person who is a data controller by virtue of s 63(3);
● 'prescribed' means prescribed by regulations made by the Secretary of State.

See table of recent ICO penalties, which indicate that substantial fines and penalties can be imposed on organisations and, importantly, upon individuals also.

Monetary Penalty Notices: Procedural Rights

22.15   Section 55B refers to monetary penalty notices and procedural rights. Section 55(B)(1) provides that before serving a monetary penalty notice, the ICO must serve the data controller with a notice of intent.

Section 55(B)(2) provides that (2)A notice of intent is a notice that the ICO proposes to serve a monetary penalty notice. Section 55(B)(3) provides that a notice of intent must:

- inform the data controller that it may make written representations in relation to the ICO's proposal within a period specified in the notice; and
- contain such other information as may be prescribed.

Section 55(B)(4) provides that the ICO may not serve a monetary penalty notice until the time within which the data controller may make representations has expired.

Section 55(B)(5) provides that a person on whom a monetary penalty notice is served may appeal to the Tribunal against:

- the issue of the monetary penalty notice;
- the amount of the penalty specified in the notice.

Section 55(B)(6) provides that in this section, 'prescribed' means prescribed by regulations made by the Secretary of State.

Guidance About Monetary Penalty Notices

22.16   Section 55C refers to guidance about monetary penalty notices. Section 55C(1) provides that the ICO must prepare and issue guidance on how he proposes to exercise his functions under sections 55A and 55B.

Section 55C(2) provides that the guidance must, in particular, deal with:

- the circumstances in which it would consider it appropriate to issue a monetary penalty notice; and
- how it will determine the amount of the penalty.

Section 55C(3) provides that the ICO may alter or replace the guidance. Section 55C(4) provides that if the guidance is altered or replaced, the ICO must issue the altered or replacement guidance. Section 55C(5) provides that the ICO may not issue guidance under this section without the approval of the Secretary of State. Section 55C(6) provides that the ICO must lay any guidance issued under this section before each House of Parliament.

Section 55C(7) provides that the ICO must arrange for the publication of any guidance issued under this section in such form and manner as it considers appropriate.

Section 55C(8) provides that in sub-s (5) to (7), 'guidance' includes altered or replacement guidance.

Monetary Penalty Notices: Enforcement

22.17 Section 55D refers to monetary penalty notices: enforcement. Section 55D(1) provides that this section applies in relation to any penalty payable to the ICO by virtue of s 55A.

Section 55D(2) provides that in England and Wales, the penalty is recoverable:

- if a county court so orders, as if it were payable under an order of that court;
- if the High Court so orders, as if it were payable under an order of that court.

Section 55D(3) provides that in Scotland, the penalty may be enforced in the same manner as an extract registered decree arbitral bearing a warrant for execution issued by the sheriff court of any sheriffdom in Scotland.

Section 55D(4) provides that in Northern Ireland, the penalty is recoverable:

- if a county court so orders, as if it were payable under an order of that court;
- if the High Court so orders, as if it were payable under an order of that court.

Notices Under Sections 55A and 55B: Supplemental Provisions

22.18 Section 55E refers to notices under ss 55A and 55B (ie ICO monetary penalty notice) and contains supplemental provisions. Section 55E(1) provides that the Secretary of State may by order make further provision in connection with monetary penalty notices and notices of intent.

Section 55E(2) provides that an order under this section may in particular:

(a) provide that a monetary penalty notice may not be served on a data controller with respect to the processing of personal data for the special purposes except in circumstances specified in the order;

(b) make provision for the cancellation or variation of monetary penalty notices;

(c) confer rights of appeal to the Tribunal against decisions of the ICO in relation to the cancellation or variation of such notices;

(d) [amended];

(e) make provision for the determination of appeals made by virtue of para (c);

(f) [amended];

(3) An order under this section may apply any provision of the DPA with such modifications as may be specified in the order;

(4) An order under this section may amend the DPA.

Prohibition of Requirement as to Production of Certain Records

22.19 Section 56 refers to a prohibition of requirement as to production of certain records. Section 56(1) provides that a person must not, in connection with:

- the recruitment of another person as an employee;
- the continued employment of another person; or
- any contract for the provision of services to them by another person,

require that other person or a third party to supply them with a relevant record or to produce a relevant record to them.

Section 56(2) provides that a person concerned with the provision (for payment or not) of goods, facilities or services to the public or a section of the public must not, as a condition of providing or offering to provide any goods, facilities or services to another person, require that other person or a third party to supply them with a relevant record or to produce a relevant record to them.

Section 56(1) provides that s 56(1) and (2) do not apply to a person who shows:

- that the imposition of the requirement was required or authorised by or under any enactment, by any rule of law or by the order of a court; or

- that in the particular circumstances the imposition of the require-ment was justified as being in the public interest.

Section 56(4) provides that having regard to the provisions of Part V of the Police Act 1997 (certificates of criminal records etc), the imposition of the requirement referred to in s 56(1) or (2) is not to be regarded as being justified as being in the public interest on the ground that it would assist in the prevention or detection of crime.

Section 56(5) provides that a person who contravenes s 56(1) or (2) is guilty of an offence.

Section 56(6) provides that in this section 'a relevant record' means any record which:

- has been or is to be obtained by a data subject from any data controller specified in the first column of the Table below in the exercise of the right conferred by s 7; and
- contains information relating to any matter specified in relation to that data controller in the second column,

and includes a copy of such a record or a part of such a record.

Conclusion

22.20 Even general personal data is considered important and sensi-tive to customers. This should be respected by organisations. Organ-isations are not permitted to collect nor process customer, etc, personal data without being data protection compliant. It is in this context that there can be severe consequences for organisations for non-compliance, whether in collecting personal data initially, or in the subsequent processing of the personal data. The ICO can impose penalties finan-cially, or can prosecute for non-compliance. Alternatively, enforcement notices can be imposed which specify certain actions that must be implemented by the organisation. Certain types of organisation can be the recipient of separate types of notices, namely assessment notices. In any of these events, customers, etc will be particularly concerned that their personal data has been collected, is being processed in a certain manner and or may have been subject to a breach event. This can have its own consequences. Overall, it should also be noted that the conse-quences of breach or non-compliance are becoming increasingly important as enforcement actions and penalties are increasing, in frequency, number and financial scale.

Chapter 23

Trans Border Data Flows/ Transfers of Personal Data

Introduction

23.01 Organisations are under ever increasing pressure to reduce costs. This can sometimes involve consideration of outsourcing to countries outside of the EEA. Any transfers of personal data, unless specifically exempted, are restricted.

In addition, the global nature of commercial activities means that organisations as part of normal business processes may seek to transfer particular sets of personal data to group entities whom may be located outside of the EEA. There can be similar situations where an organisation wishes to make trans border data flows to agents, partners or outsourced data processors.

The data protection regime controls and regulates the transfers of personal data[1] from the UK to jurisdictions outside of the EEA. The transfer of personal data outside of the EU/EEA are known as trans border data flows (TBDFs).[2] Frequently organisations would have transferred personal data to other sections within their international organisation, such as banks. This could be personal data in relation to customers as well as employees (eg where the HR or payroll section

---

1 See Nugter, A., *Transborder Flow of Personal Data within the EC* (Boston: Kluwer Law and Taxation Publishers, 1990).

2 Beling, C.T., 'Transborder Data Flows: International Privacy Protection and the Free Flow of Information,' *Boston College International and Comparative Law Review* (1983)(6), pp. 591–624; 'Declaration on Transborder Data Flows,' *International Legal Materials* (1985)(24), pp. 912–913; Council recommendation Concerning Guidelines Governing the Protection of Privacy and Transborder Flows of Personal Data,' *International Legal Materials* (1981)(20), pp. 422–450; 'Draft Recommendation of the Council Concerning Guidelines the Protection of Privacy and Transborder Flows of Personal Data,' *International Legal Materials* (1980)(19), pp. 318–324.

may be in a different country). This too is included in the default ban, unless specifically exempted.

This trend of TDBFs has increased, however, as more and more activity is carried out online, such as eCommerce and social networking. Personal data is frequently transferred or mirrored on computer servers in more than one country as a matter of apparent technical routine.

However, organisations need to be aware that any transfer of personal data of EU citizens needs to be in compliance with the EU data protection regime. One of the obligations is that TBDFs of personal data may not occur.[3] This default position can be derogated from if one of a limited number of criteria are satisfied. If none of the exemption criteria apply, the default position in the data protection regime applies and the transfer cannot take place.

Transfer Ban

23.02 Article 25 of the DPD95 prohibits the transfer of data outside of the EEA unless:

- The third country ensures appropriate levels of protection (Article 25); or
- the transfer can come within one of the exemptions (Article 26).

The regime created under DPD95 means that transfers are prohibited per se. The focus is directed upon the privacy protection elsewhere and the dangers of uncontrolled transfers of personal data.

The DPA sets out in the eight Data Protection Principle that,

> 'Personal data shall not be transferred to a country or territory outside the European Economic Area [EEA] unless that country or territory ensures an adequate level of protection for the rights and freedoms of data subjects in relation to the processing of personal data.'

Data protection compliance practice for organisations means that they will have to include a compliance assessment as well as an assessment of the risks associated with transfers of personal data outside of the EEA. This applies to transfers from parent to subsidiary

---

3   For one article noting the difficulties that the data protection regime creates in terms of trans border data flows, see Kong L., 'Data Protection and Trans Border Data Flow in the European and Global Context,' *European Journal of International Law* (2010)(21), pp. 441–456.

or to a branch office in the same way as a transfer to an unrelated company or entity. However, different exemptions can apply in different scenarios.

DPA: Adequate Protection Exception

23.03 If the recipient country has already been deemed by the UK or EU to already have an adequate level of protection for personal data, then the transfer is permitted.

The DPA, Schedule 1, Part II, refers to the eighth Data Protection Principle and provides that an adequate level of protection is one which is adequate in all the circumstances of the case, having regard in particular to:

- the nature of the personal data;
- the country or territory of origin of the information contained in the data;
- the country or territory of final destination of that information;
- the purposes for which and period during which the data are intended to be processed;
- the law in force in the country or territory in question;
- the international obligations of that country or territory;
- any relevant codes of conduct or other rules which are enforceable in that country or territory (whether generally or by arrangement in particular cases); and
- any security measures taken in respect of the data in that country or territory.

It is also provided that a transfer can occur where there has been a positive Community finding in relation to the type of transfer proposed. A Community finding means a finding of the European Commission (under the procedure provided for in Article 31(2) of the DPD95), that a country or territory outside the European Economic Area does, or does not, ensure an adequate level of protection within the meaning of Article 25(2) of the Directive.

Therefore, if there has been a positive community finding in relation to a named country outside of the EEA, this means that that country is deemed to have a level of protection in its laws comparable to the EU data protection regime. This then makes it possible for organisations to make transfers to that specific country.

The EU Commission provides a list of Commission decisions on the adequacy of the protection of personal data in named third countries.[4] The EU Commission has thus far recognised that Switzerland, Canada, Argentina, Guernsey, Isle of Man, the US Department of Commerce's Safe Harbor Privacy Principles (if signed up and adhered to), and the transfer of air passenger name record to the United States Bureau of Customs and Border Protection (as specified) as providing adequate protection for personal data. This list will expand over time.

Exceptions

23.04 If the recipient country's protection for personal data is not adequate, or not ascertainable, but it is intended that TBDFs are still commercially desired, the organisation should ascertain if the transfer is comes within one of the excepted categories. Transfers of personal data from the UK to outside of the EEA cannot occur unless it falls within one of the transfer exemptions

The exemptions from the transfer restrictions are:

- The data subject has given consent;
- The transfer is necessary for performance of contract between data subject and data controller;
- The transfer is necessary for taking steps a request of data subject with a view to entering into a contract with the data controller;
- The transfer is necessary for conclusion of a contract between data controller and a person other than data subject that is entered into at request of data subject and is in the interests of the data subject;
- The transfer is necessary for the performance of such a contract;
- The transfer is required or authorised under any enactment or instrument imposing international obligation on UK;
- The transfer is necessary for reasons of substantial public interest;
- The transfer is necessary for purposes of or in connection with legal proceedings or prospective legal proceedings;
- The transfer is necessary in order to prevent injury or damage to the health of the data subject or serious loss of or damage to the property of the data subject or otherwise to protect vital interests;
- Subject to certain conditions the transfer is only part of personal data on a register established by or under an enactment;

4   Available at http://ec.europa.eu/justice/policies/privacy/thridcountries/index_en.htm, accessed on 18 January 2013.

- The transfer has been authorised by data protection commissioners where the data controller adduces adequate safeguards;
- The transfer is made to a country that has been determined by the EU Commission as having 'adequate levels of [data] protection' ie a Community finding (see above);
- The transfer is made to a US entity that has signed up to the EU/US 'safe harbour' arrangements (although less have signed up than originally envisaged);
- EU Commission contract provisions: the Model Contracts (the EU has set out model contracts which if incorporated into the data exporter – data importer/recipient relationship can act as an exemption thus permitting the transfer to occur.

In determining whether a third country ensures an adequate level of protection one factor taken into account includes:

- 'any security measures taken in respect of the data in that country or territory';
- *the transfer is necessary for obtaining legal advice or in connection with legal proceedings or prospective proceedings;*
- *(subject to certain conditions) it is necessary in order to prevent injury or damage to the health or property of the data subject, or in order to protect his or her vital interests;*
- *the transfer is required or authorised by law;*
- *the ICO has authorised the transfer where the data controller has given or adduced adequate safeguards; or*
- *the contract relating to the transfer of the data embodies appropriate contract clauses as specified in a 'Community finding.'*

Other potential exempted categories are where:

- The transfers substantially in the public interest;
- The transfers made in connection with any (legal) claim;
- The transfers in the vital interests of the data subject;
- There are public protesters;
- The transfer is necessary for the performance of a contract. (This will depend on the nature of the goods or services provided under the contract. The transfer must be necessary for the benefit of the transferee and not just convenient for the organisation).

For example, where a customer books a hotel in New York through an agent in London and it is necessary for the ultimate performance of the contract for the personal data to be transferred to the hotel in New York from the UK. The transfer of the personal data is permitted.

However, when a UK company in processing its employee payroll personal data sends it to a US parent company, such a transfer is for the convenience of the company and is not strictly necessary for the performance of a contract.

Creating Adequacy Through Consent

23.05 One of the possible transfer solutions is "creating adequacy" through consent.

Under Article 26 of DPD95, transfers can be made to a non-EEA country where the unambiguous consent of the data subject to that transfer is obtained. This will involve establishing sufficient prior information being provided to the data subject and appropriate consent then being given to the organisation.

Creating Adequacy Through Contract

23.06 One of the other exemptions relates to transfers permitted as a result of adopting the EU model contracts into the legal relationship between the data exporter and the data importer/recipient.

Transfers of data to a third country may be made even though there is not adequate protection in place in the third country, if the data controller secures the necessary level of protection through contractual obligations.

These contractual protections are the model contract clauses emanating from Commission. The Commission has issued what it considers to be adequate clauses which are incorporated into the contract relationship of the data exporter and data importer as then provide an adequate level of consent.

Obtaining consent of pre-existing customers may pose a problem so in some cases may not be possible or practical. For example, it may not be possible to retrospectively change existing contracts and terms.

However, going forward it may be possible to include 'transfer' issues in any data protection compliance and related models.

Binding Corporate Rules

23.07 The Commission and the WP29[5] also developed a policy of recognising adequate protection of the policies of multinational organisations transferring personal data whom satisfy the determined binding corporate rules (BCR), pursuant to DPD95 Article 26 (2).[6] This relates to transfers internally between companies within a related group of large multinational companies. It therefore, differs from the model contract clauses above which generally relate to non-related companies, rather than group companies.

Organisations which have contracts, policies and procedure which satisfy the BCR and are so accepted as doing so after a review process with the Commission or one of the national Data Protection Authorities can transfer personal data outside of the EU within the group organisation.

The WP29 has issued the following documents in relation to the BCR, namely:

- Working Document on Transfers of personal data to third countries: Applying Article 26 (2) of the EU Data Protection Directive to Binding Corporate Rules for International Data Transfers, 3 June 2003, WP 74;
- Model Checklist, Application for approval of Binding Corporate Rules, 25 November 2004, WP 102;
- Working Document Setting Forth a Co-Operation Procedure for Issuing Common Opinions on Adequate Safeguards Resulting From Binding Corporate Rules, 14 April 2005, WP 107;
- Working Document Establishing a Model Checklist Application for Approval of Binding Corporate Rules, 14 April 2005, WP 108;
- Recommendation 1/2007 on the Standard Application for Approval of Binding Corporate Rules for the Transfer of Personal Data;
- Working Document setting up a table with the elements and principles to be found in Binding Corporate Rules, 24 June 2008, WP 153;

---

5   Article 29 Working Party Recommendation 1/2007 on the Standard Application for Approval of Binding Corporate Rules for the Transfer of Personal Data; Working Document setting up a table with the elements and principles to be found in Binding Corporate Rules, WP 153 (2008); Working Document Setting up a framework for the structure of Binding Corporate Rules, WP154 (2008); Working Document on Frequently Asked Questions (FAQs) related to Binding Corporate Rules, WP155 (2008).

6   See http://ec.europa.eu/justice/policies/privacy/binding_rules/index_en.htm, accessed on 18 January 2013; Moerel, L., *Binding Corporate Rules, Corporate Self-Regulation of Global Data Transfers* (Oxford: OUP, 2012).

- Working Document Setting up a framework for the structure of Binding Corporate Rules, 24 June 2008, WP 154;
- Working Document on Frequently Asked Questions (FAQs) related to Binding Corporate Rules, 24 June 2008.

The BCR[7] appear to be increasingly popular to large multinational organisation in relation to their data processing and data transfer compliance obligations. The ICO also refers to the BCR at:

- http://www.ico.gov.uk/for_organisations/data_protection/overseas/binding_corporate_rules.aspx

It is envisaged that the popularity of the BCR option for exemption from the data protection regime transfer restrictions will increase. However, the review process with the Commission or one of the national Data Protection Authorities (such as the ICO) can take a considerable time given the complexity involved.

DPD95: Transfer Ban In Detail

23.08 DPD95 Article 25 refers to the principles. Article 25 (1) provides that the Member States shall provide that the transfer to a third country of personal data which are undergoing processing or are intended for processing after transfer may take place only if, without prejudice to compliance with the national provisions, the third country in question ensures an adequate level of protection.

Article 25 (2) provides that the adequacy of the level of protection afforded by a third country shall be assessed in the light of all the circumstances surrounding a data transfer operation or set of data transfer operations. Particular consideration shall be given to the nature of the data, the purpose and duration of the proposed processing operation or operations, the country of origin and country of final destination, the rules of law, both general and sectoral, in force in the third country in question and the professional rules and security measures which are complied with in that country.

Article 25(3) provides that the Member States and the Commission shall inform each other of cases where they consider that a third country does not ensure an adequate level of protection within the meaning of Article 25(2).

Article 25 (4) provides that where the Commission finds, under the procedure provided for in Article 31(2), that a third country does not

---

7   See also Moerel, L, *Binding Corporate Rules, Corporate Self-Regulation and Global Data Transfers* (Oxford: OUP, 2012).

ensure an adequate level of protection within the meaning of Article 25(2), Member States shall take the measures necessary to prevent any transfer of data of the same type to the third country in question.

Article 25 (4) provides that at the appropriate time, the Commission shall enter into negotiations with a view to remedying the situation resulting from the finding made pursuant to Article 25(4).

Article 25(6) provides that the Commission may find, in accordance with the procedure referred to in Article 31(2), that a third country ensures an adequate level of protection within the meaning of Article 25(2), by reason of its domestic law or of the international commitments it has entered into, particularly upon conclusion of the negotiations referred to in Article 25(5), for the protection of the private lives and basic freedoms and rights of individuals. In addition, Member States shall take the measures necessary to comply with the Commission's decision.

DPR: The New Transfers Regime

23.09   Chapter V of the DPR refers to the transfer of personal data to third countries or international organisations. Article 40 refers to the general principle for transfers. It provides that any transfer of personal data which are undergoing processing or are intended for processing after transfer to a third country or to an international organisation may only take place if, subject to the other provisions of the Regulation, the conditions laid down in this Chapter are complied with by the data controller and data processor, including for onward transfers of personal data from the third country or an international organisation to another third country or to another international organisation.

Article 41 refers to transfers with an adequacy decision. Article 41(1) provides that a transfer may take place where the Commission has decided that the third country, or a territory or a processing sector within that third country, or the international organisation in question ensures an adequate level of protection. Such transfer shall not require any further authorisation.

Article 41(2) provides that when assessing the adequacy of the level of protection, the Commission shall give consideration to the following elements, namely:

● the rule of law, relevant legislation in force, both general and sectoral, including concerning public security, defence, national security and criminal law, the professional rules and security measures which are complied with in that country or by that international organisation, as well as effective and enforceable rights including effective administrative and judicial redress for data subjects, in particular for those data subjects residing in the EU whose personal data are being transferred;

- the existence and effective functioning of one or more independent Supervisory Authorities in the third country or international organisation in question responsible for ensuring compliance with the data protection rules, for assisting and advising the data subjects in exercising their rights and for co-operation with the Supervisory Authorities of the EU and of Member States; and

- the international commitments the third country or international organisation in question has entered into.

Article 41(3) provides that the Commission may decide that a third country, or a territory or a processing sector within that third country, or an international organisation ensures an adequate level of protection within the meaning of Article 41(2). Those implementing acts shall be adopted in accordance with the examination procedure referred to in Article 87 (2).

Article 41(4) provides that the implementing act shall specify its geographical and sectoral application, and, where applicable, identify the National Supervisory Authority mentioned in Article 412(b) ie the second bullet above.

Article 41(5) provides that the Commission may decide that a third country, or a territory or a processing sector within that third country, or an international organisation does not ensure an adequate level of protection within the meaning of paragraph 2 of this Article, in particular in cases where the relevant legislation, both general and sectoral, in force in the third country or international organisation, does not guarantee effective and enforceable rights including effective administrative and judicial redress for data subjects, in particular for those data subjects residing in the EU whose personal data are being transferred. Those implementing acts shall be adopted in accordance with the examination procedure referred to in Article 87(2), or, in cases of extreme urgency for individuals with respect to their right to personal data protection, in accordance with the procedure referred to in Article 87(3).

Article 41(6) provides that where the Commission decides pursuant to Article 41(5), any transfer of personal data to the third country, or a territory or a processing sector within that third country, or the international organisation in question shall be prohibited, without prejudice to Articles 42 to 44. At the appropriate time, the Commission shall enter into consultations with the third country or international organisation with a view to remedying the situation resulting from the Decision made pursuant to para 5 of this Article.

Article 41(7) provides that the Commission shall publish a list of those third countries, territories and processing sectors within a third country and international organisations where it has decided that an adequate level of protection is or is not ensured. Organisations should continually check this list as it will change over time.

Article 41(8) provides that decisions adopted by the Commission on the basis of Article 25(6) or Article 26(4) of DPD95 shall remain in force, until amended, replaced or repealed by the Commission.

Article 42 refers to transfers by way of appropriate safeguards. Article 42(1) provides that where the Commission has taken no decision pursuant to Article 41, a data controller or data processor may transfer personal data to a third country or an international organisation only if the data controller or data processor has adduced appropriate safeguards with respect to the protection of personal data in a legally binding instrument.

Article 42(2) provides that the appropriate safeguards referred to in Article 42(1) shall be provided for, in particular, by:

- binding corporate rules in accordance with Article 43; or
- standard data protection clauses adopted by the Commission. Those implementing acts shall be adopted in accordance with the examination procedure referred to in Article 87(2); or
- standard data protection clauses adopted by a National Supervisory Authority in accordance with the consistency mechanism referred to in Article 57 when declared generally valid by the Commission pursuant to Article 62(1)(b); or
- contractual clauses between the data controller or data processor and the recipient of the data authorised by a National Supervisory Authority in accordance with Article 42(4).

Article 42(3) provides that a transfer based on standard data protection clauses or binding corporate rules as referred to in points (a), (b) or (c) of Article 42(2) shall not require any further authorisation ie the first three bullets above.

Article 42(4) provides that where a transfer is based on contractual clauses as referred to in point (d) of Article 42(2) of this Article the data controller or data processor shall obtain prior authorisation of the contractual clauses according to point (a) of Article 34(1) from the National Supervisory Authority. If the transfer is related to processing activities which concern data subjects in another Member State or other Member States, or substantially affect the free movement of personal data within the EU, the National Supervisory Authority shall apply the consistency mechanism referred to in Article 57.

Article 42(5) provides that where the appropriate safeguards with respect to the protection of personal data are not provided for in a legally binding instrument, the data controller or data processor shall obtain prior authorisation for the transfer, or a set of transfers, or for provisions to be inserted into administrative arrangements providing the basis for such transfer. Such authorisation by the National Supervisory Authority shall be in accordance with point (a) of Article 34(1). If the transfer is related to processing activities which concern data subjects in another Member State or other Member States, or substantially affect the free movement of personal data within the EU, the National Supervisory Authority shall apply the consistency mechanism referred to in Article 57. Authorisations by a National Supervisory Authority on the basis of Article 26(2) of DPD95 remain valid, until amended, replaced or repealed by that National Supervisory Authority.

Article 43 refers to transfers by way of binding corporate rules. Article 43(1) provides that a National Supervisory Authority shall in accordance with the consistency mechanism set out in Article 58 approve BCR, provided that they:

- are legally binding and apply to and are enforced by every member within the data controller's or data processor's group of undertakings, and include their employees;
- expressly confer enforceable rights on data subjects;
- fulfil the requirements laid down in Article 43(2).

Article 43(2) provides that the BCR shall at least specify:

(a) the structure and contact details of the group of undertakings and its members;

(b) the data transfers or set of transfers, including the categories of personal data, the type of processing and its purposes, the type of data subjects affected and the identification of the third country or countries in question;

(c) their legally binding nature, both internally and externally;

(d) the general data protection principles, in particular purpose limitation, data quality, legal basis for the processing, processing of sensitive personal data; measures to ensure data security; and the requirements for onward transfers to organisations which are not bound by the policies;

(e) the rights of data subjects and the means to exercise these rights, including the right not to be subject to a measure based on profiling in accordance with Article 20, the right to lodge a complaint before the competent National Supervisory Authority and before the competent courts of the Member States in accordance with Article 75, and to obtain redress and, where appropriate, compensation for a breach of the binding corporate rules;

(f) the acceptance by the data controller or data processor established on the territory of a Member State of liability for any breaches of the binding corporate rules by any member of the group of undertakings not established in the EU; the data controller or the data processor may only be exempted from this liability, in whole or in part, if it proves that that member is not responsible for the event giving rise to the damage;

(g) how the information on the BCR, in particular on the provisions referred to in points (d), (e) and (f) of this paragraph is provided to the data subjects in accordance with Article 11;

(h) the tasks of the data protection officer designated in accordance with Article 35, including monitoring within the group of undertakings the compliance with the binding corporate rules, as well as monitoring the training and complaint handling;

(i) the mechanisms within the group of undertakings aiming at ensuring the verification of compliance with the binding corporate rules;

(j) the mechanisms for reporting and recording changes to the policies and reporting these changes to the National Supervisory Authority;

(k) the co-operation mechanism with the National Supervisory Authority to ensure compliance by any member of the group of undertakings, in particular by making available to the National Supervisory Authority the results of the verifications of the measures referred to in point (i) of this paragraph.

Article 43(3) provides that the Commission shall be empowered to adopt delegated acts in accordance with Article 86 for the purpose of further specifying the criteria and requirements for binding corporate rules within the meaning of this Article, in particular as regards the criteria for their approval, the application of points (b), (d), (e) and (f) of para 2 to binding corporate rules adhered to by data processors and on further necessary requirements to ensure the protection of personal data of the data subjects concerned.

Article 43(4) provides that the Commission may specify the format and procedures for the exchange of information by electronic means between data controllers, data processors and National Supervisory Authorities for BCR within the meaning of this Article. Those implementing acts shall be adopted in accordance with the examination procedure set out in Article 87(2).

Article 44 refers to derogations. Article 44 (1) provides that in the absence of an adequacy decision pursuant to Article 41 or of appropriate safeguards pursuant to Article 42, a transfer or a set of transfers of personal data to a third country or an international organisation may take place only on condition that:

(a) the data subject has consented to the proposed transfer, after having been informed of the risks of such transfers due to the absence of an adequacy decision and appropriate safeguards; or

(b) the transfer is necessary for the performance of a contract between the data subject and the data controller or the implementation of pre-contractual measures taken at the data subject's request; or

(c) the transfer is necessary for the conclusion or performance of a contract concluded in the interest of the data subject between the data controller and another natural or legal person; or

(d) the transfer is necessary for important grounds of public interest; or

(e) the transfer is necessary for the establishment, exercise or defence of legal claims; or

(f) the transfer is necessary in order to protect the vital interests of the data subject or of another person, where the data subject is physically or legally incapable of giving consent; or

(g) the transfer is made from a register which according to EU or Member State law is intended to provide information to the public and which is open to consultation either by the public in general or by any person who can demonstrate legitimate interest, to the extent that the conditions laid down in EU or Member State law for consultation are fulfilled in the particular case; or

(h) the transfer is necessary for the purposes of the legitimate interests pursued by the data controller or the data processor, which cannot be qualified as frequent or massive, and where the data controller or data processor has assessed all the circumstances surrounding the data transfer operation or the set of data transfer operations and based on this assessment adduced appropriate safeguards with respect to the protection of personal data, where necessary.

Article 44(2) provides that a transfer pursuant to point (g) of Article 44(1) shall not involve the entirety of the personal data or entire categories of the personal data contained in the register. When the register is intended for consultation by persons having a legitimate interest, the transfer shall be made only at the request of those persons or if they are to be the recipients.

Article 44(3) provides that where the processing is based on point (h) of Article 44(1), the data controller or data processor shall give particular consideration to the nature of the data, the purpose and duration of the proposed processing operation or operations, as well as the situation in the country of origin, the third country and the country of final destination, and adduced appropriate safeguards with respect to the protection of personal data, where necessary.

Article 44(4) provides that points (b), (c) and (h) of Article 44(1) shall not apply to activities carried out by public authorities in the exercise of their public powers.

Article 44(5) provides that the public interest referred to in point (d) of Article 44(1) must be recognised in EU law or in the law of the Member State to which the controller is subject.

Article 44(6) provides that the data controller or data processor shall document the assessment as well as the appropriate safeguards adduced referred to in point (h) of Article 44(1) of this Article in the documentation referred to in Article 28 and shall inform the National Supervisory Authority of the transfer.

Article 44(7) provides that the Commission shall be empowered to adopt delegated acts in accordance with Article 86 for the purpose of further specifying 'important grounds of public interest' within the meaning of point (d) of Article 44(1) as well as the criteria and requirements for appropriate safeguards referred to in point (h) of Article 44(1).

Article 45 refers to international co-operation for the protection of personal data. Article 45 (1) provides that in relation to third countries and international organisations, the Commission and Supervisory Authorities shall take appropriate steps to:

(a) develop effective international co-operation mechanisms to facilitate the enforcement of legislation for the protection of personal data;

(b) provide international mutual assistance in the enforcement of legislation for the protection of personal data, including through notification, complaint referral, investigative assistance and information exchange, subject to appropriate safeguards for the protection of personal data and other fundamental rights and freedoms;

(c) engage relevant stakeholders in discussion and activities aimed at furthering international co-operation in the enforcement of legislation for the protection of personal data;

(d) promote the exchange and documentation of personal data protection legislation and practice.

Article 45(2) provides that for the purposes of Article 45(1), the Commission shall take appropriate steps to advance the relationship with third countries or international organisations, and in particular their Supervisory Authorities, where the Commission has decided that they ensure an adequate level of protection within the meaning of Article 41 (3).

DPD95: Derogations

23.10   Article 26 of the DPD95 refers to derogations. Article 26(1) provides that by way of derogation from Article 25, Member States shall provide that a transfer or a set of transfers of personal data to a third country which does not ensure an adequate level of protection within the meaning of Article 25(2) may take place on condition that:

- data subject has given their consent unambiguously to the proposed transfer; or
- the transfer is necessary for the performance of a contract between the data subject and the data controller or the implementation of pre-contractual measures taken in response to the data subject's request; or
- the transfer is necessary for the conclusion or performance of a contract concluded in the interest of the data subject between the data controller and a third party; or
- the transfer is necessary or legally required on important public interest grounds, or for the establishment, exercise or defence of legal claims; or
- the transfer is necessary in order to protect the vital interests of the data subject; or
- the transfer is made from a register which according to laws or regulations is intended to provide information to the public and which is open to consultation either by the public in general or by any person who can demonstrate legitimate interest, to the extent that the conditions laid down in law for consultation are fulfilled in the particular case.

Article 26(2) provides that without prejudice to Article 26(1), a Member State may authorise a transfer or a set of transfers of personal data to a third country which does not ensure an adequate level of protection within the meaning of Article 25(2), where the data controller adduces adequate safeguards with respect to the protection of the privacy and fundamental rights and freedoms of individuals and as regards the exercise of the corresponding rights. Such safeguards may in particular result from appropriate contractual clauses.

Article 26(3) provides that the Member State shall inform the Commission and the other Member States of the authorisations it grants pursuant to Article 26(2). If a Member State or the Commission objects on justified grounds involving the protection of the privacy and fundamental rights and freedoms of individuals, the Commission shall take appropriate measures in accordance with the procedure laid down in Article 31(2). Member States shall take the necessary measures to comply with the Commission's decision.

Article 26(4) provides that where the Commission decides, in accordance with the procedure referred to in Article 31(2), that certain standard contractual clauses offer sufficient safeguards as required by Article 26(2), Member States shall take the necessary measures to comply with the Commission's decision.

DPR: Derogations and Restriction

23.11 Section 5 of the DPR refers to restrictions. Article 21(1) provides that EU or Member State law may restrict by way of a legislative measure the scope of the obligations and rights provided for in of Article 5(a) to (e), Articles 11 to 20 and Article 32, when such a restriction constitutes a necessary and proportionate measure in a democratic society to safeguard:

(a) public security;

(b) the prevention, investigation, detection and prosecution of criminal offences;

(c) other public interests of the EU or of a Member State, in particular an important economic or financial interest of the EU or of a Member State, including monetary, budgetary and taxation matters and the protection of market stability and integrity;

(d) the prevention, investigation, detection and prosecution of breaches of ethics for regulated professions;

(e) a monitoring, inspection or regulatory function connected, even occasionally, with the exercise of official authority in cases referred to in (a), (b), (c) and (d);

(f) the protection of the data subject or the rights and freedoms of others.

Article 21(2) provides that in particular, any legislative measure referred to in Article 22(1) shall contain specific provisions at least as to the objectives to be pursued by the processing and the determination of the data controller.

Issues

23.12 Certain issues may arise in relation to:

- What is a "transfer"? Is there a difference between transfer versus transit;
- "Data" and anonymised data, is there a restriction on TBDFs of anonymised data. For example, can certain anonymised data fall outside the definition of personal data?;
- "Third country" currently includes the EU countries and EEA countries of Iceland, Norway, Liechtenstein. The EU countries are expanding over time. In addition, the list of permitted additional third countries is also expanding over time, for example, safe harbour.

Establishing if the Ban Applies

23.13 Assessing if the export ban applies, includes asking the following questions:

- Does the organisation transfer personal data?;
- Is there a transfer?;
- Is there a transfer to a 'third country'?;
- Does that third country have an adequate level of protection?;
- Transfers to the US – safe harbour;
- White list countries;
- What constitutes adequacy?;
- The nature of the data;
- How it is to be used?;
- The laws and practices in place in the third country;
- Transfer by data controller to data processor. Under Article 7 DPD95 such a transfer requires a contract to be put in place relating to security measures to date. The data controller retains control of the personal data so that the risk to the data subject is minimal;
- Transfers within an international or multinational company or group of companies where an internal privacy code or agreement is in place;
- Transfers within a consortium established to process international transactions, for example, banking;
- Transfers between professionals such as lawyers or accountants where a clients business has on international dimension;
- The European Commission has identified core principles which must be present in the foreign laws or codes of practice or

regulations in order to achieve the requisite standard of 'adequacy' in third party countries;

- Personal data must be processed for a specific purpose;
- Personal data must be accurate and kept up to date;
- The data subject must be provided with adequate information in relation to the transfer;
- Technical and organisational security measures should be taken by the data controller;
- There must be a right of access to the data by the data subject;
- There should be a prohibition on onward transfer of data along the lines of Article 25 of the DPD95; and
- There should be an effective procedure or mode of enforcement.

Checklist for Compliance

23.14   Organisations should consider the following queries:

- Does the organisation transfer customer, etc personal data outside of that EEA?;
- Is there a transfer to the US? If so, is the recipient of the data a safe harbour recipient? If yes, then the organisation can transfer the data. If not, the organisation needs to: (i) assess the adequacy of the protection measures in place; (ii) see if that transfer is exempted; (iii) create adequacy through consent or appropriate contract;
- Is the recipient country a Commission permitted white list country? If so, transfer is permitted;
- Are there data protection rules in place or codes of practice and if so did they incorporate the adequate and equivalent protections?;
- If there is inadequate protection is it practical to obtain the consent of the data subject?;
- If not, then is it practical to enter into an appropriate contract with the recipient?;
- Are the Commission model data contract clauses is available?

The ICO also asks:

1. Does the organisation need to transfer personal data abroad?;
2. Is the organisation transferring the personal data to a country outside of the EEA or will it just be in transit through a non-EEA country?:
3. Has the organisation complied with all the other Data Protection Principles?;
4. Is the transfer to a country on the EU Commission's white list of countries or territories (per a Community finding) accepted as

providing adequate levels of protection for the rights and freedoms of data subjects in connection with the processing of their personal data?;

5. If the transfer is to the US, has the US recipient of the personal data signed up to the EU-US Department of Commerce Safe Harbor scheme?;

6. Is the personal data passenger name record information (PNR)? If so, particular rules may apply;

8. Can the organisation assess that the level of protection for data subjects' rights as 'adequate in all the circumstances of the case'?;

9. If not, can the organisation put in place adequate safeguards to protect the rights of the data subjects whose data is to be transferred?;

10. Can the organisation rely on another exception from the restriction on international transfers of personal data?[8]

Conclusion

23.15 Data protection compliance practice for organisations means that they will have to include a compliance assessment, as well as an assessment of associated risks, in relation to potential transfers of personal data outside of the EEA. This applies to transfers from parent to subsidiary or to a branch office as well as transfers to any unrelated company or entity.

The ICO also provides useful guidance in relation to:

- Assessing Adequacy;
- Model Contract Clauses;
- Binding Corporate Rules; and
- Outsourcing.[9]

There is also the following ICO guidance which can be a useful reference for organisations, namely, the,

Data Protection Act 1998,

The Eighth Data Protection Principle and International Data Transfers,

The Information Commissioner's Recommended Approach to Assessing Adequacy Including Consideration of the Issue of Contractual Solutions, Binding Corporate Rules and Safe Harbor.

---

8 ICO, available at http://www.ico.gov.uk/for_organisations/data_protection/overseas. aspx, accessed on 18 January 2013.

9 ICO, available at http://www.ico.gov.uk/for_organisations/data_protection/overseas. aspx, accessed on 18 January 2013.

Organisations should be aware that if they wish to transfer personal data outside of the EEA, that additional considerations arise and that unless there is a specific exemption, then the transfer may not be permitted. Once a transfer possibility arises, the organisation should undertake a compliance exercise to assess if the transfer can be permitted, and if so, how. Additional compliance documentation and contracts may be required.

The increasing locations and methods by which personal data may be collected by organisations, in particular internet, communications and social networking, will increasingly be scrutinised in terms of transparency, consent and compliance. Equally, cloud computing is receiving particular data protection attention. Apps are also being considered.

Chapter 24

ePrivacy and Electronic Communications

Introduction

24.01 There is increasing use of electronically transmitted personal data. This is protected and regulated, in certain respects, separate from the general data protection regime under the DPD95 (and forthcoming DPR).

While originally the regulation of telecommunications related personal data centred on telecoms companies, it is now recognised as encompassing telecoms companies and certain companies engaged in activities involving the collection or transmission of particular personal data over electronic communications networks, including the internet.

Organisations concerned with compliance relating to marketing, email marketing, text marketing, telephone marketing, fax marketing, the use of location based data, cookies, identification regarding telephone calls and other telephone issues need to consider the additional data protection rules.

Background

24.02 There has been a separation between the data protection of general personal data, in the DPD95, and the regulation of personal data in (tele)communications networks. The later were legislated for in the Data Protection Directive of 1997.[1] This was later replaced with the ePrivacy Directive (ePD). More recently, the ePD was amended by Directive 2006/24/EC and Directive 2009/136/EC.

ePD[2] concerns the processing and protection of personal data and privacy in the electronic communications sector. It is also known as the

---

1   Directive 97/66/EC.
2   Directive 2002/58/EC of 12 July 2002.

Directive on privacy and electronic communications, hence ePD. One of the concerns has been how electronic communications and electronic information are increasingly used for profiling for marketing purposes, including by electronic means.[3] (Indeed, this is also reflected in the new cookie rules mentioned earlier).

Scope of the ePD

24.03 The ePD broadly relates to and encompasses the following, namely:

- Definitions;
- Security;
- Confidentiality;
- Traffic data;
- Non itemised bills;
- Call and connected line identification;
- Location data;
- Exceptions;
- Directories;
- Unsolicited communications;
- Technical Features.

It also provides rules in relation to:

- Email marketing;
- Text marketing;
- Telephone marketing;
- Fax marketing;
- Cookies, etc. (See above also, Chapter 21).

Marketing

24.04 How should organisations go about ensuring data protection compliance for direct marketing (DM)? When is DM permitted? All organisations should carefully assess compliance issues when considering any direct marketing activities. Getting it wrong can be costly and can have ICO enforcement and investigation consequences as well as penalties.

---

3   See, for example, McGeveran, W., 'Disclosure, Endorsement, and Identity in Social Marketing,' *University of Illinois Law Review* (2009)(4), pp. 1105–1166.

Article 13 of the ePD refers to unsolicited communications. Article 13(1) in particular provides that the use of the following, namely:

- automated calling systems without human intervention (automatic calling machines);
- facsimile machines (fax); or
- electronic mail,

for the purposes of direct marketing may *only* be allowed in respect of subscribers who have given their *prior consent*.

This means that there is a default rule prohibiting DM without prior consent. Many marketing orientated organisation may be surprised, if not dismayed by this.

Existing Customers' Email

24.05 However, in the context of existing customers, there is a possibility to direct market using emails. Article 13(2) of the ePD provides that notwithstanding Article 13(1), where an organisation obtains from its customers their electronic contact details for email, in the context of the sale of a product or a service, in accordance with DPD95, the organisation may use these electronic contact details for DM of its own similar products or services provided that customers clearly and distinctly are given the opportunity to object, free of charge and in an easy manner, to such use of electronic contact details when they are collected and on the occasion of each message in case the customer has not initially refused such use.

Therefore, once the email details are obtained at the time of a product or service transaction, it will be possible to use that email for direct marketing purposes. Conditions or limitations apply however. Firstly, the organisation is only permitted to market and promote similar products or services. This, therefore, rules out unrelated, non-identical and non-similar products and services. Secondly, at the time of each subsequent act of DM, the customer must be given the opportunity in an easy manner to opt-out or cancel the DM. Effectively, they must be taken off of the DM list.

National Opt-out Registers

24.06 Article 13 (3) of ePD provides that Member States shall take appropriate measures to ensure that, free of charge, unsolicited communications for purposes of direct marketing, in cases other than those referred to in paragraphs 1 and 2, are not allowed either without the consent of the subscribers concerned or in respect of subscribers who do not wish to receive these communications, the choice between these options to be determined by national legislation. This means that each Member State must determine and provide a means for individuals to opt-out of receiving DM in advance.[4]

Marketing Emails Must Not Conceal Their Identity

24.07 Article 13(4) of ePD provides that the practice of sending electronic mail for purposes of DM disguising or concealing the identity of the sender on whose behalf the communication is made shall be prohibited. This means that organisations cannot conceal their identity if permitted to engage in direct marketing. If these are not complied with, what might otherwise be permissible DM can be deemed to be impermissible. Complaints, investigations or enforcement proceedings can thus arise.

Marketing Emails Must Have an Opt-Out

24.08 In addition, Article 13(4) of ePD provides that the practice of sending electronic mail for purposes of DM without a valid address to which the recipient may send a request that such communications cease, shall be prohibited. This means that organisations must also include an easy contact address or other details at which the recipient can contact if they wish to object to receiving any further DM. If these are not complied with, what might otherwise be permissible DM can be deemed to be impermissible. Complaints, investigations or enforcement proceedings can thus also arise.

Marketing Protection for Organisations

24.09 Article 13(5) of ePD provides that Article 13(1) and (3) shall apply to subscribers who are natural persons. Member States shall also ensure, in the framework of EU law and applicable national legislation, that the legitimate interests of subscribers other than natural persons with regard to unsolicited communications are sufficiently protected. This means that protection from unsolicited DM can also be extended to organisations.

---

4   See ICO website, available at http://www.ico.gov.uk/for_the_public/topic_specific_ guides/marketing.aspx, accessed on 18 January 2013.

Background: ePD

24.10   As with DPD95, the Recitals provide background and contextual details useful to understanding the purpose and interpretation of the
Directive. ePD Recital 1 notes that DPD94 requires Member States to
ensure the rights and freedoms of natural persons with regard to the
processing of personal data, and in particular their right to privacy, in
order to ensure the free flow of personal data in the EU.

ePD Recital 2 notes that the Directive seeks to respect the fundamental rights and observes the principles recognised in particular by the
Charter of fundamental rights of the European Union.

ePD Recital 3 notes that confidentiality of communications is guaranteed in accordance with the international instruments relating to
human rights, in particular the European Convention for the Protection
of Human Rights and Fundamental Freedoms, and the constitutions of
the Member States. ePD Recital 6 notes that the Internet is overturning
traditional market structures by providing a common, global infrastructure for the delivery of a wide range of electronic communications
services. Publicly available electronic communications services over
the Internet open new possibilities for users but also new risks for their
personal data and privacy.

ePD Recital 7 notes that in the case of public communications
networks, specific legal, regulatory and technical provisions should be
made in order to protect fundamental rights and freedoms of natural
persons and legitimate interests of legal persons, in particular with
regard to the increasing capacity for automated storage and processing
of data relating to subscribers and users.

ePD Recital 12 notes that subscribers to a publicly available electronic communications service may be natural or legal persons. By
supplementing DPD95, this Directive is aimed at protecting the fundamental rights of natural persons and particularly their right to privacy,
as well as the legitimate interests of legal persons. This Directive does
not entail an obligation for Member States to extend the application of
DPD95 to the protection of the legitimate interests of legal persons,
which is ensured within the framework of the applicable EU and
national legislation.

ePD Recital 14 notes that location data may refer to the latitude,
longitude and altitude of the user's terminal equipment, to the direction
of travel, to the level of accuracy of the location information, to the
identification of the network cell in which the terminal equipment is
located at a certain point in time and to the time the location information was recorded.

ePD Recital 15 notes that a communication may include any naming, numbering or addressing information provided by the sender of a communication or the user of a connection to carry out the communication. Traffic data may include any translation of this information by the network over which the communication is transmitted for the purpose of carrying out the transmission. Traffic data may, inter alia, consist of data referring to the routing, duration, time or volume of a communication, to the protocol used, to the location of the terminal equipment of the sender or recipient, to the network on which the communication originates or terminates, to the beginning, end or duration of a connection. They may also consist of the format in which the communication is conveyed by the network.

ePD Recital 16 notes that information that is part of a broadcasting service provided over a public communications network is intended for a potentially unlimited audience and does not constitute a communication in the sense of this Directive. However, in cases where the individual subscriber or user receiving such information can be identified, for example with video-on-demand services, the information conveyed is covered within the meaning of a communication for the purposes of this Directive.

ePD Recital 17 notes that for the purposes of this Directive, consent of a user or subscriber, regardless of whether the latter is a natural or a legal person, should have the same meaning as the data subject's consent as defined and further specified in DPD95. Consent may be given by any appropriate method enabling a freely given specific and informed indication of the user's wishes, including by ticking a box when visiting an Internet website.

ePD Recital 18 notes that value added services (VAS) may, for example, consist of advice on least expensive tariff packages, route guidance, traffic information, weather forecasts and tourist information.

ePD Recital 19 notes that the application of certain requirements relating to presentation and restriction of calling and connected line identification and to automatic call forwarding to subscriber lines connected to analogue exchanges should not be made mandatory in specific cases where such application would prove to be technically impossible or would require a disproportionate economic effort. It is important for interested parties to be informed of such cases and the Member States should therefore notify them to the Commission.

ePD Recital 20 notes that service providers should take appropriate measures to safeguard the security of their services, if necessary in conjunction with the provider of the network, and inform subscribers of any special risks of a breach of the security of the network. Such risks may especially occur for electronic communications services over an open network such as the Internet or analogue mobile telephony. It is particularly important for subscribers and users of such services to be fully informed by their service provider of the existing security risks which lie outside the scope of possible remedies by the service provider. Service providers who offer publicly available electronic communications services over the Internet should inform users and subscribers of measures they can take to protect the security of their communications for instance by using specific types of software or encryption technologies. The requirement to inform subscribers of particular security risks does not discharge a service provider from the obligation to take, at its own costs, appropriate and immediate measures to remedy any new, unforeseen security risks and restore the normal security level of the service. The provision of information about security risks to the subscriber should be free of charge except for any nominal costs which the subscriber may incur while receiving or collecting the information, for instance by downloading an electronic mail message. Security is appraised in the light of Article 17 of DPD95.

ePD Recital 21 notes that notes that measures should be taken to prevent unauthorised access to communications in order to protect the confidentiality of communications, including both the contents and any data related to such communications, by means of public communications networks and publicly available electronic communications services.

ePD Recital 22 notes that the prohibition of storage of communications and the related traffic data by persons other than the users or without their consent is not intended to prohibit any automatic, intermediate and transient storage of this information in so far as this takes place for the sole purpose of carrying out the transmission in the electronic communications network and provided that the information is not stored for any period longer than is necessary for the transmission and for traffic management purposes, and that during the period of storage the confidentiality remains guaranteed. Where this is necessary for making more efficient the onward transmission of any publicly accessible information to other recipients of the service upon their request, this Directive should not prevent such information from being further stored, provided that this information would in any case be accessible to the public without restriction and that any data referring to the individual subscribers or users requesting such information are erased.

ePD Recital 23 notes that confidentiality of communications should also be ensured in the course of lawful business practice. Where necessary and legally authorised, communications can be recorded for the purpose of providing evidence of a commercial transaction. DPD95 applies to such processing. Parties to the communications should be informed prior to the recording about the recording, its purpose and the duration of its storage. The recorded communication should be erased as soon as possible and in any case at the latest by the end of the period during which the transaction can be lawfully challenged.

ePD Recital 24 notes that terminal equipment of users of electronic communications networks and any information stored on such equipment are part of the private sphere of the users requiring protection under the European Convention for the Protection of Human Rights and Fundamental Freedoms. So-called spyware, web bugs, hidden identifiers and other similar devices can enter the user's terminal without their knowledge in order to gain access to information, to store hidden information or to trace the activities of the user and may seriously intrude upon the privacy of these users. The use of such devices should be allowed only for legitimate purposes, with the knowledge of the users concerned.

ePD Recital 25 notes, however, such devices, for instance 'cookies,' can sometimes be a legitimate and useful tool, for example, in analysing the effectiveness of website design and advertising, and in verifying the identity of users engaged in on-line transactions. Where such devices, for instance cookies, are intended for a legitimate purpose, such as to facilitate the provision of information society services, their use should be allowed on condition that users are provided with clear and precise information in accordance with DPD95 about the purposes of cookies or similar devices so as to ensure that users are made aware of information being placed on the terminal equipment they are using. Users should have the opportunity to refuse to have a cookie or similar device stored on their terminal equipment. This is particularly important where users other than the original user have access to the terminal equipment and thereby to any data containing privacy-sensitive information stored on such equipment. Information and the right to refuse may be offered once for the use of various devices to be installed on the user's terminal equipment during the same connection and also covering any further use that may be made of those devices during subsequent connections. The methods for giving information, offering a right to refuse or requesting consent should be made as user-friendly as possible. Access to specific website content may still be made conditional on the well-informed acceptance of a cookie or similar device, if it is used for a legitimate purpose.

ePD Recital 26 notes that the data relating to subscribers processed within electronic communications networks to establish connections and to transmit information contain information on the private life of natural persons and concern the right to respect for their correspond-ence or concern the legitimate interests of legal persons. Such data may only be stored to the extent that is necessary for the provision of the service for the purpose of billing and for interconnection payments, and for a limited time. Any further processing of such data which the provider of the publicly available electronic communications services may want to perform, for the marketing of electronic communications services or for the provision of value added services, may only be allowed if the subscriber has agreed to this on the basis of accurate and full information given by the provider of the publicly available elec-tronic communications services about the types of further processing it intends to perform and about the subscriber's right not to give or to withdraw his/her consent to such processing. Traffic data used for marketing communications services or for the provision of value added services should also be erased or made anonymous after the provision of the service. Service providers should always keep subscribers informed of the types of data they are processing and the purposes and duration for which this is done.

ePD Recital 27 notes that the exact moment of the completion of the transmission of a communication, after which traffic data should be erased except for billing purposes, may depend on the type of electronic communications service that is provided. For instance, for a voice telephony call the transmission will be completed as soon as either of the users terminates the connection. For electronic mail the transmis-sion is completed as soon as the addressee collects the message, typically from the server of his service provider.

ePD Recital 28 notes that the obligation to erase traffic data or to make such data anonymous when it is no longer needed for the purpose of the transmission of a communication does not conflict with such procedures on the Internet as the caching in the domain name system of IP addresses or the caching of IP addresses to physical address bindings or the use of log-in information to control the right of access to networks or services.

ePD Recital 29 notes that the service provider may process traffic data relating to subscribers and users where necessary in individual cases in order to detect technical failure or errors in the transmission of communications. Traffic data necessary for billing purposes may also be processed by the provider in order to detect and stop fraud consisting of unpaid use of the electronic communications service.

Recital 30 notes that systems for the provision of electronic commu-nications networks and services should be designed to limit the amount of personal data necessary to a strict minimum. Any activities related to the provision of the electronic communications service that go beyond the transmission of a communication and the billing thereof should be based on aggregated, traffic data that cannot be related to subscribers or users. Where such activities cannot be based on aggregated data, they should be considered as value added services for which the consent of the subscriber is required.

ePD Recital 31 notes that whether the consent to be obtained for the processing of personal data with a view to providing a particular value added service should be that of the user or of the subscriber, will depend on the data to be processed and on the type of service to be provided and on whether it is technically, procedurally and contractually possible to distinguish the individual using an electronic communications service from the legal or natural person having subscribed to it.

ePD Recital 32 notes that where the provider of an electronic communications service or of a value added service subcontracts the processing of personal data necessary for the provision of these services to another entity, such subcontracting and subsequent data processing should be in full compliance with the requirements regarding data controllers and data processors of personal data as set out in DPD95. Where the provision of a value added service requires that traffic or location data are forwarded from an electronic communications service provider to a provider of value added services, the subscribers or users to whom the data are related should also be fully informed of this forwarding before giving their consent for the processing of the data.

ePD Recital 33 notes that the introduction of itemised bills has improved the possibilities for the subscriber to check the accuracy of the fees charged by the service provider but, at the same time, it may jeopardise the privacy of the users of publicly available electronic communications services. Therefore, in order to preserve the privacy of the user, Member States should encourage the development of electronic communication service options such as alternative payment facilities which allow anonymous or strictly private access to publicly available electronic communications services, for example calling cards and facilities for payment by credit card. To the same end, Member States may ask the operators to offer their subscribers a different type of detailed bill in which a certain number of digits of the called number have been deleted.

ePD Recital 34 notes that it is necessary, as regards calling line identification, to protect the right of the calling party to withhold the presentation of the identification of the line from which the call is being made and the right of the called party to reject calls from unidentified lines.

ePD Recital 35 notes that that in digital mobile networks, location data giving the geographic position of the terminal equipment of the mobile user are processed to enable the transmission of communications. Such data are traffic data covered by Article 6 of the ePD. However, in addition, digital mobile networks may have the capacity to process location data which are more precise than is necessary for the transmission of communications and which are used for the provision of value added services such as services providing individualised traffic information and guidance to drivers. The processing of such data for value added services should only be allowed where subscribers have given their consent. Even in cases where subscribers have given their consent, they should have a simple means to temporarily deny the processing of location data, free of charge.

ePD Recital 36 notes that Member States may restrict the users' and subscribers' rights to privacy with regard to calling line identification where this is necessary to trace nuisance calls and with regard to calling line identification and location data where this is necessary to allow emergency services to carry out their tasks as effectively as possible.

ePD Recital 37 notes that safeguards should be provided for subscribers against the nuisance which may be caused by automatic call forwarding by others. It must be possible for subscribers to stop the forwarded calls being passed on to their terminals by simple request to the provider of the publicly available electronic communications service.

ePD Recital 38 notes that directories of subscribers to electronic communications services are widely distributed and public. The right to privacy of natural persons and the legitimate interest of legal persons require that subscribers are able to determine whether their personal data are published in a directory and if so, which. Providers of public directories should inform the subscribers to be included in such directories of the purposes of the directory and of any particular usage which may be made of electronic versions of public directories especially through search functions embedded in the software, such as reverse search functions enabling users of the directory to discover the name and address of the subscriber on the basis of a telephone number only.

ePD Recital 39 notes that the obligation to inform subscribers of the purpose(s) of public directories in which their personal data are to be included should be imposed on the party collecting the data for such inclusion. Where the data may be transmitted to one or more third parties, the subscriber should be informed of this possibility and of the recipient or the categories of possible recipients. Any transmission should be subject to the condition that the data may not be used for other purposes than those for which they were collected. If the party collecting the data from the subscriber or any third party to whom the data have been transmitted wishes to use the data for an additional purpose, the renewed consent of the subscriber is to be obtained either by the initial party collecting the data or by the third party to whom the data have been transmitted.

ePD Recital 40 notes that safeguards should be provided for subscribers against intrusion of their privacy by unsolicited communications for direct marketing purposes in particular by means of automated calling machines, telefaxes, and e-mails, including SMS messages. These forms of unsolicited commercial communications may on the one hand be relatively easy and cheap to send and on the other may impose a burden and/or cost on the recipient. Moreover, in some cases their volume may also cause difficulties for electronic communications networks and terminal equipment. For such forms of unsolicited communications for direct marketing, it is justified to require that prior explicit consent of the recipients is obtained before such communications are addressed to them. The single market requires a harmonised approach to ensure simple, EU-wide rules for businesses and users.

ePD Recital 41 notes that within the context of an existing customer relationship, it is reasonable to allow the use of electronic contact details for the offering of similar products or services, but only by the same company that has obtained the electronic contact details in accordance with DPD95. When electronic contact details are obtained, the customer should be informed about their further use for direct marketing in a clear and distinct manner, and be given the opportunity to refuse such usage. This opportunity should continue to be offered with each subsequent direct marketing message, free of charge, except for any costs for the transmission of this refusal.

ePD Recital 42 notes that other forms of direct marketing that are more costly for the sender and impose no financial costs on subscribers and users, such as person-to-person voice telephony calls, may justify the maintenance of a system giving subscribers or users the possibility to indicate that they do not want to receive such calls. Nevertheless, in order not to decrease existing levels of privacy protection, Member States should be entitled to uphold national systems, only allowing such calls to subscribers and users who have given their prior consent.

ePD Recital 43 notes that to facilitate effective enforcement of EU rules on unsolicited messages for direct marketing, it is necessary to prohibit the use of false identities or false return addresses or numbers while sending unsolicited messages for direct marketing purposes.

ePD Recital 44 notes that certain electronic mail systems allow subscribers to view the sender and subject line of an electronic mail, and also to delete the message, without having to download the rest of the electronic mail's content or any attachments, thereby reducing costs which could arise from downloading unsolicited electronic mails or attachments. These arrangements may continue to be useful in certain cases as an additional tool to the general obligations established in this Directive.

ePD Recital 45 notes that this Directive is without prejudice to the arrangements which Member States make to protect the legitimate interests of legal persons with regard to unsolicited communications for direct marketing purposes. Where Member States establish an opt-out register for such communications to legal persons, mostly business users, the provisions of Article 7 of Directive 2000/31/EC (Directive on electronic commerce) are fully applicable.

ePD Recital 46 notes that the functionalities for the provision of electronic communications services may be integrated in the network or in any part of the terminal equipment of the user, including the software. The protection of the personal data and the privacy of the user of publicly available electronic communications services should be independent of the configuration of the various components necessary to provide the service and of the distribution of the necessary functionalities between these components. DPD95 covers any form of processing of personal data regardless of the technology used. The existence of specific rules for electronic communications services alongside general rules for other components necessary for the provision of such services may not facilitate the protection of personal data and privacy in a technologically neutral way. It may, therefore, be necessary to adopt measures requiring manufacturers of certain types of equipment used for electronic communications services to construct their product in such a way as to incorporate safeguards to ensure that the personal data and privacy of the user and subscriber are protected. The adoption of such measures in accordance with Directive 1999/5/EC will ensure that the introduction of technical features of electronic communication equipment including software for data protection purposes is harmonised in order to be compatible with the implementation of the internal market.

ePD Recital 47 notes that where the rights of the users and subscribers are not respected, national legislation should provide for judicial remedies. Penalties should be imposed on any person, whether governed by private or public law, who fails to comply with the national measures taken under this Directive.

ePD: Scope

24.11 ePD Article 1 refers to the scope and aim of the Directive. Article 1(1) provides that the Directive harmonises the provisions of the

Member States to ensure an equivalent level of protection of fundamental rights and freedoms, and in particular the right to privacy, with respect to the processing of personal data in the electronic communication sector and to ensure the free movement of such data and of electronic communication equipment and services in the EU.

Article 1(2) provides that the provisions of the Directive particularise and complement Directive 95/46/EC for the purposes mentioned in Article 1(1). Moreover, they provide for protection of the legitimate interests of subscribers who are legal persons.

Article 1(3) provides that the ePD shall not apply to activities which fall outside the scope of the Treaty establishing the European Community, such as those covered by Titles V and VI of the Treaty on European Union, and in any case to activities concerning public security, defence, State security (including the economic well-being of the State when the activities relate to State security matters) and the activities of the State in areas of criminal law.

ePD: Definitions

24.12 Article 2 of the ePD refers to definitions. The definitions in the DPD95 and in the ePD shall apply. The following additional definitions shall also apply,

'user'	means any natural person using a publicly available electronic communications service, for private or business purposes, without necessarily having subscribed to this service;
'traffic data'	means any data processed for the purpose of the conveyance of a communication on an electronic communications network or for the billing thereof;
'location data'	means any data processed in an electronic communications network, indicating the geographic position of the terminal equipment of a user of a publicly available electronic communications service;
'communication'	means any information exchanged or conveyed between a finite number of parties by means of a publicly available electronic communications service. This does not include any information conveyed as part of a broadcasting service to the public over an electronic communications network except to the extent that the information can be related to the identifiable subscriber or user receiving the information;

'call'	means a connection established by means of a publicly available telephone service allowing two-way communication in real time;
'consent'	by a user or subscriber corresponds to the data subject's consent in DPD95;
'value added service'	means any service which requires the processing of traffic data or location data other than traffic data beyond what is necessary for the transmission of a communication or the billing thereof;
'electronic mail'	means any text, voice, sound or image message sent over a public communications network which can be stored in the network or in the recipient's terminal equipment until it is collected by the recipient.

ePD: Services

24.13 Article 3 relates to the services concerned. Article 3(1) provides that the ePD shall apply to the processing of personal data in connection with the provision of publicly available electronic communications services in public communications networks in the EU.

Article 3(2) provides that Articles 8, 10 and 11 shall apply to subscriber lines connected to digital exchanges and, where technically possible and if it does not require a disproportionate economic effort, to subscriber lines connected to analogue exchanges.

Article 3(3) provides that cases where it would be technically impossible or require a disproportionate economic effort to fulfil the requirements of Articles 8, 10 and 11 shall be notified to the Commission by the Member States.

ePD: Unsolicited Communications

24.14 Article 13 refers to unsolicited communications. Article 13(1) provides that the use of automated calling systems without human intervention (automatic calling machines), facsimile machines (fax) or electronic mail for the purposes of direct marketing may only be allowed in respect of subscribers who have given their prior consent.

Article 13(2) provides that notwithstanding Article 13(1), where a natural or legal person obtains from its customers their electronic contact details for electronic mail, in the context of the sale of a product or a service, in accordance with DPD95, the same natural or legal person may use these electronic contact details for direct marketing of its own similar products or services provided that customers clearly and distinctly are given the opportunity to object, free of charge and in an easy manner, to such use of electronic contact details when they are collected and on the occasion of each message in case the customer has not initially refused such use.

Article 13(3) provides that Member States shall take appropriate measures to ensure that, free of charge, unsolicited communications for purposes of direct marketing, in cases other than those referred to in Article 13(1) and (2), are not allowed either without the consent of the subscribers concerned or in respect of subscribers who do not wish to receive these communications, the choice between these options to be determined by national legislation.

Article 13(4) provides that in any event, the practice of sending electronic mail for purposes of direct marketing disguising or concealing the identity of the sender on whose behalf the communication is made, or without a valid address to which the recipient may send a request that such communications cease, shall be prohibited.

Article 13(5) provides that Article 13(1) and (3) shall apply to subscribers who are natural persons. Member States shall also ensure, in the framework of EU law and applicable national legislation, that the legitimate interests of subscribers other than natural persons with regard to unsolicited communications are sufficiently protected.

ePD: Security

24.15   Article 4 relates to security. Article 4(1) provides that the provider of a publicly available electronic communications service must take appropriate technical and organisational measures to safeguard security of its services, if necessary in conjunction with the provider of the public communications network with respect to network security. Having regard to the state of the art and the cost of their implementation, these measures shall ensure a level of security appropriate to the risk presented. Obviously, these can change over time as risks and as technology change.

Article 4(2) provides that in case of a particular risk of a breach of the security of the network, the provider of a publicly available electronic communications service must inform the subscribers concerning such risk and, where the risk lies outside the scope of the measures to be taken by the service provider, of any possible remedies, including an indication of the likely costs involved.

ePD: Confidentiality

24.16 Article 5 refers to confidentiality of the communications. Article 5(1) provides that Member States shall ensure the confidentiality of communications and the related traffic data by means of a public communications network and publicly available electronic communications services, through national legislation. In particular, they shall prohibit listening, tapping, storage or other kinds of interception or surveillance of communications and the related traffic data by persons other than users, without the consent of the users concerned, except when legally authorised to do so in accordance with Article 15(1). This paragraph shall not prevent technical storage which is necessary for the conveyance of a communication without prejudice to the principle of confidentiality.

Article 5(2) provides that para 1 shall not affect any legally authorised recording of communications and the related traffic data when carried out in the course of lawful business practice for the purpose of providing evidence of a commercial transaction or of any other business communication.

Article 5(3) provides that Member States shall ensure that the use of electronic communications networks to store information or to gain access to information stored in the terminal equipment of a subscriber or user is only allowed on condition that the subscriber or user concerned is provided with clear and comprehensive information in accordance with DPD95, *inter alia* about the purposes of the processing, and is offered the right to refuse such processing by the data controller. This shall not prevent any technical storage or access for the sole purpose of carrying out or facilitating the transmission of a communication over an electronic communications network, or as strictly necessary in order to provide an information society service explicitly requested by the subscriber or user.

ePD: Traffic Data

24.17 Article 6 refers to traffic data. Article 6(1) provides that traffic data relating to subscribers and users processed and stored by the provider of a public communications network or publicly available electronic communications service must be erased or made anonymous when it is no longer needed for the purpose of the transmission of a communication without prejudice to Article 6(2), (3) and (5) and Article 15(1).

Article 6(2) provides that traffic data necessary for the purposes of subscriber billing and interconnection payments may be processed.

Such processing is permissible only up to the end of the period during which the bill may lawfully be challenged or payment pursued.

Article 6(3) provides that for the purpose of marketing electronic communications services or for the provision of value added services, the provider of a publicly available electronic communications service may process the data referred to in Article 6(1) to the extent and for the duration necessary for such services or marketing, if the subscriber or user to whom the data relate has given his/her consent. Users or subscribers shall be given the possibility to withdraw their consent for the processing of traffic data at any time.

Article 6(3) provides that the service provider must inform the subscriber or user of the types of traffic data which are processed and of the duration of such processing for the purposes mentioned in Article 6(2) and, prior to obtaining consent, for the purposes mentioned in Article 6(3).

Article 6(3) provides that processing of traffic data, in accordance with Article 6(1), (2), (3) and (4), must be restricted to persons acting under the authority of providers of the public communications networks and publicly available electronic communications services handling billing or traffic management, customer enquiries, fraud detection, marketing electronic communications services or providing a value added service, and must be restricted to what is necessary for the purposes of such activities.

Article 6(6) provides that Articles 6(1), (2), (3) and (5) shall apply without prejudice to the possibility for competent bodies to be informed of traffic data in conformity with applicable legislation with a view to settling disputes, in particular interconnection or billing disputes.

ePD: Non-Itemised Billing

24.18 Article 7 relates to itemised billing. Article 7(1) provides that subscribers shall have the right to receive non-itemised bills. Article 7(2) provides that Member States shall apply national provisions in order to reconcile the rights of subscribers receiving itemised bills with the right to privacy of calling users and called subscribers, for example by ensuring that sufficient alternative privacy enhancing methods of communications or payments are available to such users and subscribers.

ePD: Calling and Connected Line Identification

24.19 Article 8 relates to presentation and restriction of calling and connected line identification. Article 8(1) provides that where presentation of calling line identification is offered, the service provider must offer the calling user the possibility, using a simple means and free of charge, of preventing the presentation of the calling line identification on a per-call basis. The calling subscriber must have this possibility on a per-line basis.

Article 8(2) provides that where presentation of calling line identification is offered, the service provider must offer the called subscriber the possibility, using a simple means and free of charge for reasonable use of this function, of preventing the presentation of the calling line identification of incoming calls.

Article 8(3) provides that where presentation of calling line identification is offered and where the calling line identification is presented prior to the call being established, the service provider must offer the called subscriber the possibility, using a simple means, of rejecting incoming calls where the presentation of the calling line identification has been prevented by the calling user or subscriber.

Article 8(4) provides that where presentation of connected line identification is offered, the service provider must offer the called subscriber the possibility, using a simple means and free of charge, of preventing the presentation of the connected line identification to the calling user.

Article 8(5) provides that Article 8(1) shall also apply with regard to calls to third countries originating in the EU. Paragraphs (2), (3) and (4) shall also apply to incoming calls originating in third countries.

Article 8(6) provides that Member States shall ensure that where presentation of calling and/or connected line identification is offered, the providers of publicly available electronic communications services inform the public thereof and of the possibilities set out in paragraphs (1), (2), (3) and (4).

ePD: Location Data other than Traffic Data

24.20 Article 9 of the ePD relates to location data other than traffic data. Article 9(1) provides that where location data other than traffic data, relating to users or subscribers of public communications networks or publicly available electronic communications services, can be processed, such data may only be processed when they are made anonymous, or with the *consent* of the users or subscribers to the extent and for the duration necessary for the provision of a value added service. The service provider must inform the users or subscribers, prior to obtaining their consent, of the type of location data other than traffic data which will be processed, of the purposes and duration of the processing and whether the data will be transmitted to a third party for the purpose of providing the value added service. Users or subscribers shall be given the possibility to withdraw their consent for the processing of location data other than traffic data at any time.

This is increasingly important as more and more smart phones and electronic devices permit the capture of location based data relating to individuals and or their personal equipment.

Article 9(1) provides that where consent of the users or subscribers has been obtained for the processing of location data other than traffic data, the user or subscriber must continue to have the possibility, using a simple means and free of charge, of temporarily refusing the processing of such data for each connection to the network or for each transmission of a communication.

Article 9(1) provides that processing of location data other than traffic data in accordance with Articles 9(1) and (2) must be restricted to persons acting under the authority of the provider of the public communications network or publicly available communications service or of the third party providing the value added service, and must be restricted to what is necessary for the purposes of providing the value added service.

ePD: Exceptions

24.21   Article 10 relates to exceptions. Member States shall ensure that there are transparent procedures governing the way in which a provider of a public communications network and/or a publicly available electronic communications service may override:

- the elimination of the presentation of calling line identification, on a temporary basis, upon application of a subscriber requesting the tracing of malicious or nuisance calls. In this case, the data containing the identification of the calling subscriber will be stored and be made available by the provider of a public communications network and/or publicly available electronic communications service;

- the elimination of the presentation of calling line identification and the temporary denial or absence of consent of a subscriber or user for the processing of location data, on a per-line basis for organisations dealing with emergency calls and recognised as such by a

Member State, including law enforcement agencies, ambulance services and fire brigades, for the purpose of responding to such calls.

Article 11 refers to automatic call forwarding. It provides that Member States shall ensure that any subscriber has the possibility, using a simple means and free of charge, of stopping automatic call forwarding by a third party to the subscriber's terminal.

ePD: Directories

24.22 Article 12 refers to directories of subscribers. Article 12(1) provides that Member States shall ensure that subscribers are informed, free of charge and before they are included in the directory, about the purpose(s) of a printed or electronic directory of subscribers available to the public or obtainable through directory enquiry services, in which their personal data can be included and of any further usage possibilities based on search functions embedded in electronic versions of the directory.

Article 12(2) provides that Member States shall ensure that subscribers are given the opportunity to determine whether their personal data are included in a public directory, and if so, which, to the extent that such data are relevant for the purpose of the directory as determined by the provider of the directory, and to verify, correct or withdraw such data. Not being included in a public subscriber directory, verifying, correcting or withdrawing personal data from it shall be free of charge.

Article 12(3) provides that Member States may require that for any purpose of a public directory other than the search of contact details of persons on the basis of their name and, where necessary, a minimum of other identifiers, additional consent be asked of the subscribers.

Article 12(4) provides that Articles 12(1) and (2) shall apply to subscribers who are natural persons. Member States shall also ensure, in the framework of EU law and applicable national legislation, that the legitimate interests of subscribers other than natural persons with regard to their entry in public directories are sufficiently protected.

ePD: Technical Features

24.23 ePD Article 14 refers to technical features and standardisation. Article 14(1) provides that in implementing the provisions of this Directive, Member States shall ensure, subject to Articles 14(2) and (3), that no mandatory requirements for specific technical features are imposed on terminal or other electronic communication equipment which could impede the placing of equipment on the market and the free circulation of such equipment in and between Member States.

Article 14(2) provides that where provisions of this Directive can be implemented only by requiring specific technical features in electronic communications networks, Member States shall inform the Commission in accordance with the procedure provided for by Directive 98/34/EC laying down a procedure for the provision of information in the field of technical standards and regulations and of rules on information society services.

Article 14(3) provides that where required, measures may be adopted to ensure that terminal equipment is constructed in a way that is compatible with the right of users to protect and control the use of their personal data, in accordance with Directive 1999/5/EC and Council Decision 87/95/EEC on standardisation in the field of information technology and communications.

ePD: Re DPD95

24.24   Article 15 refers to application of certain provisions of DPD95. Article 15(1) provides that Member States may adopt legislative measures to restrict the scope of the rights and obligations provided for in Article 5, Article 6, Article 8(1), (2), (3) and (4), and Article 9 of the ePD when such restriction constitutes a necessary, appropriate and proportionate measure within a democratic society to safeguard national security (ie State security), defence, public security, and the prevention, investigation, detection and prosecution of criminal offences or of unauthorised use of the electronic communication system, as referred to in Article 13(1) of DPD95. To this end, Member States may, inter alia, adopt legislative measures providing for the retention of data for a limited period justified on the grounds laid down in this paragraph. All the measures referred to in this paragraph shall be in accordance with the general principles of EU law, including those referred to in Article 6(1) and (2) of the Treaty on European Union.

Article 15(1) provides that the provisions of Chapter III on judicial remedies, liability and sanctions of DPD95 shall apply with regard to national provisions adopted pursuant to this Directive and with regard to the individual rights derived from this Directive.

Article 15(3) provides that the WP29 shall also carry out the tasks laid down in Article 30 of that Directive with regard to matters covered by the ePD, namely the protection of fundamental rights and freedoms and of legitimate interests in the electronic communications sector.

ePD Amended by Directive 2006/24/EC

24.25 The ePD was amended by Directive 2006/24/EC of 15 March 2006 on the retention of data generated or processed in connection with the provision of publicly available electronic communications services or of public communications networks and amending the ePD.

Directive 2006/24/EC: Background

24.26 Recital 3 notes that Articles 5, 6 and 9 of the ePD lay down the rules applicable to the processing by network and service providers of traffic and location data generated by using electronic communications services. Such data must be erased or made anonymous when no longer needed for the purpose of the transmission of a communication, except for the data necessary for billing or interconnection payments. Subject to consent, certain data may also be processed for marketing purposes and the provision of value-added services.

Recital 4 notes that Article 15(1) of the ePD sets out the conditions under which Member States may restrict the scope of the rights and obligations provided for in Article 5, Article 6, Article 8(1), (2), (3) and (4), and Article 9 of that Directive. Any such restrictions must be necessary, appropriate and proportionate within a democratic society for specific public order purposes, ie to safeguard national security (ie State security), defence, public security or the prevention, investigation, detection and prosecution of criminal offences or of unauthorised use of the electronic communications systems.

Recital 5 notes that several Member States have adopted legislation providing for the retention of data by service providers for the prevention, investigation, detection, and prosecution of criminal offences. Those national provisions vary considerably. They are also contentious.

Recital 6 notes that the legal and technical differences between national provisions concerning the retention of data for the purpose of prevention, investigation, detection and prosecution of criminal offences present obstacles to the internal market for electronic communications, since service providers are faced with different requirements regarding the types of traffic and location data to be retained and the conditions and periods of retention.

Recital 7 notes that data relating to the use of electronic communications are a valuable tool in the prevention, investigation, detection and prosecution of criminal offences, in particular organised crime.

Recital 8 notes that the Declaration on Combating Terrorism adopted by the European Council on 25 March 2004 instructed the Council to examine measures for establishing rules on the retention of communications traffic data by service providers.

Recital 9 notes that under Article 8 of the European Convention for the Protection of Human Rights and Fundamental Freedoms (ECHR), everyone has the right to respect for his private life and his correspondence. Public authorities may interfere with the exercise of that right only in accordance with the law and where necessary in a democratic society, *inter alia*, in the interests of national security or public safety, for the prevention of disorder or crime, or for the protection of the rights and freedoms of others. Because retention of data has proved to be such a necessary and effective investigative tool for law enforcement in several Member States, and in particular concerning serious matters such as organised crime and terrorism, it is necessary to ensure that retained data are made available to law enforcement authorities for a certain period, subject to the conditions provided for in this Directive. The adoption of an instrument on data retention that complies with the requirements of Article 8 of the ECHR is therefore a necessary measure.

Recital 11 notes that given the importance of traffic and location data for the investigation, detection, and prosecution of criminal offences, as demonstrated by research and the practical experience of several Member States, there is a need to ensure at European level that data that are generated or processed, in the course of the supply of communications services, by providers of publicly available electronic communications services or of a public communications network are retained for a certain period, subject to the conditions provided for in this Directive.

Recital 12 notes that Article 15(1) of the ePD continues to apply to data, including data relating to unsuccessful call attempts, the retention of which is not specifically required under the Directive and which therefore fall outside the scope thereof, and to retention for purposes, including judicial purposes, other than those covered by the Directive.

Recital 13 notes that the Directive relates only to data generated or processed as a consequence of a communication or a communication service and does not relate to data that are the content of the information communicated. Data should be retained in such a way as to avoid their being retained more than once. Data generated or processed when supplying the communications services concerned refers to data which are accessible. In particular, as regards the retention of data relating to Internet email and Internet telephony, the obligation to retain data may apply only in respect of data from the providers' or the network providers' own services.

Recital 14 notes that technologies relating to electronic communications are changing rapidly and the legitimate requirements of the competent authorities may evolve. In order to obtain advice and encourage the sharing of experience of best practice in these matters, the Commission intends to establish a group composed of Member States' law enforcement authorities, associations of the electronic communications industry, representatives of the European Parliament and data protection authorities, including the European Data Protection Supervisor.

Recital 15 notes that DPD95 and ePD are fully applicable to the data retained in accordance with this Directive.

Recital 16 notes that the obligations on service providers concerning measures to ensure data quality, derived from Article 6 of DPD95, and obligations concerning measures to ensure confidentiality and security of processing of data, which derive from Articles 16 and 17 of that Directive, apply in full to data being retained within the meaning of the Directive.

Recital 17 notes that it is essential that Member States adopt legislative measures to ensure that data retained under the Directive are provided to the competent national authorities only in accordance with national legislation in full respect of the fundamental rights of the persons concerned.

Recital 18 notes that in this context, Article 24 of DPD95 imposes an obligation on Member States to lay down sanctions for infringements of the provisions adopted pursuant to that Directive. Article 15(2) of the ePD imposes the same requirement in relation to national provisions adopted pursuant to the ePD. Council Framework Decision 2005/222/JHA of on attacks against information systems provides that the intentional illegal access to information systems, including to data retained therein, is to be made punishable as a criminal offence.

Recital 19 notes that the right of any person who has suffered damage as a result of an unlawful processing operation or of any act incompatible with national provisions adopted pursuant to DPD95 to receive compensation, which derives from Article 23 of that Directive, applies also in relation to the unlawful processing of any personal data pursuant to this Directive.

Recital 20 notes that the 2001 Council of Europe Convention on Cybercrime and the 1981 Council of Europe Convention for the Protection of Individuals with Regard to Automatic Processing of Personal Data also cover data being retained within the meaning of this Directive.

Recital 21 notes that since the objectives of this Directive, namely to harmonise the obligations on providers to retain certain data and to ensure that those data are available for the purpose of the investigation, detection and prosecution of serious crime, as defined by each Member

State in its national law, cannot be sufficiently achieved by the Member States and can, therefore, by reason of the scale and effects of this Directive, be better achieved at EU level, the EU may adopt measures, in accordance with the principle of subsidiarity as set out in Article 5 of the Treaty. In accordance with the principle of proportionality, as set out in that Article, this Directive does not go beyond what is necessary in order to achieve those objectives.

Recital 22 notes that this Directive respects the fundamental rights and observes the principles recognised, in particular, by the Charter of Fundamental Rights of the European Union. In particular, this Directive, together with the ePD, seeks to ensure full compliance with citizens' fundamental rights to respect for private life and communications and to the protection of their personal data, as enshrined in Articles 7 and 8 of the Charter.

Recital 23 notes that given that the obligations on providers of electronic communications services should be proportionate, this Directive requires that they retain only such data as are generated or processed in the process of supplying their communications services. To the extent that such data are not generated or processed by those providers, there is no obligation to retain them. This Directive is not intended to harmonise the technology for retaining data, the choice of which is a matter to be resolved at national level.

Recital 25 notes that this Directive is without prejudice to the power of Member States to adopt legislative measures concerning the right of access to, and use of, data by national authorities, as designated by them. Issues of access to data retained pursuant to this Directive by national authorities for such activities as are referred to in the first indent of Article 3(2) of DPD95 fall outside the scope of EU law. However, they may be subject to national law or action pursuant to Title VI of the Treaty on European Union. Such laws or action must fully respect fundamental rights as they result from the common constitutional traditions of the Member States and as guaranteed by the ECHR. Under Article 8 of the ECHR, as interpreted by the European Court of Human Rights, interference by public authorities with privacy rights must meet the requirements of necessity and proportionality and must therefore serve specified, explicit and legitimate purposes and be exercised in a manner that is adequate, relevant and not excessive in relation to the purpose of the interference.

Directive 2006/24/EC: Scope

24.27   Article 1 refers to subject matter and scope. Article 1(1) provides that the Directive aims to harmonise Member States' provisions concerning the obligations of the providers of publicly available electronic communications services or of public communications networks with respect to the retention of certain data which are generated or processed by them, in order to ensure that the data are available for the purpose of the investigation, detection and prosecution of serious crime, as defined by each Member State in its national law.

Article 1(2) provides that the Directive shall apply to traffic and location data on both legal entities and natural persons and to the related data necessary to identify the subscriber or registered user. It shall not apply to the content of electronic communications, including information consulted using an electronic communications network.

Directive 2006/24/EC: Definitions

24.28   Article 2 of Directive 2006/24/EC refers to definitions. The definitions in DPD95, Directive 2002/21/EC (Framework Directive), and in ePD shall apply.

Article 2(1) of Directive 2006/24/EC provides that for the purpose of the Directive,

'data'	means traffic data and location data and the related data necessary to identify the subscriber or user;
'user'	means any legal entity or natural person using a publicly available electronic communications service, for private or business purposes, without necessarily having subscribed to that service;
'telephone service'	means calls (including voice, voicemail and conference and data calls), supplementary services (including call forwarding and call transfer) and messaging and multi-media services (including short message services, enhanced media services and multi-media services);
'user ID'	means a unique identifier allocated to persons when they subscribe to or register with an internet access service or Internet communications service;
'cell ID'	means the identity of the cell from which a mobile telephony call originated or in which it terminated;

'unsuccessful call Attempt'	means a communication where a telephone call has been successfully connected but not answered or there has been a network management intervention.

Directive 2006/24/EC: Obligation to Retain Data

24.29 Article 3 of Directive 2006/24/EC refers to an obligation to retain data. Article 3(1) provides that by way of derogation from Articles 5, 6 and 9 of ePD, Member States shall adopt measures to ensure that the data specified in Article 5 of this Directive are retained in accordance with the provisions thereof, to the extent that those data are generated or processed by providers of publicly available electronic communications services or of a public communications network within their jurisdiction in the process of supplying the communications services concerned.

Article 3(2) provides that the obligation to retain data provided for in Article 3(1) shall include the retention of the data specified in Article 5 relating to unsuccessful call attempts where those data are generated or processed, and stored (as regards telephony data) or logged (as regards Internet data), by providers of publicly available electronic communications services or of a public communications network within the jurisdiction of the Member State concerned in the process of supplying the communication services concerned. This Directive shall not require data relating to unconnected calls to be retained.

Directive 2006/24/EC: Access

24.230 Article 4 of Directive 2006/24/EC refers to access to data. It provides that Member States shall adopt measures to ensure that data retained in accordance with this Directive are provided only to the competent national authorities in specific cases and in accordance with national law. The procedures to be followed and the conditions to be fulfilled in order to gain access to retained data in accordance with necessity and proportionality requirements shall be defined by each Member State in its national law, subject to the relevant provisions of EU law or public international law, and in particular the ECHR as interpreted by the European Court of Human Rights.

Directive 2006/24/EC: Data Categories

24.31   Article 5 of Directive 2006/24/EC refers to categories of data to be retained. Article 5(1) provides that Member States shall ensure that the following categories of data are retained under this Directive:

(a) data necessary to trace and identify the source of a communication;
    (1) concerning fixed network telephony and mobile telephony:
        (i) the calling telephone number;
        (ii) the name and address of the subscriber or registered user;
    (2) concerning Internet access, Internet email and Internet telephony,
        (i) the user ID(s) allocated;
        (ii) the user ID and telephone number allocated to any communication entering the public telephone network;
        (iii) the name and address of the subscriber or registered user to whom an Internet Protocol (IP) address, user ID or telephone number was allocated at the time of the communication;
(b) data necessary to identify the destination of a communication;
    (1) concerning fixed network telephony and mobile telephony:
        (i) the number(s) dialled (the telephone number(s) called), and, in cases involving supplementary services such as call forwarding or call transfer, the number or numbers to which the call is routed;
        (ii) the name(s) and address(es) of the subscriber(s) or registered user(s);
    (2) concerning internet e-mail and Internet telephony:
        (i) the user ID or telephone number of the intended recipient(s) of an internet telephony call;
        (ii) the name(s) and address(es) of the subscriber(s) or registered user(s) and user ID of the intended recipient of the communication;
(c) data necessary to identify the date, time and duration of a communication:
    (1) concerning fixed network telephony and mobile telephony, the date and time of the start and end of the communication;
    (2) concerning Internet access, internet email and Internet telephony:
        (i) the date and time of the log-in and log-off of the Internet access service, based on a certain time zone, together with the IP address, whether dynamic or static, allocated

by the Internet access service provider to a communication, and the user ID of the subscriber or registered user;

    (ii) the date and time of the log-in and log-off of the Internet email service or Internet telephony service, based on a certain time zone;

(d) data necessary to identify the type of communication:

    (1) concerning fixed network telephony and mobile telephony: the telephone service used;

    (2) concerning Internet email and Internet telephony: the internet service used;

(e) data necessary to identify users' communication equipment or what purports to be their equipment:

    (1) concerning fixed network telephony, the calling and called telephone numbers;

    (2) concerning mobile telephony:

        (i) the calling and called telephone numbers;

        (ii) the International Mobile Subscriber Identity (IMSI) of the calling party;

        (iii) the International Mobile Equipment Identity (IMEI) of the calling party;

        (iv) the IMSI of the called party;

        (v) the IMEI of the called party;

        (vi) in the case of pre-paid anonymous services, the date and time of the initial activation of the service and the location label (Cell ID) from which the service was activated;

    (3) concerning Internet access, internet email and internet telephony:

        (i) the calling telephone number for dial-up access;

        (ii) the digital subscriber line (DSL) or other end point of the originator of the communication;

(f) data necessary to identify the location of mobile communication equipment:

    (1) the location label (Cell ID) at the start of the communication;

    (2) data identifying the geographic location of cells by reference to their location labels (Cell ID) during the period for which communications data are retained.

2. No data revealing the content of the communication may be retained pursuant to this Directive.

Directive 2006/24/EC: Periods of Retention

24.32   Article 6 of Directive 2006/24/EC refers to periods of retention. Member States shall ensure that the categories of data specified in Article 5 are retained for periods of not less than six months and not more than two years from the date of the communication.

Directive 2006/24/EC: Security

24.33   Article 7 of Directive 2006/24/EC refers to data protection and data security. It provides that without prejudice to the provisions adopted pursuant to DP95 and Directive 2002/58/EC, each Member State shall ensure that providers of publicly available electronic communications services or of a public communications network respect, as a minimum, the following data security principles with respect to data retained in accordance with this Directive:

- the retained data shall be of the same quality and subject to the same security and protection as those data on the network;
- the data shall be subject to appropriate technical and organisational measures to protect the data against accidental or unlawful destruction, accidental loss or alteration, or unauthorised or unlawful storage, processing, access or disclosure;
- the data shall be subject to appropriate technical and organisational measures to ensure that they can be accessed by specially authorised personnel only; and
- the data, except those that have been accessed and preserved, shall be destroyed at the end of the period of retention.

Directive 2006/24/EC: Storage Requirements for Retained Data

24.34   Article 8 of Directive 2006/24/EC refers to storage requirements for retained data. It provides that Member States shall ensure that the data specified in Article 5 are retained in accordance with this Directive in such a way that the data retained and any other necessary information relating to such data can be transmitted upon request to the competent authorities without undue delay.

Directive 2006/24/EC: ICO

24.35   Article 9 of Directive 2006/24/EC refers to the National Supervisory Authority. Each Member State shall designate one or more public authorities to be responsible for monitoring the application within its territory of the provisions adopted by the Member States pursuant to Article 7 regarding the security of the stored data. Those authorities may be the same authorities as those referred to in Article 28 of DPD95. The authorities referred to in Article 9(1) shall act with complete independence in carrying out the monitoring referred to in that paragraph.

Directive 2006/24/EC: Statistics on Retention

24.36 Article 10 of Directive 2006/24/EC refers to statistics. Article 10(1) provides that Member States shall ensure that the Commission is provided on a yearly basis with statistics on the retention of data generated or processed in connection with the provision of publicly available electronic communications services or a public communications network. Such statistics shall include:

- the cases in which information was provided to the competent authorities in accordance with applicable national law;
- the time elapsed between the date on which the data were retained and the date on which the competent authority requested the transmission of the data;
- the cases where requests for data could not be met.

Article 10(2) provides that such statistics shall not contain personal data.

Directive 2006/24/EC: ePD

24.37 Article 11 of Directive 2006/24/EC refers to amendment of ePD. The following paragraph shall be inserted in Article 15 of ePD,

> '1a. Paragraph 1 shall not apply to data specifically required by Directive 2006/24/EC of the European Parliament and of the Council of 15 March 2006 on the retention of data generated or processed in connection with the provision of publicly available electronic communications services or of public communications networks [] to be retained for the purposes referred to in Article 1(1) of that Directive.'

Directive 2006/24/EC: Future Measures

24.38 Article 12 of Directive 2006/24/EC refers to future measures. Article 12(1) provides that a Member State facing particular circumstances that warrant an extension for a limited period of the maximum retention period referred to in Article 6 may take the necessary measures. That Member State shall immediately notify the Commission and inform the other Member States of the measures taken under this Article and shall state the grounds for introducing them.

Directive 2006/24/EC: Remedies, Liability and Penalties

24.39   Article 13 of Directive 2006/24/EC refers to remedies, liability and penalties. Article 13 (1) provides that each Member State shall take the necessary measures to ensure that the national measures implementing Chapter III of DPD95 providing for judicial remedies, liability and sanctions are fully implemented with respect to the processing of data under this Directive.

Article 13 (2) of Directive 2006/24/EC provides that each Member State shall, in particular, take the necessary measures to ensure that any intentional access to, or transfer of, data retained in accordance with the Directive that is not permitted under national law adopted pursuant to the Directive is punishable by penalties, including administrative or criminal penalties, that are effective, proportionate and dissuasive.

Conclusion

24.40   Originally envisaged as relating to telecoms type data only, this secondary aspect data protection regime has expanded in substance, scope and detail. While much of it is still specific to telecoms companies and entities involved in the transfer of electronic communications, certain issues are more generally applicable. The ePD as amended applies to all organisations who wish to engage in direct marketing through a variety of means. Compliance is necessary and needs to be planned in advance. If not specifically exempted from the default rule it is difficult envisage permissible direct marketing (DM).

Chapter 25

Electronic Direct Marketing and Spam

Introduction

25.01 Direct marketing (DM) tends to be one of the most contentious areas of data protection practice. It also receives probably most attention, with the possible exceptions of data breach/data loss and internet/social networking data protection issues.

Most organisations need to engage in (DM) at some stage, some more heavily than others. Many organisation may even go so far as to say that DM is an essential ingredient of continued commercial success.

However, DM is sometimes viewed as spam and unsolicited commercial communications which are unwanted and also unlawful. The data protection regime (and eCommerce legal regime) refers to permissible DM and sets out various obligatory requirements while at the same time setting a default position of prohibiting non-exempted or non-permitted electronic direct marketing.

Direct Marketing (DM)

25.02 If the organisation anticipates that personal data kept by it will be processed for the purposes of DM, it must inform the persons to whom the data relates that they may object by means of a request in writing to the data controller and free of charge.[1]

---

1   See, for example, Edwards, L., 'Consumer Privacy Law 1: Online Direct Marketing,' and Edwards, L., and Hatcher, J., 'Consumer Privacy Law: Data Collection, Profiling and Targeting,' each in Edwards, L., and Waelde, C., eds., *Law and the Internet* (Oxford: Hart, 2009), pp. 489 et seq, and pp. 511 *et seq* respectively; and

Unsolicited Communications in the ePD

25.03 Article 13 of the ePD refers to unsolicited communications. Article 13(1) provides that the use of automated calling systems without human intervention (automatic calling machines), facsimile machines (fax) or electronic mail for the purposes of direct marketing may only be allowed in respect of subscribers who have given their prior consent.

Article 13(2) provides that notwithstanding Article 13(1), where a natural or legal person obtains from its customers their electronic contact details for email, in the context of the sale of a product or a service, in accordance with DPD95, the same natural or legal person may use these electronic contact details for direct marketing of its own similar products or services provided that customers clearly and distinctly are given the opportunity to object, free of charge and in an easy manner, to such use of electronic contact details when they are collected and on the occasion of each message in case the customer has not initially refused such use.

Article 13(3) provides that Member States shall take appropriate measures to ensure that, free of charge, unsolicited communications for purposes of DM, in cases other than those referred to in Article 13(1) and (2), are not allowed either without the consent of the subscribers concerned or in respect of subscribers who do not wish to receive these communications, the choice between these options to be determined by national legislation.

Article 13(4) provides that in any event, the practice of sending electronic mail for purposes of DM disguising or concealing the identity of the sender on whose behalf the communication is made, or without a valid address to which the recipient may send a request that such communications cease, shall be prohibited.

Article 13(5) provides that Article 13(1) and (3) shall apply to subscribers who are natural persons. Member States shall also ensure that the legitimate interests of subscribers other than natural persons with regard to unsolicited communications are sufficiently protected.

Marketing Default Position

25.04 How should organisations go about data protection compliance DM? When is DM permitted? All organisations should carefully assess compliance issues when considering any DM activities. Getting it wrong can be costly and can have ICO enforcement and investigation consequences, not to mention penalties Indeed, a penalty of £440,000 was recently imposed in relation to spam DM (see ICO cases chart).

Article 13 of the ePD provides a number of rules in relation to unsolicited communications. Article 13(1) provides that:

- automated calling systems without human intervention (automatic calling machines);
- facsimile machines (fax); or
- electronic mail,

for the purposes of DM may *only* be allowed in respect of subscribers who have given their *prior consent.*

Therefore, there is a default rule prohibiting the forms of DM referred to above *without* prior consent. Many marketing orientated organisation may consider this a hindrance to what may have been considered legitimate marketing and business activities.

Limited Direct Marketing Permitted

25.05   Limited direct marketing is permitted, namely, of subscribers or customers whom have given their prior consent. This implies consent in advance of receiving the DM or simultaneous to the DM.

However, in terms of DM by email, this is further restricted.

Direct Marketing to Existing Customers' Email

25.06   In the context of existing customers, there is a possibility to DM using emails. Article 13(2) of the ePD provides that where an organisation obtains from its customers their electronic contact details for email, in the context of the sale of a product or a service, in accordance with DPD95, the organisation may use these electronic contact details for DM of its own similar products or services provided that customers clearly and distinctly are given the opportunity to object, free of charge and in an easy manner, to such use of electronic contact details when they are collected and on the occasion of each message in case the customer has not initially refused such use.

Therefore, once the email details are obtained at the time of a product or service transaction, it will be possible to use that email for direct marketing purposes. Conditions or limitations apply however. Firstly, the organisation is only permitted to market and promote similar products or services. This, therefore, rules out unrelated, non-identical and non-similar products and services. Secondly, at the time of each subsequent act of DM, the customer must be given the opportunity in an easy and accessible manner to opt out or cancel the DM. Effectively, they must be taken off of the organisation's DM list.

National Marketing Opt-out Registers

25.07 Article 13(3) of ePD provides that Member States shall take appropriate measures to ensure that, free of charge, unsolicited communications for purposes of direct marketing, in cases other than those referred to in Article 13(1) and (2), are not allowed either without the consent of the subscribers concerned or in respect of subscribers who do not wish to receive these communications, the choice between these options to be determined by national legislation. This means that each Member State must determine and provide a means for individuals to opt-out of receiving DM in advance.[2]

Deceptive Emails: Marketing Emails Must Not Conceal Identity

25.08 Article 13(4) of ePD provides that the practice of sending email for purposes of DM disguising or concealing the identity of the sender on whose behalf the communication is made shall be prohibited. This means that organisations cannot conceal their identity if permitted to engage in direct marketing. If these are not complied with, what might otherwise be permissible DM can be deemed to be impermissible. Complaints, investigations or enforcement proceedings can thus arise.

Marketing Emails Must Provide Opt-Out

25.09 In addition, Article 13(4) of ePD provides that the practice of sending email for purposes of DM without a valid address to which the recipient may send a request that such communications cease, shall be prohibited. This means that organisations must also include an easy contact address or other details at which the recipient can contact if they wish to object to receiving any further DM. If these are not complied with, what might otherwise be permissible DM can be deemed to be impermissible. Complaints, investigations or enforcement proceedings can thus also arise.

---

2   See ICO website, available at http://www.ico.gov.uk/for_the_public/topic_specific_ guides/marketing.aspx, accessed on 18 January 2013.

Marketing Protection for Organisations

25.10   Article 13 (5) of ePD provides that Article 13(1) and (3) shall apply to subscribers who are natural persons. Member States shall also ensure, in the framework of EU law and applicable national legislation, that the legitimate interests of subscribers other than natural persons with regard to unsolicited communications are sufficiently protected. This means that protection from unsolicited DM can also be extended to organisations.

PECR

25.11   Detailed provisions governing direct marketing by electronic communications are set out in the PECR, implementing the ePD in the UK

It provides rules in relation to automated calling machine; fax; email; unsolicited call by automated calling machine or fax; unsolicited telephone call; disguising or concealing identity; contact address; opt in/opt out; and 'soft opt in.'

PECR is also interesting in that it applies to both legal and natural persons. Generally, rights are not recognised for organisations in the data protection regime.

The PECR refers to the implementation of the rules regarding electronic communications and direct marketing DM). Regulation 22 and 23 refer to email marketing.[3]

Regulation 22 of PECR provides as follows:

'(1)   This regulation applies to the transmission of unsolicited communications by means of electronic mail to individual subscribers;

(2)   Except in the circumstances referred to in paragraph (3), a person shall neither transmit, nor instigate the transmission of, unsolicited communications for the purposes of direct marketing by means of electronic mail unless the recipient of the electronic mail has previously notified the sender that he consents for the time being to such communications being sent by, or at the instigation of, the sender;

(3)   A person may send or instigate the sending of electronic mail for the purposes of direct marketing where:

(a)   that person has obtained the contact details of the recipient of that electronic mail in the course of the sale or negotiations for the sale of a product or service to that recipient;

---

3   Privacy and Electronic Communications (EC Directive) Regulations 2003, available at http://www.legislation.gov.uk/uksi/2003/2426/contents/made, accessed on 18 January 2013.

(b)   the direct marketing is in respect of that person's similar products and services only; and

(c)   the recipient has been given a simple means of refusing (free of charge except for the costs of the transmission of the refusal) the use of his contact details for the purposes of such direct marketing, at the time that the details were initially collected, and, where he did not initially refuse the use of the details, at the time of each subsequent communication;

(4)   A subscriber shall not permit his line to be used in contravention of paragraph (2).'

Regulation 23 of PECR provides as follows,

'A person shall neither transmit, nor instigate the transmission of, a communication for the purposes of direct marketing by means of electronic mail,

(a)   where the identity of the person on whose behalf the communication has been sent has been disguised or concealed; or

(b)   where a valid address to which the recipient of the communication may send a request that such communications cease has not been provided.'

Regulation 24 of PECR is also relevant in that it provides the information which must be furnished with the direct marketing so that the recipient may contact the organisation to opt-out, namely:

- the name of the organisation; and
- either the address of the person or a telephone number on which he can be reached free of charge.

Regulation 19 of PECR prohibits the use of automated calling machines for the purposes of direct marketing.

The use of fax machines for the purposes of direct marketing is restricted in Regulation 20 of PECR.

Regulation 21 of PECR provides restrictions in relation to direct marketing by unsolicited telephone calls. An organisation cannot undertake such direct marketing if the called line is previously notified that such calls should not be made to that line; or if the called line is listed on an opt out register (referred to under Regulation 26 of PECR).

ICO PECR Guidance

25.12   The ICO guidance states as follows,

'The Regulations define electronic mail as "any text, voice, sound, or image message sent over a public electronic communications network which can be stored in the network or in the recipient's terminal equipment until it is collected by the recipient and includes messages sent using a short message service" (Regulation 2 "Interpretation" applies).

In other words, email, text, picture and video marketing messages are all considered to be "electronic mail". Marketing transmitted in WAP messages is considered to be "electronic mail". WAP Push allows a sender to send a specially formatted SMS message to a handset which, when received, allows a recipient through a single click to access and view content stored online, through the browser on the handset.

We consider this rule also applies to voicemail and answerphone messages left by marketers making marketing calls that would otherwise be "live". So there are stricter obligations placed on you if you make live calls but then wish to leave messages on a person's voicemail or answerphone.

Faxes are not considered to be "electronic mail". Fax marketing is covered elsewhere in the Regulations. These regulations also do not cover so-called silent calls or calls where a fax or other electronic signal is transmitted; this is because no marketing material is transmitted during these calls.'[4]

It adds that,

'This is what the law requires:

- You cannot transmit, or instigate the transmission of, unsolicited marketing material by electronic mail to an individual subscriber unless they have previously notified you, the sender, that they consent, for the time being, to receiving such communications. There is an exception to this rule which has been widely referred to as the soft opt in (Regulation 22 (2) refers).
- You cannot transmit, or instigate the transmission of, any marketing by electronic mail (whether solicited or unsolicited) to any subscriber (whether corporate or individual) where:
  o Your identity has been disguised or concealed; or
  o You have not provided a valid address to which the recipient can send an opt-out request.
  o That electronic mail would contravene regulations 7 or 8 of the Electronic Commerce (EC Directive) Regulations 2002 (SI 2002/2013); or
  o That electronic mail encourages recipients to visit websites which contravene those regulations (Regulation 23 refers).
- A subscriber must not allow their line to be used to breach Regulation 22 (2) (Regulation 22 (4) refers).'[5]

---

4   ICO, available at http://www.ico.gov.uk/for_organisations/privacy_and_electronic_communications/the_guide/electronic_mail.aspx, accessed on 18 January 2013.

5   ICO, available at http://www.ico.gov.uk/for_organisations/privacy_and_electronic_communications/the_guide/electronic_mail.aspx, accessed on 18 January 2013.

DPA: Offences by Direct Marketers under PECR

25.13 Offences arise in relation to activities referred to under PECR. These include:

- sending unsolicited marketing messages to individuals by fax, SMS, email or automated dialling machine;
- sending unsolicited marketing by fax, SMS, email or automated dialling machine to a business if it has objected to the receipt of such messages;
- marketing by telephone where the subscriber has objected to the receipt of such calls;
- failing to identify the caller or sender or failing to provide a physical address or a return email address;
- failing to give customers the possibility of objecting to future email and SMS marketing messages with each message sent;
- concealing the identity of the sender on whose behalf the marketing communication was made.

Fines can be significant. Organisations can be fined up to £500,000 by the ICO for unwanted marketing phone calls and emails in accordance with the updated amended PECR. It is also envisaged that fines will increase significantly in potential under the proposed DPR.

ICO Monetary Penalties

25.14 The ICO is also empowered under the Criminal Justice and Immigration Act 2008 to impose penalties of a monetary variety. Section 77 of the CJIA 2008 provides power to alter penalty for unlawfully obtaining etc personal data, as follows:

(1) The Secretary of State may by order provide for a person who is guilty of an offence under s 55 of the DPA (unlawful obtaining etc of personal data) to be liable:
    (a) on summary conviction, to imprisonment for a term not exceeding the specified period or to a fine not exceeding the statutory maximum or to both;
    (b) on conviction on indictment, to imprisonment for a term not exceeding the specified period or to a fine or to both;
(2) In subsection (1)(a) and (b) 2specified period2 means a period provided for by the order but the period must not exceed:
    (a) in the case of summary conviction, 12 months (or, in Northern Ireland, 6 months); and
    (b) in the case of conviction on indictment, two years;

(3) The Secretary of State must ensure that any specified period for England and Wales which, in the case of summary conviction, exceeds six months is to be read as a reference to six months so far as it relates to an offence committed before the commencement of s 282(1) of the Criminal Justice Act 2003 (increase in sentencing powers of magistrates' courts from 6 to 12 months for certain offences triable either way);

(4) Before making an order under this section, the Secretary of State must consult:

    (a) the Information Commissioner;

    (b) such media organisations as the Secretary of State considers appropriate; and

    (c) such other persons as the Secretary of State considers appropriate;

(5) An order under this section may, in particular, amend the DPA.

Civil Sanctions under the DPA

25.15 Individual data subjects can also sue for compensation under the DPA. Where a person suffers damage as a result of a failure by a data controller or data processor to meet their data protection obligations, then the data controller or data processor may be subject to civil sanctions by the person affected. Damage suffered by a data subject will include damage to reputation, financial loss and mental distress.

Section 13 of the DPA provides as follows:

- An individual who suffers damage by reason of any contravention by a data controller of any of the requirements of this Act is entitled to compensation from the data controller for that damage;
- An individual who suffers distress by reason of any contravention by a data controller of any of the requirements of this Act is entitled to compensation from the data controller for that distress if:
  - the individual also suffers damage by reason of the contravention; or
  - the contravention relates to the processing of personal data for the special purposes;
- In proceedings brought against a person by virtue of this section it is a defence to prove that one had taken such care as in all the circumstances was reasonably required to comply with the requirement concerned.

While there are certain conditions, the primary clause refers to 'any contravention' by the organisation. In terms of the defence, in order to be able to avail of it, an organisation will have to establish that it has 'taken such care as in all the circumstances was reasonably required.' This will vary from organisation to organisation, sector to sector, the type of personal data involved, the risks of damage, loss, etc, the nature of the security risks, the security measures and procedures adopted, the history of risk, loss and damage in the organisation and sector.

Certain types of data will convey inherent additional risks over others, such as loss of financial personal data. This can be argued to require higher obligations for the organisation.

One interesting area to consider going forward is online damage, such as viral abuse, publication, defamation, bulletin boards, discussion forums and websites (or sections of websites), and social networking websites. Where damage occurs as a result of misuse or loss of personal data or results in defamation, abuse and threats, liability could arise for the individual tortfeasors as well as the website.

While there are eCommerce defences in the eCommerce Directive, one should recall that the data protection regime (and its duty of care and liability provisions) are separate and stand alone from the eCommerce Directive legal regime. Indeed, even in terms of the eCommerce defences one should also recall that (a) an organisation must first fall within an eCommerce defence, and not lost that defence, in order to avail of it; and (b) there is no automatic entitlement to an internet service provider (ISP) or website to a global eCommerce defence, as in fact there in not one eCommerce defence but three specific defences relating to specific and technical activities. Not all or every ISP activity will fall into one of these defences. Neither will one activity fall into all three defences.

It is also possible to conceive of a website which has no take down procedures, inadequate take down defences, or non-expeditious take down procedures or remedies, and which will face potential liability under privacy and data protection as well as eCommerce liability. For example, an imposter social networking profile which contains abuse, personal data and defamatory material could attract liability for the website operator under data protection, and under normal liability if none of the eCommerce defences were unavailable or were lost. The later could occur if, for example, the false impersonating profile was notified to the website (or it was otherwise aware) but it did not do anything.[6]

---

6 This is a complex and developing area of law, common law, civil law, Directive, forthcoming Regulation (DPR) and case law, both in the UK and internationally. A full detailed analysis is beyond this current work.

PECR implemented ePD (also known as the ePrivacy Directive) regarding the protection of privacy in the electronic communications sector. In 2009 ePD was amended by Directive 2009/136/EC. This included changes to Article 5(3) of ePD requiring consent for the storage or access to information stored on a subscriber or users terminal equipment ie a requirement for organisations to obtain consent for cookies and similar technologies.[7]

The government introduced the amendments on 25 May, 2011 through the Privacy and Electronic Communications (EC Directive) (Amendment) Regulations 2011 (the PECR Amendment Regulations).[8]

Call and Fax Opt Out Registers

25.16 The Telephone Preference Service (TPS) and Fax Preference Service (FPS), operated by the Direct Marketing Association, are registers that allow people to register their numbers and their preference to opt out of receiving unsolicited calls or faxes. Therefore, organisation proposing to use call or fax for DM, must first consult these registers to ensure that no contact details are used which are already registered on these registers.

The Spam Problem

25.17 Spam is just one of a number of names taken to describe the problem of unsolicited electronic commercial marketing materials. The Spam name comes originally from a Monty Python comic sketch. However, electronic Spam is far from comic and costs industry hundreds of millions of pounds each year in employee lost time and resources, in lost bandwidth, in reduced capacity and network speed, as well as other problems.

Spam Internationally

25.18 The growing recognition of the problems caused by Spam, such as scams, viruses, lost productivity and bandwidth, has meant an increasing number of local and national laws specifically dedicated to preventing Spam.

---

7   This is a complex and developing area of law, common law, civil law, Directive, forthcoming Regulation (DPR) and case law, both in the UK and internationally. A full detailed analysis is beyond this current work.

8   *Ibid.*

In the US for example there a large number of local state laws[9] and national federal laws dedicated to tackling Spam. These include both news specific laws and Spam specific amendments to pre-existing laws. A US federal Spam act known as the CANSPAM Act was introduced.[10]

Related Issues

25.19 Certain related issues also arise, which are beyond detailed analysis presently but which may be used for specific organisations to consider further.

One example is the increasingly controversial area of profiling, advertising and direct marketing in relation to children.[11]

Online behavioural advertising (OBA) and the behavioural targeting of internet advertising is increasingly debated[12]

Commentators, and media, often focus on the issue of threats to privacy, data protection and reputation rights caused by web 2.0 activities such as social networking, search engine services, etc. The query arises as to whether revenue versus privacy is better respected by certain online services providers?[13]

Conclusion

25.20 Few organisation will not be interested in DM and advertising. The key is to get it right. The consequences of sending unlawful electronic communications can amount to offences, prosecutions official enforcement and investigations as well as being sued or prosecuted. This is one of the areas which is consistently an area of focus from ICO investigation.

---

9   See www.spamlaws.com, accessed on 18 January 2013.
10 See Reid, V.J., 'Recent Developments in Private Enforcement of the Can-Spam Act,' *Akron Intellectual Property Journal* (2010)(4), pp. 281–307.
11 Munukutla-Parker, U., 'Unsolicited Commercial E-mail, Privacy Concerns Related to Social Network Services, Online Protection of Children, and Cyberbullying,' *I/S: A Journal of Law and Policy* (2006)(2), pp. 628–650.
12 Deane-Johns, 'Behavioural Targeting of Internet Advertising,' (2009)(20), *Computers and Law*, p. 22.
13 Edwards, L., and Waelde, C., eds., *Law and the Internet* (Oxford: Hart, 2009), p. 539.

Part 4
New EU Regime

Chapter 26

EU DP Review and Update

Introduction

26.01 The EU data protection regime is being fundamentally updated and expanded.[1] Many things have changed since the introduction of the DPD95. Data processing activities have changed as well as increased in scale and complexity. New data processing activities and fields of personal data are constantly evolving. The EU undertook a review of the data protection regime. Partly on foot of the review, it was decided to propose a legal update to the DPD95. This has culminated in the drafting and publication for a proposed new EU Data Protection Regulation. Indeed, the Council of Europe Convention on data protection[2] which pre-dates the DPD95 and which was incorporated into the national law of many EU and other states (40 plus) prior to the DPD95, is also in the process of review and updating.[3]

The WP29 also refers to the need for future data protection measures in its opinion regarding *The Future of Privacy*.[4] Indeed, there have also

---

1   Graham, R., 'Prepare for European Data Protection Reform,' *SCL Computer and Law*, 30 November, 2011.

2   Convention for the Protection of Individuals with regard to Automatic Processing of Personal Data, Council of Europe (1982), available at http://conventions.coe.int/Treaty/en/Treaties/Html/108.htm, accessed on 18 January 2013.

3   See Kierkegaard, S., et al, "30 Years On – The Review of the Council of Europe Data Protection Convention 108," *Computer Law & Security Review* (2011)(27), pp. 223–231.

4   The Future of Privacy, WP29, referred to in Wong, R., "Data Protection: The Future of Privacy," *Computer Law & Security Review* (2011)(27), pp. 53–57.

been calls for greater political activism in relation to particular data protection issues.[5]

Others[6] have also highlighted new problematic developments in relation to such things as location data and location based services, which need to be dealt with. Online abuse is yet another category.

Formal Nature of Regulations and Directives

26.02 The draft DPR is still currently proceeding through the EU legislative process. However, it is important to note that an EU Regulation differs from a Directive under formal EU law.[7] A Regulation is immediately directly effective in all EU Member States – without the need for national implementing laws. Once the Regulation is passed, it will apply in the UK. It will also change the UK data protection regime as well as commercial practice. The reforms introduced are described as being 'comprehensive.'[8]

Review Policy

26.03 Rebecca Wong refers to some of the areas of concern which the DPR is proposing to address.[9] These include:

- The data protection regime in the online age;
- Social networking;
- Cloud computing;
- Minimum/maximum standards;
- The Data Protection Principles.[10]

---

5   Ripoll Servent, A., and MacKenzie, A., 'Is the EP Still a Data Protection Champion? The Case of SWIFT,' *Perspectives on European Politics & Society* (2011)(12), pp. 390–406.

6   Cuijpers, C., and Pekarek, M., 'The Regulation of Location-Based Services: Challenges to the European Union Data Protection Regime,' *Journal of Location Based Services* (2011)(5), pp. 223–241.

7   Generally see, for example, Biondi, A., and Eeckhout, P., eds., EU Law after Lisbon (2012); Foster, N., *Foster on EU Law* (2011); O'Neill, A., *EU Law for UK Lawyers* (2011); Steiner, J., *EU Law* (2011).

8   In Brief, *Communications Law* (2012)(17), p. 3.

9   Wong, R., 'The Data Protection Directive 95/46/EC: Idealisms and Realisms,' *International Review of Law, Computers & Technology* (2012)(26), pp. 229–244.

10 See *ibid.*

The Commission states[11] that the policy in reviewing the data protection regime it to:

- Modernise the EU legal system for the protection of personal data, in particular to meet the challenges resulting from globalisation and the use of new technologies;
- Strengthen individuals' rights, and at the same time reduce administrative formalities to ensure a free flow of personal data within the EU and beyond;
- Improve the clarity and coherence of the EU rules for personal data protection and achieve a consistent and effective implementation and application of the fundamental right to the protection of personal data in all areas of the EU's activities.[12]

It is also to enhance consumer confidence in eCommerce.[13] In addition, it should also bring comprehensive savings to organisations as the compliance obligations of complying with somewhat differing national data protection regimes will be reduced if not eliminated.[14]

The review process has been ongoing for some time.[15] It further summarises the need for new data protection rules, as follows,

'The current EU data protection rules date from 1995. Back then, the internet was virtually unknown to most people. Today, 250 million people use the internet daily in Europe.

Think how that has changed our personal data landscape through the explosion of ecommerce, social networks, online games and cloud computing.

The European Commission has therefore adopted proposals for updating data protection rules to meet the challenges of the digital age. In particular, the proposals will strengthen protection of your personal data online.

---

11 Reform of Data Protection legal Framework, Commission, Justice directorate, available at http://ec.europa.eu/justice/data-protection/review/index_en.htm, accessed on 18 January 2013.
12 Reform of Data Protection legal Framework, Commission, Justice directorate, available at http://ec.europa.eu/justice/data-protection/review/index_en.htm, accessed on 18 January 2013.
13 In Brief, *Communications Law* (2012)(17), p. 3.
14 See *ibid*.
15 See details of some of the steps and consultations at http://ec.europa.eu/justice/data-protection/review/actions/index_en.htm, accessed on 18 January 2013.

These proposals will now be debated by the Council and the European Parliament before they can become law.'[16]

Commentators describe the draft DPR as 'a long (and ambitious) text.'[17] In addition, the process which has arrived at this stage is described as being herculean.[18]

Some Key Changes

26.04 The key changes are referred to below. In some respects, these could also be seen as advantages of the new DPR data protection regime.

- Administrative costs are to be reduced with a single EU wide set of rules and obligations;
- There may be less need to interact with the ICO, as more responsibility and accountability is passed to the organisational level;
- The consent requirement is clarified as to mean explicit consent (whereas previously there were references to different categories of consent);
- Rights are improved with easier access to personal data, as well as its transferability;
- The enhanced right to be forgotten will improve the position of data subjects and the ability to delete data;
- The EU data protection will apply to non-EU entities operating with regard to EU personal data and EU citizens;
- The national authorities will be able to impose fines of €1,000,000 or up to two percent of global turnover.[19]

The ICO is reported as welcoming the DPR and stating that,

'In particular its strengthens the position of individuals, recognises important concepts such as privacy by design and privacy impact assessments and

---

16 See Commission, Why Do We Need New Data Protection Rules Now?, available at http://ec.europa.eu/justice/data-protection/minisite/index.html, accessed on 18 January 2013.

17 De Hert, P., and Papakonstantinou, V., 'The Proposed Data Protection Regulation Replacing Directive 95/46/EC: A Sound System for the Protection of Individuals,' *Computer Law & security Review* (2012)(28), pp. 130–142. Note also, Walden, I.N., and Savage, R.N., 'Data Protection and Privacy Laws: Should Organisations be Protected?,' *International and Comparativee Law Quarterly* (1988)(37), pp. 337–347.

18 *Ibid.*

19 In Brief, *Communications Law* (2012)(17), p. 3.

requires organisations to be able to demonstrate that they have measures in place to ensure personal information is properly protected.'[20]

DPR: Definitions

26.05   The DPR definitions are as follows,

'personal data breach'	means a breach of security leading to the accidental or unlawful destruction, loss, alteration, unauthorised disclosure of, or access to, personal data transmitted, stored or otherwise processed;
'genetic data'	means all data, of whatever type, concerning the characteristics of an individual which are inherited or acquired during early prenatal development;
'biometric data'	means any data relating to the physical, physiological or behavioural characteristics of an individual which allow their unique identification, such as facial images, or dactyloscopic data;
'data concerning health'	means any information which relates to the physical or mental health of an individual, or to the provision of health services to the individual;
'main establishment'	means as regards the data controller, the place of its establishment in the EU where the main decisions as to the purposes, conditions and means of the processing of personal data are taken; if no decisions as to the purposes, conditions and means of the processing of personal data are taken in the EU, the main establishment is the place where the main processing activities in the context of the activities of an establishment of a data controller in the EU take place. As regards the data processor, 'main establishment' means the place of its central administration in the EU;
'representative'	means any natural or legal person established in the EU who, explicitly designated by the data controller, acts and may be addressed by any National Supervisory Authority and other bodies in the EU instead of the data controller, with regard to the obligations of the data controller under the Regulation;

20   Referred to in In Brief, *Communications Law* (2012)(17), p. 3.

'enterprise'	means any entity engaged in an economic activity, irrespective of its legal form, thus including, in particular, natural and legal persons, partnerships or associations regularly engaged in an economic activity;
'group of undertakings'	means a controlling undertaking and its controlled undertakings;
'binding corporate rules'	means personal data protection policies which are adhered to by a data controller or data processor established on the territory of a Member State of the EU for transfers or a set of transfers of personal data to a data controller or data processor in one or more third countries within a group of undertakings;
'child'	means any person below the age of 18 years;
'Supervisory Authority'	means a public authority which is established by a Member State in accordance with Article 46.

DPR Recitals

26.06 The Recitals to the proposed DPR are also instructive in relation to the purposes and themes covered. They include,

Data Protection/Fundamental Right

Recital 1 states that the protection of natural persons in relation to the processing of personal data is a fundamental right. Article 8(1) of the Charter of Fundamental Rights of the EU and Article 16(1) of the Treaty lay down that everyone has the right to the protection of personal data concerning them.

Recital 2 states that the processing of personal data is designed to serve man. The principles and rules on the protection of individuals with regard to the processing of their personal data should, whatever the nationality or residence of natural persons, respect their fundamental rights and freedoms, notably their right to the protection of personal data. It should contribute to the accomplishment of an area of freedom, security and justice and of an economic union, to economic and social progress, the strengthening and the convergence of the economies within the internal market, and the well-being of individuals.

DPD

26.07 Recital 3 states that the DPD95 seeks to harmonise the protection of fundamental rights and freedoms of natural persons, in respect of processing activities and to guarantee the free flow of personal data between Member States.

Processing Increase/Technology/Co-operation

26.08 Recital 4 states that the economic and social integration resulting from the functioning of the internal market has led to a substantial increase in cross-border flows. The exchange of data between economic and social, public and private actors across the EU increased.

National authorities in the Member States are being called upon by EU law to cooperate and exchange personal data so as to be able to perform their duties or carry out tasks on behalf of an authority in another Member State.

Recital 5 states that the rapid technological developments and globalisation have brought new challenges for the protection of personal data. The scale of data sharing and collecting has increased spectacularly. Technology allows both private companies and public authorities to make use of personal data on an unprecedented scale in order to pursue their activities.

Individuals increasingly make personal information available publicly and globally.

Technology has transformed both the economy and social life, and requires to further facilitate the free flow of data within the EU and the transfer to third countries and international organisations, while ensuring an high level of the protection of personal data.

Need for Stronger Data Protection Regime Framework

26.09 Recital 6 states that the these developments require building a strong and more coherent data protection framework in the EU, backed by strong enforcement, given the importance to create the trust that will allow the digital economy to develop across the internal market.

Individuals should have control of their own personal data and legal and practical certainty for individuals, economic operators and public authorities should be reinforced.

Recital 7 states that the objectives and principles of DPD95 remain sound, but it has not prevented fragmentation in the way data protection is implemented across the EU, legal uncertainty and a widespread public perception that there are significant risks for the protection of individuals associated notably with online activity. Differences in the level of protection of the rights and freedoms of individuals, notably to the right to the protection of personal data, with regard to the processing of personal data afforded in the Member States may prevent the free flow of personal data throughout the EU.

These differences may therefore constitute an obstacle to the pursuit of economic activities at the level of the EU, distort competition and impede authorities in the discharge of their responsibilities under EU law. This difference in levels of protection is due to the existence of differences in the implementation and application of DPD95.

Recital 8 states that the in order to ensure consistent and high level of protection of individuals and to remove the obstacles to flows of personal data, the level of protection of the rights and freedoms of individuals with regard to the processing of such data should be equivalent in all Member States. Consistent and homogenous application of the rules for the protection of the fundamental rights and freedoms of natural persons with regard to the processing of personal data should be ensured throughout the EU.

Recital 9 states that the effective protection of personal data throughout the EU requires strengthening and detailing the rights of data subjects and the obligations of those who process and determine the processing of personal data, but also equivalent powers for monitoring and ensuring compliance with the rules for the protection of personal data and equivalent sanctions for offenders in the Member States.

Recital 10 states that Article 16(2) of the Treaty mandates the European Parliament and the Council to lay down the rules relating to the protection of individuals with regard to the processing of personal data and the rules relating to the free movement of personal data.

Recital 11 states that in order to ensure a consistent level of protection for individuals throughout the EU and to prevent divergences hampering the free movement of data within the internal market, a Regulation is necessary to provide legal certainty and transparency for economic operators, including micro, small and medium-sized enterprises, and to provide individuals in all Member States with the same level of legally enforceable rights and obligations and responsibilities for data controllers and data processors, to ensure consistent monitoring of the processing of personal data, and equivalent sanctions in all Member States as well as effective co-operation by the supervisory authorities of different Member States. To take account of the specific situation of micro, small and medium-sized enterprises, the Regulation includes a number of derogations. In addition, the EU institutions and bodies, Member States and their supervisory authorities are encouraged to take account of the specific needs of micro, small and medium-sized enterprises (SMEs) in the application of the Regulation.

Recital 12 states that the protection afforded by the Regulation concerns natural persons, whatever their nationality or place of residence, in relation to the processing of personal data. With regard to the processing of data which concern legal persons and in particular undertakings established as legal persons, including the name and the form of the legal person and the contact details of the legal person, the protection of the Regulation should not be claimed by any person. This should also apply where the name of the legal person contains the names of one or more natural persons.

Technologically Neutral Protection

26.10   Recital 13 states that the protection of individuals should be technologically neutral and not depend on the techniques used. Otherwise this would create a serious risk of circumvention. The protection of individuals should apply to processing of personal data by automated means as well as to manual processing, if the data are contained or are intended to be contained in a filing system. Files or sets of files as well as their cover pages, which are not structured according to specific criteria, should not fall within the scope of the Regulation.

Exclusion

26.11   Recital 14 states that the Regulation does not address issues of protection of fundamental rights and freedoms or the free flow of data related to activities which fall outside the scope of EU law, nor does it cover the processing of personal data by the EU institutions, bodies, offices and agencies, which are subject to Regulation (EC) No 45/200144, or the processing of personal data by the Member States when carrying out activities in relation to the common foreign and security policy of the EU.

Domestic

26.12   Recital 15 states that the Regulation should not apply to processing of personal data by a natural person, which are exclusively personal or domestic, such as correspondence and the holding of addresses, and without any gainful interest and thus without any connection with a professional or commercial activity. The exemption should also not apply to data controllers or data processors which provide the means for processing personal data for such personal or domestic activities.

Criminal Exemption

26.13 Recital 16 states that the protection of individuals with regard to the processing of personal data by competent authorities for the purposes of prevention, investigation, detection or prosecution of criminal offences or the execution of criminal penalties, and the free movement of such data, is subject of a specific legal instrument at EU level.

Therefore, the Regulation should not apply to the processing activities for those purposes. However, data processed by public authorities under the Regulation when used for the purposes of prevention, investigation, detection or prosecution of criminal offences or the execution of criminal penalties should be governed by the more specific legal instrument at EU level (ie future separate Directive).

ISPs

26.14 Recital 17 states that the Regulation should be without prejudice to the application of Directive 2000/31/EC (eCommerce Directive, in particular of the liability rules of intermediary service providers in Articles 12 to 15 of that Directive (the three limited defences).

Official Documents

26.15 Recital 18 states that the Regulation allows the principle of public access to official documents to be taken into account when applying the Regulation.

Location/Jurisdiction/Processing

26.16 Recital 19 states that any processing of personal data in the context of the activities of an establishment of a data controller or a data processor in the EU should be carried out in accordance with the Regulation, regardless of whether the processing itself takes place within the EU or not. Establishment implies the effective and real exercise of activity through stable arrangements. The legal form of such arrangements, whether through a branch or a subsidiary with a legal personality, is not the determining factor in this respect.

Recital 20 states that in order to ensure that individuals are not deprived of the protection to which they are entitled under the Regulation, the processing of personal data of data subjects residing in the EU by a data controller not established in the EU should be subject to the Regulation where the processing activities are related to the offering of goods or services to such data subjects, or to the monitoring of the behaviour of such data subjects.

Monitoring

26.17 Recital 21 states that in order to determine whether a processing activity can be considered to 'monitor the behaviour' of data subjects, it should be ascertained whether individuals are tracked on the internet with data processing techniques which consist of applying a 'profile' to an individual, particularly in order to take decisions concerning them or for analysing or predicting their personal preferences, behaviours and attitudes.

Public International Law

26.18 Recital 22 states that where the national law of a Member State applies by virtue of public international law, the Regulation should also apply to a data controller not established in the EU, such as in a Member State's diplomatic mission or consular post.

Any Information

26.19 Recital 23 states that the principles of protection should apply to any information concerning an identified or identifiable person. To determine whether a person is identifiable, account should be taken of all the means likely reasonably to be used either by the data controller or by any other person to identify the individual. The principles of data protection should not apply to data rendered anonymous in such a way that the data subject is no longer identifiable.

Internet

26.20 Recital 24 states that when using online services, individuals may be associated with online identifiers provided by their devices, applications, tools and protocols, such as Internet Protocol addresses or cookie identifiers. This may leave traces which, combined with unique identifiers and other information received by the servers, may be used to create profiles of the individuals and identify them. It follows that identification numbers, location data, online identifiers or other specific factors as such need not necessarily be considered as personal data in all circumstances.

Consent

26.21 Recital 25 states that the consent should be given explicitly by any appropriate method enabling a freely given specific and informed indication of the data subject's wishes, either by a statement or by a clear affirmative action by the data subject, ensuring that individuals are aware that they give their consent to the processing of personal data, including by ticking a box when visiting an Internet website or by any other statement or conduct which clearly indicates in this context the data subject's acceptance of the proposed processing of their personal data. Silence or inactivity should therefore not constitute consent. Consent should cover all processing activities carried out for the same purpose or purposes. If the data subject's consent is to be given following an electronic request, the request must be clear, concise and not unnecessarily disruptive to the use of the service for which it is provided.

Health

26.22 Recital 26 states that the personal data relating to health should include in particular all data pertaining to the health status of a data subject; information about the registration of the individual for the provision of health services; information about payments or eligibility for healthcare with respect to the individual; a number, symbol or particular assigned to an individual to uniquely identify the individual for health purposes; any information about the individual collected in the course of the provision of health services to the individual; information derived from the testing or examination of a body part or bodily substance, including biological samples; identification of a person as provider of healthcare to the individual; or any information on eg a disease, disability, disease risk, medical history, clinical treatment, or the actual physiological or biomedical state of the data subject independent of its source, such as eg from a physician or other health professional, a hospital, a medical device, or an in-vitro diagnostic test.

Establishment

26.23 Recital 27 states that the main establishment of a data controller in the EU should be determined according to objective criteria and should imply the effective and real exercise of management activities determining the main decisions as to the purposes, conditions and means of processing through stable arrangements. This criterion should not depend whether the processing of personal data is actually carried out at that location; the presence and use of technical means and technologies for processing personal data or processing activities do not, in themselves, constitute such main establishment and are therefore no determining criteria for a main establishment. The main establishment of the data processor should be the place of its central administration in the EU.

Group Companies

26.24   Recital 28 states that a group of undertakings should cover a controlling undertaking and its controlled undertakings, whereby the controlling undertaking should be the undertaking which can exercise a dominant influence over the other undertakings by virtue, for example, of ownership, financial participation or the rules which govern it or the power to have personal data protection rules implemented.

Children

26.25   Recital 29 states that the children deserve specific protection of their personal data, as they may be less aware of risks, consequences, safeguards and their rights in relation to the processing of personal data. To determine when an individual is a child, the Regulation should take over the definition laid down by the UN Convention on the Rights of the Child.

Lawful Processing

26.26   Recital 30 states that any processing of personal data should be lawful, fair and transparent in relation to the individuals concerned. In particular, the specific purposes for which the data are processed should be explicit and legitimate and determined at the time of the collection of the data. The data should be adequate, relevant and limited to the minimum necessary for the purposes for which the data are processed. This requires in particular ensuring that the data collected are not excessive and that the period for which the data are stored is limited to a strict minimum. Personal data should only be processed if the purpose of the processing could not be fulfilled by other means. Every reasonable step should be taken to ensure that personal data which are inaccurate are rectified or deleted. In order to ensure that the data are not kept longer than necessary, time limits should be established by the data controller for erasure or for a periodic review.

Recital 31 states that in order for processing to be lawful, personal data should be processed on the basis of the consent of the person concerned or some other legitimate basis, laid down by law, either in the Regulation or in other EU or Member State law as referred to in the Regulation.

Recital 35 states that the processing should be lawful where it is necessary in the context of a contract or the intended entering into of a contract.

Recital 36 states that where processing is carried out in compliance with a legal obligation to which the data controller is subject or where processing is necessary for the performance of a task carried out in the public interest or in the exercise of an official authority, the processing should have a legal basis in EU law, or in a Member State law which meets the requirements of the Charter of Fundamental Rights of the EU for any limitation of the rights and freedoms. It is also for EU or national law to determine whether the data controller performing a task carried out in the public interest or in the exercise of official authority should be a public administration or another natural or legal person governed by public law, or by private law such as a professional association.

Recital 37 states that the processing of personal data should equally be regarded as lawful where it is necessary to protect an interest which is essential for the data subject's life.

Recital 38 states that the legitimate interests of a data controller may provide a legal basis for processing, provided that the interests or the fundamental rights and freedoms of the data subject are not overriding. This would need careful assessment in particular where the data subject is a child, given that children deserve specific protection. The data subject should have the right to object to the processing, on grounds relating to their particular situation and free of charge. To ensure transparency, the controller should be obliged to explicitly inform the data subject on the legitimate interests pursued and on the right to object, and also be obliged to document these legitimate interests. Given that it is for the legislator to provide by law the legal basis for public authorities to process data, this legal ground should not apply for the processing by public authorities in the performance of their tasks.

Recital 39 states that the processing of data to the extent strictly necessary for the purposes of ensuring network and information security, ie the ability of a network or an information system to resist, at a given level of confidence, accidental events or unlawful or malicious actions that compromise the availability, authenticity, integrity and confidentiality of stored or transmitted data, and the security of the related services offered by, or accessible via, these networks and systems, by public authorities, Computer Emergency Response Teams – CERTs, Computer Security Incident Response Teams – CSIRTs, providers of electronic communications networks and services and by providers of security technologies and services, constitutes a legitimate interest of the concerned data controller. This could, for example, include preventing unauthorised access to electronic communications networks and malicious code distribution and stopping 'denial of service' attacks and damage to computer and electronic communication systems.

Recital 40 states that the processing of personal data for other purposes should be only allowed where the processing is compatible with those purposes for which the data have been initially collected, in particular where the processing is necessary for historical, statistical or scientific research purposes. Where the other purpose is not compatible with the initial one for which the data are collected, the data controller should obtain the consent of the data subject for this other purpose or should base the processing on another legitimate ground for lawful processing, in particular where provided by EU law or the law of the Member State to which the data controller is subject. In any case, the application of the principles set out by the Regulation and in particular the information of the data subject on those other purposes should be ensured.

Consent

26.27 Recital 32 states that where processing is based on the data subject's consent, the data controller should have the burden of proving that the data subject has given the consent to the processing operation. In particular in the context of a written declaration on another matter, safeguards should ensure that the data subject is aware that and to what extent consent is given.

Recital 33 states that in order to ensure free consent, it should be clarified that consent does not provide a valid legal ground where the individual has no genuine and free choice and is subsequently not able to refuse or withdraw consent without detriment.

Recital 34 states that the consent should not provide a valid legal ground for the processing of personal data, where there is a clear imbalance between the data subject and the data controller. This is especially the case where the data subject is in a situation of dependence from the data controller, among others, where personal data are processed by the employer of employees' personal data in the employment context. Where the data controller is a public authority, there would be an imbalance only in the specific data processing operations where the public authority can impose an obligation by virtue of its relevant public powers and the consent cannot be deemed as freely given, taking into account the interest of the data subject.

Sensitive Personal Data

26.28 Recital 41 states that the personal data which are, by their nature, particularly sensitive and vulnerable in relation to fundamental rights or privacy, deserve specific protection. Such data should not be processed, unless the data subject gives his explicit consent. However, derogations from this prohibition should be explicitly provided for in respect of specific needs, in particular where the processing is carried out in the course of legitimate activities by certain associations or foundations the purpose of which is to permit the exercise of fundamental freedoms.

Recital 42 states that the derogating from the prohibition on processing sensitive categories of data should also be allowed if done by a law, and subject to suitable safeguards, so as to protect personal data and other fundamental rights, where grounds of public interest so justify and in particular for health purposes, including public health and social protection and the management of healthcare services, especially in order to ensure the quality and cost-effectiveness of the procedures used for settling claims for benefits and services in the health insurance system, or for historical, statistical and scientific research purposes.

Official Processing/Religion

26.29 Recital 43 states that moreover, the processing of personal data by official authorities for achieving aims, laid down in constitutional law or international public law, of officially recognised religious associations is carried out on grounds of public interest.

Elections

26.30 Recital 44 states that the where in the course of electoral activities, the operation of the democratic system requires in a Member State that political parties compile data on people's political opinions, the processing of such data may be permitted for reasons of public interest, provided that appropriate safeguards are established.

Access

26.31 Recital 45 states that if the data processed by a data controller do not permit the controller to identify a natural person, the data controller should not be obliged to acquire additional information in order to identify the data subject for the sole purpose of complying with any provision of the Regulation. In case of a request for access, the controller should be entitled to ask the data subject for further information to enable the data controller to locate the personal data which that person seeks.

Transparency/Children

26.32 Recital 46 states that the principle of transparency requires that any information addressed to the public or to the data subject should be easily accessible and easy to understand, and that clear and plain language is used. This is particularly relevant where in situations, such as online advertising, the proliferation of actors and the technological complexity of practice makes it difficult for the data subject to know and understand if personal data relating to them are being collected, by whom and for what purpose. Given that children deserve specific protection, any information and communication, where processing is addressed specifically to a child, should be in such a clear and plain language that the child can easily understand.

Exercising Rights

26.33   Recital 47 states that the modalities should be provided for facilitating the data subject's exercise of their rights provided by the Regulation, including mechanisms to request, free of charge, in particular access to data, rectification, erasure and to exercise the right to object. The data controller should be obliged to respond to requests of the data subject within a fixed deadline and give reasons, in case he does not comply with the data subject's request. (48) The principles of fair and transparent processing require that the data subject should be informed in particular of the existence of the processing operation and its purposes, how long the data will be stored, on the existence of the right of access, rectification or erasure and on the right to lodge a complaint. Where the data are collected from the data subject, the data subject should also be informed whether they are obliged to provide the data and of the consequences, in cases they do not provide such data.

Recital 51 states that any person should have the right of access to data which has been collected concerning them, and to exercise this right easily, in order to be aware and verify the lawfulness of the processing. Every data subject should therefore have the right to know and obtain communication in particular for what purposes the data are processed, for what period, which recipients receive the data, what is the logic of the data that are undergoing the processing and what might be, at least when based on profiling, the consequences of such processing. This right should not adversely affect the rights and freedoms of others, including trade secrets or intellectual property and in particular the copyright protecting the software. However, the result of these considerations should not be that all information is refused to the data subject.

Recital 52 states that the data controller should use all reasonable measures to verify the identity of a data subject that requests access, in particular in the context of online services and online identifiers. A data controller should not retain personal data for the unique purpose of being able to react to potential requests.

Prior Information

26.34 Recital 49 states that the information in relation to the processing of personal data relating to the data subject should be given to them at the time of collection, or, where the data are not collected from the data subject, within a reasonable period, depending on the circumstances of the case. Where data can be legitimately disclosed to another recipient, the data subject should be informed when the data are first disclosed to the recipient.

Recital 50 states, however, that it is not necessary to impose this obligation where the data subject already disposes of this information, or where the recording or disclosure of the data is expressly laid down by law, or where the provision of information to the data subject proves impossible or would involve disproportionate efforts. The latter could be particularly the case where processing is for historical, statistical or scientific research purposes; in this regard, the number of data subjects, the age of the data, and any compensatory measures adopted may be taken into consideration.

Rectification

26.35 Recital 53 states that any person should have the right to have personal data concerning them rectified and an expanded 'right to be forgotten' where the retention of such data is not in compliance with the Regulation. In particular, data subjects should have the right that their personal data are erased and no longer processed, where the data are no longer necessary in relation to the purposes for which the data are collected or otherwise processed, where data subjects have withdrawn their consent for processing or where they object to the processing of personal data concerning them or where the processing of their personal data otherwise does not comply with the Regulation. This right is particularly relevant, when the data subject has given their consent as a child, when not being fully aware of the risks involved by the processing, and later wants to remove such personal data especially on the Internet. However, the further retention of the data should be allowed where it is necessary for historical, statistical and scientific research purposes, for reasons of public interest in the area of public health, for exercising the right of freedom of expression, when required by law or where there is a reason to restrict the processing of the data instead of erasing them.

Enhancing Right to Be Forgotten

26.36   Recital 54 states that to strengthen the expanded 'right to be forgotten' in the online environment, the right to erasure should also be extended in such a way that a data controller who has made the personal data public should be obliged to inform third parties which are processing such data that a data subject requests them to erase any links to, or copies or replications of that personal data. To ensure this information, the data controller should take all reasonable steps, including technical measures, in relation to data for the publication of which the data controller is responsible. In relation to a third party publication of personal data, the data controller should be considered responsible for the publication, where the controller has authorised the publication by the third party.

Electronic Access

26.37   Recital 55 states that to further strengthen the control over their own data and their right of access, data subjects should have the right, where personal data are processed by electronic means and in a structured and commonly used format, to obtain a copy of the data concerning them also in commonly used electronic format. The data subject should also be allowed to transmit those data, which they have provided, from one automated application, such as a social network, into another one. This should apply where the data subject provided the data to the automated processing system, based on their consent or in the performance of a contract.

Right to Object

26.38   Recital 56 states that in cases where personal data might lawfully be processed to protect the vital interests of the data subject, or on grounds of public interest, official authority or the legitimate interests of a data controller, any data subject should nevertheless be entitled to object to the processing of any data relating to them. The burden of proof should be on the data controller to demonstrate that their legitimate interests may override the interests or the fundamental rights and freedoms of the data subject.

Direct Marketing

26.39   Recital 57 states that where personal data are processed for the purposes of direct marketing, the data subject should have the right to object to such processing free of charge and in a manner that can be easily and effectively invoked.

Automated Processing

26.40 Recital 58 states that every natural person should have the right not to be subject to a measure which is based on profiling by means of automated processing. However, such measure should be allowed when expressly authorised by law, carried out in the course of entering or performance of a contract, or when the data subject has given his consent. In any case, such processing should be subject to suitable safeguards, including specific information of the data subject and the right to obtain human intervention and that such measure should not concern a child.

26.41 Recital 59 states that the restrictions on specific principles and on the rights of information, access, rectification and erasure or on the right to data portability, the right to object, measures based on profiling, as well as on the communication of a personal data breach to a data subject and on certain related obligations of the data controllers may be imposed by EU or Member State law, as far as necessary and proportionate in a democratic society to safeguard public security, including the protection of human life especially in response to natural or man made disasters, the prevention, investigation and prosecution of criminal offences or of breaches of ethics for regulated professions, other public interests of the EU or of a Member State, in particular an important economic or financial interest of the EU or of a Member State, or the protection of the data subject or the rights and freedoms of others. Those restrictions should be in compliance with requirements set out by the Charter of Fundamental Rights of the EU and by the European Convention for the Protection of Human Rights and Fundamental Freedoms.

Liability

26.42 Recital 60 states that the comprehensive responsibility and liability of the data controller for any processing of personal data carried out by the data controller or on the data controller's behalf should be established. In particular, the data controller should ensure and be obliged to demonstrate the compliance of each processing operation with the Regulation.

Policies and Measures

26.43 Recital 61 states that the protection of the rights and freedoms of data subjects with regard to the processing of personal data require that appropriate technical and organisational measures are taken, both at the time of the design of the processing and at the time of the processing itself, to ensure that the requirements of the Regulation are met. In order to ensure and demonstrate compliance with the Regulation, the data controller should adopt internal policies and implement appropriate measures, which meet in particular the principles of data protection by design and data protection by default.

Recital 62 states that the protection of the rights and freedoms of data subjects as well as the responsibility and liability of data controllers and data processor, also in relation to the monitoring by and measures of supervisory authorities, requires a clear attribution of the responsibilities under the Regulation, including where a data controller determines the purposes, conditions and means of the processing jointly with other data controllers or where a processing operation is carried out on behalf of a controller.

Recital 65 states that in order to demonstrate compliance with the Regulation, the data controller or data processor should document each processing operation. Each data controller and data processor should be obliged to co-operate with the Supervisory Authority and make this documentation, on request, available to it, so that it might serve for monitoring those processing operations.

Third Counties

26.44   Recital 63 states that where a data controller not established in the EU is processing personal data of data subjects residing in the EU whose processing activities are related to the offering of goods or services to such data subjects, or to the monitoring their behaviour, the data controller should designate a representative, unless the data controller is established in a third country ensuring an adequate level of protection, or the data controller is a small or medium sized enterprise or a public authority or body or where the data controller is only occasionally offering goods or services to such data subjects. The representative should act on behalf of the data controller and may be addressed by any Supervisory Authority.

Recital 64 states that in order to determine whether a data controller is only occasionally offering goods and services to data subjects residing in the EU, it should be ascertained whether it is apparent from the data controller's overall activities that the offering of goods and services to such data subjects is ancillary to those main activities.

Security

26.45   Recital 66 states that in order to maintain security and to prevent processing in breach of the Regulation, the data controller or data processor should evaluate the risks inherent to the processing and implement measures to mitigate those risks. These measures should ensure an appropriate level of security, taking into account the state of the art and the costs of their implementation in relation to the risks and the nature of the personal data to be protected. When establishing technical standards and organisational measures to ensure security of processing, the Commission should promote technological neutrality, interoperability and innovation, and, where appropriate, cooperate with third countries.

Data Breach

26.46 Recital 67 states that a personal data breach may, if not addressed in an adequate and timely manner, result in substantial economic loss and social harm, including identity fraud, to the individual concerned. Therefore, as soon as the data controller becomes aware that such a breach has occurred, the data controller should notify the breach to the Supervisory Authority without undue delay and, where feasible, within 24 hours. Where this cannot achieved within 24 hours, an explanation of the reasons for the delay should accompany the notification. The individuals whose personal data could be adversely affected by the breach should be notified without undue delay in order to allow them to take the necessary precautions. A breach should be considered as adversely affecting the personal data or privacy of a data subject where it could result in, for example, identity theft or fraud, physical harm, significant humiliation or damage to reputation. The notification should describe the nature of the personal data breach as well as recommendations as well as recommendations for the individual concerned to mitigate potential adverse effects. Notifications to data subjects should be made as soon as reasonably feasible, and in close cooperation with the Supervisory Authority and respecting guidance provided by it or other relevant authorities (eg law enforcement authorities). For example, the chance for data subjects to mitigate an immediate risk of harm would call for a prompt notification of data subjects whereas the need to implement appropriate measures against continuing or similar data breaches may justify a longer delay.

Recital 68 states that in order to determine whether a personal data breach is notified to the Supervisory Authority and to the data subject without undue delay, it should be ascertained whether the data controller has implemented and applied appropriate technological protection and organisational measures to establish immediately whether a personal data breach has taken place and to inform promptly the Supervisory Authority and the data subject, before damage to personal and economic interests occurs, taking into account in particular the nature and gravity of the personal data breach and its consequences and adverse effects for the data subject.

Recital 69 states that in setting detailed rules concerning the format and procedures applicable to the notification of personal data breaches, due consideration should be given to the circumstances of the breach, including whether or not personal data had been protected by appropriate technical protection measures, effectively limiting the likelihood of identity fraud or other forms of misuse. Moreover, such rules and procedures should take into account the legitimate interests of law enforcement authorities in cases where early disclosure could unnecessarily hamper the investigation of the circumstances of a breach.

Registration/Notification

26.47 Recital 70 states that DPD95 provided for a general obligation to notify processing of personal data to the supervisory authorities. While this obligation produces administrative and financial burdens, it did not in all cases contribute to improving the protection of personal data. Therefore, such indiscriminate general notification obligation should be abolished, and replaced by effective procedures and mechanism which focus instead on those processing operations which are likely to present specific risks to the rights and freedoms of data subjects by virtue of their nature, their scope or their purposes. In such cases, a data protection impact assessment should be carried out by the data controller or data processor prior to the processing, which should include in particular the envisaged measures, safeguards and mechanisms for ensuring the protection of personal data and for demonstrating the compliance with the Regulation.

Recital 71states that this should in particular apply to newly established large scale filing systems, which aim at processing a considerable amount of personal data at regional, national or supranational level and which could affect a large number of data subjects.

Impact Assessments

26.48 Recital 72 states that there are circumstances under which it may be sensible and economic that the subject of a data protection impact assessment should be broader than a single project, for example where public authorities or bodies intend to establish a common application or processing platform or where several data controllers plan to introduce a common application or processing environment across an industry sector or segment or for a widely used horizontal activity.

Recital 73 states that the data protection impact assessments should be carried out by a public authority or public body if such an assessment has not already been made in the context of the adoption of the national law on which the performance of the tasks of the public authority or public body is based and which regulates the specific processing operation or set of operations in question.

Recital 74 states that where a data protection impact assessment indicates that processing operations involve a high degree of specific risks to the rights and freedoms of data subjects, such as excluding individuals from their right, or by the use of specific new technologies, the Supervisory Authority should be consulted, prior to the start of operations, on a risky processing which might not be in compliance with the Regulation, and to make proposals to remedy such situation. Such consultation should equally take place in the course of the preparation either of a measure by the national parliament or of a measure based on such legislative measure which defines the nature of the processing and lays down appropriate safeguards.

Public Sector

26.49 Recital 75 states that where the processing is carried out in the public sector or where, in the private sector, processing is carried out by a large enterprise, or where its core activities, regardless of the size of the enterprise, involve processing operations which require regular and systematic monitoring, a person should assist the data controller or data processor to monitor internal compliance with the Regulation. Such data protection officers, whether or not employees of the data controller, should be in a position to perform their duties and tasks independently.

Industry Codes

26.50 Recital 76 states that the associations or other bodies representing categories of data controllers should be encouraged to draw up codes of conduct.

Certification

26.51 Recital 77 states that in order to enhance transparency and compliance with the Regulation, the establishment of certification mechanisms, data protection seals and marks should be encouraged, allowing data subjects to quickly assess the level of data protection of relevant products and services.

Recital 78 states that cross-border flows of personal data are necessary for the expansion of international trade and international co-operation. The increase in these flows has raised new challenges and concerns with respect to the protection of personal data. However, when personal data are transferred from the EU to third countries or to international organisations, the level of protection of individuals guaranteed in the EU by the Regulation should not be undermined. In any event, transfers to third countries may only be carried out in full compliance with the Regulation.

Global Data Protection

26.52 Recital 79 states that the Regulation is without prejudice to international agreements concluded between the EU and third countries regulating the transfer of personal data including appropriate safeguards for the data subjects.

Recital 80 states that the Commission may decide with effect for the entire EU that certain third countries, or a territory or a processing sector within a third country, or an international organisation, offer an adequate level of data protection, thus providing legal certainty and uniformity throughout the EU as regards the third countries or international organisations which are considered to provide such level of protection. In these cases, transfers of personal data to these countries may take place without needing to obtain any further authorisation.

Recital 81 states that in line with the fundamental values on which the EU is founded, in particular the protection of human rights, the Commission should, in its assessment of the third country, take into account how a given third country respects the rule of law, access to justice as well as international human rights norms and standards.

TCBFs, White List, etc

26.53 Recital 82 states that the Commission may equally recognise that a third country, or a territory or a processing sector within a third country, or an international organisation offers no adequate level of data protection. Consequently the transfer of personal data to that third country should be prohibited. In that case, provision should be made for consultations between the Commission and such third countries or international organisations.

Recital 83 states that in the absence of an adequacy decision, the data controller or data processor should take measures to compensate for the lack of data protection in a third country by way of appropriate safeguards for the data subject. Such appropriate safeguards may consist of making use of binding corporate rules, standard data protection clauses adopted by the Commission, standard data protection clauses adopted by a Supervisory Authority or contractual clauses authorised by a Supervisory Authority, or other suitable and proportionate measures justified in the light of all the circumstances surrounding a data transfer operation or set of data transfer operations and where authorised by a Supervisory Authority.

Recital 84 states that the possibility for the data controller or data processor to use standard data protection clauses adopted by the Commission or by a Supervisory Authority should neither prevent the possibility for data controllers or data processors to include the standard data protection clauses in a wider contract nor to add other clauses as long as they do not contradict, directly or indirectly, the standard contractual clauses adopted by the Commission or by a Supervisory Authority or prejudice the fundamental rights or freedoms of the data subjects.

Recital 85 states that a corporate group should be able to make use of approved binding corporate rules for its international transfers from the EU to organisations within the same corporate group of undertakings, as long as such corporate rules include essential principles and enforceable rights to ensure appropriate safeguards for transfers or categories of transfers of personal data.

Recital 86 states that provisions should be made for the possibility for transfers in certain circumstances where the data subject has given his consent, where the transfer is necessary in relation to a contract or a legal claim, where important grounds of public interest laid down by EU or Member State law so require or where the transfer is made from a register established by law and intended for consultation by the public or persons having a legitimate interest. In this latter case such a transfer should not involve the entirety of the data or entire categories of the data contained in the register and, when the register is intended for consultation by persons having a legitimate interest, the transfer should be made only at the request of those persons or if they are to be the recipients.

Recital 87 states that these derogations should in particular apply to data transfers required and necessary for the protection of important grounds of public interest, for example in cases of international data transfers between competition authorities, tax or customs administrations, financial supervisory authorities, between services competent for social security matters, or to competent authorities for the prevention, investigation, detection and prosecution of criminal offences.

Recital 88 states that the transfers which cannot be qualified as frequent or massive, could also be possible for the purposes of the legitimate interests pursued by the data controller or the data processor, when they have assessed all the circumstances surrounding the data transfer. For the purposes of processing for historical, statistical and scientific research purposes, the legitimate expectations of society for an increase of knowledge should be taken into consideration.

Recital 89 states that in any case, where the Commission has taken no decision on the adequate level of data protection in a third country, the data controller or data processor should make use of solutions that provide data subjects with a guarantee that they will continue to benefit from the fundamental rights and safeguards as regards processing of their data in the EU once this data has been transferred.

Recital 90 states that the some third countries enact laws, regulations and other legislative instruments which purport to directly regulate data processing activities of natural and legal persons under the jurisdiction of the Member States. The extraterritorial application of these laws, regulations and other legislative instruments may be in breach of international law and may impede the attainment of the protection of individuals guaranteed in the EU by the Regulation. Transfers should only be allowed where the conditions of the Regulation for a transfer to third countries are met. This may inter alia be the case where the disclosure is necessary for an important ground of public interest recognised in EU law or in a Member State law to which the data controller is subject. The conditions under which an important ground of public interest exists should be further specified by the Commission in a delegated act.

Information Commissioner/Supervisory Authorities

26.54   Recital 92 states that the establishment of Supervisory Authorities in Member States, exercising their functions with complete independence, is an essential component of the protection of individuals with regard to the processing of their personal data. Member States may establish more than one Supervisory Authority, to reflect their constitutional, organisational and administrative structure.

Recital 94 states that each Supervisory Authority should be provided with the adequate financial and human resources, premises and infrastructure, which is necessary for the effective performance of their tasks, including for the tasks related to mutual assistance and cooperation with other supervisory authorities throughout the EU.

Recital 96 states that the supervisory authorities should monitor the application of the provisions pursuant to the Regulation and contribute to its consistent application throughout the EU, in order to protect natural persons in relation to the processing of their personal data and to facilitate the free flow of personal data within the internal market. For that purpose, the supervisory authorities should co-operate with each other and the Commission.

Processing in More than One Member State

26.55 Recital 97 states that where the processing of personal data in the context of the activities of an establishment of a data controller or a data processor in the EU takes place in more than one Member State, one single Supervisory Authority should be competent for monitoring the activities of the data controller or data processor throughout the EU and taking the related decisions, in order to increase the consistent application, provide legal certainty and reduce administrative burden for such data controllers and data processors.

One Stop Shop

26.56 Recital 98 states that the competent authority, providing such one-stop shop, should be the Supervisory Authority of the Member State in which the data controller or data processor has its main establishment.

Recital 99 states that the while the Regulation applies also to the activities of national courts, the competence of the Supervisory Authorities should not cover the processing of personal data when courts are acting in their judicial capacity, in order to safeguard the independence of judges in the performance of their judicial tasks. However, this exemption should be strictly limited to genuine judicial activities in court cases and not apply to other activities where judges might be involved in, in accordance with national law.

Recital 100 states that in order to ensure consistent monitoring and enforcement of the Regulation throughout the EU, the Supervisory Authorities should have in each Member State the same duties and effective powers, including powers of investigation, legally binding intervention, decisions and sanctions, particularly in cases of complaints from individuals, and to engage in legal proceedings. Investigative powers of Supervisory Authorities as regards access to premises should be exercised in conformity with EU law and national law. This concerns in particular the requirement to obtain a prior judicial authorisation.

Recital 101 states that each Supervisory Authority should hear complaints lodged by any data subject and should investigate the matter. The investigation following a complaint should be carried out, subject to judicial review, to the extent that is appropriate in the specific case. The Supervisory Authority should inform the data subject of the progress and the outcome of the complaint within a reasonable period. If the case requires further investigation or coordination with another Supervisory Authority, intermediate information should be given to the data subject.

DP Awareness

26.57 Recital 102 states that the awareness raising activities by Supervisory Authorities addressed to the public should include specific measures directed at data controllers and data processors, including micro, small and medium-sized enterprises, as well as data subjects.

Recital 103 states that the Supervisory Authorities should assist each other in performing their duties and provide mutual assistance, so as to ensure the consistent application and enforcement of the Regulation in the internal market.

Recital 104 states that each Supervisory Authority should have the right to participate in joint operations between supervisory authorities. The requested Supervisory Authority should be obliged to respond to the request in a defined time period.

Recital 105 states that in order to ensure the consistent application of the Regulation throughout the EU, a consistency mechanism for co-operation between the Supervisory Authorities themselves and the Commission should be established. This mechanism should in particular apply where a Supervisory Authority intends to take a measure as regards processing operations that are related to the offering of goods or services to data subjects in several Member States, or to the monitoring such data subjects, or that might substantially affect the free flow of personal data. It should also apply where any Supervisory Authority or the Commission requests that the matter should be dealt with in the consistency mechanism. This mechanism should be without prejudice to any measures that the Commission may take in the exercise of its powers under the Treaties.

Recital 106 states that in application of the consistency mechanism, the European Data Protection Board should, within a determined period of time, issue an opinion, if a simple majority of its members so decides or if so requested by any Supervisory Authority or the Commission.

Recital 107 states that in order to ensure compliance with the Regulation, the Commission may adopt an opinion on this matter, or a decision, requiring the Supervisory Authority to suspend its draft measure.

Enforcement

26.58 Recital 108 states that there may be an urgent need to act in order to protect the interests of data subjects, in particular when the danger exists that the enforcement of a right of a data subject could be considerably impeded. Therefore, a Supervisory Authority should be able to adopt provisional measures with a specified period of validity when applying the consistency mechanism.

Recital 109 states that the application of this mechanism should be a condition for the legal validity and enforcement of the respective decision by a Supervisory Authority. In other cases of cross-border relevance, mutual assistance and joint investigations might be carried out between the concerned Supervisory Authorities on a bilateral or multilateral basis without triggering the consistency mechanism.

Recital 110 states that at EU level, a European Data Protection Board should be set up. It should replace the Working Party on the Protection of Individuals with Regard to the Processing of Personal Data established by DPD95. It should consist of a head of a Supervisory Authority of each Member State and of the European Data Protection Supervisor. The Commission should participate in its activities. The European Data Protection Board should contribute to the consistent application of the Regulation throughout the EU, including by advising the Commission and promoting cooperation of the supervisory authorities throughout the EU. The European Data Protection Board should act independently when exercising its tasks.

Complaints to Information Commissioner

26.59 Recital 111 states that every data subject should have the right to lodge a complaint with a Supervisory Authority in any Member State and have the right to a judicial remedy if they consider that their rights under the Regulation are infringed or where the Supervisory Authority does not react on a complaint or does not act where such action is necessary to protect the rights of the data subject.

Recital 112 states that any body, organisation or association which aims to protect the rights and interests of data subjects in relation to the protection of their data and is constituted according to the law of a Member State should have the right to lodge a complaint with a Supervisory Authority or exercise the right to a judicial remedy on behalf of data subjects, or to lodge, independently of a data subject's complaint, an own complaint where it considers that a personal data breach has occurred.

Court Remedies

26.60 Recital 113 states that each natural or legal person should have the right to a judicial remedy against decisions of a Supervisory Authority concerning them. Proceedings against a Supervisory Authority should be brought before the courts of the Member State, where the Supervisory Authority is established.

Recital 114 states that the in order to strengthen the judicial protection of the data subject in situations where the competent Supervisory

Authority is established in another Member State than the one where the data subject is residing, the data subject may request any body, organisation or association aiming to protect the rights and interests of data subjects in relation to the protection of their data to bring on the data subject's behalf proceedings against that Supervisory Authority to the competent court in the other Member State.

Recital 115 states that in situations where the competent Supervisory Authority established in another Member State does not act or has taken insufficient measures in relation to a complaint, the data subject may request the Supervisory Authority in the Member State of his or her habitual residence to bring proceedings against that Supervisory Authority to the competent court in the other Member State. The requested Supervisory Authority may decide, subject to judicial review, whether it is appropriate to follow the request or not.

Recital 116 states that for proceedings against a data controller or data processor, the plaintiff should have the choice to bring the action before the courts of the Member States where the data controller or data processor has an establishment or where the data subject resides, unless the data controller is a public authority acting in the exercise of its public powers.

Recital 117 states that where there are indications that parallel proceedings are pending before the courts in different Member States, the courts should be obliged to contact each other. The courts should have the possibility to suspend a case where a parallel case is pending in another Member State. Member States should ensure that court actions, in order to be effective, should allow the rapid adoption of measures to remedy or prevent an infringement of the Regulation.

Compensation

26.61   Recital 118 states that any damage which a person may suffer as a result of unlawful processing should be compensated by the data controller or data processor, who may be exempted from liability if they prove that they are not responsible for the damage, in particular where they establish fault on the part of the data subject or in case of force majeure.

Penalties

26.62   Recital 119 states that penalties should be imposed to any person, whether governed by private or public law, who fails to comply with the Regulation. Member States should ensure that the penalties should be effective, proportionate and dissuasive and should take all measures to implement the penalties.

Sanctions

26.63 Recital 120 states that in order to strengthen and harmonise administrative sanctions against infringements of the Regulation, each Supervisory Authority should have the power to sanction administrative offences. The Regulation should indicate these offences and the upper limit for the related administrative fines, which should be fixed in each individual case proportionate to the specific situation, with due regard in particular to the nature, gravity and duration of the breach. The consistency mechanism may also be used to cover divergences in the application of administrative sanctions.

Journalism

26.64 Recital 121 states that the processing of personal data solely for journalistic purposes, or for the purposes of artistic or literary expression should qualify for exemption from the requirements of certain provisions of the Regulation in order to reconcile the right to the protection of personal data with the right to freedom of expression, and notably the right to receive and impart information, as guaranteed in particular by Article 11 of the Charter of Fundamental Rights of the European Union. This should apply in particular to processing of personal data in the audiovisual field and in news archives and press libraries. Therefore, Member States should adopt legislative measures, which should lay down exemptions and derogations which are necessary for the purpose of balancing these fundamental rights. Such exemptions and derogations should be adopted by the Member States on general principles, on the rights of the data subject, on data controller and data processor, on the transfer of data to third countries or international organisations, on the independent supervisory authorities and on co-operation and consistency. This should not, however, lead Member States to lay down exemptions from the other provisions of the Regulation. In order to take account of the importance of the right to freedom of expression in every democratic society, it is necessary to interpret notions relating to that freedom, such as journalism, broadly.

Therefore, Member States should classify activities as 'journalistic' for the purpose of the exemptions and derogations to be laid down under the Regulation if the object of these activities is the disclosure to the public of information, opinions or ideas, irrespective of the medium which is used to transmit them. They should not be limited to media undertakings and may be undertaken for profit-making or for non-profit making purposes.

Health

26.65 Recital 122 states that the processing of personal data concerning health, as a special category of data which deserves higher protection, may often be justified by a number of legitimate reasons for the benefit of individuals and society as a whole, in particular in the context of ensuring continuity of cross-border healthcare. Therefore, the Regulation should provide for harmonised conditions for the processing of personal data concerning health, subject to specific and suitable safeguards so as to protect the fundamental rights and the personal data of individuals. This includes the right for individuals to have access to their personal data concerning their health, for example the data in their medical records containing such information as diagnosis, examination results, assessments by treating physicians and any treatment or interventions provided.

Recital 123 states that processing of personal data concerning health may be necessary for reasons of public interest in the areas of public health, without consent of the data subject. In that context, 'public health' should be interpreted as defined in Regulation (EC) No 1338/2008 of the European Parliament and of the Council of 16 December 2008 on EU statistics on public health and health and safety at work, meaning all elements related to health, namely health status, including morbidity and disability, the determinants having an effect on that health status, health care needs, resources allocated to health care, the provision of, and universal access to, health care as well as health care expenditure and financing, and the causes of mortality. Such processing of personal data concerning health for reasons of public interest should not result in personal data being processed for other purposes by third parties such as employers, insurance and banking companies.

Employment

26.66 Recital 124 states that the general principles on the protection of individuals with regard to the processing of personal data should also be applicable to the employment context. Therefore, in order to regulate the processing of employees' personal data in the employment context, Member States should be able, within the limits of the Regulation, to adopt by law specific rules for the processing of personal data in the employment sector.

Research

26.67 Recital 125 states that the processing of personal data for the purposes of historical, statistical or scientific research should, in order to be lawful, also respect other relevant legislation such as on clinical trials.

Recital 126 states that the scientific research for the purposes of the Regulation should include fundamental research, applied research, and privately funded research and in addition should take into account the EU's objective under Article 179(1) of the Treaty on the Functioning of the European Union of achieving a European Research Area.

Recital 127 states that as regards the powers of the Supervisory Authorities to obtain from the data controller or data processor access personal data and access to its premises, Member States may adopt by law, within the limits of the Regulation, specific rules in order to safeguard the professional or other equivalent secrecy obligations, in so far as necessary to reconcile the right to the protection of personal data with an obligation of professional secrecy.

Religious Not Effected

26.68 Recital 128 states that the Regulation respects and does not prejudice the status under national law of churches and religious associations or communities in the Member States, as recognised in Article 17 of the Treaty on the Functioning of the European Union. As a consequence, where a church in a Member State applies, at the time of entry into force of the Regulation, comprehensive rules relating to the protection of individuals with regard to the processing of personal data, these existing rules should continue to apply if they are brought in line with the Regulation. Such churches and religious associations should be required to provide for the establishment of a completely independent Supervisory Authority.

Data Protection Right and Laws

26.69 Recital 129 states that in order to fulfil the objectives of the Regulation, namely to protect the fundamental rights and freedoms of natural persons and in particular their right to the protection of personal data and to ensure the free movement of personal data within the EU, the power to adopt acts in accordance with Article 290 of the Treaty on the Functioning of the European Union should be delegated to the Commission. In particular, delegated acts should be adopted in respect of lawfulness of processing; specifying the criteria and conditions in relation to the consent of a child; processing of special categories of data; specifying the criteria and conditions for manifestly excessive requests and fees for exercising the rights of the data subject; criteria and requirements for the information to the data subject and in relation to the right of access; the enhanced right to be forgotten and to erasure; measures based on profiling; criteria and requirements in relation to the responsibility of the data controller and to data protection by design and by default; a data processor; criteria and requirements for the documentation and the security of processing; criteria and requirements for establishing a personal data breach and for its notification to the Supervisory Authority, and on the circumstances where a personal data breach is likely to adversely affect the data subject; the criteria and conditions for processing operations requiring a data protection impact assessment; the criteria and requirements for determining a high degree of specific risks which require prior consultation; designation and tasks of the data protection officer; codes of conduct; criteria and requirements for certification mechanisms; criteria and requirements for transfers by way of binding corporate rules; transfer derogations; administrative sanctions; processing for health purposes; processing in the employment context and processing for historical, statistical and scientific research purposes. It is of particular importance that the Commission carry out appropriate consultations during its preparatory work, including at expert level.

Recital 130 states that in order to ensure uniform conditions for the implementation of the Regulation, implementing powers should be conferred on the Commission for: specifying standard forms in relation to the processing of personal data of a child; standard procedures and forms for exercising the rights of data subjects; standard forms for the information to the data subject; standard forms and procedures in relation to the right of access; the right to data portability; standard forms in relation to the responsibility of the data controller to data protection by design and by default and to the documentation; specific requirements for the security of processing; the standard format and the procedures for the notification of a personal data breach to the Supervisory Authority and the communication of a personal data breach to the data subject; standards and procedures for a data protection impact assessment; forms and procedures for prior authorisation and prior consultation; technical standards and mechanisms for certification; the adequate level of protection afforded by a third country or a territory or a processing sector within that third country or an international organisation; disclosures not authorised by EU law; mutual assistance; joint operations; decisions under the consistency mechanism.

SMEs

26.70 Recital 131 states that the examination procedure should be used for the adoption of specifying standard forms in relation to the consent of a child; standard procedures and forms for exercising the rights of data subjects; standard forms for the information to the data subject; standard forms and procedures in relation to the right of access; the right to data portability; standard forms in relation to the responsibility of the data controller to data protection by design and by default and to the documentation; specific requirements for the security of processing; the standard format and the procedures for the notification of a personal data breach to the Supervisory Authority and the communication of a personal data breach to the data subject; standards and procedures for a data protection impact assessment; forms and procedures for prior authorisation and prior consultation; technical standards and mechanisms for certification; the adequate level of protection afforded by a third country or a territory or a processing sector within that third country or an international organisation; disclosures not authorised by EU law; mutual assistance; joint operations; decisions under the consistency mechanism, given that those acts are of general scope.

Third Countries

26.71 Recital 132 states that the Commission should adopt immediately applicable implementing acts where, in duly justified cases relating to a third country or a territory or a processing sector within that third country or an international organisation which does not ensure an adequate level of protection and relating to matters communicated by Supervisory Authorities under the consistency mechanism, imperative grounds of urgency so require.

Recital 133 states that since the objectives of the Regulation, namely to ensure an equivalent level of protection of individuals and the free flow of data throughout the EU, cannot be sufficiently achieved by the Member States and can therefore, by reason of the scale or effects of the action, be better achieved at EU level, the EU may adopt measures, in accordance with the principle of subsidiarity as set out in Article 5 of the Treaty on European Union. In accordance with the principle of proportionality as set out in that Article, the Regulation does not go beyond what is necessary in order to achieve that objective.

DPD Repeal

26.72   Recital 134 states that DPD95 should be repealed by the Regulation. However, Commission decisions adopted and authorisations by supervisory authorities based on DPD95 remain in force.

ePD Amended

26.73   Recital 135 states that the Regulation should apply to all matters concerning the protection of fundamental rights and freedom vis-à-vis the processing of personal data, which are not subject to specific obligations with the same objective set out in Directive 2002/58/EC, including the obligations on the data controller and the rights of individuals. In order to clarify the relationship between the Regulation and Directive 2002/58/EC, the latter Directive should be amended accordingly.

Schengen

26.74   Recital 136 states that as regards Iceland and Norway, the Regulation constitutes a development of provisions of the Schengen acquis to the extent that it applies to the processing of personal data by authorities involved in the implementation of that acquis, as provided for by the Agreement concluded by the Council of the European Union and the Republic of Iceland and the Kingdom of Norway concerning the association of those two States with the implementation, application and development of the Schengen acquis

Recital 137 states that as regards Switzerland, the Regulation constitutes a development of provisions of the Schengen acquis to the extent that it applies to the processing of personal data by authorities involved in the implementation of that acquis, as provided for by the Agreement between the European Union, the European Community and the Swiss Confederation concerning the association of the Swiss Confederation with the implementation, application and development of the Schengen acquis

Recital 138 states that as regards Liechtenstein, the Regulation constitutes a development of provisions of the Schengen acquis to the extent that it applies to the processing of personal data by authorities involved in the implementation of that acquis, as provided for by the Protocol between the European Union, the European Community, the Swiss Confederation and the Principality of Liechtenstein on the accession of the Principality of Liechtenstein to the Agreement between the European Union, the European Community and the Swiss Confederation on the Swiss Confederation's association with the implementation, application and development of the Schengen acquis.

Proportionality

26.78 Recital 139 states that in view of the fact that, as underlined by the Court of Justice of the EU (ECJ/CJEU), the right to the protection of personal data is not an absolute right, but must be considered in relation to its function in society and be balanced with other fundamental rights, in accordance with the principle of proportionality, the Regulation respects all fundamental rights and observes the principles recognised in the Charter of Fundamental Rights of the European Union as enshrined in the Treaties, notably the right to respect for private and family life, home and communications, the right to the protection of personal data, the freedom of thought, conscience and religion, the freedom of expression and information, the freedom to conduct a business, the right to an effective remedy and to a fair trial as well as cultural, religious and linguistic diversity.

DPR: Children

26.79 The issue of children in the data protection regime have been steadily rising. The increased use of social networking and Web 2.0 services enhance the exposures and risks for children and the uninitiated.[21]

This has included children's groups, regulators and also the WP29. WP29 has issued Opinion 2/2009 on the Protection of Children's Personal Data (General Guidelines and the Special Case of Schools) in 2009 and also Working Document 1/2008 on the Protection of Children's Personal Data (General Guidelines and the Special Case of Schools) in 2008. Schools are being encouraged to be proactive and to have appropriate codes and policies for childrens' social networking and internet usage.[22]

---

21 See, for example, Gourlay, D., and Gallagher, G., 'Collecting and Using Children's Information Online: the UK/US Dichotomy,' SCL *Computers and Law*, 12 December 2011.

22 Note generally, for example, Groppe, J.S., 'A Child's Playground or a Predator's Hunting Ground? – How to Protect Children on Internet Social Networking Sites, *CommLaw Conspectus* (2007)(16) pp. 215–245; Steadman, E.P., 'MySpace, But Who's Responsibility? Liability of Social Networking Websites When Offline

There is now going to be an explicit acknowledgement of children's interest in the EU data protection regime, unlike with the DPD95 which contained no explicit reference. The DPR defines a 'child' as any person below the age of 18 years. This is significant amongst other things in relation consent, contracting, etc. It is also significant for social networks which have significant numbers of children. Up until now it was common for certain social networks to purport to accept users only over the age of thirteen. Now that a child is defined as up to eighteen, it may require careful assessment in relation to social networking contracts, terms, processes, sign ups, etc.

Article 8 of the DPR contains provisions in relation to the processing of personal data of a child, Article 8(1) provides that for the purposes of the Regulation, in relation to the offering of information society services directly to a child, the processing of personal data of a child below the age of 13 years shall only be lawful if and to the extent that consent is given or authorised by the child's parent or custodian. The data controller shall make reasonable efforts to obtain verifiable consent, taking into consideration available technology.

Article 8(1) provides that Article 8(1) shall not affect the general contract law of Member States such as the rules on the validity, formation or effect of a contract in relation to a child.

Under Article 8(3) the Commission shall be empowered to adopt delegated acts in accordance with Article 86 for the purpose of further specifying the criteria and requirements for the methods to obtain verifiable consent referred to in Article 8(1). In doing so, the Commission shall consider specific measures for micro, small and medium-sized enterprises (Article 8(3)).

In addition, the Commission under may lay down standard forms for specific methods to obtain verifiable consent referred to in Article 8(1). Those implementing acts shall be adopted in accordance with the examination procedure referred to in Article 87(2) (Article 8(4)).

DPR: Processing Not Allowing Identification

26.80   Article 10 refers to processing not allowing identification, and provides that if the data processed by a data controller do not permit the data controller to identify a natural person, the data controller shall not

Sexual Assault of Minors Follows Online Interaction,' *Villanova Sports and Entertainment Law Journal* (2007)(14), pp. 363–397; Beckstrom, D.C., 'Who's Looking at Your Facebook Profile? the Use of Student Conduct Codes to Censor College Students' Online Speech,' *Willamette Law Review* (2008), pp. 261–312.

be obliged to acquire additional information in order to identify the data subject for the sole purpose of complying with any provision of the Regulation.

DPD95: Processing, Journalism, Freedom of Expression

26.81 Article 9 of the DPD95 refers to processing of personal data and freedom of expression, and provides that Member States shall provide for exemptions or derogations from the provisions of this Chapter, Chapter IV and Chapter VI for the processing of personal data carried out solely for journalistic purposes or the purpose of artistic or literary expression only if they are necessary to reconcile the right to privacy with the rules governing freedom of expression.

DPR: Processing and Freedom of Expression

26.82 Chapter IX of the DPR also makes provisions relating to specific data processing situations. Under Article 80 the heading is processing of personal data and freedom of expression.

Article 80(1) Member States shall provide for exemptions or derogations from the provisions on the general principles in Chapter II, the rights of the data subject in Chapter III, on data controller and data processor in Chapter IV, on the transfer of personal data to third countries and international organisations in Chapter V, the independent Supervisory Authorities in Chapter VI and on co-operation and consistency in Chapter VII for the processing of personal data carried out solely for journalistic purposes or the purpose of artistic or literary expression in order to reconcile the right to the protection of personal data with the rules governing freedom of expression.

In accordance with Article 80(2) each Member State shall notify to the Commission those provisions of its law which it has adopted pursuant to paragraph 1 by the date specified in Article 91(2) at the latest and, without delay, any subsequent amendment law or amendment affecting them.

DPR: Health Data

26.83 Chapter IX of the DPR makes provisions relating to specific data processing situations. Article 81 refers to processing of personal data concerning health.

Article 81(1) provides that within the limits of DPR and in accordance with point (h) of Article 9(2), processing of personal data concerning health must be on the basis of EU law or Member State law which shall provide for suitable and specific measures to safeguard the data subject's legitimate interests, and be necessary for:

- the purposes of preventive or occupational medicine, medical diagnosis, the provision of care or treatment or the management of healthcare services, and where those data are processed by a health professional subject to the obligation of professional secrecy or another person also subject to an equivalent obligation of confidentiality under Member State law or rules established by national competent bodies; or
- reasons of public interest in the area of public health, such as protecting against serious cross-border threats to health or ensuring high standards of quality and safety, inter alia for medicinal products or medical devices; or
- other reasons of public interest in areas such as social protection, especially in order to ensure the quality and cost-effectiveness of the procedures used for settling claims for benefits and services in the health insurance system.

Under Article 81(2), it is provided that processing of personal data concerning health which is necessary for historical, statistical or scientific research purposes, such as patient registries set up for improving diagnoses and differentiating between similar types of diseases and preparing studies for therapies, is subject to the conditions and safeguards referred to in Article 83.

Article 81(3) empowers the Commission to adopt delegated acts in accordance with Article 86 for the purpose of further specifying other reasons of public interest in the area of public health as referred to in Article 81(1)(b) (ie second bullet above), as well as criteria and requirements for the safeguards for the processing of personal data for the purposes referred to in Article 81(1).

DPR: Employment Data

26.84 Chapter IX of the DPR refers to provisions relating to specific data processing situations. Article 82 refers to processing in the employment context. Article 82(1) provides that within the limits of the DPR, Member States may adopt by law specific rules regulating the processing of employees' personal data in the employment context, in particular for the purposes of the recruitment, the performance of the contract of employment, including discharge of obligations laid down by law or by collective agreements, management, planning and organisation of work, health and safety at work, and for the purposes of the exercise and enjoyment, on an individual or collective basis, of rights and benefits related to employment, and for the purpose of the termination of the employment relationship.

Article 82(2) states that each Member State shall notify to the Commission those provisions of its law which it adopts pursuant to Article 82(1), by the date specified in Article 91(2) at the latest and, without delay, any subsequent amendment affecting them.

In addition, Article 82(3) provides that the Commission shall be empowered to adopt delegated acts in accordance with Article 86 for the purpose of further specifying the criteria and requirements for the safeguards for the processing of personal data for the purposes referred to in Article 82(1).

DPR: Research Data

26.85 Chapter IX refers to provisions relating to specific data processing situations. Article 83 refers to processing for historical, statistical and scientific research purposes.

Under Article 83(1) it is provided that within the limits of the DPR, personal data may be processed for historical, statistical or scientific research purposes only if:

- these purposes cannot be otherwise fulfilled by processing data which does not permit or not any longer permit the identification of the data subject;
- data enabling the attribution of information to an identified or identifiable data subject is kept separately from the other information as long as these purposes can be fulfilled in this manner.

Under Article 83(2), bodies conducting historical, statistical or scientific research may publish or otherwise publicly disclose personal data only if:

- the data subject has given consent, subject to the conditions laid down in Article 7;
- the publication of personal data is necessary to present research findings or to facilitate research insofar as the interests or the fundamental rights or freedoms of the data subject do not override these interests; or
- the data subject has made the data public.

Article 83(3) provides that the Commission shall be empowered to adopt delegated acts in accordance with Article 86 for the purpose of further specifying the criteria and requirements for the processing of personal data for the purposes referred to in Article 83(1) and (2) as well as any necessary limitations on the rights of information to and access by the data subject and detailing the conditions and safeguards for the rights of the data subject under these circumstances.

DPR: Rights of Data Subjects

26.86   Recital 1 states that the protection of natural persons in relation to the processing of personal data is a fundamental right. Article 8(1) of the Charter of Fundamental Rights of the European Union and Article 16(1) of the Treaty lay down that everyone has the right to the protection of personal data concerning them.

Recital 2 indicates that the processing of personal data is designed to serve man; the principles and rules on the protection of individuals with regard to the processing of their personal data should, whatever the nationality or residence of natural persons, respect their fundamental rights and freedoms, notably their right to the protection of personal data. It should contribute to the accomplishment of an area of freedom, security and justice and of an economic union, to economic and social progress, the strengthening and the convergence of the economies within the internal market, and the well-being of individuals.

Recital 19 states that any processing of personal data in the context of the activities of an establishment of a data controller or a data processor in the EU should be carried out in accordance with the Regulation, regardless of whether the processing itself takes place within the EU or not. Establishment implies the effective and real exercise of activity through stable arrangements. The legal form of such arrangements, whether through a branch or a subsidiary with a legal personality, is not the determining factor in this respect.

Recital 20 states that in order to ensure that individuals are not deprived of the protection to which they are entitled under the Regulation, the processing of personal data of data subjects residing in the EU by a data controller not established in the EU should be subject to the Regulation where the processing activities are related to the offering of goods or services to such data subjects, or to the monitoring of the behaviour of such data subjects.

Recital 21 states that in order to determine whether a processing activity can be considered to 'monitor the behaviour' of data subjects, it should be ascertained whether individuals are tracked on the internet with data processing techniques which consist of applying a 'profile' to an individual, particularly in order to take decisions concerning them or for analysing or predicting her or his personal preferences, behaviours and attitudes.

Recital 22 states that where the national law of a Member State applies by virtue of public international law, the Regulation should also apply to a data controller not established in the EU, such as in a Member State's diplomatic mission or consular post.

Recital 23 states that the principles of protection should apply to any information concerning an identified or identifiable person. To determine whether a person is identifiable, account should be taken of all the means likely reasonably to be used either by the data controller or by any other person to identify the individual. The principles of data protection should not apply to data rendered anonymous in such a way that the data subject is no longer identifiable.

Chapter III of the DPR refers to rights of the data subject. Section 1 refers specifically to transparency and modalities.

Article 11 is headed 'Transparent information and communication'. Under Article 11(1) the data controller shall have transparent and easily accessible policies with regard to the processing of personal data and for the exercise of data subjects' rights.

Under Article 11(2) the data controller shall provide any information and any communication relating to the processing of personal data to the data subject in an intelligible form, using clear and plain language, adapted to the data subject, in particular for any information addressed specifically to a child.

Article 12 refers to procedures and mechanisms for exercising the rights of the data subject. Article 12(1) provides that the data controller shall establish procedures for providing the information referred to in Article 14 and for the exercise of the rights of data subjects referred to in Article 13 and Articles 15 to 19. The data controller shall provide in particular mechanisms for facilitating the request for the actions referred to in Article 13 and Articles 15 to 19. Where personal data are processed by automated means, the data controller shall also provide means for requests to be made electronically (Article 12(2)).

Article 12(2) provides that the data controller shall inform the data subject without delay and, at the latest within one month of receipt of the request, whether or not any action has been taken pursuant to Article 13 and Articles 15 to 19 and shall provide the requested information. This period may be prolonged for a further month, if several data subjects exercise their rights and their cooperation is necessary to a reasonable extent to prevent an unnecessary and disproportionate effort on the part of the data controller. The information shall be given in writing. Where the data subject makes the request in electronic form, the information shall be provided in electronic form, unless otherwise requested by the data subject.

Under Article 12(3), it is provided that if the data controller refuses to take action on the request of the data subject, the data controller shall inform the data subject of the reasons for the refusal and on the possibilities of lodging a complaint to the Supervisory Authority and seeking a judicial remedy.

Under Article 12(4) the information and the actions taken on requests referred to in paragraph 1 shall be free of charge. Where requests are manifestly excessive, in particular because of their repetitive character, the data controller may charge a fee for providing the information or taking the action requested, or the data controller may not take the action requested. In that case, the data controller shall bear the burden of proving the manifestly excessive character of the request.

The Commission is empowered, under Article 12(5), to adopt delegated acts in accordance with Article 86 for the purpose of further specifying the criteria and conditions for the manifestly excessive requests and the fees referred to in Article 12(4). In addition, Article 12(6) provides that the Commission may lay down standard forms and specifying standard procedures for the communication referred to in Article 12(2), including the electronic format. In doing so, the Commission shall take the appropriate measures for micro, small and medium-sized enterprises. Those implementing acts shall be adopted in accordance with the examination procedure referred to in Article 87(2) (Article 12(6)).

Article 13 refers to rights in relation to recipients. It provides that the data controller shall communicate any rectification or erasure carried out in accordance with Articles 16 and 17 to each recipient to whom the data have been disclosed, unless this proves impossible or involves a disproportionate effort.

'Personal data breach' is defined to mean a breach of security leading to the accidental or unlawful destruction, loss, alteration, unauthorised disclosure of, or access to, personal data transmitted, stored or otherwise processed.

DPR: Secrecy

26.87 Chapter IX of the DPR refers to provisions relating to specific data processing situations. Article 84 is headed obligations of secrecy.

Under Article 84(1), it is provided that within the limits of the DPR, Member States may adopt specific rules to set out the investigative powers by the supervisory authorities laid down in Article 53(2) in relation to data controllers or data processors that are subjects under national law or rules established by national competent bodies to an obligation of professional secrecy or other equivalent obligations of secrecy, where this is necessary and proportionate to reconcile the right of the protection of personal data with the obligation of secrecy. These rules shall only apply with regard to personal data which the data controller or data processor has received from or has obtained in an activity covered by this obligation of secrecy.

Also, each Member State shall notify to the Commission the rules adopted pursuant to paragraph 1, by the date specified in Article 91(2) at the latest and, without delay, any subsequent amendment affecting them (Article 84(2)).

DPR: Religion

26.88 Chapter IX of the DPR refers to provisions relating to specific data processing situations. Article 85 refers to existing data protection rules of churches and religious associations.

Under Article 85(1), where in a Member State, churches and religious associations or communities apply, at the time of entry into force of the Regulation, comprehensive rules relating to the protection of individuals with regard to the processing of personal data, such rules may continue to apply, provided that they are brought in line with the provisions of the Regulation.

Churches and religious associations which apply comprehensive rules in accordance with paragraph 1 shall provide for the establishment of an independent Supervisory Authority in accordance with Chapter VI of the Regulation (Article 85(2)).

DPR: Impact Assessment

26.89 Section 3 of the DPR refers to data protection impact assessment and prior authorisation. Article 33 is headed data protection impact assessment. Article 33(1) states that where processing operations present specific risks to the rights and freedoms of data subjects by virtue of their nature, their scope or their purposes, the data controller or the data processor acting on the data controller's behalf shall carry out an assessment of the impact of the envisaged processing operations on the protection of personal data.

Under Article 33(2) the following processing operations in particular present specific risks referred to in Article 33(1):

- a systematic and extensive evaluation of personal aspects relating to a natural person or for analysing or predicting in particular the natural person's economic situation, location, health, personal preferences, reliability or behaviour, which is based on automated processing and on which measures are based that produce legal effects concerning the individual or significantly affect the individual;
- information on sex life, health, race and ethnic origin or for the provision of health care, epidemiological researches, or surveys of mental or infectious diseases, where the data are processed for taking measures or decisions regarding specific individuals on a large scale;
- monitoring publicly accessible areas, especially when using optic-electronic devices (video surveillance) on a large scale;
- personal data in large scale filing systems on children, genetic data or biometric data;
- other processing operations for which the consultation of the Supervisory Authority is required pursuant to Article 34(2)(b).

In accordance with Article 33(3) the assessment shall contain at least a general description of the envisaged processing operations, an assessment of the risks to the rights and freedoms of data subjects, the measures envisaged to address the risks, safeguards, security measures and mechanisms to ensure the protection of personal data and to demonstrate compliance with the DPR, taking into account the rights and legitimate interests of data subjects and other persons concerned.

Under Article 33(4) the data controller shall seek the views of data subjects or their representatives on the intended processing, without prejudice to the protection of commercial or public interests or the security of the processing operations.

If the data controller is a public authority or body and where the processing results from a legal obligation pursuant to Article 6(1)(c) providing for rules and procedures pertaining to the processing operations and regulated by EU law, Article 6(1) to (4) shall not apply, unless Member States deem it necessary to carry out such assessment prior to the processing activities (Article 33(5)).

Also, under Article 33(6), the Commission shall be empowered to adopt delegated acts in accordance with Article 86 for the purpose of further specifying the criteria and conditions for the processing operations likely to present specific risks referred to in Article 33(1) and 2 and the requirements for the assessment referred to in Article 33(3), including conditions for scalability, verification and auditability. In doing so, the Commission shall consider specific measures for micro, small and medium-sized enterprises (Article 33(6)).

Under Article 33(7), the Commission may specify standards and procedures for carrying out and verifying and auditing the assessment referred to in Article 33(3). Those implementing acts shall be adopted in accordance with the examination procedure referred to in Article 87(2)(Article 33(7)).

DPR: Data Protection Officer

26.90 Section 4 of the DPR refers to the data protection officer. Article 35 is headed the designation of the data protection officer. Article 35(1) states that the data controller and the data processor shall designate a data protection officer in any case where:

- the processing is carried out by a public authority or body; or
- the processing is carried out by an enterprise employing 250 persons or more; or
- the core activities of the data controller or the data processor consist of processing operations which, by virtue of their nature, their scope and/or their purposes, require regular and systematic monitoring of data subjects.

In the case referred to in bullet two of paragraph 1, a group of undertakings may appoint a single data protection officer (Article 35(1)).

Where the data controller or the data processor is a public authority or body, the data protection officer may be designated for several of its entities, taking account of the organisational structure of the public authority or body (Article 35(3)).

In cases other than those referred to in paragraph 1, the data controller or data processor or associations and other bodies representing categories of data controllers or data processors may designate a data protection officer Article 35(4)).

Under Article 35(5) the data controller or data processor shall designate the data protection officer on the basis of professional qualities and, in particular, expert knowledge of data protection law and practices and ability to fulfil the tasks referred to in Article 37. The necessary level of expert knowledge shall be determined in particular according to the data processing carried out and the protection required for the personal data processed by the data controller or the data processor (Article 35(5)).

The data controller or the data processor shall ensure, in accordance with Article 35(6), that any other professional duties of the data protection officer are compatible with the person's tasks and duties as data protection officer and do not result in a conflict of interests.

Also, Article 35(7) provides that the data controller or the data processor shall designate a data protection officer for a period of at least two years. The data protection officer may be reappointed for further terms. During their term of office, the data protection officer may only be dismissed, if the data protection officer no longer fulfils the conditions required for the performance of their duties.

The data protection officer may be employed by the data controller or data processor, or fulfil his or her tasks on the basis of a service contract (Article 35(8)).

The data controller or the data processor shall communicate the name and contact details of the data protection officer to the Supervisory Authority and to the public (Article 35(9)).

Article 35(10) provides that data subjects shall have the right to contact the data protection officer on all issues related to the processing of the data subject's data and to request exercising the rights under the DPR.

Also, under Article 35(11) the Commission shall be empowered to adopt delegated acts in accordance with Article 86 for the purpose of further specifying the criteria and requirements for the core activities of the data controller or the data processor referred to in Article 35(1)(c) and the criteria for the professional qualities of the data protection officer referred to in Article 35(5).

Article 36 refers to the position of the data protection officer. Article 36(1) provides that the data controller or the data processor shall ensure that the data protection officer is properly and in a timely manner involved in all issues which relate to the protection of personal data.

Article 36(2) provides that the data controller or data processor shall ensure that the data protection officer performs the duties and tasks independently and does not receive any instructions as regards the exercise of the function. The data protection officer shall directly report to the management of the data controller or the data processor. Under Article 36(3) the data controller or the data processor shall support the data protection officer in performing the tasks and shall provide staff, premises, equipment and any other resources necessary to carry out the duties and tasks referred to in Article 37.

Article 37 refers to the tasks of the data protection officer. Under Article 37(1) the data controller or the data processor shall entrust the data protection officer at least with the following tasks:

- to inform and advise the data controller or the data processor of their obligations pursuant to the DPR and to document this activity and the responses received;
- to monitor the implementation and application of the policies of the data controller or data processor in relation to the protection of personal data, including the assignment of responsibilities, the training of staff involved in the processing operations, and the related audits;
- to monitor the implementation and application of the DPR, in particular as to the requirements related to data protection by design, data protection by default and data security and to the information of data subjects and their requests in exercising their rights under the DPR;
- to ensure that the documentation referred to in Article 28 is maintained;
- to monitor the documentation, notification and communication of personal data breaches pursuant to Articles 31 and 32;
- to monitor the performance of the data protection impact assessment by the data controller or data processor and the application for prior authorisation or prior consultation, if required pursuant Articles 33 and 34;
- to monitor the response to requests from the Supervisory Authority, and, within the sphere of the data protection officer's competence, co-operating with the Supervisory Authority at the latter's request or on the data protection officer's own initiative;
- to act as the contact point for the Supervisory Authority on issues related to the processing and consult with the Supervisory Authority, if appropriate, on his/her own initiative.

Under Article 37(2) the Commission shall be empowered to adopt delegated acts in accordance with Article 86 for the purpose of further specifying the criteria and requirements for tasks, certification, status, powers and resources of the data protection officer referred to in Article 37(1).

DPR: General Obligations Data Controllers and Data Processors

26.91 Chapter IV refers to data controllers and data processors, or data controllers and data processors. Section 1 sets out general obligations. Article 22 refers to the responsibility of the data controller.

The data controller shall adopt policies and implement appropriate measures to ensure and be able to demonstrate that the processing of personal data is performed in compliance with the DPR (Article 22(1)).

The measures provided for in Article 22(1) are set out in Article 22(2), and shall in particular include:

- keeping the documentation pursuant to Article 28;
- implementing the data security requirements laid down in Article 30;
- performing a data protection impact assessment pursuant to Article 33;
- complying with the requirements for prior authorisation or prior consultation of the Supervisory Authority pursuant to Article 34(1) and (2);
- designating a data protection officer pursuant to Article 35(1).

Under Article 22(3), the data controller shall implement mechanisms to ensure the verification of the effectiveness of the measures referred to in Article 22(1) and (2). If proportionate, this verification shall be carried out by independent internal or external auditors (Article 22(3)).

Article 22(4) provides that the Commission shall be empowered to adopt delegated acts in accordance with Article 86 for the purpose of specifying any further criteria and requirements for appropriate measures referred to in Article 22(1) other than those already referred to in Article 22(2), the conditions for the verification and auditing mechanisms referred to in Article 22(3) and as regards the criteria for proportionality under Article 22(3), and considering specific measures for micro, small and medium-sized-enterprises.

DPR: Data Protection By Design (DPbD)(PbD)

26.92 Article 23 of the DPR refers to data protection by design and by default. This is an increasingly important area in data protection.

Article 23(1) introduces this topic by saying that having regard to the state of the art and the cost of implementation, the data controller shall, both at the time of the determination of the means for processing and at the time of the processing itself, implement appropriate technical and organisational measures and procedures in such a way that the processing will meet the requirements of the DPR and ensure the protection of the rights of the data subject.

Under Article 23(2), it is provided that the data controller shall implement mechanisms for ensuring that, by default, only those personal data are processed which are necessary for each specific purpose of the processing and are especially not collected or retained beyond the minimum necessary for those purposes, both in terms of the amount of the data and the time of their storage. In particular, those mechanisms shall ensure that by default personal data are not made accessible to an indefinite number of individuals.

In addition, under Article 23(3), the Commission is empowered to adopt delegated acts in accordance with Article 86 for the purpose of specifying any further criteria and requirements for appropriate measures and mechanisms referred to in Article 23(1) and (2), in particular for data protection by design requirements applicable across sectors, products and services.

Furthermore, Under Article 23(4) the Commission is also empowered to lay down technical standards for the requirements laid down in Article 23(1) and (2). Those implementing acts shall be adopted in accordance with the examination procedure referred to in Article 87(2).

DPR: Joint Data Controllers

26.93 Article 24 refers to the new concept of joint data controllers or joint data controllers. It provides that where a data controller determines the purposes, conditions and means of the processing of personal data jointly with others, the joint data controllers shall determine their respective responsibilities for compliance with the obligations under the DPR, in particular as regards the procedures and mechanisms for exercising the rights of the data subject, by means of an arrangement between them.

DPR: Non-EU Data Controllers

26.94 Article 25 of the DPR refers to representatives of data controllers not established in the EU. Article 25(1) provides that '[i]n the situation referred to in Article 3(2), the [data] controller shall designate a representative in the [EU].'

Article 25(2) explains that this obligation shall not apply to:

- a data controller established in a third country where the Commission has decided that the third country ensures an adequate level of protection in accordance with Article 41; or
- an enterprise employing fewer than 250 persons; or
- a public authority or body; or
- a data controller offering only occasionally goods or services to data subjects residing in the EU.

Under Article 25(3) the representative shall be established in one of those Member States where the data subjects whose personal data are processed in relation to the offering of goods or services to them, or whose behaviour is monitored, reside.

Article 25(4) also provides that the designation of a representative by the data controller shall be without prejudice to legal actions which could be initiated against the data controller itself.

DPR: Data Processors

26.95   Article 26 of the DPR refers to data processors. Article 26(1) provides that where a processing operation is to be carried out on behalf of a data controller, the data controller shall choose a data processor providing sufficient guarantees to implement appropriate technical and organisational measures and procedures in such a way that the processing will meet the requirements of the DPR and ensure the protection of the rights of the data subject, in particular in respect of the technical security measures and organisational measures governing the processing to be carried out and shall ensure compliance with those measures.

Under Article 26(2) the carrying out of processing by a data processor shall be governed by a contract or other legal act binding the data processor to the data controller and stipulating in particular that the data processor shall:

- act only on instructions from the data controller, in particular, where the transfer of the personal data used is prohibited;
- employ only staff who have committed themselves to confidentiality or are under a statutory obligation of confidentiality;
- take all required measures pursuant to Article 30;
- enlist another data processor only with the prior permission of the data controller;
- insofar as this is possible given the nature of the processing, create in agreement with the data controller the necessary technical and organisational requirements for the fulfilment of the data controller's obligation to respond to requests for exercising the data subject's rights laid down in Chapter III;
- assist the data controller in ensuring compliance with the obligations pursuant to Articles 30 to 34;
- hand over all results to the data controller after the end of the processing and not process the personal data otherwise;
- make available to the data controller and the Supervisory Authority all information necessary to control compliance with the obligations laid down in this Article.

Article 26(3) also sets out obligations whereby the data controller and the data processor shall document in writing the data controller's instructions and the data processor's obligations referred to in Article 26(2).

Under Article 26(4), if a data processor processes personal data other than as instructed by the data controller, the data processor shall be considered to be a data controller in respect of that processing and shall be subject to the rules on joint data controllers laid down in Article 24.

The Commission shall be empowered under Article 26(5) to adopt delegated acts in accordance with Article 86 for the purpose of further specifying the criteria and requirements for the responsibilities, duties and tasks in relation to a data processor in line with paragraph 1, and conditions which allow facilitating the processing of personal data within a group of undertakings, in particular for the purposes of control and reporting.

DPR: Processing Under Authority

26.96 Article 27 refers to processing under the authority of the data controller and data processor and provides that the data processor and any person acting under the authority of the data controller or of the data processor who has access to personal data shall not process them except on instructions from the data controller, unless required to do so by EU or Member State law.

DPR: Documentation

26.97 Article 28 of the DPR provides that each data controller and data processor and, if any, the data controller's representative, shall maintain documentation of all processing operations under its responsibility (Article 28(1)).

In accordance with Article 28(2) the documentation shall contain at least the following information:

- the name and contact details of the data controller, or any joint data controller or data processor, and of the representative, if any;
- the name and contact details of the data protection officer, if any;
- the purposes of the processing, including the legitimate interests pursued by the controller where the processing is based on Article 6(1)(f);
- a description of categories of data subjects and of the categories of personal data relating to them;

- the recipients or categories of recipients of the personal data, including the controllers to whom personal data are disclosed for the legitimate interest pursued by them;
- where applicable, transfers of data to a third country or an international organisation, including the identification of that third country or international organisation and, in case of transfers referred to in Article 44(1)(h), the documentation of appropriate safeguards;
- a general indication of the time limits for erasure of the different categories of data;
- the description of the mechanisms referred to in Article 22(3).

The data controller and the data processor and, if any, the data controller's representative, shall make the documentation available, on request, to the Supervisory Authority, in accordance with Article 28(3).

However, under Article 28(4) the obligations referred to in Article 28(1) and (2) shall not apply to the following data controllers and data processors:

- a natural person processing personal data without a commercial interest; or
- an enterprise or an organisation employing fewer than 250 persons that is processing personal data only as an activity ancillary to its main activities.

The Commission shall be empowered to adopt delegated acts in accordance with Article 86 for the purpose of further specifying the criteria and requirements for the documentation referred to in Article 28(1), to take account of in particular the responsibilities of the data controller and the data processor and, if any, the data controller's representative (Article 28(5)).

In addition, the Commission may, per Article 28(6), lay down standard forms for the documentation referred to in Article 28(1). Those implementing acts shall be adopted in accordance with the examination procedure referred to in Article 87(2).

DPD95: Codes and Certification

26.98 Chapter V of the DPD95 refers to codes of conduct. Article 27(1) provides that the Member States and the Commission shall encourage the drawing up of codes of conduct intended to contribute to the proper implementation of the national provisions adopted by the Member States pursuant to this Directive, taking account of the specific features of the various sectors.

Article 27(2) provides that Member States shall make provision for trade associations and other bodies representing other categories of data controllers which have drawn up draft national codes or which have the intention of amending or extending existing national codes to be able to submit them to the opinion of the national authority. Member States shall make provision for this authority to ascertain, among other things, whether the drafts submitted to it are in accordance with the national provisions adopted pursuant to this Directive. If it sees fit, the authority shall seek the views of data subjects or their representatives (Article 27(2)).

Under Article 27(3) draft EU codes, and amendments or extensions to existing EU codes, may be submitted to WP29. WP29 shall determine, among other things, whether the drafts submitted to it are in accordance with the national provisions adopted pursuant to the DPD95. If it sees fit, the authority shall seek the views of data subjects or their representatives. The Commission may ensure appropriate publicity for the codes which have been approved by WP95.

DPR: Codes

26.99 Section 5 refers to and is headed Codes of Conduct and Certification. Article 38 refers to codes of conduct and Article 38(1) provides that Member States, the supervisory authorities and the Commission shall encourage the drawing up of codes of conduct intended to contribute to the proper application of the Regulation, taking account of the specific features of the various data processing sectors, in particular in relation to:

- fair and transparent data processing;
- the collection of data;
- the information of the public and of data subjects;
- requests of data subjects in exercise of their rights;
- information and protection of children;
- transfer of data to third countries or international organisations;
- mechanisms for monitoring and ensuring compliance with the code by the controllers adherent to it;
- out-of-court proceedings and other dispute resolution procedures for resolving disputes between data controllers and data subjects with respect to the processing of personal data, without prejudice to the rights of the data subjects pursuant to Articles 73 and 75.

Article 38(2) provides that associations and other bodies representing categories of data controllers or data processors in one Member State which intend to draw up codes of conduct or to amend or extend existing codes of conduct may submit them to an opinion of the Supervisory Authority in that Member State. The Supervisory Authority may give an opinion whether the draft code of conduct or the amendment is in compliance with the DPR. The Supervisory Authority shall seek the views of data subjects or their representatives on these drafts.

Associations and other bodies representing categories of data controllers in several Member States may submit draft codes of conduct and amendments or extensions to existing codes of conduct to the Commission per Article 38(3).

The Commission may adopt implementing acts for deciding that the codes of conduct and amendments or extensions to existing codes of conduct submitted to it pursuant to paragraph 3 have general validity within the EU. Those implementing acts shall be adopted in accordance with the examination procedure set out in Article 87(2) (Article 38(4)). The Commission shall also ensure appropriate publicity for the codes which have been decided as having general validity in accordance with paragraph 4 (Article 38(5)).

DPR: Certification

26.100　Article 39(1) provides that the Member States and the Commission shall encourage, in particular at European level, the establishment of data protection certification mechanisms and of data protection seals and marks, allowing data subjects to quickly assess the level of data protection provided by data controllers and data processors. The data protection certifications mechanisms shall contribute to the proper application of the Regulation, taking account of the specific features of the various sectors and different processing operations.

Article 39(2) provides that the Commission shall be empowered to adopt delegated acts in accordance with Article 86 for the purpose of further specifying the criteria and requirements for the data protection certification mechanisms referred to in Article 39(1), including conditions for granting and withdrawal, and requirements for recognition within the EU and in third countries.

The Commission is also empowered by Article 39(3) to lay down technical standards for certification mechanisms and data protection seals and marks and mechanisms to promote and recognise certification mechanisms and data protection seals and marks. Those implementing acts shall be adopted in accordance with the examination procedure set out in Article 87(2).

DPD95: National Supervisory Authorities and Agencies

26.101 Chapter VI is headed Supervisory Authority and Working Party on the Protection of Individuals with regard to the Processing of Personal Data. Article 28 refers to the Supervisory Authority. Article 28(1) provides that each Member State shall provide that one or more public authorities are responsible for monitoring the application within its territory of the provisions adopted by the Member States pursuant to the Directive. These authorities shall act with complete independence in exercising the functions entrusted to them.

Each Member State shall provide that the Supervisory Authorities are consulted when drawing up administrative measures or regulations relating to the protection of individuals' rights and freedoms with regard to the processing of personal data (Article 28(2)).

In accordance with Article 28(3) each authority shall in particular be endowed with:

- investigative powers, such as powers of access to data forming the subject-matter of processing operations and powers to collect all the information necessary for the performance of its supervisory duties,
- effective powers of intervention, such as, for example, that of delivering opinions before processing operations are carried out, in accordance with Article 20, and ensuring appropriate publication of such opinions, of ordering the blocking, erasure or destruction of data, of imposing a temporary or definitive ban on processing, of warning or admonishing the data controller, or that of referring the matter to national parliaments or other political institutions,
- the power to engage in legal proceedings where the national provisions adopted pursuant to the Directive have been violated or to bring these violations to the attention of the judicial authorities.

Decisions by the Supervisory Authority which give rise to complaints may be appealed against through the courts (Article 28(3)).

Each Supervisory Authority shall hear claims lodged by any person, or by an association representing that person, concerning the protection of his rights and freedoms in regard to the processing of personal data. The person concerned shall be informed of the outcome of the claim (Article 28(4)). They shall also hear claims for checks on the lawfulness of data processing lodged by any person when the national provisions adopted pursuant to Article 13 of the Directive apply. The person shall at any rate be informed that a check has taken place (Article 28(4)).

Each Supervisory Authority shall draw up a report on its activities at regular intervals which shall be made public (Article 28(5)).

Article 28(6) provides that each Supervisory Authority is competent, whatever the national law applicable to the processing in question, to exercise, on the territory of its own Member State, the powers conferred on it in accordance with paragraph 3. Each authority may be requested to exercise its powers by an authority of another Member State. The supervisory authorities shall cooperate with one another to the extent necessary for the performance of their duties, in particular by exchanging all useful information (Article 28(6)).

Member States shall provide that the members and staff of the Supervisory Authority, even after their employment has ended, are to be subject to a duty of professional secrecy with regard to confidential information to which they have access (Article 28(7)).

DPR: National Supervisory Authorities and Agencies

26.102 Chapter VI of the DPR refers to the national independent supervisory authorities as well as their independent status.

Article 46 of the DPR refers to the Supervisory Authority of Member States. Article 46(1) provides that each Member State shall provide that one or more public authorities are responsible for monitoring the application of the Regulation and for contributing to its consistent application throughout the EU, in order to protect the fundamental rights and freedoms of natural persons in relation to the processing of their personal data and to facilitate the free flow of personal data within the EU. For these purposes, the supervisory authorities shall co-operate with each other and the Commission.

If a Member State and more than one Supervisory Authority are established, that Member State shall designate the Supervisory Authority which functions as a single contact point for the effective participation of those authorities in the European Data Protection Board and shall set out the mechanism to ensure compliance by the other authorities with the rules relating to the consistency mechanism referred to in Article 57 (Article 46(2)).

Each Member State shall notify to the Commission those provisions of its law which it adopts and any subsequent amendment affecting them (Article 46(3)).

Article 47 refers to the independence of the supervisory authorities. Article 47(1) states that the Supervisory Authority shall act with complete independence in exercising the duties and powers entrusted to it. Furthermore, Article 47(2) provides that the members of the Supervisory Authority shall, in the performance of their duties, neither seek nor take instructions from anybody. Also, the members of the Supervisory Authority shall refrain from any action incompatible with their duties and shall not, during their term of office, engage in any incompatible organisational communications usage policies, whether gainful or not, in accordance with Article 47(3). There is also an obligation after leaving office. Article 4(4) states that the members of the Supervisory Authority shall behave, after their term of office, with integrity and discretion as regards the acceptance of appointments and benefits.

Each Member State is obliged to ensure that the Supervisory Authority is provided with the adequate human, technical and financial resources, premises and infrastructure necessary for the effective performance of its duties and powers, including those to be carried out in the context of mutual assistance, co-operation and participation in the European Data Protection Board (Article 47(5). Each Member State shall ensure, in accordance with Article 47(6), that the Supervisory Authority has its own staff which shall be appointed by and be subject to the direction of the head of the Supervisory Authority. Importantly perhaps, Article 47(7) provides that Member States shall ensure that the Supervisory Authority is subject to financial control which shall not affect its independence. Member States shall ensure that the Supervisory Authority has separate annual budgets. The budgets shall be made public. One could speculate whether this includes sufficient resources to be able to properly undertake and fulfil its obligations. Many national supervisory authorities are experiencing additional workload from that which may have been originally envisaged. There is an issue, therefore, in terms of whether they are entitled to be adequately resourced.

Article 48 is headed, general conditions for the members of the Supervisory Authority. Under Article 48(1) Member States shall provide that the members of the Supervisory Authority must be appointed either by the parliament or the government of the Member State concerned, and whom must be independent, skilled and experienced (Article 48(2).

Article 49 sets out provisions regarding the rules on the establishment of the Supervisory Authority. Each Member State shall provide by law within the limits of the Regulation:

- the establishment and status of the Supervisory Authority;
- the qualifications, experience and skills required to perform the duties of the members of the Supervisory Authority;
- the rules and procedures for the appointment of the members of the

Supervisory Authority, as well the rules on actions or organisational communications usage policies incompatible with the duties of the office;

- the duration of the term of the members of the Supervisory Authority which shall be no less than four years, except for the first appointment after entry into force of the DPR, part of which may take place for a shorter period where this is necessary to protect the independence of the Supervisory Authority by means of a staggered appointment procedure;
- whether the members of the Supervisory Authority shall be eligible for reappointment;
- the regulations and common conditions governing the duties of the members and staff of the Supervisory Authority;
- the rules and procedures on the termination of the duties of the members of the Supervisory Authority, including in case that they no longer fulfil the conditions required for the performance of their duties or if they are guilty of serious misconduct.

Article 50 refers to professional secrecy. The members and the staff of the Supervisory Authority shall be subject, both during and after their term of office, to a duty of professional secrecy with regard to any confidential information which has come to their knowledge in the course of the performance of their official duties.

Section 2 refers to duties and powers. Article 51 refers to competence and provides that each Supervisory Authority shall exercise, on the territory of its own Member State, the powers conferred on it in accordance with the Regulation (Article 51(1)).

Article 51(2) provides that where the processing of personal data takes place in the context of the activities of an establishment of a data controller or a data processor in the EU, and the data controller or data processor is established in more than one Member State, the Supervisory Authority of the main establishment of the data controller or data processor shall be competent for the supervision of the processing activities of the data controller or the data processor in all Member States. This is without prejudice to the provisions of Chapter VII of the DPR.

Article 51(3) states that the Supervisory Authority shall not be competent to supervise processing operations of courts acting in their judicial capacity.

Article 52 refers to duties. It provides that the Supervisory Authority shall:

- monitor and ensure the application of the DPR;
- hear complaints lodged by any data subject, or by an association

representing that data subject in accordance with Article 73, investigate, to the extent appropriate, the matter and inform the data subject or the association of the progress and the outcome of the complaint within a reasonable period, in particular if further investigation or coordination with another Supervisory Authority is necessary;

- share information with and provide mutual assistance to other supervisory authorities and ensure the consistency of application and enforcement of the DPR;
- conduct investigations either on its own initiative or on the basis of a complaint or on request of another Supervisory Authority, and inform the data subject concerned, if the data subject has addressed a complaint to this Supervisory Authority, of the outcome of the investigations within a reasonable period;
- monitor relevant developments, insofar as they have an impact on the protection of personal data, in particular the development of information and communication technologies and commercial practices;
- be consulted by Member State institutions and bodies on legislative and administrative measures relating to the protection of individuals' rights and freedoms with regard to the processing of personal data;
- authorise and be consulted on the processing operations referred to in Article 34;
- issue an opinion on the draft codes of conduct pursuant to Article 38(2);
- approve binding corporate rules pursuant to Article 43;
- participate in the activities of the European Data Protection Board (Article 52(1)).

Article 52(2) provides that each Supervisory Authority shall promote the awareness of the public on risks, rules, safeguards and rights in relation to the processing of personal data.

Article 52(2) also specifically provides that activities addressed specifically to children shall receive specific attention. This was not explicitly mentioned before in the DPD95.

National supervisory authorities shall, upon request, advise any data subject in exercising the rights under the DPR and, if appropriate, co-operate with the supervisory authorities in other Member States to this end (Article 52(3)).

For complaints referred to in point (b) of paragraph 1, the Supervisory Authority shall provide a complaint submission form, which can be completed electronically, without excluding other means of communication (Article 52(4)). Previously, certain authorities did not require a specific form.

Importantly for individuals, Article 52(5) provides that the performance of the duties of the Supervisory Authority shall be free of charge for the data subject.

However, Article 52(6) provides that where requests are manifestly excessive, in particular due to their repetitive character, the Supervisory Authority may charge a fee or not take the action requested by the data subject. The Supervisory Authority shall bear the burden of proving the manifestly excessive character of the request (Article 52(6)).

Article 53(1) provides that each Supervisory Authority shall have the power:

- to notify the data controller or the data processor of an alleged breach of the provisions governing the processing of personal data, and, where appropriate, order the data controller or the data processor to remedy that breach, in a specific manner, in order to improve the protection of the data subject;
- to order the data controller or the data processor to comply with the data subject's requests to exercise the rights provided by the DPR;
- to order the data controller and the data processor, and, where applicable, the representative to provide any information relevant for the performance of its duties;
- to ensure the compliance with prior authorisations and prior consultations referred to in Article 34;
- to warn or admonish the data controller or the data processor;
- to order the rectification, erasure or destruction of all data when they have been processed in breach of the provisions of the DPR and the notification of such actions to third parties to whom the data have been disclosed;
- to impose a temporary or definitive ban on processing;
- to suspend data flows to a recipient in a third country or to an international organisation;
- to issue opinions on any issue related to the protection of personal data;
- to inform the national parliament, the government or other political institutions as well as the public on any issue related to the protection of personal data.

Each Supervisory Authority shall have the investigative power to obtain from the data controller or the data processor: access to all personal data and to all information necessary for the performance of its duties (Article 53(2)(a)); access to any of its premises, including to any data processing equipment and means, where there are reasonable grounds for presuming that an activity in violation of the Regulation is being carried out there (Article 53(2)(b)). The powers referred to in point (b) shall be exercised in conformity with EU law and Member State law.

Article 53(3) provides that each Supervisory Authority shall have the power to bring violations of the Regulation to the attention of the judicial authorities (ie courts) and to engage in legal proceedings, in particular pursuant to Article 74(4) and Article 75(2).

In addition Article 53(4) provides that each Supervisory Authority shall have the power to sanction administrative offences, in particular those referred to in Article 79(4), (5) and (6).

Article 54 provides for an activity report. Each Supervisory Authority must draw up an annual report on its activities. The report shall be presented to the national parliament and shall be made be available to the public, the Commission and the European Data Protection Board.

Chapter VII refers to co-operation and consistency. Article 55 makes provision as regards what is called 'mutual assistance'.

Supervisory authorities shall provide each other relevant information and mutual assistance in order to implement and apply the DPR in a consistent manner, and shall put in place measures for effective co-operation with one another. Mutual assistance shall cover, in particular, information requests and supervisory measures, such as requests to carry out prior authorisations and consultations, inspections and prompt information on the opening of cases and ensuing developments where data subjects in several Member States are likely to be affected by processing operations (Article 55(1)).

Each Supervisory Authority shall take all appropriate measures required to reply to the request of another Supervisory Authority without delay and no later than one month after having received the request. Such measures may include, in particular, the transmission of relevant information on the course of an investigation or enforcement measures to bring about the cessation or prohibition of processing operations contrary to the DPR (Article 55(2)).

Article 55(3) provides that the request for assistance shall contain all the necessary information, including the purpose of the request and reasons for the request. Information exchanged shall be used only in respect of the matter for which it was requested (Article 55(3)).

Requests must be complied with. Article 55(4) provides that a Supervisory Authority to which a request for assistance is addressed may not refuse to comply with it unless: (a) it is not competent for the request; or (b) compliance with the request would be incompatible with the provisions of the DPR.

The requested Supervisory Authority shall inform the requesting Supervisory Authority of the results or, as the case may be, of the progress or the measures taken in order to meet the request by the requesting Supervisory Authority (Article 55(5)). The information is to be supplied by electronic means and within the shortest possible period of time, using a standardised format (Article 55(6)).

There is no fee charged for any action taken following a request for mutual assistance (Article 55(7)).

Article 55(8) provides that,

'Where a Supervisory Authority does not act within one month on request of another Supervisory Authority, the requesting Supervisory Authorities shall be competent to take a provisional measure on the territory of its Member State in accordance with Article 51(1) and shall submit the matter to the European Data Protection Board in accordance with the procedure referred to in Article 57.'

The Supervisory Authority shall specify the period of validity, not exceed three months, of such provisional measure, and shall, without delay communicate those measures, with full reasons, to the European Data Protection Board and to the Commission (Article 55(9)). The Commission may specify the format and procedures for mutual assistance referred to in the article and the arrangements for the exchange of information by electronic means between supervisory authorities, and between supervisory authorities and the European Data Protection Board, in particular the standardised format (Article 55(10)).

Article 56 provides for joint operations of supervisory authorities. Article 56(1) provides that in order to step up co-operation and mutual assistance, the supervisory authorities shall carry out joint investigative tasks, joint enforcement measures and other joint operations, in which designated members or staff from other Member States' Supervisory Authorities are involved.

Article 56(2) continues that in cases where data subjects in several Member States are likely to be affected by processing operations, a Supervisory Authority of each of those Member States shall have the right to participate in the joint investigative tasks or joint operations, as appropriate. The competent Supervisory Authority shall invite the Supervisory Authority of each of those Member States to take part in the respective joint investigative tasks or joint operations and respond to the request of a Supervisory Authority to participate in the operations without delay.

In addition Article 56(3) states that each Supervisory Authority may, as a host Supervisory Authority, in compliance with its own national law, and with the seconding Supervisory Authority's authorisation, confer executive powers, including investigative tasks on the seconding Supervisory Authority's members or staff involved in joint operations or, in so far as the host Supervisory Authority's law permits, allow the seconding Supervisory Authority's members or staff to exercise their executive powers in accordance with the seconding Supervisory Authority's law. Such executive powers may be exercised only under the guidance and, as a rule, in the presence of members or staff from the host Supervisory Authority. The seconding Supervisory Authority's members or staff shall be subject to the host Supervisory Authority's national law. The host Supervisory Authority shall assume responsibility for their actions.

The supervisory authorities are obliged to set out down the practical aspects of specific co-operation actions (Article 56(4)).

If a Supervisory Authority does not comply within one month with the obligation, the other supervisory authorities shall be competent to take a provisional measure on the territory of its Member State in accordance with Article 51(1)(Article 56(5)).

The Supervisory Authority shall specify the period of validity, not exceed three months, of a provisional measure referred to in paragraph 5, and shall, without delay, communicate those measures, with full reasons, to the European Data Protection Board and to the Commission and shall submit the matter in the mechanism referred to in Article 57 (Article 56(6)).

Section 2 refers to consistency. Article 57 is headed consistency mechanism. It states that for the purposes set out in Article 46(1), the supervisory authorities shall co-operate with each other and the Commission through the consistency mechanism as set out in the section.

European Data Protection Board

26.103 Article 58 is headed opinion by the European Data Protection Board. Article 58(1) provides that before a Supervisory Authority adopts a measure referred to in paragraph 2, the Supervisory Authority shall communicate the draft measure to the European Data Protection Board and the Commission.

The obligation set out in Article 58(1) shall apply to a measure intended to produce legal effects and which:

- relates to processing activities which are related to the offering of goods or services to data subjects in several Member States, or to the monitoring of their behaviour; or
- may substantially affect the free movement of personal data within the EU; or

- aims at adopting a list of the processing operations subject to prior consultation pursuant to Article 34(5); or
- aims to determine standard data protection clauses referred to in point (c) of Article 42(2); or
- aims to authorise contractual clauses referred to in point (d) of Article 42(2); or
- aims to approve binding corporate rules within the meaning of Article 43 (Article 58(2)).

Article 58(3) provides that any Supervisory Authority or the European Data Protection Board may request that any matter shall be dealt with in the consistency mechanism, in particular where a Supervisory Authority does not submit a draft measure referred to in paragraph 2 or does not comply with the obligations for mutual assistance in accordance with Article 55 or for joint operations in accordance with Article 56.

To ensure correct and consistent application of the Regulation, the Commission may request that any matter shall be dealt with in the consistency mechanism (Article 58(4)). Both supervisory authorities and the Commission shall electronically communicate any relevant information, including as the case may be a summary of the facts, the draft measure, and the grounds which make the enactment of such measure necessary, using a standardised format (Article 58(5)).

Under Article 58(6) the European Data Protection Board chair shall immediately electronically inform the members of the European Data Protection Board and the Commission of any relevant information which has been communicated to it, using a standardised format. The chair of the European Data Protection Board shall provide translations of relevant information, where necessary.

Article 58(7) provides that the European Data Protection Board shall issue an opinion on the matter, if the European Data Protection Board so decides by simple majority of its members or any Supervisory Authority or the Commission so requests within one week after the relevant information has been provided according to Article 58(5). The opinion shall be adopted within one month by simple majority of the members of the European Data Protection Board. The chair of the European Data Protection Board shall inform, without undue delay, the Supervisory Authority referred to, as the case may be, in Article 58(1) and (3), the Commission and the Supervisory Authority competent under Article 51 of the opinion and make it public.

Finally, Article 58(8) provides that the Supervisory Authority referred to in Article 58(1) and the Supervisory Authority competent under Article 51 shall take account of the opinion of the European Data

Protection Board and shall within two weeks after the information on the opinion by the chair of the European Data Protection Board, electronically communicate to the chair of the European Data Protection Board and to the Commission whether it maintains or amends its draft measure and, if any, the amended draft measure, using a standardised format.

Article 59 refers to the opinion by the Commission. Within ten weeks after a matter has been raised under Article 58, or at the latest within six weeks in the case of Article 61, the Commission may adopt, in order to ensure correct and consistent application of the Regulation, an opinion in relation to matters raised pursuant to Articles 58 or 61 (Article 59(1)). If the Commission has adopted an opinion in accordance with paragraph 1, the Supervisory Authority concerned shall take utmost account of the Commission's opinion and inform the Commission and the European Data Protection Board whether it intends to maintain or amend its draft measure (Article 59(2)). Where the Supervisory Authority concerned intends not to follow the opinion of the Commission, it shall inform the Commission and the European Data Protection Board thereof within the period referred to in paragraph 1 and provide a justification (Article 59(4)). In this case the draft measure shall not be adopted for one further month.

Article 60 refers to the suspension of a draft measure. Under Article 60(1) it is provided that within one month after the communication referred to in Article 59(4), and where the Commission has serious doubts as to whether the draft measure would ensure the correct application of the Regulation or would otherwise result in its inconsistent application, the Commission may adopt a reasoned decision requiring the Supervisory Authority to suspend the adoption of the draft measure, taking into account the opinion issued by the European Data Protection Board pursuant to Article 58(7) or Article 61(2), where it appears necessary in order to: (a) reconcile the diverging positions of the Supervisory Authority and the European Data Protection Board, if this still appears to be possible; or (b) adopt a measure pursuant to Article 62(1)(a). The Commission shall specify the duration of the suspension which shall not exceed 12 months (Article 60(2)). During the period referred to in paragraph 2, the Supervisory Authority may not adopt the draft measure (Article 60(3)).

Article 61 refers to an urgency procedure. Article 61(1) provides that in exceptional circumstances, where a Supervisory Authority considers that there is an urgent need to act in order to protect the interests of data subjects, in particular when the danger exists that the enforcement of a right of a data subject could be considerably impeded by means of an alteration of the existing state or for averting major disadvantages or for other reasons, by way of derogation from the procedure referred to in Article 58, it may immediately adopt provisional measures with a specified period of validity. The Supervisory Authority shall, without delay, communicate those measures, with full reasons, to the European Data Protection Board and to the Commission.

Enforcement

26.104   Article 63 refers to enforcement. Article 63(1) provides that an enforceable measure of the Supervisory Authority of one Member State shall be enforced in all Member States concerned. In addition, Article 63(2) provides that where a Supervisory Authority does not submit a draft measure to the consistency mechanism in breach of Article 58(1) to (5), the measure of the Supervisory Authority shall not be legally valid and enforceable.

DPR: Cooperation with National Supervisory Authorities and Agencies

26.105   Article 29 of the DPR makes provision in relation to co-operation with the Supervisory Authority. Article 29(1) provides that the data controller and the data processor and, if any, the representative of the data controller, shall co-operate, on request, with the Supervisory Authority in the performance of its duties, in particular by providing the information referred to in Article 53(2)(a) and by granting access as provided in point (b) of that paragraph.

In response to the Supervisory Authority's exercise of its powers under Article 53(2), the data controller and the data processor shall reply to the Supervisory Authority within a reasonable period to be specified by the Supervisory Authority. The reply shall include a description of the measures taken and the results achieved, in response to the remarks of the Supervisory Authority (Article 29(2)).

DPD95:WP29

26.106   Article 29 of the DPD95 establishes the influential working group on data protection, which advised and researches EU data protection issues, and which is comprised of members of the respective national data protection authorities throughout the EU. Given that it is comprised of national authority members and is an EU working group, the decisions and recommendations are very persuasive to say the least at national level.

The official title of WP29 is the Working Party on the Protection of Individuals with regard to the Processing of Personal Data.

Article 29(1) provides as follows, 'A Working Party on the Protection of Individuals with regard to the Processing of Personal Data, hereinafter referred to as the Working Party, is hereby set up.' It shall have advisory status and act independently.

The WP29 shall be composed of a representative of the Supervisory Authority or authorities designated by each Member State and of a representative of the authority or authorities established for the EU institutions and bodies, and of a representative of the Commission (Article 29(2)). Each member of the WP29 shall be designated by the institution, authority or authorities which he represents. Where a Member State has designated more than one Supervisory Authority, they shall nominate a joint representative. The same shall apply to the authorities established for EU institutions and bodies.

The WP29 shall take decisions by a simple majority of the representatives of the supervisory authorities (Article 29(3)). A chairman shall be elected, for a renewable period of two years (Article 29(4)). The WP29's secretariat shall be provided by the Commission under Article 29(5).

The WP29 shall adopt its own rules of procedure (Article 29(6)) and shall consider items placed on its agenda by its chairman, either on his own initiative or at the request of a representative of the Supervisory Authorities or at the Commission's request (Article 20(7)).

The WP29 shall, in accordance with Article 30(1):

- examine any question covering the application of the national measures adopted under the DPD95 in order to contribute to the uniform application of such measures;
- give the Commission an opinion on the level of protection in the EU and in third countries;
- advise the Commission on any proposed amendment of the DPD95, on any additional or specific measures to safeguard the rights and freedoms of natural persons with regard to the processing of personal data and on any other proposed EU measures affecting such rights and freedoms;
- give an opinion on codes of conduct drawn up at EU level.

If the WP29 finds that divergences likely to affect the equivalence of protection for persons with regard to the processing of personal data in the EU are arising between the laws or practices of Member States, it shall inform the Commission accordingly (Article 30(2)).

In addition, the WP29 may, on its own initiative, make recommendations on all matters relating to the protection of persons with regard to the processing of personal data in the EU (Article 30(3)).

The WP29's opinions and recommendations shall be forwarded to the Commission and to the committee referred to in Article 31 (Article 30(4)).

The WP29 shall draw up an annual report on the situation regarding the protection of natural persons with regard to the processing of personal data in the EU and in third countries, which it shall transmit to the Commission, the European Parliament and the Council. The report shall be made public (Article 30(6)).

DPR: The EU Data Protection Board

26.107 Section 3 of the DPR related to the establishment of the new European Data Protection Board. This will be an EU wide data protection advisory and research board. It will take over from the previous influential WP29 established under the DPD95.

Article 64 of the DPR refers to the European Data Protection Board. Article 64(1) states that 'A European Data Protection Board is hereby set up.' Under Article 62(2) the European Data Protection Board shall be composed of the head of one Supervisory Authority of each Member State and of the European Data Protection Supervisor. If a Member State has more than one Supervisory Authority is responsible for monitoring the application of the provisions pursuant to the DPR, they shall nominate the head of one of those Supervisory Authorities as joint representative (Article 64(3)). Under Article 64(4) the Commission shall have the right to participate in the activities and meetings of the European Data Protection Board and shall designate a representative to do so. The chair of the European Data Protection Board shall also, 'without delay,' inform the Commission on all activities of the European Data Protection Board.

The various activities or tasks of the European Data Protection Board are provided for in Article 66. Article 66(1), headed Tasks of the European Data Protection Board, states that the European Data Protection Board shall ensure the 'consistent application' of the DPR. It shall, 'on its own initiative or at the request of the Commission,' in particular,

- advise the Commission on any issue related to the protection of personal data in the EU, including on any proposed amendment of the DPR;
- examine, on its own initiative or on request of one of its members or on request of the Commission, any question covering the

application of the DPR and issue guidelines, recommendations and best practices addressed to the Supervisory Authorities in order to encourage consistent application of the DPR;

- review the practical application of the guidelines, recommendations and best practices referred to in point (b) and report regularly to the Commission on these;

- issue opinions on draft decisions of Supervisory Authorities pursuant to the consistency mechanism referred to in Article 57;

- promote the co-operation and the effective bilateral and multilateral exchange of information and practices between the Supervisory Authorities;

- promote common training programmes and facilitate personnel exchanges between the Supervisory Authorities, as well as, where appropriate, with the Supervisory Authorities of third countries or of international organisations;

- promote the exchange of knowledge and documentation on data protection legislation and practice with data protection Supervisory Authorities worldwide.

DPR: Regarding DPD95 and ePD

26.108 Article 88(1) of the DPR refers to the repeal of DPD95.[23] Under Article 88(2), it states that references to the repealed DPD95 shall be construed as references to the new Regulation, the DPR Once enacted). It also provides that references to the WP29 established by Article 29 of DPD95 shall be construed as references to the European Data Protection Board established by the Regulation. WP29 shall become the European Data Protection Board.

The DPR also refers to the ePD. Article 89 refers to the relationship to an amendment of the ePD.[24] It states that the DPR shall not impose additional obligations on natural or legal persons in relation to the processing of personal data in connection with the provision of publicly available electronic communications services in public communication networks in the EU in relation to matters for which they are subject to specific obligations with the same objective set out in the ePD. Article 89(2) states that Article 1(2) of the ePD shall be deleted.

23 Directive 95/46/EC.
24 Directive 2002/58/EC.

Importance

26.109 Costa and Poullet indicate that once the DPR 'comes into force, the document will be the new general legal framework of data protection, repealing [DPD95] more than twenty-seven years after its adoption.'[25] The DPR as well as Article 8(1) of the EU Charter of fundamental rights of 2000 and Article 16(1) and reassert the importance of privacy and data protection 'as a fundamental right.'[26] '[E]ffective and more coherent protection' is required.[27]

In terms of policy as between modernising via a Directive or via a Regulation 'in order to ensure a full consistent and high level of protection equivalent in all the EU member states, a Regulation was judged as the adequate solution to ensure full harmonisation'[28] throughout the EU. The Commission may also oversee and monitor the national data protection authorities (DPAs).[29]

Individuals are rarely aware about how their data are collected and processed while they are surfing on the Internet at home, using their cell phones, walking down a video-surveyed street or with an TFID tag embedded in their clothes and so on.[30] There is a need for greater transparency. As regards data processing, 'transparency translates the widening of the knowledge about information systems ... coupled with fairness.'[31]

Transparency

26.110 Article 5 of the DPR provides that personal data shall be 'processed lawfully, fairly and in a transparent manner in relation to the data subject.' Transparency breach:

> 'requires greater awareness among citizens about the processing going on: its existence, its content and the flows generated in and out by using terminals.

> Transparency also relates to security of data and risk management.[32]

---

25 Costa, L., and Poullet, Y, "Privacy and the Regulation of 2012," *Computer Law & Security Review* (2012)(28), pp. 254–262, at 254.
26 *Ibid*, at 254.
27 *Ibid*.
28 *Ibid*, at 255.
29 *Ibid*.
30 *Ibid*, p. 256.
31 *Ibid*.
32 Costa, L., and Poullet, Y, "Privacy and the Regulation of 2012," *Computer Law & Security Review* (2012)(28), pp. 254–262, at 256.

Some commentators have suggested the DPR could go further. It is suggested that 'the greater the flow of information systems the more opaque it becomes in modern information systems and with new ICT applications. In that case the right to transparency must increase alongside these new processes.'[33]

Innovations

26.111 Commentators have indicated that parts of the DPR contain particular 'legislative innovation.'[34] Some examples of this innovation are indicated to be the:

- Data Protection Principles;
- Data subjects' rights;
- Data controllers' and data processors' obligations;
- Regulation issues regarding technologies.[35]

It has been noted that while the DPD95 emphasises protection for the fundamental right and freedoms of individuals 'and in particular their right to privacy,' the DPR in Articles 1 and 2 stresses the need to protect the fundamental right and freedoms of individuals 'and in particular their right to the protection of personal data.'[36] Further references also emphasise data protection as a stand-alone concept from privacy, such as data protection assessments and data protection by design (DPbD)

There is a new consistency mechanism whereby the national data protection authorities are obliged to cooperate with each other and with the Commission (Chapter VII, section 10).[37] Two examples given include data protection assessments and also obligation in terms of notifying data subjects in relation to data breaches.[38]

The obligations in terms of insufficient security and data breaches are more detailed in the DPR than previously.[39] The obligations are now more detailed than the obligation in relation to telcos and ISPs in

---

33 Costa, L., and Poullet, Y, "Privacy and the Regulation of 2012," *Computer Law & Security Review* (2012)(28), pp. 254–262, at 256.
34 Costa, L., and Poullet, Y., 'Privacy and the Regulation of 2012,' *Computer Law & Security Review* (2012)(28), pp. 254–292.
35 *Ibid.*
36 *Ibid*, 255.
37 Costa, L., and Poullet, Y, "Privacy and the Regulation of 2012," *Computer Law & Security Review* (2012)(28), pp. 254–262, at 255.
38 *Ibid.*
39 Costa, L., and Poullet, Y, "Privacy and the Regulation of 2012," *Computer Law & Security Review* (2012)(28), pp. 254–262, at 256.

the ePD.[40] Data breaches are referred to in Articles 4 and 9 of the DPR. In the event of a data breach the data controller must notify the ICO (Article 31). In addition the data controller must also communicate to the data subjects if there is a risk of harm to their privacy or personal data (Article 32).

Data portability is a newly expressed right. It 'implies the right of data subjects to obtain from the [data] controller a copy of their personal data in a structured and commonly used format (Article 18,1) ... data portability is a kind of right to backup and use personal information under the management of the data controller. Second, data portability grants the right to transmit personal data and other information provided by the data subject from one automated processing system to another one (Article 18,2) ... therefore the right to take personal data and leave.'[41]

The DPD95 stated that data controller must not process personal data excessively. However, this is now more limited. The DPR states that data collection and processing must be limited to the minimum.

Broader parameters are contained in the DPR in relation to consent. The definition and conditions are broader than previously. The inclusion of the words freely given, informed and explicit in Article 4 is more specific than the previous 'unambiguously' consented.

The DPD95 Article 15 protection in relation to automated individual decisions 'is considerably enlarged'[42] regarding profiling in DPR Article 20. The use of, inter alia, the word 'measure' in the DPR as opposed to 'decision' in the DPD95 makes the category of activity encompassed within the obligation is now much wider.[43] There is greater data subject protection. While there were previously two exemptions, in terms of contract and also a specific law, the DPR adds a third in terms of consent from the data subject. However, data controllers will need to ensure a standalone consent for profiling separate from any consent for data collection and processing per se.[44]

40 *Ibid.*
41 Costa, L., and Poullet, Y, "Privacy and the Regulation of 2012," *Computer Law & Security Review* (2012)(28), pp. 254–262, at 256, p. 15.
42 Costa, L., and Poullet, Y, "Privacy and the Regulation of 2012," *Computer Law & Security Review* (2012)(28), pp. 254–262, at 258. Also see Council of Europe Recommendation regarding profiling, 25 November, 2010.
43 *Ibid*, pp. 258–259.
44 Costa, L., and Poullet, Y, "Privacy and the Regulation of 2012," *Computer Law & Security Review* (2012)(28), pp. 254–262, at 258. Also see Council of Europe Recommendation regarding profiling, 25 November, 2010, p. 259.

The DPR also moves significantly further than the DPD95 in terms of creating obligations, responsibility and liability on data controllers.[45] Appropriate policies must be implemented by data controllers, as well as complaint data processing, secure data processing, the undertaking of data protection impact assessments, shared liability as between joint data controllers, appointing representatives within the EU where the data controllers are located elsewhere and provisions regarding data processors.[46]

While the DPD95 imposed compensation obligations on data controllers in the case of harm to data subjects, the DPR extends liability to data processors.[47] In addition, where harm is suffered by data subjects any joint data controller and or data processors shall be 'jointly and severally liable for the entire amount of the damage.'[48]

The concepts of data protection by design (DPD), data protection by default and impact assessments all emphasise the ability of the data protection regime to become involved in standards setting and the regulation of particular technologies and technical solutions.[49] The Ontario Data Protection Commissioner, Anne Cavoukian, refers to data protection and privacy by design.[50] The DPR describes it as follows in DPR Article 23(1), by indicating that,

> '[h]aving regard to the state of the art and the cost of implementation, the data controller shall, both at the time of the determination of the means for processing and at the time of the processing itself, implement appropriate technical and organisational measures and procedures in such a way that the processing will meet the requirements of the DPR and ensure the protection of the rights of the data subject' (Article 23(1)).

Data protection by default is referred to and defined in Article 23(2) as follows,

> 'The data controller shall implement mechanisms for ensuring that, by default, only those personal data are processed which are necessary for each specific purpose of the processing and are especially not collected or retained beyond the minimum necessary for those purposes, both in terms of the amount of the data and the time of their storage. In particular, those

---

45 *Ibid.*
46 *Ibid.*
47 *Ibid.*
48 *Ibid.*
49 *Ibid.*
50 For example, Anne Cavoukian, DPA Ontario, Privacy Guidelines for RFID Information Systems, at www.ipc.on.ca, says the privacy and security must be built into the solution from the outset, at the design stage. Referred to *ibid.*

mechanisms shall ensure that by default personal data are not made accessible to an indefinite number of individuals' (Article 23(2)).

These accord with the general principle of data minimisation, whereby non-personal data should be processed first and where the collection and processing of personal data is required, it must be the minimum data as opposed to the minimum data which is so processed. This is referred to in Article 5(c).

Data subjects have more control over their personal data. In the context of social networks, 'individual profiles should be kept private from others by default.'[51]

The concept of PbD and data protection by default as provided in the DPR are predicted to soon impact upon organisational contracts and contracting practices relating to data processing activities.[52]

As mentioned above, one of the new areas is the obligation to engage in data protection impact assessments. Article 33(1) provides that that,

'[w]here processing operations present specific risks to the rights and freedoms of data subjects by virtue of their nature, their scope or their purposes, the data controller or the data processor acting on the data controller's behalf shall carry out an assessment of the impact of the envisaged processing operations on the protection of personal data.'

This is particularly so where the envisaged processing could give rise to specific risks.

One further addition is the possibility of mass group claims or claims through representative organisations. This is referred to as 'collective redress' and allows data protection and privacy NGOs to complain to both the ICO and to the courts (see Articles 73(2), 74, 75 and 76(1)).[53] 'Civil procedure rules'[54] may also need to be introduced.

The regime as regards trans-border data flows or TBDFs will be 'significantly altered.'[55] These are included in Articles 40–45.

---

51 *Ibid*, at p. 260, and referring to European data Protection Supervisor on the Communications from Commission to the European Parliament, the Council, the Economic and Social Committee and the Committee of the Regions, 'A Comprehensive Approach on Personal Data Protection in the European Union,' at p. 23.

52 *Ibid*, at p. 260.

53 See also Commission on a common framework for collective redress, http://ec.europa.eu/consumers/redress_cons/collective_redress_en.htm, accessed 18 January 2013.

54 Costa, L., and Poullet, Y, "Privacy and the Regulation of 2012," *Computer Law & Security Review* (2012)(28), pp. 254–262, at 261.

55 Costa, L., and Poullet, Y, "Privacy and the Regulation of 2012," *Computer Law & Security Review* (2012)(28), pp. 254–262, at 261.

Enhanced Provisions

26.112 One of the more important extensions and enhancements relates to the expanded right to be forgotten. The 'right to be forgotten and to erasure, which consists of securing from the [data] controller the erasure of personal data as well prevention of any further dissemination of his data.'[56] (It is also said to interface with the new right to data portability[57]).

The right to be forgotten is even more enhances in instances where the personal data was originally disclosed when the data subject was a child. Some commentators refer to the option of an entire 'clean slate.'[58]

> 'The use of data from social networks in employment contexts is a representative example. Personal data such as photos taken in private contexts have been used to refuse job positions and fire people. But forgetfulness is larger. It is one dimension of how people deal with their own history, being related not only to leaving the past behind but also to living in the present without the threat of a kind of "Miranda" warning, where whatever you say can be used against you in the future. In this sense the right to be forgotten is closely related to entitlements of dignity and self-development. Once again, privacy appears as the pre-requisite of our liberties, assuring the possibility to freely express ourselves and move freely on the street …'[59]

The right to be forgotten is most clearly associated and related to the following in particular:

- Where the personal data is no longer necessary in relation to the purposes for which they were originally collected and processed (and the associated finality principle);
- Where the data subject has withdrawn their consent for processing;
- Where data subjects object to the processing of the personal data concerning them;
- Where the processing of the personal data does not comply with the DPR.[60]

---

56 Costa, L., and Poullet, Y, "Privacy and the Regulation of 2012," *Computer Law & Security Review* (2012)(28), pp. 254–262, at 256.

57 *Ibid.*

58 Costa, L., and Poullet, Y, "Privacy and the Regulation of 2012," *Computer Law & Security Review* (2012)(28), pp. 254–262, at 257.

59 Costa, L., and Poullet, Y, "Privacy and the Regulation of 2012," *Computer Law & Security Review* (2012)(28), pp. 254–262, at 257.

60 Costa, L., and Poullet, Y, "Privacy and the Regulation of 2012," *Computer Law & Security Review* (2012)(28), pp. 254–262, at 257.

The DPR and the right to be forgotten 'amplifies the effectiveness of data protection principles and rules.'[61]

Data subjects can have their data erased under the right to be forgotten when there is no compliance as well as where they simply withdraw their consent.[62] User control and data subject control are, therefore, enhanced.

The DPR and right to be forgotten create the following compliance obligations, namely:

* Erasing personal data and not processing it further;
* Informing third parties that the data subject has requested the deletion of the personal data;
* Taking responsibility for publication by third parties under the data controller's authority.[63] (Articles 17, 2 and 8).

The DPR also enhances and expands the various powers of the national authorities, such as the ICO.[64]

Children

26.113   The explicit reference to children is new, and some would argue overdue. Increasingly, the activities of children on the internet and on social networking poses risks and concerns.[65] This has been further emphasised of late with tragic event involving online abuse, in particular cyber bullying. Risks arise obviously from their activities online (eg inappropriate content, cyber bullying, but also from the collection and use of their personal data online and collected online, sometimes without their knowledge or consent). Their personal data and privacy is more vulnerable than that of older people.

It is important for organisation to note the definition of 'child' in the DPR. A child is defined to mean any person below the age of 18 years. This will have implications in how organisations:

* Consider the interaction with children and what personal data may be collected and processed;

---

61 *Ibid.*
62 Costa, L., and Poullet, Y, "Privacy and the Regulation of 2012," *Computer Law & Security Review* (2012)(28), pp. 254–262, at 257.
63 *Ibid.*
64 Costa, L., and Poullet, Y, "Privacy and the Regulation of 2012," Computer *Law & Security Review* (2012)(28), pp. 254–262, at 260.
65 See, for example, McDermott, L., 'Legal Issues Associated with Minors and Their Use of Social Networking Sites,' *Communications Law* (2012)(17), pp. 19–24

- Ensure that there is appropriate compliance for such collection and processing for children as distinct from adults.

Conclusion

26.114 All organisations need to become very familiar with the DPR. While not yet finalised, the current draft is close to final. It reflects the shape of the new and expanded EU date protection regime. While in some instances the current compliance mechanisms are continued, there are many new requirements to compliance. Organisations need to start now in terms of ensuring preparation and compliance. Indeed, the most prudent organisations will continually be adopting best practice, and data protection compliance is an area where best practice has positive benefits above and beyond mere compliance.

Chapter 27

Social Networking

Introduction

27.01   New technologies 'permit easy dissemination and using of
information. Current ICT allows individuals to share [sometimes
unknowingly] their personal preferences and behaviour information on
an unprecedented scale. This could lead to people losing control of
personal information.'[1] Web 2.0 is an increasing part of our daily lives.
One of its more popular examples is social networking. What are the
legal implications of social networking?[2] One of the most controversial
issues in relation to social networking websites is their data processing
and respect for privacy and personal data.[3] This is only part of the story.
There are many discrete issues, such as:

- Employers using social networks to vet and screen job applicants;[4]

---

1   Stanimir, T., "Personal Data Protection and the New Technologies," *Proceedings of
    the International Conference on Information Technologies* (2011), pp. 333–344.

2   Nelson, S., Simek, J., and Foltin, J., 'The Legal Implications of Social Networking,'
    Regent University Law Review (2009–2010)(22), pp. 1–34. Also, Viscounty, P.,
    Archie, J., Alemi, F., and and Allen, J., 'Social Networking and the Law,' *Business
    Law Today* (2008–009)(58), p. 18.

3   See, for example, Roth, P, 'Data Protection Meets Web 2.0: Two Ships Passing in the
    Night,' *UNSW Law Journal* (2010)(33), pp. 532–561. Slabbert, N.J., 'Orwell's
    Ghost: How Teletechnology is Reshaping Civil Society,' *CommLaw Conspectus*
    (2007–2008)(16), pp. 349–359.

4   Brandenburg, C., 'The Newest Way to Screen Job Applicants: A Social Networker's
    Nightmare,' Federal Communications Law Journal (2007–2008)(60), p. 597. Gersen,
    D., Your Image, Employers Investigate Job Candidates Online More than Ever. What
    can You Do to Protect Yourself?' Student Law (2007–2008)(36), p. 24; Byrnside, I.,
    'Six Degrees of Separation: The Legal Ramifications of Employers Using Social
    Networking Sites to Research Applicants,' Vanderbilt Journal of Entertainment and
    Technology Law (2008)(2), pp. 445–477.

- Employers monitoring their employees' social networking;[5]
- Recruiting through social networking;[6]
- Universities monitoring student usage of social networking;
- Universities using social networking websites to vet applicants;
- New forms of digital evidence, both criminal and civil.

A significant recent development was the Facebook investigation of particular data protection issues by one of the EU National Supervisory Authorities. The Facebook Beacon settlement, albeit in the US, can also be viewed as significant as it involves a significant financial settlement in relation to privacy, data protection and online marketing without user consent.

Facebook Investigated

27.02 The recent Facebook audit[7] investigation reviewed certain specific aspects of Facebook data protection compliance. This arose after foot of a number of complaints regarding specific aspects of Facebook. Specifically, the following issues were looked at, namely:

- Privacy policies;
- Advertising;
- Access requests;
- Retention;
- Cookies/social plug-ins;
- Third part apps;
- Disclosures to third parties;
- Facial recognition/tag suggest;
- Data security;
- Deletion of accounts;
- Friend finder;
- Tagging;
- Posting on other profiles;
- Facebook credits;
- Pseudonymous profiles;

---

5   Levinson, A.R., 'Industrial Justice: Privacy Protection for the Employed,' Cornell Journal of Law and Public Policy (2009)(18), pp. 609–688.

6   Maher, M., 'You've Got Messages, Modern Technology Recruiting Through text Messaging and the Intrusiveness of Facebook,' Texas Review of Entertainment and Sports Law (2007)(8), pp. 125–151.

7   Facebook Ireland Limited, *Report of Re-Audit, Data Protection Commissioner*, 21 September, 2012.

- Abuse reporting;
- Compliance management/governance.

That is not to suggest that every potential Facebook data protection issue was considered. It was not. Other issues and complaints can arise in future, as well as further investigations. The *Europe Against Facebook*[8] group also point out that there are particular issues and complaints outstanding. There was also a group created in the US by MoveOn.org called *Petition: Facebook, Stop Invading My Privacy*, similarly objecting to certain practices of the social networking website.[9]

The audit investigation has forced Facebook to make particular changes to particular aspects of its data protection practices. These are referred to in the reports. Facebook in the EU, the entity which was investigated, is responsible for Facebook data protection compliance for everywhere outside of the US and Canada. Therefore, these changes should see an impact even beyond the EU. In addition, it is noted that the controversial use of facial recognition technology by Facebook has had to be turned off for users in the EU. This is a direct result of the complaints and the official audit investigation.

Originally, Facebook did not permit users to delete their accounts. However, it has now been made clear to Facebook that it must permit users the right and functional ability to delete their accounts. It will be recalled that one of the Data Protection Principles refers to personal data being held no longer than is necessary. User consent to processing can also be withdrawn.

Recently also, Facebook settled litigation in the US relating to the Beacon advertising feature which it had launched and later cancelled. The case is meant to have been settled for approximately $20m. Note, also that there was a strong dissenting judgement criticising the settlement as, *inter alia*, too low.[10]

---

8   See http://www.europe-v-facebook.org/EN/en.html.
9   Morganstern, A., 'In the Spotlight: Social Network Advertising and the Right of Publicity,' Intellectual Property Law Bulletin (2007–2008)(1), pp. 181–198; Podolny, R., 'When "Friends" Become Adversaries: Litigation in the Age of Facebook,' Manitoba Law Journal (2009)(33), pp. 391–408; Hashemi, Y., 'Facebook's Privacy Policy and Its Third-Party Partnerships: Lucrativity and Liability,' BU Journal of Science & Technology Law (2009)(15), pp. 140–161.
10 See appeal and lower court in the case of McCall v Facebook. The appeal case is *McCall v Facebook*, US Court of Appeals for the Ninth Circuit. It is available at http://www.ca9.uscourts.gov/datastore/opinions/2012/09/20/10–16380.pdf, accessed on 18 January 2013. See also, for example, McGeveran, W., 'Disclosure, Endorsement, and Identity in Social marketing,' Illinois Law Review (2009)(4), PP. 1105–1166.

Social Networks at Leveson

27.03 Amongst the many witnesses at the *Leveson Inquiry* were Facebook, Google and Twitter. One of the headline issues relates to what activities and services they engage in, respectively, and what they can and cannot do in terms of specific content. These are controversial and evolving issues in terms of both data protection compliance as well as take downs and liability for material on (and via) their websites. This is an area which will continue to expand. Already it is a critical area of contention in litigation (and policy discussion). Sony has been fined £250,000 by the ICO and Google may be sued by UK Apple users.

Social Network Data Transfers: Processors

27.04 Any social network may quite legitimately need to engage third parties or outsource particular tasks. However, it is not always clear that the website will have ensured that an appropriate written contract is in place and that appropriate security measures are in place with the outsourced data processor as regards the personal data received and processed by it. Users should also be informed of such outsourcing and be assured of the security measures. Consent, transparency ad prior information are equally important compliance issues.

Social Network Data Transfers: Apps

27.05 Increasingly, social networks provide and facilitate third part apps or applications on their websites.[11] Frequently, as part of this practice, personal data is disclosed to the third party companies operating or developing the apps. Unfortunately, there appeared to be an overly loose compliance relationship as regards the transfer and protection of users' personal data. Sometimes, data would be accessible or transferred without regard to users' personal data rights, user knowledge, contracts and security. In addition, there could sometimes be no restriction on the apps develops using the personal data for more than one purpose and for activities unrelated to the initial intended purpose.

---

11 See, for example, Hashemi, Y., Facebook's Privacy Policy and its Third-Party Partnerships: Lucrativity and Liability,' *B. U. J. Science & Technology Law* (2009)(15), pp. 140–161.

Awareness

27.06 Increasingly potential employers, schools and universities use social networking profile information in making assessments on applications regarding specific individuals. Unfortunately, one of the issues relates to the consequence of this for individuals, sometimes adverse consequences.[12] In addition, many users, and particularly those of a younger age, will not (fully) appreciate that such activities and consequences can arise from their social networking.

There is arguably more to be done by social networks in terms of informing and appraising users of the issues which can arise. This is particularly emphasised when children and teenagers are concerned.

WP29 in its Opinion regarding social networking, recognises the dangers arising from apps.[13] Compliance with the DPD95 must be ensured. There is also a UK Home Office Good Practice Guidance for the Providers of Social Networks.[14] Arguably, these could be updated. This is an area where significant ongoing research is needed.

Tagging

27.07 It is possible that people are visible online in photographs uploaded to social networks which they would not want, may be unaware of and also have not consented to.

In addition, social networking websites can permit people to be tagged and labelled in uploaded photographs, without their consent.

These concerns are even more enhanced as Facebook has recently announced enhanced capacity to index and reveal information and photographs from its website. This is the new Facebook Graph Search tool.

Transparency and User Friendly Tools

27.08 Social networks frequently appear to value membership numbers over fully transparent, obvious and user friendly privacy protection and complaint tools. The on-site tools (when present) are 'frequently unobvious or difficult to use. The cynical might imagine that this is

---

12 See discussion at Edwards, L., and Waelde, C., eds., above, p. 481.

13 Opinion 5/2009 on online social networking, available at http://ec.europa.eu/justice/ policies/privacy/docs/wpdocs/2009/wp163_en.pdf, accessed on 18 January 2013.

14 Available at http://dera.ioe.ac.uk/11099/, accessed on 18 January 2013. Also, http:// police.homeoffice.gov.uk/publications/operational-policing/social-networking-guidance?view=Binary.

because ... the revenue stream from the SNS comes from third parties – advertisers – having access to as much data, on as many profiles, as possible.'[15]

One part solution is to have privacy and friend restricted access as the default model for social networking websites. This is suggested particularly in relation to children by the Home Office code of conduct for social networks in 2008.[16]

WP29 in the context of online behavioural advertising indicates that an icon in itself can be insufficient. In that context it was particularly concerned with consent issues. However, significant research remains to be undertaken in order to properly assess the adequacy of icons, notices, tools, information, information notices, report buttons, reports processes, report teams, response times, resolutions times, etc in relation to online abuse and social networking websites. There is as yet a distinct shortage of research and literature on this topic. This is despite the media reports of online abuse and many examples of tragic consequences.

Abuse, Attacks, Threats, Trolling, Victims

27.09 The Olympics in London brought to the fore the disadvantages of social networking, where social networks such as Twitter, Facebook, etc, can be used for abuse.[17] There is a growing and troubling number of instances of suicides arising as a result of abuse and threats occurring on social networking websites. Social networks, and other websites, also contain controversial material in relation to self-harm.

Recently, YouTube and Google have decided to change their policies to 'real name' posting. Users need to identify their real name or a verified email account in order to be able to post comments on

---

15 Edwards, L., and Waelde, C., eds., *Law and the Internet* (Oxford: Hart, 2009), p. 483.

16 Available at http://dera.ioe.ac.uk/11099/, accessed on 18 January 2013. Also, http://police.homeoffice.gov.uk/publications/operational-policing/social-networking-guidance?view=Binary.

17 Rosenberg, J., 'Tom Daley, Twitter Abuse and the Law,' *Guardian*, 31 July, 2012; James, S., 'Man Cautioned After Mark Halsey Twitter Abuse,' *Guardian*, 27 September, 2012; Baughmanm, L.L., 'Friend Request or Foe? Confirming the Misuse of Internet and Social Networking Sites by Domestic Violence Perpetrators,' *Widener Law Journal* (2010)(19), pp. 933–966. Generally, also see Ator, J.J., 'Got Facebook?' *GPSolo* (March, 2009), pp. 4–5.

YouTube. This may assist reducing trolling and attacks online, as well as the unfortunate consequences thereof.[18]

The problem of cyber bullying is incontrovertible, with increasing high-profile suicides recently. If anyone is still unclear about the devastation caused to victims and families, the video posted by Canadian teenager Amanda Todd is required viewing. Indeed it should be required viewing for parents, educators and policy makers.

The cyberbullying of teenagers is just one facet of online abuse, which can range from threats to defamation, harassment to stalking, grooming and breaches of privacy and data protection. There are also overlaps. The cyberbulling of children can involve harassment, threats, verbal abuse and defamation, or in the case of Amanda Todd, privacy and data-protection breaches later expanding to threats. The solutions are multifaceted. Much of the recent commentary points to education, educators and parents. While this is correct, it is only one aspect.

One point missing from the current discussion is that it is legally possible to find anonymous abusers. Victims and the police can apply to court for the disclosure of user details from relevant websites and service providers. These are frequently known as Norwich Pharmacal orders. Online abusers can face civil as well as criminal consequences, even if they are children or teenagers. It goes without saying the police must properly follow up reports. It is clear from recent media commentary that the UK police are proactive and considered in this area.

Much of this abuse occurs on social networking websites, but it does also occur via mobile telephones and smartphones. Some social networking sites provide 'tools' or 'reporting processes.' However, many of them, and indeed other Web 2.0 websites, do not do all they could to deal with these issues. Even some of the largest social networks have been slower to implement reporting procedures for certain forms of abuse than should be the case. Some websites also have particular tools available which they use for certain activities, but are reluctant to extend to abuse victims.

But no matter how many 'report buttons' there are on a given website, they are entirely useless without protocols, policies and procedures behind the scenes to follow through on reports that are made. A complaints procedure is meaningless unless there are enough people investigating abuse reports.

It would be interesting to examine and compare the number of people employed in abuse investigation teams across various social networking

---

18 Generally note, for example, Kane, B., 'Balancing Anonymity, Popularity, & Micro-Celebrity: The Crossroads of Social Networking & Privacy," Albany Law Journal of Science and Technology,' (2010)(20), pp. 327–363.

websites. Should there be a minimum number of employees assigned per number of users of a social networking website? Or should there be a minimum number of employees per amount of abuse reports made? The turnover of such websites could easily absorb hiring more staff.

A further point arises regarding social networking and related websites. Some are happy to publish statistics about the level of reports and complaints received relating to copyright infringement. This appears commercially driven. There is significantly less 'transparency' as regards the level of abuse reports and complaints made to social networking websites, and around how, and how quickly, these abuse reports are resolved.

As much as we are presently shocked by the dark side of internet abuse, cyberbullying and the terrible consequences, it may be that we would be further shocked at the scale of abuse being reported, when the facility is available to do so. That may be a useful line of pursuit for anyone who is officially concerned about this issue. It is also worth considering that whatever a website may say at first blush may not always be the whole picture.

We are now beginning to realise that, on occasion, social networking and other websites can have a dark side.

Unfortunately, there are large gaps in our knowledge, research and understanding of these developing issues. More research is needed to appraise ourselves of all potential solutions and policy decisions as well as assisting websites to fully engage their own (corporate, moral and legal) responsibilities and functional capabilities.

There are also business case advantages.

Employment and Social Networking

27.10 Employers are increasingly considering access to employee's social networking materials.[19] A general policy of such monitoring is not permitted under EU data protection law. Nor can employees be forced to disclose or permit access to their social networking accounts by way of enforced access. However, it is the case that social networking evidential material is increasingly frequent in employment disputes and employment litigation. Organisations should seek legal advice in

19 Blank, A., 'On the Precipe of e-Discovery: Can Litigants Obtain Employee Social Networking Web Site Information Through Employers?' *CommLaw Conspectus* (2009–2010)(18), pp. 487–516. Also, Byrnside, I, 'Six Clicks of Separation: The Legal Ramifications of Employers using Social Networking Sites to Research Applicants,' Vanderbilt Journal of Entertainment and Technology Law (2008)(10), pp. 445–477.

advance of seeking to utilise or rely upon such materials. Otherwise potential litigation, dismissals or disciplinary actions can be deemed to be illegal.[20]

Digital Evidence

27.11   There are growing digital evidence opportunities for litigation, and which can include personal data.[21] These can include service of documents[22] and civil discovery.[23] Social networks have been described as digital footprints.[24] This can also include employee's social networking activity.[25]

20 See also Maher, M., 'You've Got Messages: Modern technology Recruiting Through Text-Messaging and the Intrusiveness of Facebook,' Texas Review of Entertainment & Sports Law,' (2007)(8), pp. 125–151; Brandenburg, C., 'The Newest way to Screen Job Applicants: A social Networker's Nightmare,' Federal Communications Law Journal (2007–2008)(60), pp. 597–626.

21 Minotti, K., 'The Advent of Digital Diaries: Implications of Social Networking Web Sites for the Legal Profession,' *South Carolina Law Review* (2009)(60), pp. 1057–1074; Wilson, J.S., 'MySpace, Your Space or Our Space? New Frontiers in Electronic Evidence,' *Oregon Law Review* (2007)(86), pp. 1201–1240; Andrew C. Payne, A.C., 'Twitigation: Old Rules in a New World,' *Washburn Law Journal* (2010)(49), pp. 842–870.

22 Shultz, A.L., 'Superpoked and Served: Service of Process via Social Networking Sites,' 43 *University Richmond Law Review* (2008–2009)(43), pp. 1497–1528. Hedges, R.J., Rashbaum, K.N., and Losey, A.C., 'Electronic Service of Process at Home and Abroad: Allowing Domestic Electronic Service of Process in Federal Courts,' *Federal Courts Law Review* (2010)(4), pp. 54–76.

23 Bennett, S.C., Civil Discovery of Social Networking Information,' *Southwestern Law Review* (2009–2010)(39), pp. 413–431. Also, Witte, D.S., 'Your Opponent Does Not Need a Friend Request to See Your Page: Social Networking Sites and Electronic Discovery,'' McGeorge Law Review (2009–2010)(41), pp. 891–903; Ward, R.A., "Discovering Facebook: Social Network Subpoenas and the Stored Communications Act,' Harvard Journal of Law & technology (2011)(24), pp. 563–588.

24 Marsico, E.M., Jr., 'Social Networking Websites: Are Myspace andFacebook the Fingerprints of the Twenty-first Century?' *Widener Law Journal* (2010)(19), pp. 967–976. Also, North, E.E., 'Facebook Isn't Your Space Anymore: Discovery of Social Networking Website,' University of Kansa Law Review (2009–2010)(58), pp. 1279–1309; Williams, T.M., 'Facebook: Ethics, Traps, and Reminders,' Litigation News (2009–2010)(35), p. 4.

25 For example, see, Thomas, L, 'Social Networking in the Workplace: Are Private Employers Prepared to Comply With Discovery Requests for Posts and Tweets?' SMU Law Review (2010)(63), pp. 1373–1402.

The Rights of Data Subjects

27.12 It is noted that '[o]ne aspect of privacy and data protection is a remedy against intrusiveness and loss of control of the circulation of a person's informational image.'[26] In addition, '[s]uch intrusiveness and its loss do not only exist when someone is or can be identified; for instance, the acts of being observed and being traced are privacy threats, even without knowing the name of the observed or traced person.'[27]

Even with social networking, the rights of data subjects remain. The rights of data subjects, including for social networking, can be summarised as including:

- Right of access (s 7 DPA);
- Right to establish if personal data exists (s 7(1)(a) DPA);
- Right to be informed of the logic in automatic decision taking (s 7(1)(d);
- Right to prevent processing likely to cause damage or distress (s 18 DPA);
- Right to prevent processing for direct marketing (s 11 DPA);
- Right to prevent automated decision taking (s 12 DPA);
- Right in relation to exempt manual data (s 12A DPA);
- Right to compensation (s 13 DPA);
- Right to rectify inaccurate data (s 14 DPA);
- Right to rectification, blocking, erasure and destruction (s 14 DPA);
- Right to complain to ICO (see s 42 DPA);
- Right to go to court (see s 15 DPA).

These expand under the DPR.

Consent and Social Networks

27.13 It is noted that social networking websites,

'are of course data controllers, and so under [data protection] law they must, in pursuit of "fair processing," gain the consent of their users to process their personal data – and indeed, "explicit consent" in the case of sensitive personal data (which abounds on SNA [social networking service] – on almost every Facebook profile a user reveals his or her race, politics,

---

26 Costa, L., and Poullet, Y, "Privacy and the Regulation of 2012," *Computer Law & Security Review* (2012)(28), pp. 254–262, at 256.
27 *Ibid.*

sexuality or religious beliefs, since these predetermined fields in the user profile, which most users fill in without much thought).'[28]

Frequently, social networking websites seek to comply with the consent requirement by providing that it is 'required as part of registration before 'admission' to the site is granted. Consent is usually obtained by displaying a privacy policy [or privacy statement] on the site and asking the user to accede to them by ticking a box. As there is no chance to negotiate, and little or no evidence that users either read or understand these conditions, it is hard to see how this consent is "free and informed" ... yet business practice for the entire sector seems to regard this consent is satisfactory.'[29]

There are other difficulties. 'A further problem arises where SNS users display facts or images about other users – eg commonly, photographs featuring multiple persons. Such users rarely seek prior consent and such software tools as are made available usually only facilitate post factum removal, for example, of "tags" on Facebook.'[30]

'Also, the question arises as to whether ordinary users should be subject to the full panoply of [data protection] obligations vis-a-vis their peers, and if they are not, how invasions of privacy by users rather than the site itself should be controlled. One suggestion has been that sites should be subject to liability for invasion of privacy if they do not take down expediently on complaint.'[31]

Website Discretion, Liability and Obligations

27.14 On occasion certain websites will argue that they are not responsible for certain activities occurring on their websites. A particular example is user generated content. The frequent argument is the ISP limited indemnities of caching, hosting and mere conduit on the ECD.[32] There is also an argument raised by certain websites that they can target and deal with European consumers and users, yet are not responsible in relation to the collection and processing of users' personal data. This later point is based on the argument that that if the website company is

---

28 Edwards, L., and *Waelde*, C., eds., *Law and the Internet* (Oxford: Hart, 2009), p. 479.
29 Edwards, L., and Waelde, C., eds., above, p. 497.
30 Edwards, L., and *Waelde*, C., eds., *Law and the Internet* (Oxford: Hart, 2009), p. 497.
31 *Ibid.*
32 Directive 2000/31/EC of the European Parliament and of the Council of 8 June 2000 on certain legal aspects of information society services, in particular electronic commerce, in the Internal Market ('Directive on electronic commerce').

based outside of the EU, even though the users are in the EU, they do not have to comply with the data protection regime. There is an irony here. These website companies seek to avail of EU law as regards EU law defences of mere conduit, caching and hosting, yet then argue their preferred policy of ignoring EU data protection law. Are such websites immune to the EU data protection regime? Can websites pick and choose one set of EU laws to benefit them, but ignore entirely other laws which create rights for their users?

These issues in relation to websites, social networking and jurisdiction are commented upon later.

Third Party Controllers and EU Data Subjects

27.15　DPD95 Recital 20 states that the fact that the processing of data is carried out by a person established in a third country must not stand in the way of the protection of individuals provided for in this Directive. Whereas in these cases, the processing should be governed by the law of the Member State in which the means used are located, and there should be guarantees to ensure that the rights and obligations provided for in this Directive are respected in practice.

Specific Processing Risks

27.16　DPD95 Recital 53 states that certain processing operations are likely to pose specific risks to the rights and freedoms of data subjects by virtue of their nature, their scope or their purposes, such as that of excluding individuals from a right, benefit or a contract, or by virtue of the *specific use of new technologies*; whereas it is for Member States, if they so wish, to specify such risks in their legislation.

DPD95 Recital 54 states that with regard to all the processing undertaken in society, the amount posing such specific risks should be very limited. Member States must provide that the Supervisory Authority, or the data protection official in cooperation with the authority, check such processing prior to it being carried out. Following this prior check, the Supervisory Authority may, according to its national law, give an opinion or an authorisation regarding the processing. Such checking may equally take place in the course of the preparation either of a measure of the national parliament or of a measure based on such a legislative measure, which defines the nature of the processing and lays down appropriate safeguards.

DPA: Right to Prevent Data Processing Likely to Cause Damage or Distress

27.17 Section 10 of the DPA refers to the right to prevent processing likely to cause damage or distress. This can also be considered relevant to social networking.

Section 10(1) provides that subject to s 10(2), an individual is entitled at any time by notice in writing to a data controller to require the data controller at the end of such period as is reasonable in the circumstances to cease, or not to begin, processing, or processing for a specified purpose or in a specified manner, any personal data in respect of which he is the data subject, on the ground that, for specified reasons:

- the processing of those data or their processing for that purpose or in that manner is causing or is likely to cause substantial damage or substantial distress to them or to another; and
- that damage or distress is or would be unwarranted.

Section 10(2) provides that s 10(1) does not apply:

- in a case where any of the conditions in paragraphs 1 to 4 of Schedule 2 are met; or
- in such other cases as may be prescribed by the Secretary of State by order.

Section 10(3) provides that the data controller must within twenty-one days of receiving a notice under s 10(1) ('the data subject notice') give the individual who gave it a written notice:

- stating that he has complied or intends to comply with the data subject notice; or
- stating his reasons for regarding the data subject notice as to any extent unjustified and the extent (if any) to which he has complied or intends to comply with it.

Section 10(4) provides that if a court is satisfied, on the application of any person who has given a notice under s 10(1) which appears to the court to be justified (or to be justified to any extent), that the data controller in question has failed to comply with the notice, the court may order them to take such steps for complying with the notice (or for complying with it to that extent) as the court thinks fit.

Section 10(5) provides that the failure by a data subject to exercise the right conferred by s 10(1) or s 11(1) does not affect any other right conferred on them by this Part.

DPA: Right to Prevent Data Processing for DM

27.18 Section 11 of the DPA relates to the right to prevent processing for purposes of direct marketing. This can also be considered relevant to social networking.

Section 11(1) provides that an individual is entitled at any time by notice in writing to a data controller to require the data controller at the end of such period as is reasonable in the circumstances to cease, or not to begin, processing for the purposes of direct marketing personal data in respect of which he is the data subject.

Section 11(2) provides that if the court is satisfied, on the application of any person who has given a notice under s 11(1), that the data controller has failed to comply with the notice, the court may order them to take such steps for complying with the notice as the court thinks fit.

Section 11(2A) provides that this section shall not apply in relation to the processing of such data as are mentioned in paragraph (1) of Regulation 8 of the Telecommunications (Data Protection and Privacy) Regulations 1999 (processing of telecommunications billing data for certain marketing purposes) for the purposes mentioned in paragraph (2) of that regulation.

Section 11(3) provides that in this section 'direct marketing' means the communication (by whatever means) of any advertising or marketing material which is directed to particular individuals.

DPA: Compensation for Data Subjects

27.19 Section 13 of the DPA refers to compensation for failure to comply with certain requirements. This can be relevant to social networking.

Section 13(1) provides that an individual who suffers damage by reason of any contravention by a data controller of any of the requirements of the DPA is entitled to compensation from the data controller for that damage.

Article 13(2) provides that an individual who suffers distress by reason of any contravention by a data controller of any of the requirements of the DPA is entitled to compensation from the data controller for that distress if:

- the individual also suffers damage by reason of the contravention; or
- the contravention relates to the processing of personal data for the special purposes.

Section 13(3) provides that in proceedings brought against a person by virtue of the section it is a defence to prove that he had taken such care as in all the circumstances was reasonably required to comply with the requirement concerned.

DPA: Rectification, Blocking, Erasure and Destruction Rights

27.20 Section 14 of the DPA provides user rights in relation to rectification, blocking, erasure and destruction. This can also be relevant to social networking.

Section 14(1) provides that if a court is satisfied on the application of a data subject that personal data of which the applicant is the subject are inaccurate, the court may order the data controller to rectify, block, erase or destroy those data and any other personal data in respect of which he is the data controller and which contain an expression of opinion which appears to the court to be based on the inaccurate data.

Section 14(2) provides that s 14(1) applies whether or not the data accurately record information received or obtained by the data controller from the data subject or a third party but where the data accurately record such information, then:

- if the requirements mentioned in paragraph 7 of Part II of Schedule 1 have been complied with, the court may, instead of making an order under s 14(1), make an order requiring the data to be supplemented by such statement of the true facts relating to the matters dealt with by the data as the court may approve; and
- if all or any of those requirements have not been complied with, the court may, instead of making an order under that sub-section, make such order as it thinks fit for securing compliance with those requirements with or without a further order requiring the data to be supplemented by such a statement as is mentioned in the above bullet.

Section 14(3) provides that where the court:

- makes an order under s 14(1); or
- is satisfied on the application of a data subject that personal data of which he was the data subject and which have been rectified, blocked, erased or destroyed were inaccurate,

it may, where it considers it reasonably practicable, order the data controller to notify third parties to whom the data have been disclosed of the rectification, blocking, erasure or destruction.

Section 14(4) provides that if a court is satisfied on the application of a data subject:

- that he has suffered damage by reason of any contravention by a data controller of any of the requirements of the DPA in respect of any personal data, in circumstances entitling them to compensation under s 13; and
- that there is a substantial risk of further contravention in respect of those data in such circumstances,

the court may order the rectification, blocking, erasure or destruction of any of those data.

Section 14(5) provides that where the court makes an order under s 14(4) it may, where it considers it reasonably practicable, order the data controller to notify third parties to whom the data have been disclosed of the rectification, blocking, erasure or destruction.

Section 14(6) provides that in determining whether it is reasonably practicable to require such notification as is mentioned in s 14(3) or (5) the court shall have regard, in particular, to the number of persons who would have to be notified.

DPA: Automated Decision Taking/Making Processes

27.21 Automated decision can also be considered in the social networking context. Data Controllers may not take decisions which produce legal effects concerning a data subject or which otherwise significantly affect a data subject and which are based solely on processing by automatic means of personal data and which are intended to evaluate certain personal matters relating to the data subject such as, performance at work, credit worthiness, reliability of conduct.

Section 12 of the DPA provides for the rights in relation to automated decision-taking.

Section 12(1) provides that an individual is entitled at any time, by notice in writing to any data controller, to require the data controller to ensure that no decision taken by or on behalf of the data controller which significantly affects that individual is based solely on the processing by automatic means of personal data in respect of which that individual is the data subject for the purpose of evaluating matters relating to them such as, for example, his performance at work, his creditworthiness, his reliability or his conduct.

Section 12(2) provides that where, in a case where no notice under s 12(1) has effect, a decision which significantly affects an individual is based solely on such processing as is mentioned in s 12(1):

- the data controller must as soon as reasonably practicable notify the individual that the decision was taken on that basis; and
- the individual is entitled, within twenty-one days of receiving that notification from the data controller, by notice in writing to require the data controller to reconsider the decision or to take a new decision otherwise than on that basis.

Section 12(3) provides that the data controller must, within twenty-one days of receiving a notice under s 12(2)(b) ('the data subject notice') give the individual a written notice specifying the steps that he intends to take to comply with the data subject notice.

Section 12(4) provides that a notice under s 12(1) does not have effect in relation to an exempt decision; and nothing in s 12(2) applies to an exempt decision.

Section 12(5) provides that in s 12(4) 'exempt decision' means any decision:

- in respect of which the condition in s 12(6) and the condition in s 12(7) are met; or
- which is made in such other circumstances as may be prescribed by the Secretary of State by order.

Section 12(6) provides that the condition in this subsection is that the decision:

- is taken in the course of steps taken:
  - for the purpose of considering whether to enter into a contract with the data subject;
  - with a view to entering into such a contract; or
  - in the course of performing such a contract; or
- is authorised or required by or under any enactment.

Section 12(7) provides that the condition in this subsection is that either:

- the effect of the decision is to grant a request of the data subject; or
- steps have been taken to safeguard the legitimate interests of the data subject (for example, by allowing them to make representations).

Section 12(8) provides that if a court is satisfied on the application of a data subject that a person taking a decision in respect of them (the 'responsible person') has failed to comply with s 12(1) or (2)(b), the court may order the responsible person to reconsider the decision, or to take a new decision which is not based solely on such processing as is mentioned in s 12(1).

Section 12(9) provides that an order under s 12(8) shall not affect the rights of any person other than the data subject and the responsible person.

Section 12 of the DPA provides rights in relation to automated decision-taking. It states:

(1) An individual is entitled at any time, by notice in writing to any data controller, to require the data controller to ensure that no decision taken by or on behalf of the data controller which significantly affects that individual is based solely on the processing by automatic means of personal data in respect of which that individual is the data subject for the purpose of evaluating matters relating to them such as, for example, his performance at work, his creditworthiness, his reliability or his conduct;

(2) Where, in a case where no notice under s 12(1) has effect, a decision which significantly affects an individual is based solely on such processing as is mentioned in s 12(1):

   (a) the data controller must as soon as reasonably practicable notify the individual that the decision was taken on that basis; and

   (b) the individual is entitled, within twenty-one days of receiving that notification from the data controller, by notice in writing to require the data controller to reconsider the decision or to take a new decision otherwise than on that basis;

(3) The data controller must, within twenty-one days of receiving a notice under s 12(2)(b) ('the data subject notice') give the individual a written notice specifying the steps that he intends to take to comply with the data subject notice;

(4) A notice under s 12(1) does not have effect in relation to an exempt decision; and nothing in s 12(2) applies to an exempt decision;

(5) In s 12(4) 'exempt decision' means any decision:

   (a) in respect of which the condition in s 12(6) and the condition in s 12(7) are met; or

   (b) which is made in such other circumstances as may be prescribed by the Secretary of State by order;

(6) The condition in the sub-section is that the decision

   (a) is taken in the course of steps taken;

      (i) for the purpose of considering whether to enter into a contract with the data subject;

      (ii) with a view to entering into such a contract; or

      (iii) in the course of performing such a contract; or

   (b) is authorised or required by or under any enactment;

(7) The condition in the subsection is that either

    (a)   the effect of the decision is to grant a request of the data subject; or

    (b)   steps have been taken to safeguard the legitimate interests of the data subject (for example, by allowing them to make representations);

(8) If a court is satisfied on the application of a data subject that a person taking a decision in respect of them ('the responsible person') has failed to comply with s 12(1) or (2)(b), the court may order the responsible person to reconsider the decision, or to take a new decision which is not based solely on such processing as is mentioned in s 12(1);

(9) An order under s 12(8) shall not affect the rights of any person other than the data subject and the responsible person.

DPD95: Right against Automated Individual Decisions

27.22   Article 15 of the DPD95 provides for the right against automated individual decisions. This can also be considered relevant to social networking. Section 15(1) states that Member States shall grant the right to every person not to be subject to a decision which produces legal effects concerning them or significantly affects them and which is based solely on automated processing of data intended to evaluate certain personal aspects relating to them, such as his performance at work, creditworthiness, reliability, conduct, etc.

Article 15(2) states that subject to the other Articles of the Directive, Member States shall provide that a person may be subjected to a decision of the kind referred to in paragraph 1 if that decision:

- is taken in the course of the entering into or performance of a contract, provided the request for the entering into or the performance of the contract, lodged by the data subject, has been satisfied or that there are suitable measures to safeguard his legitimate interests, such as arrangements allowing them to put his point of view; or
- is authorised by a law which also lays down measures to safeguard the data subject's legitimate interests.

DPD95: Right to Object

27.23   Section VII refers to the data subject's right to object. This can also be considered relevant to social networking. Article 14 of the

DPD95 provides for the data subject's right to object. It states that, Member States shall grant the data subject to the right:

- at least in the cases referred to in Article 7(e) and (f), to object at any time on compelling legitimate grounds relating to his particular situation to the processing of data relating to them, save where otherwise provided by national legislation. Where there is a justified objection, the processing instigated by the data controller may no longer involve those data;
- to object, on request and free of charge, to the processing of personal data relating to them which the data controller anticipates being processed for the purposes of direct marketing, or to be informed before personal data are disclosed for the first time to third parties or used on their behalf for the purposes of direct marketing, and to be expressly offered the right to object free of charge to such disclosures or uses.

It also provides that Member States shall take the necessary measures to ensure that data subjects are aware of the existence of the right.

DPR: Definitions and Social Networking

27.24 The DPR is relevant to social networking. The DPR definitions include,

'personal data breach'	means a breach of security leading to the accidental or unlawful destruction, loss, alteration, unauthorised disclosure of, or access to, personal data transmitted, stored or otherwise processed;
'main establishment'	means as regards the data controller, the place of its establishment in the EU where the main decisions as to the purposes, conditions and means of the processing of personal data are taken; if no decisions as to the purposes, conditions and means of the processing of personal data are taken in the EU, the main establishment is the place where the main processing activities in the context of the activities of an establishment of a data controller in the EU take place. As regards the data processor, 'main establishment' means the place of its central administration in the EU;

'representative'	means any natural or legal person established in the EU who, explicitly designated by the data controller, acts and may be addressed by any Supervisory Authority and other bodies in the EU instead of the data controller, with regard to the obligations of the data controller under the DPR;
'enterprise'	means any entity engaged in an economic activity, irrespective of its legal form, thus including, in particular, natural and legal persons, partnerships or associations regularly engaged in an economic activity;
'group of undertakings'	means a controlling undertaking and its controlled undertakings;
'child'	means any person below the age of 18 years.

DPR: Recitals and Social Networking

27.25   The Recitals to the proposed DPR are also instructive in considering social networking issues.

Need for Stronger Data Protection Regime Framework

27.26   Recital 2 The processing of personal data is designed to serve man; the principles and rules on the protection of individuals with regard to the processing of their personal data should, *whatever the nationality or residence of natural persons*, respect their fundamental rights and freedoms, notably their right to the protection of personal data. (Emphasis added). It should contribute to the accomplishment of an area of freedom, security and justice and of an economic union, to economic and social progress, the strengthening and the convergence of the economies within the internal market, and the well-being of individuals.

Recital 6 states that individuals should have control of their own personal data.

Recital 12 states that the protection afforded by the Regulation concerns natural persons, whatever their *nationality or place of residence*, in relation to the processing of personal data. (Emphasis added). With regard to the processing of data which concern legal persons and in particular undertakings established as legal persons, including the name and the form of the legal person and the contact details of the legal person, the protection of the Regulation should not be claimed by any person. This should also apply where the name of the legal person contains the names of one or more natural persons.

ISPs

27.27 Recital 17 states that the Regulation should be without prejudice to the application of Directive 2000/31/EC, in particular of the liability rules of intermediary service providers in Articles 12 to 15 of that Directive (the three limited defences).

Monitoring

27.28 Recital 21 states that in order to determine whether a processing activity can be considered to 'monitor the behaviour' of data subjects, it should be ascertained whether individuals are tracked on the internet with data processing techniques which consist of applying a 'profile' to an individual, particularly in order to take decisions concerning them or for analysing or predicting her or his personal preferences, behaviours and attitudes.

Any Information

27.29 Recital 23 states that the principles of protection should apply to any information concerning an identified or identifiable person. To determine whether a person is identifiable, account should be taken of all the means likely reasonably to be used either by the data controller or by any other person to identify the individual. The principles of data protection should not apply to data rendered anonymous in such a way that the data subject is no longer identifiable.

Internet

27.30 Recital 24 states that when using online services, individuals may be associated with online identifiers provided by their devices, applications, tools and protocols, such as Internet Protocol addresses or cookie identifiers. This may leave traces which, combined with unique identifiers and other information received by the servers, may be used to create profiles of the individuals and identify them. It follows that identification numbers, location data, online identifiers or other specific factors as such need not necessarily be considered as personal data in all circumstances.

Consent

27.31 Recital 25 states that the consent should be given explicitly by any appropriate method enabling a freely given specific and informed indication of the data subject's wishes, either by a statement or by a clear affirmative action by the data subject, ensuring that individuals are aware that they give their consent to the processing of personal data, including by ticking a box when visiting an Internet website or by any other statement or conduct which clearly indicates in this context the data subject's acceptance of the proposed processing of their personal data. Silence or inactivity should therefore not constitute consent. Consent should cover all processing activities carried out for the same purpose or purposes. If the data subject's consent is to be given following an electronic request, the request must be clear, concise and not unnecessarily disruptive to the use of the service for which it is provided.

Recital 32 states that where processing is based on the data subject's consent, the data controller should have the burden of proving that the data subject has given the consent to the processing operation. In particular in the context of a written declaration on another matter, safeguards should ensure that the data subject is aware that and to what extent consent is given.

Recital 33 states that in order to ensure free consent, it should be clarified that consent does not provide a valid legal ground where the individual has no genuine and free choice and is subsequently not able to refuse or withdraw consent without detriment.

Recital 34 states that the consent should not provide a valid legal ground for the processing of personal data, where there is a clear imbalance between the data subject and the data controller. This is especially the case where the data subject is in a situation of dependence from the data controller, among others, where personal data are processed by the employer of employees' personal data in the employment context. Where the data controller is a public authority, there would be an imbalance only in the specific data processing operations where the public authority can impose an obligation by virtue of its relevant public powers and the consent cannot be deemed as freely given, taking into account the interest of the data subject.

Children

27.31A   Recital 29 states that the children deserve specific protection of their personal data, as they may be less aware of risks, consequences, safeguards and their rights in relation to the processing of personal data. To determine when an individual is a child, the Regulation should take over the definition laid down by the UN Convention on the Rights of the Child.

Lawful Processing

27.32   Recital 30 states that any processing of personal data should be lawful, fair and transparent in relation to the individuals concerned. In particular, the specific purposes for which the data are processed should be explicit and legitimate and determined at the time of the collection of the data. The data should be adequate, relevant and limited to the minimum necessary for the purposes for which the data are processed; this requires in particular ensuring that the data collected are not excessive and that the period for which the data are stored is limited to a strict minimum. Personal data should only be processed if the purpose of the processing could not be fulfilled by other means. Every reasonable step should be taken to ensure that personal data which are inaccurate are rectified or deleted. In order to ensure that the data are not kept longer than necessary, time limits should be established by the data controller for erasure or for a periodic review.

Recital 31 states that in order for processing to be lawful, personal data should be processed on the basis of the consent of the person concerned or some other legitimate basis, laid down by law, either in the Regulation or in other EU or Member State law as referred to in the Regulation.

Recital 35 states that the processing should be lawful where it is necessary in the context of a contract or the intended entering into a contract.

Recital 36 states that where processing is carried out in compliance with a legal obligation to which the data controller is subject or where processing is necessary for the performance of a task carried out in the public interest or in the exercise of an official authority, the processing should have a legal basis in EU law, or in a Member State law which meets the requirements of the Charter of Fundamental Rights of the European Union for any limitation of the rights and freedoms. It is also for EU or national law to determine whether the data controller performing a task carried out in the public interest or in the exercise of official authority should be a public administration or another natural or legal person governed by public law, or by private law such as a professional association.

Recital 37 states that the processing of personal data should equally be regarded as lawful where it is necessary to protect an interest which is essential for the data subject's life.

Recital 38 states that the legitimate interests of a data controller may provide a legal basis for processing, provided that the interests or the fundamental rights and freedoms of the data subject are not overriding. This would need careful assessment in particular where the data subject is a child, given that children deserve specific protection. The data subject should have the right to object to the processing, on grounds relating to their particular situation and free of charge. To ensure transparency, the controller should be obliged to explicitly inform the data subject on the legitimate interests pursued and on the right to object, and also be obliged to document these legitimate interests. Given that it is for the legislator to provide by law the legal basis for public authorities to process data, this legal ground should not apply for the processing by public authorities in the performance of their tasks.

Recital 39 states that the processing of data to the extent strictly necessary for the purposes of ensuring network and information security, ie the ability of a network or an information system to resist, at a given level of confidence, accidental events or unlawful or malicious actions that compromise the availability, authenticity, integrity and confidentiality of stored or transmitted data, and the security of the related services offered by, or accessible via, these networks and systems, by public authorities, Computer Emergency Response Teams – CERTs, Computer Security Incident Response Teams – CSIRTs, providers of electronic communications networks and services and by providers of security technologies and services, constitutes a legitimate interest of the concerned data controller. This could, for example, include preventing unauthorised access to electronic communications networks and malicious code distribution and stopping 'denial of service' attacks and damage to computer and electronic communication systems.

Recital 40 states that the processing of personal data for other purposes should be only allowed where the processing is compatible with those purposes for which the data have been initially collected, in particular where the processing is necessary for historical, statistical or scientific research purposes. Where the other purpose is not compatible with the initial one for which the data are collected, the data controller should obtain the consent of the data subject for this other purpose or should base the processing on another legitimate ground for lawful processing, in particular where provided by EU law or the law of the Member State to which the data controller is subject. In any case, the application of the principles set out by the Regulation and in particular the information of the data subject on those other purposes should be ensured.

Sensitive Personal Data

27.33   Recital 41 states that the personal data which are, by their nature, particularly sensitive and vulnerable in relation to fundamental rights or privacy, deserve specific protection. Such data should not be processed, unless the data subject gives his explicit consent. However, derogations from the prohibition should be explicitly provided for in respect of specific needs, in particular where the processing is carried out in the course of legitimate activities by certain associations or foundations the purpose of which is to permit the exercise of fundamental freedoms.

Recital 42 states that the derogating from the prohibition on processing sensitive categories of data should also be allowed if done by a law, and subject to suitable safeguards, so as to protect personal data and other fundamental rights, where grounds of public interest so justify and in particular for health purposes, including public health and social protection and the management of healthcare services, especially in order to ensure the quality and cost-effectiveness of the procedures used for settling claims for benefits and services in the health insurance system, or for historical, statistical and scientific research purposes.

Particular considerations arise for dating, sex, texting, flirting, etc, apps.

Access

27.34   Recital 45 states that if the data processed by a data controller do not permit the controller to identify a natural person, the data controller should not be obliged to acquire additional information in order to identify the data subject for the sole purpose of complying with any provision of the Regulation. In case of a request for access, the controller should be entitled to ask the data subject for further information to enable the data controller to locate the personal data which that person seeks.

Transparency/Children

27.35   Recital 46 states that the principle of transparency requires that any information addressed to the public or to the data subject should be easily accessible and easy to understand, and that clear and plain language is used. This is in particular relevant where in situations, such as online advertising, the proliferation of actors and the technological complexity of practice makes it difficult for the data subject to know and understand if personal data relating to them are being collected, by whom and for what purpose. Given that children deserve specific protection, any information and communication, where processing is addressed specifically to a child, should be in such a clear and plain language that the child can easily understand.

Exercising Rights

27.36 Recital 47 states that the modalities should be provided for facilitating the data subject's exercise of their rights provided by the Regulation, including mechanisms to request, free of charge, in particular access to data, rectification, erasure and to exercise the right to object. The data controller should be obliged to respond to requests of the data subject within a fixed deadline and give reasons, in case he does not comply with the data subject's request. Recital 48 provides that the principles of fair and transparent processing require that the data subject should be informed in particular of the existence of the processing operation and its purposes, how long the data will be stored, on the existence of the right of access, rectification or erasure and on the right to lodge a complaint. Where the data are collected from the data subject, the data subject should also be informed whether they are obliged to provide the data and of the consequences, in cases they do not provide such data.

Recital 51 states that any person should have the right of access to data which has been collected concerning them, and to exercise this right easily, in order to be aware and verify the lawfulness of the processing. Every data subject should therefore have the right to know and obtain communication in particular for what purposes the data are processed, for what period, which recipients receive the data, what is the logic of the data that are undergoing the processing and what might be, at least when based on profiling, the consequences of such processing. This right should not adversely affect the rights and freedoms of others, including trade secrets or intellectual property and in particular the copyright protecting the software. However, the result of these considerations should not be that all information is refused to the data subject.

Recital 52 states that the data controller should use all reasonable measures to verify the identity of a data subject that requests access, in particular in the context of online services and online identifiers. A data controller should not retain personal data for the unique purpose of being able to react to potential requests.

Prior Information

27.37 Recital 49 states that the information in relation to the processing of personal data relating to the data subject should be given to them at the time of collection, or, where the data are not collected from the data subject, within a reasonable period, depending on the circumstances of the case. Where data can be legitimately disclosed to another recipient, the data subject should be informed when the data are first disclosed to the recipient.

Recital 50 states, however, that it is not necessary to impose the obligation where the data subject already disposes of the information, or where the recording or disclosure of the data is expressly laid down by law, or where the provision of information to the data subject proves impossible or would involve disproportionate efforts. The latter could be particularly the case where processing is for historical, statistical or scientific research purposes; in this regard, the number of data subjects, the age of the data, and any compensatory measures adopted may be taken into consideration.

Rectification

27.38 Recital 53 states that any person should have the right to have personal data concerning them rectified. This includes where data subjects have withdrawn their consent for processing or where they object to the processing of personal data concerning them or where the processing of their personal data otherwise does not comply with the Regulation.

Right to Forget

27.39 Recital 53 states that any person should have the expanded 'right to be forgotten' where the retention of such data is not in compliance with the Regulation. In particular, data subjects should have the right that their personal data are erased and no longer processed, where the data are no longer necessary in relation to the purposes for which the data are collected or otherwise processed, where data subjects have withdrawn their consent for processing or where they object to the processing of personal data concerning them or where the processing of their personal data otherwise does not comply with the Regulation. This right is particularly relevant, when the data subject has given their consent as a child, when not being fully aware of the risks involved by the processing, and later wants to remove such personal data especially on the Internet. However, the further retention of the data should be allowed where it is necessary for historical, statistical and scientific research purposes, for reasons of public interest in the area of public health, for exercising the right of freedom of expression, when required by law or where there is a reason to restrict the processing of the data instead of erasing them.

Recital 54 states that to strengthen the 'right to be forgotten' in the online environment, the right to erasure should also be extended in such a way that a data controller who has made the personal data public should be obliged to inform third parties which are processing such data that a data subject requests them to erase any links to, or copies or replications of that personal data. To ensure this information, the data controller should take all reasonable steps, including technical measures, in relation to data for the publication of which the data controller is responsible. In relation to a third party publication of personal data, the data controller should be considered responsible for the publication, where the controller has authorised the publication by the third party.

Electronic Access

27.40 Recital 55 states that to further strengthen the control over their own data and their right of access, data subjects should have the right, where personal data are processed by electronic means and in a structured and commonly used format, to obtain a copy of the data concerning them also in commonly used electronic format. The data subject should also be allowed to transmit those data, which they have provided, from one automated application, such as a social network, into another one. This should apply where the data subject provided the data to the automated processing system, based on their consent or in the performance of a contract.

Right to Object

27.41 Recital 56 states that in cases where personal data might lawfully be processed to protect the vital interests of the data subject, or on grounds of public interest, official authority or the legitimate interests of a data controller, any data subject should nevertheless be entitled to object to the processing of any data relating to them. The burden of proof should be on the data controller to demonstrate that their legitimate interests may override the interests or the fundamental rights and freedoms of the data subject.

Direct Marketing

27.42 Recital 57 states that where personal data are processed for the purposes of direct marketing, the data subject should have the right to object to such processing free of charge and in a manner that can be easily and effectively invoked.

Automated Processing

27.43 Recital 58 states that every natural person should have the right not to be subject to a measure which is based on profiling by means of automated processing. However, such measure should be allowed when expressly authorised by law, carried out in the course of entering or performance of a contract, or when the data subject has given his consent. In any case, such processing should be subject to suitable safeguards, including specific information of the data subject and the right to obtain human intervention and that such measure should not concern a child.

Recital 59 states that the restrictions on specific principles and on the rights of information, access, rectification and erasure or on the right to data portability, the right to object, measures based on profiling, as well as on the communication of a personal data breach to a data subject and on certain related obligations of the data controllers may be imposed by EU or Member State law, as far as necessary and proportionate in a democratic society to safeguard public security, including the protection of human life especially in response to natural or man made disasters, the prevention, investigation and prosecution of criminal offences or of breaches of ethics for regulated professions, other public interests of the EU or of a Member State, in particular an important economic or financial interest of the EU or of a Member State, or the protection of the data subject or the rights and freedoms of others. Those restrictions should be in compliance with requirements set out by the Charter of Fundamental Rights of the European Union and by the European Convention for the Protection of Human Rights and Fundamental Freedoms.

Liability

27.44 Recital 60 states that the comprehensive responsibility and liability of the data controller for any processing of personal data carried out by the data controller or on the data controller's behalf should be established. In particular, the data controller should ensure and be obliged to demonstrate the compliance of each processing operation with the Regulation.

Policies and Measures

27.45 Recital 61 states that the protection of the rights and freedoms of data subjects with regard to the processing of personal data require that appropriate technical and organisational measures are taken, both at the time of the design of the processing and at the time of the processing itself, to ensure that the requirements of the Regulation are met. In order to ensure and demonstrate compliance with the Regulation, the data controller should adopt internal policies and implement appropriate measures, which meet in particular the principles of data protection by design and data protection by default.

Recital 62 states that the protection of the rights and freedoms of data subjects as well as the responsibility and liability of data controllers and data processor, also in relation to the monitoring by and measures of supervisory authorities, requires a clear attribution of the responsibilities under the Regulation, including where a data controller determines the purposes, conditions and means of the processing jointly with other data controllers or where a processing operation is carried out on behalf of a controller.

Recital 65 states that in order to demonstrate compliance with the Regulation, the data controller or data processor should document each processing operation. Each data controller and data processor should be obliged to co-operate with the Supervisory Authority and make this documentation, on request, available to it, so that it might serve for monitoring those processing operations.

Security

27.46 Recital 66 states that in order to maintain security and to prevent processing in breach of the Regulation, the data controller or data processor should evaluate the risks inherent to the processing and implement measures to mitigate those risks. These measures should ensure an appropriate level of security, taking into account the state of the art and the costs of their implementation in relation to the risks and the nature of the personal data to be protected. When establishing technical standards and organisational measures to ensure security of processing, the Commission should promote technological neutrality, interoperability and innovation, and, where appropriate, cooperate with third countries.

Data Breach

27.47 Recital 67 states that a personal data breach may, if not addressed in an adequate and timely manner, result in substantial economic loss and social harm, including identity fraud, to the individual concerned. Therefore, as soon as the data controller becomes aware that such a breach has occurred, the data controller should notify the breach to the Supervisory Authority without undue delay and, where feasible, within 24 hours. Where this cannot achieved within 24 hours, an explanation of the reasons for the delay should accompany the notification. The individuals whose personal data could be adversely affected by the breach should be notified without undue delay in order to allow them to take the necessary precautions. A breach should be considered as adversely affecting the personal data or privacy of a data subject where it could result in, for example, identity theft or fraud, physical harm, significant *humiliation or damage* (emphasis added) to reputation. The notification should describe the nature of the personal data breach as well as recommendations for the individual concerned to mitigate potential adverse effects. Notifications to data subjects should be made as soon as reasonably feasible, and in close cooperation with the Supervisory Authority and respecting guidance provided by it or other relevant authorities (eg law enforcement authorities). For example, the chance for data subjects to mitigate an immediate risk of harm would call for a prompt notification of data subjects whereas the need to implement appropriate measures against continuing or similar data breaches may justify a longer delay.

Recital 68 states that in order to determine whether a personal data breach is notified to the Supervisory Authority and to the data subject without undue delay, it should be ascertained whether the data controller has implemented and applied appropriate technological protection and organisational measures to establish immediately whether a personal data breach has taken place and to inform promptly the Supervisory Authority and the data subject, before damage to personal and economic interests occurs, taking into account in particular the nature and gravity of the personal data breach and its consequences and adverse effects for the data subject.

Recital 69 states that in setting detailed rules concerning the format and procedures applicable to the notification of personal data breaches, due consideration should be given to the circumstances of the breach, including whether or not personal data had been protected by appropriate technical protection measures, effectively limiting the likelihood of identity fraud or other forms of misuse. Moreover, such rules and procedures should take into account the legitimate interests of law enforcement authorities in cases where early disclosure could unnecessarily hamper the investigation of the circumstances of a breach.

Registration/Notification/Impact Assessments

27.48 Recital 70 states that a data protection impact assessment should be carried out by the data controller or data processor prior to the processing, which should include in particular the envisaged measures, safeguards and mechanisms for ensuring the protection of personal data and for demonstrating the compliance with the Regulation.

Recital 71 states that this should in particular apply to newly established large scale filing systems, which aim at processing a considerable amount of personal data at regional, national or supranational level and which could affect a large number of data subjects.

Recital 72 states that there are circumstances under which it may be sensible and economic that the subject of a data protection impact assessment should be broader than a single project, for example where public authorities or bodies intend to establish a common application or processing platform or where several data controllers plan to introduce a common application or processing environment across an industry sector or segment or for a widely used horizontal activity.

Recital 73 states that the data protection impact assessments should be carried out by a public authority or public body if such an assessment has not already been made in the context of the adoption of the national law on which the performance of the tasks of the public authority or public body is based and which regulates the specific processing operation or set of operations in question.

Recital 74 states that where a data protection impact assessment indicates that processing operations involve a high degree of specific risks to the rights and freedoms of data subjects, such as excluding individuals from their right, or by the use of specific new technologies, the Supervisory Authority should be consulted, prior to the start of operations, on a risky processing which might not be in compliance with the Regulation, and to make proposals to remedy such situation. Such consultation should equally take place in the course of the preparation either of a measure by the national parliament or of a measure based on such legislative measure which defines the nature of the processing and lays down appropriate safeguards.

Transfers

27.49   Recital 78 states that cross-border flows of personal data are necessary for the expansion of international trade and international co-operation. The increase in these flows has raised new challenges and concerns with respect to the protection of personal data. However, when personal data are transferred from the EU to third countries or to international organisations, the level of protection of individuals guaranteed in the EU by the Regulation should not be undermined. In any event, transfers to third countries may only be carried out in full compliance with the Regulation.

Recital 90 states that the some third countries enact laws, regulations and other legislative instruments which purport to directly regulate data processing activities of natural and legal persons under the jurisdiction of the Member States. The extraterritorial application of these laws, regulations and other legislative instruments may be in breach of international law and may impede the attainment of the protection of individuals guaranteed in the EU by the Regulation. Transfers should only be allowed where the conditions of the Regulation for a transfer to third countries are met. This may inter alia be the case where the disclosure is necessary for an important ground of public interest recognised in EU law or in a Member State law to which the data controller is subject. The conditions under which an important ground of public interest exists should be further specified by the Commission in a delegated act.

Recital 91 states that when personal data moves across borders it may put at increased risk the ability of individuals to exercise data protection rights in particular to protect themselves from the unlawful use or disclosure of that information. At the same time, supervisory authorities may find that they are unable to pursue complaints or conduct investigations relating to the activities outside their borders. Their efforts to work together in the cross-border context may also be hampered by insufficient preventative or remedial powers, inconsistent legal regimes, and practical obstacles like resource constraints. Therefore, there is a need to promote closer co-operation among data protection supervisory authorities to help them exchange information and carry out investigations with their international counterparts.

Processing in More than One Member State

27.50 Recital 97 states that where the processing of personal data in the context of the activities of an establishment of a data controller or a data processor in the EU takes place in more than one Member State, one single Supervisory Authority should be competent for monitoring the activities of the data controller or data processor throughout the EU and taking the related decisions, in order to increase the consistent application, provide legal certainty and reduce administrative burden for such data controllers and data processors.

One Stop Shop

27.51 Recital 98 states that the competent authority, providing such one-stop shop, should be the Supervisory Authority of the Member State in which the data controller or data processor has its main establishment.

Recital 99 states that while the Regulation applies also to the activities of national courts, the competence of the supervisory authorities should not cover the processing of personal data when courts are acting in their judicial capacity, in order to safeguard the independence of judges in the performance of their judicial tasks. However, the exemption should be strictly limited to genuine judicial activities in court cases and not apply to other activities where judges might be involved in, in accordance with national law.

Recital 100 states that in order to ensure consistent monitoring and enforcement of the Regulation throughout the EU, the supervisory authorities should have in each Member State the same duties and effective powers, including powers of investigation, legally binding intervention, decisions and sanctions, particularly in cases of complaints from individuals, and to engage in legal proceedings. Investigative powers of supervisory authorities as regards access to premises should be exercised in conformity with EU law and national law. This concerns in particular the requirement to obtain a prior judicial authorisation.

Recital 101 states that each Supervisory Authority should hear complaints lodged by any data subject and should investigate the matter. The investigation following a complaint should be carried out, subject to judicial review, to the extent that is appropriate in the specific case. The Supervisory Authority should inform the data subject of the progress and the outcome of the complaint within a reasonable period. If the case requires further investigation or coordination with another Supervisory Authority, intermediate information should be given to the data subject.

Complaints to Information Commissioner

27.52 Recital 111 states that every data subject should have the right to lodge a complaint with a Supervisory Authority in any Member State and also have the right to a *judicial remedy* if they consider that their rights under the Regulation are infringed or where the Supervisory Authority does not react on a complaint or does not act where such action is necessary to protect the rights of the data subject. (Emphasis added).

Recital 112 states that any body, organisation or association which aims to protects the rights and interests of data subjects in relation to the protection of their data and is constituted according to the law of a Member State should have the right to lodge a complaint with a Supervisory Authority *or* exercise the right to *a judicial remedy* on behalf of data subjects, or to lodge, independently of a data subject's complaint, its own complaint where it considers that a personal data breach has occurred. (Emphasis added).

Court Remedies/Data Protection Supervisors

27.53 Recital 113 states that each natural or legal person should have the right to a judicial remedy against decisions of a Supervisory

Authority concerning them. Proceedings against a Supervisory Authority should be brought before the courts of the Member State, where the Supervisory Authority is established.

Compensation

27.54 Recital 118 states that any damage which a person may suffer as a result of unlawful processing should be compensated by the data controller or data processor, who may be exempted from liability if they prove that they are not responsible for the damage, in particular where he establishes fault on the part of the data subject or in case of force majeure.

Penalties

27.55 Recital 119 states that penalties should be imposed to any person, whether governed by private or public law, who fails to comply with the Regulation. Member States should ensure that the penalties should be effective, proportionate and dissuasive and should take all measures to implement the penalties.

Sanctions

27.56 Recital 120 states that in order to strengthen and harmonise administrative sanctions against infringements of the Regulation, each Supervisory Authority should have the power to sanction administrative offences. The Regulation should indicate these offences and the upper limit for the related administrative fines, which should be fixed in each individual case proportionate to the specific situation, with due regard in particular to the nature, gravity and duration of the breach. The consistency mechanism may also be used to cover divergences in the application of administrative sanctions.

Third Countries

27.57 Recital 132 states that the Commission should adopt immediately applicable implementing acts where, in duly justified cases relating to a third country or a territory or a processing sector within that third country or an international organisation which does not ensure an adequate level of protection and relating to matters communicated by supervisory authorities under the consistency mechanism, imperative grounds of urgency so require.

Recital 133 states that since the objectives of the Regulation, namely to ensure an equivalent level of protection of individuals and the free flow of data throughout the EU, cannot be sufficiently achieved by the

Member States and can therefore, by reason of the scale or effects of the action, be better achieved at EU level, the EU may adopt measures, in accordance with the principle of subsidiarity as set out in Article 5 of the Treaty on European Union. In accordance with the principle of proportionality as set out in that Article, the Regulation does not go beyond what is necessary in order to achieve that objective.

Proportionality

27.58   Recital 139 states that in view of the fact that, as underlined by the Court of Justice of the EU, the right to the protection of personal data is not an absolute right, but must be considered in relation to its function in society and be balanced with other fundamental rights, in accordance with the principle of proportionality, the Regulation respects all fundamental rights and observes the principles recognised in the Charter of Fundamental Rights of the European Union as enshrined in the Treaties, notably the right to respect for *private and family life, home and communications, the right to the protection of personal data, the freedom of thought, conscience and religion, the freedom of expression and information, the freedom to conduct a business, the right to an effective remedy* and to a fair trial as well as cultural, religious and linguistic diversity. (Emphasis added).

DPR: Rectification Right

27.59   Section 3 of the DPR refers to rectification and erasure. Article 16 refers to the right to rectification. It provides that the data subject shall have the right to obtain from the data controller the rectification of personal data relating to them which are inaccurate. The data subject shall have the right to obtain completion of incomplete personal data, including by way of supplementing a corrective statement.

DPR: Right to Object, Profiling and Social Networking

27.60   Section 4 of the DPR refers to the right to object and profiling. Article 19 of the DPR refers to the right to object. Article 19(1) provides that the data subject shall have the right to object, on grounds relating to their particular situation, at any time to the processing of personal data which is based on points (d), (e) and (f) of Article 6(1), unless the data controller demonstrates compelling legitimate grounds for the processing which override the interests or fundamental rights and freedoms of the data subject.

Article 19(2) provides that where personal data are processed for direct marketing purposes, the data subject shall have the right to object free of charge to the processing of their personal data for such marketing. This right shall be explicitly offered to the data subject in an intelligible manner and shall be clearly distinguishable from other information.

Article 19(3) provides that where an objection is upheld pursuant to paragraphs 1 and 2, the data controller shall no longer use or otherwise process the personal data concerned.

Article 20 of the DPR refers to measures based on profiling. Article 20(1) provides that every natural person shall have the right not to be subject to a measure which produces legal effects concerning this natural person or significantly affects this natural person, and which is based solely on automated processing intended to evaluate certain personal aspects relating to this natural person or to analyse or predict in particular the natural person's performance at work, economic situation, location, health, personal preferences, reliability or behaviour.

Article 20(2) provides that subject to the other provisions of the Regulation, a person may be subjected to a measure of the kind referred to in paragraph 1 only if the processing:

- is carried out in the course of the entering into, or performance of, a contract, where the request for the entering into or the performance of the contract, lodged by the data subject, has been satisfied or where suitable measures to safeguard the data subject's legitimate interests have been adduced, such as the right to obtain human intervention; or
- is expressly authorised by a EU or Member State law which also lays down suitable measures to safeguard the data subject's legitimate interests; or
- is based on the data subject's consent, subject to the conditions laid down in Article 7 and to suitable safeguards.

Article 20(3) provides that automated processing of personal data intended to evaluate certain personal aspects relating to a natural person shall not be based solely on the special categories of personal data referred to in Article 9.

Article 20(4) provides that in the cases referred to in Article 20(2), the information to be provided by the data controller under Article 14 shall include information as to the existence of processing for a measure of the kind referred to in paragraph 1 and the envisaged effects of such processing on the data subject.

Article 20(5) refers to the Commission shall be empowered to adopt delegated acts in accordance with Article 86 for the purpose of further specifying the criteria and conditions for suitable measures to safeguard the data subject's legitimate interests referred to in paragraph 2.

There is also discussion and proposals in relation to the area of electronic identity or eID's.[33] For example, the European Digital Agenda refers to '[e]lectronic identity (eID) technologies and authentications services are essential for transactions on the internet in both the private and public sectors.'[34]

DPR: Erasure Right/Right to be Forgotten and Social Networking

27.61 Article 17 of the DPR refers to the right to be forgotten and to erasure. Article 17(1) provides that the data subject shall have the right to obtain from the data controller the erasure of personal data relating to them and the abstention from further dissemination of such data, especially in relation to personal data which are made available by the data subject while he or she was a child, where one of the following grounds applies:

- the data are no longer necessary in relation to the purposes for which they were collected or otherwise processed;
- the data subject withdraws consent on which the processing is based according to point (a) of Article 6(1), or when the storage period consented to has expired, and where there is no other legal ground for the processing of the data;
- the data subject objects to the processing of personal data pursuant to Article 19;
- the processing of the data does not comply with the Regulation for other reasons.

Article 17(2) provides that where the data controller referred to in paragraph 1 has made the personal data public, it shall take all reasonable steps, including technical measures, in relation to data for the publication of which the data controller is responsible, to inform third parties which are processing such data, that a data subject requests them to erase any links to, or copy or replication of that personal data.

---

33 See, for example, Norberto Nuno Gomes de Ardrade, "Regulating Electronic Identity in the European Union: An Analysis of the Lisbon Treat's Competences and Legal Basis for eID," *Computer Law and Security Review* (2012)(28), pp. 153–162, at 153.
34 European Commission, "Communication from the Commission – a Digital Agenda for Europe" (Brussels: European Commission 2010), p. 11.

Where the data controller has authorised a third party publication of personal data, the data controller shall be considered responsible for that publication.

Article 17(3) provides that the data controller shall carry out the erasure without delay, except to the extent that the retention of the personal data is necessary:

- for exercising the right of freedom of expression in accordance with Article 80;
- for reasons of public interest in the area of public health in accordance with Article 81;
- for historical, statistical and scientific research purposes in accordance with Article 83;
- for compliance with a legal obligation to retain the personal data by EU or Member State law to which the data controller is subject; Member State laws shall meet an objective of public interest, respect the essence of the right to the protection of personal data and be proportionate to the legitimate aim pursued;
- in the cases referred to in Article 17(4).

Article 17(4) provides that instead of erasure, the data controller shall restrict processing of personal data where:

- their accuracy is contested by the data subject, for a period enabling the data controller to verify the accuracy of the data;
- the data controller no longer needs the personal data for the accomplishment of its task but they have to be maintained for purposes of proof;
- the processing is unlawful and the data subject opposes their erasure and requests the restriction of their use instead;
- the data subject requests to transmit the personal data into another automated processing system in accordance with Article 18(2).

Article 17(5) provides that personal data referred to in Article 17(4) may, with the exception of storage, only be processed for purposes of proof, or with the data subject's consent, or for the protection of the rights of another natural or legal person or for an objective of public interest.

Article 17(6) provides that where processing of personal data is restricted pursuant to paragraph 4, the data controller shall inform the data subject before lifting the restriction on processing.

Article 17(7) provides that the data controller shall implement mechanisms to ensure that the time limits established for the erasure of personal data and/or for a periodic review of the need for the storage of the data are observed.

Article 17(8) provides that where the erasure is carried out, the data controller shall not otherwise process such personal data.

Article 17(9) provides that the Commission shall be empowered to adopt delegated acts in accordance with Article 86 for the purpose of further specifying:

- the criteria and requirements for the application of Article 17(1) for specific sectors and in specific data processing situations;
- the conditions for deleting links, copies or replications of personal data from publicly available communication services as referred to in Article 17(2);
- the criteria and conditions for restricting the processing of personal data referred to in Article17(4).

DPR: Right to Portability

27.62 Article 18 refers to the right to data portability. Article 18(1) provides that the data subject shall have the right, where personal data are processed by electronic means and in a structured and commonly used format, to obtain from the data controller a copy of data undergoing processing in an electronic and structured format which is commonly used and allows for further use by the data subject.

Article 18(2) provides that where the data subject has provided the personal data and the processing is based on consent or on a contract, the data subject shall have the right to transmit those personal data and any other information provided by the data subject and retained by an automated processing system, into another one, in an electronic format which is commonly used, without hindrance from the data controller from whom the personal data are withdrawn.

Article 18(3) provides that the Commission may specify the electronic format referred to in paragraph 1 and the technical standards, modalities and procedures for the transmission of personal data pursuant to paragraph 2. Those implementing acts shall be adopted in accordance with the examination procedure referred to in Article 87(2).

Conclusion

27.63 The intersection of data protection and social networking is one of the most controversial issues in contemporary data protection practice. Users are concerned as to what personal data is being collected and what it will be used for. Naturally, social networks will seek to commercialise and use profile information for advertising and marketing purposes. This tension remains. Furthermore, the tension is elevated when the individuals using social networking websites are children. Recent tragic events create a new level of sensitivity and importance. While the DPR is a welcome advancement, additional research is also needed, and on an ongoing basis.

Chapter 28

Social Networking and Access

Introduction

28.01 One of the controversial issues in relation to social networks is access to personal data. This is one of the areas of complaint relating to Facebook and the audit investigation.

Facebook

28.02 In response to the audit investigation and also the receipt of tens of thousands of access requests, Facebook developed an online tool to make personal data available to users. While this is welcome, it remains to be seen if the online tool fully complies with Facebook's compliance obligations in terms of complying with access requests. In particular, it remains to be seen if all categories or fields of personal data collected and processed are made available to users pursuant to an access request.

A separate issue is that the access tools must be constantly updated as the fields and categories of personal data also expand. Therefore, the obligation, as with all areas of data protection, is an ongoing one.

Fake Profiles

28.03 There is a large problem with fake, impersonating and identity theft profiles being set up on social networking websites.

These can be set up, without consent, by an imposter in an individual's name. They will also contain comments and statements purported to be from the real person. In addition, they may also contain photos, images or content relating to the real person being impersonated.

It appears that certain social networks are reluctant to provide full and proper access to these fake profiles despite there being personal data relating to an individual. The author is aware of one contentious example where a data access request is not being complied with by a well-known social network. This remains a developing issue of contention.

DPA: Access Right

28.04　Part II of the DPA refers to the rights of data subjects and others. In particular, s 7 refers to the right of access to personal data. This applies to data subjects. It is a data subject right.

Section 7(1) provides that subject to the following provisions of this section and to ss 8, 9 and 9A, an individual is entitled:

- to be informed by any data controller whether personal data of which that individual is the data subject are being processed by or on behalf of that data controller;
- if that is the case, to be given by the data controller a description of:
  - the personal data of which that individual is the data subject;
  - the purposes for which they are being or are to be processed; and
  - the recipients or classes of recipients to whom they are or may be disclosed;
- to have communicated to them in an intelligible form:
  - the information constituting any personal data of which that individual is the data subject; and
  - any information available to the data controller as to the source of those data; and
- where the processing by automatic means of personal data of which that individual is the data subject for the purpose of evaluating matters relating to them such as, for example, his performance at work, his creditworthiness, his reliability or his conduct, has constituted or is likely to constitute the sole basis for any decision significantly affecting them, to be informed by the data controller of the logic involved in that decision-taking.

DPA s 7(2)A provides that a data controller is not obliged to supply any information under sub-s (1) unless he has received:

- a request in writing; and
- except in prescribed cases, such fee (not exceeding the prescribed maximum) as he may require.

DPA s 7(3) provides that where a data controller:

- reasonably requires further information in order to satisfy them as to the identity of the person making a request under the section and to locate the information which that person seeks; and
- has informed them of that requirement,

the data controller is not obliged to comply with the request unless he is supplied with that further information.

DPA s 7(4) provides that where a data controller cannot comply with the request without disclosing information relating to another individual who can be identified from that information, he is not obliged to comply with the request unless:

- the other individual has consented to the disclosure of the information to the person making the request; or
- it is reasonable in all the circumstances to comply with the request without the consent of the other individual.

DPA s 7(5) provides that in sub-s (4) the reference to information relating to another individual includes a reference to information identifying that individual as the source of the information sought by the request; and that sub-section is not to be construed as excusing a data controller from communicating so much of the information sought by the request as can be communicated without disclosing the identity of the other individual concerned, whether by the omission of names or other identifying particulars or otherwise.

DPA s 7(6) provides that in determining for the purposes of sub-s (4)(b) whether it is reasonable in all the circumstances to comply with the request without the consent of the other individual concerned, regard shall be had, in particular, to:

- any duty of confidentiality owed to the other individual;
- any steps taken by the data controller with a view to seeking the consent of the other individual;
- whether the other individual is capable of giving consent; and
- any express refusal of consent by the other individual.

DPA s 7(7) provides that an individual making a request under the section may, in such cases as may be prescribed, specify that his request is limited to personal data of any prescribed description.

DPA s 7(8) provides that subject to sub-s (4), a data controller shall comply with a request under the section promptly and in any event before the end of the prescribed period beginning with the relevant day.

DPA s 7(9) provides that if a court is satisfied on the application of any person who has made a request under the foregoing provisions of the section that the data controller in question has failed to comply with the request in contravention of those provisions, the court may order them to comply with the request.

DPA s 7(10) also provides that in the section:

● 'prescribed' means prescribed by the Secretary of State by regulations;

● 'the prescribed maximum' means such amount as may be prescribed;

● 'the prescribed period' means forty days or such other period as may be prescribed;

● 'the relevant day,' in relation to a request under the section, means the day on which the data controller receives the request or, if later, the first day on which the data controller has both the required fee and the information referred to in s 7(3).

DPA s 7(11) provides that different amounts or periods may be prescribed under the section in relation to different cases.

DPA s 7(12) provides that a person is a relevant person for the purposes of s7 (4)(c) if he:

● is a person referred to in paragraph 4(a) or (b) or paragraph 8(a) or (b) of Schedule 11;

● is employed by an education authority (within the meaning of paragraph 6 of Schedule 11) in pursuance of its functions relating to education and the information relates to them, or he supplied the information in his capacity as such an employee; or

● is the person making the request.

DPA s 7(12) provides that a person is a relevant person for the purposes of sub-s (4)(c) if he:

● is a person referred to in paragraph 1(p) or (q) of the Schedule to the Data Protection (Subject Access Modification)(Social Work) Order 2000; or

● is or has been employed by any person or body referred to in paragraph 1 of that Schedule in connection with functions which are or have been exercised in relation to the data consisting of the information; or

● has provided for reward a service similar to a service provided in the exercise of any functions specified in paragraph 1(a)(i), (b), (c) or (d) of that Schedule, and the information relates to them or he supplied the information in his official capacity or, as the case may be, in connection with the provision of that service.

DPA s 8 refers to provisions supplementary to s 7. Section 8(1) provides that the Secretary of State may by regulations provide that, in such cases as may be prescribed, a request for information under any provision of sub-s (1) of s 7 is to be treated as extending also to information under other provisions of that sub-section.

Section 8(2) provides that the obligation imposed by s 7(1)(c)(i) must be complied with by supplying the data subject with a copy of the information in permanent form unless:

- the supply of such a copy is not possible or would involve disproportionate effort; or
- the data subject agrees otherwise;

and where any of the information referred to in s 7(1)(c)(i) is expressed in terms which are not intelligible without explanation the copy must be accompanied by an explanation of those terms.

DPA s 8(3) provides that where a data controller has previously complied with a request made under s 7 by an individual, the data controller is not obliged to comply with a subsequent identical or similar request under that section by that individual unless a reasonable interval has elapsed between compliance with the previous request and the making of the current request.

DPA s 8(4) provides that in determining for the purposes of sub-s (3) whether requests under s 7 are made at reasonable intervals, regard shall be had to the nature of the data, the purpose for which the data are processed and the frequency with which the data are altered.

DPA s 8(5) provides that s 7(1)(d) is not to be regarded as requiring the provision of information as to the logic involved in any decision-taking if, and to the extent that, the information constitutes a trade secret.

DPA s 8(6) provides that the information to be supplied pursuant to a request under s 7 must be supplied by reference to the data in question at the time when the request is received, except that it may take account of any amendment or deletion made between that time and the time when the information is supplied, being an amendment or deletion that would have been made regardless of the receipt of the request.

DPA s 8(7) provides that for the purposes of s 7(4) and (5) another individual can be identified from the information being disclosed if he can be identified from that information, or from that and any other information which, in the reasonable belief of the data controller, is likely to be in, or to come into, the possession of the data subject making the request.

DPD95: Access Right

28.05 Article 12 of the DPD provides for the right of access, and states, Member States shall guarantee every data subject the right to obtain from the data controller

(a) without constraint at reasonable intervals and without excessive delay or expense:
- confirmation as to whether or not data relating to them are being processed and information at least as to the purposes of the processing, the categories of data concerned, and the recipients or categories of recipients to whom the data are disclosed;
- communication to them in an intelligible form of the data undergoing processing and of any available information as to their source;
- knowledge of the logic involved in any automatic processing of data concerning them at least in the case of the automated decisions referred to in Article 15(1);

(b) as appropriate the rectification, erasure or blocking of data the processing of which does not comply with the provisions of the Directive, in particular because of the incomplete or inaccurate nature of the data;

(c) notification to third parties to whom the data have been disclosed of any rectification, erasure or blocking carried out in compliance with (b), unless this proves impossible or involves a disproportionate effort.

DPR: Access Right

28.06 Article 15 of the DPR relates to the right of access for the data subject and provides:

1. The data subject shall have the right to obtain from the data controller at any time, on request, confirmation as to whether or not personal data relating to the data subject are being processed. Where such personal data are being processed, the data controller shall provide the following information
   (a) the purposes of the processing;
   (b) the categories of personal data concerned;

(c)   the recipients or categories of recipients to whom the personal data are to be or have been disclosed, in particular to recipients in third countries;

(d)   the period for which the personal data will be stored;

(e)   the existence of the right to request from the data controller rectification or erasure of personal data concerning the data subject or to object to the processing of such personal data;

(f)   the right to lodge a complaint to the Supervisory Authority and the contact details of the Supervisory Authority;

(g)   communication of the personal data undergoing processing and of any available information as to their source;

(h)   the significance and envisaged consequences of such processing, at least in the case of measures referred to in Article 20;

2.   The data subject shall have the right to obtain from the data controller communication of the personal data undergoing processing. Where the data subject makes the request in electronic form, the information shall be provided in electronic form, unless otherwise requested by the data subject;

3.   The Commission shall be empowered to adopt delegated acts in accordance with Article 86 for the purpose of further specifying the criteria and requirements for the communication to the data subject of the content of the personal data referred to in point (g) of paragraph 1;

4.   The Commission may specify standard forms and procedures for requesting and granting access to the information referred to in paragraph 1, including for verification of the identity of the data subject and communicating the personal data to the data subject, taking into account the specific features and necessities of various sectors and data processing situations. Those implementing acts shall be adopted in accordance with the examination procedure referred to in Article 87(2).

Conclusion

28.07   The frequency of change in social networking and new ways to collect and process new categories of personal data during social networking activities means that the mechanics of complying with access requests will have to continually evolve. There is also an issue remaining with certain social networks currently as to whether they are fully or only partially compliant in terms of responding to data access requests.

Chapter 29

Jurisdiction, Internet Service Provider and Social Networks

Introduction

29.01 One of the developing and more contentious areas of internet liability relates to issues of service provider liability. There is a claim often advanced by some service providers, that they are not liable to the EU data protection regime if the companies and or parent companies are located in the US. Effectively, they are claiming to be exempt from having to comply with EU law in relation to EU citizens in Europe, and the personal data of those citizens. Other companies, however, are happy to indicate a willingness to comply with EU data protection rules. Facebook, for example, indicated that Facebook in Dublin is responsible for Facebook privacy and data protection in Europe and elsewhere (apart from the US and Canada). This position is not universal with other multinationals however.

DPA: Jurisdiction

29.02 Section 15 of the DPA refers to jurisdiction and procedure. Section 15(1) provides that the jurisdiction conferred by ss 7 to 14 is exercisable by the High Court or a county court or, in Scotland, by the Court of Session or the sheriff. Section 15(2) provides that for the purpose of determining any question whether an applicant under sub-s (9) of s 7 is entitled to the information which he seeks (including any question whether any relevant data are exempt from that section by virtue of Part IV) a court may require the information constituting any data processed by or on behalf of the data controller and any information as to the logic involved in any decision-taking as mentioned in s 7(1)(d) to be made available for its own inspection but shall not, pending the determination of that question in the applicant's favour, require the information sought by the applicant to be disclosed to them or his representatives whether by discovery (or, in Scotland, recovery) or otherwise. Certain internet companies, however, seek to avoid liability to the UK and EU data protection regimes by segregating services and seeking to suggest that the entire service and surrounding infrastructure is located outside of the UK and EU. These are ongoing issues of contention. There is a Spanish case being referred to the ECJ relating to some of these multinational arguments (see below).

DPD95: Member States/Jurisdiction

29.03 DPD95 Recital 18 states that in order to ensure that individuals are *not deprived of the protection to which they are entitled under the DPD95*, any processing of personal data in the EU must be carried out in accordance with the law of one of the Member States (emphasis added). In this connection, processing carried out under the responsibility of a data controller who is established in a Member State should be governed by the law of that State. This is where certain internet multinationals take issue. They seek to argue that a particular segregated service or activity is not located or undertaken in the EU, notwithstanding that it involves UK citizens, UK personal data, the activities of UK citizens located in the UK and personal data collected in the UK. If there are ongoing services or activities these are also used and operated by UK citizens in the UK. Yet, certain internet multinationals would claim to be exempted from EU data protection, service provider and content liability rules in the UK, Ireland and EU.

DPD95 Recital 19 states that establishment on the territory of a Member State implies the effective and real exercise of activity through stable arrangements; whereas the legal form of such an establishment, whether simply branch or a subsidiary with a legal personality, is not the determining factor in this respect. When a single data controller is established on the territory of several Member States, particularly by means of subsidiaries, they must ensure, in order to avoid any circumvention of national rules, that each of the establishments fulfils the obligations imposed by the national law applicable to its activities.

Some internet multinationals argue that a segregated service is operated by a segregated legal entity which is not an "establishment on the territory of a Member State." This seeks to ignore that the core nexus of the data subject, the personal data, the collection, the use and activity by the individual are all UK/EU related. As indicated above, these are issues which are being litigated and disputed contentiously at present.

In addition, it is noted that there are ongoing development which, at the time of writing, indicates that EU data protection regulators have found that Google is in breach of EU data protection law in its unilaterally changed privacy policies in March 2011.[1] This change occurred despite EU regulators officially requesting Google to delay the go-live of the new policy pending an official examination and review. Google refused to comply. This will be an interesting, as well as an important, issue to watch as it develops.

DPR: Recitals and Social Networking

Location/Jurisdiction/Processing

29.04 Recital 19 states that any processing of personal data in the context of the activities of an establishment of a data controller or a data processor in the EU should be carried out in accordance with the Regulation, *regardless of whether the processing itself takes place within the EU or not.* Establishment implies the effective and real exercise of activity through stable arrangements. The legal form of such arrangements, whether through a branch or a subsidiary with a legal personality, is not the determining factor in this respect (emphasis added).

This reiterates, if that was needed, that EU citizens and the personal data of EU citizens must be respected and UK/EU laws complied with. Similarly, the following Recitals also enhance this position.

Recital 20 states that in order to *ensure that individuals are not deprived of the protection* to which they are entitled under the Regulation, the processing of personal data of data subjects residing in the EU by a data controller *not established in the EU should be subject to the DPR* where the processing activities are related to the offering of goods or services to such data subjects, or to the monitoring of the behaviour of such data subjects (emphasis added).

Establishment

29.05 Recital 27 states that the main establishment of a data controller in the EU should be determined according to objective criteria and

---

1   See, for example, Pancevski, B. and Duke, S., 'Google to Face Legal Threats, The Internet Giant May Be Forced to Pay Compensation for Breach of Privacy Law,' *Sunday Times*, 14 October 2012; Arthur, C., 'Google's privacy policy: EU data protection chiefs "to act within days EU data protection commissioners are believed to have determined that pooling of data by Google breaches privacy laws,' *Guardian*, 8 October, 2012.

should imply the effective and real exercise of management activities determining the main decisions as to the purposes, conditions and means of processing through stable arrangements. This criterion should not depend whether the processing of personal data is actually carried out at that location; the presence and use of technical means and technologies for processing personal data or processing activities *do not*, in themselves, constitute such main establishment and are therefore not determining criteria for a main establishment. The main establishment of the data processor should be the place of its central administration in the EU.

Group Companies

29.06 Recital 28 states that a group of undertakings should cover a controlling undertaking and its controlled undertakings, whereby the controlling undertaking should be the undertaking which can exercise a dominant influence over the other undertakings by virtue, for example, of ownership, financial participation or the rules which govern it or the power to have personal data protection rules implemented.

Third Country Data Controllers Must Appoint Representative in EU

29.07 Recital 63 states that where a data controller not established in the EU is processing personal data of data subjects residing in the EU whose processing activities are related to the offering of goods or services to such data subjects, or to the monitoring of their behaviour, the data controller should designate a representative, unless the data controller is established in a third country ensuring an adequate level of protection, or the data controller is a small or medium sized enterprise or a public authority or body or where the data controller is only occasionally offering goods or services to such data subjects. The representative should act on behalf of the data controller and may be addressed by any Supervisory Authority.

Recital 64 states that in order to determine whether a data controller is only occasionally offering goods and services to data subjects residing in the EU, it should be ascertained whether it is apparent from the data controller's overall activities that the offering of goods and services to such data subjects is ancillary to those main activities.

Public International Law

29.08 Recital 22 states that where the national law of a Member State applies by virtue of public international law, the Regulation should also apply to a data controller not established in the EU, such as in a Member State's diplomatic mission or consular post.

DPR Covers Social Networking

29.09   In the DPR, 'main establishment' is defined to mean as regards the data controller, the place of its establishment in the EU where the main decisions as to the purposes, conditions and means of the processing of personal data are taken. If no decisions as to the purposes, conditions and means of the processing of personal data are taken in the EU, the main establishment is the place where the main processing activities in the context of the activities of an establishment of a data controller in the EU take place. As regards the data processor, 'main establishment' means the place of its central administration in the EU.

In the DPR also the concept of 'representative' is defined to mean any natural or legal person established in the EU who, explicitly designated by the data controller, acts and may be addressed by any Supervisory Authority and other bodies in the EU instead of the data controller, with regard to the obligations of the data controller under the DPR.

DPR Recital 19 states that any processing of personal data in the context of the activities of an establishment of a data controller or a data processor in the EU should be carried out in accordance with the Regulation, *regardless* of whether the processing itself takes place within the EU or not. (Emphasis added). Establishment implies the effective and real exercise of activity through stable arrangements. The legal form of such arrangements, whether through a branch or a subsidiary with a legal personality, is not the determining factor in this respect.

DPR Recital 20 states that in order to *ensure that individuals are not deprived of the protection* to which they are entitled under the Regulation, the processing of personal data of data subjects residing in the EU by a data controller not established in the EU should be subject to the DPR where the processing activities are related to the offering of goods or services to such data subjects, or to the monitoring of the behaviour of such data subjects. (Emphasis added).

DPR Recital 27 states that the main establishment of a data controller in the EU should be determined according to objective criteria and should imply the effective and real exercise of management activities determining the main decisions as to the purposes, conditions and means of processing through stable arrangements. This criterion should not depend whether the processing of personal data is actually carried out at that location; the presence and use of technical means and technologies for processing personal data or processing activities do not, in themselves, constitute such main establishment and are therefore no determining criteria for a main establishment. The main establishment of the data processor should be the place of its central administration in the EU.

Third country data controllers must appoint a Representative in EU. DPR Recital 63 states that where a data controller not established in the EU is processing personal data of data subjects residing in the EU whose processing activities are related to the offering of goods or services to such data subjects, or to the monitoring their behaviour, the data controller should designate a representative, unless the data controller is established in a third country ensuring an adequate level of protection, or the data controller is a small or medium sized enterprise or a public authority or body or where the data controller is only occasionally offering goods or services to such data subjects. The representative should act on behalf of the data controller and may be addressed by any Supervisory Authority. DPR Recital 64 also states that in order to determine whether a data controller is only occasionally offering goods and services to data subjects residing in the EU, it should be ascertained whether it is apparent from the data controller's overall activities that the offering of goods and services to such data subjects is ancillary to those main activities.

It is also noted that there is no exception made in the DPR for UGC or user generated content.

Article 3 of the DPR provides that:

- The DPR applies to the processing of personal data in the context of the activities of an establishment of a data controller or a processor in the EU;
- The DPR applies to the processing of personal data of data subjects residing in the EU by a data controller not established in the EU, where the processing activities are related to:
  - the offering of goods or services to such data subjects in the EU; or
  - the monitoring of their behaviour;
- The DPR applies to the processing of personal data by a controller not established in the EU, but in a place where the national law of a Member State applies by virtue of public international law.

ECJ and Spanish Case

29.10 An important case may be *Google Spain and Google Case* C-131/12 in the ECJ. This is a reference for a preliminary ruling from the Audiencia Nacional (Spain).

It specifically relates to the following:

- Interpretation of Arts 2(b) and (d), 4(1)(a) and (c), 12(b) and 14(a) of DPD95; and
- Art. 8 of the Charter of Fundamental Rights of the European Union (OJ 2000 C 364, p. 1);
- Concept of establishment on the territory of a Member State;
- Relevant criteria;
- Concept of 'use of equipment ... situated on the territory of a Member State';
- Temporary storage of information indexed by internet search engines;
- Right to erasure and blocking of data.

The answers to some of these questions may have potentially important implications for online business models as well as the rights of UK citizens. However, one might argue that the answers may have been partly answered by the provisions and confirmations of the DPR.

Google

29.11   Just to take a recent example of an internet multinational. In March 2012 Google combined over 60 separate and discrete products and services of Google (and other companies and brand names). Data protection authorities of the EU, as well as elsewhere around the world (including officials in the US), requested Google not to go-ahead or in the case of the EU, to delay it until officials could consider it further. Google refused.

The EU data protection authorities, under WP29 and the French data protection authority (CNIL) carried out an investigation of the new privacy policy and its implications. In *WP29 and Data Protection Authorities/Google*[2] it found various breaches and problems with the new policy. Google has been required to change the policy as well as to develop new tools for users and their personal data.

As regards jurisdictional issues the above WP29 complaint on the Google policy notes and confirms that EU data protection law applies to G (see WP29 Appendix, para 1, page 2). Footnote 1 to the complaint notes that the Google EU headquarters is located in Dublin, Ireland. It

---

2   See WP29 Letter to Google:http://www.cnil.fr/fileadmin/documents/en/20121016-letter_google-article_29-FINAL.pdf; Appendix: http://www.cnil.fr/fileadmin/documents/en/GOOGLE_PRIVACY_POLICY-_RECOMMENDATIONS-FINAL-EN.pdf; French DP regulator (CNIL) statement: http://www.cnil.fr/english/news-and-events/news/article/googles-new-privacy-policy-incomplete-information-and-uncontrolled-combination-of-data-across-ser/, respectively accesses on 18 January 2013.

further notes that Google companies are located in the EU, such as in the UK, Ireland, and France. Footnote 1 also notes that Google uses computer servers in the EU, such as in Belgium and Finland. (Google just opened another major data centre in Dublin, Ireland). It seems clear, therefore, EU law and jurisdiction could apply to Google and these products and services.

Recall also the DPD95 also refers to jurisdiction issues. It states,

'Article 4

National law applicable

1. Each Member State shall apply the national provisions it adopts pursuant to the Directive to the processing of personal data where:

(a) the processing is carried out in the context of the activities of an establishment of the controller on the territory of the Member State; when the same controller is established on the territory of several Member States, he must take the necessary measures to ensure that each of these establishments complies with the obligations laid down by the national law applicable;

(b) the controller is not established on the Member State's territory, but in a place where its national law applies by virtue of international public law;

(c) the controller is not established on EU territory and, for purposes of processing personal data makes use of equipment, automated or otherwise, situated on the territory of the said Member State, unless such equipment is used only for purposes of transit through the territory of the EU.

2. In the circumstances referred to in paragraph 1 (c), the controller must designate a representative established in the territory of that Member State, without prejudice to legal actions which could be initiated against the controller himself.'

Some non-EU entities will sometimes argue not as they are non-in EU and or are US based, they do not have to comply with EU data protection law – even despite having millions of users and customers in Europe. It is worth considering (c) above. DPD95 states that EU law applies if the service provider uses equipment in the EU. WP29 above confirms Google, for example, uses servers in EU. Google also has a new data centre in Dublin. So we can see that 1(c) above applies. Therefore, EU law and jurisdiction apply to Google and its related products and services. In any event, Google has various legal entities in the EU, so EU law would in any event applies.

Conclusion

29.12 These issues are critically important, given the number of UK citizens using the internet and social networks in particular. Yet, many will be unfamiliar with these issues given that they are often overlooked in general summaries of data protection law. General compliance and data loss/data breach incidents are more frequently highlighted instead. However, increasingly users are becoming aware of their rights, including access rights.

Chapter 30

Privacy by Design

Introduction

30.01 It has been suggested that 'law should play a more active role in establishing best practices for emerging online trends.'[1] Privacy by design is a prime example. One of the most important and developing practical areas of data protection is the concept of privacy by design or PbD or data protection by design (DPbD) as referred to in the Regulation. Originally developed as a follow on from the data protection legal regime, it is now being recognised more widely, and is also being explicitly referred to and recognised in primary legislation itself.

Background

30.02 The concept of PbD is complementary to data protection law and regulation. The idea is acknowledged to start with Dr. Ann Cavoukian, the Information & Privacy Commissioner for Ontario, Canada. She states that,

> 'the increasing complexity and interconnectedness of information technologies [requires] building privacy right into system design ... the concept of Privacy by Design (PbD), ... describe[s] the philosophy of embedding privacy proactively into technology itself – making it the default.'[2]

---

1   McGeveran, W., 'Disclosure, Endorsement, and Identity in Social marketing,' *Illinois Law Review* (2009)(4), PP. 1105–1166, at 1105.
2   Available at http://privacybydesign.ca/about/, accessed on 18 January 2013.

Principles of PbD

30.03 The Information & Privacy Commissioner for Ontario refers to seven principles of PbD.[3] These are set out below.

1 Proactive not Reactive; Preventative not Remedial
The Privacy by Design (PbD) approach is characterised by proactive rather than reactive measures. It anticipates and prevents privacy invasive events before they happen. PbD does not wait for privacy risks to materialise, nor does it offer remedies for resolving privacy infractions once they have occurred – it aims to prevent them from occurring. In short, Privacy by Design comes before-the-fact, not after.

2 Privacy as the Default Setting
We can all be certain of one thing – the default rules Privacy by Design seeks to deliver the maximum degree of privacy by ensuring that personal data are automatically protected in any given IT system or business practice. If an individual does nothing, their privacy still remains intact. No action is required on the part of the individual to protect their privacy – it is built into the system, by default.

3 Privacy Embedded into Design
Privacy by Design is embedded into the design and architecture of IT systems and business practices. It is not bolted on as an add-on, after the fact. The result is that privacy becomes an essential component of the core functionality being delivered. Privacy is integral to the system, without diminishing functionality.

4 Full Functionality – Positive-Sum, not Zero-Sum
Privacy by Design seeks to accommodate all legitimate interests and objectives in a positive-sum "win-win" manner, not through a dated, zero-sum approach, where unnecessary trade-offs are made. Privacy by Design avoids the pretence of false dichotomies, such as privacy vs. security, demonstrating that it is possible to have both.

5 End-to-End Security – Full Lifecycle Protection
Privacy by Design, having been embedded into the system prior to the first element of information being collected, extends securely throughout the entire lifecycle of the data involved – strong security measures are essential to privacy, from start to finish. This ensures that all data are securely retained, and then securely destroyed at the end of the process, in a timely fashion. Thus,

---

3 Available at http://www.privacybydesign.ca/content/uploads/2009/08/7foundational principles.pdf, accessed on 18 January 2013.

Privacy by Design ensures cradle to grave, secure lifecycle management of information, end-to-end.
6   Visibility and Transparency – Keep it Open
     Privacy by Design seeks to assure all stakeholders that whatever the business practice or technology involved, it is in fact, operating according to the stated promises and objectives, subject to independent verification. Its component parts and operations remain visible and transparent, to users and providers alike. Remember, trust but verify.
7   Respect for User Privacy – Keep it User-Centric
     Above all, Privacy by Design requires architects and operators to keep the interests of the individual uppermost by offering such measures as strong privacy defaults, appropriate notice, and empowering user-friendly options. Keep it user-centric.[4]

DPD95

30.04   DPD95 Recital 46 states that whereas the protection of the rights and freedoms of data subjects with regard to the processing of personal data requires that appropriate technical and organisational measures be taken, both at the time of the design of the processing system and at the time of the processing itself, particularly in order to maintain security and thereby to prevent any unauthorised processing; whereas it is incumbent on the Member States to ensure that data controllers comply with these measures; whereas these measures must ensure an appropriate level of security, taking into account the state of the art and the costs of their implementation in relation to the risks inherent in the processing and the nature of the data to be protected.

Specific Processing Risks

DPD95 Recital 53 states that whereas, however, certain processing operation are likely to pose specific risks to the rights and freedoms of data subjects by virtue of their nature, their scope or their purposes, such as that of excluding individuals from a right, benefit or a contract, or by virtue of the *specific use of new technologies*; whereas it is for Member States, if they so wish, to specify such risks in their legislation.

DPD95 Recital 54 states that whereas with regard to all the processing undertaken in society, the amount posing such specific risks should

---

4   Available at http://www.privacybydesign.ca/content/uploads/2009/08/7foundational principles.pdf, accessed on 18 January 2013.

be very limited; whereas Member States must provide that the Supervisory Authority, or the data protection official in cooperation with the authority, check such processing prior to it being carried out; whereas following this prior check, the Supervisory Authority may, according to its national law, give an opinion or an authorisation regarding the processing; whereas such checking may equally take place in the course of the preparation either of a measure of the national parliament or of a measure based on such a legislative measure, which defines the nature of the processing and lays down appropriate safeguards.

DPR: Data Protection by Design (DPbD)

30.05 The Commission proposed an enhanced data protection regime including PbD.[5] Article 23 of the DPR refers to data protection by design and by default. This is an increasingly important area in data protection.

Article 23(1) introduces this topic by saying that having regard to the state of the art and the cost of implementation, the data controller shall, both at the time of the determination of the means for processing and at the time of the processing itself, implement appropriate technical and organisational measures and procedures in such a way that the processing will meet the requirements of the DPR and ensure the protection of the rights of the data subject.

Under Article 23(2), it is provided that the data controller shall implement mechanisms for ensuring that, by default, only those personal data are processed which are necessary for each specific purpose of the processing and are especially not collected or retained beyond the minimum necessary for those purposes, both in terms of the amount of the data and the time of their storage. In particular, those mechanisms shall ensure that by default personal data are not made accessible to an indefinite number of individuals (Article 23(2)).

In addition, under Article 23(3), the Commission is empowered to adopt delegated acts in accordance with Article 86 for the purpose of specifying any further criteria and requirements for appropriate measures and mechanisms referred to in paragraph 1 and 2, in particular for data protection by design requirements applicable across sectors, products and services.

---

5   See DPR, Spiekermann, S., "The Challenges of Privacy by Design,' *Communications of the ACM* (2012)(55), pp. 38–40; Spiekermann, S., and Cranor, L.F., 'Engineering Privacy,' *IEEE Transactions on Software Engineering* (2009)(35), pp. 67–82.

Furthermore, Under Article 23(4) the Commission is also empowered to lay down technical standards for the requirements laid down in paragraph 1 and 2. Those implementing acts shall be adopted in accordance with the examination procedure referred to in Article 87(2) (Article 23(4)).

ICO

30.06   PbD is embraced by the ICO in the UK. The ICO refers to PbD by saying that 'Privacy by Design is an approach whereby privacy and data protection compliance is designed into systems holding information right from the start, rather than being bolted on afterwards or ignored, as has too often been the case.'[6]

It provides[7] the following documents and guidance:

- Privacy by Design report;[8]
- Privacy by Design implementation plan;[9]
- Privacy Impact Assessment (PIA) handbook;[10]
- ICO technical guidance note on Privacy Enhancing Tecnologies (PETs);[11]
- Enterprise Privacy Group paper on PETs;
- HIDE (Homeland security, biometric Identification and personal Detection Ethics);
- Glossary of privacy and data protection terms;
- Privacy Impact Assessments – international study (Loughborough University).

---

6   ICO website, available at http://www.ico.gov.uk/for_organisations/data_protection/topic_guides/privacy_by_design.aspx, accessed on 18 January 2013.

7   *Ibid.*

8   *Privacy by Design*, Information Commissioner's Office (2008). Available at http://www.ico.gov.uk/for_organisations/data_protection/topic_guides/privacy_by_design.aspx, accessed on 18 January 2013.

9   Available at http://www.ico.gov.uk/upload/documents/pdb_report_html/pbd_ico_implementation_plan.pdf, accessed on 18 January 2013.

10   Available at http://www.ico.gov.uk/for_organisations/data_protection/topic_guides/privacy_impact_assessment.aspx, accessed on 18 January 2013.

11   *Privacy by Design, An Overview of Privacy Enhancing Technologies*, 26 November, 2008. Available at http://www.ico.gov.uk/for_organisations/data_protection/topic_guides/privacy_by_design.aspx, last accessed on 18 January 2013.

Privacy by Design Report

30.07 The ICO report on Privacy by design was launched in November 2008. The Commission in the Foreword notes that,

'The capacity of organisations to acquire and use our personal details has increased dramatically since our data protection laws were first passed. There is an ever increasing amount of personal information collected and held about us as we go about our daily lives ... we have seen a dramatic change in the capability of organisations to exploit modern technology that uses our information to deliver services, this has not been accompanied by a similar drive to develop new effective technical and procedural privacy safeguards. We have seen how vulnerable our most personal of details can be and these should not be put at risk.'[12]

In the report, Toby Stevens, Director, of the Enterprise Privacy Group, adds that,

'This report is the first stage in bridging the current gap in the development and adoption of privacy-friendly solutions as part of modern information systems. It aims to address the current problems related to the handling of personal information and put into place a model for privacy by design that will ensure privacy achieves the same structured and professional recognition as information security has today.'[13]

The report describes PbD as follows,

'The purpose of privacy by design is to give due consideration to privacy needs prior to the development of new initiatives – in other words, to consider the impact of a system or process on individuals' privacy and to do this throughout the systems lifecycle, thus ensuring that appropriate controls are implemented and maintained.'[14]

The report refers to the various lifecycles that arise in an organisation.[15] These can be products, services, systems and processes.

'For a privacy by design approach to be effective, it must take into account the full lifecycle of any system or process, from the earliest stages of the system business case, through requirements gathering and design, to delivery, testing, operations, and out to the final decommissioning of the system.

---

12 *Privacy by Design*, Information Commissioner's Office (2008). Available at http://www.ico.gov.uk/for_organisations/data_protection/topic_guides/privacy_by_design.aspx, accessed on 18 January 2013.
13 *Ibid*, p. 2.
14 *Ibid*, p. 7.
15 *Ibid*.

This lifetime approach ensures that privacy controls are stronger, simpler and therefore cheaper to implement, harder to by-pass, and fully embedded in the system as part of its core functionality.

However, neither current design practices in the private and public sectors, nor existing tools tend to readily support such an approach. Current privacy practices and technologies are geared towards 'spot' implementations and 'spot' verifications to confirm that privacy designs and practices are correct at a given moment within a given scope of inspection.'[16]

ICO Recommendations

30.08 The ICO report makes a number of recommendations in relation to PbD practice in the UK.[17] These are set out below.

'Working with industry bodies to build an **executive mandate for privacy by design**, supported by sample business cases for the costs, benefits and risks associated with the processing of personal information, and promotion of executive awareness of key privacy and identity concepts so that privacy is reflected in the business cases for new systems.

Encouraging widespread use of **privacy impact assessments throughout the systems lifecycle**, and ensuring that these assessments are both maintained and published where appropriate to demonstrate transparency of privacy controls.

Supporting the development of **cross-sector standards for data sharing** both within and between organisations, so that privacy needs are harmonised with the pressures on public authorities and private organisations to share personal information.

Nurturing the development of **practical privacy standards** that will help organisations to turn the legal outcomes mandated under data protection laws into consistent, provable privacy implementations.

Promoting current and future research into PETs that deliver commercial products to manage consent and revocation, privacy-friendly identification and authentication, and prove the effectiveness of privacy controls.

Establishing more rigorous compliance and enforcement mechanisms by assigning responsibility for privacy management within organisations to nominated individuals, urging organisations to demonstrate greater clarity in their personal information processing, and empowering and providing the ICO with the ability to investigate and enforce compliance where required.

---

16 *Privacy by Design*, Information Commissioner's Office (2008). Available at http://www.ico.gov.uk/for_organisations/data_protection/topic_guides/privacy_by_design.aspx, accessed on 18 January 2013, pp. 7–8.
17 *Ibid.*, summarised at p. 3, and in detail at pp. 22–31.

The government, key industry representatives and academics, and the ICO are urged to consider, prioritise and set in motion plans to deliver these recommendations and hence make privacy by design a reality.'[18]

The report highlights the need and context for PbD in relation to the many instances of data loss in the UK (and internationally). It states that,

'Consumer trust in the ability of public authorities and private organisations to manage personal information is at an all-time low ebb. A stream of high-profile privacy incidents in the UK over the past year has shaken confidence in the data sharing agenda for government with associated impacts on high-profile data management programmes, and businesses are having to work that much harder to persuade customers to release personal information to them.'[19]

PbD is part of the solution whereby 'the evolution of a new approach to the management of personal information that ingrains privacy principles into every part of every system in every organisation.'[20]

Organisations need to address many key privacy and data protection issues, such as

'assessing information risks from the individual's perspective; adopting transparency and data minimisation principles; exploiting opportunities for differentiation through enhanced privacy practices; and ensuring that privacy needs influence their identity management agenda (since identity technologies are invariably needed to deliver effective privacy approaches).'[21]

Google

30.09 In March 2012 Google rolled out a major privacy policy change regarding users' personal data. It decided to combine the policies for over 60 separate and discrete products and services of Google (and other companies and brand names).

---

18   *Ibid*, note emphasis in original.
19   *Privacy by Design*, Information Commissioner's Office (2008). Available at http://www.ico.gov.uk/for_organisations/data_protection/topic_guides/privacy_by_design.aspx, accessed on 18 January 2013, p. 6.
20   *Ibid*.
21   *Ibid*.

The data protection authorities of the EU, as well as elsewhere around the world (including various officials in the US), requested Google to not go-ahead or in the case of the EU, to delay it until officials could consider it further.

The EU data protection authorities, under WP29 and the French data protection authority (CNIL) carried out an investigation of the new privacy policy and its implications. In *WP29 and Data Protection Authorities/Google*[22] the new Google policy change was found to be in breach of data protection law. Various changes are required. However, one of these included that Google incorporate the policy of Privacy by Design (PbD) into its products and services.

Conclusion

30.10   PbD is one of the more important innovations in data protection generally. This is reflected in the DPR. All organisations will need to appraise themselves of the concept and the regulatory compliance issues. The above Google requirement to implement PbD is also timely and reflects the importance that enterprise, both large and small, needs to engage the benefits, as well as the requirements, of PbD.

Privacy impact assessments[23] are also referred to in the DPR and may also be relevant in the context of PbD. PbD, privacy impact assessments are also relevant in the context of developing cloud services.[24] Cloud services also raise important data protection and

---

22   See WP29 Letter to Google: http://www.cnil.fr/fileadmin/documents/en/20121016-letter_google-article_29-FINAL.pdf;   Appendix: http://www.cnil.fr/fileadmin/documents/en/GOOGLE_PRIVACY_POLICY-_RECOMMENDATIONS-FINAL-EN.pdf; French DP regulator (CNIL) statement: http://www.cnil.fr/english/news-and-events/news/article/googles-new-privacy-policy-incomplete-information-and-uncontrolled-combination-of-data-across-ser/, respectively accesses on 18 January 2013.

23   Wright, D., "The State of the Art in Privacy Impact Assessments," *Computer Law & Security Review* (2012)(28), pp. 54–61.

24   Cloud and data protection reliability and compliance issues are referred to Clarke R., "How Reliable is Cloudsourcing? A Review of Articles in the Technical Media 2005–11," *Computer Law & Security Review* (2012)(28), pp. 90–95. Kind and Rajy also research the area of the protections of sensitive personal data and cloud computing, see King, N.J., and Raja, V.T., "Protecting the Privacy and Security of Sensitive Customer Data in the Cloud," *Computer Law & Security Review* (2012)(28), pp. 308–319.

security considerations and these should be carefully considered by customers as well as providers.[25]

---

25 See, for example ICO, *Guidance on the Use of Cloud Computing*, available at http://www.ico.gov.uk/for_organisations/data_protection/topic_guides/online/cloud_computing.aspx, accessed on 18 January 2013; Article 29 Working Party, *Opinion 05/2012 on Cloud Computing*, WP 196, 1 July 2012; Lanois, P., 'Caught in the Clouds: The Web 2.0, Cloud Computing, and Privacy?,' *Northwestern Journal of Technology and Intellectual Property* (2010)(9), pp. 29–49; Pinguelo, F.M., and Muller, B.W., 'Avoid the Rainy Day: Survey of US Cloud Computing Caselaw,' *Boston College Intellectual Property & Technology Forum* (2011), 1–7; Kattan, I.R., 'Cloudy Privacy Protections: Why the Stored Communications Act Fails to Protect the Privacy of Communications Stored in the Cloud," *Vandenburg Journal of Entertainment and Technology Law* (2010–2011)(13), pp. 617–656.

Chapter 31

Leveson, the Press and Data Protection

Introduction

31.01 The UK Leveson Report deals with (certain) data protection issues in detail, namely the recommendations relating to data protection and journalism. The evidence and issues are more fully described in Part H, 5 of the actual Report.

Section 32 UK DPA

31.02 The current s 32 of the UK DPA 1998 refers to journalism activities. It provides

> "(1) Personal data which are processed only for the special purposes are exempt from any provision to which this subsection relates if—
>
> (a) the processing is undertaken with a view to the publication by any person of any journalistic, literary or artistic material,
>
> (b) the data controller reasonably believes that, having regard in particular to the special importance of the public interest in freedom of expression, publication would be in the public interest, and
>
> (c) the data controller reasonably believes that, in all the circumstances, compliance with that provision is incompatible with the special purposes.
>
> (2) Subsection (1) relates to the provisions of—
>
> (a) the data protection principles except the seventh data protection principle,
>
> (b) section 7,
>
> (c) section 10,
>
> (d) section 12, and
>
> (e) section 14(1) to (3).
>
> (3) In considering for the purposes of subsection (1)(b) whether the belief of a data controller that publication would be in the public interest was

or is a reasonable one, regard may be had to his compliance with any code of practice which—

(a) is relevant to the publication in question, and

(b) is designated by the [Secretary of State] by order for the purposes of this subsection.

(4) Where at any time ('the relevant time') in any proceedings against a data controller under section 7(9), 10(4), 12(8) or 14 or by virtue of section 13 the data controller claims, or it appears to the court, that any personal data to which the proceedings relate are being processed—

(a) only for the special purposes, and

(b) with a view to the publication by any person of any journalistic, literary or artistic material which, at the time twenty-four hours immediately before the relevant time, had not previously been published by the data controller,

the court shall stay the proceedings until either of the conditions in subsection (5) is met.

(5) Those conditions are—

(a) that a determination of the Commissioner under section 45 with respect to the data in question takes effect, or

(b) in a case where the proceedings were stayed on the making of a claim, that the claim is withdrawn.

(6) For the purposes of this Act 'publish', in relation to journalistic, literary or artistic material, means make available to the public or any section of the public."

Lord Lester of Herne Hill is referred to in the Report (p 1067) as having "warned at length that, as drafted and because of cl 31, the DPA failed to implement the Directive and authorised interference by the press with the right to privacy in breach of Art 8 of the ECHR."

At page 1068 of the Report, it refers to,

"Mr Coppel's arguments ... would be that on the current state of the UK authorities, s32 fails to implement the Directive from which it derives, and is inconsistent with the relevant parts of the ECHR to which it is intended to give effect, because the relationship between privacy and expression rights has got out of balance. A proper balance is a fundamental obligation. The UK is therefore positively *required* to change the law to restore the balance. That is indeed Mr Coppel's own contention: that UK data protection law currently fails to implement our obligations, and that Lord Lester's concerns had proved to be prescient."

The Report itself then states,

"2.11 Without going so far as that, even if the current balance were within the spectrum permitted by our international obligations, the argument could be expressed in terms that it is at an extreme end of that spectrum, and the UK can as a matter of law, and should as a matter of policy, restore a more even-handed approach, not least given the asymmetry of risks and harms as between the individual and the press.

2.12 Put at its very lowest, the point could be made that the effect of the development of the case law has been to push personal privacy law in media cases out of the data protection regime and into the more open seas of the Human Rights Act. This has happened for no better reason than the slowness of the legal profession to assimilate data protection law and, in the case of the judiciary, its greater familiarity with (and, he suggests, perhaps a preference for) the latitude afforded by the human rights regime over the specificity of data protection. But this, the argument goes, is undesirable because the data protection regime is much more predictable, detailed and sophisticated in the way it protects and balances rights, and significantly reduces the risks, uncertainties and expense of litigation concomitant on more open-textured law dependent on a court's discretion. Where the law has provided specific answers, the fine-nibbed pen should be grasped and not the broad brush. The balancing of competing rights in a free democracy is a highly sophisticated exercise; appropriate tools have been provided for the job and should be used."

Leveson Recommendations to the Ministry of Justice

31.03   The Leveson Report makes the following recommendations, namely,

"48. The exemption in section 32 of the Data Protection Act 1998 should be amended so as to make it available only where:49 (a) the processing of data is necessary for publication, rather than simply being in fact undertaken with a view to publication; (b) the data controller reasonably believes that the relevant publication would be or is in the public interest, with no special weighting of the balance between the public interest in freedom of expression and in privacy; and (c) objectively, that the likely interference with privacy resulting from the processing of the data is outweighed by the public interest in publication.

49. The exemption in section 32 of the Data Protection Act 1998 should be narrowed in scope, so that it no longer allows, by itself, for exemption from:50 (a) the requirement of the first data protection principle to process personal data fairly (except in relation to the provision of information to the data subject under paragraph 2(1)(a) of Part II Schedule 1 to the 1998 Act) and in accordance with statute law; (b) the second data protection principle (personal data to be obtained only for specific purposes and not processed incompatibly with those purposes); (c) the fourth data protection principle (personal data to be accurate and kept up to date); (d) the sixth data protection principle (personal data to be processed in accordance with the rights of individuals under the Act); (e) the eighth data protection principle (restrictions on exporting personal data); and (f) the right of subject access.

The recommendation on the removal of the right of subject access from the scope of section 32 is subject to any necessary clarification that the law relating to the protection of journalists' sources is not affected by the Act.

50. It should be made clear that the right to compensation for distress conferred by section 13 of the Data Protection Act 1998 is not restricted to cases of pecuniary loss, but should include compensation for pure distress.

51. The procedural provisions of the Data Protection Act 1998 with special application to journalism in: (a) section 32(4) and (5) (b) sections 44 to 46 inclusive should be repealed.52

51. In conjunction with the repeal of those procedural provisions, consideration should be given to the desirability of including in the Data Protection Act 1998 a provision to the effect that, in considering the exercise of any powers in relation to the media or other publishers, the Information Commissioner's Office should have special regard to the obligation in law to balance the public interest in freedom of expression alongside the public interest in upholding the data protection regime.

53. Specific provision should be made to the effect that, in considering the exercise of any of its powers in relation to the media or other publishers, the Information Commissioner's Office must have regard to the application to a data controller of any relevant system of regulation or standards enforcement which is contained in or recognised by statute.

54. The necessary steps should be taken to bring into force the amendments made to section 55 of the Data Protection Act 1998 by section 77 of the Criminal Justice and Immigration Act 2008 (increase of sentence maxima) to the extent of the maximum specified period; and by section 78 of the 2008 Act (enhanced defence for public interest journalism).

55. The prosecution powers of the Information Commissioner should be extended to include any offence which also constitutes a breach of the data protection principles.

56. A new duty should be introduced (whether formal or informal) for the Information Commissioner's Office to consult with the Crown Prosecution Service in relation to the exercise of its powers to undertake criminal proceedings.

57. The opportunity should be taken to consider amending the Data Protection Act 1998 formally to reconstitute the Information Commissioner's Office as an Information Commission, led by a Board of Commissioners with suitable expertise drawn from the worlds of regulation, public administration, law and business, and active consideration should be given in that context to the desirability of including on the Board a Commissioner from the media sector."

Recommendations to the Information Commissioner

31.04   The Leveson Report also makes recommendation to the ICO. These are,

"58. The Information Commissioner's Office should take immediate steps to prepare, adopt and publish a policy on the exercise of its formal regulatory functions in order to ensure that the press complies with the legal requirements of the data protection regime.

59. In discharge of its functions and duties to promote good practice in areas of public concern, the Information Commissioner's Office should take immediate steps, in consultation with the industry, to prepare and issue comprehensive good practice guidelines and advice on appropriate principles and standards to be observed by the press in the processing of personal data. This should be prepared and implemented within six months from the date of this Report.

60. The Information Commissioner's Office should take steps to prepare and issue guidance to the public on their individual rights in relation to the obtaining and use by the press of their personal data, and how to exercise those rights.

61. In particular, the Information Commissioner's Office should take immediate steps to publish advice aimed at individuals (data subjects) concerned that their data have or may have been processed by the press unlawfully or otherwise than in accordance with good practice.

62. The Information Commissioner's Office, in the Annual Report to Parliament which it is required to make by virtue of section 52(1) of the Act, should include regular updates on the effectiveness of the foregoing measures, and on the culture, practices and ethics of the press in relation to the processing of personal data.

63. The Information Commissioner's Office should immediately adopt the Guidelines for Prosecutors on assessing the public interest in cases affecting the media, issued by the Director of Public Prosecutions in September 2012.

64. The Information Commissioner's Office should take immediate steps to engage with the Metropolitan Police on the preparation of a long-term strategy in relation to alleged media crime with a view to ensuring that the Office is well placed to fulfil any necessary role in this respect in the future, and in particular in the aftermath of Operations Weeting, Tuleta and Elveden.

65. The Information Commissioner's Office should take the opportunity to review the availability to it of specialist legal and practical knowledge of the application of the data protection regime to the press, and to any extent necessary address it.

66. The Information Commissioner's Office should take the opportunity to review its organisation and decision-making processes to ensure that large-scale issues, with both strategic and operational dimensions (including the relationship between the culture, practices and ethics of the press in relation to personal information on the one hand, and the application of the data protection regime to the press on the other) can be satisfactorily considered and addressed in the round."

Increased Sentencing for Data Breach

31.05 The Leveson Report also makes other law recommendations. These are,

"67. On the basis that the provisions of s77–78 of the Criminal Justice and Immigration Act 2008 are brought into effect, so that increased sentencing powers are available for breaches of s55 of the Data Protection Act 1998,68 the Secretary of State for Justice should use the power vested in him by s124(1)(a)(i) of the Coroners and Justice Act 2009 to invite the Sentencing Council of England and Wales to prepare guidelines in relation to data protection offences (including computer misuse)."

Comparison

31.06 A comparison of the DPA and the Leveson comments is set out below.

UK (s 32)	Leveson
(1) Personal data which are processed only for the special purposes are exempt from any provision to which this subsection relates if— (a) the processing is undertaken with a view to the publication by any person of any journalistic, literary or artistic material, (b) the data controller reasonably believes that, having regard in particular to the special importance of the public interest in freedom of expression, publication would be in the public interest, and (c) the data controller reasonably believes that, in	48 The exemption in s 32 of the Data Protection Act 1998 should be amended so as to make it available only where:(a) the processing of data is necessary for publication, rather than simply being in fact undertaken with a view to publication; (b) the data controller reasonably believes that the relevant publication would be or is in the public interest, with no special weighting of the balance between the public interest in freedom of expression and in privacy; and (c) objectively, that the likely interference with privacy resulting from the processing of the data is outweighed by the public interest in publication. 49 The exemption in s 32 of the Data Protection Act 1998 should be

all the circumstances, compliance with that provision is incompatible with the special purposes.	narrowed in scope, so that it no longer allows, by itself, for exemption from: (a) the requirement of the first data protection principle to process personal data fairly (except in relation to the provision of information to the data subject under paragraph 2(1)(a) of Part II Schedule 1 to the 1998 Act) and in accordance with statute law; (b) the second data protection principle (personal data to be obtained only for specific purposes and not processed incompatibly with those purposes); (c) the fourth data protection principle (personal data to be accurate and kept up to date); (d) the sixth data protection principle (personal data to be processed in accordance with the rights of individuals under the Act); (e) the eighth data protection principle (restrictions on exporting personal data); and (f) the right of subject access. The recommendation on the removal of the right of subject access from the scope of s 32 is subject to any necessary clarification that the law relating to the protection of journalists' sources is not affected by the Act.
(2) Sub-s (1) relates to the provisions of—	
(a) the data protection principles except the seventh data protection principle,	
(b) s 7,	
(c) s 10,	
(d) s 12, and	
(e) s 14(1) to (3).	
(3) In considering for the purposes of sub-s (1)(b) whether the belief of a data controller that publication would be in the public interest was or is a reasonable one, regard may be had to his compliance with any code of practice which—	
(a) is relevant to the publication in question, and	
(b) is designated by the[Secretary of State]by order for the purposes of this sub-section.	
(4) Where at any time ('the relevant time') in any proceedings against a data controller under s 7(9), 10(4), 12(8) or 14 or by virtue of s 13 the data controller claims, or it appears to the court, that any personal data to which the proceedings relate are being processed—	50 It should be made clear that the right to compensation for distress conferred by s 13 of the Data Protection Act 1998 is not restricted to cases of pecuniary loss, but should include compensation for pure distress.
(a) only for the special purposes, and	51 The procedural provisions of the Data Protection Act 1998 with special application to journalism in: (a) s 32(4) and (5); (b) ss 44 – 46 inclusive should be repealed.52
(b) with a view to the publication by any person of any journalistic, literary or artistic material which, at the time twenty-four hours immediately before the relevant time, had not previously been published by the data controller, the court shall stay the proceedings until either of the conditions in sub-s (5) is met.	51 In conjunction with the repeal of those procedural provisions, consideration should be given to the desirability of including in the Data Protection Act 1998 a provision to the effect that, in considering the exercise of any powers in relation to the media or other publishers, the Information Commissioner's Office should have special regard to the obligation in law to balance the public interest in freedom of expression alongside the
(5) Those conditions are—	
(a) that a determination of the Commissioner under s 45 with respect to the data in	

<table>
<tr>
<td>

          question takes effect, or
  (b) in a case where the
        proceedings were stayed on
        the making of a claim, that
        the claim is withdrawn.
(6) For the purposes of this Act
     'publish', in relation to
     journalistic, literary or artistic
     material, means make available to
     the public or any section of the
     public.

</td>
<td>

    public interest in upholding the data
    protection regime.
53 Specific provision should be made to the
    effect that, in considering the exercise of
    any of its powers in relation to the media
    or other publishers, the Information
    Commissioner's Office must have regard
    to the application to a data controller of
    any relevant system of regulation or
    standards enforcement which is con-
    tained in or recognised by statute.

</td>
</tr>
</table>

Conclusion

31.07 The recommendations of the Leveson Report appear to have been accepted at a political level in the UK. The exact nature of the amendments to be introduced remains to be finalised at the time of writing. It remains to be seen what effect this will have.

Appendices

Reference Links

Information Commissioner's Office:
http://www.ico.gov.uk/

Article 29 Working Party:
http://ec.europa.eu/justice/policies/privacy/workinggroup/index_en.htm

Society of Computers and Law:
http://www.scl.org

Legislative Links

Data Protection Act 1998:
http://www.legislation.gov.uk/ukpga/1998/29/contents

Data Protection Directive 1995:
http://eur-lex.europa.eu/LexUriServ/LexUriServ.do?uri=CELEX:
31995L0046:en:HTML

Proposed Data Protection Regulation:
http://ec.europa.eu/justice/data-protection/document/review2012/com_
2012_11_en.pdf

Forms and Document Links

ICO section on notifications:
http://www.ico.gov.uk/for_organisations/data_protection/notification.
aspx

Appendices

Notification Handbook, A Complete Guide, ICO:
http://www.ico.gov.uk/for_organisations/data_protection/notification.
aspx

Notification self assessment guides:
http://www.ico.gov.uk/for_organisations/data_protection/notification/
need_to_notify.aspx

ICO online notification form:
https://www.ico.gov.uk/onlinenotification/?page=7.html

Complying with Data Protection

All organisations collect and process at least some personal data as
defined under the DPA and the data protection regime. Therefore, an
organisation must ensure it only collects and processes personal data if
complying with:

- The obligation to only collect and process personal data if in
  compliance with the DPA;
- the Data Protection Principles;
- the Legitimate Processing Conditions;
- the Sensitive Personal Data Legitimate Processing Conditions;
- the security conditions;
- the notification and registration conditions;
- the data breach notification conditions;
- the personal data outsourcing and data processor conditions;
- the personal data transfer ban or trans border data flow restrictions;
- the individual data subject rights, including access, deletion, etc;
- queries, audits and investigation orders from the ICO;
- the time limits for undertaking various tasks and obligations.

Data Protection Principles

All organisations with personal data must comply with the following
Data Protection Principles, namely:

- Personal data shall be obtained only for one or more specified and
  lawful purposes, and shall not be further processed in any manner
  incompatible with that purpose or those purposes;
- Personal data shall be adequate, relevant and not excessive in
  relation to the purpose or purposes for which they are processed;
- Personal data shall be accurate and, where necessary, kept up to
  date;

- Personal data processed for any purpose or purposes shall not be kept for longer than is necessary for that purpose or those purposes;
- Personal data shall be processed in accordance with the rights of data subjects under this Act;
- Appropriate technical and organisational measures shall be taken against unauthorised or unlawful processing of personal data and against accidental loss or destruction of, or damage to, personal data;
- Personal data shall not be transferred to a country or territory outside the EEA unless that country or territory ensures an adequate level of protection for the rights and freedoms of data subjects in relation to the processing of personal data.

The eight Data Protection Principles can be summarised as:

1. fairly and lawfully processed;
2. processed for limited purposes;
3. adequate, relevant and not excessive;
4. accurate and up to date;
5. not kept for longer than is necessary;
6. processed in line with individual data subject rights;
7. secure; and
8. not transferred to other countries without adequate protection.

All eight of the principled must be complied with. Compliance with the Data Protection Principles applies to all employee and inward-facing personal data collected and or processed by an organisation. It also applied regardless of registration requirements.

Ordinary Personal Data Legitimate Processing Conditions

When dealing with the above inward-facing categories of employees, agents, contractors, etc, the Legitimate Processing Conditions are required to be complied with, *in addition* to the Data Protection Principles.

Schedule 2 of the DPA contains the general Legitimate Processing Conditions eg employee non sensitive personal data. In order to comply with the general personal data Legitimate Processing Conditions, the organisation must fall within *one* of the following conditions, namely:

- The individual who the personal data is about has consented to the processing.

- The processing is necessary:
  - o   in relation to a contract which the individual has entered into; or
  - o   because the individual has asked for something to be done so they can enter into a contract.
- The processing is necessary because of a legal obligation that applies to the organisation (except an obligation imposed by a contract);
- The processing is necessary to protect the individual's 'vital interests.' This condition only applies in cases of life or death, such as where an employee's medical history is disclosed to a hospital's A&E department treating them after a serious road accident;
- The processing is necessary for administering justice, or for exercising statutory, governmental, or other public functions;
- The processing is in accordance with the 'legitimate interests' condition.

DPA Schedule 2C of the DPA contains conditions relevant for the purposes of the first Data Protection Principle, in particular the processing of personal data. It states:

1   The data subject has given his consent to the processing;
2   The processing is necessary:
  (a)   for the performance of a contract to which the data subject is a party; or
  (b)   for the taking of steps at the request of the data subject with a view to entering into a contract;
3   The processing is necessary for compliance with any legal obligation to which the data controller is subject, other than an obligation imposed by contract;
4   The processing is necessary in order to protect the vital interests of the data subject;
5   The processing is necessary:
  (a)   for the administration of justice;
  (aa)   for the exercise of any functions of either House of Parliament;
  (b)   for the exercise of any functions conferred on any person by or under any enactment;
  (c)   for the exercise of any functions of the Crown, a Minister of the Crown or a government department; or
  (d)   for the exercise of any other functions of a public nature exercised in the public interest by any person.
6(1) The processing is necessary for the purposes of legitimate interests pursued by the data controller or by the third party or parties to

whom the data are disclosed, except where the processing is unwarranted in any particular case by reason of prejudice to the rights and freedoms or legitimate interests of the data subject;

(2) The Secretary of State may by order specify particular circumstances in which this condition is, or is not, to be taken to be satisfied.

There are, therefore, six general Legitimate Processing Conditions. Frequently, an organisation would seek to fall within the legitimate interests condition above. These might be summarised as follows:

- The employee has given explicit consent;
- Processing necessary for performance of *contract* to which the employee is a party;
- Processing is necessary to take steps at request of the employee prior to entering into contract;
- Processing is necessary for compliance with legal obligation (other than contractual obligation);
- Necessary to prevent injury or other damage to health of the employee or serious loss or damage to property of the employee or to protect vital interests;
- Necessary for the administration of justice, performance of statutory function or function of public nature performed in public interest;
- Processing necessary for *legitimate interests* pursued by data controller except where unwarranted.

Unlike certain other areas, the legitimate processing of employee personal data does not require employee consent. However, many organisations would have originally expected and proceeded on the basis that consent was so required. They would have incorporated (deemed) consent clauses into employment contracts, etc.

As indicated above, DPA Schedule 2C of the DPA enables organisations to rely upon the legitimate processing condition that processing is necessary for the purposes of *legitimate interests* pursued by the data controller or by the third party or parties to whom the data are disclosed, except where the processing is unwarranted in any particular case by reason of prejudice to the rights and freedoms or legitimate interests of the data subject.

An alternative would be to say that the processing is necessary as part of a contract to which the employee is a party, in particular the employment contract.

Sensitive Personal Data Legitimate Processing Conditions

Organisation may also feel the need on occasion to store and use sensitive personal data in relation to employees, such as medical and health data. In the case of sensitive personal data, an organisation must in addition to satisfying all of the Data Protection Principles, be able to comply or fall within *one* of the Sensitive Personal Data Legitimate Processing Conditions.

Schedule 3C of the DPA sets out conditions relevant for the purposes of the first Data Protection Principle in particular in relation to the processing of Sensitive Personal Data. In the context of employees and inward-facing personal data, it provides:

1 The employee data subject has given his or her explicit consent to the processing of the personal data;

2(1) The processing is necessary for the purposes of exercising or performing any right or obligation which is conferred or imposed by law on the data controller in connection with employment;

(2) The Secretary of State may by order:

    (a) exclude the application of sub-paragraph (1) in such cases as may be specified; or

    (b) provide that, in such cases as may be specified, the condition in sub-paragraph (1) is not to be regarded as satisfied unless such further conditions as may be specified in the order are also satisfied;

3 The processing is necessary:

    (a) in order to protect the vital interests of the employee data subject or another person, in a case where,

       (i) consent cannot be given by or on behalf of the employee data subject; or

       (ii) the data controller cannot reasonably be expected to obtain the consent of the employee data subject; or

    (b) in order to protect the vital interests of another person, in a case where consent by or on behalf of the employee data subject has been unreasonably withheld;

4 The processing:

    (a) is carried out in the course of its legitimate activities by any body or association which,

       (i) is not established or conducted for profit; and

       (ii) exists for political, philosophical, religious or trade-union purposes;

    (b) is carried out with appropriate safeguards for the rights and freedoms of data subjects;

    (c) relates only to individuals who either are members of the body or association or have regular contact with it in connection with its purposes; and

(d) does not involve disclosure of the employee personal data to a third party without the consent of the employee data subject;

5 The information contained in the personal data has been made public as a result of steps deliberately taken by the employee data subject;

6 The processing:

(a) is necessary for the purpose of, or in connection with, any legal proceedings (including prospective legal proceedings);

(b) is necessary for the purpose of obtaining legal advice; or

(c) is otherwise necessary for the purposes of establishing, exercising or defending legal rights;

7(1) The processing is necessary:

(a) for the administration of justice;

(aa) for the exercise of any functions of either House of Parliament;

(b) for the exercise of any functions conferred on any person by or under an enactment; or

(c) for the exercise of any functions of the Crown, a Minister of the Crown or a government department;

(2) The Secretary of State may by order:

(a) exclude the application of sub-paragraph (1) in such cases as may be specified; or

(b) provide that, in such cases as may be specified, the condition in sub-paragraph (1) is not to be regarded as satisfied unless such further conditions as may be specified in the order are also satisfied;

7A(1) The processing:

(a) is either,

(i) the disclosure of sensitive personal data by a person as a member of an anti-fraud organisation or otherwise in accordance with any arrangements made by such an organisation; or

(ii) any other processing by that person or another person of sensitive personal data so disclosed; and

(b) is necessary for the purposes of preventing fraud or a particular kind of fraud;

(2) In this paragraph 'an anti-fraud organisation' means any unincorporated association, body corporate or other person which enables or facilitates any sharing of information to prevent fraud or a particular kind of fraud or which has any of these functions as its purpose or one of its purposes;

8(1) The processing is necessary for medical purposes and is undertaken by:

  (a) a health professional; or

  (b) a person who in the circumstances owes a duty of confidentiality which is equivalent to that which would arise if that person were a health professional;

(2) In this paragraph 'medical purposes' includes the purposes of preventative medicine, medical diagnosis, medical research, the provision of care and treatment and the management of healthcare services;

9(1) The processing:

  (a) is of sensitive personal data consisting of information as to racial or ethnic origin;

  (b) is necessary for the purpose of identifying or keeping under review the existence or absence of equality of opportunity or treatment between persons of different racial or ethnic origins, with a view to enabling such equality to be promoted or maintained; and

  (c) is carried out with appropriate safeguards for the rights and freedoms of employee data subjects;

(2) The Secretary of State may by order specify circumstances in which processing falling within sub-paragraph (1)(a) and (b) is, or is not, to be taken for the purposes of sub-paragraph (1)(c) to be carried out with appropriate safeguards for the rights and freedoms of data subjects.

These Sensitive Personal Data Legitimate Processing conditions may be summarised as follows:

- The employee whom the sensitive personal data is about has given explicit consent to the processing;
- The processing is necessary so that the organisation can comply with employment law;
- The processing is necessary to protect the vital interests of,
  - o the employee (in a case where the employee's consent cannot be given or reasonably obtained); or
  - o another person (in a case where the individual's consent has been unreasonably withheld);
- The processing is carried out by a not-for-profit organisation and does not involve disclosing personal data to a third party, unless the employee consents. Extra limitations apply to this condition;
- The employee has deliberately made the information public;
- The processing is necessary in relation to legal proceedings, for obtaining legal advice; or otherwise for establishing, exercising or defending legal rights;

- The processing is necessary for administering justice, or for exercising statutory or governmental functions;
- The processing is necessary for medical purposes, and is undertaken by a health professional or by someone who is subject to an equivalent duty of confidentiality;
- The processing is necessary for monitoring equality of opportunity, and is carried out with appropriate safeguards for the rights of individuals.

Furthermore, regulations also set out further obligations in relation to the processing of sensitive personal data.

Access Request Flows

Morgan and Boardman[1] refer to the access request. The following flow description is a further adapted of same.

1 Data subject access request

3 Organisation sends access request for to data subject

3 Completed access request for returned to organisation (plus fee (if applicable))

4 Personal data located by legal department/Data Protection Officers/Third parties

5 Information reviewed by legal department

6 Personal data sent to data subject

---

1 Morgan, R,. and Boardman, R., *Data Protection Strategy, Implementing Data Protection Compliance* (London: Sweet and Maxwell, 2012), p. 335.

Objections to Marketing

Jay[2] provides the following suggestions for organisations when dealing with access requests/marketing objections, namely:

- Does the objection relate to marketing or another form or processing?
- Does it relate to direct marketing within the definition?
- Is it in writing or sent electronically or oral?
- If it is not in writing or electronic is it appropriate to deal with it as sent or should the individual be require to put it in writing or send it by electronic means?
- At which branch or office was it received?
- On what date was the request received?
- Has the individual making the request given an intelligible name and address to which the controller can respond?
- When does the period for response expire?
- What time scale has the individual specified to stop marketing processing on a notice?
- What marketing processing is affected?
- Is more time needed to comply with the requirement?
- How is the marketing data held? Is it manual or automated or some of both?
- Does the objection apply to manual or automated?
- Has the individual described the data?
- Has the individual described the processing?
- Has the individual explained why unwarranted damage and distress would be caused?
- On what grounds are the data being processing?
- Can one of the primary grounds be claimed?
- Does the notice amount to a revocation of an existing consent?
- Is it possible to comply with the objection?
- Is processing about others affected?
- Would compliance mean system changes?

---

2   Jay and Hamilton, *Data Protection: Law and Practice* (London: Sweet and Maxwell, 2007), pp. 436–437.

Audit Checklist

Morgan and Boardman[3] refer to the audits. There checklists include for example,

Extent of Audit

- What parts of the organisation and its files and systems have been audits and for what reason?
- Are they likely to be sufficient to give an indication of the organisation's overall data protection compliance or not?

Classes of Personal Data Audited

- Computer?
- Email?
- Other letter/memo files?
- Internet?
- Intranet?
- Manual (relevant filing system)
- Video (scanned images, CCTV, photographic, film)
- Audio (contract, training, voicemail)
- Biometric
- Other categories of personal data (eg tachograph)
- Types of Personal Data
- Is there personal data or not?
- If yes, is the personal data sensitive personal data?
- Or accessible personal data?
- Is any of the personal data confidential? Eg medical/financial? If so, what are the consequences of this and what are individuals told about this?
- Is there any automatic or automated processing of personal data? If so, what are the consequences of this and what are individuals told about this?
- Are there any cookies? If so, how are they used?

Types of Data Subject

- Staff
- Retires Staff
- Staff spouses or other family members
- Members of the public
- Customers

---

3   Morgan, R., and Boardman, R., *Data Protection Strategy, Implementing Data Protection Compliance* (London: Sweet and Maxwell, 2012), pp. 78 *et seq.*

- Prospective customers
- Business contacts, which may include:
  - o Sole traders or partnerships, who are identifiable individuals and so data subjects; or
  - o Managers or other individual office holders in those bodies the organisation has contracts with?

'Owner' of Personal Data

- Who?
- Any 'private' files?
- How are private emails handled?
- What, if any, of the data is processed by a data processor?
- What personal data is received from another organisation?
- What personal data is shared with one or more other organisations?
- Does the organisation process data itself on behalf of others, as a data processor?

Purposes of Processing

- How and why is the personal data collected?
- What information is given to individuals about this, how and when?
- How well does the data's use match the purposes for which it is collected?
- Does the organisation carry out direct marketing? If so, how?
- Does it subscribe to 'preference' service?
- What or whom ensures that the personal data are accurate?
- What are the consequences if the personal data is inaccurate?
- How long is it kept?
- What happens to it when it is no longer used?
- What are the criteria for its destruction?
- Is it in fact destroyed: if so, who does this and how do they do it?

Contracts

- Data processing contracts
- Data sharing contracts
- Contracts involving personal data outside of the EEA
- Fair obtaining warranties

Security of Personal Data

- Physical security
- Staff security
- What standards accreditation does the organisation have?

- System security – eg passwords, firewalls, etc.
- What about portable media eg Laptops, memory sticks, CDs, etc?
- Procedures for sending secure faxes – and emails – for sensitive personal data?
- Is there any use of wireless transmission wi-fi?
- Security with data processors
- How were they selected?
- Was their security checked?
- How is it guaranteed by the data processor and documented?
- Is there any ongoing review processing?

Sending Outside EEA?

- Files?
- Emails?
- Internet material?
- Intranet material?

Cookies

- Which?
- From where?
- How intrusive?

Procedures

Morgan and Boardman[4] refer to processes and procedures in relation compliance and ongoing compliance. The queries checklist includes for example,

Procedures and Procedures

- What industry/trade association guidance is available?
- What published processed and procedures are there in respect of personal data?
- How are they brought to the attention of staff others?
- How enforced?
- How updated?
- Who is responsible for this?
- How does he/she fit into the organisations structure?

Data Protection Notification/Registration

---

4   Morgan, R., and Boardman, R., *Data Protection Strategy, Implementing Data Protection Compliance* (London: Sweet and Maxwell, 2012), pp. 80 *et seq.*

- Has the organisation notified?
- If not, why does it consider itself exempt?
- Is the notification consistent with the personal data identified by the audit?
- Purposes?
- Is the notification up to date?
- How is the notification kept up to date?

Data Subjects' Rights

- What Procedures are in place to deal with requests in connection with data subjects rights?
- How has it worked so far?
- Any problems with identifying a particular individual in the personal data?
- Are the Information Commissioner's Codes (eg CCTV, employment practice, data sharing) followed?

People

- Who is in charge of data protection?
- What resources does he/she have?
- How is he/she supported by senior management?
- What if any disciplinary action has been taken in respect of data protection?

Information Commissioner Office (ICO)

- Apart from notification/registration, has the organisation ever had any dealings with the ICO? If so, what and when and with what particular results?

Recent ICO Data Loss/Breaches/Fines/Convictions

Issue	Date	Party	Breach	Penalty
Data breach	2 January 2013	Sony	Hack breach	£250,000
Unlawful access Customer financial data Bank employee	6 November 2012	Lara Davies	Bank employee obtained unlawfully access to bank statements of her partner's ex-wife. Court prosecution. Pleaded guilty to 11 DPA offences.	Court conviction. Fined. Lost job.
Spam	28 November 2012	Christopher Niebel and Gary McNeish, joint owners ofTetrus Telecoms.	An ICO monetary penaltywas issued. The company had sent millions of unlawful spam texts to the public over the past three years.	£300,000 £140,000
Data Loss/Data Breach Unlawful disclosure Sensitive data	22 November 2012	Plymouth City Council	An ICO monetary penaltyissuedfor a serious breach of the seventh data protection principle. A social worker sentpart of a reportrelating to family A, to familyB due to printing issues. The photocopied report contained confidential andhighly sensitive personal data relating to the two parents and their four children, including of allegations of child neglect in on-goingcare proceedings.	£60,000

Appendices

Incorrect storage and processing Potential loss and damage Financial institution	6 November 2012	Prudential	An ICO monetary penalty issued after a mix-up over the administration of two customers' accounts led to tens of thousands of pounds, meant for an individual's retirement fund, ending up in the wrong account.	£50,000
Data Loss/Data Breach Unlawful disclosure Sensitive data	25 October 2012	Stoke-on-Trent City Council	An ICO monetary penalty issued following a serious breach of the Data Protection Act that led to sensitive information about a child protection legal case being emailed to the wrong person.	£120,000
Data Loss/Data Breach Police	16 October 2012	Greater Manchester Police	An ICO monetary penalty issued after the theft of a memory stick containing sensitive personal data from an officer's home. The device, which had no password protection, contained details of more than a thousand people with links to serious crime investigations.	£150,000
Data Loss/Data Breach Charity	10 October 2012	Norwood Ravenswood Ltd	An ICO monetary penalty issued after highly sensitive information about the care of four young children was lost after being left outside a London home. This was a charity which was fined.	£70,000

Data Loss/Data Breach	11 September 2012	Scottish Borders Council	An ICO monetary penaltyissuedafter former employees' pension records were found in an over-filled paper recycle bank in a supermarket car park.	£250,000
Unlawful disclosure Sensitive data	6 August 2012	Torbay Care Trust	An ICO monetary penaltyissuedafter sensitive personal information relating to 1,373 employees was published on the Trust's website.	£175,000
Unlawful disclosure Sensitive data	12 July 2012	St George's Healthcare NHS Trust	An ICO monetary penaltyissuedafter a vulnerable individual's sensitive medical details were sent to the wrong address.	£60,000
Data Loss/Data Breach	5 July 2012	Welcome Financial Services Limited	An ICO monetary penaltyissuedfollowing a serious breach of the Data Protection Act. The breach led to the personal data of more than half a million customers being lost.	£150,000
Data Loss/Data Breach Sensitive data	19 June 2012	Belfast Health and Social Care Trust	An ICO monetary penaltyissuedfollowing a serious breach of the Data Protection Act. The breach led to the sensitive personal data of thousands of patients and staff being compromised. The Trust also failed to report the incident to the ICO.	£225,000

Unlawful disclosure Sensitive data	6 June 2012	Telford & Wrekin Council	An ICO monetary penaltyissuedfor two serious breaches of the seventh data protection principle. A Social Worker sent a core assessment report to the child's sibling instead of the mother. The assessment contained confidential and highly sensitive personal data. Whilst investigating the first incident, a second incident was reported to the ICO involving the inappropriate disclosure of foster carer names and addresses to the children's mother. Both children had to be re-homed.	£90,000
Unlawful disclosure Sensitive data Security	1 June 2012	Brighton and Sussex University Hospitals NHS Trust	An ICO monetary penaltyissuedfollowing the discovery of highly sensitive personal data belonging to tens of thousands of patients and staff – including some relating to HIV and Genito Urinary Medicine patients – on hard drives sold on an Internet auction site in October and November 2010.	£325,000

Unlawful disclosure Sensitive data	21 May 2012	Central London Community Healthcare NHS Trust	An ICO monetary penalty issued for a serious contravention of the DPA, which occurred when sensitive personal data was faxed to an incorrect and unidentified number. The contravention was repeated on 45 occasions over a number of weeks and compromised 59 data subjects' personal data.	£90,000
Data Loss/Data Breach Sensitive data	15 May 2012	London Borough of Barnet	An ICO monetary penalty issued following the loss of sensitive information relating to 15 vulnerable children or young people, during a burglary at an employee's home.	£70,000
Unlawful disclosure Sensitive data	30 April 2012	Aneurin Bevan Health Board	An ICO monetary penalty issued following an incident where a sensitive report – containing explicit details relating to a patient's health – was sent to the wrong person.	£70,000
Unlawful disclosure Sensitive data	14 March 2012	Lancashire Constabulary	An ICO monetary penalty issued following the discovery of a missing person's report containing sensitive personal information about a missing 15 year old girl.	£70,000

Appendices

Unlawful disclosure Sensitive data	15 February 2012	Cheshire East Council	An ICO monetary penaltyissuedafter an email containing sensitive personal information about an individual of concern to the police was distributed to 180 unintended recipients.	£80,000
Data Loss/Data Breach Sensitive data	13 February 2012	Croydon Council	An ICO monetary penaltyissuedafter a bag containing papers relating to the care of a child sex abuse victim was stolen from a London pub.	£100,000
Unlawful disclosure Sensitive data	13 February 2012	Norfolk County Council	An ICO monetary penaltyissuedfor disclosing information about allegations against a parent and the welfare of their child to the wrong recipient.	£80,000
Unlawful disclosure Sensitive data	30 January 2012	Midlothian Council	An ICO monetary penaltyissuedfor disclosing sensitive personal data relating to children and their carers to the wrong recipients on five separate occasions. The penalty is the first that the ICO has served against an organisation in Scotland.	£140,000
Unlawful disclosure Sensitive data	6 December 2011	Powys County Council	An ICO monetary penaltyissuedfor a serious breach of the Data Protection Act after the details of a child protection case were sent to the wrong recipient.	£130,000

Unlawful disclosure Sensitive data	28 November 2011	North Somerset Council	An ICO monetary penaltyissuedfor a serious breach of the Data Protection Act where a council employee sent five emails, two of which contained highly sensitive and confidential information about a child's serious case review, to the wrong NHS employee.	£60,000
Unlawful disclosure Sensitive data	28 November 2011	Worcestershire County Council	An ICO monetary penaltyissuedfor an incident where a member of staff emailed highly sensitive personal information about a large number of vulnerable people to 23 unintended recipients.	£80,000
Unlawful disclosure Sensitive data	9 June 2011	Surrey County Council	An ICO monetary penaltyissuedfor a serious breach of the Data Protection Act after sensitive personal information was emailed to the wrong recipients on three separate occasions.	£120,000
Unlawful disclosure Sensitive data Security	10 May 2011	Andrew Jonathan Crossley, formerly trading as solicitors firmACS Law	An ICO monetary penaltyissuedfor failing to keep sensitive personal information relating to around 6,000 people secure.	£1,000

Appendices

Data Loss/Data Breach Laptop Encryption	8 February 2011	Ealing Council	An ICO monetary penaltyissuedfollowing the loss of an unencrypted laptop which contained personal information. Ealing Council breached the Data Protection Act by issuing an unencrypted laptop to a member of staff in breach of its own policies.	£80,000
Data Loss/Data Breach Laptop Encryption	8 February 2011	Hounslow Council	An ICO monetary penaltyissuedfollowing the loss of an unencrypted laptop which contained personal information. Hounslow Council breached the Act by failing to have a written contract in place with Ealing Council. Hounslow Council also did not monitor Ealing Council's procedures for operating the service securely.	£70,000

Sample of Cases

Asda v Thompson (2004) IRLR 598
Employment. Unfair dismissal. Allegations of drug use. Witness statements relied on. Dismissal. Employers not able to disclose witness statements. Promises of confidentiality to informants. Informants afraid. Held: EAT could order documents to be anonymised.

Asociación Nacional de Establecimientos Financieros de Crédito (ASNEF) (C–468/10), Federación de Comercio Electrónico y Marketing Directo (FECEMD)(C–469/10) v Administración del Estado ECJ (Third Chamber). Joined Cases C–468/10 and C–469/10, 24 November 2011

Processing of personal data. DPD95. Article 7(f). Direct effect. References for a preliminary ruling from the Tribunal Supremo (Spain).

Attorney General v Guardian Newspapers Ltd (No. 1) HL 13–Aug–1987; *AG v Guardian (No. 2)* [1990] 1 AC 109; [1990] 1 AC 109 HL; *AG v Observer and Others*; *AG v Times and Another* [on appeal from *AG v Guardian (No. 2)*]; *Case of Observer and Guardian v UK*, ECHR (application no. 13585/88) (Spycatcher case)
Confidential information. Breach of confidence. Public interest. Disclosure by former Crown servant of alleged illegal activities of British security service. Information freely available outside UK. Balancing public interest in freedom of speech against public interest in maintaining confidentiality. Whether injunction against publication to be granted.

Baker v Secretary of State for the Home Office (Information Tribunal) [2001] UKHRR 1275
National security. Freedom of information. Held: Ministerial certificate that certified personal data as national security-sensitive quashed.

BKM Limited v BBC [2009] EWHC 3151 (Ch).
Injunctions. Privacy. Article 8. Freedom of expression. Article 10. Human Rights Act 1998, ss 12(3) and (4). Whether injunction to restrain broadcasting of secret footage. BKM care home in Wales. Sought to restrain BBC footage surreptitiously obtained from the home. Contents unknown. Programme about standards at the care home. BBC agreed to pixelate the faces of residents.
Held: Injunction refused. Residents' Article 8 were engaged and were not removed by obscuring identities. Invasion of privacy was likely to be relatively slight. Serious factors justified or out-balanced infringement of privacy rights. Public interest in care standards.

Brian Reid Beetson Robertson v Wakefield Metropolitan Council, Secretary of State for the Home Department [2001] EWHC Admin 915
Sale of electoral register. Challenge to refusal of Electoral Registration Officer (ERO) of Wakefield Council. Request to prevent electoral register details being supplied to marketing organisations.
Held: ERO refusal breach of DPD95, Article 8 and Protocol 1 Article 3 of Convention.

British Gas v Data Protection Registrar [1998] UKIT DA98–3/49/2 (4 March 1998)
Enforcement notice appeal. Utility. Leaflet to gas customers. Present and future range of products and services. Passing customer details to group companies. Opt-out. Forced to give their personal data.

Held: Processing for gas-related marketing purposes would be fair. Processing for wider than obvious purposes at the time of supply of information without consent would not be fair. Expectations as to scope of goods and services may change over time.

Campbell v MGN [2002] EWHC 299; EMLR 2 (CA); [2004] UKHL 22; [2004] AC 457; [2002] EWHC 499 (QB); [2002] EWCA Civ 1373, [2003] QB 633
Privacy. Confidence. Data protection. Actress. Photos. Going to Narcotics Anonymous.
Held: Damages were awarded for breach of confidence and compensation under DPA.

CCN Systems v Data Protection Registrar (1991) Case DA/90 5/49/19, Data Protection Tribunal
Application for credit card. Judgement recorded. Previous non-connected debtor at same address. No connection.
Held: Breach.

Charleston v News Group Newspapers [1995] 2 AC 65; [1995] 2 WLR 450; [1995] 2 All ER 313, House of Lords
Defamation. Headline. Photographs. Meaning. Manipulated images. Superimposed pornographic
images. Text made clear superimposing without knowledge or consent.
Held: Needed to look at headline, photograph and text to evaluate defamatory meaning. Whether text of article or a disclaimer was sufficient to neutralise otherwise defamatory headline or photograph was a jury matter. On the facts, appears no defamation.

Chief Constable of Humberside v Information Commissioner & Another [2009] EWCA Civ 1079
Data protection. Data Protection Principles. Human Rights. Whether Data Protection Principles under oblige police to delete certain old minor convictions from Police National Computer (PNC).
Held: Data controllers must identify the purpose for which the data is retained so data subjects know the purposes for which the data is being retained and so the ICO and data subjects can test the principles to the purposes identified. Data retention on the PN to enable the police to assist the public in accordance with force policies. This included the supply of accurate records to the CPS, the courts and the CRB. Broad purpose. Retaining minor conviction information for this purpose did not breach Data Protection Principles 3 and 5. Deletion may prejudice prevention and detection of crime.

Clark v Associated Newspapers [1998] RPC 261; [1998] 1 WLR 1558
Ex-politician. Spoof diaries.
Held: Successful claim for false attribution.

Coco v AN Clark (Engineers) [1968] FSR 415; [1969] RPC 49
Joint venture. Production of a new moped engine. Allegation of use of
information imparted earlier. No contract. Equitable doctrine of confidence. Unaffected by contract.
Held: Three essential elements for breach of confidence. Information
must be of a confidential character. Imparting of information in circumstances where the confidant ought reasonably to have known that the
information was confidential. Information used or disclosed in an
unauthorised manner causing detriment.

*Commission of the European Communities v The Bavarian
Lager Co Ltd*, Case C–28/08 P
Access to documents. Regulation (EC) No 1049/2001. Documents
relating to proceedings for failure to fulfil obligations. Access refused.
Protection of physical persons in relation to processing of personal
data. Regulation (EC) No 45/2001. Concept of private life.
Held: Decision to annul Commission's decision rejecting application
for access to the full minutes of the meeting, containing all the names.

Common Services Agency v Scottish Information Commissioner [2008]
UKHL 47
Freedom of information. Data protection. Whether information held at
time requested. Whether personal data. Whether sensitive personal data.
s 1(1), Schedules 1, 2, and 3, DPA. Disclosure of medical information.
Anonymous data. Barnardisation. Member of the Scottish Parliament.
Request for details of all incidents of childhood leukaemia 1990 to
2003 for Dumfries and Galloway areas. CSA refused. Significant risk
of indirect identification of living individuals. Personal data. Exempt
for Freedom of Information. Duty of confidence to patients. Scottish
ICO agreed it was personal data. But ruled that the CSA should disclose
after barnardisation to disguise personal information. CSA appealed.
Whether the information in barnardised form was information held by
the CSA at the time of the request. If so, whether it was personal data.
If so, whether release would accords with Data Protection Principles.
Conditions for processing in Schedule 2 DPA. If so, whether sensitive
personal data. Whether release satisfies one of Sensitive Personal Data
Legitimate Processing Conditions in Sch 3 DPA.
Held: Appeal allowed. Remitted to SIC. Information held by CSA at
time requested. This part of DPD given wide interpretation. Barnardis-
ing was reasonable in the circumstances. Whether barnardisation

achieved that was a question of fact for the SIC. Barnardisation effectively anonymises the data, condition 6(1) of Sch 2 (processing necessary for the purposes of legitimate interests and not unwarranted by prejudice to the data subject) would be met. Whether sensitive personal data and whether any Sch 3 conditions satisfied were questions of fact for SIC.

CTB v News Group Newspapers & Another [2011] EWHC 1326 (QB) 23 May 2011
Injunction. Soccer player. Extra-marital relationship. The *Sun*. Kiss and tell story. Photograph 'set up.' Alleged demand for money. Injunction to restrain publication of plaintiff identity and relationship. Married. Family. Well established court needs to take into account interests of the family and their Article 8 of Convention rights. Apprehension of selling story. 'Needed' £50,000. Possible request for £100,000. Human Rights Act. Claimant entitled to anonymity at the first occasion. Injunction continuing. Denies causing publication or asking for money. Balancing exercise. Competing Convention rights. Article 8 and Article 10. Kiss and tell. Court obligation to afford remedies to such individuals, to discourage blackmailers and to give protection to personal or private information where there is a threat of revelation. Two-stage process. Whether subject matter of threatened publication such as to give rise to 'reasonable expectation of privacy.' Next stage is to weigh claimant's Article 8 rights, and any traditional law of confidence duty. Whether those rights overridden by any countervailing considerations. Whether legitimate public interest in revealing information already in the public domain.
Held: Plaintiff likely to obtain a permanent injunction at trial. Uncontradicted. Reasonable expectation of privacy. No countervailing argument advanced to suggest Article 10 rights of the defendants, or anyone else, should prevail. No suggestion of any legitimate public interest in publishing.

Denco Ltd v Joinson [1991] 1 WLR 330
Employment. Unfair dismissal. Damages. Reasonableness of dismissal. Misconduct. Computer. Deliberate and unauthorised access to computer files. Using another employee password. Summary dismissal for gross misconduct. Whether purpose for access relevant.
Held: Tribunal erred in requiring employers to show reasonable grounds for believing access was illegitimate. The motive was irrelevant in law. Though the misuse of computers is a serious offence, companies advised to put appropriate policies in place.

Department of Health v (1) Information Commissioner (2) Pro Life Alliance, EA/2008/0074, Court Information Tribunal
Freedom of information. Data protection. s 40 Freedom of Information Act 2000 (personal information exemption). s 44 Freedom of Information Act 2000 (disclosure prohibited by an enactment). Abortion statistics. Anonymisation. Abortion Regulations 1991. Pro Life Alliance. Whether low cell count statistics were personal data because a person could be identified from that data (a) together with data in the hands of DH or (b) together with information publicly available. Whether personal data exemption under s 40(2) FOIA applied. Whether zero cell counts should be suppressed as may lead to identification. Whether s 44 FOIA provided an exemption for disclosure by virtue of the Abortion Regulations 1991 (which prohibit disclosure of abortion information provided mandatorily to the Chief Medical Officer).
Held: Appeal allowed, but failure to disclose was breach of FOIA. Was personal data in the hands of DH pursuant to s 1(1)(b) DPA following *Common Services Agency v Scottish Information Commissioner*. Disclosure would not contravene Data Protection Principles. s 40 FOIA exemption did not apply. Zero cell counts were capable of adding information to the totality of data such as to reveal personal data. Disclosure would not be in breach of the Abortion Regulations 1991 and therefore the s 44 FOIA exemption did not apply.

Douglas v Hello! Ltd [2001] QB 967; [2001] 2 WLR 992; [2001] 2 All ER 289; [2001] EMLR 199; [2001] FSR 732
Breach of confidence. Injunction. Privacy. Human Rights Act 1998, s 12(3). ECHR. Article 10, Article 8. Whether injunction should be discharged.
Held: s 12(3) Human Rights Act required, when considering whether to grant an injunction likely to affect freedom of expression, court to consider Article 10(2) as well as Article 10(1), and all relevant Convention rights, such as Article 8, and merits of the case. Although plaintiffs might establish at trial that publication should not be allowed, the organised publicity surrounding wedding tipped balance in favour of allowing publication. Damages would be an adequate remedy. Balance of convenience favoured defendant. Injunction discharged.

Douglas and Jones v Hello Hello! Ltd (No. 2) (2003) UKHC 55; [2003] 1 AER 1087; UKSC (2005)
Privacy. Confidence. Secret photos of wedding was published.
Held: Privacy and commercial interests were infringed.

Appendices

Douglas v Hello! Ltd (*No. 2*) [2003] EWCA Civ 139; [2003] EMLR 585
Breach of confidence. Privacy. ECHR, Article 10, Article 8. Service out of jurisdiction. DPA. Interference with rights and business. Unlawful means. Conspiracy. Photographs.
Held: There was a good arguable case that Ramey was a joint tortfeasor. If he took or arranged the photographs, it was arguable he was jointly liable as an author is jointly liable in libel. Good arguable claims of breach of statutory duty under DPA, interference with rights and business and unlawful means conspiracy. Appeal allowed.

Douglas v Hello! Ltd (*No. 5*) [2003] EWHC 786 (Ch); [2003] 3 All ER 996; [2003] EMLR 641
Human Rights. Intellectual property. Breach of confidence. Privacy. ECHR. Article 8. Freedom of expression. ECHR. Article 10. DPA. Use of covert photographs.
Held: Applying the three elements in *Coco v Clark* [1969] RPC 41, the plaintiffs succeeded in claim for breach of confidence. This claim adequately protected the claimants' Article 8 rights, so there was no need to address the question of any breach of privacy. Breach of DPA, as the Act applied to the publication of the photographs. The s 32 journalistic purposes exemption did not apply. Processing was not done 'fairly and lawfully.'

Douglas v Hello! Ltd (*No. 8*) (*CA*) [2005] EWCA Civ 595; [2006] QB 125; [2005] 3 WLR 881; [2005] EMLR 609; *The Times*, 24 May 2005; *The Times*, 26 May 2005, Court Court of Appeal
Privacy. Confidence. Transferability of rights of privacy/confidence. Economic torts. Test of intention as an ingredient of economic torts. Test of causation of damage. Interim injunctions. Whether damages adequate remedy.
Held: Privacy rights in photographs of a private occasion can survive commercial sale of controlled and authorised photographs. Privacy rights are capable of exploitation by the subject as a commercial confidence. Whether commercial confidence rights are transferred to a publication on sale, so as to enable the publisher to sue, depends on the nature and terms of contract. In this case, no such right was acquired by *OK!*. *Hello!* published unauthorised pictures. The authorised images were not truly in the public domain when they published. Economic torts require that the conduct causing the harm be aimed and directed at the plaintiff, and the purpose or object of the conduct must be to cause the economic loss. *Hello!* would, had liability been established, have been responsible for republication. Notional licence fee was not appropriate.

Durant v Financial Services Authority (2003) EWCA Civ 1746; [2004]
FSR 28; B2/2002/2636 (A), 20 March 2002
Data protection. Access request. Minutes of meting. Applicant names in
minutes. Data Protection. Manual Filing System. Subject Access
Requests. Definition of 'data.' DPA, ss 1 and 7, DPD95. Subject access
request. Respondent provided some documents but refused others.
'Personal data.' 'Relevant filing system.'
Held: Not all information retrieved from a computer against an individual's name was personal data within the DPA. The mere mention of
the data subject in a document did not make that information personal
data of the data subject. To be personal data the information had to be
significantly biographical and/or such that the data subject was the
focus of attention. The purpose of DPA was to apply the same standard
of accessibility to personal data in manual filing systems as to computerised records. Protection aimed at data and not the documents. The
Structured filing system was to ensure the information was readily
accessible. Disproportionate to search unstructured filing systems. The
That a document could be retrieved using the plaintiff name was not
sufficient to make the information contained therein personal data. But
Durant criticised by WP29 for being too narrow. Also revision of ICO
guidance on this issue. Caution needed with *Durant*.

Durham County Council v Dunn [2012] EWCA Civ 1654
Access

Guardian News & Media Ltd v Information Commissioner
EA/2008/0084, Court Information Tribunal
Freedom of Information Act 2000. Privacy. DPA. Disciplinary action.
Judges. Publication. Public interest. Administration of justice. Constitutional Reform Act 2005. Reasonable expectation of privacy. Whether
the exemptions under s 40 (personal data) and s 31 (administration of
justice) of the FOIA applied. If so, whether they exempted disclosure of
the requested information to the media.
Held: Appeal dismissed. Disclosure was in breach of first Data Protection Principle on grounds of unfairness. The Tribunal took into account
the individual data subjects' reasonable expectations of what would
happen to the information, whether disclosure would cause unnecessary
or unjustified damage to the individuals and the legitimate interests of
the public in seeing the withheld information. The Tribunal held that
judges had a reasonable expectation of privacy that may be breached by
disclosure of the information, especially as complaints leading to
disciplinary action often involved personal, not professional, misconduct. In relation to s 31, it held disclosure would prejudice administration of justice as it would risk undermining a judge's authority while

carrying out judicial functions. The public interest in withholding the information sought outweighed public interest in disclosure.

Halford v UK (1997) IRLR 471; (1997) 24 EHRR 523
Assistant Chief Constable Merseyside Police. Refusal to promote. Proceedings re sex discrimination. Campaign in response to complaint. Press leaks. Interception of telephone calls. Home and office calls intercepted. Obtaining information to defend discrimination proceedings. Breach of Article 8 of Convention.
Held: ECHR held telephone conversations within scope of private life and correspondence in Article 8(1). ECHR case law adopts a broad construction.

Hartmut Eifert v Land Hessen (Case C–93/09)
Preliminary ruling. Publication of information on the beneficiaries of funds deriving from the European Agricultural Guarantee Fund (EAGF) and the European Agricultural Fund for Rural Development (EAFRD). Processing of personal data of beneficiaries of the European agricultural funds consisting in publishing the data on a website with a search tool. Validity in the light of the right to protection of personal data of the provisions of EU law prescribing that publication and laying down the detailed rules for publication. Conditions under which publication may be carried out.
Held: Provisions invalid insofar as, with regard to natural persons who are beneficiaries of EAGF and EAFRD aid, those provisions impose an obligation to publish personal data relating to each beneficiary without drawing a distinction based on relevant criteria such as the periods during which those persons have received such aid, the frequency of such aid or the nature and amount thereof. The invalidity does not allow any action to be brought to challenge the effects of the publication of the lists of beneficiaries of EAGF and EAFRD aid carried out by the national authorities on the basis of those provisions during the period prior to the date on which the present judgment is delivered. The second indent of Article 18(2) of DPD95 must be interpreted as not placing the personal data protection official under an obligation to keep the register provided for by that provision before an operation for the processing of personal data, such as that resulting from articles 42(8b) and 44a of Regulation No. 1290/2005, as amended by Regulation No. 1437/2007, and from Regulation No. 259/2008, is carried out. Article 20 of DPD95 must be interpreted as not imposing an obligation on the Member States to make the publication of information resulting from Articles 42(8b) and 44a of Regulation No. 1290/2005, as amended by Regulation No. 1437/2007, and from Regulation No. 259/2008 subject to the prior checks for which that Article 20 provides.

Equifax Europe v Data Protection Registrar (28 February 1992, Case DA/90/5/49/7) Data Protection Tribunal
Equifax. Credit reference agency. Appeal of enforcement notice re provision to those making searches. Third-party information relating not to the subject of the search, the applicant for credit, but to persons who lived at same address. Enforcement notice prohibited supply. One ground of appeal on s 28(4) DPA exempting data from the Registrar's powers 'in any case in which [their exercise] would be likely to prejudice' either the prevention or detection of crime or the apprehension or prosecution of offenders. s 28(1) exempted data 'in any case in which [disclosure] would be likely to prejudice' either the prevention or detection of crime or the apprehension or prosecution of offenders. Re 'in any case' the Registrar argued, and the Tribunal accepted, it meant 'in any particular case.' Agency argued and the Tribunal accepted that one of the functions of a credit reference agency is the prevention of crime and fraud. Searches by credit reference agency may help to prevent or detect fraud. The agency further argued that Registrar powers would prejudice this. If searches restricted in the manner required by the Registrar 'some cases of fraud or suspected fraud might not be exposed.'
Held: Argument rejected. Majority of applicants for credit were not fraudulent. Criminals only a tiny proportion of applicants for credit. Personal data are exempt from the provisions referred to in any case in which the application of those provisions to the data would be likely to prejudice the prevention or detection of crime or the apprehension of offenders. Exemption applies only in particular cases where one can talk about the data, the personal data to which one may or may not apply the provisions.

Ezsias v Welsh Ministers [2007] EWHC B15 (QB); [2007] AER (D) 65
Personal data. Access request. Data disclosure.
Held: Welsh National Assembly acted reasonably disclosing personal information to subject-access request. Presumption requested documents did not contain personal data, as per Court of Appeal in *Durant v Financial Services Authority*. But Durant criticised by WP29 for being too narrow. Also revision of ICO guidance on this issue. Caution needed with *Ezsias* and *Durant*.

Ferdinand v MGN Limited [2011] EWHC 2454 (QB)
Soccer player. *Sunday Mirror*. Alleged affair. Claim of misuse of private information and breach of confidence.
Held: Claim dismissed. Publication justified in the public interest. Portrayed image of reformed character and family man. Legitimate public interest to correct false image portrayed, and suitability as

England captain. Publication of relationship, texts and a photograph did not excessively intrude into private life.

Gaskin v UK (A/160) [1990] 1 FLR 167; (1990) 12 EHRR 36
In care by a local authority. Ill-treated. Wishing to claim against local authority for damages for negligence. Discovery of records. Discovery refused as private and confidential. Confirmed by Court of Appeal.
Held: Procedures followed in relation to access to his case records failed to secure respect for his private and family life as required by Article 8 of Convention. No violation of Article 10.

H v Associated Newspapers Ltd [2002] EWCA Civ 195
Confidence. Privacy. Human rights. Injunction. HIV. Medical records. DPA. Health worker. Diagnosed with HIV. Attempt to prevent previous employer obtaining medical records to notify his private patients. Seeking declaration that notification contrary to DPA and injunction to prohibit obtaining records. Master ordered that the parties should be anonymised. *Mail on Sunday* restrained by injunction of Scott Baker J. Newspaper applied to vary. Publication of identity, whereabouts and professional specialism of heath worker forbidden.
Held: Revelation of authority identity would lead to the identification of health worker. In order not to pre-empt the determination of the issues raised, order that both should only be identified by initials was appropriate and Gross J's modification of the orders to permit the identification of authority was set aside. Order restricting further journalistic investigation into health worker's identity was not upheld for being unjustifiably wide.

Hughes v Carratu International plc [2006] EWHC 1791 (QB)
DPA. Confidence/privacy. CPR 31.16. *Norwich Pharmacal*. Personal financial information. Legal professional privilege. Search of documents containing personal financial information relating to applicant. Application to disclose all documents containing applicant's personal data and to identity instructing party.
Held: Disclosure order. Under the *Norwich Pharmacal* jurisdiction the Court to be satisfied, first, that a wrong had been carried out or arguably carried out, by an ultimate wrongdoer: *Mitsui & Co Ltd v Neeun Petrolium UK Ltd* [2005] 3 All ER 511 followed. Court could not rule out possibility that respondent had acted unlawfully. Arguable cause of action against both parties in confidence or privacy and under the DPA s 7(9)(right of access to personal data), s 14(4)(rectification and destruction), 13(1)(compensation for any contravention of the requirements of the Act) and s 55. Under CPR 31.16 applicant had to show, *inter alia*, the respondent was likely to be a party to the proceedings.

Despite the absence of any clear evidence to this effect, the Court was satisfied that this was the case.

Hutcheson (formerly KGM) v News Group Newspapers [2012] EMLR 2 CA
Plaintiff Gordon Ramsay's father-in-law. Former chief executive of Gordon Ramsay Holdings Ltd and Gordon Ramsay Holdings International Ltd. Married with four children. Second relationship. Two children. *The Sun* saying he was dismissed for using company monies to fund his second family. Injunction. Refused. Appeal.
Held: Appeal dismissed.

Innovations (Mail Order) v Data Protection Registrar (DA92 31/49/1)
First principle of data protection. Obtain information fairly. Enforcement notice. Innovations was a mail-order business providing lists of customers, including names and addresses, to other companies for direct marketing purposes. Registrar held obtaining customer information unfairly. Whether or not fairness required the customer be notified of secondary uses. Court decided customer was to be notified. Insufficient to notify customers of this intended use by means of the company's entry in the data protection registry. Accepted by both parties that notification by the data protection register was not sufficient.

Johnson v Medical Union [2004] EWHC 347; [2007] EWCA Civ 262
Data protection. Subject Access request. s 7 DPA. Disclosure. Claim for improper processing of personal data under s 13 DPA. MDU decided not to renew claimant's membership. Subject access request to ascertain basis of decision. Disclosed certain documents, some redacted. Challenged adequacy of disclosure. Applying under s 7(9) of DPA for an order that MDU provide further documents and unredacted versions of documents already disclosed. Application rejected by Laddie J. Application for specific disclosure in his compensation claim to obtain disclosure of the same documents refused earlier. MDU argued that this application was an impermissible attempt to circumvent the subject access provisions of DPA.
Held: Allowing the application. Section 15(2) DPA has no direct effect on a claimant's right to CPR disclosure where claim based on breaches of Data Protection Principles. The provision does not prevent data subject obtaining disclosure in the ordinary way. Section 15(2) and orders for disclosure serve different ends. s 15(2) is concerned with whether subject access requests under s 7 are properly considered and complied with or not, whereas disclosure under CPR is an ordinary incident of civil proceedings. Section 15 has an indirect influence on

disclosure under the CPR: 's 15(2), like s 7(4) to (6), emphasises the concern of the legislature that confidential information relating to third parties should not be disclosed to a data subject. When a court exercises its discretion to order specific disclosure, this concern must be borne in mind.'

Leander v Sweden (A/116) (1987) 9 EHRR 433
Secret police files. Private life. Used for assessing suitability for employment. Access request refused. Violation Convention Article 8 right to private life. ECHR.
Held: No violation of Article 8. The use of confidential information in government files was not obstruction of access to information.

Lindqvist v Kammaraklagaren (C–101/01) [2004] 1 CMLR 0 (ECJ)
DPD95. Scope. Publication of personal data on the internet. Place of publication. Definition of transfer of personal data to third countries. Freedom of expression. Compatibility with DP Directive 95 of greater protection for personal data under the national legislation of a Member State.
Held: The act of referring, on an internet page, to various persons and identifying them by name or by other means, for instance by giving their telephone number or information regarding their working conditions and hobbies, constitutes 'the processing of personal data wholly or partly by automatic means' within Article 3(1) DPD95. Such processing of personal data is not covered by any of the exceptions in Article 3(2) DPD95. Reference to the fact that an individual has injured her foot and is on half-time on medical grounds constitutes personal data concerning health within the meaning of Article 8(1) DPD95. There is no 'transfer [of data] to a third country' within the meaning of Article 25 DPD95 where an individual in a Member State loads personal data onto an internet page that is stored on an internet site on which the page can be consulted and that is hosted by a natural or legal person who is established in that State or in another Member State, thereby making those data accessible to anyone who connects to the internet, including people in a third country. The provisions of DPD95 do not, in themselves, bring about a restriction that conflicts with the general principles of freedom of expression or other freedoms and rights, which are applicable within the EU and are enshrined *inter alia* in Article 10 of Convention. It is for the national authorities and courts responsible for applying the national legislation implementing DPD95 to ensure a fair balance between the rights and interests in question, including the fundamental rights protected by the EU legal order. Measures taken by the Member States to ensure the protection of personal data must be consistent both with the provisions of DPD95

and with its objective of maintaining a balance between freedom of movement of personal data and the protection of private life. However, nothing prevents a Member State from extending the scope of the national legislation implementing the provisions of DPD95 to areas not included in the scope thereof provided that no other provision of EU law precludes it.

Lion Laboratories v Evans [1984] AER 414
Confidential Information. Breach of confidence. Public interest. Disclosure of confidential information for purpose of criticism. Internal memoranda. Ex-employees taking memoranda without authority. Publication. Breach of confidence and copyright. Memoranda relating to functioning of electronic breathalyser. Public interest. Whether public interest in publication outweighing confidentiality.
Held: Allowing appeal. Conflict between two public interests. Right to protect internal, confidential documents and their copyright in them. Public's entitlement to information raising serious doubts about reliability of an instrument which was providing the sole evidence on which members of the public had been or were being prosecuted; and that in actions for breach of confidence, the defence of disclosure in the public interest, where just cause or excuse for breaking confidence, did not depend on any 'iniquity' on the part of plaintiffs. Defendants in interlocutory proceedings had to show a serious defence of public interest that might succeed at trial and did not have to show that the plaintiffs were guilty of iniquitous conduct. That the information contained in the documents was so important to the public as to outweigh the plaintiffs' interests and that accordingly, the court was entitled to overrule the judge's exercise of discretion and would permit publication of specified documents.

Lord Ashcroft v Attorney General & Others, 5 June 2003
Data Protection. Subject access request. Section 7 DPA. Manual files. Exemptions. Privacy. Breach of confidence. Right of access to information on manual government files. Exemptions. DPD95. ECHR. If access was not available under the DPA, could it be obtained directly under DPD95 or by Article 8 rights, under s 7 HRA?
Details: Case settled. Public apology from government and payment of substantial costs.

Mensah v Jones [2004] EWHC 2699 (Ch)
Confidence. DPA. Access to Health Records Act 1990. Disclosure of medical records. Course of legal proceedings. Obligation of disclosure. Legal advice. Applicant's (M's) doctor. Damages for assault. Disclosure. Medical records set to solicitors. Further action. Alleging

breaches of law. Granted summary judgment. Appeal. Whether real prospect of success that disclosure was unlawful under: DPA; Access to Health Records Act 1990; law of confidence.

Held: Dismissed application. No real prospect of appeal succeeding. No other reason why permission to appeal should be given. Disclosure necessary for purpose and in connection with legal proceedings within s 35(2) DPA. Needed legal advice re extent of obligation of disclosure. Access to Health Records Act 1990 did not require a court order before sending health records to solicitor. Law of confidence did not preclude seeking legal advice re obligation of disclosure. Obligation of disclosure may override obligation of confidentiality. Here, law and common sense required doctor disclose to his solicitor confidential material that might be relevant for advices.

Midlands Electrical v Data Information Registrar [1999] UKIT DA99–B1 (7 May 1999); [1999] Info TLR 217

Information. Utilities. Degree to which an electricity supplier was able to use names and addresses acquired in its main activity. Whether such uses complied with the first Data Protection Principle that personal data shall be processed fairly.

Held: In assessing fairness of processing, it was relevant to take into account the purpose of the processing. Marketing material would be sent with a bill even though customer had requested it not to be sent. Evidence that many consumers felt direct mailings intrusive and a nuisance. The Direct Marketing Association's Code of Practice did not prevent marketing to existing customers. A supplier of an essential utility is in a different position to other companies. The use of the list for marketing was a use not for the purpose for which the addresses had been given. The use of the addresses for non-electrical marketing would be unfair without consent.

MG v UK (1999) (application no. 44657/98) *Times*, 3 February 2003, ECHR

In care. Access request to social service records. Risk register. Whether father had been investigated or convicted of crimes against children. Responsibility of local authority for abuse. Inadequate disclosure by local authority. Plaintiff was only given limited access to his records in 1995, compared to the records submitted to the court by the UK government. No statutory right of access. No appeal against a refusal of access to any independent body.

Held: Violation of Article 8 in respect of the applicant's access, between April 1995 and 1 March 2000 (pre-DPA), to his social service records. Violation of Article 8 of Convention.

Motion Picture Association v BT
Filtering. Blocking. Linking. Copyright. Pirate Bay. Newzbin. Application for an order requiring BT to block access.
Held: Blocking orders granted.

Murray v Big Pictures (UK) Ltd (CA) [2008] EWCA Civ 446; [2008] 3 WLR 1360; [2008] EMLR 399; [2008] EHRR 736; [2008] 2 FLR 599; [2008] HRLR 33; [2008] UKHRR 736
Photographs of infant son of JK Rowling, while walking. Covert. Long range lens. Published in *Sunday Express*. Proceedings for misuse of private information and breach DPA. The claim against Express Newspapers was settled. Struck out against other defendant. Appealed. Whether claims for misuse of private information and under DPA were arguable.
Held: Appeal allowed. Reinstating claims and directing a trial. The 'question of whether there is a reasonable expectation of privacy is a broad one, which takes account of all the circumstances of the case. They include the attributes of the claimant, the nature of the activity in which the claimant was engaged, the place at which it was happening, the nature and purpose of the intrusion, the absence of consent and whether it was known or could be inferred, the effect on the claimant and the circumstances in which and the purposes for which the information came into the hands of the publisher.' Applying test, 'it is at least arguable that [there was] a reasonable expectation of privacy. The fact that he is a child is in our view of greater significance than the judge thought.' Since the striking out of the DPA claim was based on the erroneous conclusion that Article 8 rights were not arguably engaged, it was reinstated and tried.

Murray v Express Newspapers plc & Another Case Reference [2007] EWHC 1908 (Ch); [2007] EMLR 583; [2007] 3 FCR 331; [2007] HRLR 44; [2007] UKHRR 1322; [2007] Fam Law 1073; (2007) 157 NLJ 1199; (2008) 1 FLR 704
Privacy. Confidentiality. Data protection. Human Rights. Photographs. Paparazzi. Reasonable expectation of privacy. Public place. Child. Photographs of JK Rowling being pushed in a buggy. with Covertly long lens. Published in *Sunday Express*. Proceedings against the publisher of *Sunday Express* and agent for breach of privacy/confidence and under the DPA. The claim against Express Newspapers was settled. Agent applied to strike out C's claim as disclosing no reasonable cause of action.
Held: claims for breach of privacy/confidence and under the DPA were struck out. As regards the former claim: 'on my understanding of the law including *Von Hannover* there remains an area of innocuous

conduct in a public place which does not raise a reasonable expectation of privacy; and secondly, that even if the ECHR in Von Hannover has extended the scope of protection into areas which conflict with the principles and decision in Campbell, I am bound to follow Campbell in preference. Because I regard this case as materially indistinguishable from the facts in *Hosking v Runting* I am satisfied that on that test it has no realistic prospect of success' (para 68). The DPA claim was dismissed on grounds that plaintitff was unable to establish causation or damage of a species that s 13 allowed to be recovered.

Ntuli v Donald [2011] 1 WLR 294 CA
Privacy. Injunctions. Articles 8 and 10 Convention. Anonymity of parties. Non-disclosure of fact of injunction. Whether (1) the superinjunction should be discharged in its entirety; (2) the additional orders to protect privacy should be made; (3) orders for anonymity of the parties and non-disclosure of the application and injunction were necessary. 1980's boyband. Relationship. Ex-parte on notice interim injunction. Superinjunction anonymising the parties and restraining the defendant and third parties from referring to the fact of the injunction was sought and obtained. Defendant appealed seeking the discharge of the injunction and, in the alternative complaining that the orders for anonymity and non-disclosure of the fact the application had been obtained were unnecessary. Reference to the fact of the relationship was permitted. Cross-appealed. Injunction did not go far enough.
Held: Dismissing cross-appeal and the appeal in part. Substantive injunction remained in force. Argument that publication of non-core information ought not to be restricted was rejected. The judge had rightly considered within the intense focus on competing rights the claimant's past admissions and the defendant's interest in telling her story but placed a relatively low value on it. The injunction did not lack clarity. The word 'intimate' from the prohibition on disclosure did not have merely sexual connotation but referred to non-sexual but personal information about the relationship that the claimant was likely to establish was covered by a reasonable expectation of privacy at trial. No grounds for extending the prohibition on disclosure and communication to the fact that a relationship took place. No evidence that relationship was entirely secret. Disclosure had no particularly grave adverse consequence. The orders for non-disclosure of the fact that an injunction had been obtained was unnecessary in view of the terms of the substantive injunction and circumstances of the case. Orders for non-disclosure of the proceedings are essentially case-sensitive. The test is one of necessity. Anonymity was unnecessary. It would have been possible and appropriate for the judge to have written a judgment in

publishable form. The benefit of not anonymising was removing the risk of misidentification of the parties, although continued anonymity may be justified where identification risked serious consequences for a person's private life.

O'Flynn v Airlinks (2002) EAT 10269/01
Unfair dismissal. Reasons justifying dismissal. Whether employer acted reasonably. Gross misconduct. Employment tribunal finding decision to dismiss within band of reasonable responses. Whether tribunal erring.
Held: On the facts the decision to dismiss the appellant employee for gross misconduct fell within the band of reasonable responses that a reasonable employer might apply.

P v Wozencroft [2002] EWHC 1724
Keywords: Data controllers. Data protection. Disclosure and inspection. Expert witnesses. Family proceedings. Data protection. Disclosure and accuracy of expert evidence. Claimant sought disclosure and rectification under the DPA ss 7 and 14 of documents created by a psychiatrist, instructed to prepare reports on claimant and his wife and child. Claimant requesting disclosure of all relevant documents to show that the report filed was inaccurate.
Held: Application dismissed. Application was an abuse of process. The time for questioning the accuracy of report was at the family proceedings hearing.

Pal v General Medical Council and others [2004] EWHC 1485 (QB)
Defamation. Libel. DPA. Human Rights Act 1998. Article 8. General Medical Council. Summary Judgment. CPR Part 24. Costs.
Held: Application dismissed. Could not be said that there were no reasonable prospects of plaintiff succeeding. Data protection was an important and developing area of law. In respect of the defamation claim the test for summary judgment was higher and it would not be perverse for the jury to find that the words complained of bore the defamatory meaning alleged by the claimant. *Alexander v The Arts Council of Wales* [2001] 1 WLR 1840 and *Jameel v The Wall Street Journal* [2003] EWCA Civ 1694 applied.

Pennwell v Isles (2007) IRLR 700
Contract of employment. Confidential information. Ownership of contacts. Commencement of employment. Brought a list of contacts. Uploaded onto new employer's email system. During the course of employment he added details to this list. Employment ended. He downloaded the list. Set up a new business in competition. Whether breached the express terms of his contract with his employer. Whether entitled to retain the contacts he had created. Contract. In breach of his

contract, removed substantial quantities of confidential information detailing lists of customers, suppliers and advertisers. Interim injunction to return property. Computer examination. Created a list of contacts through the outlook system. Proceedings were compromised. Whether entitled to retain the list or not. Argued list contained his personal contacts as well as contacts which pre-dated his employment and only 20% of contacts added while an employee and therefore his personal information. To deprive would breach Article 10.

Held: Breach of contract. Address list contained on the employer's email and backed up the employer. Database list belongs to employer. Consequently, it could not be copied or removed in their entirety by employees for use after employment. Employer entitled to retain database and to a permanent injunction preventing use of it.

The Queen on the Application of Brian Reid Beetson Robertson v City of Wakefield Metropolitan Council and Secretary of State of the Home Department

Sale of electoral register to companies. Without affording individual right of objection. Interfered with rights under Article 8 and Protocol 1 Article 3. Refusal by Electoral Registration Officer of defendant council to block name. Claimed unlawful under Article 14 DPD95 (in particular Article 14(b)); the right to respect for privacy under Article 8 of Convention; Protocol 1 Article 3 of Convention made it an unlawful interference with the right to vote to make eligibility to vote conditional upon consent to, or acquiescence in, the sale of personal particulars to commercial organisations.

Held: Article 14(b) of DPD95 clearly capable of having direct effect, although the court concluded that domestic law (s 11 DPA) complied with the first limb of Article 14(b) of DPD95 and in principle an elector had a remedy by notice in writing and, if necessary by application to the court, pursuant to s 11(2). However, Electoral Registration Officers were wrong to disregard DPD95 and s 11 DPA. It was incumbent on courts to construe the 1986 and 2001 Regulations in a manner that was Directive compliant and constructive with the DPA. The plaintiff had had a remedy since March 2000, the commencement date of the DPA, albeit not by way of an application for judicial review. Selling the register to companies without affording individual electors a right of objection was a disproportionate way to give effect to the legitimate objective in question, particularly in view of technological advance. Held unjustifiable interference with the claimant's rights under Article 8. The right to vote conditional upon acquiescence in the sale of the Register to companies for marketing purposes with no individual right of objection. Contravened Protocol 1 Article 3 of the Convention. Since there was no individual right of objection it could not be said that these procedures were justifiable.

Quinton v Peirce & Cooper [2009] EWHC 912 (QB); [2009] FSR 17
Malicious falsehood. DPA. Election leaflet. Meaning. Malice. Falsity. s 3 Defamation Act 1952. Remedies. Rectification. Accuracy. Causation. Publication. Sued for malicious falsehood and breach of DPA re three allegations in leaflet.
Held: The words did not bear the meanings contended. No false meanings found. Did not act maliciously. The words were actionable per se as they were likely to have caused plainitff to lose income linked to the office of councillor. It was neither necessary nor proportionate to interpret the scope of the DPA so as to provide a parallel set of remedies for the publication of information that was neither defamatory nor malicious. Remedy of rectification sought. The publication complained of did not cause plaintiff to lose the election.

R (on the Application of Addinell) v Sheffield City Council [2001] ACD 61, QBD (Admin Ct)
Confidential information. Disclosure. Public interest. Adult in local authority's guardianship. Adult's mother seeking disclosure of confidential information before deciding whether or not to discharge guardianship. Risk of local authority applying to displace claimant as nearest relative. Whether or not refusal to disclose information infringed Convention rights. Whether or not right of access to information outweighed interest in confidentiality. Whether or not disclosure to be ordered. Mental Health Act 1983 (c 0), s 29(3). Human Rights Act 1998 (c 42), Sch I, Pt I, arts 6, 8.

Roberts v Nottinghamshire Healthcare, NHS Trust
A psychiatric patient not entitled under DPA to full disclosure by an NHS trust of a psychology report or disclosure only to his legal representatives. Claimant applied for disclosure on the grounds that (1) he was entitled to disclosure of the report under the DPA and the Convention; and (2) even if the report could not be disclosed to claimant, it should be disclosed to his legal representatives.
Held: Application rejected.

Rugby Football Union v Viagogo Limited [2012] UKSC 55
Keywords:Norwich

Smith v Lloyd TSB Bank [2005] EWHC 246
Data protection. Data. Section 1(1) DPA. Information previously processed. Information capable of conversion to digital format. Personal data. Information about company. Section 7(9) DPA. Whether data in

s 1(1) of the DPA ought to be construed to include information once but no longer held on computer. Whether data in s 1(1) DPA ought to be construed to include information in documents. Documents could rapidly be turned into a digital format. Whether personal data.

Held: Whether information was personal data had to be answered at the time of the request. At that time Lloyds did not hold any information about Smith wholly or partly on automatic equipment. The reference to and definition of a relevant filing system in s 1(1) would be meaningless if any documents capable of being converted into a digital format were to be treated as if they were in a computer database. Smith was not entitled to disclosure of such material under DPA. Documents related to the company rather than Smith. As such, they did not contain personal data.

Smith v Trafford Housing Trust [2012] EWHC 3221 (Ch)
Employee comments of social networking website. Discipline.

Sofola v Lloyds TSB Bank [2005] EWHC 1335 QBD
DPA. Sub-section 13 and 14. Leave to appeal. New information.
Held: Right to appeal allowed on basis of new information, but exceptional circumstances.

Spring v Guardian Assurance [1995] AC 96
Dismissal. Reference for ex-employee. Negative references. Adversely affected employment applications. Claim for damages and economic loss.
Held: Previous employer liable to damages, as duty of care if it agrees to provide a reference.

Sunderland Housing Company & another v Baines & others [2006] EWHC 2359 (QB)
Defamation. Harassment. Data protection. Injunctive relief. Responsibility for website. Whether or not injunctive relief should be granted. John Doe order. C1, a company responsible for public housing in Sunderland and C2, its chief executive (together with representative parties), sought interim injunctive relief in respect of allegations published on an anonymous website called Dad's Place. C1 and C2 relied upon defamation, harassment and data protection. D1 admitted responsibility for the website but stated an intention to justify. D2 and D4 denied in witness statements any responsibility for the website. D3 did not attend. D5 was a John Doe Defendant.
Held: P1 not entitled to injunction. It was a corporate entity and arguably a public body: *Derbyshire County Council v Times Newspapers* considered. P2 entitled to injunction in defamation, harassment and data protection against D1, D3 and D5. P2 had produced a witness

statement stating that the allegations were untrue and it was not sufficient for D1 to merely assert an intention to justify without identifying the extent to which he proposes and intends to do so and supports it with a statement of truth: *Bonnard v Perryman* distinguished. Anonymous postings were particularly distressing form of harassment and D1 was not a registered data processor and was hence processing data improperly. No injunction against D2 and D4. While there were suspicions, there was a clear conflict on the evidence that could not be determined on paper nor was there evidence of further publication.

Theakston v MGN Limited [2002] EWHC 137 (QB); [2002] EMLR 398
Breach of confidence. Privacy. DPA. Interim injunction. Photographs. Section 12 Human Rights Act 1998. Plaintiff photographed without consent in a brothel in Mayfair. Drinking with friends that night. Could not remember what happened. Text messages. Threats to sell pictures to press unless he paid money. Prostitutes took their story to the *Sunday People*. Injunction to prevent publication both of details of the claimant's activities and the photographs, taken without consent.
Held: Plaintiff had previously placed certain aspects of his love and sexual life in the press. Not all relationships of a sexual nature should be afforded the same quality of confidence. Even more so where, as here, the claimant did not at the time he entered the brothel stipulate that his activities in the brothel should be kept confidential. Further, there was a public interest in publishing the fact that he had behaved in the manner he had, given his public role as a television presenter who was perceived as a respectable figure to present programmes aimed at young people. The photographs, however, merited special consideration as the details contained in them were likely to be of an especially intimate, personal and intrusive nature. Plaintiff right to keep the details private outweighed papers and prostitutes rights of freedom of expression.

Tournier v National Provincial and Union Bank of England [1924] 1 KB 461
Bank. Disclosure of customer data. Four areas or situations where a bank can disclose customer data. If (1) bank compelled by law, (2) public duty to disclose, (3) bank's interest requires disclosure, and (4) customer agrees to the disclosure.

Volker und Markus Schecke GbR v Land Hessen (Case C–92/09) Joined Cases C–92/09 and C–93/09
Protection of individuals regarding the treatment of personal data. Publication of information on beneficiaries of funds deriving from the

European Agricultural Guarantee Fund and the European Agricultural Fund for rural development. Validity of the legal provisions that provide for such publication and the manner in which it is to be made. Reference for a preliminary ruling from the Verwaltungsgericht Wiesbaden (Germany).

Von Hannover v Germany (No 1) ECHR, (2004), (application no. 59320/00), [2005] 40 EHRR 1
Princess Caroline. Privacy. Related rights. Tabloid press photos (including of her children). Media and privacy arguments. Convention.
Held: ECHR held breach of Article 8 of Convention.

Springer and Von Hannover v Germany (*Von Hannover No. 2*), 07.02.12 [2012] EMLR 16. Also note *Axel Springer AG v Germany* (application no. 39954/08)
Princess Caroline. Privacy. Related rights. Tabloid press photos. Media and privacy arguments. Convention. Argument that national lay not sufficiently protective.
Held: National law sufficient.

Smith v Lloyds TSB Bank Plc [2005] EWHC 246 (Ch)
Data protection. Data. Section 1(1) DPA. Information previously processed. Information capable of conversion to digital format. Personal data. Information about company. S 7(9) DPA. Claimant controlling shareholder of a company involved in a development project funded by loans from the defendant (Lloyds). Both the company's borrowings and claimant's personal borrowings were secured on the development and by a mortgage on home. The company became unable to repay the loan and went into liquidation. Lloyds petitioned to bankrupt Smith. Plaintiff asserted Lloyds had entered into an oral agreement with him to the effect that Lloyds would make available to the company long-term finance in a substantial amount. He claimed that documentation held by Lloyds would prove that contention and sought an order for its disclosure under s 7(9) DPA. It was not in dispute that Lloyds did not hold any information about Smith on computer at the time of his request.
Held: Whether or not information was data had to be answered at the time of the request, *Johnson v Medical Defence Union* [2004] EWHC 347 applied. At that time Lloyds did not hold any information about Smith wholly or partly on automatic equipment. The reference to and definition of a 'relevant filing system' in s 1(1) would be meaningless if any documents capable of being converted into a digital format were to be treated as if they were in a computer database. Smith was not entitled to disclosure of such material under DPA. The documents

related to the company rather than Smith. As such they did not contain personal data, *Durant v Financial Services Authority* [2003] EWCA Civ 1746 applied.

Sofola v Lloyds TSB Bank plc [2005] EWHC 1335 (QB)
Defamation qualified privilege. Sections 13 and 14 DPA. Civil Procedure. CPR Part 3.4. CPR Part 24. CPR Part 52(3)(6). Appeal against a decision of Master Tennant, of whose reasons there was no record, to strike out claims for slander and under ss 13 and 14 of the DPA (claims for compensation and an order for relief respectively). Claims in relation to a visit to a bank where a photocopied driving license was suspected to be a forgery when an erroneous note on account warned staff of previous fraud. The police were called but no action was taken. Plaintiff requested the bank remove the erroneous note and a later note suggesting he withdraw money using the driving license, which it failed to do. Mitting J gave permission to appeal only on the slander point.
Held: Allowing the appeal in part. Slander claim allowed to proceed. There was nothing to contradict Plaintiff account of the facts and nothing that indicated why the bank had called the police. This case was exceptional and Plaintiff application for permission to appeal the DPA points should be reopened. There was no record of the Master's reasons why the DPA claims should be struck out and Mitting J had not given reasons why they were bound to fail. Tugendhat J accepted that the bank's non-compliance with the deletion request gave rise to an arguable claim under s 13. This matter had not been addressed properly by Mitting J, which was a compelling reason to allow the appeal within CPR Part 52(3)(6).

Webster & Ors v the Governors of the Ridgway Foundation School [2009] EWHC 1140 (QB)
Privacy. Proportionality. Specific disclosure. Redaction. Witness statements. CPR rr 31.3, 31.12, 31.14. Article 8, ECHR. Data protection. Pupil assaulted at school. He was white. Assailants non-white. Whether the family were entitled to specific disclosure of (1) the unredacted versions of the documents already disclosed; and (2) the computer database of pupil misbehaviour.
Held: The request for disclosure of names of pupils in memos relating to the 'climate of racial tension' could not be objected to on the grounds of proportionality as the application was focussed and the numbers of pupils involved was small. However, disclosure of their identities would be an interference with their private lives, especially as the matters discussed had caused many of them upset. In any event, it was not necessary for the applicants to know their identities to have a fair trial. Identifiers were sufficient. Under CPR r 31.14, mention of a document

in a witness statement would usually trigger a right to inspection. However, this position was subject to qualifications in CPR r 31.3. Allowing inspection of the whole database would be disproportionate in this case. Furthermore, requiring the governors to provide a redacted version of the database would be a very substantial task, which was disproportionate to the issues in the case.

W v JH & A County Council Limited [2008] EWHC 399 (QB); [2009] EMLR11
Libel. Summary judgment. Qualified privilege. 'Off the peg' privilege. Lapse of time. DPA. Plaintiff worked as a social worker for the Second Defendant. In 1994 a disciplinary panel found him guilty of sexual harassment, and gave him a final written warning. Second Defendant assured the claimant that after 18 months the written warning would be reviewed. In 1996 the Claimant was made redundant. In July 2005 the claimant agreed to act as an assessor for a University. In September 2005 the First Defendant informed the University that the claimant had 'left in a hurry' before a hearing into allegations of sexual harassment. Claimant sued the Defendants for slander. Defendants applied for summary judgment. Criminal Justice Act 2003.
Held: The relationship between the parties was not such that it was clear that this was an 'off the peg' case where no investigation of the circumstances was required in order to determine whether publication was privileged; *Kearns v General Council of the Bar* applied. The historic nature of the information was a relevant factor in considering whether or not a duty to publish arose; *Ley v Hamilton* [1935] 153 LTR 384 considered. There may be no duty where an ex-employer had given the employee an assurance of the sort given in this case, or where it had held the information on file for an unreasonably long period of time. DPA, Criminal Justice Act 2003 and Article 8 ECHR may be relevant in this context. Given the pleaded context of publication, the words were capable of bearing the meanings pleaded by the plaintiff.

WP29 and Data Protection Authorities/Google (re Google policy change and breaches)
Google. Data protection. Policy change. Data protection authority request to delay. Refused. Go live. Investigation. Breaches of data protection regime. Official questions to Google. Not happy with replies. Breaches. Changes required. Compliance required. New privacy tools required. Privacy by design (PbD). Data Protection Privacy by Design (DPbD). [*Note: ongoing*].

Index

Index

Index

Index

Index

Index

Index

Index

Index